CW01203279

Oxford Bibliographical Society
Publications

NEW SERIES VOLUME XVIII

ADVERTISEMENT

THIS VOLUME is offered to GRAHAM POLLARD as a tribute from his friends and admirers within and without the Oxford Bibliographical Society. It could not have come into being without a generous response to the Society's appeal for donations towards the cost of production and for subscriptions before publication.

To the donors and subscribers: to the contributors of the studies: to M. L. Turner who undertook much of the preliminary work of preparing the book for press, Rosemary Morgan who compiled the index, S. Nowell-Smith and Gwen Hampshire who helped to see the volume through to its final stages: to Hugh Williamson of the Alden Press – to all who have combined to honour GRAHAM POLLARD the editors would express appreciation and gratitude.

We sadly record the deaths, while the volume was in preparation, of two of the contributors, JOHN CARTER and A. N. L. MUNBY.

R. W. HUNT, I. G. PHILIP, R. J. ROBERTS

STUDIES IN THE BOOK TRADE

IN HONOUR OF
GRAHAM POLLARD

OXFORD
THE OXFORD BIBLIOGRAPHICAL SOCIETY
1975

Inquiries about the Society and its publications
should be addressed to the Honorary Secretary
The Oxford Bibliographical Society
care of The Bodleian Library, Oxford

© Oxford Bibliographical Society 1975

ISBN 0 901420 30 1

Set in Monotype Bembo and printed in Great Britain
at the Alden Press, Oxford

Contents

JOHN CARTER

Graham Pollard   3

NICOLAS BARKER

Quiring and the binder: quire-marks in some
manuscripts in fifteenth-century blind-stamped bindings   11

ANTHONY HOBSON

The *iter italicum* of Jean Matal   33

RICHARD HUNT

Donors of manuscripts to St. John's College, Oxford,
during the Presidency of William Laud, 1611–1621   63

PAUL MORGAN

Letters relating to the Oxford book trade
found in bindings in Oxford college libraries, *c.* 1611–1647   71

D. G. VAISEY

Anthony Stephens: the rise and fall of an Oxford bookseller   91

HARRY CARTER

Early accounts of the University Press, Oxford:
an introduction   119

MICHAEL HARRIS

Newspaper distribution during Queen Anne's reign:
Charles Delafaye and the Secretary of State's office   139

CONTENTS

HOWARD NIXON
Harleian bindings — 153

TERRY BELANGER
Tonson, Wellington and the Shakespeare copyrights — 195

J. D. FLEEMAN
The revenue of a writer: Samuel Johnson's literary earnings — 211

GILES BARBER
Pendred abroad: a view of the
late eighteenth-century book trade in Europe — 231

A. N. L. MUNBY
Dibdin's reference library: the sale of 26–28 June 1817 — 279

DAVID ROGERS
Francis Duoce's manuscripts:
some hitherto unrecognised provenances — 315

JOHN DREYFUS and **PETER C. G. ISAAC**
William Bulmer's will — 341

MICHAEL TURNER
Tillotson's Fiction Bureau: agreements with authors — 351

Writings of Graham Pollard — 379

Index — 387

Plates

Facing page 2
1 Graham Pollard 1975

Between pages 48 and 49
2 Matal's catalogue of the Vatican's Bibliotheca Publica Graeca
3 Matal's catalogue of Greek legal manuscripts in the Laurentian Library
4 Matal's 'Canones Ecclesiastici diversorum auctorum' in the Laurentian Library

Facing page 72
5 Tools used by Damian Cope

Between pages 144 and 145
6 Delafaye's customers and publications supplied
7 Delafaye's list of customers
8 London coffee-house proprietors and foreign papers supplied

Between pages 184 and 185
9 Binding by Jane Steel 1717
10 Tools used by Jane Steel
11 Binding by Thomas Elliott 1724
12 Binding by Christopher Chapman 1720
13 Binding by Christopher Chapman 1724
14 Rolls used by T. Elliott and C. Chapman
15 Tools used by T. Elliott and C. Chapman
16 Binding by John Brindley

STUDIES IN
THE BOOK TRADE

PLATE 1. Graham Pollard 1975.

JOHN CARTER

Graham Pollard

BIOGRAPHY

GRAHAM POLLARD's entry in *Who's Who*, though it includes one misprint among the titles of his published books, is presumably accurate in stating that his first name is Henry; that he was born 7th March 1903; and that his parents were A. F. Pollard, the Oxford historian, first director of the Institute of Historical Research, and Catherine Susannah Lucy.

He was educated at Shrewsbury, where he came under the influence of J. B. Oldham, the authority on early English bindings; a subject to which he was later to make important contributions himself. Oldham was then the school librarian and subsequently a Gold Medallist of the Bibliographical Society, and it was at least partly a difference of opinion as to the direction of Graham's future studies between Oldham and his father, who wanted him to become a professional historian, which led to his leaving Shrewsbury early for a year at University College London. He then put in for an Oxford scholarship. Balliol was his first choice, and I sometimes wonder what effect the Balliol atmosphere would have had on an already idiosyncratic temperament. But in the event he was offered the top scholarship at Jesus (the two colleges used the same examination), which he was advised to accept, as a bird in the hand, with the promise to his father that he would sit for the Brackenbury Scholarship (Balliol), as he duly did, but without success.

It was a brilliant period at Oxford, and the Jesus man who was the first to introduce corduroy trousers to polite society (purchased on Gloucester Green for ten shillings) soon numbered amongst his acquaintance such noticeable and in later life notable figures as Harold Acton, who was editing the short-lived *Oxford Museum*, Peter Quennell, Cyril Connolly, Robert Byron, Brian Howard, Anthony Powell, David Talbot Rice and Evelyn Waugh; the last of whom, as he remembers with satisfaction, he beat for the (unofficial) half-blue at spitting (target at ten feet).

His political affiliations were already in evidence; he held party card No. 1 of the Young Communist League of Great Britain; he edited *The New Oxford*, the organ of the University's Labour Club, in which Malcolm MacDonald was one of his successors; and in one of a series of murals executed by Oliver Messel, Graham was represented in a punt accompanied by a load of bombs.

By way of forecast to his future career he formed the habit of scouring the bookshops of the Charing Cross Road for secondhand textbooks, which could be bought at one-third of the published price and then sold for two-thirds at Blackwell's or Parker's. He had earlier been introduced to the habits of the antiquarian trade, when, as a boy on holiday near Freshwater, I.O.W., he had been observed thumbing through a set of the *Hudson River Portfolio*, even then worth a couple of hundred pounds, and was approached by a bookseller who gave him a fiver to go away and not come back. The books in his own collection were sufficiently interesting to cause a mutual friend (could it have been C. H. Wilkinson) to bring Thomas J. Wise, the great panjandrum of those days, to see them, and Graham has recorded[1] that when he displayed with some pride one of the three known copies of George Crabbe's earliest separate publication, *Inebriety*, Ipswich 1775, Wise's only comment was to reprove him for buying imperfect books (it lacks the title page but has a note in Crabbe's handwriting; it had cost him two guineas; it is now in the Bodleian). Before he went down from Oxford Graham Pollard's immediate future was decided; he had bought David Garnett's shares in the Birrell & Garnett bookshop.

He sat for his finals and got a third but he never took his degree, since he regarded the expenditure of five pounds as a waste of money for anyone not proceding to an academic career.

Birrell & Garnett's bookshop had started in Taviton Street, W.C.1., and even later, as I remember it in Gerrard Street, Soho, in the late 20s, it still retained, especially in the front room (new books), a strong 'Bloomsbury' flavour. Francis Birrell, son of Augustine, had been a founder-member of the group in its Cambridge days and Jane Norton, the bibliographer of Gibbon, who succeeded Ralph Wright (also a Bloomsbury) in the business was the sister of Harry Norton, another founder-member. Furthermore in the early Gerrard Street days the Nonesuch Press, before it set up in Great James Street, occupied the basement area below the shop.

Here Graham remained as Jane Norton's partner, from 1924 until

[1] *Bodleian Library Record*, v (1954–6), p. 149.

1938 when Birrell & Garnett closed its doors, doubling it with a Leverhulme Research Fellowship for a history of the book trade from 1934 to 1937; and one must hope that he will some day write his own reminiscences of his days as an antiquarian bookseller. I myself remember him, in the years following my own entry into the rare book business in 1927, as one of the three most stimulating, imaginative and learned ports of call for any tyro in the trade (the others being A. W. Evans of Elkin Mathews and E. P. Goldschmidt). And of course our joint investigation of the nineteenth-century pamphlets brought us much more closely together from 1931 onwards, with lunch once or twice a week at Brice's restaurant in Wardour Street and a solid day on Saturdays at the British Museum (with a tea break at the Express Dairy among the other bibliographers). This was an invigorating period for me. In addition to the excitement of the chase, which we shared, I got to know my collaborator pretty well. I learned to appreciate the width and depth of his powers of research and his lucid analysis of its results, and in particular to admire, without ever being able to emulate, his uncannily accurate eye for type-design.

One of the most important evenings in Graham's life at Birrell & Garnett was on some unrecorded date in 1926 when, working late with the lights on, he heard a knock at the door and opened it to find an unknown character who was 'travelling', among the London booksellers, Frederic Warde's facsimile edition of the Arrighi writing books, the introduction to which, set in Arrighi's own newly recut italic, had been contributed by the 'traveller' himself. Yes, it was Stanley Morison. And this fortunate chance initiated one of the strongest and most fruitful friendships in the lives of both men. They had in common not only marxist politics but a discriminating taste in food and drink and a passion for railway engines: they differed in that Morison was a devout Roman Catholic and a dedicated Londoner, whereas Graham depends for his physical as well as spiritual well-being on fairly frequent bouts of long country walking. Each respected the other's powerful intelligence, and Graham was one of the handful of Morison's friends who could always stand up to him in an argument. In the professional area it was Birrell & Garnett's purchase of Morison's remarkable collection of early writing books which introduced Graham to a field that he made peculiarly his own, and it was Morison who introduced to him that splendidly convivial character, William S. Ivins of the Metropolitan Museum of New York, who not only bought the whole collection but gave him a free hand for purchases additional to it.

Morison was also influential in the studies which in due course resulted in Birrell & Garnett's famous catalogue of typefounders' specimens.

The years in Gerrard Street were followed by a period (1939-42) as Reader in the History of Newspapers in the University of London: a post initiated, I think, by Stanley Morison and financed by the Astors; and much of Graham's time at this stage was spent in the University's wartime exile, at Aberystwyth or Bangor, out of reach of his London friends. In 1942 he joined the Board of Trade, where he stayed (in due course becoming 'established') until 1959. During the war years he managed—contrary, I fancy, to all the rules—to keep a bed in his office, which he often used; but at other times he slept above an inn somewhere in the East End where they somehow could always produce a steak for his dinner and eggs and bacon for breakfast. At one time, about the end of the war, he was seconded to the Organisation and Methods Division of the Treasury, and one of the *rariora* in my own collection is a copy (No. 1090, For Official Use Only) of an eighty-page foolscap size memorandum *On the Design of Forms*, dated October 1945, from which, in defiance of the Official Secrets Act, I quote the following characteristic sentences: 'Aim at a design which does not *look* complicated (e.g. by avoiding large areas of print)'; 'Help the eye to enter and read (e.g. by choosing suitable colours of ink or paper; by the arrangement of entries)'; 'It is doubtful if generous entry spaces for unskilled persons are an advantage; they tend to encourage scribbling'.

In 1959, the year of his retirement from the Government service, Graham delivered the Sandars Lectures at Cambridge, and in 1960/61 the Lyell Lectures at Oxford, in which years also he served as President of the Bibliographical Society. He was now a bibliographer at large, and although neither his Sandars nor his Lyell Lectures, nor certain other projects on which he is known to be working, have yet been completed for publication, he has remained more than ever generous to his fellow-workers (as the contributions to the present volume bear ample witness); and his eminence was recognised in 1969 by the award of the Gold Medal of the Bibliographical Society.

ACHIEVEMENTS

In summarising the achievements which justified that award I cannot do better than to repeat, with a little updating, the citation which I had the honour of delivering, as President, on 6 May 1969.

'In presenting to you Mr. Graham Pollard, I take a more than special satisfaction; it is indeed a sensation so intimate as to be almost incestuous. For in half a dozen of his minor published works my own name is joined with his on the title-page. Of these, one is directly pertinent to this evening's exercise, for it was a joint tribute, on his sixtieth birthday, to an earlier Gold Medallist, Stanley Morison, to whom both of us were for many years deeply indebted and affectionately attached. Of the others (most of them concerned with the doings of an earlier President of this Society) I shall say no more than that, despite a certain tendency to procrastination in recent years (known to our publisher as "Pollard's pace"), no collaboration in a series of technical memoranda can ever have been more harmonious; nor, I think, has any co-author been more comfortably conscious of his debts than I am.

'If the British Museum catalogue is to be trusted, Graham Pollard's earliest publication between hard covers—I charitably overlook that notorious rarity, *Public School Verse* 1920—approximately coincided with my first acquaintance with him. We were both, in the year 1928, engaged in the rare book business; and Messrs. Birrell & Garnett's now historic catalogue of *Typefounders' Specimens, Books printed in founts of historic importance*, etc., served impressive notice to the cognoscenti of those distant days that E. P. Goldschmidt was not the only learned man to have hung his hat behind a tradesman's sign. Its logical successor never got printed, since the collection it described—perhaps the finest of its kind ever assembled—was sold *en bloc* to the Metropolitan Museum of New York; but there survives in typescript in the British Museum the scrupulously annotated *List of Writing Books offered for sale by Birrell & Garnett*, ff. 125, with manuscript prices and additions, dated c. 1935.

'Two years later there was lodged in the same repository—Oxonians may care to make a note of the pressmark, 010368. i. 88—Graham Pollard's *Notes for a Directory of Cat Street, Oxford, before A.D. 1500*, 4to, ff. xv, 73, manuscript additions, typescript, no. 2 of three copies. Its author's loyalty to Oxford was further expressed in a concisely argued paper proving—well, virtually proving—that the thirteenth-century miniaturist William de Brailles, first identified by Sydney Cockerell in 1908, had practised his craft on the site of what is now All Souls Chapel. Secluded in the pages of the 1966 volume of *Oxoniensia* is a paper of formidable erudition on "The Medieval Town Clerks of Oxford". Only the other day Mr. Pollard established the authorship of his university's oldest statute book and proved it to be forty years earlier than even Strickland Gibson had supposed. And back in 1961 his Lyell Lectures, delivered to standing room only (as the Warden of All Souls and I discovered to our discomfort), were devoted to "The Medieval Book Trade in Oxford". This masterful series, like Mr. Pollard's Sandars Lectures of two years earlier on 'The English Market for Printed Books", has not as yet been printed.

'Yet if too large a proportion of Graham Pollard's bibliographical work still awaits those final revisions to which perfectionists, and also those who have too many irons in the fire, are unfortunately prone, he has enriched the pages of *The Library* with a number of papers of the first quality; as well as his edition, no. 14 of our series of *Supplements*, of Pendred's earliest directory of the English book trade (1955). In 1937 we had *The Company of Stationers before 1557* and *The Early Constitution of the Stationers' Company*. A second linked group comprised *Changes in the Style of Bookbinding, 1530–1830*, (1956), *The Construction of English Twelfth-century Bindings*, (1962), and *The Names of some English Fifteenth-century Binders* (1970), a trio of excursions into the technical, as distinct from the merely decorative, history of bookbinding which, along with an equally pregnant paper, *Notes on the Size of the Sheet* (1941), have introduced what is virtually a new dimension into our study of books and their bindings as physical objects.

'Graham Pollard's interests, as expressed in print, have ranged from *Medieval Loan Chests in Cambridge* to a bibliography of John Meade Falkner, from *The Bibliographical History of Hall's Chronicle 1542*, to a dissertation on the early poems of George Crabbe and a pioneer essay on *Serial Fiction*. For *CBEL* he not only dealt more than faithfully with such dauntingly prolific and bibliographically nightmarish authors as Byron and Ruskin: his articles on book production and distribution, on libraries, on newspaper and periodical publication, are perhaps the most illuminating components of the entire work.

'But, of course, the culmination—to date (I repeat, to date)—of Mr. Pollard's output is the 450-page profusely illustrated folio which Mr. Albert Ehrman, who furnished the first chapter, presented to the fortunate, and one hopes appreciative, members of the Roxburghe Club in 1964: *The Distribution of Books by Catalogue, from the Invention of Printing to A.D. 1800*. This extraordinary and fascinating book—learned, imaginative, cosmopolitan, profoundly significant for the future direction of bibliographical studies—displays at their capacious best those qualities which we are formally recognising this evening: a feeling for history, the understanding to relate the science of bibliography to prevailing economic and social conditions (as well as to technical factors); the capacity for research in depth, and a scholarly relish for human detail; a sense of order in the marshalling of evidence and a sense of proportion in the advancing of theory; clarity and economy in exposition; and finally the ability to be precise without pedantry, decisive without dogmatism.'

NICOLAS BARKER

Quiring and the binder

Quire-marks in some manuscripts in fifteenth-century blind-stamped bindings

A recent account of the Scales Binder's work has pointed to a singular characteristic in it, his 'unusual technique of signing the quires of a number of the books he bound'.[1] This was not his universal habit; only 8 out of the 15 manuscripts at present identified as his work are quired thus. In the others, an adequate series of scribal catchwords may have obviated the need, or the quiring may have been put in and later trimmed away. The system was regularly and precisely used. Minuscule letters and roman figures are invariable; red ink alternates with black for preliminary leaves, or to indicate a change of work within the whole book; a + sign sometimes appears, either as the signature mark of the first quire or on the first leaf after the middle of the quire, perhaps as an indication to help the left hand in sewing. It is noticeable that the manuscripts with the fullest set of quire marks are those which were old and had to be rebound, or were in an unfamiliar script.

The hand itself is homogeneous but not quite uniform. The number of samples of it is so small that identification would be difficult, it if were not for the similar bindings, which provide a certain link. This alone justifies the assumption that the hand is the same in each book, and that it is the binder's or that of a close associate.

But if, it was further suggested, 'the Scales Binder's practice in this respect is sufficiently individual and methodical to be recognizable, he was not the only binder of the period to mark the quiring of manuscripts sent to him for binding'. An example was advanced to support this assertion, to which we will return, but the subject itself seemed unfamiliar and interesting enough to justify further examination on its own.

From this point, it seemed best to pursue the work of other binders, following Graham Pollard's article on 'The Names of Some English

[1] Notes begin on page 30.

Fifteenth-Century Binders[2] as a guide. Like him, so now I must acknowledge how much I owe to the earlier work of Strickland Gibson, G. D. Hobson and J. B. Oldham.[3] But without Pollard's article, I should have entirely lacked any sense of direction. Not for the first time, his peculiar mixture of thorough physical examination with archival expertise has reduced apparent chaos to something close to order. Where before there was a confused mass of craftsmen identified by and nick-named from their tools, there is now a chronological framework, identified both stylistically and by documents, with a surprising number of named binders to fill it out. It was, and is, a brilliant and stimulating piece of work.

If, however, the reader is expecting something, if only a lunar reflection, of the same sort now, he will be disappointed. The pursuit of other binders using the same technique of quire-signature as the Scales Binder (whose name is still to be found) has been largely fruitless. What follows is based on examination of a considerable number of manuscripts in fifteenth-century English blind-stamped bindings. It is not by any means complete, but the sample is large enough to show that the binder did not normally sign the quires, and that the Scales Binder's practice was rarely imitated; no evidence of the use of his rather complicated 'full' system has yet been discovered. This is not to say that it did not exist: only a small proportion of the books bound in the fifteenth-century, perhaps less than ten per cent,[4] have survived. Hence conclusions can only be tentative.

The material is set out in the order given in Pollard's Appendix I. If it tells us a little more about the technique and practice of bookbinding in England in the fifteenth century, it is interesting to look at one aspect of the books which the binder must himself have considered before setting to work.

The first thing that would strike him might very well be the large number of marks of quiring already there. It is very difficult to prove that any of the books were bound for the first time in their present fifteenth-century binding, although it is probable that a few were. Many of them were old books, however, and in some cases works previously bound separately were brought together. Many of the books have scribal catchwords, a tiresome convention for the binders, since it involved comparison of the quire just sewn with the next to be sewn. The original scribe may have added quiring, or it may be scribbled in plumbago or red chalk (often erased; perhaps this was a rough marking put on when the blank vellum was issued), or written in by the rubricator (who may or may not be the scribe), or by an earlier binder or stationer. Often this process may have extended over several hundred years; different and conflicting quire-marks show how often a group of quires may have been bound and rebound in different company over the years. On the other hand, all these systems may be found in a book bound as soon as it was written. Sometimes the quiring (particularly if by the text scribe) seems to be an intended part of the text page; more often it is written so close to the foot foredge that part, usually a large part (and in some cases perhaps all), of the quiring has been trimmed off. But there is a lot to be found and a lot more to be found out about the systems used.

The first exponent of the 'all-over' style employed by the early binders is the Scales Binder, whose work can be traced back to the early 1450s; he worked in London. It is probable that the binder of Pembroke College, Cambridge, MS. 204, was also a London man. One of his tools is a double (in both senses of the word) of one of the Scales Binder's and two others are in very much the same style, although his method of applying them was quite different.[5] It is confusing that the book consists of two different works, which were probably imperfect when bound (the second surviving quire of the second work, although lettered 'd', is also marked '2·q̃·' in a fifteenth-century hand), and that it was worse damaged when rebound *c.* 1880. More than half the first work is lost (*teste* the list of contents on the original flyleaf), and an unknown amount of the second. The first sequence, however, is almost certainly the scribe's, and although the quiring of the second part does not seem to be scribal, it is unlikely to be the binder's; much more likely that he wrote the '2·q̃·'.

No other work with the same stamps as Pembroke MS. 204 is known, and the same is true of Magdalen College, Oxford MS. 196, which has a binding in the same style. It is a book well known to amateurs of early humanistic writing in this country because it was written by a distinguished scribe who signed it, but the signature is damaged and all that can be read of his name is 'Thomas S'.[6] It is a Boethius written for John Neele, who took his M.A. in 1454 and was later chaplain to William of Waynflete; he left all his books to Magdalen when he died in 1498.

Another binder who also probably worked in London bound three manuscripts in the all-over style. Pollard has called him the Sheen Binder. The name and the London connection are suggested by MS. Bodley 117, an unassuming paper book, written by William Mede, a monk of the Carthusian House of Jesus of Bethlehem at Sheen, who died in 1474. Only a few of the quire marks survive; the rest have been erased or cut away. Those that remain indicate that the leaves of the first half of each quire were numbered in roman numerals, but the quires are not serially lettered; the final 'j' of the numerals slopes from right to left. Very similar numerals are found in Magdalen MS. 145, a much larger vellum book (the *Distinctiones theologicae* of Nicholas Byard) also bound by the Sheen Binder. Here the quires are lettered as well; the last, which should be n, is in fact zz, perhaps to indicate that it is the last. The third book, Isocrates in Latin with other tracts written in 1445 by Theodoricus Nicolaus Werken,[7] a Dutch scribe in the service of William Gray, Bishop of Ely, then in northern Italy, has been rebound. Although the covers have been preserved, the book has been re-trimmed in binding, and all traces of quire-marks have vanished. This is unfortunate: two books with similar numerals may be a coincidence; a third could not be.

Outside London, there were three early centres of blind-stamped binding where the 'all-over' style was used. At Oxford, we can now put names to the two binders who successively used tools copied from those used on romanesque bindings from Winchester, Thomas Hokyns (d. 1465) and John More (d. 1472). The manuscripts they bound varied from a Vergil of c. 1200 from Cirencester, later in the hands of Sir John Prise and now All Souls MS. 82, to new books such as Richard Rotheram's *De pluralitate beneficiorum*, now British Library Egerton MS. 2892. (This last, Mr. Pollard now maintains, cannot be claimed as the earliest datable example from Oxford; it may not be the dedication copy prepared before Rotheram's death, but a fine copy written for William of Waynflete.)

Egerton 2892, probably by design, has no quire marks. All Souls 82, which is in the odd 'agenda' format used for small classical texts in hexameters or elegiac couplets, has clear scribal catchwords but no signatures, possibly because its earlier sewing and bands were retained. But a book of sermons by John Felton (Bodleian, Lat.th.e.7), written at Oxford on 5 July 1460 and then bound by Hokyns, shows an unusual system. Arabic figures are used for both quire and leaf, although roman numerals are occasionally substituted for the leaf numbers (but 6 is always used, never vi, even in roman sequences). It is unlikely that a system like this, with all the risks of confusion that it involves, would be devised by anyone for other than his own use; it may be Hokyns's hand.

The system is quite different from that used in at least three manuscripts bound by Moore. Two of these were written by John Goold, fellow of Magdalen College, who wrote the date 1 February 1471 at the end of the first work in a Latin translation of Aristotle *Ethics* and *Politics* which he later gave to the college (Magdalen MS. 49). It looks as if he quired the first work (the letters are unlike his text hand, but the ink colour changes with the text), but the second is quired in a different hand, probably the same as that which marked University College MS. 110, a Duns Scotus also written by Goold. Finally, Magdalen MS. 189, another Aristotle, is also quired by two hands; the first seems to be that which was also responsible for copious marginal notes; the second that already noticed (the second hand has also written in 'g 4', omitted by the first hand due to a defect in the vellum at the foot foredge).

It is not easy to decide if the hand that quired the second parts of Magdalen 49 and 189 and the whole of University 110 is the same. The system is the same, and the letter forms are similar. But the forms are commonplace at the time, and there are divergences in size, formality, height-to-width, and so on. If it is the same, it is certainly not as deliberate as the Scales Binder's style, although its unselfconsciousness could account for the disparities.

Matters are not made easier by the other manuscripts in Oxford bindings with different or no quiring. MS. Bodley 141, Albertus Magnus *Parva naturalia* and other works, written in England[8] not long before it was bound, is fully quired in a neat small hand with a very individual 'g', quite unlike that described above. But All Souls 82 has none. A fourteenth-century manuscript of Petrus Ruffensis *In summula viciorum* and other tracts (Bodleian MS. Lyell 16), in a binding close to All Souls 82 in style, has only a partial quiring in plumbago, almost certainly contemporary with the text. It belonged to a Durham monk, John Manby, who was at Durham College, Oxford, from 1471 to 1477, a *terminus ante* for the binding. One of the stamps on it, the bird with a bearded man's head wearing a cap, is one of the 'romanesque' tools used early, and then again *c.* 1480. Bodleian MS. Auct.D. infra 2.4, a thirteenth-century Anglo-Norman bible with the erased remains of a more complex contemporary plumbago quiring, has a binding with stamps which also bridge the twenty years or more.

Hobson's valiant attempt to group surviving Oxford bindings on a basis of common tools[9] was vitiated by this factor: of 11 groups, the first contained 18 bindings from *c.* 1455 to 1486, while no other contained more than four and most only one. MS. Bodley 95, a fifteenth-century collection of English sermons, spoils the picture still further. Its stamps include one from Group A and also another from Group I (three books, one not earlier than 1482), which must therefore be added to the omnium gatherum of Group A. Interestingly, the quiring in Bodley 95, simple perhaps because it is on paper not vellum, is in a hand not dissimilar from that common to the early John More bindings.

The final impression can only be that the early Oxford binders cannot be firmly identified either on the basis of common stamps or of quiring. They seem to have taken manuscript books as they found them, and quire-marks were added by binder or stationer in a much more casual way than that adopted by the Scales Binder (and perhaps also the Sheen Binder).

The Salisbury books bound in the all-over style present a complete contrast. Two of them were written by Herman Zurke, a German scribe who was working in Oxford during Gilbert Kymer's second term as Chancellor of the university from 1447 to 1453. Kymer took Zurke with him when he went to Salisbury as Dean in 1453. The earliest book that Zurke wrote there is bound in the old style of tawed leather, but a binder capable of working with stamps on tanned leather was at work by about 1460. Together, binder and scribe produced some very individual-looking books: it looks as if Kymer had, so to speak, a private press. Although the production of these books was constricted in time and place, they abound in marks. The full quota seems to be as follows:

1. A large scrawly hand noted the quiring in plumbago (later erased) in the foot margin, the leaf number in the centre and the quire letter in the foredge.
2. Elaborately framed catchwords were written by the scribe on the last verso of each quire.
3. Quire letter and leaf number, in black ink, are also found centred between the text columns.
4. Careful small ink signatures, using three different coloured inks, appear at the foot foredge.

The elaborate treatment of the catchwords is commonplace, if Zurke was perhaps unusually extravagant in this respect. Exuberance was clearly a tolerated relief after the discipline of writing a quire of text. It is possible that the first sequence was put in by the stationer or, less likely, by the binder as a first step towards binding; 2 and 3 may be the scribe's work. The coloured ink section is likely to have been added by the rubricator or binder (the use of colour is clearly an extension of the rubrication and initialling and is another instance of the close integration of the production of the books), and some very idiosyncratic forms are used. The use of symbols instead of letters is a continental practice, and its systematic use suggests foreign rather than local use. The writing may therefore be by Zurke, although he was certainly also responsible for the fine catchword with their elaborate frames. The full system is not used elsewhere, which strongly suggests that both scribe and binder were working to the order of Kymer (who died in 1463).

John Kemsyn, the Canterbury Binder, bound a fair number of manuscripts, if the surviving examples reflect his work properly. This is doubtful, however; his style varies considerably, from the fine overall designs like that on the book containing Gulielmus Alvernus *Cur deus homo* and other tracts written by the Canterbury scribe (MS. Bodley 281) to the extremely simple patterns which he used for an early Canterbury Hugh of St. Victor *De sacramentis* (MS. Bodley 379) or a small paper manuscript of contemporary tracts (Society of Antiquaries, MS. 287). Equally, no continuity can be seen in the quire-marks. Some have none (e.g. Magdalen MS. 88 and Bodleian, Selden supra 25), some have partial quiring by the scribe. It is possible that Bodley 281 and 379 were marked by the same hand. The fantastic scheme in Bodley 379 (which deserves to be recorded on that score alone) clearly replaces an earlier quiring; there will be no mistaking a second example of its use, if it should turn up. The quiring in Canterbury books no longer in early bindings may reveal whether Kemsyn did quire some of his books.

With Kemsyn we come to the end of the early all-over style. The later fifteenth-century binders had inevitably fewer manuscripts to bind, and the evidence of quiring is correspondingly slighter. Among those who used the 'central block' design (Mr. Pollard's next stylistic group), the Crucifer Binder, in all probability a London man, bound a number of manuscripts. In some of these (e.g. BL. Add. MS. 22573 and Magdalen MS. 166), the quiring is missing. On the tract *De astrorum succincte vi fatali* written by an astrologer from Piacenza, Gulielmus Parronus, as a New Year's Day present for Henry VII in 1500 (Bodleian, MS. Selden supra 77), traces of quiring in a neat small hand, quite unlike the text, can just be seen on some leaves. The very irregular quiring in Fitzwilliam Museum MS. 375, a Sarum Hours, is due to the fact that the numerous decorated pages were inserted separately, in all probability after the main text had been written, gathered and quired.

At the beginning of the book, the collation is too disturbed and the marks too infrequent for the quiring to be reconstructed with certainty, but at quire 17 there is one sequence which has already reached 'k' while another begins with 'a'. The first sequence, in the centre of the leaf, has been more frequently cut away; it probably represents part of a complete sequence for the book before the decorated pages were put in, and may be by the same hand as the text. I think the second sequence is in the same hand as the quiring in Selden supra 77, and that it represents the binder's attempt to re-quire, taking account of the added pages and starting a new set for each main section of the book (now distinguished by a miniature and decorated page). It is at least possible that the '+' and '×' quires and the arabic figures are in the same hand.

It would be useful to localise the atelier that Oldham called 'Binder J', but the surviving examples of his work do not suggest that he quired his manuscripts. Two mid-fifteenth-century manuscripts, a copy of Bruni's letters and a primer (Bodleian, MSS. Laud misc. 701 and Douce 246), have quiring which is certainly scribal. A book by the same binder, containing the churchwardens' accounts of Horley in Surrey (BL. Add. MS. 6173) has no trace of quire-marks.[10]

None of the bindings characterised by Pollard as 'transitional' designs has been found on a manuscript with quire-marks, but some of the 'diaper design' binders bound manuscripts with marked quires. The Floral, Fishtail, and Fruit and Flower Binders, now rejoicing in their new-found names, Thomas Uffington, Christopher Coke and George Chastelaine, all Oxford men, inevitably had manuscripts to bind for their college patrons.

Thomas Uffington was faced with the problem of binding some new Greek manuscripts written in Italy, which John Claimond, the first President, later gave to Bishop Richard Fox's new Corpus Christi College (Corpus MSS. 96, 112–13). The elaborate Greek notation of quire and leaf was clearly beyond him, and he (or someone for him) simply lettered the first leaf of each quire in a quick informal cursive minuscule, with capital forms of R and T. Two outran the alphabet by two quires, which were lettered g and R, a fairly common professional way of expanding the collational alphabet, which suggests the binder rather than a scholar. On the other hand, Magdalen MS. 63, which he also bound, is only quired in the first part in a hand contemporary with the text not the binding, and Corpus MS. 227, a new book when bound, has not only a statement in words of quaternion and leaf but also quire numbers in the foredge margin, as if to guide a numerate but illiterate binder.

Christopher Coke bound the fine early fifteenth-century copy of Bartholomeus de Urbino *Memoriale milicie spiritualis*, now MS. Bodley 460, which is fully quired in red and black in a hand which must (since the pen widths are the same as in the text) be the scribe's. George Chastelaine bound a number of manuscripts for Merton (MSS. 119, 175–7); the first has the page numbers marked i–vi in plummet, and MS. 175 is similarly marked in arabic figures in ink. The hands are quite different, and there is nothing to connect them with the binding.

The Greyhound Binder remains unidentified. He bound five manuscripts which were among Bishop Fox's original donation to Corpus. They have the large clasps and studs characteristic of his work, and plain vellum ends, which suggest that he may have been a London man. Oxford binders tended to use old manuscript waste; besides, Fox is known to have bought some of his books in London. These books are of various dates and sizes. MS. 58 is a thirteenth-century Statius in agenda format, like the All Souls Vergil, inscribed 'Iste liber est conventus Jernemute' (the Benedictine priory of St Nicolas at Yarmouth, a cell of Norwich) in a fifteenth-century hand. MS. 49 Petrus Cantor *Glossae in psalterium* is another thirteenth-century book which belonged to John Sherwood, bishop of Durham, before Fox. Both are quired in roman numerals by the scribe on the last verso of the quire. MS. 49 also has a rather unusual (and mainly erased) lettered sequence, in which the quire letter is repeated on the verso of the leaves in the first half of the quire, together with the catchword for the next recto; it looks to be contemporary with the text. Magdalen MS. 58, a thirteenth-century text of Peter Lombard also bound by the Greyhound Binder, is more interesting. The trick of numbering the leaves by multiplying the quire letter is peculiar. The hand is certainly English; it may be the binder's notation.

Before turning to Pollard's final group, something may be gained from examining the fifteenth-century stamped bindings which do not fall into his first three categories, most of which are unique: that is to say, they cannot be grouped, on the basis of common tools, with any other binding. Some of them are plain and rough in a way that suggests provincial work (as some are), but they could equally well be plain work from Oxford or London.

The Eton binder, Andrew Lisleie, who had a wholly original large saltire tool and a rather similar *oeuvre* to the Oxford binders, seems to have had no special quiring habits. Neither his books still at Eton, nor the volume containing extracts from Grosseteste's *De lingua* with Gilbert de la Porrée's commentary on the Epistles of St. Paul, now University College MS. 62-3 (a gift in memory of Herbert Elmhurst, an Old Etonian who died as an undergraduate in the 1670s), nor Winchester College Register O (an unusually elaborate binding) have any common features in their quiring.

One of these, Magdalen MS. 71, is a plain book, containing various works attributed to Richard Rolle. The binding seems to be contemporary with the text. On each board is a panel made up with a double dotted fillet in slightly different diaper patterns, each diamond with a ring in the centre. The diaper work is inexpertly done, although the manuscript itself is a professional piece of work. It is consistently quired in a hand different from the text; there are no early indications of provenance. Bodleian, MS. Tanner 4, St. Augustine *Sermones de verbis domini* and other pieces, is a 'central block' binding, but its one stamp is unrecorded elsewhere. Its quiring may have been consistent but it has been too frequently cut away for one to be sure. Like Lyell 16, it belonged to a Durham monk, Richard Byllyngham, who was at Durham College in Oxford from 1446/7 to 1456/7.

Another unique binding is that on MS. Laud Misc. 602, an early fifteenth-century English manuscript. The upper cover has a plain pattern of coarse diagonal fillets, with a diaper pattern on the back enclosing a roughly-cut mermaid stamp. It is possible that part of the quiring is contemporary with the binding, although the main sequence antedates it. It has no early ownership indication, the endpapers include a contemporary deed relating to the abbey of Barking. On the other hand, the design is remarkably similar to that on a printed book in the Bodleian, Auct. R. supra 10, an Oxford incunable of 1481, even down to the poor cutting of the stamp, unique in both cases. The last and in some ways most distinguished of the *adespota* is a small English manuscript of Nicolas de Lyra *Expositio decem praeceptorum* and other pieces (MS. Laud Misc. 12) in a fine 'all-over' binding. No fewer than five stamps are used on it, none of which is recorded elsewhere. It is fully and neatly quired in a hand quite different from the text. The style of the stamps suggests London rather than any of the early provincial centres, but there is nothing to reveal its provenance.

After 1490, the proportion of manuscripts to printed books drops suddenly and predictably. Despite this, two manuscript books with claims to notice survive. The first of these is University College 123,

QUIRING AND THE BINDER

Bonaventure *The mirrour of the blessid lyf of Jhesu Crist*, bound in the diaper style by a binder who also bound a printed book now in Shrewsbury School Library about 1520. But the full and careful quiring in it is almost certainly the scribe's work.

The very fine manuscript of Adam of Eynsham *Magna vita Sancti Hugonis* (*c.* 1500) probably of Carthusian origin (it may have been written for the house at Sheen) and now Huntington Library MS. 36336 is very different. It was bound, almost certainly as a new book, by John Reynes, in the second decade of the sixteenth-century. The scribe who wrote the text on thick but very good vellum carefully lettered each quire and numbered the leaves in the first half of it, in the centre at the foot of the text panel. These marks have been discreetly sanded down; they are not fully erased, nor is the surface of the vellum damaged. Another hand has re-quired the manuscript, marking the first half of the quire by lettering the leaves in it a,b,c,d in black ink close to the foredge. The forms and the fine pen used distinguish these marks sharply from the text. It is difficult to imagine anyone but the binder having an interest in putting new quire marks near the foredge. But more confirmatory evidence would be useful.[11]

It is difficult to resist the feeling that only one conclusion can be drawn from all this: that the Scales Binder's quiring technique was, like other aspects of his work, unique. But perhaps this is too harsh a judgement. Far more manuscripts bound by the Scales Binder survive than of any of the binders here considered. Further, only 8 of the 17 manuscripts bound by Scales Binder were quired by him, so that there is no reason to suppose that there is a better than fifty-fifty chance that his contemporaries' books were similarly treated. Statistically, therefore, it would not be surprising if none of these books contained evidence of quiring by the binder, even if he had once quired other books now lost.

But it looks as if, in one or two cases, we have examples of quiring by other binders, and it may not be fanciful to notice that the best attested seeming cases are by binders with known or probable links with London: the Sheen, Crucifer and Greyhound Binders, the binder of Pembroke MS. 204, and John Reynes. The best that can be said of the Oxford bindings decorated with tools that at some point belonged to John More is that they are tenuously linked by a similar quiring system. If this is so, it suggests that the London binder was the professional who made his own arrangements for preparing his work while his provincial contemporary was an amateur who expected guidance from the client, such as Thomas Kymer may have given to the staff of his 'private press', or the Oxford binders acquired from the members of the halls and colleges of which they were also stewards or manciples.[12]

But this is speculation: the hard facts do no more than add a detail to the 'chronological and topographical framework for the early development of English stamped binding' which Pollard has already so vividly provided.

LIST OF BOOKS

Not all the manuscripts discussed above are listed here, but fuller details are given where the quiring seems of particular interest. The books are set out in the order of Pollard's Appendix I, which indicates the type of design used. Details of the stamps are given by reference to Gibson's *Early Oxford Bindings* (S.G.) or Oldham's *English Blind-Stamped Bindings* (Oldham); stamps not there listed are described. Full details of quiring contemporary with the binding are given, but not of earlier quiring. References are given to standard catalogues: for manuscripts in the Bodleian Library, to the *Summary Catalogue of Western Manuscripts* (S.C.) or the Quarto Catalogue (Coxe); for manuscripts in Oxford College libraries, to *Catalogus codicum MSS. qui in collegiis aulisque Oxoniensibus hodie adservantur*, confecit H. O. Coxe (Oxford, 1852), (Coxe, by page number for each college). The notes include details of early provenance.

SHEEN BINDER

Bodleian, Bodley 117: St. Augustine, De dignitate condicionis humanae, and other tracts, written by William Mede, monk of the Carthusian house of Jesus of Bethlehem at Sheen, *ante* 1474, on paper, 223 × 166 mm, 133 ff.

Stamps: a fleur-de-lys between two affronted birds; pig in front of tree in roundel in square, small lozenges in corners; foliage spray in figure of eight; two sphinxes.

Quiring: 8s, some leaves numbered i–iiij in black ink, at foot foredge (cf. ff. 3, 55).

References: Pollard, p. 201; S.C. 1929.

Notes: Mede died in 1474. Given by Nicholas Limbye or Lymbe, B.D. of St. John's College, in 1602.

Magdalen 145: N. Byard, Distinctiones theologicae, English, s.15, 430 × 280 mm, 105 ff.

Stamps: as Bodley 117, plus medallion enclosing orb.

Quiring: 8s, a–e (2nd and 3rd leaves only numbered ii and iij), f–h i–iiij, m i–iiij, i–l i–iiij, zz i–iiij, plus one single unsigned leaf.

References: Pollard, p. 201 and pl. II; Coxe.

QUIRING AND THE BINDER

UNKNOWN BINDER 1

Pembroke (Cambridge) 204: Albertus Magnus, De caelo et mundo and other tracts (imperfect at beginning and end), both English, s.15 med, 320×235 mm, 84 ff.

Stamps: double tool of squares divided diagonally into four triangular compartments, each containing a rose with two leaves (cf. Scales Binder Stamp 15); continuous strip tool with 3 central roundels containing 7-point flower and 2 half roundels, surrounded by leaves; double tool of squares with triangular cornerpieces containing two birds with fleur-de-lys on stalk between; continuous strip, two cinquefoil flowers on S-shaped stem, tulip-shaped leaves between; continuous strip, 8-shaped fillet.

Quiring: first part in 12s, signed [a]-f, 3, 5 and 6 numbered in [a], b and c signed $-$6, d and e -6, f 1-6 signed in full including f 1, all probably by the scribe; second part in 8s, signed c j-iiij, d j-iiij 2·q̄ (first recto also), e j, imperfect thereafter.

References: M. R. James, *Catalogue of the Manuscripts of Pembroke College Cambridge* (1905). *E.B.B. 1500*, p. 53 and pl. 38; Pollard, p. 201.

Notes: According to James, MS. 204 was rebound *c.* 1880, when the original leather cover was removed and kept separately. It must have been in bad state then, since the surviving leaves of the first quire were bound in the wrong order; possibly imperfect when bound in the 15th century.

THOMAS HOKYNS

Bodleian, Lat.th.e.7: Sermones dominicales by John Felton, written at Oxford, 5 July 1460, 205×130 mm, 313 ff.

Stamps: S.G. 1, 2, 6.

Quiring: 12s; quires numbered in arabic figures, leaves also numbered in arabic figures 1-6 (roman numerals i-v alternate for 1-5, but 6 is constant); first leaf of quire fully signed (e.g. 3 i).

References: *E.O.B.* no. 1, pl. 1; *E.B.B. 1500*, p. 58; Pollard, p. 212. S.C. 31831.

JOHN MORE

Magdalen 49: Aristotle, Ethics and Politics, in Leonardo Bruni's translation, written by John Goulde on or after 1 February 1471, 245×170 mm, 242 ff.

Stamps: S.G. 3, 6, 11, 13-15.

Quiring: 8s; a–n^8, o^{10}, +^{8}, a–p^8, leaves numbered 1-4 before the quire letter in the first sequence (to the end of k), after it from l to the end; + numbered 1-3[4]; second sequence with arabic figures after letter, in a different hand, although text runs on.

References: *E.O.B.*, no. 5; Coxe, 29.

Notes: The first part ends 'quod Goold' and is dated at the foot of the last leaf as above. A later inscription records the gift of the book by Goulde to Magdalen.

23

University College 110: Duns Scotus, Quaestiones quodlibetales, written by John Goolde, 212×136 mm, 139 ff.
Stamps: S.G. 6, 10–15.
Quiring: 12s; a–l[m]¹², leaves numbered 1–6.
References: *E.O.B.*, no. 3, pl. III; Coxe, 33.

Magdalen 189: Aristotle, Ethics, Economics and Politics, translated by Durandus de Alvernia, and other pieces, s.15, English, 326×225 mm, 177 ff.
Stamps: S.G. 3–6, 11, 13–16.
Quiring: 8s; a–h (ends f. 68); then a–n, leaves numbered 1–4 or i–iiij; the two sequences in different hands, the first perhaps that of the text annotator, but note 'g 4' inserted by second hand, who has also written in some partly erased marks in the first part.
Note: Belonged to Nicholas Good, Fellow of Magdalen College, *c.* 1470, and bought after his death by William Atwater who gave it to the College, 1502/3.
References: *E.O.B.*, no. 4, pl. iv; Coxe, 86–7.

Bodleian, Bodley 141: Albertus Magnus, Parva naturalia, English, *c.* 1440–50, 278×178 mm, 354 ff.
Stamps: S.G. 6–9.
Quiring: 12s; unsigned quire, leaves numbered 1–6, then a–[e], a–z, HH, leaves numbered i–vj after letters.
References: *E.O.B.*, no. 2, pl. 2; S.C. 1911.
Note: Given by the Dean and Canons of Windsor, 1612.

?SUCCESSOR TO JOHN MORE

Bodleian, Auct. D. infra 2.4: Vulgate bible, French, s.13, 263×177 mm, 360 ff.
Stamps: S.G. 18, 55, 73, 77–9.
Quiring: Catchwords erased; 12s, pencil quiring also erased at foot of outer column, in form a–aa i–vj or 1–6, etc.
References: *E.O.B.*, no. 28; S.C. 4089.
Notes: Early signature of T. Lynley; pledged by the monk Bennet in 1482 (*cautio* T. Reve); later at Worcester, whence acquired by Bodley, *c.* 1605–11.

Bodleian, Bodley 95: English sermons for every Sunday in the year, s.15, 220×152 mm, 113 ff.
Stamps: S.G. 68, 79, plus lamb and flag in square (different from S.G. 12).
Quiring: Mainly 12s; ff. 1–60, quires numbered 1–5; ff. 61–4, quaternion numbered 'vj'; ff. 65–100, 8s numbered 7–9 (the odd quaternion may be signed by the scribe; the rest are in the same different hand, very like the figures in University College MS. 110).
References: S.C. 1905.
Notes: Belonged to John Jessye (s.15); 'Robert Walter dwells in Fairford' (*c.* 1530); presented to the Bodleian, *c.* 1630.

QUIRING AND THE BINDER

SALISBURY BINDER

Bodleian, Laud Misc. 558: Quaestiones super Hippocratis aphorismos, written at Salisbury by Herman Zurke of Greifswald, 1459–60, 292×191 mm, 320 ff.
  Stamps: gothic MON/BIEN/MON/DAIN and IHV/MCY/LADI/HELP, the latter in roundels; fleur-de-lis in lozenge in square, paschal lamb (?), three small circles as triangle.
  Quiring: 8s, a–p 1–4 in red ink (only g 1–4 = ff. 48–51 clear); a [1] 6 (?) in blue ink, ff. 120–7; b 1–[6] (e red, f black); f. 169 signed Ω.
  References: S. Gibson *Some Notable Bodleian Bindings* 1901–4, no. 5 and pl. 5; S.C. 1577; Pollard, p. 204.

British Library, Add. 28870: Register of Vallis Scholarium at Salisbury, s.15.
  Stamps: see above.
  Quiring: 8s, signatured 3–23 in centre of first leaf, subsequent leaves signed 2–4 in pencil; quires 1–4 also marked '2 q̄tniʒ'–'5 q̄'tniʒ in foot foredge margin.
  References: Pollard, p. 204.

Merton 268: Isagoge in Johannitium with Quaestiones in Galeni Tegni, written at Salisbury by Herman Zurke, 1458–60, 292×203 mm, 299 ff.
  Stamps: see above.
  Quiring: 8s, a 1–4, etc., in red ink with fine pen at foredge foot corner; occasional black ink marks (e.g. y 1) centred at foot; some pencil signatures, leaf number in centre foot margin, quire letter parallel on foredge.
  References: Coxe, 106; Hobson *E.B.B. 1500*, pl. 34.

JOHN KEMSYN (Canterbury Binder)

Bodleian, Bodley 281: Gulielmus Alvernus, Cur deus homo, and other tracts, written by the Canterbury scribe, Henry Mere, s.15[1], 393×302 mm, 166 ff.
  Stamps: Oldham 209, 211–13, 216, 218, 222, 224–6, 228–9.
  Quiring: 8s, [a]–s 1–4 or i–iiij; all in red ink in the same rough hand, using a fine pen and some anglicana and secretary forms, with old forms of 4 and 5; first visible signature on f 85 (g 3).
  References: Hobson, *E.B.B. 1500*, pp. 15–16, pl. 33; M. B. Parkes, 'A 15th century scribe: Henry Mere', *Bodleian Library Record*, 6 (1957–61), 654–9.
  Notes: From Christ Church Priory, Canterbury; S.C. 2331 given by Abraham, Isaac and Jacob Colfe in 1616.

Bodleian, Bodley 379: Hugh of St. Victor, De sacramentis, English, S. 12, 377×258 mm, 157 ff.
  Stamps: Overall diaper of double fillets, with ring (cf. Oldham 19) in centres.
  Quiring: 12s; 1, I–VI in pencil; 2, ‾ ‾ ≡ ≡ ≣ ≣ in pencil; 3, 1–6 in pencil; 4, 0 00 000 0000 Vo VIo in pencil; 5, I–VI in red ink; 6, a–f in red ink; 7, ‾ – ≡ in red ink; 8, Ī–ō in red ink; 9, I–ṼI in blue ink; 10, a–f in blue ink; 11, I–VI in blue ink; 12, I–VI in pencil (old forms of 4 and 5). From quire 5 onwards, these signatures are

written over a partially erased (and possibly older) sequence a–f iiij, a–f v, etc. (the quire numbers always one behind those given above).

References: S.C. 2434.

Notes: From Christ Church Priory, Canterbury; given by Abraham, Isaac and Jacob Colfe in 1616.

Society of Antiquaries 47: Revelations of Methodius, and other tracts, English (Kent ?). s.15, 230×148 mm, 214 ff.

Stamps: Oldham 209, 210, 212, 216, 225, 226, 229.

Quiring: 8s (with some 6s, 10s and 12s), signed i– in inner margin, 1″ up, outside outer bounding line. In text hand.

References: N. R. Ker, *Medieval Manuscripts in British Libraries*, I (1969), pp. 301–2; *E.B.S.B.*, p. 34.

Notes: Belonged to Canon John Ramsey, O.S.A., prior of Merton 1530–8.

Society of Antiquaries 287: various tracts in English, s.15^2, 226×144 mm, 126 ff.

Stamps: 209, 211–13, 231.

Quiring: 1^{20} 2–11^8, 12^4, 13^{12}, 14^8; 1–12 unsigned; outer pair of 13 unsigned, inner 10 signed ·ȧ· to ·ė· on outer edge, 1″ up from tail edge; 14 signed i–iiij in same position.

References: N. R. Ker, *Medieval Manuscripts in British Libraries*, I (1969), p. 309; *E.B.S.B.*, p. 24.

Notes: Written after 1465 (reference to 'stallacion' of Archbishop Neville in that year); ownership inscription of John Frodsham (s.16).

CRUCIFER BINDER

Bodleian, Selden supra 77: Gulielmus Parronus (of Piacenza), De astrorum succincte vi fatali, Flanders (?) or England. s.15, 174×133 mm, 58 ff.

Stamps: Oldham 256, 258, bough with flowers, lion passant regardant, small crescent of ropework.

Quiring: 6s, presumably a–i i–iij (traces on ff. 23, 24, 36, 46, 47, 48) in ink with thin pen, secretary minuscule forms.

Reference: S.C. 3456.

Notes: the dedication manuscript given to Henry VII, New Year's day 1500; belonged c. 1580–9 to Philip Howard, Earl of Arundel.

Fitzwilliam Museum 375: Hours (Use of Sarum), with London Calendar, s.15 med., 145×100 mm, 248 ff.

Stamps: Oldham 253, 255, 257, 259, 261–4.

Quiring: irregular, mainly 8s and 10s, with much cancellation and substitutions; 1^8 (−8 cut away) unsigned, 2^8 3 signed '× iij', 3^8 unsigned, 4^4 (−4 cut away, bifolium guarded to stub), 4^{10} (−9, 10 cut away) '2 3 4 5' signed in arabic figures in red ink with trace of black mark cut away at foot of 5, 5^1 (inserted leaf), 6^8 1–4 signed '+ i–iiij' as $2, 7^8 unsigned, 8^8 remains of black signatures '3' '4', 9^{10} (−10 cut away) unsigned, 10^8 (+1) unsigned, 11^{10} 3 signed 'f iii' (lower part cut away), 12^{10} trace of

QUIRING AND THE BINDER

'v' on 5, 13^8 (−8 cut away) traces on 3 and 4, 14^6 (−6 cut away) unsigned, 15^{10} signed 'd 1–5' on foredge in black with thin pen, 16^8 (+1 pasted on) 1–4 signed '[i] i–iiij' in centre of leaf, 17^8 signed 'k i–iiij' in centre and 'a i–[iiij]' at foredge, 18^8 (+9 pasted on) signed 'l i–iiij' centre, 19^8 unsigned, 20^8 signed 'd i–iiij' at foredge. 21^8 signed 'e i–iiij' at edge and 'o i–iiij' centre, 22–29^8 ($23 and 26+1) signed 'p–v i–iiij' centre and 'f–n i–iiij' at edge, 30^8 unsigned, 31^8 (−8 cut away) unsigned.

References: E. G. Millar, *English Illuminated Manuscripts of the XIVth and XVth Centuries* (1928), pp. 40–1; *E.B.S.B.*, p. 28 and pl. XXI; F. Wormald and P. M. Giles, 'A Handlist of the Additional Manuscripts in the Fitzwilliam Museum' in *Transactions of the Cambridge Bibliographical Society*, no. 163; Wormald and Giles, *Illuminated Manuscripts in the Fitzwilliam Museum* (1966), no. 74 and pl. 22; Pollard, p. 212.

Notes: On f96 in margin 'per Robertum morrite'; bought by Sir A. Chester Beatty in 1929 and given by him to the Museum in 1936.

BINDER J

Bodleian, Laud Misc 701: L. Bruni, Epistolarum libri novem priores, English, s.15, 220×150 mm, 214 ff.
 Stamps: Oldham 407, quatrefoil with centre and points between petals.
 Quiring: 12s, 1–6Ā, 1–6 a–s, written in a changeable and scribbly hand but in the same ink as the text, changing colour with it.
 Reference: Coxe, 502.
 Note: Pre-Laud ownership inscription of Edmund Jonson.

Bodleian, Douce 246: Primer, English, *ante* 1446, 185×137 mm, 110 ff.
 Stamps: 408, 409; oblong wreath with 3 roses; double-headed eagle.
 Quiring: 8s, some signatures signed i–iiij in black ink, points of i, j in red (and therefore scribal; the same hand has written the black text and the many rubrics).
 References: Pollard, p. 212; S.C. 21820.
 Note: Contains obit of Agnes Orges, 1446.

THOMAS UFFINGTON (Floral Binder)

Corpus Christi, Oxford, 96: Plato, Republic, Timaeus, de legibus, Philosophus, Proclus in Alcibiadem, in Greek (written in Italy?), s.15^2, 350×248 mm, 253 ff.
 Stamps: Oldham 166–9, 177.
 Quiring: 10s, scribal Greek notation of quire and leaf, first leaf of each quire lettered A–Z, ꝗ, ℟, in hasty minuscule.
 Reference: Coxe, 34; *E.B.S.B.*, 22–3.
 Note: Given by John Claimond (*c.* 1468–1537), first President of the College (1517).

Corpus Christi, Oxford, 112–13: Aristotle and Theophrastus, various tracts, in Greek (by the same hand as 96), s.15^2, 350×348 mm, 174 ff. and 233 ff.
 Stamps: Oldham 166–9, 172, 177, 178.

Quiring: as 96; a–T (cap R & T); a–Z, R̷, g.
Reference: Coxe, 39; *E.B.S.B.*, 22–3.
Note: Given by John Claimond

CHRISTOPHER COKE (Fishtail Binder)

Bodleian, Bodley 460: Bartholomeus de Urbino, Memoriale milicie spiritualis, English, s.15^1, 318×220 mm, 134 ff.
Stamps: SG 6, 10 (= Oldham 164), elongated fleur-de-lys in lozenge.
Quiring: 10s, a 1–5 in black ink, b 1–5 in red ink with fine pen, c–n 1–5 in black ink.
Reference: S.C. 2417.
Note: Acquired between 1605 and 1616.

THE GREYHOUND BINDER

Magdalen 58: Peter Lombard, Sententie, English, s.14, 290×210 mm, 154 ff.
Stamps: Oldham 136, 140, 141, 144, 145, and one corresponding to half 141, divided across the short diagonal of the lozenge.
Quiring: 12s, a–p (q has 6 leaves), in red ink, foredge foot. Each leaf in the quire is numbered by repeating the letter, thus a1 = a a2 = aa ... a6 = aaaaaa (q is signed to qqq).
Reference: Coxe, 36.
Notes: Coxe notes that the endpapers are leaves from a canon law treatise De rescriptis et de consuetudinibus by a Bolognese doctor of canon law, perhaps Johannes Andreae or Antonius de Butrio (Italian, s.13).

ANDREW LISLEIE (?)

University College 62, 63: Extracts from Robert Grosseteste, De lingua et corde, English, s.15, with Gilbert de la Porrée, Commentarius in S. Pauli epistolas, English, s.13, 265×190 mm, 197 ff.
Stamp: Saltire in quatrefoil.
Quiring: 12s; first quire 1–6 in ink, second 1 b–6 b in ink, third c 1–6 in pencil partially; sporadically thereafter (f 60 = e 5). No signatures in second work.
References: Coxe, 19; Robert Birley, *The History of Eton College Library*, 1970, pp. 8–9 and also in *The Library*, 5th ser., xi (1957).
Note: Given by Maria Elmhurst in memory of her son, Herbert Elmhurst (matric. 1670, died as undergraduate).

UNKNOWN BINDER 2

Magdalen 71: Richard Rolle, De emendatione peccatoris, etc., English, s.15, 274×203 mm, 135 ff.

QUIRING AND THE BINDER

Stamps: plain ring, 2·2 mm diam. double dotted fillet.

Quiring: 8s; unsigned quire, leaves numbered 1–4 in black ink then a–z^8, n^{12}, i^{10}, k–l^8, leaves numbered i–iiij in black ink; then one unsigned $_2$ gathering, a–d i–iiij in similar hands.

Reference: Coxe, 41.

Note: Given by Arthur Throckmorton, 1626.

UNKNOWN BINDER 3

Bodleian, Tanner 4: St. Augustine, Sermones de verbis domini, and other tracts various hands and dates, English s.13 ex–s.14 med., 275×195 mm, 219 ff.

Stamps: five cinquefoils, with centres, joined with sprays of foliage, in square.

Quiring: 8s (some 12s), first quire numbered iij in red ink on f. 3; some cut away thereafter; a (ii, iii, iiij) in black ink from f. 118, and similarly thereafter (both minuscule and capital forms used for signature letters).

References: S.C. 9824; Coxe, 4–7.

Note: fol. 4; 'Iste liber constat . . . Ricardo Byllyngham ex dono domini W. Seton'. (See A. B. Emden, *Biographical Register of the University of Oxford before 1500*, I.189.)

UNKNOWN BINDER 4

Bodleian, Laud Misc. 602: Richard Hampole (Walter Hilton), The boke maad . . . of an heremyte to an ankeresse, English, written by a scribe called Raynes (f. 74v), s.15 in., 302×210 mm, 75 ff.

Stamps: mermaid in circular wreath (back only).

Quiring: 12s, recent quiring from f. 28 (f. 40 bj, 43 biiij, 44 bv, 67 c (sic) iiij). The original quiring (probably scribal) shows that this MS was part of a larger work; at present it opens with last 3 leaves of original quire 18, and from then on runs 1[–6] fo.q.19 up to 6.fo.q.24.

References; Coxe, 11, S.C. 1499.

Notes: Ownership inscription of R. Hedrington, 1577. The front paste down is part of an old deed relating to the convent of Barking 'anno reg 2do'.

UNKNOWN BINDER 5

Bodleian, Laud Misc 12: Nicolas de Lyra, Expositio decem praeceptorum, and other tracts, English, s.15, 154×105 mm, 126 ff.

Stamps: 8-petalled flower with large 9-point centre in square, trefoils in corners; small wyvern; dragon (?) in narrow oblong; 2-headed spread eagle (note straight vertical pinions): fleur-de-lys in lozenge in square, two leaves conjoined in corners.

Quiring: 8s, a–p i–iiij in black ink in neat thin spiky hand with several identifiable letters (cf. f. 52), quite different from text.

Reference: Coxe, 60–1.

UNKNOWN BINDER 6

University College 123: Bonaventura, The mirrour of the blessid lyf of Jhesu Crist, and other tracts, s.15, 208×145 mm, 77 ff.
Stamps: S.S.L.B. 97, 100 (= E.B.S.B. 569), 307.
Quiring: 10s, a–g i–iiiij, almost certainly by scribe.
References: Coxe 36–7; compare Oldham, S.S.L.B., pp. 36, 116, pls L and LXI for another book by the same binder (Shrewsbury School A.X. 13, c. 1520).
Notes: Given by William Rogers (matriculated 1663).

JOHN REYNES

Huntington Library 36336: Adam of Eynsham, Magna Vita Sancti Hugonis English, c. 1500, 274×203 mm, 99 ff.
Stamps: Oldham 433, 969 (with both half-pieces).
Quiring: 8s, signed a–m i–iiij by the text hand; these marks partially erased and the first four leaves of each quire marked 'a, b, c, d' with a fine pen in black ink at the foredge, lining with the foot of the text.
References: Sotheby's Catalogue of Western Miniatures and Manuscripts, 6 December 1971, lot 15 (Maggs); N. Barker in the *Book Collector* XXI.3 (1972), p. 369.

NOTES

1. 'A Register of Writs and the Scales Binder', part II, *The Book Collector*, XXI (1972), no. 3, pp. 368–9.
2. *The Library*, 5th series, XXV (1970), no. 3, pp. 193–218.
3. In particular, Strickland Gibson's *Early Oxford Bindings*, 1903 (hereafter *E.O.B.*); Hobson's *English Binding before 1500*, 1929 (*E.B.B. 1500*); and Oldham's *English Blind-Stamped Bindings*, 1952 (*E.B.S.B.*).
4. *E.B.S.B.*, p. 38.
5. 'A Register of Writs,' p. 361.
6. *Duke Humfrey and English Humanism in the Fifteenth Century*, cotologue of an exhibition held in the Bodleian Library, Oxford, 1970, pp. 32–5.
7. R. A. B. Mynors, 'A fifteenth-century scribe, T. Werken' in *Transactions of the Cambridge Bibliographical Society*, I (1949–53), pp. 97–104.
8. Dr. Hunt has pointed out to me the oddness of the ruling, a single bounding line for vertical and horizontal lines although the text is laid out in two columns.
9. *E.B.B. 1500*, Appendix G, p. 48.
10. This binding (on which three tools are employed, Oldham 407 and 408 and a narrow oblong tool with a stylised thistle) has recently been substantially repaired, and the contents reinserted upside down. It was probably in a poor way when found: a note on the front endleaf, probably by the antiquary John Brand (1744–1806),

reads 'B^t of Mr Waight who told me he bought it at a sale by Sheriffs distress in the Borough'. It is possible that the contents are not original, since the accounts seem to begin in 1518; but the vellum leaves must belong to the paper text, since the lower part of the foredge is pricked through.

11. Three continental examples may be noted. MS. Bodley 478 is a Dutch manuscript of St. Ambrose, s.14 ex., in a later binding with a characteristically Flemish diaper work binding, punctuated with open-work flower stamps (it was liberated from Doesborch by John Gibson and passed on to Thomas James before 1602); it is in 12s, with the fourth leaf signed a 4, b 4, etc. A north French binder bound Bodleian MS. Selden supra 70, an early fourteenth-century customary of Normandy, which is quired with a succession of horizontal bars, like Bodley 379, the exotically-quired manuscript bound by John Kemsyn.

12. Pollard, p. 210.

ANTHONY HOBSON

The *iter italicum* of Jean Matal[1]

A large part of the great Spanish scholar Antonio Agustín's fame rests on his work in restoring the text of Justinian's *Pandects* and *Codex*. Soon after obtaining his doctorate in civil and canon law at Bologna University at the age of twenty-four, he travelled to Florence to study the famous sixth-century codex of the *Pandects*. The manuscript was jealously guarded as a national treasure in the Palazzo Vecchio; for his edition published in Nuremberg in 1529 its previous editor, Gregor Haloander, had preferred to work from a transcript of Poliziano's collation of the manuscript by Luigi Bolognini in the library of S. Domenico in Bologna.[2] Through the generosity of Lelio Torelli, the distinguished jurist and Chancellor of the Duchy of Florence who was himself planning a new edition, Agustín was granted access to the original. He collated the Florentine manuscript during the early months of 1542 in company with his fellow-student from Bologna and *fidus Achates*, Jean Matal (Johannes Metellus). His proposed emendations and opinions on the text were published in Venice in 1543 and won him immediate recognition.[3]

From the *Pandects* Agustín turned his attention to the *Codex* and the *Novellae*. In a long letter of 1 August 1544[4] from Bologna to the Imperial Ambassador to the Venetian Republic, Diego Hurtado de Mendoza, his host in Venice a year earlier and the owner of a famous collection of Greek manuscripts, he explained his plans for future research. He had two projects in mind. The primary one was to recover the missing *Novellae Constitutiones* that were unknown in the West; he had already examined one manuscript in the Marciana Library in Venice and compared it with another which Lelio Torelli had arranged for him to be sent from Florence; and he had used two manuscripts of the Latin *Epitome* of Julianus, one obtained through Hurtado de Mendoza, the other a present from Jean Matal who had acquired it

[1] Notes begin on page 60.

from their former tutor at Bologna, the celebrated jurist Andrea Alciati.[5] He hoped to be assisted in his task by the *Basilica*, which he had not yet seen but knew of through Viglius van Zwichem's observations in his edition of the *Institutes* of Theophilus (Basle: H. Froben and N. Episcopius, 1534). He believed that a manuscript of them existed in Rome.[6] Secondly, he had already started a work on ecclesiastical law but could not complete it until he had time to work in the Vatican Library.

Eighteen months later, on 1 February 1546, he wrote from Rome to Lelio Torelli to announce a notable series of discoveries.[7] 'You will not only receive [a copy of] the constitutions that Metellus found in your Medici Library among the Greek books of ecclesiastical law, but others too which here in the Vatican and in other libraries we observed were lacking in Justinian's *Codex*. . . . Many passages of the *Digest* and of Haloander's edition of the Greek *Novellae* have been restored to their pristine splendour. The same Haloander carefully noted in the titles of many constitutions where the text of the Greek law was defective. Stimulated by these challenges I began by my own efforts and with the help of friends to search in the libraries of Greek books for the roving wild animals we were tracking, in case they were lying hidden somewhere among the Greek commentators on civil law, which I had learned were very numerous. . . .' And after relating some details of the quest he claimed that 'all the laws concerning sacred matters which Justinian collected in the first book of the *Codex* and the first book of the *Novellae* are [now] contained in one volume . . .' Unfortunately he delayed publishing the results of his researches for twenty-one years. By then most of them had been anticipated.

The events of these three years of exploration are illuminated by a manuscript in Cambridge University Library (Add. 565), which contains Matal's notes on the contents of the libraries he visited between late 1542 or early 1543 and 1546, with more detailed records of particular manuscripts. The volume consists of thirty-five separate sections, now bound together but written at different times, in different places and generally on different paper, and varying in length from a bifolium, only the first leaf of which has been used, to a substantial work of fourteen signed gatherings totalling eighty leaves. All are in Matal's humanistic cursive hand with two exceptions, but the writing varies from a hasty scrawl to a formal calligraphy.[8] The volume gives a fascinating glimpse of the many public libraries accessible to scholars, especially in Florence and Rome, and of some private collections. The object of this essay is to place it in the context of Matal's and Agustín's lives and to give enough description of the contents for historians of libraries to judge which may be of interest to them. I am not qualified to comment on the manuscript's value, if any, to historians of Byzantine law.

The contents serve to identify some of the friends who helped Agustín in his search. It can no longer be claimed that it was Agustín who 'examined everything in Florence, Venice and Rome in his hunt for manuscripts'.[9] The main burden of the quest, it is now clear, fell on Jean Matal. Matal, a slightly younger contemporary of Agustín's in the law school at Bologna, was a native of Franche Comté, born in Poligny (Jura), and so, like the Spanish scholar, a subject of Charles V. He still enjoys a modest degree of fame, both for his finds in Florentine libraries and for his epigraphic collections.

Another helper was Juan de Arce, doctor of theology and Canon of Palencia Cathedral. Born in 1510, he studied in Alcalá de Henares and Paris, acquiring a reputation for unusual intelligence and learning. In 1545 he was in Rome and compiled lists of manuscripts in the Vatican Library. By the following year he was back in Spain, but paid a second visit to Italy in 1551–2 as one of the Spanish delegates to the Council of Trent before returning home for good. Residence in Palencia brought on a severe attack of depression. He wrote to Agustín lamenting his 'unhappy exile' from the intellectual life of Rome; his only solace was corresponding with him and with Francisco Torres about art, literature and scholarship. He died in Palencia in 1564 and was buried in the chapel of S. Gregorio in the cathedral, which had been sumptuously decorated and handsomely endowed at his expense. His 'large and curious' library of 2000 works was bequeathed to the Chapter, but had already been dispersed by 1680.[10]

The third associate named in the volume was the celebrated Greek scholar, Francisco Torres (Turrianus). A native of the diocese of Palencia, like Juan de Arce, he spent his entire working life in Italy, for many years in the household of Cardinal Giovanni Salviati, though he probably lodged for a time with Agustín after his patron's death in 1553. In later life he joined the Society of Jesus and bequeathed his collection of Greek manuscripts to the Jesuit Collegio Romano. He was the author of numerous polemical works on the questions at issue between Catholics and Protestants.[11]

After spending the first months of 1542 together collating the Florentine *Pandects*, Agustín and Matal separated, the former returning to Bologna while the latter proceeded to Padua to continue his study of Greek. Before the end of this year, or early in 1543 he paid his first visit to Venice, where the most considerable private library was that of Agustín's host, Diego Hurtado de Mendoza. The latter's collection seems then to have been divided into four categories, each separately numbered in Arabic numerals: Greek manuscripts, Greek printed books, printed books in Latin and modern languages, and Arabic manuscripts.[12] Matal's notes include a list of all the Greek manuscripts, which are numbered from 1 to 259. This was no doubt the numeration given by Hurtado de Mendoza's Flemish librarian, Arnoldus Arlenius, and evidently corresponded to the shelf order, as it agrees with the numbers surviving on the spines of some volumes.[13] The collection at the time of Matal's list had thus more than doubled from the 102 titles listed by an anonymous scholar a few years earlier.[14]

Selections follow of twenty-three of the Greek printed books, 'corrected and collated with ancient manuscripts', and of eleven works on civil or canon law from the Latin and vernacular printed books. Each has a pressmark consisting of an Arabic number preceded by a sign: 'g' or ⲅ for the Greek books, a cross above a circle for the Latin ones.[15] The Arabic manuscripts were not fully arranged or catalogued. Matal listed eighty-three, remarked that the titles of many had not been set down, and added a second list of seventy, ending with a record of their provenance, 'All these Arabic books, and the ones immediately preceding, were bought in Venice by Jacobus Mendoza. It is said also that at the capture of Tunis in 1536 he bought as many as he could, up to 2000 volumes, and sent them to Granada; but I have not seen the catalogue of them'—a greatly exaggerated report, as Mendoza's Arabic manuscripts numbered only 268 when they reached the Escorial in 1576.[16]

Matal seems to have had difficulty in gaining access to the books themselves.[17] He evidently compiled the lists some years later from Arlenius's catalogue, which Conrad Gesner was shown in 1543.[18] In Florence in 1544 or 1545 Matal wrote down a list of printed books which Arlenius had annotated with variant readings:

Arnoldus Arlenius haec correxit:
    Catullum, ex libro Pontani[19]
    Gazae gram[m]aticam, ex codice Guarini Veronensis[20] et Jul. Caesarem, ex codice dominicano Bononiensi.[21]
    Plutarchi moralia, ex codice Martiani Rotae;[22] Polybium[23] etc. aliquod
    Aristotelem, ex libris Mendozianis[24]

Habet ipse non edita: Polybii fragmenta multa, Greg[orii] Naz[ianzeni] or[ati]o[n]es xvi. et alia satis multa.[25]

Matal's Venetian notes include four much shorter lists: twelve Greek legal manuscripts from Bessarion's legacy to the Marciana[26] (f. 63b, lower half); short titles of sixty-seven works in the same library, a copy of a selection listed by Francisco Torres in 1543 (ff. 333-4); a selection of manuscripts in the Greek Library of the Vatican, taken from a lost index that belonged to Hurtado de Mendoza[27] (ff. 76-82); and a brief record of works by the Patriarch Photius and other Greek authors extant in Mendoza's collection, jotted down when he was in Florence (f. 176b).

Matal spent the winter in Padua except for a brief visit to Venice at the beginning of February 1543. From there he wrote to Agustín on 6 February, as he was about to set off on the return journey to Padua, offering to come back at any time to make transcripts of any Greek legal manuscripts that his friend would not himself have leisure for. The same letter reported that Arlenius had undertaken to collate Mendoza's manuscript of the *Novellae* with one in the Marciana, provided that he did not have to accompany the ambassador on a journey to see Cardinal Granvelle. Matal had taken an opportunity of urging the Greek scholar and scribe, Nicolas Sophianos, whom Mendoza had sent to Mount Athos in search of unpublished manuscripts, to make particular enquiries for copies of the Byzantine jurists and of Justinian's *Codex* and *Pandects*.[28]

A letter of 12 April from Padua to Agustín conveyed his ardent desire to be allowed to collaborate in Lelio Torelli's edition of the *Pandects*. He hoped that Froben would be chosen as the printer, as he had great authority in publishing ancient books of all kinds, and his type-faces were more elegant and less tiring to the eye than those of Robert Estienne. Matal was willing to come to Florence to receive Torelli's instructions and then to remain in Basle as corrector until printing was completed. He was still anxious to help, even if Torelli insisted on employing Robert Estienne. As for Agustín's book, he would send it, if the author approved, to be printed by his close friend, Gabriel Giolito, who owned beautiful founts of type, and he was willing to see it through the press himself. Nevertheless his advice was to publish it as part of Torelli's edition of the *Pandects*.[29]

Shortly after the date of this letter Matal fell victim to an illness lasting six months.[30] He was prevented from meeting Agustín in

Venice to help him correct the proofs of his book, which appeared there on 13 September from the press, not of Gabriel Giolito, but of Lucantonio Giunta's heirs.[31]

Proof-correcting occupied only part of Agustín's time in Venice, which was chiefly devoted to research. Mendoza arranged for the Marciana to place Bessarion's manuscript of the *Novellae* at his guest's disposal. With the help of Arlenius and 'another Greek bookseller' (perhaps Anthony the Eparch) he collated it in the ambassador's palace against Haloander's edition (Nuremberg, 1531) and arranged for a transcript to be made of the constitutions lacking in the printed book.[32] At the end of the summer Matal was startled to learn the extent of his friend's activities and wrote with evident surprise from Padua on 21 September: 'When you say that you have had all the Constitutions transcribed, both pontifical and royal, as well as the part Eusebius published of the laws of Constantine, and that you are going to collate all these with the printed texts, I hardly understand which ones you mean. So please inform me of the contents of every single book . . .'.[33]

It was probably during the early part of his stay in Padua that Matal visited Pietro Bembo's library. His notes occupy thirteen pages.[34] Most of the titles are of printed books, which are recorded in unusually full detail, with printers' names as well as places and dates of publication.[35] But the famous antique Virgil and Terence[36] were noticed, together with other Latin and Greek manuscripts, two Chaldean—both untitled—and a few Italian. The notes are arranged under five headings: 'Editi' (i.e. printed), a category that contains, illogically, six Latin manuscripts; 'Hebraei', including a copy of the five-volume Complutensian Polyglot Bible; books with manuscript annotations by Bembo or others (14 titles); 'Manuscripti'; and 'Volgari', all but one in Italian, the exception being in Spanish.[37] Matal recorded that he saw the Terence and the annotated books; but he probably copied many of the other titles from a catalogue, as the bindings are described in the terms characteristic of Italian inventories.[38]

In November Matal went to join Andrea Alciati in Ferrara, where he stayed until the following February. Scraps of news or gossip reached him, to be relayed in letters to Agustín. He heard that Lelio Torelli intended to entrust his edition of the *Pandects* to be printed in Rome by Francesco Priscianese, the Tuscan humanist who had recently acquired a press. Alciati had shown him an ancient manuscript of Justinian's *Novellae* written in a pre-gothic hand ('manu langobardica'); unfortunately it lacked some leaves, or more probably gatherings, at the end. The presentation copy to Alciati of Agustín's book arrived on 20 December. Francisco Torres passed through Ferrara at the beginning of February and sent greetings.[39]

Matal left Ferrara in February 1544.[40] By the first week in August he had made one stay in Florence, discovered a new and, he thought, more correct manuscript of the *Institutes* of Theophilus in the Medici Library,[41] toured western Tuscany, and was back in Florence preparing to join Agustín in Bologna. Before he could set out a letter reached him from the latter with the news that Pope Paul III had appointed him an Auditor of the Rota. The appointment entailed a complete change in his plans as his duties would not leave him time to continue the search for the missing constitutions. Accordingly he wrote to invite Matal to become his secretary with the principal task of pursuing the quest. In January 1545 the two friends again visited Florence. This time, when the Spaniard returned to Rome, the Franc-Comtois remained behind to carry out a thorough reconnaissance of Florentine libraries.[42]

The next two months were active ones. Matal visited twelve public collections in Florence and Fiesole and at least one private one, and noted some of the holdings of each. They were as follows:

The Badia (ff. 174, 185, 185b). Short titles noted of 123 Greek manuscripts or printed books (with slightly fuller notes of a few 'libri selectiores') and five Latin manuscripts.[43]

San Marco (ff. 176, 178–84b, 186–7b, 188, 191b–192b). The titles of about 240 Greek manuscripts and of about 160 Latin manuscripts and printed books are given. Three manuscripts in the hand of Niccolo Niccoli were pointed out to him, also a Cicero, *Epistolae ad familiares*, believed to be in Petrarch's hand,[44] and two printed books annotated by Poliziano.[45] Desk numbers are given.

Santa Maria Novella (ff. 177b, 188b–189). Forty-two manuscripts, all Latin, and one printed book (Gilbertus de Hoilandia, *Sermones super cantica canticorum*, Florence: Nicolaus Laurenti, Alamanus, 1485[46]).

Santa Maria della Annunziata (f. 189b). About forty titles are given, with desk numbers (the highest is 'XIV') 'ad dextram' and 'ad sinistram', showing that it was a chained library of the usual Florentine kind. Towards the end of the Florentine section (f. 196) Matal has noted a manuscript of Chrysostom's *De Poenitentia* 'in Florence, but in which library I don't remember, unless perhaps that of the Servite Fathers', i.e. the Annunziata.[47]

San Gallo (ff. 191–3*b*).⁴⁸ About sixty-six manuscripts; no pressmarks.
Santo Spirito (f. 193*b*).⁴⁹ Thirty-seven manuscripts; no pressmarks.
Santa Maria del Carmine (f. 194). Eight manuscripts only noted, without pressmarks but with the indication 'ad dextram' or 'ad sinistram'.⁵⁰
Santa Croce⁵¹ (ff. 194–6). Titles of upwards of a hundred manuscripts are given, with desk numbers.

Matal inspected two works in the church of San Domenico on the way to Fiesole. In Fiesole itself he recorded over fifty titles in the library given by Cosimo 'pater patriae' to the Badia and thirteen in the Hieronymite convent (ff. 190–1). He also inspected the collection of a German doctor in Florence, Johannes de Rubeis (Roth?), and noted the titles of nine Greek manuscripts (f. 174*b*).

For Matal's purpose the most important collection in Florence was the Medici library in San Lorenzo. He listed sixty-seven of its Greek manuscripts (noting in particular the Homer copied by Theodore Gaza and with his interlinear gloss, from which he believed that Francesco Filelfo had intended to prepare a Latin translation for Nicholas V[52]) and five of its most famous Latin codices (ff. 175–175*b*, 176*b*, 177–177*b*). These were the uncial Orosius,[53] which resembled the Pisan Pandects, he observed, in having no divisions between words or sentences, the eleventh-century Tacitus[54] and *Letters* of the younger Pliny,[55] 'both in very ancient letters, mixed with a few Lombard letters' (i.e. caroline minuscule), the ninth-century Cicero, *Epistolae ad Familiares*,[56] 'in the same characters as' the Pliny, and the tenth-century Celsus,[57] which he was told about but did not see.

Matal's discoveries in the Laurenziana were the crown of his Florentine researches. His catalogue of sixteen of its Greek juridical manuscripts[58] (ff. 198–203) is written in his most formal hand[59] and dated at the end of his stay in the city, 'Flor[entiae] M.D.XLV M[ense] Martio'. Detailed notes of the contents of fifteen of them follow.[58] The latter occupy 160 pages and represent a major labour of investigation, as Matal not only recorded what he saw. He tells us (f. 224) that he collated one manuscript with the 'Basiliense', in other words with Viglius van Zwichem's edition of the *Institutes* of Theophilus, besides comparing others with the Paris edition of the four general Church Councils (*Conciliorum quatuor generalium tomi duo*, Paris: F. Regnault, 1535) and with Haloander's edition of the *Novellae Constitutiones*, for which he used the second, amended, edition printed at Basle by Herwagen in

1541. Agustín's letter to Torelli implies that in addition he may have transcribed at least parts of one or more manuscripts.[60]

Matal was the first savant to use the Laurenziana's Greek legal texts, and he prefixed summaries of contents to eight volumes. In the course of time the greater fame of the scholar for whom his researches were carried out eclipsed the memory of his work. His visit was forgotten and the summaries were ascribed to the hand of Antonio Agustín.[61] Matal's notes are of value for their glosses, added in Rome and giving the ownership of other copies of the same texts, for their descriptions of original bindings that fell victim to the wholesale rebinding in uniform morocco thirty years later, and for two records of provenance, the evidence for which disappeared when the old covers were removed. Theodore Gaza's note of ownership survives in Constantine Harmenopulos's legal manual,[62] but Matal's is the only record that two copies of the *Institutes* of Theophilus used to contain Poliziano's name.[63]

Little is known about the Laurenziana at the time of Matal's visit. Michelangelo's and Ammanati's great library-room had not yet been completed, but part at least of the holdings was available to scholars, and Conrad Gesner was another northern *Gelehrter* who consulted the collection when preparing his *Bibliotheca Universalis* (Zürich 1545). Matal's notes provide evidence that the books had pressmarks, apparently in the form of a continuous numeration—the highest figure he cites is '774', but he only quotes them for five or six manuscripts. The library was already in the care of its first *Custos*, Pier Francesco Giambullari, Canon of S. Lorenzo (1495-1555).[64] Son of the vernacular poet, Bernardo Giambullari, he was a learned man, expert in Greek and Latin and with some knowledge of Hebrew and Aramaic, and author of the earliest Florentine grammar and of a popular history of Europe. We learn from Matal that the titles of at least some of the manuscripts had been supplied in his hand, and it is evident that he was responsible for the first organisation of the library. Baccio Bandini, the Grand-Duke's doctor who succeeded as 'Custos' after his death, seems to have been at pains to deny his predecessor any credit for his pioneer work.

Some incidental scraps of book news found their way into the notes. Piero Vettori, whom Matal must have met with Agustín on his first visit to Florence, owned 'a very ancient Terence',[65] another Terence corrected by Poliziano from Pietro Bembo's manuscript,[66] a 'very ancient Aristotle'[67] and much else (f. 174b). The Duke's tutor, who is given his Christian names only, 'Petrus Franciscus', had a 'very ancient Homer' and other texts (ff. 174, 174b).[68] Giannozzo Manetti's heir had a collection of Greek and Latin manuscripts and ancient codices,[69] and Francesco Campana[70] owned a fair number of manuscripts (f. 174). Antonio Lapini[71] used to be the owner of a manuscript containing a great number of commentators on Aristotle[72] (f. 177*b*). A very ancient Greek New Testament[73] was kept with the Pisan Pandects in the Palazzo Vecchio, and used at one time to be shown to the public by the light of candles, like a holy relic (f. 174*b*).

One of the gatherings that record Florentine holdings contains a few lines written upside down in an odd mixture of Latin and French (f. 174). All the places mentioned lie between Bourges and Dole, and the information no doubt came from Charles de Lamoignon, of Nevers, who is named as the owner of a manuscript of the *Codex Theodosianus* with many scholia. He was the first of that celebrated family of magistrates to adopt the legal profession. Matal had known him in Padua and had sent him with a letter of introduction to Agustín.[74] The notes record that another copy of the *Codex* of Theodosius was in Dole, that in the fifth chapel (presumably of the cathedral) of Bourges there was a volume containing both Justinian's *Digest* and *Codex*, and that the *Pandects* in one volume were privately owned in the same city.[75]

In the spring or early summer of 1545 Matal left Florence for Rome to continue his researches in the third of the great Italian repositories of Greek manuscripts, Agustín, who had investigated the Marciana himself, having confided to him the exploration of the Laurenziana and the Vatican. The last-named then contained four libraries, two public and two 'secret'. The former, Matal informs us (f. 83), were open for two hours daily or during the whole time that the college of cardinals was in session. Access to the latter was presumably by special permit. The largest of the four was the Bibliotheca Latina, with sixteen desks. It was divided by a line of columns, and gave the impression, Matal remarks (f. 89), of being two rooms. One wall was decorated with a portrait of Sixtus IV, with a six-line verse by Platina below.[76] The other public library was the Bibliotheca Graeca, with eight desks. Matal calls the two reserve collections the Secreta Major, with twelve desks, containing only Latin manuscripts, and the Parva Secreta, with three Latin (numbered I–III) and three Greek desks (IV–VI), as well as cupboards ('armaria') and small chests ('capsulae').

By 1 September 1545 Matal had completed a catalogue of the Bibliotheca Graeca. Written in his formal hand and occupying pride of place at the beginning of the volume, it is the only list to bear his name. The colophon reads, 'Romae, in Vaticana bibliotheca [ego ipse (*erased*)] ex ipsis libris, hunc indicem Metellus confeci, Cal. Septemb. M.D.XLV'. Four hundred and eighty manuscripts are listed on the upper and lower shelves ('ordine superiore' and 'inferiore') of eight desks. The descriptions are unusually full and include pressmark, author, title and details of material, format, script, age and whether or not the text was a correct one. The Vatican owns an incomplete contemporary transcript which breaks off in Pluteus IV and omits the Greek words.[77]

Matal started to catalogue the Greek desks of the Parva Secreta, but reached only the middle of the centre shelf of Pluteus V. Here the catalogue ends with a note that he had got so far by 1 September 1545; there still remained to be listed half the manuscripts of the centre shelf, and all those on the lower one, as well as those on Pluteus VI[78] and in the cupboards and chests (ff. 49–60b). Lack of time and a summons from Agustín prevented him from completing his index. Instead he later copied much briefer notes of the principal manuscripts only in the rest of the Parva Secreta (ff. 69b–70b, 64, 66b, 67), and in the Secreta Major (ff. 68–9) from lists compiled by Juan de Arce. He also recorded titles obtained from three indices: seventeen legal manuscripts, extracted from Girolamo Aleandro's index of the Library's Greek holdings (f. 63);[79] the contents of the second *armarium* in the Parva Secreta, taken from an index by Agostino Steuco (ff. 99–101);[80] and the 'principal Latin authors' in the Bibliotheca Latina and the two 'secret' libraries, copied from an index compiled by Juan de Arce in 1545 (ff. 83–97).

The volume contains records of ten other libraries in Rome, as follows:

San Marcello (ff. 103–4).[81] There are brief notes in a hurried hand of some titles in this library which contained two rows each of not less than twelve desks or shelves.

Santa Maria del Popolo (ff. 105–6).[82] Notes of a few titles with desk numbers, to right and left, which run as high as XXVIII.

Santa Maria sopra Minerva (ff. 105–7).[83] A few books are noted, with desk numbers up to XXVII, 'ad dextram', 'ad sinistram'.

Santa Maria della Pace (ff. 109–10). Four titles only noted.

Santa Maria in Ara Coeli (ff. 162b–163b).[84] Titles are given of fifty-seven manuscripts with pressmarks in various forms: 'Scamno VII F', 'Bancho C [to P]' or a roman numeral (I to XV) followed by the letter 'a' or 'b', the last evidently denoting a line of desks or wall-cases each with two shelves.

Sant' Agostino (ff. 97b, 164-5). There are separate notes, evidently made at different times, of the library and books in the sacristy. The library was on two rows each of six desks; one desk held a collection of Hebrew manuscripts and printed books, presented by Leo X but little used. 'All of them lie there neglected', Matal observed. The sacristy contained books given by Egidio Canisio, Cardinal of Viterdo.[85] Matal has noted eleven Latin manuscripts, one of which—the decrees of the Council of Basle—had belonged to the Cardinal of Rouen,[86] and three printed books.[87]

In addition to these six public libraries four private ones are mentioned:

Cardinal Giovanni Salviati (ff. 133-4). An alphabetical list, dated 1546, of about 170 Greek and Latin manuscripts and three works in Spanish, two of the latter probably printed.[88] Elsewhere Matal has remarked that the collection of Greek ecclesiastical laws the Cardinal owned was to be distinguished from a different collection extant in a manuscript brought back from Crete by Carlo Cappello, the island's Venetian governor (f. 61b);[89] and that his copy of Theodorus Hermopolites's commentary on the first ten books of the *Basilica* had been a present from Hermodorus [Listarchus], the Greek reader (ἀναγνώστης) in his household (f. 267b).[90] Although the list appears to be copied from an inventory, Matal evidently knew the books, as he sometimes makes comparisons between them and texts in other libraries. Many manuscripts from the collection were acquired by the Vatican in 1821.[91]

Cardinal Niccolò Ridolfi (ff. 121-32b). About 460 manuscripts are listed (not in Matal's hand) under different headings: Greek philosophy, medicine, grammar, poetry, rhetoric and other prose, mathematics and tactics, theology, law, and various; Latin, and *Volgari*.[92]

Basilio Zanchi of Bergamo (ff. 156-8b). He was a man of vast culture, a friend of Agustín's, *Custos* of the Vatican Library from 1550 and author of several works of classical philology and biblical exegesis. His *In omnes divinos libros notationes* (Rome: Antonio Blado, 1553) was dedicated to Agustín. He was arrested by order of Paul IV in 1558 and died soon afterwards in Castel Sant' Angelo. Cardinal Alfonso Carafa was believed to have acquired his library.[93] The list gives only the authors' names (or titles, e.g. 'Homiliarum', in the case of miscellanies or anonyma) of 157 printed books.

Jacob Apozeller (Apocellus), a German notary living in Rome from 1515 to 1550 (f. 162).[94] Ten Greek manuscripts can now be added to the single one he was previously recorded to have owned, among them Eusebius, *De preparatione evangelica*, in the hand of Michael Apostolis, which earlier had belonged to Janus Parrhasius and Antonio Seripandi and later formed part of Fulvio Orsini's library.[95] The books are described as 'Romae in banchis'. No doubt the collector lived in the *banchi*, presumably the Via dei Nuovi Banchi, near the German church of Santa Maria dell'Anima.

One other list (ff. 331-2) probably dates from the same period. It is of seventy-one Greek manuscripts which the City Council of Augsburg had bought in Venice 'at great expense'.[96] Matal comments, 'All these Greek books are manuscripts, and quite old, but really most of them are wormeaten and useless'. He derived his information from a letter of 1544—and therefore a year or more old when he saw it—from the Augsburg reformer Wolfgang Musculus (1497-1563) to the Greek and Hebrew scholar, Andreas Masius (1513-73). Masius was secretary to Johann von Weze, Bishop of Constance, but spent much time in Rome where he was well acquainted with the circle round Agustín.[97] At the end of the list Matal has noted that a manuscript of Chrysostom's commentaries on the psalms was at Cesena in the Romagna.[98]

Matal's long and numerous notes on Greek juristic manuscripts, principally in the Laurenziana and the Vatican, and his list of maps and of printed commentators on Aristotle fall outside the scope of this account. It remains only to notice some fragments of information about Spanish collections. To his list of manuscripts in the Bibliotheca Secreta Major of the Vatican Matal has appended two notes (f. 69): 'Agustín told me that he [had seen] a complete *Decretals* in the possession of some private owner at Salamanca. . . . Perhaps they had been stolen from the Vatican Library when Rome was captured by [the Constable de] Bourbon. But he has no idea where they are now, as their owner is dead.' The source of the second piece of information was probably again Agustín: 'The Emperor's chaplain, Juan de Rojas, has many Greek and Latin manuscripts'.[99]

Letters written in 1546 by Juan de Arce to Agustín provided other news (f. 170). A friend of the writer, a certain Hernan Díaz de Pastrana who was living in the Collège des Lombards in the University of Paris, had compiled an index of 'all printed books' and of some manuscripts.[100] The library of Cardinal Don Pedro González in Valladolid was rich in manuscripts collected from various places in Italy.[101] Finally Juan de Arce supplied a list of sixteen manuscripts owned by the Chapter of his own cathedral of Palencia. They are mostly legal, but include a copy of Bede's *Historia ecclesiastica Angliae* in two volumes.[102]

Apart from lists of Mendoza's library and of the books mentioned in Photius's *Bibliotheca*, the latest contents of the volume belong to 1546. A list of titles of the sixty books of the *Basilica* has a Greek colophon (f. 321) giving the date and place of completion as 'Rome, May 1546'. Notes on a manuscript belonging to Pietro Donato Cesi describe him as Bishop of Narni, a see to which he was elected in June 1546. Juan de Arce's letters, from which Matal extracted the literary information, are dated in the same year. By this time Agustín evidently considered that the quest for the missing constitutions had been successfully concluded. As early as February 1546 he had informed Torelli, 'All the laws concerning sacred matters which Justinian collected in the first book of the *Codex* and the first of the *Novellae*, are [now] contained in one volume'.[103] Matal gave up the search for manuscripts and devoted himself instead to assembling Roman inscriptions, a task in which he was helped and encouraged by his patron. His epigraphic collections were principally formed in the years 1546-51, partly from his own observations, partly with the help of friends and correspondents, who included Lelio Torelli, the engraver and map-publisher Antonio Lafreri, the architect Pirro Ligorio, and naturally Agustín. They fill five volumes in the Vatican Library,[104] which also possesses a copy of the *Epigrammata antiquae Urbis* (Rome: J. Mazochius, 1521), with marginal notes by both Matal and Agustín.[105]

The two savants remained together in Rome until 1555. These were no doubt happy years. Agustín's international reputation for learning made his establishment a natural focus for humanist scholars, both Italian and foreign: one of them being the young Fulvio Orsini, with whom he subsequently collaborated in two books. But Matal too enjoyed his share of recognition. Benedetto Egio of Spoleto's *editio princeps* of the *Bibliotheca* of Apollodorus (Rome: A. Blado, 1555) was dedicated to him,[106] and Pierre Gilles, the French traveller, gave him a manuscript of his *Elephanti tam terrestris quam marini... recens descriptio*.[107]

The later history of the friendship makes melancholy reading. In 1555 Agustín was sent as Papal Nuncio to Philip and Mary in England. Matal accompanied him, but in England their ways separated. Agustín returned to Spain to become Bishop, first of Alife, later of Lérida, and finally Archbishop of Tarragona. He died in 1586. His Greek manuscripts were acquired by Philip II for the Escorial.[108] Matal evidently intended to return to Rome as he left his books there, the Cambridge manuscript among them.[109] But something occurred to change his plans and he remained in Northern Europe, settling in Cologne as a pensioner both of the Emperor and of the Archbishop of Salzburg. In his later years he exchanged numerous letters with other savants which reveal an increasing preoccupation with contemporary politics. He died at Cologne in June 1598.[110] A world atlas edited by him was first published as late as 1600–02 (*Speculum orbis terrarum*, Cologne).

The two friends may have corresponded again when Agustín was attending the Council of Trent in 1561–3. But a coldness had arisen between them. When dedicating the 1574 Cologne edition of the account of Manuel I's reign by their Portuguese fellow-student at Bologna, Jeronimo Osorio da Fonseca, Bishop of Silves,[111] to his former patron, Matal observed that he had heard nothing from him for ten years. The reason is perhaps to be found in Agustín's preface to his *Constitutionum Graecarum Codicis Justiniani Imperatoris collectio et interpretatio* (Lérida, 1567), the work which at last contained his findings on the text of the *Codex*. Part of the praise for his discoveries, he acknowledged, was due to Matal for unearthing a manuscript of the Byzantine ecclesiastical constitutions in Florence;[112] but he qualified his thanks by remarking that the Franc-Comtois had been induced to communicate part of the information to the booksellers of Lyons.[113] Agustín had delayed more than twenty years before publishing the results of his researches, but he did not forgive his old friend for what he believed to be his share in causing them to be anticipated. The two men never again met, though they corresponded in 1577.[114]

When Agustín was sixty, an archbishop and immensely eminent, he recalled with nostalgia his happy years in Rome, when every day had been bright with the prospect of a fresh discovery in the city's libraries or among its ruins. 'O mihi felices', he addressed Latino Latini:

> O mihi felices (frustra suspiria duco)
>   Praeteritosque dies!
> Viximus, antiquas cum Urbis lustrare ruinas
>   Romuleae licuit . . . [115]

ANTHONY HOBSON

DESCRIPTION OF CAMBRIDGE UNIVERSITY LIBRARY ADD. MS. 565

Paper. 4to (varying from 209 × 140 mm. to 220 × 145 mm.). 359 leaves + inserted f. 68* and 8 endleaves. Modern foliation. The foliator has omitted the leaf following f. 133.[116] Humanistic cursive script (autograph of Jean Matal except ff. 121–32 and 337–58). Sixteenth-century vellum; spine lettered in ink 'BIBLIOTHECAE', and in an untidy later hand 'Index Auct. Grae [corum]'. Edges uncut.

Ownership: Abate Prospero Petroni, with inscription on endleaf 'Ex Bibliotheca MSS. Petroniana Nº. 57' and pressmark 'P 5732'; Avvocato Augusto Mariotti, with ownership inscription on f. 1 and note that he bought it from the Libreria Pagliarini; Henry Bradshaw; presented by the last named to the University Library in 1869.

Contents: 35 parts bound together:

I. ff. 1–48; f. 1 'INDEX BIBLIOTHECAE VATICANAE'; f. 2 blank; f. 3 'INDEX BIBLIOTHECAE PVBLICAE GRAECAE VATICANAE'; f. 47 'ROMAE, in Vaticana bibliotheca, [ego ipse, *crossed out*] ex ipsis libris, hunc indicem Metellus confeci, Cal. Septemb. M.D.XLV.'; f. 48 blank. Three gatherings (20, 16, 12). Watermarks: first gathering—angel (close to Briquet 613), Farnese arms (type of Briquet 1860); other gatherings, fleur-de-lys in circle (not in Briquet, but type of 7099–108).

II. ff. 49–62; ff. 49–50 blank; f. 51 'INDEX AUCTORUM GRAECORUM BIBLIOTHECAE PARVAE SECRETAE VATICANAE'; ff. 61–2 are occupied by notes on three MSS. in the Bibliotheca Parva Secreta. One gathering (12). Watermark: fleur-de-lys in circle (as in I).

III. ff. 63–70; f. 63 'Ex indice Graecorum librorum Vaticanae bibliothecae ab Hieronymo Aleandro bibliothecario Leonis X collecto'; f. 63b 'Venetis Bessarionis graeci libri'; f. 64 'INDEX CAPSVLARVM bibliothecae Vaticanae parvae secretae, sed insignium tantum librorum, non omnium; latinor[um] quidem'; f. 65 'INDEX PVBLICAE LATINAE BIBLIOTHECAE VATICANAE, LIBRORUM QVIDEM insignium vel vetustate, vel quod non exstant'; f. 66b 'PARVAE SECRETAE armaria graecorum librorum: Insignium tantum index'; f. 67 'Index insignium librorum latinorum bibliothecae Vaticanae (nempe vetustissimorum, aut non editorum) BIBLIOTHECAE parvae secretae quidem'; f. 68 'INDEX BIBLIOTHECAE SECRETAE MAIORIS, latinorum libror[um] quidem . . .'; f. 69b 'BIBLIOTHECAE PARVAE SECRETAE INDEX praecipuorum librorum . . .'. One gathering (8). Watermarks: five-pointed star in circle below cross (cf. Briquet 6088), fleur-de-lys (no close equivalent in Briquet). The outer bifolio (ff. 63, 70) is of a different paper without watermark.

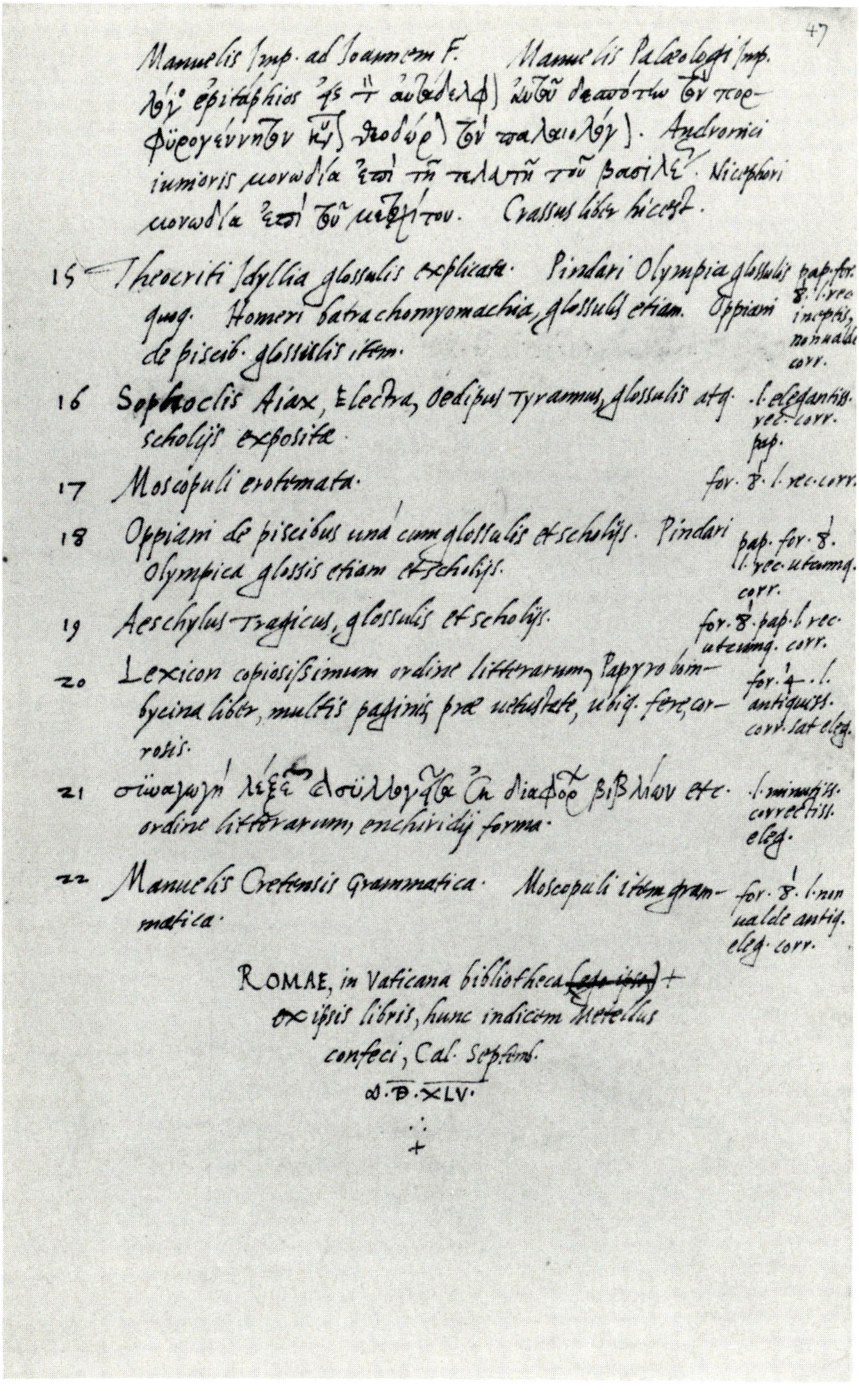

Manuelis [imp.] ad Ioannem F.   Manuelis Palaeologi [imp.]
λόγ' ἐπιτάφιος [ἐς † ἀδελφὸν] τοῦ δεσπότου ἐν πορ-
φυρογεννητῶν κ[αὶ] Θεοδώρο[υ] τοῦ παλαιολόγ[ου]. Andronici
iunioris μονωδία ἐπὶ τῇ τελευτῇ τοῦ βασιλέ[ως]. Nicephori
μονωδία ἐπὶ τοῦ ἀδελφοῦ. Crassus liber hic est.

15 — Theocriti Idyllia glossulis explicata. Pindari Olympia glossulis — pap. for. 8. l. rec. inceptis, nonnulla corr.
Homeri batrachomyomachia, glossulis etiam. Oppiani de pisciis glossulis item.

16 Sophoclis Aiax, Electra, Oedipus Tyrannus, glossulis atq[ue] scholijs exposita. — l. elegantis. rec. corr. pap.

17 Moschopuli erotemata. — for. 8. l. rec. corr.

18 Oppiani de piscibus una cum glossulis et scholiis. Pindari Olympica glossis etiam et scholiis. — pap. for. 8. l. rec. utcumq[ue] corr.

19 Aeschylus Tragicus, glossulis et scholiis. — for. 8. pap. l. rec. utcumq[ue] corr.

20 Lexicon copiosissimum ordine litterarum, papyro bombycina liber, multis paginis prae vetustate, ubiq[ue] fere, corrosis. — for. 4. l. antiquiss. corr. sat eleg.

21 συναγωγὴ λέξε[ων] ἀοὐλλόγη[ς] ἐκ διαφόρ[ων] βιβλίων etc. ordine litterarum, enchiridij forma. — l. minutiss. correctiss. eleg.

22 Manuelis Cretensis Grammatica. Moschopuli item grammatica. — for. 8. l. non valde antiq. eleg. corr.

ROMAE, in Vaticana bibliotheca ~~et ipsis~~ †
~~ex~~ ipsis libris, hunc indicem Metellus
confeci, Cal. Septemb.
ⅭⅠƆ·Ⅰ·ƆⅬⅤ·
†

PLATE 2. University Library, Cambridge, Add. MS. 565, f. 47. The end of Matal's catalogue of the Vatican's Bibliotheca Publica Graeca.

1. Epitome libror. LX. Leontis Cæsaris (quos LX libros βασιλικοὺς et ἑξάβιβλον appellant) in libris distincta; auctore Constantino Harmenopolo iudice Thessalonicense.

2. Eiusdem Constantini compendium Canonum Conciliorum septem, in cuius extremo de omnis generis hæreticis quam breuissime. Hic liber fuit Theodori Gazæ.

II
1. Epitome legum, hac inscriptione, περὶ ἴδεος τῶν νόμων, auctoris incerti. Fortasse est Seleri, aut Nicolai, aut Magni Droṇgarij, quorum postrema Nouella inscriptione mentio.

2. Aliud compendium Michaelis Iudicis hoc titulo: μιχαὴλ κριτοῦ τοῦ ἀνθυπάτου τοῦ ἀλαλδάστου περὶ ἴδεος.

3. Aliud compendium τῶν πολιτικῶν τίτλων τοῦ ἀνθυδένλων παρὰ ἐμβάτου:— Hic, initio, scripta est quædam Constantini Leontisq. præfatio. In extremo quædam de quibusdam legib. καὶ περὶ ἀγωγῶν ἐννόμων, καὶ περὶ ἐγκλήτων καὶ κανόνων. Deinde ἀλφάβητος ῥωμαϊκός: Item περὶ ἐκάστου κλημάτων etc. Alius ἀλφάβητος ῥωμαϊκός.

4. Institutionum Justinianarum lib. IV. de latinis, expressi græcis Theophili antecessoris uerbis: in quib. adscripta margini nonnulla scholia. Illis coniunguntur quædam de nuptijs fragmenta.

5. Epitome quædam legum: τοῦ βασιλέως κῦ Λέοντα τοῦ φιλοσόφου, ἐν ἐπιτομῇ τῶν νόμων: auctoris incerti.

6. Aliud compendium Michaelis Pselli: τοῦ σοφωτάτου μιχαὴλ τοῦ ψελλοῦ ὑπερεξ, σύνοψις τῶν νόμων διὰ στίχων ἰάμβων καὶ πολιτικῶν, πρὸς τὸν βασιλέα κῦ μιχαὴλ τὸν δούκα, ἐν προτάξει τοῦ περὶ αὐτοῦ βασιλέως:— Illic, in fine, περὶ δικῶν ἀγωγῶν.

PLATE 3. University Library, Cambridge, Add. MS. 565, f. 198. Matal's catalogue of Greek legal manuscripts in the Laurentian Library.

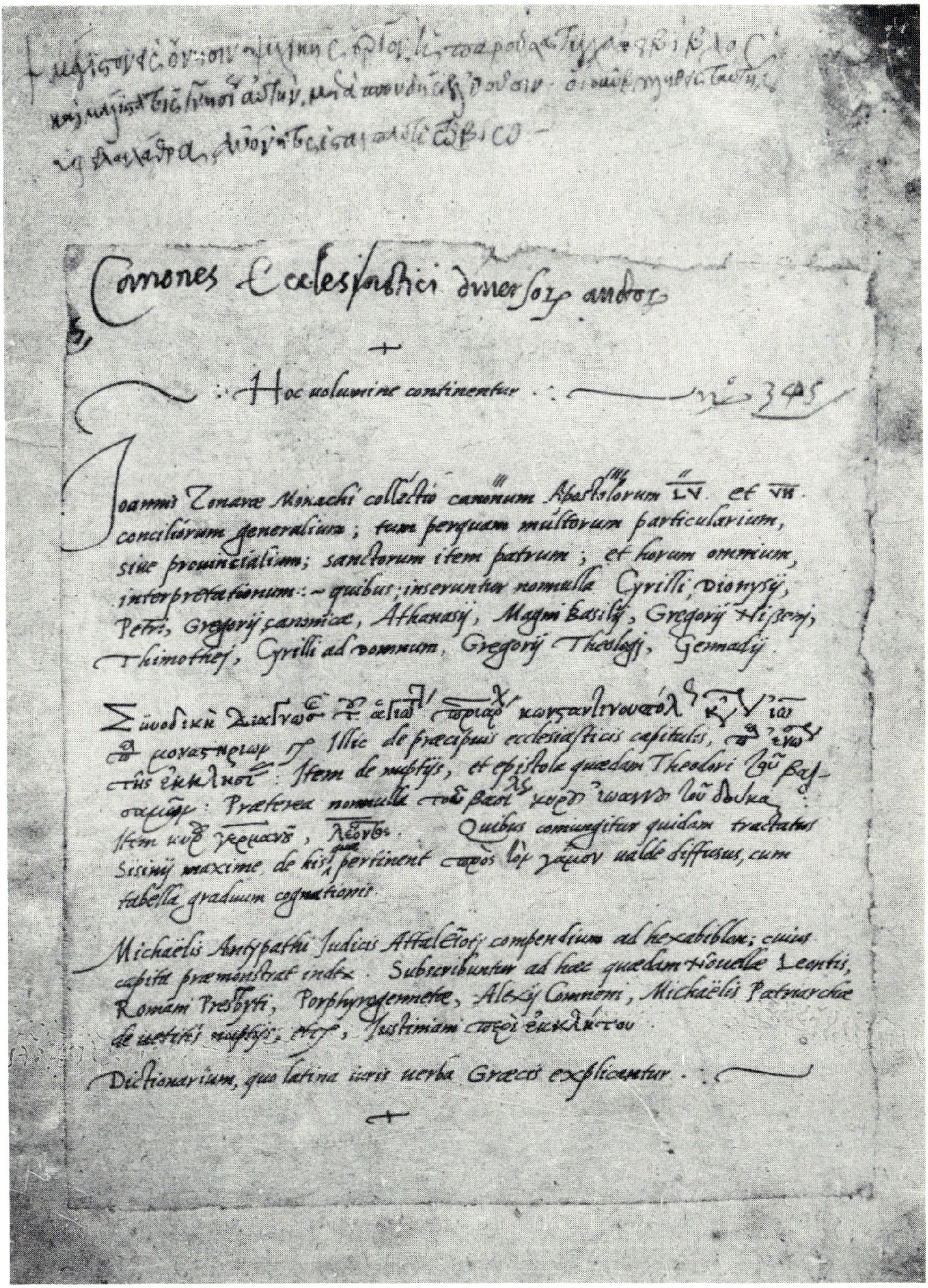

Canones Ecclesiastici diversorum auctorum

Hoc volumine continentur ... n° 345

Joannis Zonarae Monachi collectio canonum Apostolorum LV et VII conciliorum generalium; tum perquam multorum particularium, sive provincialium; sanctorum item patrum; et horum omnium interpretationum: ~ quibus inseruntur nonnulla Cyrilli, Dionysii, Petri, Gregorii canonicae, Athanasii, Magni Basilii, Gregorii Nisseni, Thimothei, Cyrilli ad Domnum, Gregorii Theologi, Gennadii.

Michaëlis Antypathi Iudicis ... compendium ad hexabiblon; cuius capita praemonstrat index. Subscribuntur ad haec quaedam Novellae Leontis, Romani Presbyti, Porphyrogenetae, Alexii Comneni, Michaëlis Patriarchae ... Justiniani περὶ ἐκκλήτου

Dictionarium, quo latina iuris verba Graecis explicantur.

PLATE 4. Biblioteca Laurenziana V, 40, flyleaf. The heading 'Canones Ecclesiastici diversorum auctorum' is in the hand of Pier Francesco Giambullari, the list of contents in Jean Matal's hand.

IV. f. 68*; 'Jurisconsultorum Graecorum; bibliothecae Bessarionis, quam Marcianam appellant, index'. One leaf inserted horizontally. Watermark: anchor in circle below star (cf. Briquet 485).

V. ff. 71–4; f. 71 'Canones Zonarae, qui omnes uno papyraceo bombycino volumine continentur, [non conglutinato, *crossed out*]; in quodam parvae Vaticanae armario' [Vat. gr. 828]. Two gatherings (2, 2). No watermark.

VI. ff. 75–82; f. 75. 'Aristotelis interpretes editi'; f. 75*b* 'Appiani historiae'; f. 76 'Romanae Index libror[um] Vaticanae bibliothecae graecae: selectorum ex indice Iacobi Mendozae'. One gathering (8). Watermark: Agnus Dei in double circle surmounted by a crown (close to Briquet 59).[117]

VII. ff. 83–98; f. 83 'INDEX PRAECIPVOR. AVCTOR. LATINOR. BIBLIOTHECAE VATICANAE (Collectore Ioanne Arce, Theol. Canonico Palentino, Hispano. M.D.XLV.)'; f. 97*b* 'Index precipuor. libror. bibliothecae Augustinor. prope Pacis'; f. 98 blank; f. 98*b* 'Adde ad bibliothecam Pontificiam'. Two gatherings (12, 4). Watermark: five-pointed star in double circle below a cross (not in Briquet).

VIII. ff. 99–102; f. 99 'Armarium II bibliothecae secretae parvae Vaticanae ex indice librarij Eugubini; Episcopi'; f. 102 blank. One gathering, ff. 101–2, unopened. Watermark uncertain.[118]

IX. ff. 103–4; f. 103 'In Marcelli'; f. 104 blank. One gathering (2). Watermark: triple flower in circle below a star (similar to Briquet 6684).

X. ff. 105–8; f. 105 'In Mariae populi'; f. 105*b* 'in Mariae Minervae'; f. 106 'In Mariae populi'; f. 106*b* 'Romae, in Minervae'; f. 108 blank. One gathering (4), ff. 106–7 half sheets. Watermark: five-pointed star in circle below a cross (as in III).

XI. ff. 109–10; f. 109 'Index libror. bibliothecae Pacis. R'; f. 110 blank. One gathering (2). No watermark.

XII. ff. 111–20; f. 111 'Ex bibliothecae P. Bembi, editi'; f. 113*b* blank; f. 114 no title; f. 115 blank; f. 116 'Hebraei libri bibliothecae P. Bembi'; f. 118 'Libri quos vidimus P. Bembi manu aut alterius notatos'; f. 118*b* blank; f. 119 'Manuscripti libri ex bibliotheca Bembi'; f. 120 blank; f. 120*b* 'Volgari'. One gathering (8), ff. 114–15 a loosely inserted bifolium. Watermark uncertain,[118] ff. 114–15 on thinner paper than the remainder.

XIII. ff. 121–32; f. 121 'Compendium indicis libror. m.s. R^{mi}. Domini Nicolai Cardin[a]lis Rodulphi. Catalogus Graecor. in philosophia'. One gathering (12). Not in Matal's hand. Watermark: Agnus Dei in double circle below a cross (type of Briquet 60).

XIV. ff. 133–5; f. 133 'Index libror. graecor. et latinor. manuscriptorum, Cardinalis Salviati Florentini 1546'; f. 135 blank. One gathering (4), leaf after f. 133 unfoliated. Watermark: Farnese arms (cf. I).

XV. ff. 136–55; f. 136 'INDEX BIBLIOTHECAE IAC. HURTADI MENDOZAE. Libri Graeci manuscripti'; f. 147 'Libri Graeci impressi, castigati et cum vetustis codicib[us] manuscriptis collati'; ff. 148–9 blank;

f. 150 'Libri iuris Pontificii et Caesaris editi'; f. 151 blank; f. 152 'Libri Arabici manuscripti'; f. 153*b* 'Alii libri Arabici'; f. 155 blank. Five gatherings (6, 6, 2, 2, 4), ff. 147–8 inserted into the second gathering. Watermark: shield charged with a bird below a star (type of Briquet 12235–6).

XVI. ff. 156–161; f. 156 'Ex libris Basilii Zanchi Bergomensis, editis'; ff. 159–61 blank. One gathering (6), ff. 159–60 unopened. Watermark: dog in double circle below crown (not in Briquet).

XVII. ff. 162–5; f. 162 'Ex bibliotheca Jacobi Apocelli Germani, Romae in banchis'; f. 162*b* 'In ara coeli'; f. 164 'Libri Aegidii Cardinalis Viterbiensis in Augustini sacristia'; f. 165 'Libri Aegidii Cardinalis hebraei'; f. 165*b* blank. One gathering (4). Watermark: walking man in circle (cf. Briquet 757 ff.).

XVIII. ff. 166–9; f. 166 note on a manuscript belonging to Pietro Donato Cesi, Bishop of Narni; ff. 168–9 blank. One gathering (4). Watermark: bat (not in Briquet).

XIX. ff. 170–1; f. 170 'Ex litteris Jo. Arcei Canonici Palentini ad A. Aug. 1546'; f. 171 blank. One gathering (2), loose. No watermark.

XX. ff. 172–3; f. 172 'Tabellae Cosmographicae'; f. 173 blank. One gathering (2). Watermark: angel (as in I).

XXI. ff. 174–7; f. 174 'Abbatiae' and other notes; f. 175 'S. Lorenzo'; f. 176 'IN MARCI. LATINI'; f. 176*b* 'In Jacobi Mendozae bibliotheca Graeci ... IN LAURENTII Florentiae Latini'; f. 177 'GRAECI S. LAURENTII'. One gathering (4). Watermark: Agnus Dei (type of Briquet 50).

XXII. ff. 178–89; f. 178 'Florentiae in Marciana bibliotheca haec sunt. In latina bibliotheca'; f. 179*b* 'Flor. in Graeca Marciana bibliotheca'; f. 185 'Fl. Abbatiae libri Graeci'; f. 186 'Flor. in Marci ad dextram: in bibliotheca Graeca ...'; f. 188 'Flor. in Marci: in lat. biblioth.'; f. 188*b* 'Flor. Sanctae Mariae Novellae'; f. 189*b* 'Flor. in S[er]vorum id est A[n]nu[n]tiate'. Four gatherings (2, 2, 4, 4). Watermark: Agnus Dei in double circle below crown (as in VI), and unidentified.

XXIII. ff. 190–7; f. 190 'FAESVLIS ad tertium Florentia lapidem. In Abbatiae'; f. 191 'In monte; Faesulis; in Hieronymianorum'; f. 191*b* 'Faesulis: Ad pedem montis in dominici ... FLOR. in Sancti Galli'; f. 193*b* 'FLOR. S[anc]ti Spiritus'; f. 194 'Flor. in Carmelitarum ... Flor. in S. Crucis'; ff. 196*b*–197 blank. Two gatherings (4, 4). Watermark: Agnus Dei in double circle below crown (as in VI and XXII).

XXIV. ff. 198–203; f. 198 no title; f. 203 'Finis indicis librorum de iure civili Graecor. bibliothecae Mediceae. Flor. M.D.XLV.M.Martio' (see Appendix); f. 203*b* note beginning 'Pontificii Graecorum iuris volumina ...'. Two gatherings (4, 2). Watermark: uncertain (anvil?).

XXV. ff. 204–83; notes on manuscripts in the Laurenziana (see Appendix). Fourteen gatherings, with signatures: A⁶ B⁸ C⁶ D⁸ E–G⁴ H–L⁶ M⁸ N–O⁴. Watermark: shield charged with two chevrons in a circle (not in Briquet), bow and arrow (not in Briquet), and unidentified.

XXVI. ff. 284-5; titles of the first ten books of the *Basilica* copied from Laur. LXXX, 12. One gathering (2). Watermark: Agnus Dei in double circle below crown (as in VI, XXII and XXIII).

XXVII. ff. 286-90; notes on a manuscript of the *Basilica* belonging to Cardinal Ridolfi (= Paris, B.N., ms. grec 1349). One gathering (5, lacks the first leaf, presumably blank). Watermark: uncertain.

XXVIII. ff. 291-4; f. 291 'Quaestiones et problemata περὶ τῶν βασιλικων'; ff. 293 blank except for some names in French written horizontally; f. 294 blank except for an Italian name, not in Matal's hand. One gathering (4). No watermark.

XXIX. ff. 295-6; notes on a manuscript of the *Basilica* in the 'Bibliotheca privata Graeca' of the Vatican (Vat. gr. 2075?); f. 296b blank. One gathering (2). Watermark: Piccolomini arms (Briquet 5377).

XXX. ff. 297-8; index of books of the *Basilica* taken from Cardinal Ridolfi's manuscript (cf. XXVIII); f. 298 blank. One gathering (2), in red ink. No watermark.

XXXI. ff. 299-318; f. 299 ΠΙΝΑΞ των τιτλ[ων] των ξ βιβλι[ων] των βασιλικ[ων], from a Vatican manuscript; f. 318 blank except for imitations of a decorated majuscule epsilon. One gathering (20). Watermark: fleur-de-lys in circle (as in I, II and III).[119]

XXXII. ff. 319-30; lists of paratitla of the *Basilica* and of the *Novellae* of Leo; ff. 329b-330 blank. One gathering (12). Watermark: fleur-de-lys in circle (as in I, II, IIII and XXXI);[119] and shield charged with a crowned eagle (not in Briquet).

XXXIII. ff. 331-2; f. 331 'Index librorum quos emit senatus Augustanus Venetiis grandi pecunia, ut Jo. Musculus scribit ad And. Matium (1544)'; f. 332b blank. One gathering (2). No watermark.

XXXIV. ff. 333-6; f. 333 'Ex Marciana Veneta bibliotheca hos excerpsit Franc. Turrensis. 1543'; ff. 335-6 blank. One gathering (4), ff. 335-6 unopened. Watermark: uncertain (coat of arms in circle below star?).

XXXV. ff. 337-58; f. 337 'Index librorum ex Photii Patriarchae Byzantii bibliotheca, sub compendio, excerptus; ordine litterarum'; f. 342b blank; f. 343 'Epitome Bibliothecae Photii, eo, quo ipse, ordine, collecta'; f. 358b blank. Three gatherings (8, 8, 6). Only the headings, corrections and part of the numeration are in Matal's hand. Watermarks: shield charged with a bird below a star (as in XV); and fleur-de-lys in circle.

Endleaves: four at each end, blank except for Petroni's record of ownership on i.

APPENDIX

Laurentian manuscripts described by Matal

A star after the pressmark means that the volume contains
a list of contents in Matal's hand

Number in list (Add. 565, ff. 198–203)	Notes Add. 565, ff.	Contents	Pressmark	Bandini Reference
I	207b–211	Constantine Harmenopulos, *Promptuarium juris*	LXXXI, 19*	III, 230-3
II	211–230b	*Epitome Legum*, containing fragments of six books of the *Basilica*	LXXX, 6*	III, 178-85
III	205–207b	Institutes of Theophilus	LXXX, 2	III, 172-3
IV	204–5	Institutes of Theophilus	LXXX, 1	III, 171
V	230b–239b	Collection of expositions of laws relating to the clergy, ecclesiastical affairs, Jews and heretics	LVI, 13	II, 307-11
VI	240–246b	*Syntagma* of Photius	IX, 8*	I, 395-403
VII	246b–249b	*Synopsis Basilicorum secundae classis*	LXXX, 8*	III, 186-92
VIII	249b–256	Joannes Zonaras, Commentary on the *Collectio canonum*	V, 40*	I, 70-82
IX	256–257b	*Synopsis minor Basilicorum*	LXXX, 16	III, 205-6
X	257b–262	*Basilica*, bks. 28 and 29	LXXX, 11	III, 199
XI	262–264b	*Novellae* of Emperors Constantine Porphyrogennitus, Nicephorus Phocas, etc.	LXXX, 10	III, 194-8
XII	264b–267b	*Collectio canonum*	V, 22*	I, 45-8
XIII	267b–277b	Commentary on the first ten books of the *Basilica*	LXXX, 12*	III, 200-2
XIV	—	Institutes of Theophilus	X, 16	I, 485
XV	277b–278b	Alphabetical epitome of the *Basilica*	LXXX, 20	III, 208-9
XVI	278b–283b	*Syntagma* of Photius, with commentaries of Zonaras and Theodore Balsamon	V, 2*	I, 1-11

NOTES

1. I am much indebted to my friend, the late Dr. A. N. L. Munby, for drawing my attention to Add. MS. 565 in Cambridge University Library, on which this essay is based, and to Dr. R. W. Hunt and Miss A. C. de la Mare for their help with several details. M. Pierre Petitmengin, who had independently been working on the manuscript, unreservedly placed his notes at my disposal. I am deeply grateful to him for

this act of generosity. The essay has greatly profited from his comments and he has saved me from at least one gross error.

2. An earlier edition using Bolognini's notes had been printed in Lyons by François Fradin in 1511.

3. F. de Zulueta, *Don Antonio Agustín*, Glasgow, 1939 (a Spanish translation appeared in *Boletín Arqueológico de la Real Sociedad Arqueológica Tarraconense*, Año XLVI, Época IV, fasc. 3-4, Tarragona, July-December 1946); C. Gutiérrez, *Españoles en Trento*, Valladolid, 1951, 96-9. H. E. Troje, *Graeca leguntur*, Cologne, 1971, gives a helpful account of the study of Byzantine law in the 16th century.

4. Juan Andrés, *Antonii Augustini epistolae*, Parma, 1804, 11-26.

5. For the Marciana MS. see below n. 32. The Florentine MS. is now Biblioteca Laurenziana LXXX, 4, but then belonged to the Dominican convent of San Marco. (It is no. 101 in a 16th-century inventory printed by Berthold L. Ullman and Philip A. Stadter, *The Public Library of Renaissance Florence*, Padua, 1972, 278.) Alciati's copy of the *Epitome* of Julianus may be Madrid, Biblioteca Nacional, ms. 629, a handsome 13th-century manuscript on vellum with miniatures, which, by a tradition going back to the seventeenth century, is said to contain notes in Agustín's hand (cf. Antonio Rodríguez Moñino, *La Colección de Manuscritos del marqués de Montealegre en 1677*, 1951, 57, ms. 193).

6. Viglius van Zwichem's manuscript is Paris, Bibl. Nat., ms. gr. 1345. The manuscript in Rome belonged to Cardinal Ridolfi; it is now Paris, B.N., ms. gr. 1349.

7. Juan Andrés, *Epistolae*, 148-52.

8. A description of the manuscript is given at p. 48.

9. F. de Zulueta, 'Don Antonio Agustín'.

10. Pedro Fernández de Pulgar, *Teatro clerical, apostólico y secular*, Madrid: Viuda de Francisco Nieto, 1680, II, 309-10; Gutiérrez, *Españoles en Trento*, 574-81. Two letters to Agustín are printed in Melchor de Azagra, *Cartas eruditas de algunos literatos españoles*, Madrid: J. Ibarra, 1775. For the dating of the second (actually earlier) letter, see F. Miguel Rosell, 'Epistolario Antonio Agustín', *Analecta Sacra Tarraconensia*, XIII, 1937-40, 9. The letter of 1554 sent greetings to Matal: 'Al Senor Metello *saluto in Christo*, y deseo saber de su buen suceso, estudios, y santas ocupaciones'. For his Vatican Library lists, see p. 43. When in Rome he borrowed three works on church councils from the Vatican: M. Bertòla, *I due primi registri di prestito della Biblioteca Apostolica Vaticana*, Città del Vaticano, 1932 (Codices e Vaticanis selecti 27), 96.

11. Nicolas Antonio, *Bibliotheca Hispana*, Rome, 1672, 371-4; Gutiérrez, *Españoles en Trento*, 446-73. That Francisco Torres received 'charity'—and presumably lodging —from Agustín is stated in Juan de Arce's letter of 16 June 1554; Melchor de Azagra, *Cartas*, 12-13. For the bequest of his books: P. Jacob, *Traité des plus belles bibliothèques*, Paris, 1644, 106; B. G. Struvius, *Introductio in notitiam rei litterariae*, 6th edn., Frankfurt and Leipzig, 1754, 287. Antonio Possevino, *Apparatus sacer*, 2 vols., Cologne, 1608, appendix 23-6, prints a list of the texts contained in his Greek MSS. They were dispersed after the suppression of the Society: cf. O. Kresten, 'Zu griechischen Handschriften des Francisco Torres SJ', *Römische historische Mitteilungen*, 12, Rome-Vienna, 1970, 179-96.

12. Latin manuscripts, not noted by Matal, presumably formed a fifth category.

13. E.g. 33 Psalterium, 2 Jo. Cantacuzenus, 42 Eusebius, 15 Xenophon. Charles Graux, *Essai sur les origines du fonds grec de l'Escurial*, Paris, 1880, 252 ff.; P. Gregoiro

de Andrés, O.S.A., 'Dos listas inéditas de manuscritos griegos de Hurtado de Mendoza', *La Ciudad de Dios*, CLXXIV (1961), 393, 395. Mendoza's books were evidently shelved spines outwards in accordance with what Graham Pollard has observed was the general rule in Italy: 'Changes in the style of bookbinding', *Transactions of the Bibliographical Society*, 5th Series, XI (1956), 73.

14. Gregorio de Andrés, *'Dos listas'*, 384–9. For other lists of Hurtado de Mendoza's Greek manuscripts see P. Alejo Revilla, O.S.A., *Catálogo de los codices griegos de la Biblioteca de El Escorial*, Madrid, 1936, and P. Gregorio de Andrés, *Documentos para la historia del Monasterio de San Lorenzo el Real de El Escorial*, VII, Madrid, 1964, 237–323. The latter list, taken from Besançon ms. 1284, appears to be complete, but was made after the manuscripts reached the Escorial and does not preserve Arlenius's order.

15. The latter include one book in Italian, 'Statuta Venetorum italice', probably the octavo edition of 1537.

16. Gregorio de Andrés, *Documentos*, 240. Cf. Nemesio Morata, 'Un catálogo de los fondos árabes primitivos de El Escorial,' *Al-Andalus*, II, 1934, 87–181.

17. Juan Andrés, *Epistolae*, 160. Matal was evidently better received by Anthony the Eparch (ibid.).

18. Angel González Palencia and Eugenio Mele, *Vida y obras de Don Diego Hurtado de Mendoza*, Madrid, 1941, I, 260; B. R. Jenny, 'Arlenius in Basel', *Basler Zeitschrift für Geschichte und Altertumskunde*, 64, 1964, 18. Matal's lists of the Mendoza collection cannot be earlier than 1549 as they include a book printed in that year.

19. Catullus, *Carmina*, Brescia: Boninus de Boninis, 1486 (GKW 6301), annotated by Pontano and Angelo Colocci. This copy belonged afterward to Fulvio Orsini and entered the Vatican Library with his collection, but it is now lost. P. de Nolhac, *La bibliothèque de Fulvio Orsini*, 1887, 232.

20. The inventory of Guarino's Greek manuscripts, printed by H. Omont in *Revue des bibliothèques*, II, 1892, 78–81, includes no copy of Theodore Gaza's grammar. Probably the manuscript Arlenius used was no. 50 in the list, 'Lexicon graecum ejusdem Baptistae Guarini, ab eo confectum anno 1440, et in eodem volumine multae observationes in litteris graecis'. Aubrey Diller (*Journal of the Warburg and Courtauld Institutes*, XXIV, 1961, 319) proposes various identifications for the manuscript. If Arlenius owned it in Venice, it may be the one afterwards in the library of S. Francesco della Vigna.

21. An early sixteenth-century inventory of the library of S. Domenico in Bologna records this manuscript, now vanished: M. H. Laurent, O.P., *Fabio Vigili et les bibliothèques de Bologne au début du XVIe siècle*, Citta del Vaticano, 1943 (Studi e Testi 105), 91–2.

22. Martianus Rota edited Boethius's *Dialectica* (Venice, 1556) and Joannes Philoponus's commentary on Aristotle's *Posteriora Analytica* (ibid., 1559) and wrote a life of Boethius prefixed to Pietro Berti's edition of the *De Consolatione* printed in Padua at the Stamperia Cominiana in 1721: Cosenza, *Dictionary of the Italian Humanists*, IV, 3100.

23. Arlenius's edition of Polybius was printed in Basle by Johann Herwagen in March 1549, with a dedication to Hurtado de Mendoza and a Latin translation of the second part by Wolfgang Musculus.

24. For Hurtado de Mendoza's collection of manuscripts and printed editions of

Aristotle, which he had taken special pains to make as complete as possible, see Gregorio de Andrés, *Documentos*, 264–8, 308, and Juan Andrés, *Epistolae*, 25.

25. The *Orations* of St. Gregory Nazianzen appear again in a later list of Arlenius's Greek manuscripts: Giovanni Mercati, *Opere minori*, IV, Città del Vaticano, 1937 (Studi e Testi 79), 366. They were probably copied from a manuscript in the monastery of S. Salvatore in Bologna (Laurent, *Fabio Vigili*, 277)—Arlenius had used a manuscript of Lycophron in the same library in 1541-2 for his edition published in Basle in 1546—unless indeed he obtained possession of the original, which is not now in Bologna University Library.

26. Probably a copy of the list sent to Agustín on 30 November 1542: Juan Andrés, *Epistolae*, 160.

27. Subsequently E.II.18 in the Escorial, presumably destroyed in the fire of 1671. Graux, *Essai*, p. 270, no. 262; P. Gregorio de Andrés, O.S.A., *Catálogo de los códices griegos desaparecidos de la Real Biblioteca de El Escorial*, El Escorial, 1968, 131.

28. Juan Andrés, *Epistolae*, 164–7.

29. Juan Andrés, *Epistolae*, 175–6. Matal played no part in Torelli's edition of the Pandects, which was printed in Florence by Lorenzo Torrentino in 1553.

30. Matal's six-month illness must have occurred at this time and not later, as González Palencia and Mele suggest (I, 277–8). In November he reported that his health was improved and that he had left Padua (Juan Andrés, *Epistolae*, 178–9).

31. Antonio Agustín, *Emendationes et Opiniones*, Venice: heirs of Lucantonio Giunta, idibus Septembris 1543.

32. Juan Andrés, *Epistolae*, 13. The exemplar is Bibl. Marciana Cod. graec. 179. The copy is El Escorial o.1.7., ff. 4–68 (Gregorio de Andrés, *Catálogo de los códices griegos de la Real Biblioteca de El Escorial*, II, Madrid, 1965, 10–13). The Escorial also possesses Agustín's annotated copy of Haloander, 1531, pressmark 82-VI-4 (G. de Andrés, ibid.). The Marciana MS. had already been studied in 1533 by Viglius van Zwichem (J. A. B. Mortreuil, *Histoire du droit byzantin*, 1843, I, 37–8).

33. Juan Andrés, *Epistolae*, 177–8. Agustín presumably used the Marciana MS., Cod. graec. 339, of Eusebius's *Vita Constantini* and *Laus Constantini*.

34. Folios 111–20. Folios 114–15, containing the titles of three printed books, followed by a list of the works of Rodericus Zamorensis (whose *Compendiosa historia Hispanica*, Rome: Ulrich Han, not after 4 October 1470, Bembo owned), are loosely inserted and on different paper from the remainder, but have the same full details of printers, places and dates of printing, and evidently refer to the same collection.

35. Agustín's catalogue of his own printed books is similarly detailed: A. Agustín, *Opera omnia*, VII, Lucca, 1772, 119–61.

36. Vat. lat. 3225 and 3226; cf. P. de Nolhac, *La Bibliothèque de Fulvio Orsini*, Paris, 1887, ch. III.

37. Pedro Jiménez de Préjano, Bishop of Coria, *Luzero de la vida cristiana*, Salamanca: [Juan de Porras?], 1501. Mr. F. J. Norton (to whom I am indebted for identifying the book) tells me that he knows only one (imperfect) copy of this edition, in the Österreichische Nationalbibliothek, Vienna.

38. 'Coperto di bianco [rosso, pauonazo, uerde, coro negro, pergamena, uelutto rosso]', 'con tauole' [over wooden boards], 'sciolto' [unbound]. For Bembo's library cf. Cecil H. Clough, *Pietro Bembo's Library as represented particularly in the British*

Museum, revised edition, 1971, and the same author's note in 'Notes and News', *Bulletin of the John Rylands University Library of Manchester*, 55, 2 (1973), 253-8.

39. Juan Andrés, *Epistolae*, 178-83.
40. Cf. Agustín, *Opera omnia*, VII, 181.
41. Perhaps Laur. X, 16.
42. Juan Andrés, *Epistolae*, 185-9.
43. The list on ff. 185-185b is a much abbreviated version of 'Tabula librorum Graecorum' in the sixteenth-century catalogue in the Laurenziana, Conv. Sopp. 151 (published by R. Blum, *La biblioteca della Badia Fiorentina e i codici di Antonio Corbinelli*, Città del Vaticano, 1951 (Studi e Testi 155), 114-19). It omits nos. 28, 39, 112-16 and 126 of Blum's list but adds five manuscripts, including 'Thucydides antiquissimus' and 'Historia Herodoti antiquissima'.
44. Niccoli's three are Ammianus Marcellinus (Florence, BN, Conv. Sopp. J.V.43), Aulus Gellius (ibid., Conv. Sopp. J.IV.26) and Plautus (ibid., Conv. Sopp. J.I.12). See Ullman and Stadter, *The public library*, nos. 830, 900 and 918; A. C. de la Mare, *The handwriting of Italian humanists*, I, 1, 1973, 56. The Cicero is Laur. XLIX, 7. The mistaken belief that it was in Petrarch's hand originated from Poliziano; cf. A. M. Bandini, *Catalogus codd. lat. Bibl. Med. Laur.*, II, 1775, 464; B. L. Ullman, *The humanism of Coluccio Salutati*, 1963, 146, and *The Origin and Development of humanist script*, 1960, 76.
45. Ovid, *Opera*, Parma: Stephanus Corallus, 1477 (Bodleian Library Auct. P.2.2) and Aristotle, *De historia animalium*, translated by Theodore Gaza, Venice: Johannes de Colonia and Johannes Manthen, 1476 (unlocated). San Marco had two copies (or two editions) of the latter: Ullman and Stadter, nos. 612 and 810. The copy annotated by Poliziano is said by Matal to have been on Ordo XXIV 'ad sinistram', which does not agree with either copy. Cf. Alessandro Perosa, *Mostra del Poliziano*, Florence, 1954, no. 34.
46. Not recorded by P. Stefano Orlandi, O.P., *La biblioteca di S. Maria Novella in Firenze*, Florence, 1952.
47. Montfaucon, *Bibliotheca bibliothecarum manuscriptorum nova*, Paris, 1739, I, 429, records various manuscripts of Chrysostom in the Annunziata.
48. A convent of Augustinian hermit friars where Egidio da Viterbo probably lectured in 1497: G. Signorelli, *Egidio da Viterbo*, Florence, 1929, 127.
49. An inventory of the lesser library, to which Boccaccio had left his books, is printed by A. Mazza, 'L'inventario della "parva libreria" di Santo Spirito e la biblioteca di Boccaccio', *Italia medioevale e umanistica*, IX (1966), 1-74. For the 'bibliotheca maior', see D. Gutierrez, 'La biblioteca di Santo Spirito in Firenze nella metà del secolo XV', *Analecta Augustiniana*, 25, 1962, 5-88.
50. The Carmelites' library was very extensive; cf. K. W. Humphreys, *The Library of the Carmelites of Florence*, Amsterdam, 1964, and L. Perini, 'L'inventario dei codici di S. Maria del Carmine di Firenze del 1461', *Studi Medievali*, X/3, 1969, 461-561.
51. The library contained 781 manuscripts on seventy desks in 1426; C. Mazzi, 'L'inventario quattrocentistico della biblioteca di S. Croce in Firenze', *Rivista dello Biblioteche e degli Archivi*, VIII (1897), 16 ff. Cf. Charles T. Davis, 'The early collection of books of S. Croce in Florence', *Proceedings of the American Philosophical Society*, 107, no. 5, 1963, 399-414.

52. Laur. XXXII, 1.
53. Laur. LXV, 1.
54. Laur. LXVIII, 1, from which the *editio princeps* was printed.
55. Laur. XLVII, 36.
56. Laur. XLIX, 9, from Vercelli.
57. Laur. LXXIII, 1, from Sant'Ambrogio, Milan.
58. See the Appendix, p. 52.
59. Resembling the hand in his letter of 1564 to Georg Cassander in B.L. Add. MS. 5018 (printed in P. Burmannus, *Sylloges epistolarum a viris illustribus scriptarum*, Leiden, 1727, II, 288) and that in his letter of 1563 to Cornelius Wouters in B.L. Add. MS. 38,846. The page of Vat. lat. 6038 reproduced by C. Leonardi, 'Per la storia dell' edizione romana dei concili ecumenici', *Mélanges Eugène Tisserand*, VI (Studi e Testi 236), Tav. III, seems to me to be in Matal's hand, not Agustín's.
60. Agustín owned transcripts of many of the Laurentian manuscripts Matal noted, e.g. Laur. LXXX, 11, the transcript of which was afterwards Z.I.17 in the Escorial: G. de Andrés, *Códices griegos desaparecidos*, no. 322. For Agustín's letter, see above p. 34, n. 7.
61. Photographs kindly supplied by Dott. ssa Morandini show that the notes are in Matal's hand. A later annotator of Laur. V, 22, has added the erroneous attribution, 'manus Antonii Augustini', which misled Bandini into believing Agustín to have been 'omnium primus': *Catalogus codicum manuscriptorum Bibl. Med. Laurentianae*, Florence, 1764, I, xvi. See the Appendix for the manuscripts in question.
62. Laur. LXXXI, 19.
63. Laur. LXXX, 1 and 2. Of the latter Matal observes (f. 205), 'Hic liber priore tabula Politani nomen adscriptum habet et numerum quo fuit fortasse in eius bibliotheca, hoc modo: N°. 608', but the number is more probably Giambullari's press-mark (see below, p. 41). The manuscripts are not recorded by Ida Maïer, *Les manuscrits d'Ange Politien*, Geneva, 1965 (*Travaux d'Humanisme et Renaissance*, LXX).
64. Add. 565, f. 230b. The author of the biographical note prefixed to P. F. Giambullari, *Storia dell'Europa*, Parma, 1846, is therefore mistaken in saying that he was appointed *Custos*, c. 1552.
65. The tenth-century 'Victorianus', now Laur. XXXVIII, 24. Matal adds the interesting remark that it had belonged to St. Gall ('ex S. Gallo'). Vettori presented the volume to the Grand-Duke in 1567; see Giovanni Ghinassi, *Lettere di Piero Vettori*, Bologna, 1870, 52–3.
66. Terence, *Comoediae*, Milan: Antonius Zarotus, 1475: Florence, B.N., B.R.97. Perosa, *Mostra del Poliziano*, no. 61. Vettori lent the volume to Fulvio Orsini in 1567: Ghinassi, ibid.
67. Probably Cod. Riccardianus 46. Vettori published an edition of the Nicomachean Ethics (Florence, Giunta) in 1547 based largely on this manuscript.
68. 'Petrus Franciscus Ducis Flo. praeceptor'. Baccio Bandini, *Vita di Cosimo Medici* (Florence, 1579), 9, says that Cosimo was taught such good Latin that he could follow ambassadors' orations, as well as a little Greek, but does not name his teacher. Perhaps the Homer he owned is the tenth-century Iliad in the Laurenziana, XXXII, 3.
69. Later sold to Ulrich Fugger, through whom they reached the Heidelberg Library, and now among the Codices Palatini in the Vatican: Giuseppe M. Cagni, 'I

codici Vaticani Palatino-Latini appartenuti alla biblioteca di Giannozzo Manetti', *La Bibliofilia*, LXII (1960), 1-43.

70. Chief secretary of Cosimo de' Medici, the first Grand-Duke, *d.* 1546.

71. A correspondent of Piero Vettori (B.L. Add. MS. 10267). His name was put forward as a possible tutor for Giuliano della Rovere: Vittorio Cian, *Un medaglione del Rinascimento*, Florence, 1891, 92.

72. Transcribed, if I understand Matal correctly, from a borrowed copy of the Laurentian manuscript known on account of its size as the 'Oceanus' (i.e. Laur. LXXXV, 1, as Mr. Paul Quarrie kindly pointed out to me).

73. Possibly Laur. VI, 18?

74. Juan Andrés, *Epistolae*, 163-4, 167, 169.

75. Apparently in the possession of a certain Germain Calladon; but my reading of this sentence is at best conjectural.

76. The portrait is the famous one by Melozzo da Forlì, showing the Pope handing the bull of foundation of the Library to Platina, its first librarian. The verse as quoted by Matal differs slightly from that printed by Eugène Müntz, *Les arts à la cour des papes pendant le XVe et le XVIe siècle*, Bibliothèque des Écoles françaises d'Athènes et de Rome, XXVIII (1882), 117-18. The first line reads:

Templa domum expositis, vicos, fora, moenia, fontes . . .

The four rooms of Sixtus IV's library still exist and have recently been restored.

77. Vat. gr. 7132; published by Mgr. Robert Devreesse, *Le fonds grec de la Bibliothèque Vaticane des origines à Paul V*, Città del Vaticano, 1965 (Studi e Testi 244), 362-79.

78. Desks IV and V each had manuscripts on three shelves, Desk VI only on two, the lowest being empty.

79. Vat. gr. 1483. Jeanne Bignami Odier and José Ruysschaert, *La Bibliothèque Vaticane de Sixte IV à Pie XI*, Città del Vaticano, 1973 (Studi e Testi 272), 30. Girolamo Aleandro was Librarian from 1519 to 1538.

80. Cf. Bignami Odier and Ruysschaert, p. 56, n. 6. Agostino Steuco, of Gubbio, Bishop of Kissanos (here called 'Eugubinus Episcopus'), was Librarian from 1538 to 1548. His catalogue was widely disseminated as a bibliographical tool: cf. Pierre Petitmengin in *Bibliothèque de l'École des Chartes*, CXXV, 1967, 459.

81. The library, founded in 1382 (P. Jacob, *Traicté des plus belles bibliothèques*, Paris, 1644, 103), had benefited by a bequest from Antonio Orso, Bishop of Canea (*d.* 1511), whose monument in the church shows him reclining on bound volumes.

82. This library, together with those of Sta. Maria sopra Minerva and Ara Coeli is mentioned by Franciscus Schottus, *Itinerario, ovvero nova descrittione de' viaggi principali d'Italia*, II, Vicenza, 1615, f. 10b. A group of its manuscripts remains intact in the Biblioteca Angelica, to which they were transferred in 1849: H. Narducci, *Catalogus codicum manuscriptorum . . . in Bibliotheca Angelica*, Rome, 1893, 233 (no. 524); C. Frati, 'Evasio Leone e le sue ricerche intorno a Niccolò vescovo Modrussiense', *La Bibliofilia*, XVIII (1916-17), 86-90.

83. The most famous library in Rome after the Vatican, with a history going back to the late 13th century. Pietro Bembo and Paolo Manuzio were both buried in the convent. The catalogue of its manuscripts has been published from Vat. lat. 3958 by G. Meersseman, 'La bibliothèque des Frères Prêcheurs de la Minerve à la fin du XVIe siècle', *Mélanges Auguste Pelzer*, Louvain, 1947, 605-31. Bignami Odier and Ruysschaert, 114 and 134, n.142.

84. The library had probably recently acquired a group of manuscripts from the Franciscan Pietro Galatino (*d.* 1540). These later entered the Vatican Library. Bignami Odier and Ruysschaert, 102, 120 n. 30, 218 n. 7.

85. 1470–1532, General of the Augustinian order, created Cardinal 1517. He is said to have known Hebrew, Aramaic, Turkish, Persian and Arabic. One book from his gift to Sant'Agostino, an Aristotle, *Ethica*, in Greek, inscribed 'xxv aprilis 1514 Egidius dedit', is Vatican Library, Rossiano 412: Giovanni Mercati, 'Nota per la storia di alcune bibliothece romane nei secoli XVI–XIX', Città del Vaticano, 1952 (Studi e Testi 164), 31. A list of his books is printed from Paris, B.N., ms. grec 3074 by Charles Astruc and Jacques Monfrin in *Bibliothèque d'Humanisme et Renaissance*, XXIII (1961), 551–4.

86. Guillaume d'Estouteville, *d.* 1483. On his legacy to Sant'Agostino, cf. D. Gutierrez, 'La biblioteca di Sant'Agostino di Roma nel secolo XV', *Analecta Augustiniana*, 27 (1964), 5–58, and 28 (1965), 57–153. The manuscript mentioned by Matal is no. 475 on p. 122 of the latter article. Other manuscripts had been acquired for the Vatican: E. Müntz and Paul Fabre, *La bibliothèque du Vatican au XVe siècle*, Bibliothèque des Écoles françaises d'Athènes et de Rome, XLVIII (1887), 261–4. They are identified by Bignami Odier and Ruysschaert, 36, n. 41.

87. Johann Reuchlin, *De accentibus et orthographia linguae hebraicae*, Hagenau: Thomas Anshelm, 1518; Janus Vitalis, *De divina trinitate versu heroico*, Rome: Marcello Silber, 1521; and the Genoese Polyglot Psalter of 1516.

88. 'Libro de falconeria, en lengua española. Naharro, en lengua española. Agonia, en lengua española'. The first is a manuscript of Pero López de Ayala's *Libro de cetrería* (Vatican Library, Ottobon. lat. 3324). Profesor E. M. Wilson has kindly identified the others as Bartolomé de Torres Naharro, *Propalladia*, Naples, 1517 (reprinted Naples, 1524; Seville, 1520, 1526?, 1533–4, 1545; Toledo, 1535, etc.), and Alejo Vanegas de Busto, *Agonia del transito dela muerte*, Toledo, 1537 (reprinted Toledo, 1543, etc.).

89. Carlo Cappello became governor of Crete in 1540 and collected manuscripts on ecclesiastical history, some of which he brought home: R. Sabbadini, *Le scoperte dei codici latini e greci*, I, 1905, 62, n.119; Giovanni Mercati, *Codici latini Pico Grimani Pio*, Città del Vaticano, 1938 (Studi e Testi 75), 72 n. 2; Giulio Coggiola in *Zentralblatt für Bibliothekswesen*, XXV (1908), 66.

90. A. M. Bandini, *Clarorum Italorum et Germanorum epistolae ad P. Victorium*, Florence, 1758, I, 38–9; Ph. K. Bouboulides, Μιχαὴλ-Ἑρμόδωρος Λῄσταρχος, Athens, 1959.

91. Giovanni Mercati, 'Il Plutarcho di Bartolomeo di Montepulciano', *Opere minori*, Città del Vaticano, 1937, IV (Studi e Testi 79), 201, n. 1.

92. Many lists exist of this famous collection, which passed through the ownership of Piero Strozzi and Caterine de Médicis into the Bibliothèque Nationale, Paris. See Montfaucon, *Bibliotheca bibliothecarum*, II, 766–82; Léopold Delisle, *Le Cabinet des manuscrits de la Bibliothèque Impériale*, Paris, 1868, I, 209–10; Giovanni Mercati, 'Indice di manoscritti greci del cardinale N. Ridolfi', *Opere minori*, III, Città del Vaticano, 1937 (Studi e Testi 78), 126–9; Roberto Ridolfi, 'La biblioteca del cardinale Niccolò Ridolfi', *La Bibliofilia*, XXXI (1929), 173–93.

93. Romeo de Maio, *Alfonso Carafa cardinale di Napoli, 1540–1565*, Città del Vaticano, 1961 (Studi e Testi 210), 119; idem, 'La Biblioteca apostolica sotto Paolo IV e Pio V,

1555–1565', *Collectanea Vaticana in honorem Anselmi card. Albareda*, I, Città del Vaticano, 1962 (Studi e Testi 219), 285; Andreas Schott, 'Vita di Monsignore Don Antonio Agostini', in Agustín, *Dialoghi sopra le medaglie*, Rome, 1698.

94. Giovanni Mercati, *Note per la storia di alcune biblioteche romane nei secoli XVI–XIX*, Città del Vaticano, 1952 (Studi e Testi 164), 136 ff. Vatican Library Ottobon. lat. 2191, a Latin vocabulary of the 16th century, is dedicated to him: G. Mercati, *Codici latini Pico Grimani Pio*, 256, n. 191.

95. Vat. gr. 1303: Vogel-Gardthausen, *Die griechischen Schreiber des Mittelalters und der Renaissance*, reprint 1966, 309; Nolhac, *Fulvio Orsini*, 148.

96. This was the group of manuscripts bought from the patriotic Corfiote dealer, Anthony the Eparch, for 800 *scudi d'oro*: Legrand, *Bibliothèque Hellénique*, I, ccxviii, who postdates the purchase, on the authority of Schwaighaeuser, to 1545; Graham Pollard, *The distribution of books by catalogue*, Roxburghe Club, 1965, 253; Graux, *Essai*, 413–17; W. Weinberger, 'Greichische Handschriften des Antonios Eparchos', *Festschrift Theodor Gompertz*, Vienna, 1903, 305–10.

97. Max Lossen (ed.) *Briefe von Andreas Masius und seinen Freunden*, Leipzig, 1886 (*Publikationen der Gesellschaft für Rheinische Geschichtskunde*, II), 22–3.

98. Cesena, Bibl. Malatestiana, D. XXVIII, 2–3.

99. He is mentioned in a letter of Fernan Nuñez de Guzmán ('el Comendador Griego') to Gerónimo Zurita printed by Dormer, *Progresos de la Historia en el Reyno de Aragon*, Saragossa, 1680, 544; cited by Graux, 52, n. 1.

100. This early project for a universal bibliography—contemporary with Gesner's—seems to be otherwise unrecorded. It is not mentioned by Theodore Besterman, *The beginnings of systematic bibliography*, 1940 (reprint 1968). The first Jesuits in Paris were at this time installed in the Collège des Lombards (Crevier, *Histoire de l'Université de Paris*, Paris, 1761, VI, 3).

101. Cardinal D. Pedro González de Mendoza (1428–95) was Archbishop of Toledo 1483–95.

102. The only manuscript of the *History* that M. L. W. Laistner (*A hand-list of Bede manuscripts*, Ithaca, N.Y., 1943, 98) records in Spain is in the Royal Library (i.e. Biblioteca de Palacio), Madrid, but B. Colgrave and R. A. B. Mynors (*Bede's Ecclesiastical History of the English People*, Oxford, 1969) mention another in Valencia Cathedral.

103. Juan Andrés, *Epistolae*, 152.

104. Vat. lat. 6034, 6037, 6038, 6039, 6040. Cf. A. Silvagni, *Inscriptiones christianae Urbis Romae*, nova series, I, Rome, 1922, xlii; *C.I.L.*, VI, 1, xlix; 11, x.

105. Vat. lat. 8495 (Kristeller, *Iter italicum*, II, 345).

106. Nolhac, *Fulvio Orsini*, 6.

107. Naples, B.N., MS. XVI.A.11 (Kristeller, *Iter italicum*, I, 434). Pierre Gilles died in Rome in 1555. The work was printed in 1562 (Lyons, Guillaume Rouillé) with an edition of his translation of Aelian. The elephant was Matal's crest or badge. M. François Avril tells me that a letter of his in the Bibliothèque Nationale, Paris (ms. lat. 8583, ff. 10–17) bears a seal with the impression of a shield charged with an elephant.

108. Graham Pollard, *Distribution*, 201–2. The archbishop's nephew, D. Rodrigo Zapata y Palafox, had tried to dissuade his uncle from leaving his books to the Escorial by emphasising the quantity already there: F. Miquel Rosell, 'Epistolario', 57.

109. Besides the volumes mentioned in notes 104, 105 and 107, they include manuscripts of works by Hippocrates (Vat. gr. 276 and Barb. gr. 11), Joannes Tzetzes (Barb. gr. 11) and Arrian (Pius gr. 43), also a 14th-century astronomical miscellany (Vat. gr. 318) and a transcript of the late 9th-century MS. of the *Corpus Agrimensorum* in Florence, Laur. XXIX, 32 (Barb. lat. 164; cf. C. Thulin, 'Humanistische Handschriften des Corpus Agrimensorum Romanorum', *Rheinisches Museum für Philologie*, 66 (1911), 423–4, 441–3). Cambridge Add. MS. 565 belonged in the late 18th century to Abate Prospero Petroni, librarian of the Sapienza from 1784. Petroni's heirs sold it to a bookseller Pagliarini, from whom it was bought by a certain Avvocato Augusto Mariotti. It was given to the University Library by Henry Bradshaw in 1869. The most celebrated MS. Matal owned was the 9th-century Holkham codex of Cicero, now B.L. Add. MS. 47,678: cf. W. Peterson, *Anecdota Oxoniensia*, Classical Series, IX (1901), pp. xxxiv–xxxviii.

110. Letters of Matal are printed in Max Rooses and J. Denucé, *Correspondance de Christophe Plantin*, Antwerp-Ghent, 1883–1918, VI, 310; J. H. Hessels, *Abrahami Orteli ... et virorum eruditorum ad eundem ... epistulae*, Cambridge, 1887, nos. 60 and 101; *Epistolae Io. Sturmii ... ad R. Ascham*, Hanover, 1707, 84–6; and Burmannus, *Sylloges* (see p. 57, n. 59). A letter to him from Latino Latini is printed in the latter's *Epistolae, Coniecturae, et Observationes*, Rome, 1659, II, 92. Unpublished letters (besides the one noticed in n. 59) are in B. L. Harley 7011, f. 170 (to Ortelius), Paris, B.N., ms. lat. 8583, ff. 10–17 and 243 (to Hubert Languet and his brother), ibid., Dupuy 490, f. 38, and Dupuy 348, ff. 200–203 (to Pierre Pithou), Vat. lat. 4103, f. 112 (to Fulvio Orsini: cf. Nolhac, *Fulvio Orsini*, 62), Vat. lat. 6193, II, f. 411 (to Guglielmo Sirleto: cf. Nolhac, ibid.), Reg. lat. 2023, f. 444 (cf. Ch. Dejob, *De l'influence du Concile de Trente*, Paris, 1884, 374) and Munich BSB, Clm. 10364 (= Collectio Camerariana 14, to Joachim Camerarius II). The date of Matal's death is taken from Dupuy 348, ff. 200–3. A letter of one of his executors, Henricus Botterus (ibid., f. 201), provides the information that he owned only few books, but among them were manuscripts and rare works.

111. Hieronymus Osorius, *De rebus gestis Emmanuelis regis Lusitaniae ... domi forisque gestis*, Cologne: heirs of Arnold Birckmann, 1574.

112. This sounds grudging, as Matal discovered four such manuscripts in the Laurenziana; but the reference is to Laur. IX, 8, the most valuable.

113. According to G. Haenel (*Juliani epitome*, xxiv–xxv) he was referring to *Justiniani novellae constitutiones*, ed. Ludovicus Miraeus, Lyons: Jean de Tournes and Gulielmus Gazeius, 1561, but Mortreuil, *Histoire*, I, 21, believed that the reference was to the 1551 Lyons edition of the *Codex*.

114. Nolhac, *Fulvio Orsini*, 62, n.3; Rooses and Denucé, *Correspondance de Plantin*, V, 274.

115. Nicolas Antonio, *Bibliotheca Hispana*, 79.

116. The (incorrect) foliation in the manuscript has been followed in this description.

117. The watermark suggests that this section was written in Florence; cf. XXII, XXIII and XXVI.

118. M. Petitmengin detects a watermark of a letter (B or R?) in VIII, and possibly also in XII.

119. The watermarks suggest that these two sections were written in Rome in the autumn of 1545. Cf. I, II and III.

RICHARD HUNT

St. John's College donors

Donors of manuscripts to St. John's College Oxford during the presidency of William Laud 1611–1621

Archbishop Laud is remembered as a great benefactor of the Bodleian Library and of the Library of his college, St John's. These benefactions were made after he became Archbishop of Canterbury and commanded considerable resources. They have overshadowed the modest gifts of manuscripts which he made to the College when he was President (1611–21). It is the purpose of this paper to examine these latter, together with some others made to the College during the same period. They show unexpected links between men of common ecclesiastical interests, and illustrate the way in which small groups of books from medieval libraries survived.

    I shall begin with the largest of the gifts. In 1613 nineteen manuscripts came to the College from Richard Butler, archdeacon of Northampton, through John, Bishop of Rochester (procurante reverendo in Christo patre Johanne episcopo Roffensi).[1] John, Bishop of Rochester, is John Buckeridge, Laud's tutor, and President of St. John's from 1605 to 1611. Among his other preferments was the archdeaconry of Northampton, which he held from 1604 to 1611. Richard Butler succeeded him as archdeacon on 9 July 1611, but died in September of the following year. Butler was a Northamptonshire man[2] who went up to St. John's College, Cambridge, as sizar in 1580, proceeded B.A. in 1584 and M.A. in 1587. In 1591 he became vicar of Spratton, Northants, a living he continued to hold until his death. In 1594 he proceeded B.D. at Cambridge. In 1602 he was presented by Alban Butler to the living of Aston-le-Walls, Northants. He incorporated D.D. at Oxford on 30 May 1608, as a member of St. John's College, the same day that Laud supplicated for his D.D.[3] He was a Chaplain in ordinary to King James I. We know nothing of him beyond the bare facts of his career,

[1] Notes begin on p. 69.

which suggest that he was a man of a certain note. His will, dated 10 September 1612, which survives among State Papers Domestic in the Public Record Office,[4] gives us a little more information about him. It begins rather sadly: 'Whereas I have many friends to whom I am much oblidge and should to each leave some testimony of my love, upon a view of my estate it comes very short that I cannot express my love and therefore crave pardon of them'. After bequests of 40s. to the poor of each of the parishes of which he had held the benefice he continues: 'To Mrs. Neale my Lord Bishop of Lichfielde wife as a small remembrance an unite of gold.'[5] Richard Neile, Bishop of Lichfield, who was an early patron of Laud, had been admitted scholar of St. John's College, Cambridge, in 1580, the same year that Butler had entered as sizar. Butler's will continues: 'Item. I give to my Lord of Rochester all my Books.' 'My Lord of Rochester' is, as we have already seen, John Buckeridge. The sole executor of the will was John Lambe, the notorious ecclesiastical lawyer, at that time registrar of the diocese of Peterborough. Lambe also had been a sizar of St. John's College, Cambridge, three years junior to Butler. With the will is a paper of Lambe:[6] 'The estate of the recknings between Mr Dr Butler and me this 6th of Sept. 1612'. From this it appears that Lambe and his brother (Thomas) had been living at Spratton with Butler, who was unmarried, since 1605.[7] By Lambe's reckoning Butler was £150 to £200 in his debt.

There is no list of the books bequeathed to Buckeridge, and we do not know how many more there were than the nineteen manuscripts and two printed books[8] which Buckeridge sent to St. John's College, Oxford. Among the manuscripts are two groups which Butler had obtained *en bloc*. The first group contains the inscription: 'Liber Ricardi Butler rectoris de Aston in le Walles ex dono magistri Albani Butler senioris 21 Dec. 1607.'[9] Alban Butler was, as we have seen, the patron who presented Richard Butler to the living of Aston-le-Walls. Whether they were kinsfolk I have been unable to discover.[10] Alban Butler is called 'senior' to distinguish him from the grandson of the same name who succeeded him.[11] The manuscripts are as follows:

MS. St. John's Coll. 118: Philip the Chancellor on the Psalms. 13th cent. The lines are numbered by 5s between the columns.

MS. St. John's Coll. 136:[12] Dogma laicorum, Sermons, etc. 13th, 14th cent. A volume with Northamptonshire connections.

MS. St. John's Coll. 147: Richard Rolle, *Parce michi*, Saints' lives, etc. 15th cent. From Westminster Abbey.

MS. St. John's Coll. 171: Wyclif, Postilla on parts of the Old Testament.

15th cent. On fol. 1 is 'Condam fui libellus domini Thome Graunte sacerdotis. Et nunc sum libellus Nicholai Sykys', and 'Christopherus Pollein nunc me possidet.' Both 16th cent.

MS. St. John's Coll. 190: Bonaventura, Breviloquium, etc. 13th cent. From Westminster Abbey. On fol. 307 is 'Graunte', in red ink.

MS. St. John's Coll. 206: Flores Bernardi, etc. 13th, 14th cent. On fol. 310ᵛ is 'Thomas Graunte,' in red ink, cf. fol. 5. In books I–III of the Flores lines by 5s and columns are numbered. Similarly on fol. 283–94.

With these should be associated MS. 178, a well-known miscellany of teaching texts of the thirteenth century, which bears the *ex libris* of Westminster Abbey, and the names of Nicholas Sykys and George Whalley. There is no indication how it came to the College.

The second group consists of seven manuscripts that had belonged to John Backhouse. They are:

MS. St. John's Coll. 16: Joshua, Judges, Tobit, Esther, Acts, glossed. 13th cent. On fol. 1 is 'J.B.'

MS. St. John's Coll. 20: Haymo on Isaiah. 12th cent. With a pressmark assigned by Mr. Ker to St. Andrew's Northampton.[13] Fine penwork initials. 'John Backhous me possidet xiiij l. 4 s. (*sic*).'

MS. St. John's Coll. 26: Isaiah, Daniel, glossed. Second half of 12th cent. Good quality initials. Chapter numbering in the untidy hand of Backhouse.

MS. St. John's Coll. 27: Ezechiel, glossed. Second half of 12th cent. Good quality initials. 'Johannes Bacchus me possidet precium iij s. 4 d.'

MS. St. John's Coll. 38: Jerome on the Psalms. 12th cent. On Ps. 138 is a note in the hand of Backhouse. Both this manuscript and MS. 26 have a strip cut off the top of the first leaf where there was, no doubt, an *ex libris*.

MS. St. John's Coll. 39: Matthew, Mark, glossed. 13th cent. With the pressmark assigned to St. Andrew's Northampton. Until 1921 it was in wrappers, which consisted of a bifolium and a single leaf from a manuscript of Jerome on Isaiah (bks. xiv–xv), written in England in the third quarter of the twelfth century, and a list of inhabitants of Newark-on-Trent, *c*. 1175.[14] There are verse jottings by Backhouse on the verso of the front flyleaf.[15]

MS. St. John's Coll. 42: Jeremiah, glossed. 14th cent. There is an erased *ex libris* at the top of fol. 1. 'Johannes Backhus me possidet precium ij s.'

John Backhouse (or Bacchus)[16] was ordained priest by Cuthbert Tunstall, Bishop of Durham, at Chester on 25 March 1559 on the title of lands of Thomas Parker, gent. He was not a graduate, and before his ordination had been a schoolmaster (*pedagogus*). He became Rector of Thorpe Achurch, Northants, in 1563, and of Aldwinkle All Souls in 1568. The latter benefice he resigned in 1580, since he had become

Rector of Haselbeach in December 1579. He was still there in 1591. He is recorded as Rural Dean of Oundle in 1574. Another manuscript at St. John's is connected with him. At the end of MS. 56, a paper copy of Lydgate's Life of the Virgin, are bound in two letters written by Thomas Elmes from Cambridge. One is addressed 'To his ryght worshypfull and singular good frend Mr Bachous Deane of Oundhill and person of Acruch.' It is a letter recommending the bearer who is not named. The manuscript came to the College in 1619 from Richard Tileslye, Archdeacon of Rochester and a former fellow, and 'custos' of the College Library.[17] Tileslye at the same time gave four other manuscripts.[18] Three had belonged in the Middle Ages to the Abbey of Lesnes, which was in his Archdeaconry.

The remainder of the manuscripts which came from Richard Butler is as follows:

MS. St. John's Coll. 8: Job, glossed. 13th cent. Bequeathed by Henry of Walton, Archdeacon of Richmond, to his nephew in 1359.

MS. St. John's Coll. 47: Sarum Manual. 15th cent.

MS. St. John's Coll. 50: Peter Lombard, Sentences. 13th cent. (writing above the top line). From Hurley, a cell of Westminster Abbey.

MS. St. John's Coll. 100: Bible. (262 × 160 mm.) 13th cent. (writing above the top line). On fol. 1 is 'Liber Johannis Ryngrosii ex dono domini Ricardi Westowre' 16th cent.

MS. St. John's Coll. 138: Prick of Conscience. 15th cent.

MS. St. John's Coll. 141: Gregory the Great, Homilies on the Gospels. 14th cent.

This is a miscellaneous lot. The books had probably not been in institutional hands in the middle ages, except for the Peter Lombard from Hurley.

John Lambe, Butler's executor, gave one manuscript to the College: Peter Comestor, Historia scholastica, late 12th cent. (MS. 34). The date of the gift is not entered in the inscription, but since Lambe is described as Registrar of the diocese of Peterborough, it cannot be later than February 1616, when he became Vicar-General.[19] This is the earliest evidence of an association between Laud and Lambe. Later, in 1632, Lambe gave Laud twenty-one manuscripts, twelve of which can be identified among the Laudian manuscripts in the Bodleian Library.

In 1620 Buckeridge gave three manuscripts. One is a folio Bible (MS. 4), of the thirteenth century, of which the medieval provenance is Rochester, his see. The other two are works on medieval political theory (MSS. 69, Ocham's Dialogi, and 71, Augustinus Anconitanus) of unknown provenance.[20] I include Thomas Walker here, though his gift cannot be dated,[21] because he was a connection of Laud, who bequeathed to him 'my ring with a sapphire in it. I having interest in the Master of Univ. Coll.' The manuscripts are:

MS. St. John's Coll. 67: Petrus Cantor, Verbum abbreviatum. Early 13th cent.

MS. St. John's Coll. 77: Miscellanea theologica. 15th cent. From Exeter College, Oxford.

MS. St. John's Coll. 169: Liber de septem sacramentis, etc. 15th cent. From Magdalen College, Oxford.[22]

Walker had presumably picked up the last two in Oxford. He also gave manuscripts to University College.

Lastly we come to Laud's own gifts. The first two had been received in 1610 when he resigned his fellowship (MSS. 117, 207).[23] While he was President he gave one in 1613 (MS. 111), two in 1617 (MSS. 49, 64), one in 1618 (MS. 98), and three in 1620 (MSS. 9, 60, 99). We only know for certain how he came by one of them (MS. 64), a gift from an unidentified friend ('Chr: M:'). Of the others, one was a local book (MS. 60), the Sarum Hymnal given by Robert King, last Abbot of Oseney and first Bishop of Oxford to the Cathedral in 1542. A monastic provenance is known for three: Jervaulx (MS. 95), Chichester (MS. 49), and the Isle of May, co. Fife, at one time a cell of Reading, Laud's birthplace (MS. 111). It is worth noting that there are two other Chichester books at St. John's (MSS. 88, 95) which contain no indication of donor, and that William Juxon, who was a close friend of Laud, and who succeeded him as President, was born at Chichester where his father was receiver-general of the estates of the Bishop.

The Fellows of St. John's were very active in building up their Library at the end of the sixteenth and beginning of the seventeenth century. In Mr. Ker's words, it 'surpasses that of other Oxford Colleges'.[24] The moving spirits in the College behind this growth cannot at present be discerned, and we have only the circumstantial evidence, here set out, that Laud as President furthered the work. Evidence of this kind is admittedly not proof, but as I gathered together the facts I could discover about these donors, and as their connections with Laud became apparent, it seemed worth while to set them down.

The main lines of the descent of medieval manuscripts from monastic and other libraries to the institutions where they are now preserved are well established,[25] but much remains to be discovered in detail. Many books remained in the neighbourhood of the monastic houses to which they had belonged. The Lesnes books which Richard Tileslye gave belong to this class, as also probably the Bible from Rochester given by Buckeridge. A possible line of connection with Chichester has been suggested for two of Laud's gifts. One might have expected the books that belonged to John Backhouse to belong to this class, but there is only evidence of earlier provenance for two of them which are probably from the Priory of St. Andrew's, Northampton. Sometimes little groups of books appear to have remained together since the Reformation. Part of the manuscripts given by Alban Butler to Richard Butler appears to be an example, although the evidence is not as clear as one could wish. Three of the volumes (MSS. 171, 190, 206) belonged to Thomas Graunte, priest, whose name is written in red in a hand of the sixteenth century difficult to date.[26] In only one of them (MS. 171) are there further names of the sixteenth century, Nicholas Sykys and Christopher Pollein. It would be of considerable interest to identify these men, since the manuscript is one of the very few surviving witnesses to the text of Wyclif's Postilla on the Old Testament. It is not likely to have belonged to an institution. The name of Nicholas Sykys is also found in another of the College manuscripts (MS. 178) from an unknown donor. It formerly belonged to Westminster Abbey which was also the medieval home of one of Graunte's books (MS. 190) and of one of the other books from Alban Butler (MS. 147).

These two ways of transmission cover only a minority of manuscripts, and the second does not exclude the intervention of a bookseller. To complete our picture of the way medieval manuscripts have come down to us we need above all evidence of the activity of booksellers, and it is notoriously hard to obtain such evidence. The College records do not help us. Only once, in 1610, the Register of Benefactors records the gift of a bookseller, Stephen Pott, 'bibliopola Londinensis', who gave the College an early fifteenth-century Sarum Breviary (MS. 179) together with a 'Psalterium Moscovitice'.[27] About 1626 Sir Roger Twysden bought from a bookseller of the same name a manuscript of the Golden Legend (now British Library, MS. Stowe 49), which had belonged to St. Stephen's Chapel, Westminster.[28] A man of the same name is mentioned in a list returned to the Privy Council in 1628 of thirty-nine booksellers in London who dealt 'in old libraries, mart books or any other'.[29] The absence of evidence for the activities of booksellers equally confronts us when we try to discover the ways in which large collections, like that of Sir Robert Cotton, were built up. The earliest collection for which we have firm evidence for the part they played is the Harleian, thanks to the Diary kept by Humfrey Wanley. Nevertheless we should surely keep them in mind when studying the history of collections of the earlier seventeenth century.[30]

NOTES

1. The inscriptions are indicated in H. O. Coxe, *Catalogus Codicum MSS ... in Collegiis Aulisque Oxoniensibus*, pars II (1852).

2. For his career see H. I. Longden, *Northamptonshire and Rutland clergy from 1500*, Northampton, 1938, ii. 339.

3. *Register of the University of Oxford*, ed. A. Clark (O.H.S. X, XII), II. i, p. 348; iii, p. 183.

4. S. P. Dom. 14/70/66. I owe my knowledge of it to the unpublished Oxford B.Litt. thesis of Miss D. M. Slatter, 'A biographical study of Sir John Lambe, c. 1566–1646'. Miss Slatter there drew attention to the manuscripts from Butler at St John's College. I have to thank Miss D. M. Barratt for the extracts from the will, as well as for much other help.

5. A gold coin issued by King James I, worth 22s; see *OED* s.v. Unite *numism*.

6. S.P. Dom. 14/70/66.

7. The connection probably goes back further. Butler and Mr. John Lambe, senior, that is, the father of our John Lambe, each received a bequest of £5 from Thomas Bellamy, rector of St. Peter's, Northampton, who died in 1606, as overseers of his will. Longden, op. cit., ii. 63.

8. The printed books are the Oxford Lathbury, 1482, and Joh. Arboreus, *Primus (Secundus) Tomus Theosophiae*, Paris, 1540.

9. MS. St. John's Coll. 190 has the date 24 Dec. 1607.

10. In his will Butler bequeathed the residue of his estate to his mother for life. It was then to be divided into four parts, one to Thomas Butler, the other three equally between his brother, John, and his sister, Edith Deacon.

11. J. Bridges, *Hist. and antiquities of Northamptonshire*, Oxford, 1791, i, 101–102; G. Baker, *Hist. and antiquities of the county of Northampton*, London, 1822–30, i. 471.

12. Coxe does not record the inscription.

13. *Medieval libraries of Great Britain*, 2nd ed. (Royal Hist. Soc., 1964), p. 135.

14. Printed in *Documents relating to the manor and soke of Newark-on-Trent*, edited by M. W. Barley, with contributions by W. H. Stevenson and Kenneth Cameron (Thoroton Society, Record series, xvi), 1956. W. H. Stevenson identified the jottings of Backhouse.

15. The re-binding was done by Messrs. Maltby of Oxford in pigskin elaborately ornamented with revived 15–16th cent. stamps and rolls.

16. Longden, op. cit., ii. 129, 131. For his ordination by Tunstall see the *Register of Cuthbert Tunstall* ... Surtees Soc. 161 (1952), 122. In the addenda to Longden (xvi. 7) is a reference which comes from Bishop Richard Howland's Clergy Book, 1586 (Northants County Record Office, Peterborough Diocesan Records, Misc. Book 9),

under Haselbeche R(ectoria): 'Johannes Bacchus rector ibidem, nullius gradus, ordinatus per dominum Robertum (sic) episcopum xxv^{to} Martii 1559, et ante admissionem suam ad ordines fuit pedagogus. Predicator.' I am indebted to the archivist, Mr. P. I. King, for a photocopy of the entry.

17. W. C. Costin, *The history of St. John's College 1598-1860* (O.H.S. N.S. XII, 1958), p. 73.

18. MSS. 19 (his gift is recorded in the Register of Benefactors and not in the MS.), 31, 134 are from Lesnes. MS. 93 is of unknown medieval provenance.

19. Slatter, op. cit., p. 22.

20. Both volumes have pastedown from a commentary on Aristotle, De generations et corruptione, 15th cent.

21. In the inscriptions he is described as M.A. and fellow, i.e. between 1619 and 1631; see Costin, pp. 49-50.

22. Emden, *B.R.U.O.*, ii. 1107 under Laugharne, Richard.

23. I have given more details on them in the catalogue of the Laudian commemorative exhibition held in the Bodleian Library, 1973.

24. *Bodleian Library Record*, 6 (1959), 511.

25. See especially the magisterial survey by N. R. Ker in *Medieval Libraries of Great Britain*, pp. x-xv.

26. A man of this name was a member of the Dominican Convent at Dartford, and, in Nov. 1539, was granted a dispensation to hold a benefice with change of habit; see *Faculty Office Register, 1534-49* ed. D.S. Chambers, Oxford, 1966, pp. 199, 220.

27. This is the Psalter, printed at Vilna, 1596; see J. S. G. Simmons, *Times Literary Supplement*, 27 September 1963. The Breviary has an inscription 'Found by me Hugh Fortescu, in the house of John Roberts of Comb Martin' [co. Devon].

28. Hist. MSS. Commission, 8th Report iii. 26, no. 16: 'Ego Rogerus Twysden emi hunc librum a Stephano Potts librario publico circa annum domini 1626 tunc commorante in vico vocato Aldersgate St.' I owe the reference to the card index (kept in the Bodleian Library) on which Mr. Ker's *Medieval Libraries* is based.

29. *A companion to Arber*, ed. W. W. Greg. Oxford, 1966, pp. 240-1; in H. R. Plomer, *Dictionary of booksellers and printers* ... *1557-1640* (Bibliographical Society), 1910, p. 220, this document is the only evidence cited.

30. I have to thank Mr. H. M. Colvin, librarian of St. John's College and his assistant, Mr. C. Morgenstern, for giving me every facility to work on the manuscripts in their charge. I have also to thank Miss C. Starks for much help in the preparation of this paper.

PAUL MORGAN

The Oxford book trade

Letters relating to the Oxford book trade found in bindings in Oxford college libraries c. 1611–1647

When calling attention to the importance of wills for giving biographical details of early members of the Oxford book trade, Strickland Gibson wrote: 'There is one other likely source of information, and that is in the fragments found lining the boards of bindings',[1] and then mentioned part of an account-book of Henry Cripps, now removed from several Jesus College books.[2] Leaves from account or daybooks from bookshops, as well as lists of books, are fairly numerous, but other documents such as letters can also be found. Those described here are all from bindings in Oxford college libraries and are concerned with the Oxford book trade during the first half of the seventeenth century.

The bindings in which these letters were used vary in style. The first three all come from a single volume in Magdalen College, bound in dark calf over pasteboards, tooled with a centrepiece and a small ornament in blind which can now safely be ascribed to Damian Cope, one of the correspondents and an Oxford binder in the reign of James I. Nos. IV–VI all come from books bound similarly in plain, dark calf over pasteboards, undecorated except for a frame of three lines in blind, and spines with diagonal hatching at the top and bottom. Dr. N. R. Ker has noted that these 'plain, unadorned covers hardly occur before *c*. 1615'[3] and the books in which these letters were used were bound in the 1630s; this style is associated with Thomas Huggins and William Webb who started business in Oxford in 1609 and 1625 respectively. No. VII comes from a volume which has been re-backed but the covers, though they have the frame of three lines in blind as in Nos. IV–VI, are in mottled calf and would seem to be a very early example of this way of treating leather.[4] No. VIII was formerly in a book that has since been completely rebound.

1. Notes begin on p. 86.

All the letters have inevitably been cropped to a greater or less extent during binding, but some of the lost text can be supplied. Some are very fragmentary, but others throw considerable light on personal and business concerns. The first three are rather full of family affairs, though they also reveal how closely London tradesmen kept in touch with their native districts and how their Oxford counterparts obtained supplies, with some details of prices. How the West Country and Wales looked to Oxford for books and printing is shown in No. IV and No. VII. The fifth and sixth retail book-trade gossip, while the former is also important for the background to the production of a second edition. The last throws light on the careers of some Oxford and London booksellers, with financial details about profits and costs, besides revealing that a name found on imprints over forty years, formerly thought to be one man, in reality indicates a father and a son.

In the following transcriptions, a stroke (/) is used to indicate the ends of lines, whether cropped or not; missing parts of the text are shown by square brackets ([ ]), and inferred readings added where possible, but otherwise left blank.

The practice of historians in adding punctuation, capitalisation and expanding contractions has been adopted, in order to make the letters as readable as possible. It was thought that the method used in Sir Walter Greg's *Companion to Arber* is too literal and cumbersome for such fragmentary documents.

I am most grateful to the college librarians of Brasenose, Jesus, Magdalen, Merton, Queen's and Worcester for permission to publish these letters and, where necessary, to allow them to be extracted temporarily[5] so that concealed parts could be read. I am also indebted, as always, both to my colleague Dr. D. M. Barratt for help with transcription, and to Dr. N. R. Ker for advice.

I

Damian Cope, bookbinder, of Oxford, to his brother John, baker, of London, c. 1611

To my verie lovinge/brother John Cope, baker,/at Mr. Smithe's in Puddinge/ Lane, give this.

Brother John, I commend me un to you & your wife/[and all] of our frends in London. This is to sertifie unto you t/[hat Mr.] Nickcoles hath delivered me a note of the charges betw/[een Mr.] [Furnis ?] & you, and he hath had of

PLATE 5. Tools used by Damian Cope.

OXFORD BOOK-TRADE LETTERS

me xs. that the charg/[ges] too. Like wise I have spoken with Mr. Nickcoles about Mr. B/[oone?] They are both satisfied for that you may speake/[to] Mr. Boone when you have conwenient tyme and soe end/[the matter] about the charges, because the monie he hath had of you/[in Mr.] Nickcoles' words is more then he should have but/[I asked] Mr. Nickcoles to speake to him & he saith some thinges si/[nce] that was done made up the even monie wich you may kn/[ow of.] If anie thinge may be saved by it, it is better then lost/[of the] monie I have paid. I received the over pluse monie of good/ [wife] Kensall becase Mr. Nickcoles was ernest with me for it/ & the rest I would have sent you before, but I looked for/you rite in your letter that you would send word/. I cold not tell where to deliver it, but your monie is as/[safe] for you as if it were in your owne hands and shall be, an/[d] that I receive by God's helpe and for the receivinge of you/[r money] out of Kensall's hand, it is not possible I thincke. For/[do] not pay it at your apoint-mentment [sic] but pay it to th/[e land]lord himselfe, and all to [currie ?] favor with the landlo/[rd] is the truth of the matter, I well perceive and all the money/[ ] makethe to hir, as I beleve you shall heare ere longe; soe[I] thinck thinck [sic] good you may come or send Mr. Holloway/[ ] minde and that will serve. So I end to you for that and I p/[ray] thee doe soe much if you see Gorge Edwards com[mend me] to/[him]. [*Tear*] and pray him if he can poss[ibly] tie/[ ] sheete of the Bible & the last sheets of the Psallmes/[*At least one line trimmed away*]

   Your brother, Damian Cope.[6]
[*Postscript put vertically in margin*] But the monie will/[ ] his dates must be p/[ ] be Richard Osboond/[ ]

This letter is written on a single sheet used originally as the front paste-down, but now lifted, in Martin Chemnitz, *Loci theologici* (Wittenberg, 1610, fol.) in Magdalen College (shelf-mark: l.11.12). The book is bound in dark calf over pasteboards; the covers are blind-tooled with three frames, each of three lines, the centre one being 15 mm. from the outer, and the innermost 20 mm. from the centre one; a triangular ornament of a vase with flowers is used twice in each corner between the frames. There is a blind, arabesque centre-piece stylistically similar to, but different from, N. R. Ker's Centrepiece No. 2. Stubs of two leather thongs remain. The spine has five bands with diagonal hatching at its top and bottom.

There is no indication of provenance, though the figures 13 and 9 flank the imprint on the title; it was probably acquired by the College early in the seventeenth century.

The letter has been cropped at its top, bottom and right, removing some words. The address is opposite the text. The verso contains John

Cope's letter. It was probably written about 1611, judging from the reference to Goodwife Jennings in Letter II.

Damian Cope was born about 1581 and was admitted a privileged member of the University at the age of 28 in October 1609.[7] He was one of the eight sons of Hugh Cope, of Merton, Oxon., husbandman, whose will was proved in November 1590.[8] Both he and his brother John were left £4, to be paid when they reached 18. Hugh's brother John, of Blackthorn, possibly the uncle mentioned in Letter II, was one of the overseers, and John Osborne, of Merton, possibly a connection of Richard 'Osboond', was another. The father's estate was valued at £47.15s. Damian's binding career is unknown beyond these letters, and the absence of references to him in the Bodleian and other records suggests that he either died young, or failed in business.

Few of the various people named can be definitely identified; there were more than one Nicholls or Kensall in Oxford at this time, for instance. George Edwards was an Oxfordshire man, the son of Richard Edwards of 'Sybbert', Oxon. (possibly one of the Sibfords, or Shifford), yeoman, and apprenticed to the bookseller and bookbinder Manasses Bloome, from 1600 to 1608. He was possibly first in partnership with Jacob Bloome, but had an independent business in Green Arbour from 1616 to 1640.[9]

Letters I and II obviously form part of a series; the references to Kensall, and the commissions to Edwards suggest that Damian's was the earlier. The contacts between men from the same area in London, and those between the Londoners and provincial tradesmen, are interesting.

II

John Cope to his brother, Damian, c. 1611

To my very loving/brother, Damyan Cope/bookbinder in Oxford,/give this./Brother Damyan, Yr. letter on t/[   ] second day of Maye. The conttentes/[I] have receved xxiijs. iiijd. of Kensall/[; she gave it] me at our Ladey Day last and you have/[   ] [*Tear*] feel that I am well contented but I p/[   ] to aney body of my money for g/[   ] my selfe, but send it to me by the next/[carrier]. Provid me my money you owe me I p/[ray] now so sonne as is posibull another tyme/[   ] with you for twise so much if God mak/[   ] Mr. Holloway; I have sent him a letter an/[d] a boke. I pray comend me to my mothe/[r; tell] hir, if it please

God to send me life,/[   ] I will be at Marton betwene this a[nd
near, if it be posibull to recefe my unkell/[10][   ] that he hath geven me.
So I end for that fo/[   ] the prise is xijs. a hundred for peney borde/
[s, and] for a hundred of eight peney bordes[11] he a/[   ] peney, so if you
[send][12] me word howe manye/[you want] and send me money to pay
for them I w/[ill get as] maney as I can by for your money/[from] Gorge
Edwardes, and if he can helpe y/[ou] of the Bybell and the rest you write for.
So/[many] hartey comendaciones to all our frendse th/[*At least one line trimmed away*].
[*Postscript on verso*] Brother Damyan, I pray inquire whether goodwif/
Jenninges in All Hollowes have let hir backhouse/or if she will let it or not;
if she will I will/geve hir as much for it as it is worth & I pray/send me word
by the next carriar/

Written on the verso of Damian's letter, this reply is similarly cropped on the right and bottom, removing some of the text. John's offer to get boards for his brother was not accepted, judging from Letter III, which shows Damian directly dealing with George Edwards. These pasteboards, used for book covers, were available in various thicknesses distinguished (until the 1950s) by a number before the penny; the eightpenny boards would be thicker than the penny ones. Goodwife Jennings, mentioned in the postscript, would seem to have been Joan Jennings, buried at All Saints, Oxford, on 8 June 1612;[13] she was the widow of Edward Jennings buried on 11 October 1608,[14] so these letters were written some time after October 1608 and before June 1612.

III

George Edwards to Damian Cope, c. 1611

This to be given to Damian Cope/bookebinder in Saint Mary's Lane/in Oxford[15] with speede/
[Wor]shepful and well beloved Damian Cope, I commende me and/[all o]f your frindes in Greene Arbar[16] to you. I received your letter, and you sent/
[   ] and iij$d$. The carrier had and xs and a jd I had whereof Egelston had viij$s$–viij$d$/[for boa]rdes and the carriege to the Sargin's Head.[17] I got him to take iiij$s$ vj$d$ for the halfe/hundred of jd bordes and the quarter of xd ij$s$ and the viij$d$ bordes xx$d$ and vi$d$/the carrige, that is viij$s$ viij$d$ then I had xv[ii]d [in] hand wherof a iiij$d$ is to [buy a] drink at Mtris. Tayler's to the health of all the good fellues in Oxford. Then there is xiij$d$/behinde so I will have xij$d$ and the other id shall paye for the carriege of this letter. So you owe me iiij$s$ stil, and I

will get you halfe a C of goulde shortly. Send iiij*s*/and the munny for the goulde together; but for the print which you speeke of tel me/whether of[18] them you would have that with the doges[19] heades or the other and I will/ [find] the price of the cutinge of it and sende you worde. And you must wringe the/[   ]her when you have washed them in allem water. I forgout to tel you of your lime/water; you must take a peck of lime and put it in to your water and let it stand/a daye and a night, and then it will be reddy for you to take it out with a bowle/safely, that you doo not stur the lime, and then you may put mowre water to it, and/take a staf and stur the lime up and downe, and then let it settel tel you have yuse for it/for it [*sic*] againe, and it will serve you a mounth, and then put another peck in it./ I went to Egelston on Sunday and gave him the munny, and he saye faithfully he yould bring/them to the the [*sic*] carrier on Tusday nyght without faile as I hoope he did. When you send/up munny you shoulde send ij*d* or iij*d* moore then the sum because the carrier will have so[me]/and then wee shall make wright account and at your next letter I will send your gould./So wrighting it in hast when all our folkes were asleepe. I commit you to God,/
                Your frind,/
               George Edwardes

This letter was the back pastedown in the book in which the first two letters were used at the front; it is now lifted. Written on one side of a single sheet, it shows creases from folding; the top left corner has been cut off and there is some mutilation, especially in lines 5–7.

   George Edwards' connections with Oxfordshire were mentioned under Letter I. The hearty tone of this letter to Damian Cope suggests the friendship of near contemporaries, with Edwards as the senior dispensing advice to one starting a career; confirmation of this comes from the fact that Cope was admitted a privileged person at Oxford in 1609, the year after Edwards completed his apprenticeship to a bookseller and binder. Edwards implies in this letter that Cope was known in London, and may have learnt his craft there. These connections may explain why he wanted boards sent from London to Oxford instead of buying local products, since other Oxford binders owned presses and moulds at this period,[20] and so avoiding costs of carriage.

   The financial transactions recounted are obscure and complex, but there were apparently two principal sums involved: (i) an unknown amount ending in 3*d* (the first figure has been trimmed away), sent by Cope to Edwards; (ii) 10*s* 1*d* sent with the carrier of which 8*s* 8*d* was paid for boards and carriage, leaving 1*s* 5*d* of which a groat went as a tip, leaving 1*s* 1*d* with Edwards. The outstanding debt of 4*s* presumably refers to the unknown sum first mentioned.

In Letter II, John Cope quoted the price of 12s for a hundred penny boards, but Edwards actually paid at the rate of 9s a hundred. Prices for boards are difficult to determine on account of their varying thicknesses, but in the 1580s boards of unspecified sizes were valued in Cambridge at 3s and 5s the hundred;[21] contemporary Oxford inventories unfortunately do not mention quantities.

Alum had several uses in binders' shops such as in making paste, but it is not known exactly what has first to be washed in alum water and then wrung out. Lime water was used in preparing and washing vellum.[22] Presumably gold-leaf for tooled decoration on leather, or for gilt-edges, is meant by 'goulde'.

IV

John Langley to Thomas Huggins, 15 December c. 1622–3

To his loving freind Mr/Thomas Huggins at/Mrs Garbrand's shoppe/in Oxon. these/Mr Huggins (after my love remembered), I h/[ope] the carrier sent you 13° desiring you [to] send mee/[   ] his Lexicon in folio; & also what the price of Tilen/[us his] Syntagma bound in two pts. is. I desired Mr Potter to/[tell me] the price, but having this occasion to write[23] I ha/[ve] now seconded him if hee have already bin with you/[. Will] you bind up the booke that it take no hurt; & for/[the care] of it I perswade my selfe you will not sent[*sic*]one faul/[ty my] way. Thus in hast I committ you to God & r/[est]
                      Your assured freind

Coll Gloucr.   Jo. Langley
Decemb: 15

This letter, written on one side of a single sheet, is the front pastedown of Theodore Balsamon, *Canones ss. apostolorum conciliorum generalium et provincialium* (Paris, 1620, fol.) in Brasenose College (shelf-mark: Lath.H.1.5). Printed waste from an edition of the *Dissertationes* of Maximus Tyrius is used at the back. The book is bound in dark calf, undecorated except for a frame of three lines in blind on each cover; the spine has five bands, without hatching. Marks of chaining remain on the top of the upper cover. There is no indication of provenance. Trimming on the right has removed a little of the text of the letter, which was probably written about 1622 or 1623, since an edition of the *Syntagma* of Daniel Tilenus, in two parts, was published in Geneva in 1622.

Thomas Huggins was admitted as a privileged person in the University of Oxford in November 1609 (a month after Damian Cope) when he was described as a servant of 'Master Garbrand, bookseller'.[24] He worked independently as an Oxford bookseller and stationer from 1609 to 1636,[25] probably taking over the business of Richard Herkes *alias* Garbrand, who died in 1602 and whose widow, Anne's, will was proved in December 1609.[26] The identity of 'Mr Potter' is not clear; it could be George Potter, a London bookseller who might call at Oxford and Gloucester when visiting his native Shropshire,[27] or equally an academic such as Christopher Potter of Queen's College.

John Langley, a native of Banbury, graduated from Magdalen Hall in 1616, the year he was appointed usher of the College (now the King's) School, Gloucester. In 1620 he became the headmaster, but his strong Puritanical leanings caused his resignation in 1635, though he apparently continued to teach elsewhere in Gloucester until he was appointed High Master of St. Paul's School, London, in 1640 where he remained until his death in 1657.[28] In a sermon preached at his funeral by Edward Reynolds, Langley was extolled as 'a *Learned man* ... not onely an excellent *Linguist* and *Grammarian, Historian, Cosmographer, Artist*, but a most judicious *Divine* and a great *Antiquary*'.[29]

This letter gives an interesting glimpse of a young scholar in the provinces keeping in touch with new publications through a friendly relationship with a bookseller. The sphere of influence of the Oxford book trade in the western parts of Britain is further illustrated in Letter VII.

V

To Thomas Huggins, 20 April 1631

To my very loving brother/Mr. Thomas Huggins, bookseller/in Oxford,/ these.
[*Beginning of letter missing*]/care and [   ]/right, and me content, if you would admitt/[   ] of pay and satisfaction for Matt's dyett so long/[   ] a time. I doe heartily desire it may be so; and/[then] our obligation wilbe nere the lesse to you and/[   ] my sister for your great love and tendernes/ [spent] over him. For under God you have been the/instruments and meanes of his life. I have rec/[eived] your bills, but perceive you have forgott to set/ downe for making his breeches we lately sent: I/pray doe not wrong yourself so apparently./I have a desire, that you speedily reprint Bree/[wood] for feare that in these disquiet times, it be prohibit/[ed] for I feare lest violent

spirits prevayle too fa/[r.] And if you dout of selling it off I will for m/[y] owne particular take *5=hundred of them off of y/[our] hand, at those rates, that you can with good ben/[efit] to yourselfe afford them. But then let me tell y/[ou] I would have you have speceall care of your presse; it/[will] be for your creditt and the author's that is dead; and/[let] it be printed by the copie that I have exa/[mined and] corrected. For the manuscript I writ to you/[   ] afore, there is no great dout, but you shall have/[it.] I am told at London house a week since (b/[ut] keepe it to yourselfe) that Turner your neighb/[our] is the man that printed Prin's last booke;/[if] it be so, it wilbe his undoing. Thus wit/[h] love to yourselfe and my sister, and Ma/[tt. Tell] Mr. Chellingworth when you see him I comme/[nd . . .]

Aprill 20. 1631

[*Marginal note on left*] * If you will/800 fo/[r] I know I ca/[n] sell them well/

This letter is written on a single sheet folded to form bifolium endleaves at the back of R. Goclenius, *Lexicon philosophicum Graecum* (Frankfurt, 1634, 4°) in Worcester College (shelf-mark: S.10.3). Bound in dark calf over pasteboards, there is a frame of three lines blind-tooled on the covers and the spine, with diagonal hatching at the top and bottom, has four bands. There is no indication of provenance or of chaining, but '5.' has been written on the right of the imprint. At the front there is a bifolium containing in manuscript parts of A to E of an unpriced inventory of books published in Europe between 1502 and 1598.

Trimming at the top, bottom and on the right has unfortunately removed both the beginning and end of the letter with the writer's name, though the text suggests a London bookseller whose sister was married to Thomas Huggins (also the recipient of Letter IV) and whose son or dependant was lodging in the Huggins household. Furthermore, it is particularly unfortunate that the unknown editor behind Brerewood's book remains unidentified. The first edition of Edward Brerewood, *A learned treatise of the Sabaoth* appeared in 1630[30] with the imprint: Oxford, John Lichfield for Thomas Huggins, and the second, with the same imprint but *Sabaoth* in the title changed to *Sabbath* in 1631:[31] Brerewood, a Brasenose man later the first professor of astronomy at Gresham College in London, had died in 1613; in this *Treatise*, taking the form of a letter to Nicholas Byfield, a Chester preacher, he advocated a less strict attitude to Sunday observance than that adopted by Byfield and other Puritans; Byfield's answer and Brerewood's reply were also appended.

Since Byfield had died in 1622, posthumous publication without naming the editor was presumably a device to escape any adverse consequences. The number of copies this unknown person could dispose of, 500 or 800, represents about a third or a half of an average-sized edition.[32] The warning to take special care was caused by the presence of many errors in the first edition in which the *errata* states 'Many misprintings and lesser faultes there are, by the darknesse of the copy and oversight of the Printer, which the iudicious reader may easily correct'. It would appear that the second edition was set from manuscript copy, and not from the first corrected by hand.

That Huggins' correspondent was concerned with the London book trade is strengthened by the reference to 'London house', a former residence of the bishops of London at the north-west corner of St. Paul's Churchyard where there is now a yard called after it.[33] 'Prin's last booke' probably refers to *Lame Giles his haultings*, 1630, with a false imprint naming 'Giles Widdowes'.[34] William Turner, printer and vintner in Oxford 1610–43,[35] on 6 May 1631 denied any connection with this tract when in trouble with the High Commission together with Michael Sparke, the London bookseller, for unlicensed printing.[36] The typographical evidence supports Turner's denial since the poor and damaged printer's flowers and a capital 'A' with a distinctive nick used in *Lame Giles* have not been found elsewhere in works printed by Turner. This case naturally would have been the subject of gossip around St. Paul's Churchyard during April and May 1631.

VI

To William Webb, 24 February 1635/6

To his loving frende/Mr. Webb, bookseller/in Oxford, these/Mr. Webb, my love u/[nto you   ] your letter a[nd] the 12 G/[rotius] as for Reynolds and have ha/[   ] 5 yeares and your Cycle/[   ] last Commensment from lo/[   ] have them still by me, and/[   ] for the other bookes I hav/[e   ] and too many of some of th/[em   ] De umbra if you please/[   ] 12 Grotius poems, and if/[   ] use more I shall give y/[   ] the Bible in 4°. They giv/[e out at   ] the printing house that/[   ] there is not a bookseller/[   ] out as yet neither can get/[   ] I end and rest/
            Your/[   ]
Feb. 24. 1635

This very fragmentary letter is used as the back end-leaf of Johannes Scharpius, *Cursus theologicus* (Geneva, 1620, 4°) in Merton College (shelf-mark: 83.e.3), bound in dark calf in the same manner as the Goclenius described in Letter V. Printed waste from a contemporary English work is at the front. Marks of chaining remain on the lower front cover. The provenance is unknown, but 'h' and 'd' flank the imprint.

So much of the right half of the latter has been trimmed away that it is impossible to reconstruct the text. The recipient, William Webb *alias* Richmond, was a stationer, bookseller, publisher and binder in Oxford between 1625 and his death in 1652;[37] he was binding for the Bodleian in 1636–7.[38] Whether he actually had a binder's shop himself is uncertain; there is no equipment mentioned in his administration bond.[39]

The writer of the letter (only a loop remains of his signature) would appear to be another bookseller, ordering forthcoming publications and declining to replenish stock, and in view of Webb's contacts shown in Letter VII, possibly living in the provinces though the scrap of news at the end suggests London. The duodecimo Grotius probably refers to *Defensio fidei catholicae de satisfactione Christi adversus Faustum Socinum*, printed by William Turner for Webb in 1636.[40] What is meant by the reference to Reynolds cannot be exactly determined. *De umbra* indicates Johannes Wouwerus, *Dies aestiva sive de umbra paegnion*, also printed by Turner for Webb in the same year.[41] What edition of the poems of Grotius is meant is not clear; it could refer to the *Poemata collecta* printed at Leiden in 1617; more likely it could indicate a projected edition, later published in 1639, also probably printed in Leiden but with a London imprint;[42] an issue is known naming Francis Bowman of Oxford on the imprint as a publisher.[43] But the figure '12' in the letter could mean either duodecimo or 12 copies, and these editions of the poems are all in octavo.

VII

Francis Harvey to William Webb, August 1637

Too my verie good/freind Mr. Webb/in Oxford, bookseller/give this [*Beginning of letter missing*] thanking you for your last kinde book when you we/[re] in Bristoll and in Baith here; I have sent too you o/[ne] of the copies and for the others, the gentelman hath/not don but it will be redie by the next returne of/the carrier; which, if you doe mistrust the saile/[of] this impression of this copie, I will taike it up/[on] me and pay you for the

printing of it and se/[nd] you over paper if you please, for I doe thinke/that I sall [sic] sell 600 in his owne towne of Card/[iff] of them. And I pray rememer [sic] myne and my wife's/love too my sister Pardis, and I give hir much/thanks for hir token that she sent hir since/you were here, so desiring aunswer from y/[ou] so soone as you cann, I rest your freind to/use, Francis Harvey, from Bristoll, August the/[   ] 1637/
If the book cannot be printed unless his n/[ame] bee too it, his name is William Erberie.

This letter is written on a single folio used as the front free end-leaf in Cardinal Domenico Toschi, *Practicarum conclusionum iuris in omni foro frequentiorum tomus quartus* (Lyons, 1634, fol.) in Queen's College (shelf-mark: 40.E.15). The volume is bound in contemporary mottled brown calf, recently re-backed, with a frame of three lines in blind on each cover; marks of chaining are on the upper cover, but there is no indication of provenance. At the back of the volume there is a bifolium, signed *** 2-3, of Guillaume Ranchin, *A review of the Councell of Trent*, printed at Oxford by William Turner in 1638 for himself, Edward Forrest and William Webb,[44] containing part of the contents list set in roman type unlike the italic of the published version.[45] The letter has had its beginning trimmed off, and cropping on the right has removed a few words; traces of a wax seal remain.

What Harvey writes is particularly interesting, not least in showing the sphere of influence of the Oxford book trade in the seventeenth century extending to Wales and the West Country, as the need to serve these areas was mentioned in a petition of 1584 seeking permission to start a learned press.[46] Printing was not established in Wales until the eighteenth century.[47] The number of copies likely to be sold in a provincial town by a local author—600 in Cardiff in the present case, representing about half an average edition[48]—is informative. No book written by Erbery and published by Webb has been traced.

The author of the proposed book, William Erbery (1604-54),[49] was a Glamorganshire man who graduated from Brasenose College in 1623. He was first curate of Newport, Mon., and then became Vicar of St. Mary's, Cardiff, in 1633. But he adopted the views of Jacob Boehme, was pronounced a schismatic by the Bishop of Llandaff in 1635 and forced to resign his living in 1638, becoming an independent Puritan divine. The book Harvey wanted printed, therefore, came at a time when Erbery was in trouble with his ecclesiastical superiors. It is possible that Webb in consequence declined to act, as the case was in the Court of High Commission until 1638. It seems probable that the work projected by Harvey was actually Erbery's first publication, *The great mystery of Godlinesse*, entered in the Stationers' Registers by Robert Milbourne on 24 January 1638/9 as *The misticall union of Christ with his church*.[50] Although not listed in *STC*, there are editions of *The great mystery* dated 1639 in duodecimo,[51] and dated 1640 in octavo;[52] the running-title of the first part of this work, *The mysticall union of/Christ and his church*, is so like the title entered by Milbourne that it must be the same book. In it, Erbery shows orthodox Puritan views. There is neither dedication nor any clue to when it was actually written; when reprinted in his *Testimony* in 1658, there was again no indication of date.

Milbourne already had some contact with the Bristol book trade as he acted as publisher for William Purser, *Compound interest and annuities*, dated 1634, which names Roger Roydon of Bristol in the imprint.[53] But on the next recorded occasion when Bristol is mentioned on a book, in 1639, it is interesting to find Leonard Lichfield of Oxford acting for Thomas Thomas of Bristol,[54] thereby giving evidence of the Oxford–West Country connection. It is, of course, possible that Webb passed Harvey's proposition on to Milbourne.

VIII

Livewell Chapman to Henry Cripps, senior, 23 March 1647/8

For his loveing freind/Mr. Henry Cripps/bookseller/in/Oxford.
[Sir][55]/To fulfill your sonn's desire, I make bold (by y/[our] leave & permission) to tender some satisfaction/about his designe; truly there is an observable/[e pro-]vidence of God to be seene in bringing about a p[ro-]ballity of so faire a way for your son's setleme/[nt] beyond his expectation; I am confident, which I hop/[e] the end will be for his abundant good, & prove/[by] the providentiall care of the Almighty, who is the/rewarde of a faithfull servant. But to the busine/[ss in] hand; as concerning the prices; considering all circum/[stances] that he comes into a faire share ready furnisht,/[(as] large as any in the Ally)[56] into a good custome, (f/[or] my master got £300 per annum, & my mistris got/[that] much the last yeare if not more, (which if you d/[esire] the truth of, I am able to satisfy you or any, of the/[truth] of it). The conveniency of the seate of it, being/[a]mongst his acquaintance: other circumstan/[ces] which may aggrevate the advantage of it to him/[I] leave to your owne thoughts, without mentioning/[that] I say these things being considered, (also that the s/[tock] of books is wholly vendible, there being nou/[ght] or very little rubbish amongst it/[(I] meane

such bookes as are little better than w/[aste] paper. My mistris deserves more, then she des/[ires] to have, or will aske; she will have (to ma/[ke] but few words) 15s per reame for the large p/[aper] & 13s 4d per reame for the pot paper:s/[   ] the stocke being cast up att that rate (except [for] Crisp's Workes, which are priced by the booke att/[a] reasonable rate) with consideration for the/[   ]pys; it will (as I guesse) amount to about £850:[57] so that he may buy a third part of the s/[tock] & have a third part of the profitt (which it/[   ] refuse (if my mistriss please) shee must hav/[e a] partner presently, I am confident before/[I] see two days past) it wilbe sufficien/[t] for him; he will have £100 per annum/disbursing not £300, which wilbe a pritty r/[ate of] interest. And where as you may say its no/[t] certaine whether he will get so much or/[less] I answer: it's as certaine, as certainty/[can] be in a trade; for, we have the custome th/[at][58] that will yeild so much if bad times hinder not,/(& that you know is a generall callamity) for that we must/ depend uppon God. The husband-man may have/ground in a good soile, but if the weather & other/circumstances prove not good, he may be deceived/of his expectations, so it's here. Thus, I have endea-/voured to satisfy both your sonne & your selfe; I/leave it to both your wills & pleasures to/act accordingly. So, makeing bold to present my/respects to you, though unknowne, I take my leave/& remaine/

 Sr, both yours & your sonn's/well-wisher,/
London this/   Livewell Chapman/
23d of March/   servant to Mrs. Hanna Allen/
1647

Post-script/
Sr, I thought good to certify you, that/those obstructions which usually make men/affraid of partner-ship wilbe quite obliterated/here, for she with whome he will have to/deale with, is a woeman of a mild, meeke/spirit, who for piety & naturall disposition/hath few fellows. Vale/
           L C

 Written on a bifolium removed from Joannes Dicastillo, *Tractatus duo de iuramento* (Antwerp, 1662, fol.) in Jesus College (shelf-mark: D.3.16 Gall.), this letter is now in a guard-book of fragments from bindings in that College (MS. (B) 147, ff. 16–17). Some leaves from a bookseller's day-book of the 1650s, ascribed to Henry Cripps, were found by Gordon Duff and Strickland Gibson at Jesus about 1906, and removed, but this letter was not mentioned.[59] The Dicastillo, which bears no indication of provenance, has been rebound since the fragments were taken out. The letter is cropped at the top, losing most of the superscription, and on the right, losing a little of the text on the recto only of the second leaf. Creases from folding remain and also a red wax seal embossed with a swan, possibly formerly owned by Benjamin Allen, though it is reminiscent of the device used by Valentine Simms, *c.* 1595–1605;[60] a swan was used as a sign by at least eight London booksellers at this period.[61]

This letter throws light on the careers of both Oxford and London booksellers, besides providing details about the economics of the book trade in the middle of the seventeenth century. It had been thought that there was only one man called Henry Cripps,[62] born in 1596, a bookseller in Oxford from 1620 with another shop in London from about 1650 to 1660, until D. F. McKenzie published his *Stationers' Company apprentices 1605–1640* in 1961; here the record shows that Henry Cripps had a son of the same name apprenticed to the London bookseller Henry Overton in October 1639 and made free in December 1647.[63] Overton had a shop at the entrance to Pope's Head Alley out of Lombard Street from 1629 to 1648,[64] and it is significant that Benjamin Allen, Livewell Chapman's master, was at the Crown in this Alley;[65] Cripps later used the same address that Overton had. Henry Cripps, junior, would naturally learn of a neighbour's death and the consequent plight of the widow; and would at least have been acquainted with, if not a friend of, another apprentice like Livewell Chapman. After he was made free in December 1647, he would have been looking out for a business of his own and so presumably asked Chapman to write to his father about acquiring a share.

The mistress on whose behalf Chapman[66] was writing was Mrs. Hanna Allen, widow of Benjamin Allen, bookseller, who had died in May 1646 leaving an estate valued at £300, half to go to his widow and half to his two children, a total the same as one year's profits according to this letter. Chapman, son of a London scrivener, had been apprenticed to Allen in November 1643[67] and so was not free until 1650, but as the only apprentice in this comparatively small business he presumably had to manage it when his master died. What is unknown is whether Cripps bought a share in the Allen shop or not; since the son is found at Overton's address from about 1650, an interest in it was presumably acquired; but the inhabitants of Pope's Head Alley seem to have been a closely-knit group.

Mrs. Allen did not remain a widow very long; before 1652 she married Livewell Chapman, not surprisingly perhaps in view of the glowing testimony to her virtues in the postscript to this letter. Since the late Miss Rostenberg has already dealt with Chapman's career in detail, it need only be said here that both he and Allen were in sympathy with non-conformists, especially Baptists and Fifth Monarchy Men, whose works they published. Consequently, Chapman was in trouble with the authorities in 1655, and was in gaol *c.* 1661–64, disappearing from the book-trade scene after his release. His rather sanctimonious style in this letter has a Puritan ring about it. Henry Cripps, junior, also published books with a Puritan bias; nothing is known of him after 1661, though his widow was named on imprints in 1664–5.

'Crisp's Workes' mentioned in the letter refer to Tobias Crisp, an Antinomian, and may indicate either the second volume of his *Christ alone exalted*, which has only *Printed 1643* in the imprint,[68] or the third volume published by Henry Overton in 1648,[69] implying connections between the neighbouring shops.

The way Chapman has set out his description of the stock implies that everything was in sheets, except for the books by Crisp, possibly already bound. The prices quoted, 15s a ream for large paper and 13s 4d a ream for pot paper are, of course, for printed sheets, but in a list of papers offered to Bishop Fell of Oxford in 1674, the prices are near those for Royal paper,[70] while 13s 4d a ream was what was being paid for ruled paper in 1636.[71] Mrs. Allen must have had about 1,250 reams in stock, excluding Crisp's *Workes*.

When this letter was written, Benjamin Allen's estate had been settled for ten months and perhaps his widow felt she could not carry on alone with only an apprentice to help, so she needed a partner badly, though the reason for Chapman's confidence about one appearing within two days is not clear. Some significance can be attached to the fact that, judging from the date of the book in which the letter was bound, it was not put for waste, probably in Oxford, until after both the Cripps had ceased their active careers, so its retention may have some importance, perhaps implying that Cripps did become a partner of Mrs. Allen.

NOTES

1. *Abstracts from the wills and testamentary documents of binders, printers, and stationers of Oxford from 1493 to 1638* (Bibliographical Society, 1907), xxiii.
2. Now Jesus College MS. (B) 147, ff. 1–15.
3. N. R. Ker, *Fragments of medieval manuscripts used as pastedowns in Oxford bindings* Oxford Bibliographical Society publications, new series v, 1954), 215, note 2.
4. Cf. Graham Pollard, 'Changes in the style of bookbinding, 1550–1830', *The Library*, 5th series, xi (1956), where it is suggested that this style dates from between 1655 and 1685.

5. The wisdom of following Dr. Ker's advice that it is best to leave pastedowns *in situ* (*Pastedowns*, xv) is illustrated by the fact that a letter to John Crosley in 1606 mentioned on p. 217 as in a book at Oriel College, has since been lifted and removed and cannot now be located.

6. Subscription added in the margin at the top of the letter.

7. A. Clark, *Register of the University of Oxford*, II, ii (Oxford Historical Society, xi, 1887), 401.

8. Bodleian Library, MS. Wills Oxon. 188, f. 124.

9. R. B. McKerrow, *A dictionary of printers and booksellers in England . . . 1557–1640* (Bibliographical Society, 1910), 38–9, 97–8. D. F. McKenzie, *Stationers' Company apprentices, 1605–1640* (Bibliographical Society of the University of Virginia, 1961), nos. 797, 1233–44.

10. Possibly John Cope, of Blackthorn, one of the overseers of Hugh Cope's will.

11. See Letter III.

12. Omitted.

13. All Saints, Oxford, parish register, f. 85v (Bodleian Library, MS D.D. Par. Oxford All Saints, c. 1). Nuncupatory will proved 27 June 1612; estate valued at £41. 6d. (MS. Wills Oxon. 37/2/37).

14. All Saints parish register, f. 84v.

15. St. Mary's Lane (if not a variant of St. Mary Hall Lane) was apparently at the eastern end of St. Mary's Church. Anthony Wood said in 1662 that Richard Davis, stationer, was living in the lane commonly called St. Mary Lane, which he elsewhere calls 'Schydyarde Street' (*Life and times*, ed. A. Clark, i (Oxford Historical Society, xix, 1891), 440, 495–6).

16. In London, where George Edwards had his shop from 1616 onwards.

17. *i.e.* The Saracen's Head, a well-known coaching inn on the north side of Snow Hill.

18. 'it' deleted.

19. Not identified, but possibly meaning the Doges of Venice.

20. *E.g.* Robert Cavey, died 1593; Francis Peerse, died 1623; Roger Barnes, died 1631; Henry Bluett, died 1633 (Gibson, *Abstracts*, 18, 28, 30–1).

21. G. J. Gray and W. Palmer, *Abstracts from the wills and testamentary documents of printers, binders and stationers of Cambridge from 1504 to 1699* (Bibliographical Society, 1915), 62, 70.

22. I am greatly indebted to Mr. H. M. Nixon formerly of the British Museum, and to Mr. R. E. Harvey of the Bodleian Bindery, for technical advice.

23. 'I desire' deleted.

24. A. Clark, *Register*, loc. cit.

25. Gibson, *Abstracts*, 46. McKerrow, *Dictionary 1557–1640*, 145.

26. Gibson, *Abstracts*, 23–4. F. Madan, *Oxford books*, i (1895), 276; ii (1912), 511.

27. McKerrow, *Dictionary 1557–1640*, 220.

28. A full acount of his career, correcting *DNB*, is in J. N. Langston, 'Headmasters and ushers of the King's (College) School, Gloucester, 1541–1841', *Records of Gloucester Cathedral*, iii, 2 (1927), 176–82.

29. E. Reynolds, *Sermon touching the use of humane learning* (1658), 29 (Wing R 1287).

30. *STC* 3622.

31. *STC* 3623.

32. Sir W. W. Greg, *A Companion to Arber*, 1967, 94-5.

33. C. L. Kingsford, 'Historical notes on medieval London houses', *London Topographical Record*, xi (1917), 35-8.

34. *STC* 20465.

35. Gibson, *Abstracts*, 28, 35-6, 51.

36. Madan, *Oxford books*, ii, 523-4. Sir W. W. Greg, *A companion to Arber*, 1967, 82-3, 268-73.

37. Madan, *Oxford books* i, 277; ii, 512, etc.; Gibson, *Abstracts*, 52, where the dating of the start of Webb's career in 1616 would seem to be an error, as he was not admitted as a privileged person until February 1625, aged 22 (J. Foster, *Alumni Oxonienses*, iv, 1591).

38. W. D. Macray, *Annals of the Bodleian Library*. 2nd. edn., 1890, 77.

39. University Archives, Hyp.B.44. His widow Joan was the administratrix and the estate valued at £400; the inventory has not survived.

40. *STC* 12401; Webb's widow issued another edition in 1660; see Madan, *Oxford books* iii, 128.

41. *STC* 26013.

42. *STC* 12402, 12402a.

43. Not in *STC;* copy at Magdalene College, Cambridge.

44. *STC* 20667.

45. Twelve copies of this bifolium are used in the bindings of the other volumes of this set of Toschi at Queen's, while copies of Ranchin's *Review* at Christ Church, Trinity and Worcester have this variant used in their bindings.

46. Strickland Gibson and D. M. Rogers, 'The Earl of Leicester and printing at Oxford', *Bodleian Library Record*, ii (1949), 240, 242.

47. Ifano Jones, *History of printing and printers in Wales*, 1925, 35.

48. Cf. Note 32.

49. Honourable Society of Cymmrodorion, *Dictionary of Welsh biography*, 1959, 216-17; J. I. Morgans, *The life and works of William Erbery* (Oxford B.Litt. thesis, 1968), especially 215-16. I am indebted to Miss Eiluned Rees of the National Library of Wales, and to Dr. Glyn Ashton of the University College of South Wales, Cardiff, for help with Erbery.

50. E. Arber, *Transcript of the registers of the Company of Stationers of London* iv (1877), 452.

51. At Magdalene College, Cambridge, and Harvard University.

52. At the Folger Shakespeare Library.

53. *STC* 20513 (where Roydon is incorrectly spelt).

54. On G. Foxle, *Groanes of the spirit (STC* 11250); three variant imprints are known: Lichfield for (1) J. Allen of Leicester; (2) Thomas Thomas of Bristol; (3) G. Hutton of London. See Madan, *Oxford books*, ii, 142, no. 913.

55. Cropping has removed all except the lower part of this line.

56. *i.e.* Pope's Head Alley.

57. '£850' is repeated in the margin in Chapman's hand.

58. End of recto of second leaf; continued on verso.

59. Gibson, *Abstracts*, xxiii.

60. R. B. McKerrow, *Printers' and publishers' devices in England and Scotland, 1485-1640*, 1913, no. 303.

61. McKerrow, *Dictionary 1557–1640*, 318.
62. Cf. Gibson, *Abstracts*, 43; Madan, *Oxford books*, iii, nos. 2164, 2275; H. R. Plomer, *Dictionary of the booksellers and printers who were at work in England . . . 1641 to 1667*, 1907, 55–6; Foster, *Alumni Oxonienses* i, 349.
63. No. 2092.
64. Plomer, *Dictionary 1641 to 1667*, 142.
65. Ibid., 1.
66. Leona Rostenberg, 'Sectarianism & revolt; Livewell Chapman, publisher to the Fifth Monarchy', in her *Literary, political, scientific, religious & legal publishing, printing & bookselling in England, 1551–1700*, 1965, 203–36.
67. Plomer, *Dictionary 1641 to 1667*, 44.
68. Wing^2 C 6958.
69. Ibid., C 6959.
70. R. W. Chapman, 'An inventory of paper, 1674', *The Library*, 4th series, vii (1927), 405–6.
71. Sir W. H. Beveridge, *Prices and wages in England* i (1939), 141.

D. G. VAISEY

Anthony Stephens

The rise and fall of an Oxford bookseller

In the standard works devoted to English bookselling in the seventeenth century, and to the intellectual, trading and social life of Oxford in the same period, the name of Anthony Stephens does not loom large. One will search in vain for his name in the pages of Anthony Wood's *Life and Times* though he was active at the time that Wood was both writing his diary and buying books. Falconer Madan's volumes on the Oxford book trade stop at 1680, just before Stephens entered it on his own account; though Madan did include him in his *Chart of Oxford Printing*. H. R. Plomer recorded him only as the publisher of *Miscellany Poems and Translations by Oxford Hands* in 1685. He figures three times only in the *Term Catalogues*. The deficiencies of Wing's *Short Title Catalogue* ensure that sometimes Stephens's imprint is recorded and sometimes not. It may be that this portrayal of Stephens's position as one of comparative insignificance is right and proper. But if his position in the history of bookselling is not a major one, the circumstances of his leaving the trade and the documents which his departure produced do add to our knowledge of the Oxford trade and of the sources of credit available to booksellers there in the second half of the seventeenth century. It may therefore be appropriate to put together in one place what can be discovered about the man and his shop.

Anthony Stephens was born on 11 February 1656/7 at Appleton, in Berkshire, where his father, the Rev. Anthony Stephens, an Oxford M.A. and an ex-fellow of Magdalen College, was the intruded rector, and where the date of his birth was recorded by his father in the parish register.[1] A year later the family moved to Great Haseley in Oxfordshire where the Rev. Anthony Stephens became rector, a position from which he was removed at the Restoration. He next appears, having presumably conformed to the teachings of the established church, as curate of Appleshaw in Hampshire in September 1663. He obtained the

[1] Notes begin on p. 114.

rectory of Avington in the same county in April 1670 but was not to enjoy this position for long, for it was there that he died early in 1672 when the young Anthony was fifteen years old.[2] He died intestate but administration of his estate was granted on 3 April 1672 in the Winchester consistory court to his widow, Martha. The probate inventory which accompanies the grant and which was taken on 25 March shows, interestingly, that amongst goods valued at a total of £46 2s. 8d. in the rector's eight-roomed house were books to the value of £11.[3]

Following his father's death Anthony Stephens returned to Oxford and in August 1672 bound himself apprentice to Thomas Gilbert, bookseller and bookbinder of the University of Oxford, for an eight-year term beginning at 1 July. As members of a 'privileged' trade in Oxford booksellers enjoyed the protection of the Chancellor's court, and it is amongst the papers of that court that the record of Stephens's apprenticeship is to be found.[4] Gilbert was himself a young man of 24 only three years out of his apprenticeship and was, like Stephens, the son of a nonconformist minister who had probably known the elder Stephens at Magdalen but who, unlike him, did not conform after the Restoration.[5] The younger Stephens had served little more than a year of his apprenticeship when Gilbert died,[6] and so it was that on 18 May 1674 a second note was sent to the registrar of the Chancellor's court recording that Stephens had bound himself to serve the remaining seven years of his term as apprentice to James Good, another Oxford bookseller and bookbinder who had matriculated as a privileged person two years previously.[7] Seven years later Stephens duly emerged from his apprenticeship at the age of 24 and, styling himself *bibliopola*, was matriculated as a privileged person on 9 December 1681, signing the subscription register at the same time as Thomas Fickus, another bookseller with whom he was subsequently to be associated in the marketing of the fourth edition of Thomas Tully's *Enchiridion* in 1683.[8]

Where Stephens set up shop is not absolutely clear. Imprints which bear his name describe him as 'bookseller near the Theatre'. The name 'Stevens' appears among the poor-rate assessments of the parish of St. Mary the Virgin in 1683 in such a position as to lead one to suppose that the premises being rated were in the Catte Street area, and the rate paid is always twice as much as that paid by his neighbours indicating that he was occupying a double tenement.[9] Assuming that this 'Stevens' is our Anthony Stephens it seems likely that the bookseller's shop was one of that block of tenements which straddled the line of the old city wall to the east of the Sheldonian Theatre between it and

Catte Street[10] and which was cleared for the erection of the Clarendon Building in 1712–13.[11]

In the three years which followed his admission to the privileges of the University, Stephens's name appeared in some capacity on the imprints of the following 21 items:

1682

1. *T. Lucretius Carus The Epicurean Philosopher, His Six Books De Natura Rerum Done into English Verse* [by Thomas Creech].[12]
   Oxford. Printed by L. Lichfield for Anthony Stephens. [Wing L.3447]

1683

2. *T. Lucretius Carus.* 2nd edn., corrected and enlarged.
   Oxford. Printed by L. Lichfield for Anthony Stephens. [Wing L.3448]
3. *T. Lucretius Carus.* 3rd edn.
   London. Printed for Anthony Stephens. [Wing L.3449^B]
4. *T. Lucretius Carus.* Another '3rd edn.'. Reset.
   London. Printed for Thomas Sawbridge and Anthony Stephens.
   [Wing L.3449^A]
5. *Anacreon Done into English Out of the Original Greek*
   [by Francis Willis and Thomas Wood].[13]
   Oxford. Printed by L. Lichfield for Anthony Stephens.
   [Wing² A.3046]
6. Thomas Tully, *Praecipuorum Theologiae Capitum Enchiridion Didactum: De Coena Domini.* 4th edn.
   Oxford. Printed by L. Lichfield, *impensis* F. Oxlad sen. *& vaeneunt apud* Tho. Fickus & Ant. Stephens. [Wing T.3249]
7. *Witt against Wisdom, or A Panegyrick upon Folly: Penn'd in Latin by Desiderius Erasmus, Render'd into English* [by White Kennet].[14]
   Oxford. Printed by L. Lichfield for Anthony Stephens.[15]
   [Wing E.3215]
8. John Dowel, *The Leviathan Heretical: Or The Charge Exhibited in Parliament against M. Hobbs.*
   Oxford. Printed by L. Lichfield and to be sold by Anthony Stephens.
   [Wing² D.2056]

1684

9. *The Speech of S^r. George Pudsey K^t. At the Time of his being Sworn Recorder of the City of Oxford . . . the Eightth day of January* 168$\frac{3}{4}$.
   Oxford. Printed for Anthony Stephens. [Wing P.4167]

10. *The Speech of S^r. George Pudsey K^t.* Another ed. London. Printed for Anthony Stephens and to be sold by Thomas Sawbridge.
 [Wing P.4166]
11. *The Lives of Illustrious Men. Written in Latin by Corn. Nepos, And Done into English By Several Hands.*
 Oxford. Printed for Hen. Cruttenden, and are to be sold by Anthony Stephens.[16] [Wing N.428]
12. *The Odes, Satyrs, and Epistles of Horace. Done into English* [by Thomas Creech].
 London. Printed for Jacob Tonson ... in Chancery Lane ... and Anthony Stephens ... in Oxford.[17] [Wing H.2774]
13. *The Idylliums of Theocritus with Rapin's Discourse of Pastorals Done into English* [by Thomas Creech].
 Oxford. Printed by L. Lichfield for Anthony Stephens. [Wing T.855]
14. *The Idylliums of Theocritus.* Another issue.
 Oxford. Printed by L. Lichfield for Anthony Stephens and are to be sold in London by Abel Swalle. [Wing T.854]
15. Humphrey Hody, *Contra Historiam Aristeae de LXX Interpretibus Dissertatio.*
 Oxford. Printed by L. Lichfield *impensis* Anthony Stephens.[18]
 [Wing H.2340]
16. John Walker, *The Antidote: Or, A Seasonable Discourse on Rom. 13. 1.*
 London. Printed by Th. Hodgkin for Anthony Stephens.[19]
 [Wing W.392]

1685

17. *A Pindarick Ode, Upon the Death of His late Sacred Majesty King Charles the Second* [by Thomas Wood].[20]
 Oxford. Printed by L. Lichfield for Anthony Stephens. [Wing P.2256]
18. J. B[rowne], *Catholick Schismatology: or An Account of Schism and Schismaticks.*
 London. Printed for Anthony Steevens. [Wing B.5116]
19. William Pemble, *A Briefe Introduction to Geography.*
 Oxford. Printed by L. Lichfield for Anthony Stephens.
 [Wing P.1113^A][21]
20. [William Halifax],[22] *The Elements of Euclid Explain'd.*
 Oxford. Printed by L. Lichfield for Anthony Stephens.
 [Wing E.3400]
21. *Miscellany Poems and Translations By Oxford Hands.*
 [With an address from the publisher to the reader signed by Stephens].
 London. Printed for Anthony Stephens.[23]
 [Wing M.2232]

During the second half of 1684 and the beginning of 1685 Stephens appears as the Oxford bookseller from whom might be had catalogues of Edward Millington's book sales. He seems to have succeeded Henry Cruttenden and was himself succeeded at some point in 1685 by Henry Clements.[24]

In 1684, too, Stephens married. His bride was Elizabeth Johnson, an Eynsham spinster, and the marriage took place at Eynsham on 17 April 1684.[25] Elizabeth was almost certainly a member of that Johnson family who were millers in the Eynsham, Cassington and Hanborough area of Oxfordshire in the seventeenth and early eighteenth centuries.

By mid-1685, therefore, Stephens was a married man of 28, not yet four years out of his apprenticeship, who from premises near the Theatre in Oxford had been connected in some way or other with the publication or distribution of at least sixteen items, ranging from the single sheet *Pindarick Ode* to the 570 pages of Creech's *Horace*. Three of these items had been issued in more than one edition, and he may well have had a stake in other publications.[26] He was not, so far as is known, a man of substantial means nor is there any evidence that his wife's family was wealthy enough for her to have brought any great amount of capital into his concern. He does not seem to have broadened the base of his business by engaging in any activity other than the production and selling of books. It was normal practice for booksellers in provincial towns to have a stake in some other commercial activity, and even in Oxford the presence of a university did not mean that the business of making and selling books was one which could survive unaided by finance from other sources. In particular the connection between the trade and that of food and drink in Oxford requires closer examination. In the earlier part of the century both Joseph Barnes and William Turner, university printers and booksellers, had held wine-licences from the university—Turner succeeding Barnes in the print-house and tavern in the High Street. Turner at his death was known as a vintner rather than as a printer or bookseller. Others, too, such as Thomas Pembroke, a bookbinder who died in 1673, were innkeepers. No doubt Stephens derived some income from his retail activities as well as from publishing, but over these three and a half years he had found himself short of capital and had had to borrow money. How much he borrowed and repaid is not known but it is apparent that he overstretched himself, for in 1685 a series of cases were brought against him in the Chancellor's court of the university which broke him and eventually drove him out of the trade. The cases all arose from bonds into which he had entered in order to repay debts and these bonds reveal the sources of capital available to a man in Stephens's position at this period.[27]

On 7 September 1683 Stephens and Henry Cruttenden[28] bound themselves in the penal sum of £100 to repay £51 10s. to Benjamin Cutler, butler of New College, on 8 March 1683/4. Stephens paid £3 by way of interest on 8 September 1684 but nothing else was paid. On 20 March 1683/4 Stephens bound himself in £60 to repay £30 9s. to Nathaniel New, an innkeeper of Holywell parish; and on 18 November 1684 Stephens, again with Cruttenden the printer, entered into a similar bond to repay £30 18s. to George Thomson, gentleman, the manciple of All Souls' College. Meanwhile, on 24 April 1684, Stephens had bound himself in £100 to repay £58 6s. 8d. to George Edwards, manciple of New Inn Hall. It is interesting that he raised money from an innkeeper, a college butler and two manciples—all men in the business of food and drink. Innkeepers at this period are known to have been the credit financiers for other traders, notably in agriculture,[29] and perhaps in Oxford the college manciples stood in the position occupied by innkeepers in smaller market towns. Their position and influence as entrepreneurs at this period would repay a serious study. Many were substantial traders on their own account[30] and, indeed, the manciple of New Inn Hall who lent money to Stephens was the same George Edwards who is known as the left-handed engraver and 'cutter of great letters' and the man who with Fell's encouragement set up the paper mill at Wolvercote.[31] In the case of this bond we know what the money was for: it was to represent 20d. each for 700 copies of *The Elements of Euclid Explain'd* which Edwards was to 'print and deliver or cause to be printed and delivered' to Stephens by 1 September 1684.[32] Edwards in this transaction thus appears as the 'undertaker' coming between Leonard Lichfield, the printer, and Stephens, the bookseller for whom the book was printed.

Benjamin Cutler was the first to sue for repayment and on 14 September 1685 the court issued a warrant to the bedels to seize goods belonging to Stephens within the university precincts and to keep them as security until Stephens answered Cutler's action. Two days later a quantity of goods, mainly household effects, were seized and valued by two of Stephens's colleagues in the book trade, George West and Henry Clements, at £31 7s. 10d. This sum included a valuation of £18 put upon eight parcels of unspecified books in quires from the warehouse.[33] It is not altogether clear whether Stephens put in an appearance or not, but judgment was eventually given for Cutler on 6 November 1685.

There then followed a year's peace for Stephens—though by this time he and his wife seem to have left the city—until 12 November 1686 when the other three claimants, acting together and using the same proctor but bringing three separate cases, petitioned for and were granted a warrant to seize the remaining goods and books belonging to Stephens within the university. New sued for his £30 9s. plus unpaid interest amounting to £5;[34] Edwards, having delivered the copies of *Euclid* on time, sued for his £58 6s. 8d. plus unpaid interest amounting to £6 3s.;[35] and Thomson for his £30 18s. plus unpaid interest of £4.[36] In all, therefore, the three claimants sought satisfaction for debts of £133 18s. 8d.

A warrant against Stephens's goods was duly issued and was executed on 23 November by the yeoman bedel of arts, Peter Cox, who arrested the goods and cited anyone with an interest in or right to them to appear in court. On the following three court days Stephens was summoned but failed to appear and judgment therefore went to the plaintiffs. The goods seized consisted wholly of books and a catalogue of them was made and produced to the court. On 20 January 1686/7 the books themselves were viewed by William Colier, bedel of law, and Richard Davis, the verger and university stationer. It is not clear if the books represent Stephens's entire remaining stock. The catalogue does not read like a select list, yet the fact that Davis called them 'certain of ye books apperteining to Mr. Anthony Stevens bookseller' and that the valuation of £130 almost exactly equals the amount claimed might lead one to suspect that some of the stock was left behind. However, taking the two seizures together, a stock of books worth £148 in a total household value of £161 7s. 10d. would have been about normal for an Oxford bookseller of that period. Thomas Gilbert, Stephens's first master, left stock in 1673 valued for probate at £100 in an estate of just over £121; John Forrest's stock in the same year was valued at £120 in an estate of just over £131; and John Barnes's stock in 1674 was reckoned to be worth £120 in a probate inventory totalling just over £136.[37] But even if the whole of Stephens's stock is not given in it, the list, which is reproduced below, provides a good idea of the range of material available from his shop.

The books were divided *pro rata* among the three claimants, and New, Edwards and Thomson left bonds in the court that if Stephens should ever reappear to answer their claims they would make their action good. But Stephens never reappeared. From the ending of these cases onwards he is not heard of again in Oxford, and it has not been possible to discover where he went.[38] His career in the university had been short and troubled. By no stretch of the imagination could he be considered an important bookseller; indeed his prime importance to subsequent students of the book trade lies in the manner of his leaving it and in the collapse of his business which resulted in the preservation amongst the legal records of the catalogue of an Oxford bookseller's establishment in 1686.

The catalogue is here transcribed literally, though the use of capitals and abbreviation marks has been standardised. There are obvious spelling mistakes in the names of the authors (Abbon for Abbot, Combdrey for Cawdrey, Symon for Simson, Sckeker for Secker, Hillom for Hilduin for example) perpetrated in all probability by the scribe who made the fair copy of the list for the court; but the short titles given in the list are sufficient in most cases for the works to be identified with little difficulty in the standard works of reference. The cataloguers drew up the list in two sections—bound volumes and books in quires—and in each section the books are grouped by size. Within each size group the books are in no logical order, the cataloguers having apparently worked along the presses or through the chests in which they found the books, and within any one group the same title can appear more than once. Where the bookseller had several copies of the same work, however, normally only one or two were bound, others being available for binding to the customer's specification. He carried very large numbers of some titles, but these are almost always his own publications or those for which he was the Oxford agent. Others may represent publications in which he had some kind of financial stake. His own titles have been here marked with an asterisk, and the fact that there are so many copies of some of these (582 copies of the work by John Walker, for instance) may indicate one reason for the failure of his business. The range of the titles is wide: standard university texts, editions of the fathers and of classical authors, works of philosophy and theology, scientific, medical and mathematical treatises, sermons, novels, editions of poets (Oldham and Donne amongst them), political tracts and pamphlets, practical manuals for lawyers, justices of the peace and others filled his shelves. It is a matter for great regret that the appraisers ran out of time or patience and failed to list by title the 43 plays and 31 pamphlets which are grouped together at the foot of the catalogue.

ANTHONY STEPHENS

THE CATALOGUE

FOLIOS

Aristotelis opera omnia. Graec: Lat: 4 vol.
3 Rushworth's hist: coll:
Dr. Allestree's sermons
2 Polyanthea
Kendall's doctrine of perseverans
Mayer's many comments on one
D'Avenant's theolog: quaestions
Aphorisms civil & militarie
The expiation of a sinner
Boys works
Cassandra a romance
Tremellii 5 lib: politici
3 Scotia illustrata
Bp. Wilkins universal caract:
Simpson's lex: Graec: Lat: Eng.
2 Wright's exposition of ye psalms
Rogers on ye Judges
Byfield's com: on ye 3 1st chap: of St. Peter
Mayne's Lucian
Baker's cronicle
Homer's Iliads. Eng.
Lightfoot's works. 2 vol.
Top's com: on ye psalms
Greenham's works
Theophrastus works. Graec:
Williams compleate statesman
Monmouth's politick discourses
Hispani logica. 4°
Lee's annot: upon Job
The Dutchess of Newcastle's letters
Ostio Franco on Averroes

Tyra quellius
Geo: Majoris homil: in ep: dic: domin:
Burnet's memoires of D: Hamilt:
Gelii lex: Arab:
Moscen: tract: philos:
Clarke's lives
Plempii medicina
Wilcock's works
Mat: Paris Eng: hist:
Musculus in psalmos
3 Mendoza in lib: Regum
Sandys Ovid
2 Magini prim: mobile
2 Suarez metaph:
Sennerti op: med: 2 vol.
5 Scibaldi hist: naturae
Ingelo's urania
Cammerarii disput: phil:
Alphonsi in Arist: de animâ
Severinus contra Aristot:
Wilson on ye Romans
Duke of Newcasle's exp: phil:
2 Common prayer book. 1 old
Zanchius de nat: Dei. 4°
2 Eusebius
Clelia a romance
Tavernier's travells
Erasmus on ye new test:
Socrates & Sozomen
Calvisii cronologium
Nalson's collections
Riverii praxis med:
Aretius in nov: test:
Stella com: on St. Luke
Dowland's book of songs
Schindleri polyglott lex:
Dutches of Newcast: phil: opin:
Tulii epistolae

Concordance
Cary's cronologie
Zwinger's theatrum vitae
    humanae
Innocentii epistolae
Velasquez in psalmum 100^{mum}
Polybii hist: Engl.
Bunny's head corners stone
Schoner's opera
Burgess on the Corinth:
Cocceius in Hieremiam & Ezek:
Seneca's works. Eng.
Cocceius on Job
Boccasio's novells
Burton's melancholy
Plyny's naturall hist:
Bonett's practical phis: Eng.
Theophilact on St. Math: Lat.
Gorraeum definitiones opera
    med:
Pemble's works
Turner's military essays
Bonett's epit: of Sennert:
Fisher of baptisme
Howel's dictionary
Annales of Eng:
Stella's com: on St. Luke
Kendall against Goodwyn
Pharmacop: Augustina
Musculus com: on St. John
Jandunus in Arist:
Davis of ye uniform: of church
Dr. Taylour's serm:
Erasmi adagia
Beza's new testament
Frigvirus com: on psalms
Zabarella
Sibbs on ye Corinthians
Guiberti opera theol:

QUARTOS

2 Crandon against Baxter

Christian policy
Coxei apologia
3 Robrough of justification
Smith's Essex dove
Brancker's introd: to algebra
Culverwell's light of nature
Holyday's motive to a good life
Euclid de coenâ dom:
The Xtian sacrifice
Paraeus in 1^{mam} epistolam &
    Corinthios
Baronius de meiendo
Abra d'Raconis summa phil:
Fontseca in lib: metaph: Arist:
2 Ruvius in Arist: de coelo
England's emprovement
Alstedii prob: theol:
Wottonus de recon: peccatoris
Wright's paradox
Altingii theol: problem:
2 Primrose de feb:
Baxter's plain scripture proof
Ramsey's sermons
Deering on the Hebrews
Collins works
Downham's treatise of
    antichrist
An exposition on ye 10
    command:
Stephens vindiciae fundamenti
Buxhomii historia universalis
2 Duport's psalms
Arist: organon
Quaestiones geometricae
Canones ecclesiastici
Randol on the church
Riolani opusc: anat:
Holland on ye Revelat:
The Graecian history
The mistery of self deceiving
Deusingii naturae theatrum
2 Baxter's confession of faith
2 Coll: conimbricence

Johan: Weidenfeild de secretis adeptorum
Duns Scotus natural: philos:
Petavii elenchus Theriaci
Rivetus on ye 20th cap: of Exod:
Clark's praxis
Purchase his hist: of flying insects
Burroughs exposition of Hosea
Hudson's vindication of ye essense of the church catholick
Elsted's theologia scholastica
Zabarell's log:
Tyco Bra's astronomy
2 Fontseca's metaph:
Soto's physicks
La bible de poets: metamorphose
Toleti com: in Arist: de gen: & cor:
Bartholomaeus in psalmos
Wendelin's physicks
2 Dr. Pierce nature of sin
Scapii cursus theologicus
2 Vanderlinden's med: physiolog:
2 Struy's travells
Ecce sponsus venit
Cowdry on ye sabbaoth
Heerbord's metaph:
Behme's aurora
Rollock's lect: on ye 1st & 2d of ye Thess:
Pitsaeus in 4 evangelia
Willan's sermons
Erpennii tyro: in ling: Arab:
Timplar's metaph:
2 Buridani polit:
Seldeni de synedriis
Malphigius de Bombyce
Waller's naturall experiments
2 Ruvii log:

Regii fundamenta med:
Weckenii antid: generale
Warren of justification
Luke's theolog: probe
Hopkins on St. John
Barriff's military discipline
Hayter on ye Revelations
Bull contra Tullium
Calvins's lectures
Scrivelii lex: Graec: Lat:
Cotton's sermons
2 Plautus
Clagett's abuse of God's grace
2 Biddle's faith confuted
2 Causinus de eloquentiâ
Heerbord's meletemata
Maccovii opusc: philos:
Alstedii theol: catech:
Munsteri horologiographia
Practicall catechism
Pierce's sermons
Guadalupension on Hosea
Cotton on ye Revelations
Thesaurus theologiae Sedanensis
Anony: upon ye evangelists
2 Tichbourn's sermons
Comment: on Habbackuk
Derwit's mirror
Tully's justificatio Paulina
Keckerman's anatomy
Vossii log: & rhet:
Des'Cartes epistolae
Coll: metaph:
Rogers parable of ye fast friend
Rutgersii lexicon
Disquisitiones criticae
3 History of ye buaccaniers
Vorsii annales
Wendelyn's phys:
Rivetus in psalmos
Zodiacus medico Gallicus
Ursini trigonometria
Harpocration Vallessii. Graec:

Willis de animâ brutorum
Fordge de mente humanâ
Burges defence of Dr. Morton
Watts vindication of ye church
Wharton's refinement of Sion
Mori metaphisica
Arist: eth:
Petili miscelanea
Scheineri optica
Godwyn's Roman antiq:
Scrivenerus contra Dallaeum
Sibelii de drachmis
Beati pauperes
Holland's hist: of Adam
Horn against Owen
Symon's sacred septinary
The holy table
Baker's algebra
Seldeni uxor Hebraica
2 Casii philos:
Craddock's ghospell libertie
Luther on ye Galatians
2 Molinaei paraenesis
2 Alstedii encyclopaidia
Busaeus de ch: virtutib:
Glissonii metaph:
Poema Lat: ad regem
Casi lapis philos:
Licetus de monstris
Holyday's sermons
Faulkner's 2 tract: of censur: & repro:
Concordance
Bythner's lyra
Smith's select discourses
Bolton's arraignment or error
2 Buxtorf's lexicon Caldaicum
Raynolds upon Haggai
Apologia pro Joan: Ersonio
Stierii philos:
Rider's dictionary
Sennerti med: pract:
Conimb: de gen: & cor:

Zanchii de operib: diei
Zanchii l: in epist: ad Eph:
Discouse de la guerre
Morisani log:
Scapii cursus theol:
Fromond de anim:
Baxter of justification
Junii de sacris parallelis. L. 3
Abbon on Job
Jus divinum
2 Becanus enervatus
Conimbrisense coll: de animâ
Causinus de symbolis Aegypt:
Sandaei theol: myst:
Holsworth's serm:
Tarnovius in Hosaeam
Bruce's way to true peace
Hewett on Daniel
Godly expositions on ye script:
Combdry's Xtian sabboth
Ruvius
Tarnovii medulla evangelii
4 Weidenfeildt

OCTAVOS

Answer to fiat lux
34 Hody against Aristaeus*
Hartman's praxis
Gore's nomenclatour
Plutarch's moralls
Ward's astronomia
2 Theocritus idilliums*
Conquest of China
9 Catholick schismatology*
Galtruchius poeticall hist:
9 Oldham's poems
Althameri sylva nom: bib:
The guide unto true blessedness
Ruland de copia verborum
Jaccaei metaph:
Praesent state of Europe
2 Caesar's commentaries

Promptuarius exaequialis
2 Martialis epig:
Galtruchius mathem:
2 Wase's dictionary
Burton's discourses
2 Culpep: Eng: dispensat:
Epigrammatum delectus
Baxter's 2 coevenants
La bible françois
3 Janua linguarum
Carpentarii philosop:
Arist: eth:
Occasionall reflections
Middleton's pract: astrol:
Galhard of travells
Secrets revealed
Petty's discourse of prayer
Buchanani historia an: human:
The last efforts of aflict: innoc:
Reusenii symbla:
2 Isocrat: orat: Graec: Lat:
Decay of Xtian piety
Bacon's cure of old age
Anacreon in Eng:*
Beauty of holyness
2 Lessius de medicam
Homerus Ἑβραιζων
Tullii enchiridion*
Rodus gordius sophistarum solutus
Sckeker's sanctified Xtian
Winchester phrases
Goveani logica
The purchase of grace
Soul's delight
Arist: phys:
Quercetani pharm:
Timpson on ye sac:
Aristot: prop: Graec:
Riverii prax: med:
Basson cont: Arist:
5 Oliveri dissert: acad:
Euclide's elem: Eng:*

Dr. Willis workes epit:
Gale philosop: gen:
Heinsii orat:
5 Rolloci analysis log:
5 Gallantry alamode
Alamod phlebotom:
Livius cum variis notis
3 Robotham's mistery of ye 2 wittnesses
Shipman's poems
Aquinas de ente & essentia
2 Leybourn's arethmetick
Divine Epicurus
Tillingshast's sermons
The yearnings of Xt's bowells
Netherland hist:
3 Parei calligraphia
Platerus de febribus
Confessio fidei
Paraphras pharm:
Cartwright's poems
Quercetani pestis Alexicacus
Erasmi apotheg:
Erasmus psalms
Dutrieus log:
2 Owen against Parker
Thilon: exer: orat:
Casi eth:
Topica theolog:
Alstedii rhetorica
2 Johannis Audoeni diatriba
Vossii rhetorica
Pagnini thesaurus
Devotions for families
Lucretius. Eng:*
Xtianae pietatis prima instit:
The lively oracles
Drummond's hist: of Scotland
The young man's instructor
Aesop's fables. Eng: & Lat:
Ryff's geometry
Bullingeri apocalipsis
Lovell's hist: of animals

Sanderson's episcopacy
　　Medulla his: Scot:
8　Euclid elem: Eng:*
　　Tombes treatise of scandal
　　Justini hist: cum notis Stabii
2　Flavel de demonstratione
　　Theophrasti notationes morum
　　Picus's explications
　　Tully
7　Miscellany poems by Oxford
　　　　hands*
　　Turkish history
　　Keckermanni ethica
2　Wit against wisdom*
2　Schnii opera theol:
　　Comment: in Aristotelem
　　Eutropius in Eng:
　　Laurence's interest of Ireland
　　Borlaei epistolae
　　Parker's case of the church
2　Golii ethica
2　Natalis comes
　　Tabidorum theatrum
　　Carmina proverbialia
　　Williams imago saeculi
　　Don's poems
　　The Graeck testament
　　Detregines harmony
　　Doughtei analect:
2　Homeri od:
2　Pererii phys:
　　Matt: Senensis med:
　　Zenophontis phil: hist:
　　Ciceronis epist:
　　Arist: op: G:
2　Hanmour of confirmation
　　The common prayer & testam:
2　Record's arithmetick
　　Puller's moderations
　　Cartesii meditationes
　　Wilkins sermons
4　Dr. Heylin's life
　　Bastingius upon ye catechism

　　The art of speaking
4　Tullii enchiridion*
3　Epicteti enchiridion
　　Horace. Eng:*
　　Mirror of fortune
　　Gore's nomenclator
　　Sincerity & hypocrisie
　　Horwood on the Lord's prayer
　　Jeanes on ye sacrament
　　Medela medicorum
　　Hunnerii prodidagmata
　　Spiritual treasure
　　Willis's diatriba
　　The reward of religion
　　Broom's Horace
　　The songs of Moses & Deborah
　　Martinii gram: Heb:
　　Sciblerus de top:
　　Arrianus in Epictetum
　　The life of Julian
　　Cleonardi Graecae ling: instit:
　　Parker against Marvell
　　Theophrastus de plantis
　　Incarnation of God
　　Harsnet's touchstone of grace
　　Historicall remarkes
　　Isocratis orat: 2
2　Sphinx theologico philosophica
　　Watson's divine cordial
2　Molinaei corollarium
　　Coudry of independency
　　Wharton's workes
　　Treatises of the gout
　　Bertii logica
　　Young's armour of proof
　　The fugitive statesman
　　Hillom's Dionisius
　　Barronis lectiones mathem:
　　Erasmus de copia verborum
　　Grotii poemata
　　Trahern's Xtian eth:
　　Posselii calligraphia
　　Erasmi colloquia

Rulandus cum notis Heesch
Sr. Thomas More's eutopia
Fabii cursus phisicus
3 plays
Weckius concordance
Anonym: de demonstratione
Rhaenodaei inst:
Wilkinson's caracter of a true heart
Machiavel's disputationes. Ital:
Meinserus
Eustachii summa phil:
Erasmi adagia
2 Arminii distinctiones theol:
2 Hunnaei log:
Cuthberti log:
Gale's anatomy of infidelity
Arist: de caelo
2 Keckerman's log:
3 Eng: rogue
The power of sin
Livii hist: Lat:
Minores poet
Duncane's log:
Isoc: orations
Gardneri gemmulae ling:
Kendal's examen
2 Lushington's log:
Javelli metaph:
Sozinus. Eng:
Fides Xtiana
Praxis medica
Answer to Dr. Stillingfleet
4 Rami log:
Articuli fidei
Eutropius by sev: hands
Garthius lex: Graec: Lat:
The spirituall house
Contraventions of France
Caesar nomismaticus
Lieus pattern of piety
Laerig's tracts of insep: of bodys
Ball's meditations
3 Mollinaei log:
The breaches of France
An essay of fluid bodys
Smith's art of gaging
A treatise of Aristippus. French
Terrentius cum notis Fabii
Doelittle on the sacrament
10 Curcellaeus ethicks
A touchstone for phisick
Astrologicall opticks
Martinii gram: Hebraeum
Pavonii ethica
Commenii jan: ling:
Owen's defens agt: Cotton
Milk for children
Godfrey's knowledg of things unknown
Graeck common prayer
Tractatus de peste
Gallenus de scorbuto
Gallataeus de morib:
Ramus olivae
Raynoldi orationes
2 Govean's log:
Plutarch's moralls
Tasso's letters. French
Anacreon. Eng:*
Balzack letters
Commenii vest: ling: Lat:
Statii opera cum not: variorum
Wither's fragments
Legrand's Epicurus
2 Occham's log:
E: of Roch: life
2 Wendelyn's mor: phil:
Bolton's true bounds of Xtian freedome
Continuation off ecc: politie
Boyl's memoirs
Walker antidote*
Cognaeus sure guide to ye French tongue
Frith's tombe of righteousness

Herbert's carefull father
2 Bainbridge's astron:
  Zenophon's Κυροπειδεια
  Hornbechii apologia
  Melancthon loci communes
  Digbey's receipts
  Loyalty of popish principles
  Fernuss's fables
  Lipsius de constantiâ
2 The k's praerogative
  A whip for ye divel
  Newhewsii fatidica sacra
  Hyperi opera theol:
  Herbert's temple
  May's hist: of the parliam: of Eng:
  Paraei com: on ye Rom:
  Barns's Αυλικοκατοπτρον
  Aulus gellius
  Middleton's practical astrol:
  Blagrave's astrolog: pract: of phys:
  Quinta pars Geo: Majoris
  Newport's poems
  Waterhouse his gent: monitor
  Sheepherd of deeds
  Lubin's clavis Graec: ling:
  Cowlaei poemata de plantis
  London's resurrection
  Du Verge's humble reflections
  Catechismus major
2 Heildebrandi antiquitates
  Thesaurus ling: Graec:
  The beauty of holyness
  Stedman's mysticall union
  Selden de diis Syris
  Thompson de gratiâ & reformatione
2 The weeks praeparative
2 Piccolominaei phil:
  Dufricus log:
  Ingelo's sermons

  Boyl's reflections
  Bp. of Down's discours of confirm:
  Powell's analysis
  Horn's Xtian governor
  Xtian consolations
  Melius inquirendum
  Graec: gram: anonym:
  The interest of England
  Missi evangelici
  Flosculi historici
  Schellii eth:
  Reebii distinctiones phil:
  Magirus in phys: Arist:
  Lucius de causâ meritoriâ
  Balthazer Mentz coll: polit:
  Junii gram: Heb:
2 Baber's arithmetick
  A discourse of monarchie
  Vellesius de sacrâ philos:
  Brownrig's funerall serm:
  Wendelyn's phys:
  Quercenani op: medica
  Ceporinus's Graec: gram:
  Cluverii introduc: geog:
  Cato's distick construed grammatically
2 Magnetica magnalia
  Ferus in Matheum
  Biblia Lat:
  Castanaei distinctiones
  The new distemper
  Stephen's dictionary
  Peccettii op: chir:
  Playford's psalms
  A narrative of the fire of Lond:
  Zenophon. Graec: Oxon:
  Breviary of ye Roman hist:
  Lipsius of constancy. Eng:
2 Monck unveiled
  Memoirs on ye family of ye Stewarts
  Lucian's works

Crocio in Jonam
A commentary on Ecclesiastes
Woolsey of scripture beleif
Paraeus on ye Romans
Stedman's sober singularity
Resburie's gangreen
Vegerius thesaus: theol:
Triumph of Xtianity
Sherrif's accounts
Barrow's lectiones math:
Historical observations
Symon's discourses
Bible. French
Isocratis sententiae
Laurence hist: of Ireland
Molinaei poemata
Spencer de Urim & Thummim
4 Fasciculus praecept: log:
Steeno de motu musculorum
2 Anthologia
Aphthonii progymnasmata
Burnett's letters
Dares de bello Trojano
Du Veil on ye Acts
Walker's art of teaching
Leusden's onomasticon
Austin of fruit trees
Zenophontis Cyrus
Amiraldi irenicon
Hunt's arithmetick
Aristotle de animâ
Wharton's workes
Christ crucified
Erasmus new testament. G: & L:
Bezae epistolae ad Rom:
Chrisologi serm:
The hist: of the house of Este
Freitagio's Sennerto:
Avega in Hippocratem
Baxter's posing quaestions
Arrianus in Epictetum
Diosiclis amorum. Lib: 9
Lublini tract: summularum

Hist: of ye Eng: & Scotch presbitery
Zwelferii pharmacop:
Grew's idaea
Ciceronis epistolae
Quintilliani institutiones
Boscobell
Whitby against Stillingfleet
Buckle of state & justice
Roberts on ye Ld's supper
Doughtey analect: sacra
Barrow's math:
Brow on ye k's evil
Retorfort praetext
Cartesii metaph:
Burnet's vindication
Plutarck's eth: & moralls
Smetii prosodia
Liturgia françois
Mischeifs or rebellion
Frith's monuments
Le Grand divine Epicurus
Causini thesaurus
Symon of ecclesiastical revenues
Statius de sylvis
Senolt on ye passion
2 Winstanly's historical rarities
Johnstoni lex: chimic:
Wilson of monarchie
Ritchel's metaph:
Orano exilium
Hesiod
Arist: op: G: & Lat:
Lovell's hist:
Carpenter's phil:
Methodica inst: ling: sanct:
Aristot: op:
Skinner's rise & prog:
Assert: meth: Cart:
Erasmi adagia
Sacraledg arraigned
Tully Tusc: quaest:
Paccesii op: chir:

Baxter of Xtian beleif
Balthazar Castilio
2 Hortense callendarium
Owen of scism
Pharmacopeia Belg:
Du Trieu's log:
Gazii pia hillaria
2 Imago seculi
New distemper
Cowdry's defence of Cotton

DUODECIMOS

4 A discription of Feroe
2 The hist: of Aristella
2 Cassimire
Comenii scenographia
Buchanani poemata
Bisco's glorious mistery
3 Strada de bello Belgico
Anthologia poemata
Brian prophet
2 Ritchell's metaph:
The Graeck bible
Heurnii institutiones med:
Taylor of contentment
Fleckno's poems
Claudian
Ecclesiae Ang: θρηνωδία
3 Justini hist:
Justinus cum not: Vinnii
3 Combachius metaph:
Solerius de philos:
5 Burgersdicii idaea phil: mor:
Bellarminus de ascension: ment:
    ad Deum
The ruine of Rome
Cornelius Tacit:
Bedae axiom:
Becker's philos:
The feare of God & ye king
Combachii phis:
3 Pharmocop: Lond:

Galtruchii metaph:
Crucii medulla logica
Hippocratis defensio
Ορθοτονία
Institutio missionariorum
Selecta poemata Italorum
2 Trelcatii loci communes
Angelus Politianus in Sueton:
Robotham on ye Revelat:
Politiani epist:
4 David's blessed man
Corvini jurisprud:
Stockeri praxis aurea
2 Barclai arg:
2 Flavell's navig:
Waters for a thirsty soul
3 Lucius Florus
3 Santi Josephi cursus philos:
6 Senecae trag:
4 Rami dialect:
Hogersii poem:
Rolloci vocatio efficax
The unfortunate policque
Elenchus motuum
Gordwin's return of prayers
2 Vox clamantis
Sin agt: ye Holy Ghost
3 Heerbord's log:
Heinsii orat:
4 Burgersdicii coll: phys:
Baker's metaph:
Euphormionis. Lat:
2 Plauti com:
Burgersdicii pol:
Praxis med:
Singing psalms
Sidelii manuale
Lucii log:
Alstedii method: metaph:
Frambesarii scholae medicae
2 Amesii scripta antisynodalia
Aelianus de variâ historiâ in
    lib: 14

Schisme unmask't
5 Dowell agt: Hobbs*
2 Gerrard's devotions
Bekkar de phil: Cartesianâ
4 Tozer's directions
Pastime royall
2 Bartholini anat:
Usher's catechism
Dury's reform'd schoole
2 Fournier in Euclide
2 Ovid met:
Pindar. G: & L:
Flores de religione
Alstedii log:
Method: theol:
Plutor's idaea theol:
Common prayer
Hunt's indwelling sin
Sherman's white salt
Baxter's confirmation
Smith's sermon
2 Effigies amoris in Eng:
Lipsii epist:
The greate propitiation
Enchir: cap: praecip: theol:
Bogan's mirth of a Xtian life
Castaneus distinctions
Buskeri eth:
Lloyd's phrases
2 Everard hom: ort:
4 Quintus Curtius
Lyford's legacie
Epit: vit: Plut:
Secundi op:
2 Andrews devotions
Reduni ars oratoriae
Catechesis elenctica
2 Quevedo's travells
2 Sancti Romani phys: nat:
Jaccaei metap:
Nowell's catech: G: & L:
Wittichii veritas
Muralti clavis med:

Pemble de orig: form:
2 Biblia septuagint
Aphthonii progymnasmata
Textoris colloquia
3 Amesius de conscientiâ
Flores poet:
May's praxis chirurg:
Claubergii log:
2 Aristophanes
Virgil
Hollinsworth's Holy Ghost
Europaei monarchia
Senguerdii astrologia
Prayers of intercession
Pinker's love to Christ
Butleri rhetorica
Puteanus de Laconismo
Variorum authorum
    sententiae
Pincieri aenigmata
Hortus Anglicus
Angelii politica gen:
Laelii epitome
Evelin's lib: & serv:
Ausonii opera
The perplexed princess
Gaul's holy madness
Bp. Usher's epit: of ye bod: of
    div:
Controversialis log:
Hist: remarks
4 Pavonii eth:
Lipsii epist:
A discourse of ye mercy of
    having godly parents
Rutcovii eth:
6 Ciceronis orat:
2 Rous interreg: Dei
Boyl de orig: gemmarum
Lemnios med:
Portius in Hippocratem
The Italian convert
Vossii rhetorica

Dee's fasciculus chim:
Tudor prince of Wales
2 Pelling's reg: Christian:
Regnorum descriptio nova
Riolani compendius phys:
A guide for constables
Aphthonii apophtheg:
Bartholini enchir: phys:
Gulinzi log:
2 Ovid de trist:
The cirugs: directory
2 Univ: stat: books
Amesii eth:
Rulandi med: pract:
2 Caesar's comment:
Dr. Hewit's prayers of intercession
Prayers & meditations
Billaei loqutiones Graecae
Medulla orat:
Gerbyar's advice to builders
2 Isocrates
Univ: poems
Arist: metaph:
Horni arca Mosis
Capell of temptations
Paradise of piety
Tullius de oratore
Farnaby on Juv:
Grammer quaest:
More's enchir: eth:
Wall's comm: on ye times
Hornbeck's apol:
Abbasius de nat: viperis
Colloquia familiaria
Jewellii apol: eccl: Ang:
Marrow's phys:
The divine Epicurus
Jessy's cases of conscience
Formulae orat:
Vane's animad:
Magnenus de manna
Kerknerii orationes

Clifford's apologie
Downham's covenant of grace
The first last
De gemitu columbae
2 Thomas a Kempis
Watsonii synop: phil:
Seidelii manuale G: & Lat:
Bruges vade mecum
2 Everard of gaging
Tullii rhet:
Rome no rule
God a good master
Musae sacrae
Salust
Dyonius
Soph: trag:
Barlaei orat:
Burgersdicii oecon:
Councell of wisdome
Rex platonicus
Medulla hist: Scot:
Carmina prov:
Herle's wisdom's tripos
Monarchie of Spain
Guthy's Xtian treatice
Children's disseases
2 Axiomata phil:
Bartholinus de mor:
Setoni dialect:
Corvini jus feudale
Colvinus de justificatione
Pleas for toleration disgor:
2 Eustachii eth:
Bp. of York's manual
Alstenius de inst: nob:
Catalogus plantarum Cantab:
Fraus honesta
Ausonii opera
Galtruchii phil: & math:
2 Galataeus de morib:
8 Verny's secret services
2 Smith's log:

ANTHONY STEPHENS

BOOKS IN QUIRES

FOLIOS

- 1 Selden's tracts
- 1 Index expurgatorius
- 3 Setts of Dr. Lightfoot's works
- 13 Dr. Alestry's serm:
- 52 Dugdale of the late troubles
- 1 Scotia illustrata
- 36 Cousin's tables
- 2 Towerson's explic: on ye catechism
- 5 Boccatio's novells
- 1 Pallas armata
- 5 Agathocles
- 1 Carleton's exercitations
- 1 Collection of memorable events
- 2 Comber on the commod: pray:
- 1 Irenaeus
- 2 Constantia & Philetus
- 2 Cary of time chronology

QUARTOS

- 334 Pemble's introduction to geography*
- 11 Cluver's geo:
- 8 Crellii eth:
- 1 Webster on minerals
- 2 Clarendon agt: Hobs
- 6 Macovii opusc: philos:
- 14 Attick antiq:
- 1 Ars gymnastica
- 5 Walker's nat: essays
- 2 Thomas praeservat: of piety
- 1 Goad's refreshing drops
- 1 Holyday sermons
- 1 Bithner's lyra
- 8 King's supremacy asserted
- 17 Jewell's apollogy
- 1 Roman antiquities
- 1 Evangelical harmony
- 5 Jackson consec: of ye son of God
- 2 Digby of bodies
- 1 Griffith's one thing necess:
- 1 Borellus de motu anim: pt. 1st
- 1 Struy's travells
- 1 Falkner of reproaching
- 2 Disquisitiones criticae
- 11 Stierii log:
- 1 Animad: on ye Rabb: talmud
- 1 Cousin's canon of scripture
- 1 Scrivener's apology
- 1 Littleton's dictionary

OCTAVOS

- 184 Hody contra Aristaeum*
- 8 Gassendi astron:
- 9 Boyl of bloud
- 9 Divine Epicurus
- 2 How's blessedness of ye right:
- 3 Bp. Wilkins sermons
- 6 Gallantry alamode
- 7 Eng: midwife
- 10 Cave's antient ch: govern:
- 4 Filmer's power of ks:
- 581 Walker's disc: of govern:*
- 85 Catholick scismatologie*
- 31 Sherlock's vind: of eccl: authorit:
- 32 Jenner of primogeniture
- 28 Gibson's anatomy
- 1 Troubles of Eng: compos'd
- 2 Boscobel
- 2 The courtier's manual oracle
- 1 Tillotson's rule of faith
- 12 Tully's enchiridion*
- 10 Ashwell's gestus eucharisticus
- 16 Wood's sermons
- 19 Abercrombius de pulsu
- 186 Euclid's elem: Eng:*
- 57 Cornelius Nepos. Eng:*
- 64 Curcellaeus eth:
- 38 Theocritus. Eng:*
- 12 Pharmacop: Lond:

172	Juvenalis redivivus	1	Miracles & works above nature
18	Anacreon. Eng:*	7	Fulwood's case of the times
22	Lovil of plants & minerals	2	Barclai poemata
4	Randolph's poems	2	Oliveri dissert: accad:
1	Hobbs humane nature	2	Euclid. Lat:
2	Interest of Ireland	2	Ray's Eng: prov:
29	Divine poems	3	Rise & power of parl:
2	Improvement of ye art of teach:	2	Eromena
2	Gailhard's 2 discourses	1	Hyworth's bagnio
26	Anthologia	3	Scrivelius lex
1	Wilkins disc: of a new world	1	How's delight in God
8	Hist: of Peter D'Aubusson	1	Justice's calling
7	Painter voyage to Italy	1	Imago seculi
2	Observ: of the princip: of nat: mot:	1	Sallius eth:
1	Sheriff's accts:	1	Anat: of humane bodys
4	Pasquin's risen from ye dead	2	Taylor's ch: catech:
1	Light in the way to paradise	1	Ten Rhyne's dissert: de Arthitides
2	Observ: on plants mention'd in ye script:	2	Long's popish & phanat: plots
1	Tuscul: quaest:	2	Heylin's life
5	Cure of old age	3	Downham's brief sum of divin:
2	Doct: of the ch: of Eng:	3	Boyl of min: waters
1	Antid: agt: distraction	7	Galtruchii math:
1	Looking glass for ladys	1	Anatomy of insects
1	Spectical chymist	19	Norris of religious assembly
1	Production of chim: princip:	2	Cave's prim: Christianity
1	Observ: on ye prot: reconc:	2	Moor's eutopia
6	Introd: ad log:	1	Minor poets
2	Occasional reflect:	1	Sanderson de solenni foed:
7	Vareni geog:	2	Whitby's eth:
2	Hale's contemplations	1	Necessary companion
2	Med: de $1^{mâ}$ philos:	1	Puffendorf de off: hom:
4	Log:	1	Rhodii eth:
1	Diaconi Epist:	1	Barclay Argenis
2	Historicall act: of ye troub: in Eng:	5	Lossius de morbis
2	Burnett's letter	1	Filmer's grand inquest
3	Vindic: of ye ord: of ye ch: of Eng:	10	Barrow's lect: math:
1	Defens of Dr. Stillingfleet	3	Elem: geom:
3	Vindic: of episcopacy	18	Epigrammatum delectus
11	Ashmel's fides apostolica	3	Church cat: expounded
		12	Discourses concern: conventic:
		18	Oldham's in 3 pts.
		5	Rochester's poems

ANTHONY STEPHENS

- 4 Hale's provision for ye poor
- 4 Creeche's Lucretius*
- 4 Graecian story
- 4 Meth: leg: hist:
- 3 Rami dialectica
- 7 Eustachii eth:
- 3 Tate's collection of poems
- 4 Theocritus idil: Eng:*
- 1 Touchstone of ye spirit
- 1 Laver of regeneration
- 236 Miscellany poems by Oxford hands*

DUODECIMOS

- 1 Eng: rogue in 4 pts.
- 16 Disc: of ye gift of preaching
- 3 Bithner's ling: eruditorum
- 4 Gassendus in French
- 2 Pandaemonium
- 1 Hobbs Homer
- 4 Use of coffee
- 2 Duty of a Christian
- 5 Epit: of the hist: of Scotland
- 2 Dialogues of health
- 1 Of arbitrary gov:
- 33 Burgersd: coll: phys:
- 1 Spirituall bee
- 2 Spence's defence of his mistress
- 3 David's blessed man
- 3 Ye Dutch rogue
- 2 Eff: amoris. Eng:
- 1 Bisterfieldus redivivus
- 1 Lomierus on ye 16th chap: of St. Luke
- 4 Councells of wisdome
- 1 Bossius de togâ Romanâ
- 4 Self examination
- 2 Terence with Minaelius notes
- 3 Hobbs de cive
- 1 Zouch civil law quaestions
- 1 Aphthonii progymnasmata
- 7 Valor ben: ecc:
- 3 Remarks on ye treatise of hum: reason
- 46 Colbert's ghost
- 6 Lucius Florus
- 3 True meth: of curing consumpt:
- 1 Countess of Salisbury, a novel
- 1 Idaea of a person of honour
- 8 Puteani diatriba
- 1 Disquisitio de repub: monst:
- 8 Galataeus
- 2 Abercrombius protest: to be emb:
- 5 Ye 10 pleasures of marriage
- 1 Thom: Kempis
- 1 Flosculi historici
- 1 Ferrarii orationes
- 1 The posie of godly prayers
- 2 Amesius de conscientia
- 1 Terence
- 1 Glanvil's invitation to ye sacmnt:
- 8 Bradshaw's dissert: de doct: justif:
- 1 Tully de nat: Deorum. Eng:
- 2 Kettlewell's help to a worthy com:
- 2 Sparrow's rationale
- 26 Dr's physitian
- 20 Novells amours
- 12 Heerbord's log:
- 21 Burgersdicius's logick
- 50 Moriae encomium
- 18 Cassimiri poemata
- 2 French intrigues
- 3 Fatherly instructions
- 3 Chamberain's compend: of geog:
- 4 Quevedo's travells
- 6 Andrews priv: devotion
- 123 Leviathan hereticall*
- 6 Grotius de veritate religionis Christianae

24s

1 Gerhard's meditations

BOOKS STICHT

Plays 43
Sermons 16
Pamphletts 31
Hody 2*
Pemble 1*

Upon ye viewing of this catalogue and ye books therein mentioned we whose names are underwritten do value them (with some imperfect and sticht) at ye summe of one hundred & thirty pounds being certain of ye books apperteining to Mr. Anthony Stevens bookseller.

 Will. Colier, beedle of
  lawe, and
 Ric. Davis, verger.

Jan. ye 20th 1686/7.

NOTES

1. The original register is in the Berkshire County Record Office and a microfilm of it is deposited in the Bodleian Library, Oxford, MS. Film dep. 21.

2. A. G. Matthews, *Calamy Revised*, 1934, p. 462. Here the Rev. Anthony Stephens is identified with a cleric of the same name but apparently without a university degree who was ordained priest at Winchester in September 1669. This, however, seems unlikely.

3. These probate papers are now in the Hampshire County Record Office.

4. O.U. Archives, Chancellor's Court papers, bundle 130. Most of the records of apprenticeship to 'privileged' trades are lost, but this miscellaneous bundle contains two files of notifications of apprenticeships apparently sent to the registrar of the court for enrolment. They cover the period from 1667 to 1685 and are mainly for members of the book trade.

5. *D.N.B.*, *sub* Thomas Gilbert (1613–94); Matthews, *Calamy Revised*, p. 221–2; J. Foster, *Alumni Oxonienses, 1500–1714*, p. 565.

6. He was buried on 13 October 1673: Bodleian Library, MS. D.D. Par. Oxf. St. Mary Virgin b. 16, p. 53. His administration papers and probate inventory are in O.U. Archives.

7. O.U. Archives, Chancellor's Court papers, bundle 130. For Good's matriculation see Foster, *Alumni Oxonienses, 1500–1714*, p. 581.

8. O.U. Archives, Matriculation Register, 1662–93, fol. 779^v; Subscription Register, 1660–93, *sub* date.

9. Bodleian Library, MS. D.D. Par. Oxf. St. Mary Virgin b. 4 and 5. The name is not present in the rate for 9 January 1682/3 but it appears in that for 11 September 1683. The intervening two-rate assessments have not survived. It remains in the lists until the rate for 23 September 1685 when it appears and is not assessed. It is not in the

rate for 29 October 1685 and does not reappear. These dates fit very well with what is known from other sources of Anthony Stephens's activities.

10. Shown in plate II of David Loggan's *Oxonia Illustrata*, Oxford, 1675.

11. A plan of the area is in J. Skelton, *Oxonia antiqua restaurata*, 1823, and an adaptation of it is in J. Johnson and S. Gibson, *Print and Privilege at Oxford to the year 1700*, Oxford, 1946, p. 137.

12. This book was evidently a great success which must have encouraged a young man in his first publishing venture. See Anthony Wood, *Athenae Oxonienses*, IV, p. 739.

13. See Wood, *Athenae*, IV, pp. 557–9.

14. Ibid., p. 793.

15. The final page is a list of 'Books printed, and sold by' Stephens. The list contains thirteen titles: nos. 3, 5 and 6 above, together with 11 and 13 below which are stated to be in the press. The other works are J. Crellius, *Ethica Christiana*, the *Geographia* of Cluverius, J. Stier, *Philosophia* and an Amsterdam printing of Hugo Grotius, *De Veritate Religionis Christianae*; J. Oldham, *Poems and Translations* (Brooks, 10), the third edition (1683) of Pierre Gassendi, *Institutio Astronomica*, the second edition (1681) of W. Howell, *Medulla Historiae Anglicanae*; and *Juvenalis Redivivus* (1683). This last item, a political satire, has the imprint 'Printed in the year 1683, and are to be sold by most Booksellers'. It was by Thomas Wood, many of whose works were published by Stephens. Stephens may have had a financial stake in this work, for there were no fewer than 172 copies in quires in his shop in 1686.

16. This book brought Cruttenden, though not apparently Stephens, into trouble. Anthony Wood noted on 12 January 1683/4 that it was forbidden to be sold because the preface, written by Leopold Finch of All Souls' College, contained more than was licensed by Dr. Timothy Halton the pro-vice-chancellor whose *imprimatur* the book carried. The objectionable passages apparently referred to the exclusion struggle and the Oxford parliament of 1681. Halton began a suit against Cruttenden in the Chancellor's court. No case-papers survive in the university's archives, however, so that there are only the bare entries in the act books to show that the case went on from February until Trinity term, and these give no indication of the substance of the case. Wood, *Life and Times*, III, 86; O.U. Archives, Chancellor's Court act books, 1679–84, 1684–5. A second edition of the work, unchanged as to content, appeared in 1685 when James II was on the throne, bearing the imprint 'London: Printed for John Weld'.

17. Another issue of the same year bears the imprint 'London. Printed for Jacob Tonson, and Sold by Tim. Goodwin . . .'.

18. The same edition reappeared in 1685 with a reset title-page and the imprint 'Oxonii, Typis Leon. Lichfield, Prostant venales Londini apud Sam. Smith . . .'.

19. The Bodleian copy is annotated '1684. Dono dedit Anth. Stephens Bibliopola Univers. Oxon.'

20. See Wood, *Athenae*, IV, 557.

21. This imprint is not recorded by Wing where all editions including that of 1685 are for members of the Forrest family. A copy in the Folger Library, however, has the Stephens imprint and he had no fewer than 334 copies of the work in quires in his shop in 1686.

22. See Wood, *Athenae*, IV, 619.

23. The final page is a list of 'Books Printed for, and Sold by' Stephens. The list comprises seventeen titles: nos. 3, 5, 6, 7, 11, 12, 13, 15, 16, 19, and 20 above; Stier, Cluverius and Grotius as in 1683 (see above, n. 15); and J. Oldham, *Works* (Brooks, 18), T. Gibson, *The Anatomy of Humane Bodies Epitomized*, 2nd edn., and ΑΝΘΟΛΟΓΙΑ *Seu Selecta Quaedam Poemata Italorum*. The inventory of his shop in 1686 shows that he had 18, 28, and 26 copies respectively of these last works in quires.

24. The latest catalogue seen by the present writer on which Stephens's name appears is that of the libraries of Dr. Ambrose Atfield and others, 25 May 1685.

25. Index to the Eynsham parish registers, Bodleian Library, MS. Top. Oxon. e. 173, fol. 355. The marriage was by licence dated 15 April 1684, Bodleian Library, MS. Oxf. Dioc. pps. d. 80, fol. 134.

26. See above, n. 15 and n. 23.

27. All the information about the court cases is taken from the following Chancellor's Court papers in O.U. Archives: the act books for 1684–5 and 1685–91, and the surviving loose papers for Michaelmas 1685 (bundle 51), Michaelmas 1686 (bundle 52) and Hilary 1686/7 (ibid).

28. The association of Cruttenden in this bond may imply that this money was borrowed towards the cost of the troublesome *Lives of Illustrious Men* or some other venture in which both men were involved, though it may just mean that Cruttenden was merely acting as a friend to Stephens since he was again a surety in November 1684. Cruttenden subsequently aided Obadiah Walker in setting up his Roman Catholic press at University College, Oxford, and was at the end of his life employed by the Delegates of the University Press. He was reckoned to be, at least by Dr. Arthur Charlett, 'A fool in his own business'. F. Madan, *A Chart of Oxford Printing: '1468'–1900*, 1903, 19; Johnson and Gibson, *Print and Privilege*, 138–9.

29. See A. Everitt in *The Agrarian History of England and Wales*, IV, 1500–1640, ed. Joan Thirsk, 1967, p. 559.

30. Thomas Wood, the master mason and architect, was manciple of Balliol College, for example. D. G. Vaisey, 'Thomas Wood and his Workshop', *Oxoniensia*, XXXVI (1971), 55–8.

31. F. Madan, *Oxford Books*, II, nos. 2997–8, 3092, 3295, 3141, 3147; H. Carter, *Wolvercote Mill*, 1957, 14–15. The signature on the bonds in O.U. Archives is the same as that on a 1675 receipt signed by the engraver. Bodleian Library, MS. Savile 101, fol. 10. I am grateful to Mr. Harry Carter for this reference.

32. This 20d. brought Stephens a small 8° book printed on 24 sheets (A–3B^4).

33. The inventory of these goods shows that Stephens occupied three-storey premises with the shop and a kitchen on the ground floor, two rooms on the first floor, and a small room and two garrets on the second floor. The goods seized included the full range of household effects: kitchen ware, beds, chairs, tables, linen, and wall-hangings.

34. Altered from £6 15s. in the libel.

35. Altered from £9 10s. in the libel.

36. The total sought by Thomson was altered in the libel from £34 18s. to £34. It is not clear why the sums were all reduced in this manner: perhaps the interest rate was deemed too high, or an adjustment was made *pro rata* in order to bring the total claimed nearer to the value of the goods available to meet the claims.

37. Probate inventories in O.U. Archives.

38. No indication has been found that he moved to Eynsham, his wife's native parish. Farther west in the county at Langford an Anthony Stevens, described as a yeoman, died in 1723 leaving a widow named Elizabeth and at least four children, two of whom were married. He would have been about the right age to have been the erstwhile bookseller, but the signature on his will (Bodleian Library, MS. Wills Peculiars 78/5/13) bears no resemblance to surviving examples of that of the bookseller from the 1680s, even allowing for deterioration due to the passage of some 40 years and possible feebleness at the time of making the will.

HARRY CARTER

Early accounts of the University Press, Oxford

An introduction

Regular accounts of expenditure and receipts for the University's printing began with the assumption of management by the board of Delegates of the Press in 1690. They are the oldest continuous set of accounts for this trade in England, older by six years than those of the University Press at Cambridge. They lack the bibliographical interest of the Cambridge accounts inasmuch as they do not preserve the vouchers on which individual workmen based their claims for pay at piecework rates,[1] and it must be admitted that until Blackstone reformed the accounting at Oxford in 1758 they reveal much less of the balance of debit or credit.

The Oxford Delegates were obliged by the terms of their appointment since 1662 to render annual accounts for publishing and printing (*res typographica*) to Convocation, and to do it in time for the Vice-Chancellor to include a figure for their gain or loss in his Computus.[2] All that the Delegates did before 1758 was to adopt the 'Account for Printing' drawn up by the Warehouse-Keeper in charge at the Press, or in some years by an Architypographus relying on him, and certify it to the Vice-Chancellor. At least they did that ideally; but in the early part of the eighteenth century there is reason to suppose that the Warehouseman's accounts went directly to the Vice-Chancellor as chairman of the Delegates and other members of the board did not see them. That was one of the grievances that made Blackstone write his open letter '*To the Reverend Doctor Randolph*' in 1757.

The Account for Printing has to be read in association with the Computus of the Vice-Chancellor. He paid or received sums in respect of the Press that did not pass through the Warehouse-Keeper's hands, repair and maintenance of the building. Rates and taxes, fees of authors, editors, artists, and engravers were paid by him, and income of the Press from endowments voted by Convocation as well as compensation

[1] Notes are on p. 138.

from the King's Printer and the Stationers' Company for forbearance to print books covered by their patents went to him. After 1708 he undertook the buying of paper, evidently because the Warehouse-Keeper was suspected of being on too good terms with a supplier, John Baskett, and of buying too much.

I shall not deal with the Computus, because it is available to researchers in the University Archives. There also, or among Bodleian manuscripts, are some accounts for printing of a date earlier than 1690, that is to say before the University corporately owned and managed a press. The oldest, apart from the Computus, is a notebook in which Samuel Clarke, Architypographus 1658–69, wrote the sums that he received and spent in the exercise of his functions.[3] It is interesting because it shows that the University regarded the money that Convocation voted to printing as a chest: the Architypographus might withdraw from it on giving, or finding, security for repayment and lend to an Oxford printer or bookseller-publisher. There was no question of usury: only the amount borrowed was paid back. Until the loan was repaid Clarke noted the number of the subsidised books in the publisher's stock, presumably because he had a lien on them in the event of failure to repay.

For the first year of the tenure of the Sheldonian Press by Fell and his partners, 1672–3, there are very interesting figures in the University Archives (S.E.P. P17^b(1)). When they entered on their lease of the University's privilege of printing at Lady Day 1672 they intended to exercise to the full the powers of comprinting on monopolists given by the charters of 1632–6, though not without misgivings about the force of these royal favours if tried at common law. They had taken on themselves the annual payments previously made by the monopolists for forbearance to comprint.

The Archives preserve calculations, estimates, and accounts by Thomas Yate for printing in despite of the Company of Stationers, text-books for schools and almanacs, as well as rough estimates for a Bible to challenge the opposition of the King's Printers.

He begins by computing the capacity of the Press and the cost to the partners of its output.[4]

6 Compositors—18 sheets per week at 2s.6d. per diem. soe charge of Printing 3000 of a sheet is to the Compositor for 2 dayes	0: 5: 0
to two Presse men for two dayes	0: 8: 0
for Correcting per sheet	0: 2: 0

for Use of Letter, Ink, Rent &c. per sheet   0:10: 0

    1: 5: 0

50 Weeks 18 sheets per week is 900 sheets per
Annum abate for Holydayes (besides the 2 weeks)
10 dayes 3 sheets per diem 30 sheets there will
be 870 sheets printed in the yeare.
870 sheets at 10s. per sheet for Use Letter,
    Ink, rent &c.   435: 0: 0

if but 4 Compositors & 8 Pressmen they will
print but 560 sheets per Annum, which at 10s.
    per sheet is   290: 0: 0

He also reckons the amounts of type of several sizes that will be needed. Where the 'Grammar' was concerned, that is to say the *Short Introduction of Grammar generally to be Used*, the partners were on relatively safe ground, because a decree of the Privy Council of 9 March 1636 had authorized the two Universities to print up to 3,000 a year each, though it was a monopoly of the King's Printer in Latin.[5] Yate contemplated keeping it standing.[6]

Long Primer 2000 li. 600 will keepe the Grammar on the Frame without Accidence.

The 'Accidence' (*Brevissima institutio grammatices cognoscendae*) was always printed at Oxford following the Grammar in one volume. Yate's reason for not reserving type for it may have been that he was not sure of being able to print it often enough because it was not covered by the Privy Council's order.

Where school books and almanacs were concerned Fell and his most active partner were extremely optimistic. In one of his letters Yate wrote that they were determined to print better than the Stationers and sell more cheaply.[7] As soon as they took charge they put in hand six texts for schools in editions of 3000 and 15,000 of a sheet almanac. These they finished, and Yate records the costs of them.

In fact, as it soon became clear, Fell's partnership was quite unequal to competing in the market for cheap school books, a kind of work for which the Stationers' English Stock must have employed poor printers at cut prices. A few examples, assuming that my calculations are right, will show it all too clearly.

Ovid's *Tristia*, for which the partners estimated for an edition of 3000 £13 5s., cost them £16 10s 6d or 1s. 2d. a copy, while the Stationers sold it in quarterns of 25 for 9d. The so-called Cato's *Disticha*, estimated at £12 for 3000, cost £12 17s. 6d, while the Stationers' price was 2½d a copy, as compared with Oxford's 9½d. Aesop, estimated at £25 5s., cost the partners £30 18s. or 2s. 7d. a copy, while the Stationers charged 12s. for a quartern. The *Sententiae pueriles* printed at Oxford worked out at 7d. a copy, and the Stationers charged 1¾d.; the *Pueriles confabulatiunculae* 6½d. as against 2d. And the buyer of a quartern got a 26th copy free.[8]

The consequence was that the confident mood lasted a short time. By October 1672 Fell had received overtures from the Stationers and agreed to hand over to them the six school books and the almanacs, pocket-book and sheet, that he had printed at something like cost price. The editions have vanished: only the copper plate for printing the title of Aesop's fables, preserved at the Press, remains of the school books; of the little book almanac for 1673 two copies are known, and of the one in sheet-form a single, very imperfect, copy has only lately been discovered.[9]

The costs of printing these books and almanacs are the oldest we have. They were written by Yate as follows.[10]

```
    1672
March 28    Sententiae Pueriles
            3 sheets. 3000 printed
            Pott paper 15 Ri ē at 4s 4d              4.  6.  8
            Composeing at 5s per sheet               0. 15.  0
            Presse worke at 2d per houre             1.  7.  0
            Correcting & charges                     (blank)
                                                     ─────────
                                                     9. 19.  0

            Sold to the Company at 10s per Reame

            Pueriles Confabulatiunculae
            8°. 4 sheets. 3000 printed.
            Pott paper 24 Reames ¼ Re at
            4s 4d per Reame                          5. 13.  9
            Composeing at 5s per sheet               1.  0.  0
            Presse worke at 2d per houre             1. 16.  0
            Correcting & charges                     1.  4.  0
                                                     ─────────
                                                     9.  2.  9

            Sold to the Company at 10s per Reame
```

UNIVERSITY PRESS ACCOUNTS

Pica	Cato. 8°. 5 sheets, 3000 printed			
	Pott paper. 30 R. 3./R. at 4s 4d	7.	3.	6
	Composeing at 6s per sheet	1.	10.	0
	Presse worke at 2d per houre	2.	5.	0
	Correcting	0.	10.	0
	Charges	1.	10.	0
		12.	17.	6
	Sold to the Company at 10s per Ream			
Long Primer	Corderius 8°. 10 sheets ¼. 3000 printed			
	Pott paper 61 R.½ 6½ (3 Quir)			
	R at 4s 4d	14.	11.	4
	Composeing at 6s per sheet	3.	1.	6
	Presse work at 2d per houre	4.	12.	3
	Correcting	1.	0.	0
	Charges	3.	0.	0
		24.	6.	9
	Sold to the Company at 10s per Ream.	24.	0.	7
	Æsops Fab. 8°. 12 sheets. 3000 printed			
Long Primer	Pott paper. 72 R.7.R. at 4s 4d	17.	2.	10
	Composeing at 6s per sheet	3.	12.	0
	Presse worke at 2d per houre	5.	8.	0
	Correcting	1.	4.	0
	Charges at 2s per 1000	3.	12.	0
		30.	18.	0
	Sold to the Company at 10s per Ream			
	Ovid de Tristibus 12mo. 4 sheets. 3000 printed.			
Small Pica	Lumbard paper 24 R. 2 R. ½ at 7s 6d	9.	18.	11
	per Reame			
	Composing at 9s (. . . .) per sheet	2.	6.	0
	Presse workes 3¼d per houre	2.	18.	6
	at 14s 7½d per houre			
	Correcting	0.	8.	0
	Charges	1.	4.	0
		16.	10.	6
	Sold to the Company at 10s per Ream			
1672				
July 6th	Dr Brevint. Missale Roman. 12 sht. ½			
	1000 printed. Eng. Rom.			

English Rom.	Lumbard paper 25 R. 2 R. ½ at 7s. 6d per Reame	10.	5.	9
	Composeing at 6s 9¼d. per sheet	4.	4.	4
	Presse worke at 3d per houre	2.	16.	3
	Correcting	1.	5.	0
	Charges at 2s per 1000	1.	4.	0
		19.	17.	11
	Sold to the Stationers 900 at 13s 9d per Booke. 100 given some few sold.			
October 1672	Almanacks sheet in 15000 printed Lumbard Paper. 30 R. 3 R.	12.	17.	6
	Composeing	(blank)		
	Presse worke at 3d per houre	3.	7.	6
	Correcting	0.	4.	0
	Charges	1.	0.	0
October 1672	Almanack Book in 12° 2 sheetes 20500 printed			
	Wolvercote Paper 20000 40 R. 8 R. 16	17.	13.	0
	Genoa Paper 2 Reames at 6s 6d	0.	13.	0
	Composeing per Sheet 30s	3.	0.	0
	Press work at 2s per houre	9.	3.	9
	Correcting	0.	8.	6
	Charges	2.	0.	0
		32.	3.	9
	Sold to the Stationers at 10s per Ream			

The brief account for printing the pocket-book *Oxford Almanack* for 1673, edited by Maurice Wheeler, is the earliest record of paper being made at Wolvercote. It is proof that a decent white paper was manufactured at that mill two years before Robert Plot noted in his diary that 'a coarse paper' was being made there[11] and six years before the next record of Wolvercote paper being used at Fell's press, for Faustinus in 1678.

The terms of the sell-out to the Stationers were not unduly harsh: in some instances Fell and Yate got a little more than their money back, which is surprising if the Company meant only to waste the whole of its purchase, as it apparently did. There is another sign of a desire for an accommodation with the Oxford partners. It appears from one of

Yate's calculations[12] that before agreeing to buy up the stock of school books more or less at cost the Stationers had offered to employ the Sheldonian Press to print 22 of such books every year, a total of 377 sheets. That would have solved the problem of providing bread-and-butter work for the printers; but the rates offered were no more than a third of the cost of producing the books at Oxford, and Yate had no difficulty in showing that acceptance would have been disastrous.

Our next set of accounts are for a period after the signing of an agreement with the Stationers of 9 March 1674/5 relinquishing by the partners any claim to print books of which the Company had a monopoly excepting the works of Virgil, Terence, Ovid and Cicero with notes or paraphrase in a form not prejudicial to the sale of the Stationers' editions, 'alsoe to print a broad Almanacke with a large border conteyning a large sheet of paper to be engraven upon a Copper plate and to be wrought of at the Roleing press not exceeding five thousand and likewise power to print singing psalmes with such Bibles as they shall see cause to be printed according to the Order of the Councill Table March the ninth Anno Domini 1635'.[13] The order in Council of 1636 (N.S.) limited the Universities to Bibles in Medium folio or in quarto.[14]

For the years 1674-6 we have only Fell's accounts for his own expenditure on the Press written on some leaves of a notebook which are preserved among the Cause Papers of the Chancellor's Court for Hilary Term 1677/8 (they had been produced as evidence in a suit by the typefounder Peter de Walpergen against Fell's executors).

Fell paid for editing, correcting, engraving, and typefounding. Expense on paper or printing does not come into his accounts at all. The part of his record from December 1675 onwards is also written by his partner, Thomas Yate, on a leaf of the Rawlinson MSS.[15] under the heading, 'Moneys layd out at the Workhouse and for the Presse By my Lor(d) Bishop of Oxon. since Christmas 1675'. His wording of the items differs from Fell's, but the amounts are the same, totalling £191 10s. by the end of 1676 Yate's version has the advantage of giving the months in which the payments were made.

'The Workhouse' was the name that Fell used for a part of the Dean's Lodging in Christ Church where the typefounding was done. His accounts mention the first typefounder, Harman Harmansz., as late as March 1675 and on 28 November following the payment of £1 to his successor, Peter de Walpergen, 'for his journey'. Yate enters £12 9s. 10d. in October 1676 for 'Diet for the Founders boyes', and in January 1676/7 £9 1s. for 'Diet for the Founder and boyes'. One of the boys, William Hall, had bound himself apprentice on 19 October 1672 'to the worshipful Dr. Fell &c. to learne the Art of Letter founding for 7 yeares',[16] and was still there in November 1674.

Fell's account-book is rich in references to engravers, and it is not, I hope, irrelevant to note that a number of the copper plates that he mentions existed at the Press until 1918 and a few still do.

Richard Rawlinson came by some accounts for receipts and expenditure of the Sheldonian Press extending from August 1676 until October 1679. They are among the MSS. at the Bodleian (Rawl. D397). The sheets, which do not form a complete sequence, are numbered (in ink) 310–29, but are not arranged in chronological order, and three lack a large part of the written area, therefore are only partly and uncertainly legible. Leaving out of account leaves that record receipts only, there are 13 that give sums paid for composing and printing books. I think they should be read in this order:

327 (1676), 328, 330, X, 313, 312 (1677), 315, 311 (1678), 318, 320, 323, 324 (1679).

The year 1678 is evidently poorly represented. X stands for half a leaf without a number.

The two that I have put first in order are wholly in the writing of Thomas Yate. The others are alike in their handwriting, and may be presumed to be those described by Yate in endorsements that have become detached as John Hall's Accounts. On the left-hand half of 323 Yate reduplicated some items that Hall put on leaves 313, 330, and one (Sallust) on 315 and dated them 1677. Sallust's title-page, however, is dated 1678.

These accounts all omit the cost of paper. Hall gives the cost of composing and presswork of some books per quire, of others per sheet, and of others per forme, and works out the total. Costs of setting and printing quires always relate to folios (quartos are reckoned per sheet), and the quires were of two sheets. So far as I can judge, the Press had type enough for all eight pages of the sections of the books for which Hall charged by the quire. I can see no indication to the contrary.

Work done at the rolling press by John Cheyney, the copperplate printer, in adding engraved title-pages, illustrations, and 'Theaters' on title-pages is charged for separately and not put down to particular books.

What chiefly interests me about Hall's accounts is the number of books for which he quotes the charge by formes. There are eight of them, and in two instances Hall makes it clear that forme and sheet were equivalent.

> (leaf 315) Herodian at case, the whole book
> makes 18 sheets and half at 20s. a sheet   £18   8s.   0d.
> for laying a Greek case and setting up the greek   5s.   0d.
> At Press the formes I.K.L.M.N.O.P.Q.R.S.T.U.X.
> Y.Z.Aaa.Bbb.Cc.Dd.Ee.Ff.Gg.Hh.Ii.Kk.Ll.Mm.Nn.
> and the title forme at 2s a form   £2   18s.   0d.
> (leaf 311) For composing in the Psalter the
> sheets Iii.Kkk.Lll and the title form at 6s.
> the form   £1   4s.   0d.
> At Press the same forms at 2s. 6d.   10s.   0d.

There is another instance in Yate's handwriting:

> (leaf 327) Homer's Iliades Gr. 8° 54 sheetes
> 1100 printed. Composeing at 18s. per sheet,
> Presswork at 6s. per sheet And for 2 formes
> printed twice 24s. in tot.   £66   0s.   ?d.

—which, if you work it out, means that a sheet was printed from one forme.

In other words, a good many books were printed half-sheet, work and turn. Of those for which Hall charges by the forme some were octavo gathered in fours:

Psalterium, 1678 (Madan 3201)
Willis, *Pharmaceutice rationalis*, 1677 (Madan 3239)
Oughtred, *Opuscula*, 1677 (Madan 3147)
Herodian, 1678 (Madan 3177)
Xenophon, 1679 (Madan 3240)
Zosimus, 1679 (Madan 3242)

—others were duodecimo in sixes:

Clement, *Epistola*, 1677 (Madan 3138)
Maximus Tyrius, 1677 (Madan 3146)
Walker, *Of Education*, 1677 (Madan 3161)

Madan made use of these accounts for Volume iii of *Oxford Books*. He describes the Clement and the Maximus as 16mo., an adjective favoured by librarians of an older generation for books that struck them as small; but the chain-lines go crossways.

The reason for working half sheets may have been the want of type enough to print a whole sheet or a belief that a book in sections of four or six leaves binds better than one in sections of twice as many. But who did the folding in two and slitting? There is no charge for it in the accounts. Most of the octavos printed at the Press in the eighteenth century were gathered in fours; but the accounts for that time give no clue to the method of working them.

One item of a converse kind in Hall's accounts is perplexing:

(leaf 320) The Catechism at case the forms
* A.B.C.D.E.F.G. at 3s. the forme £1 4s. 0d.
The same at press at 10s. the sheet £2 0s. 0d.

Thomas Marshall's *Catechism*, 1680 (Madan 3270) is a booklet of 56 pages, Pott 8vo., gathered in fours. It would certainly have been printed work and turn. They must have printed two formes at a time, lying side-by-side on the press. Perhaps the chases that would take eight pages were in use for something else.

Comparative prices for setting Latin and Greek are given in the charge for Cornelius Nepos, 1678 (Madan 3185). Sheets in Latin cost 9s., those in Greek 10s. (leaf 315).

In some memoranda doubtless written in 1671[17] Yate noted 'To enter all Bookes as ours'. He might be understood to mean enter at Stationers' Hall, but an item in Hall's accounts (leaf 318) suggests a different meaning:

For entring Dr Willis 8° English at Mr Witts   1s. 0d.

Richard Witt was registrar of the Chancellor's Court at Oxford. *Pharmaceutice rationalis* translated into English would be a valuable copy, and it is rather surprising that entry in the records of that Court should be thought to give it much protection.

For the years 1690 to 1780 we have at the Press 'The Account for Printing' in three stout volumes, 1690–1708, 1709–46, and 1747–80. The accounts should have been rendered annually to the Vice-Chancellor, who was given a copy of each year's on a quarto diploma, and have run from one Michaelmas to another, but there were many lapses from regularity.

Until Michaelmas 1706 the accounts were signed by, or for, John Hall, whom the Delegates, on taking control in 1690, had continued in the post of Warehouse-Keeper. As such he was in day-to-day charge of the learned press. Hall's widow kept the accounts for two years, and then the architypographus, Giles Thistlethwaite, took over the duty until he died early in 1715. The Delegates felt unable to face dealings

UNIVERSITY PRESS ACCOUNTS

with Thomas Hearne, the antiquary, elected to succeed Thistlethwaite, and entrusted the accounting to Stephen Richardson, the compositor whom they made Warehouse-Keeper. In any case, Hearne, after many acrimonious passages, resigned his office a few months later.

To gain a complete grasp of the University's expenditure on the learned press, or profit from it, involves reading the Warehouse-Keeper's accounts in combination with the Computus of the Vice-Chancellor. I shall not undertake here to state the result of doing so: I make some attempt at it in my forthcoming history of the Press. The Warehouse-Keeper's accounts read in isolation, with all their defects are a great improvement on the fragmentary statements of earlier years. For one thing they are a sequence, with few deliberate omissions, covering ninety years. Moreover, they are comprehensive inasmuch as they deal to some extent with every element in the production and sale of books. No other continuous and comprehensive accounts for printing in England are quite as old as these: those of the Cambridge University Press run from 1698 to 1712;[18] William Bowyer's from 1710 to 1773;[19] those of Charles Ackers from 1732 to 1748;[20] William Strahan's from 1739 to 1768.[21]

To give an idea of the kind of information to be found in the Oxford 'Account for Printing' the first year's, ending at Michaelmas 1691, is set out below.

The Account for printing from Mich. 90 to Mich. 91 by John Hall, Warehouse-keeper to the University

(p. 1) 1691. *The University Creditor.* The Reverd. Dr. Jonathan Edwards, Vice Chan.

	£	s	d
For the Plate and Graveing the Almanack (1)	13	00	00
For 2500 Almanacks sold at £1 12s. per Hundred	40	00	00
For 500 more at £1 12s. per Hundred	08	00	00
150 Almanacks for presents upon Imperial paper (2)			
For 365 Books of Verses (3) at 2s. per Book	38	08	00
138 sent to London and given to Heads of Houses and 100 left in the Warehouse			
For the use of Letter (4) to print Musae Anglicanae	01	17	06
For the use of Letter to print Dr. Spark's Sermon (5)	00	05	04
For 4 Comment on Hosea (6) sold at 13s. per Book	02	12	00
For 8 Comment on Hosea at 7s. per Book (7)	02	16	00
For 11 Josephus's (8) at 5s. per Book	02	15	00
For 51 Lactantius's (9) at 2s. per Book	05	02	00
For 462 Dr. Marshalls Catechismes (10) at 3½d.	06	14	09

	£	s	d
For 125 Dr. Hoddys Tracts (11) at 9d.	04	13	09
For one Wase (12), one Didasculus (13), one Brevint on the Mase (14)	00	01	06
For 6 Setts of Answers to Mr. Walker (15)	00	07	06
For 8 Reames of Dutch Demie fine paper for the Verses (16)	08	00	00
For 23 Reames of Fooles-Cap to print part of the Comment on Joel (17)	06	06	09
	140	14	01

(p. 2) *Per Contra*

	£	s	d
Payd Mr. Burghers for the Plate and Graveing the Alman. (18)	13	00	00
For 6 Reame of Almanack paper at 26s. per Reame	07	16	00
For one Reame more and 6 Quire of Imperial	02	10	00
For Printing at the Roleing Press 3000 Almanacks	07	17	06
For Printing 30 Sheets and halfe of Verses upon the Kings returne from Ireland 500 Books (19) upon 35 Reames of Fools-cap at 7s. 6d. per Ream	13	05	00
Composeing 4s. per sheet £6 2s. 0d.			
Presswork 3s. per Sheet 4 11 6			
Necessaries (20) 1 10 6	12	04	00
For Printing the Theatre in the Title and Border in the first page (21)	00	12	00
For 8 Reames of Dutch Demie to Print fine paper Bookes	08	00	00
For Printing 47 Sheets of Dr. Pococks Comment on Joel (22), 500 printed on 53 Reames of Fools-Cap at 5s. 3d. per Reame	13	18	03
Composeing 7s. 6d. per sheet £17 12s. 6d.			
Presswork 2s. 6d. per sheet 5 17 6			
Necessaries 2 7 0			
Correcting 1s. 6d. per sheet 3 10 6	29	07	06
For Printing a Plate and Theatre in the Title	00	12	00
For Printing 7 Sheets and halfe of Mr. Hoddy's Tract de nova &c. (23)			
Composeing 4s. 0d. per sheet £1 10s. d.			
Presswork 2s. 6d. per sheet 0 19 0			
Necessaries 7s. 6d. 0 7 6	02	16	06
For Printing 4 sheets of the Grammar (24)			
Composeing 20s. per sheet £4 0s. 0d.			
Presswork 16s. per sheet 3 4 0			

UNIVERSITY PRESS ACCOUNTS

				£	s	d
Necessaries [per sheet]	1	4	5	08	08	00
For 27 Reames of Lumber paper at 12s.				16	04	00
For binding 255 Statutes (25)				03	03	09
For Printing a Specimen for Dr. Hyde (26)				00	10	00
For Printing 2 Sheets of Josephus (27)				01	10	00
For 1 C. weight of Antimony (28)				01	08	00
For 11 melting Potts for the Founder				00	14	06
For Refineing 7½lb. of Mettle				01	02	06
				144	19	06

This years Account was adjusted and made even with Mr. Vice-Chancellor

(p. 3) These Bookes were sent to Mr. Wetstein in Holland (29) in Exchange for Bookes which he sent to the publique Library
  2 Dr. Morrisons Herbal
 12 Josephus's
 10 Misna pars Zeraim
  6 Wases Senarius
  6 Gothick Grammars
  3 Dr. Pocock on Hosea
  8 Aristarchus
  8 Aristeus

The accounts obviously need editing; this one particularly: gradually they came to be arranged in a more orderly and intelligible way.

They are essentially designed to show a balance of debit and credit as between the Vice-Chancellor (acting for the Delegates of the Press) and the Warehouse-Keeper for current expenditure on printing. Overheads hardly come into it: the Vice-Chancellor paid for rent, repairs, and maintenance of buildings and rates and taxes, besides editors' and artists' fees.

With reference to the figures within parentheses that I have added I offer the following notes.

(1) That this item appears as a debt of the Warehouse-Keeper may be explained by the Vice-Chancellor's having paid for it.

(2) There is no profit from these gift copies.

(3) Either *Vota Oxoniensia pro Guillielmo rege* of 1689 or *Academiae Oxoniensis gratulatio* of 1690 on King William's victories in Ireland and safe return from there.

(4) A charge, later called 'poundage', was added to the printers' bills

as a contribution to the University for profit, overheads, and wear and tear of type and other equipment. It was regularly imposed on charges for printing books for customers other than the University, and graduates were given a reduced rate. The entry of receipt of poundage in the accounts is enough to show that a book was not published by the Delegates, a fact which is often impossible to tell by the imprint. Books printed for 'outside' customers make no other appearance in the accounts than the receipt of poundage, and some make no appearance at all, either because the work was of such merit (e.g. Mill's New Testament or Hickes's *Thesaurus*) that the University forbore to charge, or because the amount (generally for sermons) was so small that the Warehouse-Keeper felt justified in pocketing it. When Stephen Richardson, Warehouse-Keeper, died and Blackstone was active in the affairs of the Press, Richardson's executor was required to pay for the poundage on 34 sermons printed in the previous three years and not brought to account. The sum involved was £12 1s. 10½d.

Musarum Anglicanarum analecta was a collection of Latin verses never before published or printed only sporadically. A second volume came out in 1699, and a third in 1717. All three were printed for Oxford booksellers. In this instance the accounts give no clue to the identity of the anonymous editor.

(5) Thomas Sparke's sermon at Guildford for the Bishop of Winchester's visitation was dated 1691 and printed for John Crossley of Oxford. There is a copy in the British Library.

(6 and 7) Edward Pococke's *Commentary on the Prophecy of Hosea* was published by the Delegates in 1685. We have no accounts for 1680-9, and I cannot explain why some copies cost much more than others. Differences were often due to a higher price for large paper copies.

(8) See note (27) below.

(9) Lactantius *De divinis institutionibus* of 1684, edited by Thomas Sparke.

(10) This edition is not comparable with that of 1680, noticed on an earlier page, because 56 pages of questions and answers and epilogue had been added. It was dated 1689.

(11) Humfrey Hody, *Anglicani novi schismatis redargutio*, published by the Delegates in 1691.

(12) Christopher Wase, *Senarius, sive de legibus et licentia veterum poetarum*, 1687.

(13) *Didascalophocus, or the Deaf and Dumb Man's Tutor*, 1680, by George Dalgardno (Madan, *Oxford Books*, iii, No. 3263).

UNIVERSITY PRESS ACCOUNTS

(14) Daniel Brevint, *Missale Romanum, or the Depth and Mystery of the Roman Mass*, 2nd edn., 1673 (Madan, op. cit., No. 2972).

(15) The collected volume of 'Oxford Anti-Popery Tracts' published by the Delegates in 1687 and 1688 controverting the publications of Obadiah Walker's press written by Abraham Woodhead but edited by Walker. The anonymous Protestant tracts had their own title-pages but are found bound together.

(16) *Academiae Oxoniensis gratulatio pro exoptato serenissimi Regis Gulielmi ex Hibernia reditu*, 1690.

(17) Edward Pococke, *A Commentary on the Prophecy of Joel*, 1691.

(18) That this item occurs twice in the accounts for the year may be explained by the *Oxford Almanack*'s being printed from duplicate plates as, in some years, from triplicates.

(19) The book referred to in note (16) above.

(20) A list of the consumable stores and usual services coming under this head is written at the end of the volume of accounts for 1708–47:

Ordinary Necessaries incident to printing

Fire, Candle, and Ink	Lye-Brushes
Wool	Lye
Balls	Past
Ball-stockes	Postage of Letters and parcells
Nails	Gathering, Collating, and drying of Books
Parchment	
Blanketts	Packing, Cordage, packing paper, and spunge

Considering the want of any sign that the Warehouse-Keeper received a salary, I think that he made his living by this charge. In some years he charged 'For extra help in the Warehouse'.

(21) 'Theatre' means the engraving of the Sheldonian Theatre used as a publisher's device. 'Border' generally means a headband, as here.

(22) The book referred to in note (17) above. The charge for composing is high, reflecting the abundance of quotations in exotic scripts.

(23) The book referred to in note (11) above.

(24) This is the 5th edition of the work known as the 'Oxford Grammar', the so-called 'Lily's Grammar' revised at the behest of Fell by Thomas Bennett and first issued in 1673. It was a volume made up of two books separately signed and paginated; the first *A Short Introduction of Grammar generally to be used* with a preface attributable to Fell; the second, *Brevissima institutio grammatices cognoscendae*. The

edition of 1692 referred to here is a duodecimo collating π^4/ A–C^{12} (the *Short Introduction*), A–H^{12}/I^8 (the *Brevissima institutio*). In his account for 1691–2 the Warehouse-Keeper charged the Vice-Chancellor:

> For Printing 8 Sheets more to finish the Grammar 3000 Bookes upon 55 Reams of Paper at 13s. per Reame. £35 15s. od.

Later editions were octavo. The last printed here was of 1733. It does not appear from the accounts that either of the constituent books was sold without the other.

(25) *Parecbolae, sive excerpta e statutis Universitatis ... in usum juventutis academicae*. There were editions of 1682 and 1691 (the latter of 2,000). The Printer to the University has them in poor leather bindings, square-backed, and without lettering. So far as I can tell, the Press contracted out all its binding until 1859.

(26) The Bodleian Library has a folio sheet headed 'Proponitur Maimonidis More Nevochim typis mandandum lingua Arabica ... Dicti operis sequitur hujusmodi specimen' (shelfmark 4° M 13(2) Th.). A MS. note, dated 10 December 1690, attributes it to Thomas Hyde and adds that the Delegates had declined to publish it. Anthony Wood (*Athenae*, iv, 526) includes the book among the works that Hyde had begun. It was one of the many that he abandoned. *More Nevochim* was among the works of which Fell wrote a list early in 1672 headed 'We purpose to print if we may be encouraged' (All Souls MS. 239, fol. 641).

(27) Edward Bernard had agreed with the Delegates to edit the *Jewish Antiquities* and the *Jewish War* of Flavius Josephus, and Fell announced the forthcoming publication of the book in 1672 (All Souls MS., loc. cit.). Fell became so ashamed of his inability to fulfil his promise because of Bernard's slow and intermittent progress that he had Book I and part of Book II of the *Jewish War* with notes by Bernard and an old Latin translation put to press in charge of Henry Aldrich (Bodleian MS. d'Orville 470, p. 238), and the volume appeared in 1687. The sheets to which the account for 1690–1 refers were presumably part of *Flavii Josephi Antiquitatum Judaicarum libri quatuor priores, et pars magna quinti* published in 1700, after Bernard's death. The only other mention of that book in the accounts is the receipt of £16 poundage in 1697 'For Printing both parts of the Greek Antiquities'; so it would appear that the Delegates abandoned the *Antiquities* after printing two sheets, and Bernard's unfinished work was taken over by a partnership of Oxford booksellers, who issued a prospectus in 1694 announcing it (Bodl. Wood 658(774)).

UNIVERSITY PRESS ACCOUNTS

(28) For the business of making typemetal, see the contemporary account of it by Joseph Moxon (*Mechanick Exercises on the Whole Art of Printing*, ed. Davis and Carter, 2nd edn., 1962, pp. 165 ff., 379-80).

(29) Johann Heinrich Wetstein (1649-1746), first of the dynasty of bookseller-publishers of that name at Amsterdam.

The accounts witness to a stability of prices in the first half of the eighteenth century. The 'Oxford Grammar' may be taken as one example.

			£ s d
1699.	For printing the Grammar which made 18 sheets in 8vo 2000 printed upon Demie paper 10s.		
	Composeing 14s. per sheet		12 12 00
	Press-work 10s. per sheet		09 00 00
	Correcting 2.6 per sheet		02 05 00
	Necessaries 8s. per sheet		07 04 00
	For printing the Title-plate		01 00 00
	Paper 44s. per sheet		
	To the University 15s. per sheet[22]		
1709.	Printing the Oxford Grammar 2000 Books on 86 Reams of paper at 9s. per Ream. I payd for		£ s d
	Payd Beckford for the paper		38 14 00
	Composeing 18 sheets at 16s per sheet		14 08 00
	Pressworke 10s ditto		09 00 00
	Necessaries 8s per sheet		07 04 00
	Title-plate at 12d. per C		01 00 00
	Printing the Theater 1 C		01 00 00
	Correcting		02 14 00
1714.	The charge of Printing the Grammar 2000 18 sheets		£ s d
	Composeing at 16s per sheet		14 08 00
	Press-work att 10s per sheet		09 09 00
	Necessaries att 8s per sheet		07 04 00
	86 Reams of Paper (Beckford) at 10s per Ream		43 00 00
	Printing two plates at the Roleing press		02 07 00
	Correcting		02 14 00

1733. For Printing the Grammar making 18 sheets No. 2000

	£	s	d
Composing 16s per sheet	14	08	00
Press at 10s per sheet	09	00	00
Necessaries 8s per sheet	07	04	00
Correcting 3s per sheet	02	14	00
Printing two Plates at the Rolling Press	02	07	00
Paid Mr Beckford for 85 Rms of Demy Paper at 10s. per Rm	42	10	00
	78	03	00

John Beckford was the paper-maker at Wolvercote Mill. The man mentioned in 1733 was the second of the name.

Another recurring item in the accounts is Thomas Marshall's book on the Catechism.

	£	s	d	reams
1704	23	10	6	52
1709	25	12	3	52
1719	26	1	0	53
1731	26	1	0	53
1746	26	1	0	53

From 1696 onwards the Warehouse-Keeper normally included in his account a list of 'Books remaining in the Warehouse'. He gives the number of copies in stock and their value in terms of their prices when published. These lists are useful records because they comprise only Delegates' publications, and so distinguish them from the other books printed at the Press, and because the diminishing number of copies in successive lists is a measure of the commercial success of these publications. However, in 1713 the Delegates cleared the whole of their stock at a sadly low price as a help towards paying for the Clarendon Building, excepting only the few remaining copies of Anthony Wood's *Historia et antiquitates Universitatis Oxoniensis*.

The earliest of these lists is the following.

	£	s	d
1000 Dr. Marshalls Catechismes	12	10	0
184 Comment on Joel	41	8	0
156 Comment on Micha and Mal[achi]	39	0	0

		£	s	d
170	Dr. Hoddy's Redargutio	6	7	6
170	Defence of the University Charter	8	10	0
80	Aristeus	4	0	0
470	Homers Illiads	94	0	0
1000	Small Statute Books	25	0	0
4	Oxford Antiquities best paper	8	0	0
29	Antiquities Ordinary paper	29	0	0
240	Cottons Catal.	60	0	0
200	Slavonian Grammars	10	0	0
71	Sheets of Zenophon	134	18	0
130	Sheets of Pindar	244	5	0
220	Sheets of the Catal. of Mss.	495	0	0
20	Dr. Wallis's two first Vol.	35	0	0
60	Sheets of the Herball	165	0	0
6	Mr. Kennett's Antiq.	3	0	0
50	Sheets of Dr. Wallis's Ptolomy	75	0	0
80	Sheets of Lycophron	128	0	0
28	Sheets of Sr. Harry Spelman	37	16	0
12	Sheets of Mr. Wormes[23]	24	0	0

I take it that the absence of the word 'sheets' means that the books were folded and collated, and 'sheets' usually means books in flat sheets. The 'Herball' was Robert Morison's unfinished *Historia plantarum Oxoniensis*.

I believe that the Account for Printing is the only means of telling that Volumes i and ii of the first (folio) edition of Clarendon's *History of the Rebellion* were reprinted with their dates unaltered.

Volume i was printed in 1701–2, 1,100 copies
                    in 1702–3, 500 and 10 large paper
                    in 1704–5, (1,300?)
                    in 1707, 71
Volume ii was printed in 1702–3, 1,300 and 250 large paper
                    in 1704–5, 700 and 100 large paper
                    in 1707, 71
All copies of Volume iii were printed in 1704, 2,000 and 350 large paper.

Since all reported copies are dated alike on their title-pages, Vol. i 1702, Vol. ii 1703, it is safe to assume that the reprints bear the dates of the first printings. Composing, at the rate of 8s. a sheet for Vol. i and 6s. a sheet for Vol. ii, is charged in each instance. Late printings are distinguishable by having press figures in the tail margins. In Vol. iii these are asterisks, daggers, and similar signs, and occur only in the index. The (learned) Press[24] began using press figures in 1704 and ceased to do so in 1710.

NOTES

1. D. F. McKenzie, *The Cambridge University Press, 1696–1712, a Bibliographical Study* (Cambridge, 1966), vol. ii, pp. 73 ff. In Bodleian MS. Grabe 53 there are some interesting bills from compositors and pressmen at the Oxford University Press of the years 1700–10.
2. Univ. Archives, Reg. Conv. Ta 154 (1662).
3. Bodl. MS. Rawl. D 1188.
4. Univ. Archives, S.E.P. P17^b(1)^q.
5. W. W. Greg, *A Companion to Arber* (Oxford, 1967), pp. 76–7, No. 232, 100, No. 310.
6. Univ. Archives, S.E.P. P17^b(1)^k verso.
7. Public Record Office, S.P. (Dom.), Car. II, 292, No. 38.
8. The cost of these books to the partners is given in Univ. Archives, S.E.P. P17^b(1)^e. The Stationers' prices are given in the same bundle at (1)^h.
9. By Miss H. M. Petter in Bodleian MS. Carte 114 (546).
10. R is evidently used as an abbreviation for ream. Where it occurs a second time it may stand for retree (imperfect). 'Charges' would cover overheads and consumable stores, such as ink, lye, pelts, etc., and wear of type.
11. Transcribed in Bodleian MS. Hearne's Diaries 158, p. 15.
12. Univ. Archives, S.E.P. P17^b(1)^b.
13. The agreement is printed by J. Johnson and S. Gibson in *Print and Privilege at Oxford to the year 1700* (1946), pp. 165–7.
14. Printed in W. W. Greg., *A Companion to Arber* (Oxford, 1967), p. 100, No. 310.
15. D 397, fol. 328.
16. Univ. Archives, Chancellor's Court Papers, Bundle 130.
17. Univ. Archives, S.E.P. P17^b(1)^m.
18. D. F. McKenzie, *The Cambridge University Press*, ii, pp. 41 ff.
19. 'The ledgers span the years 1710 to 1773 or so, but are much fuller and better kept from 1716 to about 1740'; Keith Maslen in *The Library*, 5th ser. xxvii (1972), at p. 303.
20. *A Ledger of Charles Ackers, Printer of the* London Magazine, ed. D. F. McKenzie and J. C. Ross (Oxford, 1968).
21. R. A. Austen-Leigh, *William Strahan and his Ledgers* (1924), p. 15.
22. 'Poundage' to cover overheads was sometimes (as here) reckoned in the charges for Delegates' publications in the first few years of their management of the Press, but it was evidently not expected to be paid. There would be no sense in the University's paying itself.
23. 500 copies of 12 sheets, part of *Ara Multiscus de Islandia* edited by Christian Worm, were printed in 1696. Worm vanished, and the 12 sheets were published by the Delegates as an incomplete book in 1716.
24. As distinct from the Oxford Bible Press, then let to London Stationers.

MICHAEL HARRIS

Newspaper distribution during Queen Anne's reign

Charles Delafaye and the Secretary of State's Office

The importance of the newspaper in the social, political and economic life of the nation during the first half of the eighteenth century is now generally acknowledged by historians. The lapse of the Licensing Act in 1695, which meant the end of direct government censorship, was followed by an extension in the number of papers published, a higher level of sales and a wider range of reading matter, and it was during Queen Anne's reign that the newspaper began to establish its position as the principal vehicle for information and opinion. Recent discoveries of some of the accounts of the *London Gazette* and of an early run of stamp tax returns have thrown light on circulation during the early years of the century;[1] but there have been no substantial finds to reveal the actual processes of distribution. The newspapers themselves have yielded some information on methods of supply in London,[2] but the channels by which subscribers outside the capital received their copies, and the character of newspaper readership remain largely speculative. The newly discovered ledger which is described here is therefore of considerable value, providing a unique view of the activity of a single distributor whose official position and personal contacts gave him particular importance as an intermediary.[3]

The ledger itself, preserved in the Public Record Office among the State Papers Domestic,[4] consists of 180 quarto-size pages in a vellum binding which is marked on the spine with the letter 'B'. The content clearly indicates that it was the work of a government employee involved in the dispersal of newspapers under frank, and the distinctive hand finally established that the accounts were those of Charles Delafaye, an official in the Secretary of State's Office.[5] Delafaye died in 1762 and under an unusual provision of his will his papers passed to the State

[1] Notes begin on p. 149.

Paper Office.[6] Subsequently they were dispersed among the records of several government departments and it was probably during this process that the ledger was separated from the other material and was placed in its present miscellaneous category.

The chronology of its contents reflects a variety of Delafaye's personal and political circumstances. On several occasions he makes oblique reference to his father who had preceded him in the business and who perhaps kept the ledger 'A' which does not seem to have survived. Lewis Delafaye, a Huguenot emigré,[7] came to England in the late 1670s and was appointed translator of the French edition of the *London Gazette*.[8] The first agreement noted in the ledger was made in February 1703, but Lewis Delafaye seems to have been involved in newspaper distribution for a considerable time before this and in a letter to the Duke of Ormonde in June 1704 remarked that he had supplied 'his Grace with foreign news for twelve years without any reward'.[9] His son Charles joined the office as a clerk in the 1690s, was promoted chief clerk under the Earl of Sunderland in 1706 and acted as gazetteer from May 1702 to May 1707.[10] Although entries refer back to a series of earlier agreements the ledger itself was not apparently in use before 22 September 1710, the date placed at the head of a large proportion of the individual accounts.[11] The last recorded payment to Lewis Delafaye was made in May 1709 and it seems possible that his son took over the business following the dismissal of Sunderland in the summer of 1710.[12] The latest entry in the ledger is dated 20 July 1714, less than two weeks before Queen Anne's death, but developments in Delafaye's career may already have curtailed his interest in newspaper distribution. In September 1713 he took up the post of Private Secretary to the Duke of Shrewsbury, newly appointed Lord Lieutenant of Ireland, and presumably remained out of England until he became Under Secretary to Sunderland in 1717.[13]

The contents of the ledger, which is concerned only with newspapers and related publications, are divided into several overlapping and not altogether consistent sections. The first consists of a partially alphabetical list of individual customers to which other names have been added in an apparently random order both before and after a list of coffee-houses. The second section is made up of a series of five schedules indicating which customers received which papers. These are apparently based on the nature of the papers supplied, but while schedules one to four seem to have been drawn up at the same time, probably in 1710, the fifth is in a rougher hand and the duplication of names suggests that it superseded other lists and that it perhaps dates from the end of the period. The third section contains a long run of scrappy individual accounts, in many cases two to an opening, drawn up under debit and credit. These are followed by a short list of customers who had apparently settled their accounts when the book was compiled, and the ledger ends with several fragmentary entries concerned with the supply of foreign gazettes and an incomplete index.

The seventy individual customers whose names and addresses were listed by Delafaye, together with the sixteen who appeared only in the schedules, were geographically very widely scattered. About thirty-two lived in Ireland, the majority in the Dublin area, with a further substantial number in or around Cork. This concentration may to some extent have resulted from the Delafayes' personal contacts. Charles's brother, Captain Lewis Delafaye, lived in Ireland and married a girl from Kilkenny, while his father's long-standing connection with Ormonde may itself have produced an accumulation of other orders.[14] Although none of his customers lived in Wales, and only two in Scotland, his list included one from Guernsey and thirty-three others living in sixteen English counties, the largest number of five in Yorkshire followed by four in Kent. Delafaye also supplied about seventeen individuals in London as well as eighteen coffee-houses, all located at the west end of town within reasonable proximity to the Whitehall office.

The composition of the list of customers, while of very considerable interest, provides no major surprises. Among the occupational groupings government officials formed a major element. In Ireland the Duke of Ormonde, reappointed Lord Lieutenant in September 1710, William Lingen, a minor employee at Dublin Castle, and two Post Office clerks formed a small but important group. However, the bulk of this category was composed of officials attached to the Secretaries' office and consequently within Delafaye's immediate compass. Two previous Secretaries, Sir Charles Hedges and the Earl of Sunderland, were included while the current heads of both the Southern and Scottish departments, Lord Dartmouth and the Duke of Queensberry, were listed with their respective Under Secretaries. Delafaye's fellow clerks, James Payzant and John Brocas, also appeared among his customers as did Richard Steele, his successor as Gazetteer. Steele was himself replaced in October 1710, but Delafaye's distribution of the *Tatler* and *Guardian* in preference to the more successful *Spectator* suggests a continuing personal link. As well as several current office holders and a group of local representatives made up of four English M.P.s.[15] and three mayors, the list of customers contained a large group of members of the professions. Two judges and an attorney from Ireland, two bishops, eight other members of the clergy, and a major-general and five junior army officers were all supplied with papers. In general, as one would expect, the customers, particularly outside London, were drawn largely from the upper and middle ranks of society. This emphasis was underlined by the inclusion not only of thirteen peers and four knights but also of a block of nineteen individuals with the style of 'Esquire', a major grouping which included such substantial local figures as George Sayer and John Taylor of Kent[16] and Richard Thompson of Yorkshire.[17]

The papers sent to the listed customers fall into two main categories. With regard to those published in London, Delafaye's position probably influenced the character of the supply, for a large proportion of the London papers he distributed was produced with official backing. The 'Letter' referred to in schedules one and two was presumably the office 'circular' which continued to be sent out by the Secretaries' clerks at least into the 1720s.[18] At the same time while Samuel Waring was supplied with *Dawkes' News-Letter* until July 1710 and Delafaye himself received a coffee-house letter, it seems possible that there were occasional variations. Forty-five of the sixty-one customers took the 'Letter' and an unclear entry in the fifth schedule suggests that five of the eight receiving the London papers were also supplied with copies. However, the most widely received of the official publications was the *London Gazette*. In spite of a declining popularity, over 8000 copies of each twice-weekly issue were still being produced in 1710,[19] and sixty-three of the seventy-two customers listed in schedules one, two and five received the paper, while sixteen of the eighteen coffee-houses took up to five copies. The case of the *Gazette de Londres*, the French language version of the same paper, was quite different. Yielding virtually no profit during the middle years of Queen Anne's reign[20] it probably had a very small circulation. Only ten customers in schedules one and two received copies and although it was sent to four coffee-houses its disappearance from the fifth schedule may imply that production had ceased. The third official item was the *Votes* which appeared daily during the parliamentary session and provided a brief outline of proceedings. In the first two schedules thirty-one customers were supplied with copies and in the last five.

Delafaye also distributed a variable number of commercial papers covering a wide political spectrum. The majority of these were thrice-weeklies, published in London each post-day to facilitate the supply to country readers. The schedules reflect the dominance in this area of De Fonvive's *Post-Man* which, on the strength of its reputation as a source of foreign and domestic news, had achieved a circulation of over 4000 copies per issue by 1712.[21] In schedules one, two and five fifty-one of the customers were supplied with copies. The *Post-Man* was politically neutral and this numerical emphasis may indicate not only the paper's general appeal but also Delafaye's caution in handling more biased publications. The Tory papers, the *Post Boy* and the *Evening Post*, were both produced in editions of over 3000 copies by 1712,[22] but only sixteen and ten of his customers respectively were supplied with them. Similarly the Whig *Flying Post*, with a circulation of about half its Tory rivals,[23] was sent to twelve individuals and its supplementary *Postscript*, probably killed by the tax, to only one. Of the other forms of commercial London paper no more than a handful was distributed by Delafaye. The *Daily Courant*, also appearing in support of the Whigs and the sole London daily of the period, was produced in editions of about 1,000 copies at the time of the tax,[24] but while problems of distribution alone probably restricted its appeal, only ten of Delafaye's customers were sent copies. Among the essay papers listed, the whig *Observator* seems to have ceased publication with the imposition of the tax[25] and although the Tory *Examiner*, which replaced it in the schedule, continued to be produced in editions of over 1500 copies[26] both papers were sent to a total of four individuals. Steele's successful *Tatler*,[27] which ceased publication on 2 January 1711, and its successor the *Guardian*, which first appeared on 12 March 1713, were sent to the comparatively large number of nineteen. Any assessment of Delafaye's weekly turnover of London papers is complicated by the fact that a large number of the names in the schedules is crossed through, as are individual papers, and there is no indication of the timing of these apparent cancellations. However, referring only to the uncrossed names in schedules one and two and only the uncrossed papers against them, it seems possible to suggest a rough minimum figure during the parliamentary session of between four and five hundred copies per week.

The second major category of papers supplied by Delafaye was made up of gazettes published in France and Holland and listed separately in the schedules. The *Paris-à-la-Main* and the *Amsterdam Gazette* were the most widely distributed and in schedules two, four and five, thirty of the forty-nine individuals took the former and twenty-eight the latter.

Although three other Dutch papers were listed Delafaye supplied few of his individual customers with copies. Eleven received the *Leyden*, five the *Rotterdam* and only two the *Haarlem Gazette* which was omitted altogether from the fifth schedule. This pattern varied slightly with the coffee-houses listed in schedule three and while nine received the Amsterdam paper seven took the *Leyden Gazette* and only six the *Paris-à-la-Main*, with three receiving copies of the *Haarlem Gazette*. This emphasis on the Dutch papers may reflect a personal element in the supply or alternatively the greater popularity of these publications among the trading community.

The organisation which supported Delafaye's role as a newspaper distributor emerges only vaguely from the oblique entries scattered through the ledger. However it is possible to draw together some of the strands and to suggest the way in which the copies were obtained and distributed. A key figure in the first of these processes was Peter Merignac who recurs throughout the ledger and who had been associated with the business at least since 1708. His name suggests a Huguenot origin and possibly this shared background led to an initial contact, perhaps with Lewis Delafaye. A number of Merignacs crop up in the records of the London Huguenots of the late seventeenth and early eighteenth century and in one instance a very tenuous link can be postulated. In April 1688 a Pierre Merignac and his wife Marie from Cleriac in France joined the Huguenot church in the Savoy,[28] where by the end of the century Lewis Delafaye was acting as a churchwarden.[29] Although in the mid-1690s the children of the same Pierre Merignac were baptised at the Tabernacle Church, in the neighbourhood of Leicester Fields,[30] it is conceivable that this was Delafaye's associate and that some early contact had been made through the church. Whether or not this was the case the Huguenot connection was clearly of importance. The links created by the movement of the protestant emigrés were undoubtedly instrumental in developing the international exchange of news and consequently in extending the role of the press. John De Fonvive, and Abel Boyer, for example, who compiled the principal London newspaper of the period both came from Huguenot stock and while the Delafayes' own background probably stimulated their interest in the distribution of news, the composition of the list of customers suggests that it may also have promoted some individual supply. James Payzant, a clerk at the Secretaries' office, was a fellow Huguenot and the French names of at least six of the coffee-house proprietors may indicate a further link. At the same time five of the six

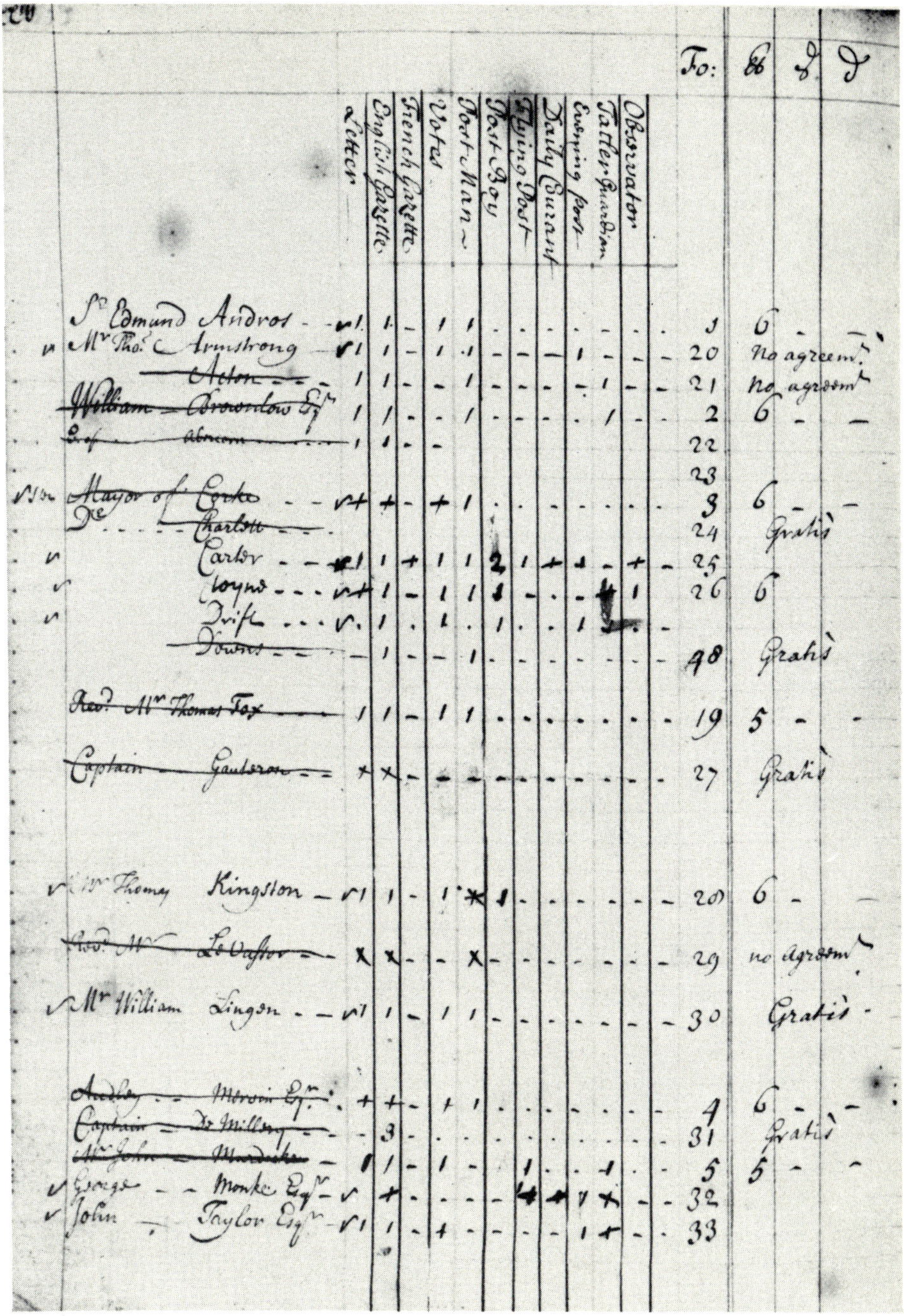

PLATE 6. The first section of schedule 1, listing Delafaye's customers and showing the publications supplied.

Began	To Mr Jn.º Fell at Attercliffe, To be left w.th Mr Nevill Simmons at Sheffield Yorks.	10	
26 Nov.r 1706	To the Rev.d Mr Fox at Tullo in y.e Co.ty of Catherlo in Irel.d	19	
21.th May 1706	To the R.t Hon.ble the Marq.s of Granby at Belvoir Castle Lincolnsh.r p Grantham Bagg. When in Town p̃ for.m Print. Sent to his house & y.e Lre to y.e D. of Rutland in the Country.	40	
15 July 1706	To Cap.t Guyon at Portarlington To be left at Mountmelick in the Queen's County. Ireland.	42	
15 Aug.t 1704	To John Harvey Esq.r at Hickwell Berry Bedfordsh Bigg's Bagg	19	
12 June 1703. Left of. for ag.n 12 Dec.r 1711.	To the R.t Hon.ble the Earl of Inchiquin at Rostellan by Tallow. Ireland (By Floyn)	44	
	To Mr W.m Lingen at Dublin Castle.	30	
	To the Rev.d Mr Lockier at Hansworth To be left w.th Mr Nevill Simmons at Sheffield Yorks.	10	
25 Dec.r	To Mr Jn.º Murdocke at Birmingham Warwicksh.	5	

PLATE 7. The first page of Delafaye's list of customers.

Coffee houses.		English Gazette	French Gazette	Paris	Amsterdam	Leyden	Rotterdam	Haerlem	Fo.	£	s	d
Marginal Charges m.d ts Violet marked thus O												
	Bordeaux			4			1		40	Gratis		
	Bolloc	Grafton Street	m. ?	1		1				49	3		
	LeBlanc	Greyhound	m. 1	1		1				50	3		
O	Geo Taunton	George	1			1				1	4		
	Cantlope	Guillard	1		1					2	4		
O	Bernard	Hanover	2		1	1			1	3	8		
	Jenny Man	George Man's	m.			1				4	4		
	Thomas	Nye	3				1			5	4		
	Isaac Norris	Norss Chocolate	m.1		1					6	3		
	Jacob Bernard	Orange	m. 2			1				7	4		
	Lodwic	Ormond Coff. Off. X @			@				0	3		
		Paris	m. 2	1		1				39	6		
	Dogory	Pyramid or 7 Dyals	m. 1	1		1				10	3		
	Pork	Presbyterian	2			1				11	3		
O		Power	2			1				12	3		
										13			
	Mitchell	Rainbow	m. 2	1	1				1	14	6		
										15			
		Smirna	m. 1		1	1			1	16	10		
O	ffrance	Tilt Yard	1		1	1				17	6		
				6	9	7	–	3	Ormond Coff.Off	77/74			

PLATE 8. Schedule 4 complete, listing the London coffee-house proprietors and showing the foreign papers supplied.

army officers in Ireland also had French names, two of them, Colonel Boissond and Captain Guyon, appearing in the register of the Huguenot church at Portarlington.[31]

Merignac's precise position in the business of distribution is almost equally obscure. Since the previous century Treasury officials had obtained their copies of the foreign gazettes through Huguenots living in London[32] and Delafaye apparently relied on Merignac in a similar way. An entry made in June 1714 stated

Merignac owns he is to allow me 5 Amsterd^m
Gazettes for my Cover
   I shall want 4 Paris
           3 Amsterd^m
           1 Leyden
           1 Rotterdam

and some time earlier Delafaye noted that £40 16s. had been 'Remitted for him to Amsterdam'. The only direct reference to their commercial relationship appears in a personal account under Merignac's name compiled towards the end of the ledger. However the entries are sketchy and their organisation under debit and credit gives no clear indication of the direction of the payments.[33] These included instalments of a salary of £24 per annum, several sums for 'Domestick prints' and £2 8s. and £2 13s. for 'New Years Guifts to ye Office and Coffee house Servants'.[34] The debit side showed only money owed for papers supplied to the coffee-houses and it seems that Merignac had a special concern with these centres, perhaps collecting the payment for copies originally sent to Delafaye. The supply to coffee-houses subsequently gave rise to a protracted and peculiarly ambiguous dispute. The last entry in Merignac's account was dated January 1711 while a large majority of the individual coffee-house accounts ended with a payment for 24 June followed by slight variations on the statement 'Merignac's pretended Claim begins here'. The nature of this claim is not specified, although in a later note Delafaye alluded to the fact that Merignac 'pretends to have taken ye Coffee houses in his Care'. This may imply that Merignac had attempted to by-pass Delafaye and to deal directly with some, if not all, the listed houses or simply that some confusion had arisen over payment.[35] The final account in the ledger embodied Merignac's 'charge' that Delafaye had received money from four coffee-houses after 24 June.[36] All were dated 25 December but in the case of the Hanover and Powers' each six-monthly total has been crossed through and replaced by one covering a full three-year period, amounting to £33. On the opposite page Delafaye noted 'by his last account he brings me in debt to £16. 17s. 6d. It appears on the other side he should owe me £33.' No further reference was made to the matter and the division of responsibilities giving rise to the dispute must remain in doubt.

Delafaye's personal role in the process of distribution which required a ready access to a source of continental papers, depended very largely on his possession of franking privileges. Through his position at the Secretaries' office he was able to offer a cut-price service to customers throughout the British Isles. Various devices, such as the amalgamation of editions, were attempted by commercial distributors but the high graduated charges of ordinary postage, increased in 1711,[37] and the slowness of such cheap alternatives as the carriers inevitably handicapped their efforts at supply. At the same time Delafaye faced a certain amount of competition from other government officials. His fellow clerks, as well as those at the War Office and more particularly at the Post Office, also had franking privileges and sometimes at least a similar access to the foreign gazettes. A note in Lord Weymouth's account, settled in March 1710, stated 'has left off ever since and is furnish't by Mr. Goslin of ye post Office',[38] while a more direct reference to a clash in the process of supply appeared at the front of a ledger. It stated 'Mr. Frowde at ye post Office stopt 16 Paris Gazettes for wch he never pd. he said he furnisht one Turney a Coffee house near ye Royal Exchange in pl. of paymt.'[39] The only medium of supply referred to in the ledger was the Post Office and there is no evidence that Delafaye's customers were sent copies through any other channel. The initial list occasionally specified the particular bag to be employed and the papers were in several cases directed to provincial post houses for collection and in one to a Scottish customs house. At the same time the Dublin Post Office was evidently used as a major centre for redistribution. John Tyrrel, who was employed at this office, appears to have been receiving about 120 papers a week during the parliamentary session for six customers and this number was increased in March 1711.[40] The ledger indicates that this sort of secondary distribution to customers outside London was very widespread. At least two, for example, received copies through the Sheffield bookseller Nevill Simmons who also had 'the News to sell', while in Dublin the perfumier Peter Raffa received copies on behalf of Armantieres. The postal service was also used in London itself although this may have been supplemented by some other process, in delivery or collection. Sir Thomas Neville received his copies at his house in Red Lion Square by way of the penny post and the Marquis of Granby when in town had copies 'sent to his house', perhaps a reference to the use of the same method.

The charges made by Delafaye and recorded in the five schedules show that the annual rate for his services was fixed by agreement and that this had little to do with the number of newspapers supplied and nothing to do with distance. It is therefore impossible to break down the costs in detail. The *London Gazette*, in both English and French versions, may have been distributed free of charge as part of the service,[41] but while there is no direct evidence for this the references in the ledger to single items are ambiguous. John Murdocke seems to have paid £1 for the *Votes* published during the parliamentary session of 1709–10, while George Sayer was charged £3 for half a year's supply of 'one Letter' in spite of the agreement by which he paid £6 for a year's supply of a cross-section of London papers. At the same time the difficulty of assessing exactly what the agreed sums covered, arising most often from the cancellations, is compounded by the occasional variations in individual orders. Sir Charles Hedges, for example, received only the foreign papers when in residence at Richmond or St. James's Mews, though also taking in the London papers when at his country house at Calne in Wiltshire. While the most usual order seems to have been for about four or five papers, usually including the *London Gazette*, the minimum charge throughout to an individual was £4 and to a coffee-house £3. The rate was apparently very flexible and seems to have risen most steeply when the foreign gazettes formed part of the order. £6 was the maximum for a variable number of London papers although in the second schedule the maximum rose to £10 and the same amount was paid by a coffee-house. Among the individuals receiving only the continental gazettes £8. 12s. was the ceiling.

Delafaye's total income also remains obscure not only because of an absence of any general account, but because of the incompleteness of many of the entries. On the one hand several charges are omitted altogether. This does not appear necessarily to have implied a waiving of payment and George Monke and the Lord Mayor of Tiverton who appear as blanks in schedules one and two respectively were charged £5 and £6. 9s. in the fifth. On the other hand Delafaye frequently noted the absence of an agreement, presumably implying that this was to be the subject of future negotiation, entering against the Marquis of Dorchester the reminder, 'No agreement used to give my fath[r] 5 G.'

However, it seems likely that in both cases payment was sometimes lost or made not in cash but in kind. John Traile of Worcester received copies of the London papers in return for an annual hogshead of cider or perry. At the same time Delafaye sent out a quite large number of papers totally free of charge. This gratis supply was usually for some clearly specified service, most often for passing on copies, but also, in the case of William Lingen, for collecting payments, and, in that of the coffee-house keeper 'Mr. Borderie', for the supply of his news-letter. It also seems likely that a free supply of papers was sometimes undertaken for purely political or professional reasons.

Payment for copies by individual customers seems often to have been made direct to Delafaye. However a number of intermediaries were also involved in the process which was complicated by the distances involved. The most important of these was William Lingen, who by September 1714 was acting as Delafaye's chief clerk in Ireland.[42] The individual accounts indicate that Lingen had been involved in the business at least since 1707 and, during the period covered by the ledger, received payments from twelve of Delafaye's Irish customers, including Tyrrel and the five French officers. Several individuals crop up in the ledger as agents for the settling of accounts; a 'Mr. Stowe', for example, paid for George Sayer's papers in 1711 and it seems possible that at least some of those appearing in brackets in the list of customers provided a similar service.[43] Whatever the arrangements for payment a very variable degree of regularity was observed. The coffee-houses seem either to have paid quarterly or in two unequal stages during the year. The individual customers were apparently much more erratic and although some, including Tyrrel, settled at regular intervals, the majority did not. Mervin and Newenham, among others, apparently owed for three years' supply and the typically scrappy account of Richard Thompson suggests that a very wide latitude was accepted.

		£	s.	d.
	Richard Thompson Esqr. Dr.			
1710				
Mar. 25	1½ yr. or 2 yrs. Suppose ye least at £5 per ann.	7.	10.	–
1714				
Mar. 25	4 years	20.	–	–

The credit side remained blank. Delafaye's evident lack of concern with unpaid bills and his failure to keep adequate financial records may in itself have prompted or at least aggravated the dispute which developed with Merignac.

In spite of its shortcomings Delafaye's ledger illuminates several areas of special interest in the history of the press. The list of customers and the newspaper schedules (Plates 6, 7 and 8)[44] provide not only a guide to the intake by a substantial number of individuals but also the first detailed information on the range and character of readership during an early period of press expansion. The question of who received the newspapers sent out of London in increasing numbers is one which can only be answered through the sort of direct evidence available here. At the same time the ledger indicates the way in which the government offices were already, by the early years of the eighteenth century becoming large-scale centres of distribution. The role of government employees and other privileged individuals in the distribution of London and continental papers was clearly of considerable importance; Delafaye himself illustrates this development which led to a major extension in the influence of the press.

NOTES

1. These items, preserved among the papers of Robert Harley, were published with a useful commentary in H. L. Snyder, 'The Circulation of Newspapers in the Reign of Queen Anne', *Library*, 5th Ser., XXIII, 1968, pp. 206–35. For details of subsequent circulation levels and an indication of the general rate of growth during the first half of the century see Michael Harris, 'The London Newspaper Press, 1725-1746', unpublished Ph.D. thesis, University College London, 1973.

2. See W. F. Belcher, 'The Sale and Distribution of the *British Apollo* in *Studies in the English Periodical*, ed. R. P. Bond, Chapel Hill, 1957.

3. For an account of the available evidence in this and subsequent periods see Harris, op. cit., pp. 31–63. Among the most interesting records of a slightly later period are those analysed in D. H. Couvée, 'The Administration of the "Oprechte Haarlemse Courant" 1738-1742', *Leyden Gazette: International Journal of the Science of the Press*, III, 1958, pp. 91-110. They contain a full account of the paper's news sources and its commercial outlets in Holland.

4. P.R.O., S.P.D. 9, 217.

5. I am grateful to Mr. John Sainty, not only for supplying the final link in the chain of identification but also for providing several valuable pieces of biographical information.

6. P.R.O., Prob. II, 884, p. 52.

7. Professor Snyder has confused Lewis the father with his second son also named Lewis who is referred to below, H. L. Snyder, op. cit., p. 219, n. 2.

8. J. C. Sainty, *Officials of the Secretaries of State, 1660–1782*, London, 1973, p. 45.

9. Historical Manuscript Commission, *Ormonde*, VIII, p. 89.
10. Sainty, loc. cit.
11. A substantial number of the listed agreements were made in 1710, three beginning on 23 September.
12. P.R.O., S.P.D. 34, 12, p. 165.
13. Sainty, op. cit., p. 29.
14. H.M.C., *Ormonde*, VIII, p. 89.
15. Sir Charles Hedges (Westlow), Marquis of Granby (Stamford), Thomas White (East-Retford), Sir Robert Danvers (Suffolk).
16. Edward Hastead, *The History of Topographical Survey of the County of Kent*, London, 1797, VII, p. 437; IX, pp. 280–1.
17. Thomas Allen, *A New and Complete History of the County of York*, 3 vols., London, 1831, II, pp. 349–50.
18. P.R.O., S.P.D. 36, 16, p. 27.
19. Snyder, op. cit., pp. 216–17.
20. Ibid., p. 230.
21. Ibid., pp. 211–12. The *Post-Man's* circulation, like that of most London papers, fell away sharply with the introduction of the Stamp Tax in August.
22. Ibid., p. 211.
23. Ibid., p. 211.
24. Ibid., p. 210.
25. Ibid., p. 208.
26. Ibid., p. 210.
27. It has been suggested that this paper's circulation was maintained at about 3000 copies and that it may sometimes have reached over 4000 per issue. See R. P. Bond, *The Tatler*, Cambridge' Mass., 1971, pp. 38–9.
28. *Publications of the Huguenot Society*, XXII, 1914, 'Conversions et Reconnoisances de l'Eglise de la Savoye, 1684–1702', p. 34.
29. H.M.C., *House of Lords 1697–1699*, pp. 369, 370, 371.
30. *Publications of the Huguenot Society*, XXIX, 1926, 'Registers of the Churches of the Tabernacle, Glasshouse Street and Leicester Fields', ed. W. Minet, pp. 49, 54.
31. Ibid., XIX, 1908, 'Registers of the French Church of Portarlington, Ireland', pp. 91, 112.
32. *Calendar of Treasury Books and Papers*, XVIII, pp. 716, 721, 933; XXVII, pp. 451, 459, *passim*. In 1704 Peter Dusouley, who took over as Treasury supplier in 1707, attempted to smear Lewis Delafaye's character, perhaps in an attempt to get his job as translator. See H.M.C., *Portland*, IV, p. 118.
33. In the customers' accounts the debit entries showed the amounts owed for papers and the credit the amounts paid. In Merienac's account there is no apparent correspondence.
34. Some payments, one stated to be from Merienac, were for unspecified purposes.
35. The individual coffee-house accounts continuing after June 1711 refer to an intermediary named 'Mobileau' who passed on money to Merienac.
36. Those marked with an 'M' in schedule three.
37. H. Robinson, *The British Post Office*, Princeton, 1948, pp. 96–7.
38. William Goslin, Clerk of the Foreign Office, see John Chamberlayne *Magnae Britanniae Notitia*, London, 1710, p. 658.

39. Ashburnham Frowde, comptroller of the Foreign Office; ibid.
40. His individual account showed that at this point he began to receive five London and two continental papers on behalf of one 'Fensham'.
41. Snyder, op. cit., pp. 220, 230.
42. P.R.O., S.P.D. 44, 326, p. 48.
43. These included Lewis Delafaye and another of the clerks at the Secretaries' office, George Tilson.
44. When this paper was planned it was assumed that the complete ledger would be reproduced in facsimile. To the author's regret this proved to be too costly, but the editors hope that the selected specimens will illustrate the general character of the entries.

HOWARD NIXON

Harleian bindings

For someone who has spent part of his career sending the books of a great library to be bound and dealing with bookbinders, it is fascinating to watch the same problems being faced two hundred and fifty years ago by Humfrey Wanley, library-keeper to the first and second Earls of Oxford, the successive owners of the Harleian Library. This is one of the reasons for my choice of subject. A second is that it throws a little light on the otherwise shadowy forms of some English eighteenth-century binders. And the third is that it identifies bindings which are admittedly elaborate, but were produced in considerable numbers as the standard clothing of the finer books in a nobleman's library, and therefore has a certain utilitarian purpose. This I feel is proper in a book of studies dedicated to Graham Pollard whose published works on the history of bookbinding have particularly stressed the bibliographical rather than the art-historical approach, although of late the glories of the French eighteenth-century bindings in the library at Waddesdon have seemingly put temptation in his way.

The Harleian Library, of which the manuscripts were to form one of the foundation collections of the British Museum while the printed books were sold in the 1740s, was founded by Robert, 1st Earl of Oxford, who died in 1724. But when he was confined to the Tower of London after his fall from office in 1715, his son Edward, Lord Harley (1689–1741), took over its management so that its true greatness, with over 7000 manuscripts and 50,000 printed books and a remarkably high average quality in both fields, was due to him and to his extremely learned and efficient librarian, Humfrey Wanley. The growth of the library between 1720 and 1726, when Wanley died, can be studied in great detail in the splendid edition of his diary by Dr. and Mrs. C. E. Wright.[1] Much that I shall have to say is taken from the diary or culled from the Wrights' introduction and footnotes, but there exists another source which has not been tapped. Among the Harley family papers which were preserved at Welbeck as a result of the marriage of the

[1] Notes begin on p. 187.

second Earl's only daughter Margaret to the second Duke of Portland, and which have been deposited on loan at the British Library by the present Duke, are a remarkable series of bookbinders' bills covering the years 1707 to 1738. They are not complete—in particular there are none at all for Christopher Chapman, shown by Wanley's diary to have been one of the two principal binders for the library—but they throw new light on the period covered by the diary[2] and extend our knowledge back to the start of Edward Harley's undergraduate career at Christ Church, Oxford, and carry it on to 1738, three years before his death. They show also that others besides Elliott and Chapman worked for Harley and that he had books bound in Oxford and Cambridge as well as in London.

Edward Harley's taste for expensive bindings must have been a contributory factor towards the grave financial difficulties in which he found himself towards the end of his life and which eventually, in 1741, involved the sale of his Cambridgeshire home at Wimpole where the printed books were kept. His binding bills begin in his first term at Christ Church in 1707 when he was eighteen years old. One of the canons, Dr. William Stratford, had been asked to keep an eye on him and on 19 December 1708 he felt constrained to write a letter to Harley's father accompanying a half year's account. This started modestly enough with:

	£	s	d
Commons—Michs. Qr.	1	10	4
Xmas. Qr.	1	6	0
Buttery — Michs. Qr.	1	10	0
Xmas. Qr.	1	9	10
Tutors, ½ year	20	0	0

and escalated to:

Bookseller's bill	25	15	9
Bookbinder's bill	16	3	4

In all it totalled £112 15s 7d.[3]

'I am afraid', wrote Stratford, 'that you will be surprised, as I was, at the bookseller's and bookbinder's bills ... two-thirds of the bookseller's bills are for very trash, and I am afraid at least half of the bookbinder's is for gilding and Turkey leather'. The bookseller's bill is presumably that amounting to £25 19s. 9d. from Henry Clements, who apparently had shops both in Oxford and London, which survives among the Welbeck papers,[4] covering the period 24 December 1707 to

15 December 1708. If so the suggestion that two-thirds were 'for very trash' seems a little unkind. It is a very miscellaneous assemblage and not at all the kind of books that Harley would be buying in a few years' time. 'A Ballad' (29 July 1708—1d.) and 'Hickelty-Pickelty' (4 Dec. 1708—6d.) may, perhaps, have caught Stratford's eye, but there are some good solid editions of the classics, a suitable quantity of theology, and some history and travels to offset a considerable number of modern plays, together with John Gay's 'Wine Poem fol.' (3 June 1708—6d.) and two copies of John Philips's 'Cyder a Poem' (8 May, 29 July 1708—both at 1s. 4d.).

RICHARD SEDGLEY

This particular bookbinder's bill for £16 3s. 4d. does not appear to have survived, but it is likely to have been from Richard Sedgley of Oxford, who had the distinction of being described by the usually cantankerous Thomas Hearne as 'an extraordinary good Binder', when recording his death at the age of 71 on 22 October 1719.[5] There are five surviving accounts from Sedgley among the Welbeck papers,[6] the first of which begins on 28 November 1707 and was finally settled on 10 March 1707/8. It totals £4 2s. 4d. It contains some 70 items, and there is certainly a good deal of gilding, but no great quantity of turkey leather. It is true that there are entries such as the following:

Testamentum Gr. per Buck. 8° Gilt Leaves, Gilt Back, double filleted, Letterd double Rold & bound in red Turkey — 0 5 0

which would be for one of the octavo Greek Testaments printed by Thomas Buck at Cambridge, bound in red turkey leather, with a two-line gold fillet round the covers enclosing a gilt double roll-tooled border, and with lettering in one panel of the spine—or conceivably with a single roll-tooled border and lettering in two panels. There was a quarto Bible bound similarly in 'blew Turkey' for 8s. 6d., while a 16° Greek Psalter was bound in gold-tooled red turkey for 3s. 6d. with 'all the writings & blots taken out with aquafortis'. There were two more octavos in gold-tooled turkey at 2s. 6d. each; two 24°s in gilt red calf at 1s. 2d. each; and a few books bound in calf, such as:

Senecae opera, Elz[evir].3 vol:12° Calves Leather, Gilt Leaves Gilt back, double filleted, Letter'd & Rould — 0 6 0

A few books are described as being bound in pasteboards, pasteboards and parchment, or pasteboards and marbled paper, at from 3d. to 6d. according to size, but much of the account is made up of lettering and gilding the spines of earlier leather-bound books dating from the period when books stood on the shelf with their fore-edges facing outwards. Where Samuel Pepys in the autumn of 1666 had been a trend-setter in having all his books 'gilt upon the backs, very handsome to the eye', no undergraduate bibliophile of 1707 could fail to follow the mode, and the commonest items are in the form:

Valerius Maximus 8° Lett[ered]: & filleted between yᵉ bands   0   0   5[7]

More extravagantly we find:

Dryden's Juvenal & Persius Folio Gilt Back & Letterd   0   1   6

 The Bill for £16 3s. 4d. which Edward Harley ran up between March 1707/8 and December 1708 must certainly have contained more books bound in turkey leather and may be compared with the last surviving Sedgley bill of 1715–16 discussed below. The fact that it had to be sent to his father for payment certainly shook Harley, who wrote to him: 'I am extremely ashamed of the two articles that have so great a share in it; I mean what's paid to the bookseller and bookbinder. I have nothing to say in excuse for my fault but only that as it is the first of this sort that ever I was guilty of, so I assure you it shall be the last.' It was not.

 It is possible that Harley had been patronising other Oxford binders during the period March to December 1708, for among these bills is a modest one of 15s. 9d. receipted by Richard Sedgley on 21 December 1708. This contains little besides lettering or the sewing of pamphlets except for six shillings for 'Fields Bible 24° in blew Turky wrought over' and a further ninepence for 'The Cover for the bible'. It is at least as likely that this was a supplementary bill submitted at the time of settlement of the outstanding £16 3s. 4d.

 Harley's good resolutions may have lasted for a whole year, since there are no bookbinder's bills for 1709, but he had certainly succumbed to temptation once more by the middle of 1710. The next bill from Sedgley for 'Bookes bound & Letter'd for Mr Harley of Christ-Church' had totalled £2 14s. 10d. for thirty-one items, when on 7 December 1710 a line was drawn across the page and a new heading written: 'Bookes bound & Lett: for yᵉ Honble the Ld Harley of Xt-Church'. Before this recognition of his courtesy title (his father had been created Earl of Oxford in May), Edward Harley had been indulging in such extravagances as a 32° Sedan Greek Testament bound in morocco 'Wrought over ye Cover & Inlay'd' for nine shillings, including one shilling for a case. During 1711 he was more restrained and, when on 2 January 1711/12 this account was settled, a further 142 items—mostly for lettering—had only brought the total to £6 14s. 7d.

The next bill, covering most of 1712, and totalling £9 17s. 8d. when it was paid on 4 December of that year, contains little of interest. The main expenditure took place in the first part of the year and is covered by the words 'Given in a bill of ye first of May 1712 of £7 17s. 6d.'. We have a detailed account only from May to December, totalling a meagre £2 0s. 2d. for 42 items, mostly for lettering and with no books bound in turkey or morocco.

There is no surviving Sedgley bill for 1713, the year in which Edward Harley married on 31 August Lady Henrietta Cavendish Holles (1694–1755), only daughter and heiress of the first Duke of Newcastle, through whom he acquired Wimpole Hall. But the last of the accounts, dated at the beginning July ye 19th 1714, and paid on 16 March 1715/6 to Henry Sedgley[8] 'for the use of my Father Richard Sedgley' totals £16 10s. 7d. for 51 items. It begins with twenty-seven volumes of classics—nearly all Aldines—bound in morocco, with gilt leaves, the covers with a single fillet and double roll borders. These are almost all octavos at 2s. 10d. or 3s. per volume, with a quarto Horace, *De arte poetica*, at 3s. 8d. and the Giunta quarto of Columella, *De re rustica* costing 4s. A seven-volume octavo Plutarch 'bound in Red Turkey' also cost 4s. a volume. The folios in this bill are mostly described as being bound in 'black marble'—which I take to be brown calf spotted with black—filleted on the back and sides. The bindings of *Orationes Aristidis*, Herodotus and Xenophon cost 6s. 6d., while the Aldine folios of Pausanias and Lucian cost 7s. 6d. each. Quartos in this style cost 4s. 8d. for a Laurentius Valla or 4s. for an Aldine Aelian. The most expensive binding—at £1 10s.—was 'A Comon prayer book fol: ye Royal Paper, Gilt Leaves, Gilt Back, Double Rold, finisht extraordinary on the sides in Blew Turkey Leather'. This seems cheap compared with the £4 13s. Sedgley charged in 1699 for binding 'the 3d Vol: of Dr Wallis's works to present ye King' and suggests that the payment may have been for all three uniformly bound volumes now in the King's Library at the British Library and not just for the third volume.[9]

All the books in Richard Sedgley's bills appear to be printed, and so none should have reached the British Museum with the Harleian

Manuscripts. As Edward Harley—unlike his father—never used an armorial block, the only means of identification is likely to be the Osborne catalogue price in the form 2–2–0 (it is nearly always in guineas) in pencil at the top right hand corner of the first white free end leaf. I am afraid I have not yet succeeded in identifying any of them, and in the absence of imprints from the descriptions of the books it may prove difficult to do so.

JOHN GRAVES

There is evidence that Harley was patronising at least one other binder in the period when Sedgley was working for him. Among the Welbeck papers is a bill from John Graves for £1 15s., paid on 11 February 1712/3.[10] It is for 18 volumes, including '3 Voll of Pamphlets 8°' for 3s., '3 Voll of Plays 4°. for 7s. 6d. and '7 Voll of Pamphlets 4°' for 15s. 'Stairs Institutes f° fill[eted]' cost 5s. and '1 Peerage of Engl^d 8°' was bound in parchment for 1s. Ellic Howe's *List of London Bookbinders, 1648–1815* records no John Graves, although he does note a Graves in 1785. A possible candidate is the John Graves, recorded by Plomer[11] as 'bookseller in London, Bible in Salisbury Street in the Strand, 1681–1715'. There is no evidence that he was a bookbinder, but he may either have employed one on his premises, or—as quite frequently happened —sent the work out to be bound and submitted the bill in his own name. By October 1712 when the bill was submitted, Harley had come down from Oxford and it may have been convenient to have a binder in London as well as Oxford.

THOMAS DAWSON

It was equally convenient to patronise Cambridge bookbinders when he acquired Wimpole Hall on the Royston–Huntingdon road by his marriage in 1713. The Welbeck papers do not include any bills from Cambridge binders of this period, but there are one or two interesting references among the bills and letters of Cornelius Crownfield, the Cambridge bookseller and University Printer, which span the years 1713 to 1720. The bills[12] are mostly for the supply of printed books, although Crownfield was not above performing other useful tasks—on 27 November 1713 he charged 6s. 6d. for 'A Pair of Rackets and

Shuttlecocks, bought in London' and a further sixpence 'paid for ye buying and Carriage from London to Cambridge'. A letter of 30 January 1713/14 records that 'I sent immediately ye Paper y^u desir'd to ye binders to get it edged black' and in the accompanying bill it is described as 'black-edged with antimony'.[13] A letter from Crownfield to Wanley dated 13 October 1716 shows that one of the best Cambridge binders of the day, Thomas Dawson, bound books for Wimpole. 'Sir', wrote Crownfield, 'I herewith send you ye following Books, which were bound before your Order came to send them to be bound by Dawson; I had no more of 'em left unbound, otherwise I would have sent 'em, with ye others he has now a binding ... [Here follow details of two books, Maimonides Yad Hazaka, 4 vols. folio, and Hus Opera 2 vols: folio, both with gilt backs, bound by someone other than Dawson] As soon as Mr Dawson has bound ye 3 others, they shall be sent'.[14] Unfortunately details of the books which Dawson did bind are not given. There is, however, among Wanley's miscellaneous papers a list of 19 volumes 'sent to Mr Dawson of Cambridge to be bound, 19 Septr 1716' and returned on 9 October 1716. There is no indication of the style in which these books were to be bound, but as those of the volumes which contain sale catalogues could prove identifiable, the list is given in Appendix A.

JANE STEEL

In 1715 Edward Harley was also having books bound by one of the best London shops of the day, that of Mrs. Jane Steel, the widow of Robert Steel, who was apprenticed to Samuel Mearne, bookbinder, stationer and bookseller to Charles II, from 1668 to 1675. Robert Steel was in business on his own by 1677, when he took the first of his eight apprentices, and he took his last one in 1710. He probably bound the royal chapel books for William III and Mary, which were supplied by Samuel Carr the Royal Stationer and Bookseller, and he owned some of the Mearne tools. Jane Steel was evidently succeeded by Thomas Elliott, who had been apprenticed to Robert in 1703 and was to become one of the two principal binders for the Harleian Library.

The first of these bills[15]—'The Right Honble the Lord Harley D^r to Mrs. Steele'—is for one book bound on August 13 and for thirteen on September 31 [sic] 1715. Most of these appear to be in calf, filleted, with folios at 6s. and 5s., quartos as 2s. 6d. and octavos as 1s. 6d., but there are two books in red turkey, an Aldine Quintilian, which must be the quarto of either 1514 or 1521, for 5s., and a duodecimo Aldine Oppian for 3s. The second bill is for five folios, probably all incunabula, bound in 'Red turkey Exter:' or as a binder would now say, 'extra'. The books are:

1716/17	Durandus Rationale Div. Offic	01:05– 0
Jan 13	Just[in]iani Institut	01:05– 0
	2 Tullij Officijs at 15s.	01:10– 0
Feb: 2	Boecius de Consolatione	01:05– 0
		05 05– 0

The bill was receipted on 2 February 1716/17 by John Neal 'for yᵉ use of Jane Steel'. The two 'Tullij Officijs' can be identified, since they are similar in style to, and have tools found on other firmly identifiable Jane Steel bindings for the Harleian Library. One is in the King's Library at the British Library (C.1.b.6). It is lettered TULIU DE OFFICII / MOGUN 1466;[16] and covers a copy of Cicero's *De officiis* and *Paradoxa* printed at Mainz by Fust & Schoeffer in 1466. That it is the Harleian copy is confirmed by the pencil Osborne price 6–6–0 not quite erased above the King's Library bibliographical references on the first white end leaf. The other is another copy of the same edition, now in the Hunterian Library at Glasgow University (Bg.2.24). Osborne's catalogue (vol. III, p. 67—part of lot 866) records two copies of this edition. They are described as quartos, but are actually small folios, 10½ inches tall. It seems likely that the Durandus and Justinian mentioned in this bill are also early Mainz printed books—respectively the *Rationale divinorum officiorum* by Fust and Schoeffer of 1459 and the *Institutiones* by Peter Schoeffer alone of 1468.

The most interesting of the extant Jane Steel bills is the third, totalling £41 13s. 6d. It is dated April 30th, 1717, but the receipt, on the recto of the second folio, reads:

> Feb: 7: 1717/18
> Received then of the Lord Harley the
> sum of sixty one pounds eight shillings
> in full of all accounts to this Day
> bi me
> Jane Steele

This suggests the existence of another bill for £19 14s. 6d. which was settled at the same time. On 26 November 1717 Harley wrote to Wanley from 'Wimple'—he did not start calling it Wimpole until 1721—'I sent you a Box by the last Higler directed for you at Dover Street there was in it . . . some MSS. to be bound. I desire they may be carefully bound, you will give directions for their being bound fine or plain as you shall see the book to deserve it, I would have them all lettered' and in his next letter on 1 December he wrote 'I would have Mrs. Steel bind my Books'.[17] Perhaps these MSS. accounted for the £19 14s. 6d.

The surviving bill, like the other Jane Steel accounts, appears to be entirely for printed books, and for £41 13s. 6d. she supplied 36 books bound in gold-tooled red turkey and 53 in 'C[al]f Gilt Lett[ere]d & fil[lette]d'. It is more detailed than any of the others among the Portland papers, normally giving either the printer's name or the place of printing together with the date and sometimes the format. It has been possible, therefore, to identify some of the books and to establish the styles of the morocco bindings, and I have also found one of the calf bindings. This is among the books bequeathed to St. John's College, Cambridge, by John Newcome in 1765, a fine collection of incunabula about twenty of which are in red morocco bindings in the Harleian style. They are nearly all bound by Chapman and are in remarkably fine condition. The book bound in calf (Ii.1.15) appears in the bill as 'Senecae opera 1478' at a cost of 4s. The sides are decorated with a panel outlined by a two-line gold fillet within which is a roll of flower heads within circles alternating with ferns. The spine is gilt, with a red title-label, reading exactly as in the bill, and in each panel between the raised bands four acorns arranged as a cross and French corner tools. These calf bindings vary considerably in price. Duodecimos cost 1s. 6d. per volume, octavos 1s. 8d. or 2s. 9d., and quartos 2s. 9d. or 3s. 6d. For folios bound in calf the usual price was 4s., and, if it has not been rebound, the book lettered 'Boellij Philosoph.', which I suspect contains an edition of the *De Consolatione philosophiae* of Boethius, may prove identifiable. Three small folios only cost 3s. 6d. each, but a few others cost considerably more. The two volumes of *Commentaria linguae latinae* of Stephanus Doletus, Lyon, 1536, together cost 10s. (They appear in Osborne's catalogue of the Harleian printed books as vol. I, 15130 and again in vol. III, 1186.) The Pliny edited by Hermolaus Barbarus, Venice 1498, cost 10s. for a single volume. The famous Landino Dante, Florence 1481, with the illustrations after Botticelli, cost 12s., and another 3s. for mending, while the binding of the oblong folio (14 × 29 inches) of Dorigny's engravings of the Raphael Cartoons then at Hampton Court and now at the Victoria & Albert Museum, came to 15s.

The bindings in red turkey leather—it is slightly pinkish in colour and is of more substance with a more marked grain than 'My Lord's Morocco leather' to be discussed later—are of two distinct designs. These differ from the typical Harleian bindings produced by both Elliott and Chapman in the 1720s, and since it is possible to identify examples of both types I have reproduced all the entries for books bound in turkey in Appendix B in the hope that other bindings may be identified.

The first design, described as 'Red.turk.fill. & side tools' appears on the Lucan printed by Sweynheim and Pannartz at Rome in 1469, which is no. 6 on the bill and cost 18s. to bind. The book was no. 3914 in vol. I of Osborne's catalogue ('*Tegm.Maur.deaurat*'),[18] and is now in the King's Library at the British Library (167.i.15). On the flyleaf is Osborne's price 8–8–0. It was illustrated in the *Book Collector*, Summer 1971, and has (like the British Library Cicero from Jane Steel's first bill mentioned above, C.1.b.6) a narrow centre panel outlined with a roll within a three-line fillet, outside which is a larger panel made by a two-line fillet, with fleurons at the angles and triangular masses of small floral volutes bounded by 'drawer-handle' tools—the 'side tools' of the bill—in the centre of each side of the panel.[19] The bill starts with eleven folio volumes bound in red turkey in this style, priced apparently according to height. The Jenson Pliny (no. 1), measuring about $15\frac{1}{2}$ inches tall, cost £1 5s. The four volumes of the Giunta Cicero of 1534–7 (2–5), priced at £1 a volume, were probably about $14\frac{1}{4}$ inches tall. The British Library Lucan (6), at 18s., is 13 inches tall, and this would seem to have been the price for folios between 12 and 13 inches (7 and 8). The Silius Italicus (10) at 16s. would be likely to measure about $11\frac{3}{4}$ inches and the Diogenes Laertius at 15s. about $11\frac{1}{2}$ inches judging by non-Harleian copies in the British Library.

After four octavos in 'Red Turk[ey]' at 5s. each comes a Justinus & Florus, probably Osborne's vol. I, 4740, Milan 1502, since this is the only folio Justinus & Florus described as *Tegm.Maurit.deaurat*. On the bill it is described as 'Mid.Piece & Corners Ditto'. The 'Ditto' presumably refers to 'Red Turk.Extr', and as all the items down to no. 37 are described just as 'Ditto' it might be expected that all these would have middle pieces and corners and no side tools. But three of them can be identified and they are all without corners, but with side tools, as was evidently the penultimate item on the bill, after the calf bindings, the Mainz 1467 edition of Thomas Aquinas, *Secunda Secundae*, which is described as 'Red Turk[ey] Middle Piece and Side tools'.[20] In this design there are again two panels outlined by gilt fillets, one within the other and 'mitred' or joined by a two-line fillet at the angles. As before, there are fleurons at each angle of the outer panel, and triangular massed tooling in the centre of each side, but there is also a diamond-shaped mass of tools in the centre of the inner panel, which constitutes the 'middle piece'. No. 28 in the Jane Steel bill, the Venice *Etymologicon magnum Graecum* of 1499 from the Hamilton Palace and Herschel V. Jones collections was lot 85A (not illustrated in the catalogue) at Sotheby's on 23 June 1969 and is in this style. It was no. 878 in vol. III of Osborne's catalogue—'*Corio Turcico deaurat*'. As a folio 16 inches tall the price was £1 6s. No. 34 'Isocrates Orationes Gr.' must be wrongly dated '1485' on the bill, for the first Greek edition is that of 1493. Osborne's vol. I 5266—'*Tegm.maurit.deaurat.*'—is a copy of the 1493 Isocrates and may be identified with the copy which belonged to John Newcome in the library of St. John's College, Cambridge (Ii.1.18) which is bound in this style (plate 9). It has Osborne's 4-4-0 on a fly leaf. No. 35 in the bill, Celsus, *De re medica*, Milan 1481, is now in the Hunterian Library at Glasgow (Be.3.27). As the spine correctly reads 'Celsus', while the bill has 'Selsuss', it may be that the writer of the bill had someone dictating to him. In Osborne's entry in vol. III, 1916, this appears as '*cor. Turc.deaurat*'. The Celsus, which is just under 13 inches tall, and the Isocrates, just over twelve inches, are both priced at 19s. as against 18s. for nos. 6, 7 and 8 on the bill which are also in the 12- to 13-inch range, but lack middle pieces.

This 'side-pieces' style was becoming slightly old-fashioned by 1717. It succeeded the 'cottage-roof' as the standard design for bindings for the royal chapels at the turn of the century, but may have been used elsewhere as early as 1686. A presentation copy of Moses Pitt's edition of Sir John Chardin's *Journal du voyage en Perse* of that year in the Huntington Library (121800) was bound in pinkish-red turkey to this design. Royal bindings include lot 146 in the Corfield Sale, with the arms of Queen Anne, and G. D. Hobson illustrates an example for George I as no. 73 of *English Bindings in the Library of J. R. Abbey*, and cites other examples. Judging from the tools used all these (including the Huntington Chardin) are the work of the Steel bindery. Some of these tools are illustrated on plate 10 and nos. 2, 3 and 4 are to be found in use by Elliott in the 1720s.

ELLIOTT and CHAPMAN

The next bills among the Portland papers are those from Thomas Elliott.[21] They appear to be complete from April 1721 until August 1727, but Elliott had been binding for Edward Harley at least as early as 1719, for on 1 May 1721, Wanley records in his diary 'Mr Elliot the Binder came, & was paid off to 1 Septr. 1719'. He was in business on his own by 1718, in which year he took his first apprentice.

The belief—perhaps first held by the indexer of Joseph Cundall's *On Bookbindings Ancient and Modern, 1881*—that the Harleian bindings were the work of the firm of Elliott and Chapman[22] was thoroughly exploded by J. B. Oldham in his *Shrewsbury School Library Bindings*. But Oldham was working from the manuscript diary, and lacked the assistance of the admirable editing of the printed version. In consequence, although he was able to stress that Elliott and Chapman were rival binders, he failed to grasp that they were doing work of equal importance and made the erroneous assumption that 'for more important work [Harley] employed Elliot and for less important Chapman'. He also failed to distinguish between the two groups of tools that were used on the Harleian bindings in the diary period, and so attributed to Elliott the binding in the Shrewsbury School Library which is certainly by Chapman.

The clearest evidence of the equal importance of the two binders may be derived from a study of what Wanley always refers to as 'My Lords Marocco-Leather'. This consisted of 288 skins, for which Harley paid £72,[23] i.e. five shillings a skin. They were obtained from Morocco through the agency of John Beaver, the husband of Wanley's stepdaughter, on a visit to Gibraltar in 1720-1. The previous time he had been there he had been 'Judge Advocate of the Place'.[24] On this occasion, he wrote to Wanley on 22 January 1720/1[25] 'I was in great hopes amongst the vast quantities of Cordouan Skinns there were in this place, to have found at least as many as would have served My Lorde Harley, but, tis allmost incredible, I turnd over near two hundred dozen with my own hands, and did not meet with one that was fit for his purpose, so was forced to employ a Merchant in Barbary, who has sent me the cream of the Countrey—but they are something dearer than usual as well for that reason as that the Spanish invasion has withdrawn all sorts of tradesmen and so interrupted the Trade of those parts that it was with great difficulty, they were got down from Fez, however I am perswaded the excellence of them will make amends, being govern'd by this rule, that the best is the best cheap'. On 9 May 1721 Wanley wrote in the diary: 'I went to the Custome House in Order to clear-off the Parcel of Marocco-Goat-skins which my Lord lately bought abroad; & were sent by Mr Beaver from Gibraltar', and in his memorandum book[26] on May 15 noted: 'I d[elivere]d Mr Serra's Bill about the Morocco Skins to Mr Croce, that he may add a Rec'. to it, I have paid the Money instantly'. This bill was evidently only for the skins and it was nearly a year later on 25 April 1722 that the diary records the payment for shipping them to England.

The first reference to the use of this leather is in the diary on 13 July 1721: 'Mr Elliot having clothed the CODEX AVREVS[27] in My Lords Marocco-Leather', but it looks as if they were not supplied regularly to the two binders before January 1721/2. The 8 MSS. sent 'to the Binder'[28] on 7 November 1721 appear to be bound in morocco and not turkey, but this was presumably supplied by the binder. In the Memorandum Book for 30 November 1721[29] is a note: 'Marocco Leather being dear: Noel would have my Lord to Supply Chapman'. But it was January 1721/2 before the use of the skins was discussed with the binders. On the twentieth 'Mr Chapman came, & received 3 Books for present Binding. And, upon his Request, I deliver'd (by Order) Six Marocco-Skins to be used in my Lords Service (all of which, by mistake, he left behind him). He desire's to have them at a cheap price, & to Bind as before. I [Wanley] say, that my Lord will not turn Leather-Seller; & therefore he must on Wednesday morning next bring hither his Proposals for Binding with my Lords Marocco-Skins; otherwise, his Lordship will appoint some other Binder to do so'. On 24 January Chapman duly 'gave in his Proposal', picked up the skins he had left behind, and took a parcel of books to bind. 'My Lord' was 'willing to consider upon' the proposal 'and in some time His Lordship will come to a Resolution' says the diary. Presumably Harley was satisfied as Chapman continued to bind with the leather. Two days later Wanley 'discoursed' with Elliott upon the same topic, and on 27 January 1721/2 'Mr Elliot brought in his Proposal about Binding with my Lords own Marocco-Leather, which not agreeing with the Method I desired him to proceed by; he rated another which I drew up, & signed the same.' The first note of the issue of any of this leather to him is on 19 February, when Wanley recorded 'Mr Elliot came for some [of] my Lords Marocco Leather for Binding'. From 26 February 1721/2 there are regular entries in the diary of the numbers of skins issued to the two binders and by my reckoning 101 skins were issued between then and December 1726 to Elliott (together with one for the Codex Aureus and 'some' on 19 February 1721/2) as against 99 to Chapman. As morocco was only used for the more important manuscripts and the more valuable printed books—usually the incunabula—it is clear that Chapman as well as Elliott was employed on top-class work and the evidence of the tools supports this.[30]

In September 1725 Harley also had two doe skins and Elliott and Chapman were given one each 'to make tryal of in the way of Binding' on the 7th and 8th respectively. On 17 September Elliott reported 'that he ha's used my Lords Doe-Skin upon Six Books, and that they may serve instead of Calf; only the Grain is courser [sic] like that of Sheep, & this Skin was tanned too much'. Chapman said on 30 September 'that it work's as well as Calf, only the Grain is not so smooth'. Elliott's comments show that the skins were tanned, and not tawed, and the three[31] which I have identified look very similar to the standard Harleian calf bindings of this date. Like the calf, the deer leather has been sprinkled, but it looks a slightly darker brown. The sides on all three deer-skin bindings seem in slightly better condition than calf ones of the period, but the gilding on the spines is rather worn, headcaps are damaged and the joints in the top panel are weak. After Wánley's death on 6 July 1726 and the discontinuation of the diary further books were bound by Elliott in the doeskin or deerskin, but the problem of accounting for them seems never to have been settled. His bill from 9 July 1726 to 28 September 1727 contains twenty-one further deerskin items, if I interpret 'Dr S' correctly, the most interesting of which was 'St Wenefrydes life of Caxton' bound on 18 March 1726/7 for 4s. This is the copy now in the Pierpont Morgan Library which Mr. Paul Needham tells me retains its Elliott binding.[32] At the end of the bill is 'Deduct for Deer Skins ... [nil]' followed by a note 'The acct of Deerskins to be refer'd to the next bill.' I regret to say Elliott's final surviving bill contains no such reference. He would not have got away with this in Wanley's lifetime.

THOMAS ELLIOTT

Thomas Elliott, according to Ellic Howe's *List of London Bookbinders*, was the son of Robert Elliott of the Inner Temple.[33] He was apprenticed to Robert Steel on 3 May 1703, was free of his indentures on 1 September 1712 and was admitted to the livery of the Stationers' Company on 7 May 1722. His business address is noted at the beginning of Wanley's diary as 'at the Bible next the Blewposts-Tavern in Portugal-street, neare Lincolns Inne Back-gate', but towards the end of his life—he was dead by 1763—he seems to have lived in Edmonton. He was in financial difficulties in 1752, when he was awarded five guineas by the Court of the Stationers' Company. In his prime, however, he was probably one of the leading London bookbinders, and he is known to have worked for the Society of Antiquaries in 1721,[34] and for Richard Rawlinson in 1727.[35]

He is first mentioned in the diary as having visited the library on 20 January 1719/20, but it is the second entry, on 25 January, which sets the tone for the somewhat strained relations he enjoyed with his patron's librarian. 'This day,' wrote Wanley, 'having Inspected Mr Elliots Bill,[36] I found him exceedingly dear in all the Work of Marocco- Turkey- & Russia-Leather: besides that of Velvet.' On the 28th there was a somewhat stormy interview. 'Mr Elliot the Bookbinder came; to whom I produced the Observations I made upon his last Bill [which unfortunately does not survive], Shewing him, that (without catching at every little Matter) my Lord might have had the same Work done as well, and cheaper by above £31'—which suggests that this must have been a stiffish bill. The first point in Elliott's reply 'that He could have saved above 8 pounds in the fine Books and yet they should have looked well' presumably meant that he could have saved this sum by skimping the workmanship where it would not show. His other points have a familiar ring: 'that he now cannot do them so cheap as he rated them at: that no man can do so well as Himself: or near the Rates I sett against His. But upon the whole, said He would write to my Lord, upon the Subject of this Our Conference'. On 13 February 'Mr Elliott came about his Accompt' without effect for, as mentioned above, it was to be well over a year, on 1 May 1721, that he was even 'paid off to 1 Septr. 1719'. It was apparently 1 September 1720 before he next visited the library and then it was to bring 'a small parcel my Lord [and not Wanley] had given him to bind'.[37] It was not until 24 January 1720/1 that we find 'I deliver'd 23 Books, with their Titles, to Mr Elliot the binder', although Chapman had been taking a parcel to bind almost every month during 1720.

By June 1721 however, Elliott was evidently restored to favour and was entrusted with the rebinding of one of the library's most precious possessions, always referred to by Wanley in capitals as the CODEX

AVREVS. It was considered so valuable that it was bound in the library at Harley's Dover Street house. This manuscript of the four Gospels written in gold, *c.* 800, for the court of Charlemagne is now Harl. 2788 and is still in its Elliott binding, although some unpleasant red leather doublures were added when it was rebacked (apparently in close imitation of the original spine) at the Museum in the nineteenth century. It is now interleaved throughout with paper with a very glossy finish. At some stage the edges of the leaves (but not of the interleaving paper) have been gilt. It is illustrated opposite page 194 in the *Book Collector*, Autumn 1964.

Humphry Wanley first mentions the binding project on 27 June 1721 'Mr Elliot begun to work about the CODEX AVREVS, in Order to the New Binding of it, the Cover it had in the Second Binding of it perhaps about 90 years ago, being worn out, and the whole sewing gone to decay'. In Elliott's bill for 1720-2, totalling £30 which was settled on 26 April 1722, we can follow the work more closely. Here are the details from the bill:

1721			
June 24	A day to work in the Library and to buy paper for the golden booke	—	5 0
	for a large Skin of Vellum	6	6
	Gilt paper, and Silk twist	—	5 —
26, 27	Worke in the Library	—	10 —
	Chinees paper 30 Sheets	—	15 —
29, 30	2 days Worke	—	10 —
July 4, 5	2 days Worke	—	10 —
	leather for lettering and gold	—	3 —
7, 8	2 days worke	—	10 —
10	a day my Wife and Selfe	—	10 —
	for Gold and Silver twist for headbanding	1	6
12	a day	—	5 —
	3 days to finish the golden booke and gold and other materials for the same	—2	2 —
22	2 yards of Persian Silk to line the case and Ribon for binding of edges and Making	—	11 6

The total cost therefore was £7 4s. 6d., with no charge for the leather for binding since one of Harley's morocco skins was used. The day's work in the library on June 24 may perhaps have been on 'my Lords Catalogue of his old Latin Books' (Harl. 7627A, 7627B—both rebound) of which Wanley had 'finished the Copie ... in order to Mr Elliot's binding' on 22 June. The vellum was probably required for endleaves, the gilt paper might have been for the pastedowns and the silk twist for sewing thread although it is now sewn with a coarse hemp thread. The Chinese paper was probably for interleaving, but as there are now over 200 inserted leaves and Elliott only bought 30 sheets of Chinese paper, I suspect that the present interleaving paper dates from the nineteenth century. Since the old binding was 'worn out, and the whole sewing gone to decay', the backs of the sections probably needed repair and Elliott may have done this on June 26, 27, 29, 30 and July 4, 5, 7 and 8. The arrival of his wife on the 10th and the purchase of gold and silver twist for headbanding suggest that she sewed and headbanded the book on that day,[38] with Elliott glueing up, rounding and backing, and attaching the boards between these operations, and he would then have been able to cover it on 12 July. On 13 July the diary records that 'Mr Elliot having clothed the CODEX AVREVS in My Lords Marocco-Leather, took the same from hence this day, in Order to work upon it with his Best Tools; which he say's he can do with much more Conveniency at his house than here'. We know from Elliott's earliest surviving bill that he had supplied to the library 'A french press for binding' for 10s. 6d. and 'a sewing press' for 5s. on 22 April 1721 and these would have served him so far. But he would obviously have found it easier to heat his finishing tools in his shop than in the library, and the bill shows that he spent three days executing the elaborate quadruple borders and 'middle-piece' on each cover, and the tooling on the spine with the lettering on the leather piece he had acquired on 5 July. To preserve his masterpiece—it is the most elaborate of all the Harleian bindings and is much better tooled than many of them—he provided a silk-lined case which has not survived.

Wanley, meanwhile, departed on a 'speedy Journey to Oxford', where he apparently remained until 28 October, so that we have no comment from him on the binding when it was returned. It would perhaps even have earned something like the unaccustomed eulogy of the entry for 17 October 1724: 'Mr Elliot's Servant brought the old Copie of S. Isidori Etymologiae, with great Labor repaired, & finely bound'. The Wrights' suggestion that this is Harl. 2686 is confirmed by the fact that the tools used on it are Elliott's, and it has one of the most elaborate 'middle pieces' to be found in these bindings (plate 11). Elliott's bill under that date records:

> Oct. 17, 1724
>   S. Isidori Etymologiae   morocco   10 –
>   Mending   1 1 –

Some of the same tools are found on two other volumes which needed a great deal of repair work. 'As to the old Missale Ecclesiae Nivernensis', noted Wanley on 3 November 1724, Elliott 'said that he hath had great trouble with the later part of it; and that so much of it is utterly perished, & a great part of what remains is so rotten, that he think's he can save but little. I encouraged him, however, to do all in [his] power'. This second volume was repaired with vellum in 1966, being rebound with the old sides of Elliott's binding mounted as doublures. Fortunately the Wrights noted (p. 320, note 2) 'the upper portions of almost all the leaves are wanting and have been crudely supplied with paper of 18th-cent. date'. Elliott did not complete his work on this book until 26 February 1725/6: 'On Saturday last Mr Elliot came to my Lodging & said that he had brought-back the so long detained Missale Nivernensis Ecclesiae, bound in two Volumes in 4to.' wrote Wanley on the 28th. Elliott charged 10s. for binding the two volumes and 'Mending the rotten part 1–1–0'. The volumes are Harl. 2991, 2992.

In general Wanley was presumably satisfied with Elliott's workmanship, but he firmly noted any shortcomings in the diary, which was kept on Harley's instructions, and in which Wanley liked to show that he was watching My Lord's interests. Typical of many is the entry on 4 March 1721/2 'Mr Elliot sent in most of the Books of the last Parcel which he was to have brought in on the 17th of the last Month, and in looking upon them, I approve not either of the Leather or Workmanship of several of them'. Another common grievance is aired by Wanley on 24 May when 'Mr Elliot brought in the Parcel last d[elivere]d to him to be Bound, 5 days before the Time by him appointed; but then by setting his Servants about them, divers Books are not so well Lettered as they might have been'. The parcel of manuscripts brought in by Elliott on 11 August, 1722 were 'pretty well done except as to the Lettering, about which he will still employ his Men notwithstanding all that I have been able to say'. On 3 December of the same year Wanley 'made him take back five of the Books in Order to amend their Vicious Lettering' and the librarian's pent-up irritation explodes in his entry on 21 May 1723. 'Mr Elliot said he had brought-in the parcel last d[elivere]d to him; where-upon I observe, 1. that nº. 7 is not brought in, so that without my check-Note, it might have been lost. 2. This parcel hath been kept too long. 3. He must take back 5 books, which are Letter'd too falsely although my Titles were accurate & plain.[39] 5[sic]. He did not bring-back half of my Titles for this parcel; but to make up, brought 3 Titles which belonged to a former parcel. 6. His Excuse for not binding my Lords fine Virgil & Tullies Epistles printed upon Velum, is an idle pretence of wanting my Lords Marocco-Leather, which he might have had of me any day.' It is difficult to avoid the impression that Elliott must have been a somewhat happy-go-lucky character, but he in turn must sometimes have been provoked by Wanley's self-righteous zeal. On 29 September 1722 Wanley found a new cause for complaint: 'Mr Elliot the Binder brought-in only 8 of the Greek MSS.[40] I last d[elivere]d unto him; all these without mid[d]le Pieces'. A month later, on 29 October, after Elliott had delivered another parcel, we read: 'A Letter sent to Mr Elliot, upon Occasion of his Neglect in not putting in Mid[d]le pieces into the Covers of such Books as he Binds for my Lord in Marocco.' Elliott's bill for that day lists twenty-two books including the manuscripts received on 5 May 1722[41] by Wanley from Mr. Gibson. Among them are two particularly interesting bindings which Dr. Wright first noticed as having the letters of Elliott's name tooled sideways in a small circle, one in the centre of each panel of the spine. If the books are laid on their lower cover the name can be read quite easily, but if they are standing upright on a shelf the letters are not very noticeable. The manuscripts are the *Cosmographia* of Pope Pius II (Aeneas Sylvius Piccolomini) billed by Elliott as 'Pii II.P.P. Cosmogr. lib.1' for 8s. 4d.[42] and an Aulus Gellius, said to have belonged to the same Pope, bound for 6s. This method of signing is very unusual at any time and particularly so for books bound for a nobleman's library in the 1720s. It seems almost as if Elliott, anticipating the complaint about the absence of middle pieces, was playing a trick on Wanley and seeing if he could get this past his eagle eye. Had Wanley spotted them, one would expect him to have returned them as 'vicious lettering' for amendment. But there is no reference to them in the diary and yet Elliott never seems to have repeated the practice.

After complaining about the absence of middle pieces, Wanley's next protest, on 12 November 1722, was that in the parcel which Elliott had returned on the 10th 'the Midle-pieces of the Marocco-work are all too small'. The bill gives sixteen items all apparently bound in morocco and nearly all printed books. Two of these can be identified, having Elliott's tools. One is in the Bodleian, a 12-inch folio by Omnibonus Leonicenus, *In Lucanum*, Venice 1475,[43] which cost 8s. to bind. The other, in the King's Library in the British Library, is a quarto containing Nicolaus Perrotus, *Liber de metris*, Bologna 1471.[44] The binding cost 4s. and the book has Osborne's price 2–2–0.

Cutting down the size of the middle-pieces, or, still better, omitting them altogether paid Elliott well, since they were comprised of impressions of single tools. It looks as if he had an agreement with Wanley based on the height of the volume. In his bill for books delivered on 30 November 1722, after enumerating six incunabula bound in morocco at 10s. each he writes 'all 13 insh'. Against two of the next three items, priced at 8s. is written $12\frac{1}{2}$, and this seems to have been the standard price for 12-inch books bound in morocco. This pricing by size may have encouraged both Elliott and Chapman to give their bindings the rather large 'squares'—the projections of the boards beyond the edges of the leaves—which characterise them, together with rather thicker boards than was usual at the time. On the other hand Harley—or Wanley—may have liked this style and insisted on it, and I incline to think that this is so. It is found on Mrs. Steel's morocco bindings—accompanied by the same type of red, white and blue (or occasionally green) silk headbands, which are double (with a bead) to accommodate the extra height of the headcap. It would be natural for Elliott to copy his predecessor's habits, but the fact that Chapman also always had exaggerated squares and the same style and colours for his headbands suggests that Wanley specified them. Another peculiarity found on Steel, Elliott and Chapman morocco bindings is that the normal practice was to leave the edges of the leaves plain and not gilt. I have not succeeded in finding the Harleian copies of these six '13 insh' incunabula, but judging by the size of non-Harleian copies in the British Library,[45] two of them at least had vast margins—or Elliott lengthened them in his bill submitted some time after they were bound, and in the knowledge that they, as printed books, were down at Wimpole, while Wanley was usually in London.

Elliott's prices for morocco work were naturally lower than Jane Steel's, since Lord Harley was supplying the skins, but Wanley had evidently struck a hard bargain over the rates to be paid. The price of eight shillings for a 12-inch folio or sixteen shillings for the largest ones,[46] which Elliott received for morocco compares very unfavourably with the eighteen and twenty-five shillings paid to Mrs. Steel for similar bindings in turkey.[47] His middle pieces would have taken as long to tool as her side tools and it is unlikely that turkey leather was so very much more expensive than morocco. On 12 October 1726 Elliott billed Harley for two sets of the new quarto five-volume translation of the Odyssey by Alexander Pope. One in blue turkey cost £3; the other, 'Maroq', was £2—a difference of four shillings for the leather for each of the five volumes. If the turkey ones were—as one would expect—large paper, it would need a very large skin to produce the covers for two volumes, although there could be enough left over to use on another smaller book. One might perhaps estimate the cost of a turkey skin at five to six shillings.

All the reprimands Elliott received did not originate with Wanley. On 17 December 1721 Harley wrote to Wanley 'I desire you will send to Elliot and let him know that I expect my portfolios down here this week without fail & that I do not take it well he should delay the doing them and that I will never employ him again if he did not send them this week'. After which thunderbolt it is not surprising that on 24 December Harley, before 'wishing you & Mrs Wanley a merry Christmas & many' was able to report that at least some of the portfolios had arrived.[48]

The next noble rocket was discharged not at Elliott but at Wanley in a letter of 1 January 1722/3 from Wimpole beginning disarmingly 'A happy new year to you and many is my hearty wish'. After reporting damage to some of the bindings in both morocco and calf in two cases which he had just opened, Harley continued 'I did many weeks if not months ago give my directions for the binding of the Virgil & Tullies Epistles. I did say that you & Elliot should consult about the method to make the leaves of vellum lye smooth & that the work should be gone upon as soon as you two had fixed upon a method. I expected the work had been done before this time'. Wanley had clearly forgotten all about this instruction and records his first action in the diary on 9 January. 'Mr Elliot came, & after much Conversation about the best way of getting out the Cockles risen in my Lords Virgil, & Tullies Epistles, both Printed upon Velum: I deliver'd them to him, & he thinks they may be both done in about Six Weeks time; and promise's to use all possible Care about them.' They took over six months. On 18 March the diary reads 'Mr Elliot brought the two Velum-printed books last deliver'd to him to shew me. I find that he ha's laid many of the Leaves smooth, & can do so by the Rest. But, through Negligence, he ha's damaged some of the principal Painted letters'. It was 9 July 1723 before

'Mr Elliot having brought home the two Velum books which had been so long in his Hands; My Lord', recorded Wanley smugly, 'made him take them both back to amend their Lettering; first one, & then the other'. In Elliott's bill, dated 6 July, we find:

Prose MS 4° royal Morocco	0 6 0
Tul. Epist e Famil. demi d°	0 10 0
Virgillius cum Servii Comentar d°	0 10 0

Judging from the books on vellum in Osborne's catalogue, the Tully could be his vol. III 3229, Ciceronis Epistolae Familiares.*cor. Turc. deaur. Venet. per Joan Spiram* 1469, but more probably is 3204, 'Ciceronis Epistolae Familiares, *Literis cujusque Libri initialibus auratis coloratisque mire exornatus cor. Turc. deaurat. Venet. per Nic. Jenson* 1471'; the Virgil is likely to be Osborne's III 3222. 'Virgilii Opera, *mira elegantia excusus et pulcherrime depictus, cor Turc. fol. deaurat. Edit. antiq.*' (Cremona, 1472), but might be 3234 'Virgilii Opera, cum Comment. Servii & aliorum. *cor Turc. deaurat. Venet.* 1486'. The latter book is possibly British Library C.19.e.14, purchased at West's sale in 1773 and now rebound.

We have already observed Elliott binding the Codex Aureus in the library, and there are quite a number of other entries in the bills for a day's work there. But he forgot to charge for 6 April 1723, when Wanley recorded that 'Mr Elliot came to Bind some Books in the Closet'. This small room at Dover Street is mentioned by Harley to Wanley in a letter of 16 November 1721, 'I desire you will send me down the peices of Antiquity that remain in the bookbinders closet'. It is just possible that Elliott may have also gone down to bind at Wimpole. On 10 November 1724 Harley wrote to Wanley, 'Upon looking over my books I find that a great many want binding very many want lettering and several have their leaves transposed by the negligence of the Binders. I think it would be much the best way to have a bookbinder here. I desire therefore that you will take an opportunity to talk with both Elliot and Chapman upon this matter and know their Terms. I design to have a binder here not above six weeks or two months at a time, and that only to be between Ladyday and Mich[ael]mas. Pray let me know what you do in this affair'. Wanley did nothing immediately, either because he was distracted by the death of his 'Good Landlady' on the day this letter was written or because, as Harley suggested in a letter of 28 November, this section of the previous letter had been written on the second page '& though I wrote at the bottom of the first page *turn over* it has escaped your eye'. The messages were duly delivered to the binders on 1 December and on the 3rd Wanley 'sent to Mr Elliot to apprise me touching his Mind about serving my Lord at Wimpole; which he is willing to do, hoping that my Lord will no[t] suffer him to be a Loser'. The combined evidence of the diary and Elliott's bills make it just possible that he could have been at Wimpole between 31 May 1725, when he entered five books on his bill, and 26 June, when he delivered three more. The diary on 3 June records that 'Mr Elliots man came for a parcel to bind' and not Mr. Elliott. But this happened on other occasions when he was in London. On 2 August Elliott went to the library in Dover Street in person.

Between 1720 and 1729 Elliott's bills for the library amount to £609 16s. 5d. After the difficulties with the 'extravagant' bill of 1719, he was paid at fairly regular intervals and there are receipts for £571 13s. On the final surviving bill for £111 14s. 1d., there is only a receipt for £60 paid in part. When Elliott got the rest of his money and whether he did any more binding for the Harleian Library is not known.

As a binder Elliott was not as original as the best binders of Charles II's reign and was apparently not an outstanding craftsman, although Wanley thought his work superior to that of his journeymen. Nor can we be sure that to him should go the credit for the development of the 'Harleian style' with its central lozenge of massed small tools surrounded by a border—often double or triple—but without any tooling in the angles. The earliest example identified so far is Elliott's binding of the Codex Aureus, which was tooled in July 1721, but it may well have been developed for some of the books in the missing 'extravagant' bill of 1719. At the moment this is pure speculation, however, and although the Eusebius which Chapman bound in June 1720 is not in the Harleian style, he was using this style on bindings in the parcel of books returned by him to Wanley on 9 November 1721.

So many manuscripts and printed books are named in Elliott's bills that I have only identified comparatively few. A high proportion of the manuscripts which he bound still remain in his bindings (or at least with his covers preserved) in the Harleian Library, despite a rather drastic rebinding programme in the last decade, and there are many more to be identified with the aid of the Wrights' notes to Wanley's diary.

CHRISTOPHER CHAPMAN

The absence of any bills from Christopher Chapman makes it much less easy to identify his work, but there is enough information in Wanley's diary, in the correspondence between Harley and Wanley and in the bindings themselves to establish him as the equal of Elliott in his work for the library. It has also been possible to recognise his bindings in the Harleian style by their distinctive although similar kit of tools to those used by Elliott and the existence of two groups of them among the Harleian manuscripts which can be linked with diary entries.

Christopher Chapman was the son of a journeyman bookbinder, George Chapman of St. Martin's-in-the-Fields, and was apprenticed to William Sparkes of Fetter Lane on 7 February 1704. (Elliott had been apprenticed to Robert Steel 9 months earlier.) He did not become free until 1718, and Ellic Howe[49] records him as being in business in Duck Lane by 1720. He was there until at least 1731, having five apprentices in the eleven years. From 1736-42 he took three more apprentices, with his shop in Paternoster Row, and between 1745-50 yet another three at Stationers' Court. On 6 August 1751 his son Nathaniel became free by patrimony and probably took over the business, he in turn taking three apprentices at the Stationers' Court address from 1751 to 1759. An apprentice of Christopher's was 'turned over' in 1756, suggesting that he may have died in that year.

He makes his first appearance in Wanley's diary on the same day as Elliott, 20 January 1719/20. 'Mr Chapman & Mr Elliot the Bookbinders came; & my Lord gave Mr Chapman two Books to Bind, & to be brought back by this day Sennight.' This may well have been his first visit. Elliott was in some disfavour as the result of his last bill and giving Chapman only two books to bind seems a likely way of testing his ability. He started in the way in which he was to continue. The two books he was to bind within a week took nearly three, being returned on 8 February. Harley, however, was evidently satisfied with the two samples and on 13 February 1719/20, Chapman received the first of many parcels of books which he was to bind. By 20 October 1720 he had bound nine such parcels and there had been adverse comments on his work on only one occasion, when Wanley noted on 6 June 'But he having blunder'd in Titling one of them: I sent him off with it, and did neither pay him, nor give him any more Work; but on Thursdaymorning he is to bring the book again, amended; & then to be paid, & to have another Parcel of Work'. In a letter of 18 September 1720 Harley wrote from Wimpole[50] to Wanley 'Chapman has sent down mr Gays Poems Milton &c but there still wants several, I am glad he has sent these because they were for my Wife & she wanted them' and on the 26th 'Keep Chapman employed allways if there is work for him because he is but slow. Pray send down the books yt came last from him'.

On 25 October 1720 Harley wrote again to Wanley 'I desire you would ask Chapman what he would have to come down and bind books here and to bring a man with him, I would have the whole expence set down and sent to me here'. Wanley asked Chapman on 29 October and recorded on 1 November 'Mr Chapman gave me his Answer as to the Terms whereupon he is willing to Bind or Letter for my Lord at Wympole'. It seems likely that he went, for it was 18 January 1720/1 before Wanley delivered him another parcel to bind. When, however, in December 1724 Wanley passed on Harley's messages to both Elliott and Chapman about working at Wimpole[51] Wanley noted in the diary on the 2nd 'Mr Chapman came to me, & desired to be excused from going down to Wimpole'. On two occasions in May 1721 Chapman did some work in the library at Dover Street. On the 1st, 'Mr Chapman came, mended two books, & was paid off, in full', and on the 23rd 'Mr Chapman came & divided some Books of Tracts'. Chapman at this period was being paid quite frequently, sometimes as on this 1 May 1721 just for his last parcel. Wanley's *Memorandum Book*[52] records that on this occasion his bill was £8 8s. 6d. Ironically this was the day on which poor Elliott was paid off to 1 September 1719.

Throughout 1721 Chapman worked steadily, binding eight parcels without any adverse comments being recorded, but by 10 March 1721/2 trouble was brewing and Wanley recorded 'A Letter written to Chapman the Binder, expostulating with him upon the account of his great Neglect toward my Lord: & requiring him to bring in such of my Lords Books as now remain in his Hands, on Tuesday next by 12 of the Clock, upon pain of my Lords Displeasure, & Loss of his Business'. This letter was dispatched on Saturday and brought results by Monday 12 March when 'Mr Chapman brought home the remaining Books of the last Parcel, well done. Part of his Excuse for their long detention, was his late Illness. That he ha's not been out of the House, these Ten days until now; & that he will be more punctual for the future'. He did amend his ways and between 13 March and 27 December 1722 bound nine parcels very satisfactorily, apart from four or five 'Blunders in the Lettering'. One parcel was described as 'all well done' and another 'very well done in the main', and a third as 'well done' and this was at a time when Wanley was complaining about nearly every batch which he received from Elliott.

Wanley failed to note the return of the parcel of MSS. which he gave to Chapman on 27 December, and it was not until 9 April 1723 that he received another parcel and was paid £20 5s. 'in part of his Accompt'. The last entry in the diary for payment to Chapman had been on 17 April in the previous year, when he 'was paid his whole Accompt'. The library-keeper may have failed to record other occasions when payments were made. But failure to meet his bills may have resulted in the marked slackening of Chapman's efforts which is now discernible. A parcel given to him on 11 May 1723 was not returned until 7 October and, although Chapman asked for more work on 16 October, he did not receive any until 28 January 1723/4. He returned these books on 24 February, but did not deliver the 'parcel of Greek MSS. to be bound all in Marocco' which he received that day until 10 August 1724. Wanley had sent him two letters hastening the return of these Greek MSS. and it may be that Chapman had only returned them on promise of payment. Five days later 'Mr Chapman the binder came, & I paid him off entirely; d[elivere]d to him a new parcell, with 5 of my Lords Marocco-Skins'. This parcel was returned on 22 September and a parcel of '25 books all printed upon Velum issued that day was returned 'indifferently well done, a day before I expected' on 12 October. The next day 'Mr Chapman came, and took-away a fine Parcel of old Printed Books, and twelve of my Lords Marocco-Skins. He said, that having postponed some other Work, for the dispatching of the last Parcel, he cannot finish this under Six Weeks time'. He was as good as his word on this occasion returning the books on 24 November 1724 and taking a further parcel, but it was to be 27 March 1725 before 'Mr Chapman brought the Parcel I deliver'd unto him the 24th of November last; & when I chode him for this delay, he pleaded the want of Hands to assist him, & laid the blame upon his idle & unfaithful Journeymen: an insufficient Excuse'. Two more parcels were returned during 1725, including, on 30 September, the one in which he used 'my Lords Doe-skin'. Wanley noted that the books were 'not so well Letter'd as I expected'. He did not give Chapman any more work on this occasion, and we hear no more until the final entry concerning him on 23 December of that year 'Mr Chapman came, but I gave him no Work; chiding him for being so slow in my Lords former business, which he had frequently postponed, that he might serve the Booksellers the sooner'. The diary—and Wanley's life—had another six months to run, but during this period only Elliott was binding for the Harleian Library.

Only two books are specifically mentioned in the diary as having been sent to Chapman to be bound, but fortunately the first of these can be identified. On 8 June 1720 'Mr Chapman came, & was bidden to take the Rufinus's Eusebius he lately bound, back with him, & find the first Leaf (which was loose) & fix it to its proper place'. This is quite certainly Harl. 3452, described in the catalogue as: 'Eusebii Pamphili, Caesariensis ep. Historiae Ecclesiasticae libri 10: ex versione Ruffini. XV. Codex membranaceus, olim elegans, sed maculis deformatus, et multis in locis carie exesus'. The edges of this manuscript were evidently so eaten away with decay that Chapman—or a previous binder—had cropped the margins so that the manuscript is now only 245 mm tall. But the edges of the first leaf, with its once elegant white-vine border, were in reasonable condition and in order not to cut into the border it was left its original size, 277 mm tall. When Chapman returned on 11 June 'having found the lost Leaf & fix'd it in it's place' he had to fold the leaf to insert it. The manuscript was rebound in 1962, preserving the original covers, but not unfortunately the backstrip, with the first leaf at full size in a separate volume. The creases can still be seen. The binding (plate 12) is not in the Harleian style, but has a double panel with distinctive corner fleurons. Neither of the tools nor the roll used on the covers seem to have been used on any bindings in the Harleian style. The other book, which I have not traced, is mentioned in the diary on 30 September 1720 'Mr Bowyer sent hither the Dr Clagetts Sermons, &c. which I sent forthwith to Mr Chapman the Binder, & a Letter desiring him to go about them out of hand, that they may be sent to my Lord the next Week'. The Wrights plausibly identify this with William Clagett's *Sermons on the following subjects. viz. Concerning Christ's not appearing to all the people after his resurrection . . . now first published from the originals by N. Clagett*, London, 1720, 2 vols. It is in vol. iv of Osborne's catalogue as no. 14931. As its binding is not mentioned it was very probably bound in calf and not turkey or morocco.

My original identification of Chapman's bindings in the Harleian style[53] was based on the knowledge that two different binders were at work and that both were binding manuscripts and early printed books in morocco; on the realisation that two different groups of tools were being used on these bindings; and on the hope that when, on 9 November 1721 Wanley recorded 'The 7th Instant I agreed with Mr Gibson, for his 8 MSS. lately arrived from Italy; & gave them to the Binder', that the binder would prove to be Chapman. These eight MSS. were duly listed by Wanley and identified by the Wrights. I found that six were in gold-tooled red morocco bindings with two different types of diamond-shaped middle-pieces, which employed non-Elliott tools; a seventh (Harl. 2554), a rather insignificant paper MS. of Lucretius, was bound in sprinkled calf with no middle-piece, but with a blind roll on the covers which was also part of the non-Elliott group of tools. The first manuscript on Wanley's list was, however, disturbing. He described it as 'C. Plinij Historia Naturalis, membr. fol. mag. man. Ital. nitidissime script. & inlum. cum Insig. Medicaeorum' and the Wrights had identified it as 'Probably Harl. 2677, which has at foot of f. 1, however, the arms *not* of Medici but Piccolomini'. This proved to be decorated with the tools I associated with Elliott. It was a relief to find that there was another fine large folio illuminated Pliny manuscript, Harl. 2676, finely bound in red morocco and tooled with a triple border and the characteristic non-Elliott tools in the middle-piece; and that on f. 1 of this manuscript were the familiar arms of the Medici family. The bindings of these eight[54] manuscripts were thus all from the same workshop, and none of them can be identified in Elliott's bills for 1721 and 1722 among the Portland papers, which are complete from April 1721. The other fine Pliny manuscript with the Piccolomini arms (Harl. 2677), brought to the library by Gibson on 4 April 1723, but not paid for until 13 February 1723/4, is to be found in Elliott's bill dated 17 March of that year, together with most of the rest of Gibson's parcel. Being over 17 inches tall it cost his top price of 16s.

Confirmation of the identification of Chapman's tools comes from two other entries in Wanley's diary. On 27 December 1722 he wrote 'I being about to make up a Parcel of MSS. for Mr Chapman to Bind, some of them will be part of those which Mr Noel sent-in, without Order, 13 September last. These lay long in his Sacks, with the Printed Books, untill that at length my Lord sent for the said Sacks to him; and keeping the Printed Books, and some of the MSS. he sent down to me these only whose Titles do here follow'. This list comprises twenty-nine manuscripts, six of which the Wrights were not able to identify, while five are described as being in Corio Turcico and one in Corio Russico and presumably would not have required rebinding. The remaining seventeen manuscripts are in a variety of bindings, most of them bound at different times at the British Museum in the eighteenth, nineteenth and twentieth centuries. But four of them are recognisably Harleian bindings, two in red morocco with middle-pieces[55] and two in calf, with a doublt gilt fillet and blind roll.[56] On all four the tools are Chapman's.

The other piece of evidence is based on the diary entry for 24 February 1723/4. 'Mr Chapman brought-in the parcel last deliver'd to him, well done in the Main; & I deliver'd to him a parcel of Greek MSS. to be bound all in Marocco'. Elliott's bills show that it was Wanley's custom when a batch of books had been brought into the library to send them off for binding quite soon after they had been paid for.[57] Looking backwards in the diary we find that three 'Codices Graeci', Harl. 5792, 5576 and 5588, were listed on 24 August, 1723. All bear the purchase date '18 die Januarii A.D. 1723/4' in Wanley's hand. Harl. 5576 has been rebound, but the other two are in red morocco with identical middle-pieces and Chapman tools. The previous batch of Greek manuscripts, also acquired from Noel, were listed by Wanley on 13 June 1723 and were also paid for on 18 January 1723/4. I have checked the more expensive items in this list, as being the likely ones to be bound in morocco, and find that nos. 30 (Harl. 5601), 31 (Harl. 5697), 32 (Harl. 5685), 43 (Harl. 5621) and 44 (Harl. 5732—plate 13) are not only in red morocco but have exactly the same middle-piece of Chapman tools as Harl. 5792 and 5588. Again none of these Greek MSS. appears in Elliott's 1724 bills.

As has been mentioned earlier[58] both Elliott and Chapman were probably binding to a pattern laid down for them, using the same batch of skins for their red morocco bindings, with rather thick boards and projecting squares, and even the same type and colour of headbands. Superficially, therefore, their bindings are remarkably similar and anyone studying only their forwarding techniques would conclude that they all came from the same workshop. The tools used on them, however, tell quite a different story (plates 14 & 15). Harley (& Wanley) did not at all insist on complete uniformity in the finishing on the morocco work. The diamond-shaped middle-pieces show quite a wide variety, with each binder having his favourite patterns, and they had quite distinctive kits of tools, only a few of which are at all closely similar, while none of them are indistinguishable. Elliott showed more originality in the designs of his middle-pieces, the majority of which include either a border or a massed centre of 'drawer-handle' tools, first introduced in the 1670s, but used by him in new combinations. He does not, however, seem to have used the spirals or volutes, again first used in Charles II's reign, which form the centre of so many of Chapman's middle-pieces. Most of the rolls they used are of different designs, and again the ones that are similar can be fairly easily distinguished. They both had a narrow roll (no. 1) with alternating fleur-de-lis and three-petalled flowers for use on the inside of a border or frame. On Elliott's version the alternation was perfect, but the engraver of Chapman's got his calculations wrong and wherever the full length of the roll can be seen two fleur-de-lis can be seen side by side. The other similar rolls (no. 2) provide the easiest method of distinguishing an Elliott morocco binding from one of Chapman's. Elliott's bindings for Harley seem always to be decorated on both the turn-ins and the edges of the boards with an alternation of flower heads within nearly complete circles and a fern. Chapman's are usually tooled with a similar roll in which the three-quarter circles contain alternately a sun and anthemion. Some of the Chapman bindings, however, have a zig-zag roll on the edges of the boards.

The design of the calf bindings was also evidently dictated to the two binders. Spines have raised bands and are gilt in similar style to the morocco bindings. On the covers there is a two-line gilt fillet tooled round the edge, within which a roll has been tooled in blind. This roll is often quite difficult to see on the calf bindings which have survived, but was no doubt much more obvious when the binding was new. The rolls used here and on the edges of the boards are those found on the morocco bindings.

JOHN STEPHENS

Only two other bookbinders are mentioned in Wanley's diary. One is John Brindley, who will be discussed below. The other, John Stephens, makes a brief and not very glorious appearance in the summer of 1723. On 21 June 'One John Stephens a Book-binder brought a pretty copy of a Latin Comedy called EPHIGENIA, written fairly upon Velum in 8vo. which [I] bought of him for a Crown. . . .[59] He said he ha's about a dozen of old Printed books to shew me, but I bad him not give himself the trouble'. Undeterred he returned with four incunables on 8 July, offering them for two guineas and leaving them at the library. On 13 July 'Mr Stephens the Bookbinder came about the four books he left here at 2 Guineas. He (foolish Man) offer'd me a Gratuity, to help him off with them. I told him he did not know me'. When Stephens returned on 18 July he was probably surprised to find that Harley had bought the books.[60] He received his two guineas, but he never called again. Nothing else seems to be known about him.

WILLIAM BONNOR

While Elliott—as his bills show—was working for Harley in London after Wanley's death until at least 1729, a Cambridge binder was also doing some work for Wimpole. The Portland papers contain three bills from one William Bonnor covering the years 1727 to 1732,[61] and the second of these locates the binder, for it is endorsed 'Mr Bonner's Bill pd. at Cambridge'.[62] Finding no mention of him in the literature on binding or the book-trade in Cambridge, I naturally appealed to Mr. J. C. T. Oates, who promptly produced twenty-four bindings in the University Library which he had identified as Bonnor's work from two bills for binding submitted by him which are now preserved in that library. He also allowed me to publish his discovery in *The Book Collector* for Winter 1973. The Cambridge bills are rather later than the Harleian ones, covering the years 1736 to 1739. All the books were evidently bound in calf, and all but two of those identified are very properly in the style known as 'Cambridge calf', in which a central rectangular panel and a wide outer border are sprinkled with copperas, but a frame around the panel is left plain.[63]

This style had been developed by about 1700, for a considerable number of the latest additions to Samuel Pepys's library, now at Magdalene College, Cambridge, were bound in London in this manner. But until some of the books bound for Harley by Bonnor have been identified, it may be wiser to look for something in the style of the calf bindings of Elliott and Chapman. The second bill for fifty-three items, totalling £9. 1s. 3d. and paid on 13 November 1730, has a note which might assist identification 'My Lord all the Directions for the Lettering is pasted to the first Lefe in Each Book & I hope your Honour will NOT think the binding over charged'. If the directions for the lettering were accurately copied on to the bill, they were not very good —two successive items are 'Portiforum ad usum sarum 0–5–0' and 'Portiforum ad usum aestivalis 0–5–0', presumably representing a Sarum Breviary bound in two parts. But the frequent misspellings suggest that Bonnor—if he wrote out the bill himself—was completely out of his depth in any language but his own, and the entry 'St Seyprian on ye Lords Prayer 0–1–6' suggests that someone read him that title at least. Almost all the books seem to be printed, but there is hardly ever a clue to the edition. 'Goodmaners Lond: by wynkyn 0–2–3' clearly refers to one of the editions of Le Grand's Book of Good Manners printed by Wynkyn de Worde (STC 15394–9) but none of the recorded copies of any of these editions appears to be in an eighteenth century binding. The third bill, covering work done from 2 December 1730 until 14 March 1732 and totalling £25, contains a few specified books such as:

Jan 25 [1731/2] the 5th & 6 vol of the Stat Tryals Grand Paper B[o]und Gilt & fillited	1 4 0
Dugdale's Warwickshire Grand Paper 2v Do	1 4 0
Dr Humphreys Translation of Montfaucon with the Suppliment in 15 Parts Royal Paper Bound in 6 vol. Books & Binding	15 15 0

but much of it is for lettering and gilding of backs. A rather baffling entry on 21 December 1731 which I first read as '26 Books New Sprouted & pollished' for 4s 4d, was fortunately explained later in the bill when on 3 February 1731/2 a further 12 books were 'New Spruced & pollished'; they were spruced or smartened up or, as we should now say, refurbished.

JOHN BRINDLEY

The remaining binder to be mentioned in this series of bills is a well-known figure in the London book trade, John Brindley. The son of Joshua Brindley of Chadleton, Staffordshire, clerk, he was apprenticed in 1705 to a member of the Merchant Taylors' Company, John Smith, whose trade is unknown. In 1723 he is recorded by Howe as being a binder in Little Britain. By 1728 he was in New Bond Street as a bookbinder and bookseller.[64] Binder to George II's consort, Queen Caroline of Anspach, he subsequently became a bookseller of importance—he founded the book-selling firm which finished as Ellis—although he continued to run his binding business. He was early on the scene at Dover Street and Wanley reports on 3 February 1719/20 'Mr Brindley came to know if my Lord had any work for him; & say's that his Lordship lately gave him a Book to Bind. I referred him to his Lordship'. There is no evidence that Harley gave him any more books to bind. He may have done, but Wanley certainly did not, for his name does not occur again in the diary. Four of his bills survive among the

PLATE 9 (p. 163). Binding by Jane Steel, 1717, with middle-piece and side pieces. Red turkey, gilt. Isocrates, Milan 1493. St. John's College, Cambridge, Ii.1.18.

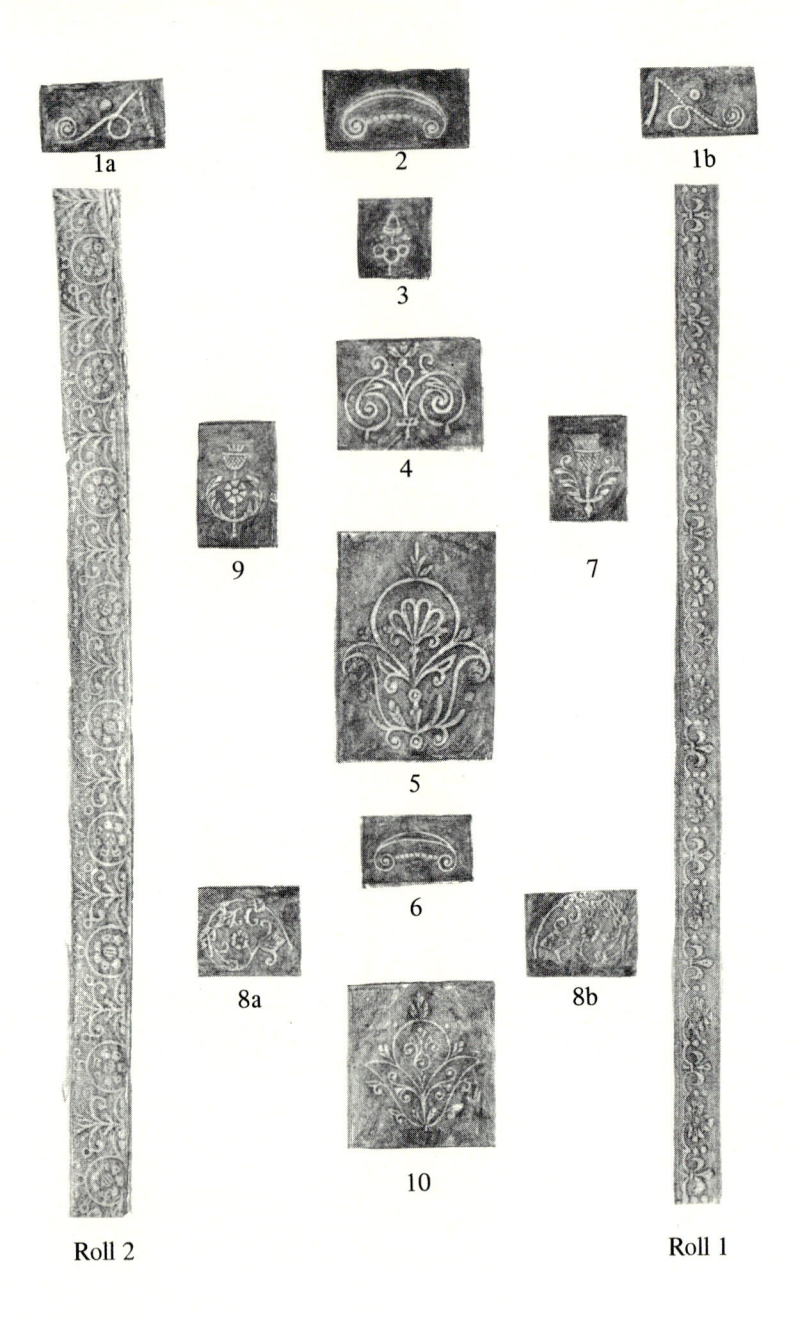

PLATE 10 (p. 163). Tools used by Jane Steel.

PLATE 11 (p. 170). Binding by Thomas Elliott, 1724, in 'Harleian' style. Red morocco, gilt. St. Isidore, *Etymologiae*. MS. 9th century. British Library, Harl. MS. 2686.

PLATE 12 (p. 179). Binding by Christopher Chapman, 1720, with double panel design. Red turkey, gilt. Eusebius, *Historiae ecclesiasticae, ex versione Rufini*. MS. 15th century. British Library, Harl. MS. 3452.

PLATE 13 (p. 181). Binding by Christopher Chapman, 1724, in 'Harleian' style. Red morocco, gilt. Apollodorus, *Bibliotheca*. MS. 16th century. British Library, Harl. MS. 5732.

1	2	3	4	5	1	2	4	5
		Elliott					Chapman	

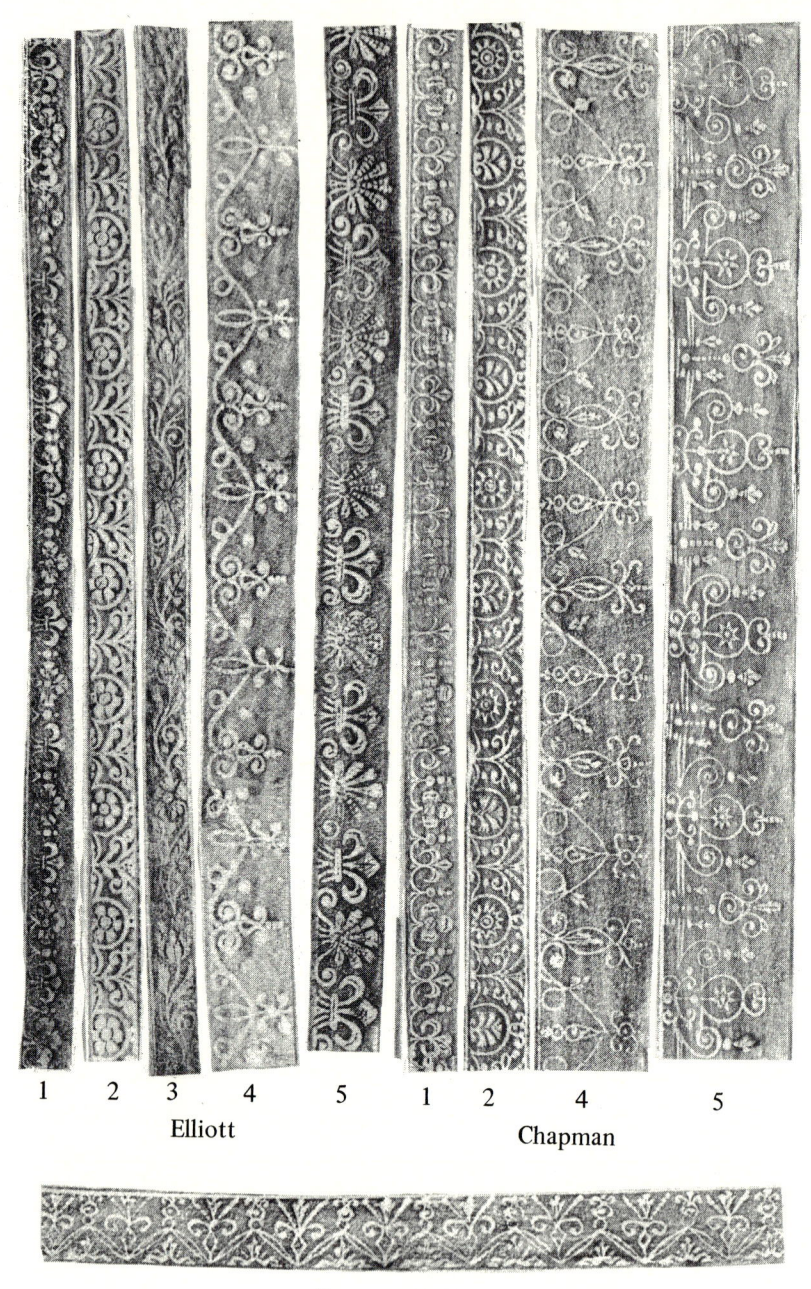

Chapman Roll 3

PLATE 14 (p. 181). Rolls used by T. Elliott and C. Chapman. The rubbings do not show the full length of most of the rolls.

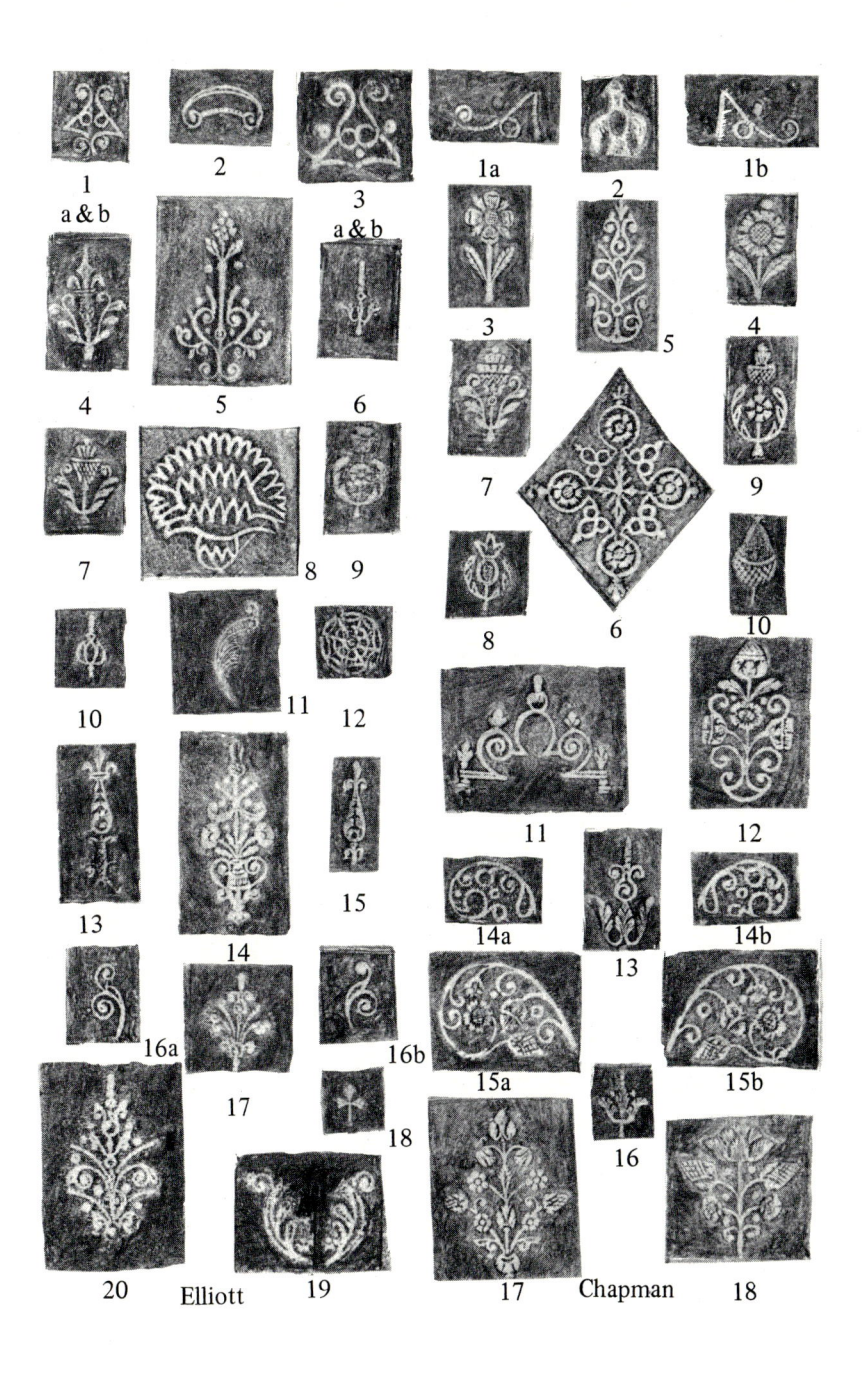

PLATE 15 (p. 181). Tools used by T. Elliott and C. Chapman.

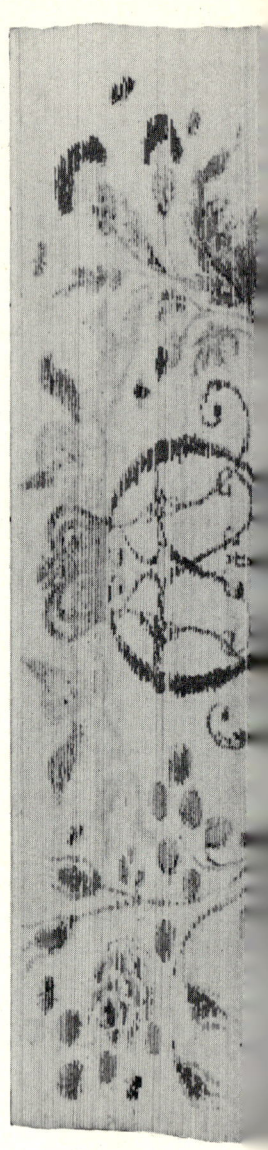

PLATE 16 (p. 186). Binding by John Brindley, *c.* 1728. Gilt red morocco covers with blue morocco doublures fore-edge painted under the gold. Richard Holland, *Observations on the small pox*. London, 1728. British Library, 43.f.16. *Left*, doublure: *right*, fore-edge.

HARLEIAN BINDINGS

Portland papers[65] covering the years 1733 to 1738, and totalling £129 7s. 9d. They are mainly for printed books sold to Harley, but there are quite a number of entries which show Brindley acting in his capacity as bookbinder. In September 1734 he lettered eleven octavos for 2s. 9d.; lettered and gilded two more octavos for 1s.; and lettered one folio, one quarto and ten octavos for 3s. Several items were sewn in blue paper for sixpence and the second and third volumes of the Musaeum Florentinum were bound in calf with a gilt back as they came out for 16s. each.[66] The most interesting items, however, occur on 11 October 1736.

Oricellarius de Bello Italico 4° bd morocco & the leaves Illuminated with ye Kings Arms	1 1 0
Holland on the Small Pox bd. morocco, blue Turky insides, Border'd ye Queens Cyphers with two Angels holding ye Crown over it and the Rose and Thistle, &c	1 1 0

A copy of each of these books exists in a binding which corresponds exactly with the description given here. In the Royal Library at Windsor there is a copy of Bernardus Oricellarius, *De bello italico*, printed at London by William Bowyer for John Brindley in 1724. It is on large paper and is bound in gold tooled red morocco with a gilt border and diamond-shaped centrepiece, and has comb-marbled paper ends. The fore-edge is painted under the gold with the Hanoverian royal arms as used by George I. Brindley seems to have been the only English binder in the first half of the eighteenth century who carried on the practice, quite common during the Restoration period, of decorating the fore-edge under the gold. There are several bindings in the King's Library (formed by George III) in the British Library with Queen Caroline's arms painted in this way.[67] Among these is a copy of the second book in Brindley's 1736 bill. This is Richard Holland's *Observations on the Small Pox*, printed for John Brindley, bookbinder to Her Majesty, at the King's Arms in New-Bond-Street, 1728 (43.f.16). The title and the words TO THE QUEEN at the beginning of the dedication are picked out in gold; the initials are illuminated, and all the headpieces and ornaments are coloured in red, yellow, and blue paint. The red morocco covers bear Queen Caroline's cypher in the centre and at the four corners; the 'insides' or doublures are of blue turkey, with the Queen's cypher above her motto DECUS ET TUTAMEN, and they are bordered with gilt tools; and the fore-edge is painted under the gold with the Queen's cypher under a crown supported by two angels, with a rose bush on the left and a clump of thistles on the right. It has always been assumed that this was Queen Caroline's copy (plate 16).

The problem remains whether these two books at Windsor and Bloomsbury are the two which Lord Oxford bought from Brindley in 1736. Osborne's sale catalogue of the Harleian Library records them both. No. 6509 in volume I is 'Oricellarii (Bernardi) de Bello Italico Commentarius, *Tegm.Maurit.deaurat.fol.deaurat.Lond.*1724' and no. 12970 in volume II is 'Observations on the Small Pox, or an Essay to discover a more effectuall Method of Cure, by Richard Holland, M.D. *bound in red Morocco, gilt on the Leaves.* 1728'. The only shred of evidence is that neither has an Osborne pencilled price on the fly-leaf, nor can I discern any trace in either book of its having been in any but royal ownership at any time.

There seem to be only two possible solutions. The first, which I slightly favour because of the absence of Osborne's prices, is that neither of the surviving copies is the one mentioned in the 1736 bill, but that they are the copies sent respectively by Brindley (who wrote the dedication to Henry D'Avenant in the Oricellarius) to George I in 1724 and by Dr. Holland (who died in 1730) to Queen Caroline in 1728. Brindley may have made a second copy of each, either as a trial or as a memento of the occasion and kept them in his shop, where Harley saw them and took a fancy to them.

Alternatively the existing bindings could be the original presentation copies, given away—as so often happens with royalty—to a member of their household or to a friend who died before 1736. They may then have been bought back by Brindley, and sold to Harley. The price of one guinea each suggests they were from stock or second-hand. It would certainly not cover both the price of a new book and its elaborate decoration and binding, had Harley been considering offering them as gifts to the King and Queen.

Harley seems in fact never to have moved in Court circles and is never referred to in Hervey's diary. His friendships were with literary figures such as Prior and Pope. His name has been perpetuated through his library of manuscripts. He may now also be remembered for services to the history of English bookbinding through the medium of his binding bills, the diary of his Library-Keeper and the able editors of that diary.

NOTES

1. *The Diary of Humfrey Wanley, 1715–26*, London, Bibliographical Society, 1966. I am greatly indebted to the editors for permission to quote freely from their book and my obligation to it and to them will be only too obvious in what follows.
2. For which see an admirable section in the Wrights' Introduction, pp. lxx–lxxi, and under Elliot, Thomas, and Chapman, Christopher, in their biographical index.
3. Historical Manuscripts Commission. *Report on the manuscripts of the Duke of Portland*, vol. vii, p. xvii. The original account and letter are in B.M. Loan 29/225.
4. B.M. Loan 29/111, Miscellanea 1(d).
5. *Remarks & Collections of Thomas Hearne*, vol. 7 (Oxford Hist. Soc. Pubns. vol. xlviii), p. 58. See my article in *The Book Collector*, Spring 1969, p. 62.
6. B.M. Loan 29/112, Miscellanea. (r).
7. The filleting between the bands involved marking the raised bands on the spine with a gold line above and below each band.
8. On the back of the bill is a note: 'Henry Sedgley at Mr. Tothams a marchant in Mark Lane near Great Tower Street'.
9. Illustrated in *The Book Collector*, Spring 1969, p. 62.
10. B.M. Loan 29/112, Miscellanea 1 (x).
11. *A Dictionary of Printers and Booksellers . . . 1668 to 1725*, 1922, p. 131.
12. B.M. Loan 29/113, Miscellanea no. 13.
13. This confirms my suggestion in 'The Memorandum Book of James Coghlan' in the *Journal of the Printing Historical Society*, no. 6, p. 44.
14. Harl. MS. 3778, f. 150. For Dawson see G. D. Hobson, *Bindings in Cambridge Libraries*, 1929, p. 168, pl. LXX.
15. B.M. Loan 29/112, Miscellanea 1(r).
16. Identification of books mentioned in binders' bills is helped by the fact that they were normally prepared by noting down the spine lettering, which is very much quicker than picking each book up, opening it, and copying from the title-page. In the Elliott bills to be discussed below there are several occasions where a finisher's mistake in lettering the spine is faithfully copied in the bill, e.g. Harl. MS. 5005, St. Cyprian's works lettered on the spine 'Opera Sancti Apriani' and recorded in the same words in Elliott's bill of 2 January 1727/8. On other occasions, however, spellings suggest dictation.
17. Both letters are in B.M. Loan 29/249.
18. Osborne's cataloguers do not seem to have been very good at distinguishing between Harleian bindings in morocco leather, imported from Africa, and turkey leather (of finer quality) from the Levant. Quite a number of books described in the binding bills as bound in gilt turkey leather (correctly 'corio turcico deaurat') appear in the catalogue as 'Tegm.Maurit.deaurat.', gilt morocco covers.
19. On both these two British Library Jane Steel bindings the arms of George III have been subsequently added to the covers.
20. On 1 August 1717 Harley wrote to Wanley (B.M. Loan 29/249) 'I have sent up the Thomas Aquinas directed to you which I desire may be bound in Red Turkey Leather by Steel'.

21. With praiseworthy consistency Wanley invariably uses the spelling 'Elliot' in the diary, and the Wrights in their edition have naturally followed him. But on the eight receipts and one letter of his which I have seen Thomas Elliott was quite convinced that his name had two 't's.

22. The text says—quite accurately—that the binders employed [in the Harleian Library] were Elliott and Chapman, who attained to some eminence in their day, but they appear in the index as 'Elliot and Chapman' and not separately. J. A. Arnett in his *An Inquiry into the nature and form of the books of the ancients*, 1837, p. 148, after describing Harleian bindings says 'the artist by whom they were bound is not known'. Extracts from Wanley's diary published in *Notes and Queries*, 1st series, viii, p. 335, in 1853, over the signature 'µ', make it quite clear that they were two distinct binders, and Cundall's information no doubt came from this source, or from the quotation of it in the chapter on bookbinding in Edward Edwards, *Memoirs of Libraries*, 1859, ii, 972.

23. B.M. Loan 29/259. Misc. 31. Letter from John Beaver to Lord Harley from Gibraltar dated 22 January 1720/1; Misc. 49. Wanley's Accounts to Lord Harley. 1720/21, March 8. Paid Mr Priverau for Mr Beavers Marocco Skins 72. –. –.

24. Letter of 11 Aug. 1721 in Harl. MS. 3777, f. 183.

25. Harl. MS. 3777, f. 179.

26. p. 431 of the Wrights' edition of the Diary.

27. See below, p. 168.

28. I believe Chapman; see below, p. 179.

29. Diary, p. 435.

30. The skins must have been quite big. On 16 October 1722 Wanley delivered to Elliott 'two more Skins, & a good piece of a Skin remaining of that wherein he Bound the CODEX AUREUS, as he say's'. The binding of the Codex Aureus, Harl. 2788, measures $15 \times 11 \times 4\frac{1}{2}$ inches ($380 \times 280 \times 110$ mm), so that it would require a piece of leather about $17 \times 27\frac{1}{2}$ inches (430×700 mm).

31. The six are listed thus in Elliott's bill among the Portland papers, B.M. Loan 29/112 Miscellanea 1(u):

Sept 16 [1725]
[1] Annales Iuridici Regium Edw^{do} I & II — 2 6
[2] Theorica Testam. Raymundi Lullii — 2 6
[3] Ysaac de Urinis 6 l. — 4 in Deer Skin
[4] Trotta Kirandes 4 l. — 3 6
[5] Tractatus Medicinales — 2 6
[6] Festivale or Sermons &c. — 2 6

[2] Harl. 3369, [3] Harl. 3371, and [5] Harl. 3372 retain their original bindings, with a gilt two-line fillet border to the covers outside a blind roll. This is the normal Harleian style for calf bindings. [4] Harl. 3407 has been rebound. '6 l.' and '4 l.' refer to the numbers of panels with lettering on the spine. In [3] Harl. 3371 there are six separate medical manuscripts, and each title is lettered. This would account for the extra price, the four books identified being all much the same size, about 9×6 inches. [6] might be Harl. 3368, but the lettering does not agree.

32. The binding bill confirms a conclusion which my colleague, Mr. George D. Painter, had reached on other grounds. Seymour de Ricci in his *Census of Caxtons* says that the Harleian copy (his 100.1) came from the Richard Rawlinson collection. But

Rawlinson's copy was not sold until 16 October 1727 (Part IX, p. 41, lot 953) over six months after the Harleian copy was bound. Rawlinson's copy is De Ricci 100.2, which is now in the British Library.

33. Robert Elliott is not described as 'Gent.' in the Apprentice Register and he does not appear among the admissions in *The Records of... Lincoln's Inn*, 1896. It is likely therefore that he was an employee of the Inn.

34. Diary, p. 446.

35. *The Library*, 5th Ser., XI, 1956, p. 32.

36. As early as 10 September 1719 Harley had written to Wanley, 'Elliots Bill very extravagant I will send it up to you to examine', but he may have failed to do so. All Harley's letters to Wanley are in B.M. Loan 29/249-51, arranged by date.

37. On 2 September 1720 Harley asked Wanley to 'send me down the books had from Mr Elliot'.

38. Elliott might have done the sewing himself and only employed his wife for the headbanding, for on 25 June 1723 the diary reports 'Mr Elliot came & sewed up a MS. for my Lord'.

39. Wanley always supplied the lettering for the binders.

40. The Greek MSS. had been given to Elliott on 14 September 1722, being most of those acquired from Mr. Gibson the day before and listed in the diary on 10 September. The eight returned by Elliott on 29 September may be identified from Elliott's bill as Harl. 5786, 6318, 6325, 5696, 5667, 5680, 5535 and 5668. All except 6325 are bound in red morocco (or have their original red morocco covers preserved) with Elliott's tools and none have middle pieces.

41. The list is on p. 143 in the Wrights' edition of the diary and the MSS. are identified there.

42. Illustrated by Dr. C. E. Wright as plate 1 in his *Fontes Harleiani*, 1972.

43. Auct.O.inf.2.16, Osborne's catalogue I. 3919 & III 932. '*Tegm.Maurit.deaurat.*'

44. C.2.a.6. Osborne II. 15709. '*Tegm.Maurit.deaurat.*'

45. 'Seneca Philos.Opera.Ven.1492' (IB.23442) and 'Homeri Ilias lat.per L.Vallam Brix.[1474] (C.1.c.1) both $11\frac{3}{4}$ inches.

46. e.g. Harl. 3481. Bill, 12 September 1723.

47. See p. 162, above.

48. In Elliott's bill for 22 December 1721, £3 is charged for 'A Ream of blew elephant paper' and £1. 4s. for binding this in four books, 22 × 18 inches, 'raised with guards to receive prints', together with 15s for 'Halfe a ream Royal blew' and 10s. for binding this in two books, 18 × 14 inches.

49. *A List of London Bookbinders*, 1950, pp. 20-1.

50. As in the section on Elliott all the letters quoted from Harley to Wanley are in BM Loan 29/249-51.

51. See above, p. 174.

52. Diary, p. 432.

53. *The Book Collector*, Autumn 1966, pp. 321-2, pl. i, ii.

54. Harl. 2676, 2657, 3110, 2771, 2628, 2554, 5741, 3925.

55. No. 5, Harl. 3015; no. 3, Harl. 3006 (covers only preserved).

56. No. 2, Harl. 3137; no. 7, Harl. 3122.

57. A good example of this is provided by the 'two little parcels of MSS.' which Gibson sent in on 4 April 1723. Wanley listed the 51 items on that date, but they were

not paid for until 13 February 1723/4. Numbers 1–11 and 15 must have been given to Elliott to bind four days later, for they are all in his bill for 17 March 1723/4, when he returned that parcel.

58. See p. 172, above.
59. This is Harl. 3328. It is bound in 18th-century vellum.
60. Wanley lists them in his entry for 13 July 1723—Bartholomaeus [Anglicus], De proprietatibus rerum, Lyon, 1482 (BMC.viii.268); Terentius cum commentis Donati & Guidonis, Venice, 1494 (BMC.v.518); Juvenalis cum Comment. Calderini, Vallae & Mancinelli, Venice, 1494 (BMC.v.529); Virgillii Opera cum Math.Vegij Addit., &c., Nuremberg, 1492 (BMC.ii.436.) None of Harley's copies are in the British Library.
61. B.M. Loan 29, 112 Miscellanea 1 (w)
62. The Harleian practice of misspelling binders' names whenever possible was still being carried on. All three bills are receipted by the binder as 'Wm Bonnor' and endorsed 'Mr Bonner's bill'.
63. The binder attaches a paper mask to the covers before sprinkling, and removes it afterwards.
64. *The Book Collector*, Winter 1962, p. 466.
65. B.M. Loan 29/111, Miscellanea 1(c).
66. 14 February 1733/4 and 16 May 1735.
67. 13.b.6, W. Wollaston, *The Religion of Nature delineated*, 1726; 31.e.12, H. Pemberton, *A View of Sir Isaac Newton's Philosophy*, 1728, 47.i.12, W. Chesledon, *Osteographia*, 1733.

APPENDIX A

B.M. Loan 29/259, Miscellanea 8.

Books sent to Mr Dawson of Cambridge, to be Bound. 19 Septr 1716.
(Brought back 9 Octob. 1716)

1. Ten Volumes of Houghtons Trade-Papers. fol.
2. Joan-Trithemij Chronicon Hirsaugiense. Bas. 1559. fol.
3. Gottofr. Viterbiensis Pantheon. Bas. 1559. fol.
4. Ugolinus Verinus de Illustratione Florentiae. *Lut.ap.Patisson*. 1583.fol.
5. Històría de las Missiones de Japon. Segunda Parte. (por Luis de Guzman) en *Alcala*. 1601.fol.
6. Vite de Pittori Bolognesi de Felsina Pittrice. in *Bologna*. 1678.4^{to}. 2 Voll.
7. I.B. Veri Res Venetae. *Venet*. 1678.4^{to}.
8. I. Labardaeus de Rebus Gallicis. Paris. 1671. 4to.
9. Clementis Epistola 1 ad Corinthios. Gr.Lat.Oxon. 1633.4^{to}.
10. Herodianus Graece. *Lovan*. 1525. 4to.
11. Dr Charleton of Stoneheng. *Lond*. 1663. 4to.
12. Ling. Belg. Idea Grammatica. Amst. 1707. 8vo.
13. Guainerie delle Fontane & Acque de Ritorbio. In Lione. 1577. 8vo.
14. Catalogue of P. Varenne's Auction, with the Appendix—Another.—

HARLEIAN BINDINGS

Another, 4 Apr. 1709. Sr Edm. Kings Catalogue 28 Nov. 1709—Bibl. Fergusoniana & Mottoccina 14 May 1711—Cat of Vincent Barry. 1709—Bibl. Sharrockiana.—Dr Mortiers Catalogue.—Bibl. Triplex.—Eminent Divines Cat.—Bibl. Goodwiniana Pars I. 27 Nov. 1710—Bibl. Cotterelliana. Jan 8. 1710/11. 8vo.

15. Catalogus Libb.Frid.Spanhemij F.F. Lug.Bat. 1701 8vo.—Bibl. Triglandiana. Lug.Bat. 1706.8^{vo}.

16. Mrs Humphrey's Auction Cat.22.Oct.1707—Mr Thornton's Cat. 10 Nov. 1707—Mr Parr's Cat. 7 Jun. 1708—Bibl. Selectissiam [sic]. 9 Nov. 1708.—Dr. Marten's Cat. 20 Oct. 1709—Mr Ford's Cat. 21 March 1708/9—Dr Pierce's Cat. 22 Jun. 1709.—Dr Royle's Cat. 13 March 1709/10—Mr Jones's Cat. 7 July 1710.—Bibl. Procesleana. 6 Nov. 1710. 8vo.

17. Bibl. Laughtoniana—Fowlkiana—Gamblyn—(ignot.) 28 Nov. 1715.—Wyrley—Higden—Hardeslee—Thompson—Burnet.—Ignot.—Southouse—Salkeld. 8vo.

18. Bibl. Westrenen. *Lug. Bat.* 1692.—Bibl. Blockiana. *Amst.* 1702.—Francij. Amst. 1705—Selectissima. Hag. 1716. 8vo.

19. Bibl. Bernardiana 22 March 1710/1. 12mo.

10 October 1716
Delivered to Mr Dawson, folios 2: & 8^{vos}. 4 to be bound: with Orders to Bind the books now bought of Mr Crownfield.

APPENDIX B

Books bound for Lord Harley in red turkey by Jane Steel.
(BM Loan, 29/112, Miscellanea 1(r))

1717
Apr. 30th   Lo^d Harley D^r to Jane Steel

[1]	Plinij Historia Nat: 1476 Red turk fill. & side tools		1- 5- 0
[2-5]	M:T: Cicer. Opera 4 vol Juntae	Ditto	4- 0- 0
[6]	Lucanus Romae 1469	Ditto	0-18- 0
[7]	Opera Collumella var. 1494	Ditto	0-18- 0
[8]	Angeli Jolitiares [sic for Politiani] opera aldi 1498	Ditto	0-18- 0
[9]	M.T. Ciceronis Prol:	Ditto	0-16- 0
[10]	Sillius Itallicus 1481	Ditto	0-16- 0
[11]	Diog Laertius. Lat. 1475	Ditto	0-15- 0
[12]	Plautus Florent. 8°	Red Turk. Extr.	0- 5- 0
[13]	Caesaris Coment. Aldi 1519	Ditto	0- 5- 0
[14]	Ausonius aldi 1517	Ditto	0- 5- 0
[15]	Juvenal and Persius Florent.	Ditto	0- 5- 0

[16]	Just. hist. Mediol. L:Florus Mid. Piece and Corners		
		Ditto	0–15– 0
[17]	Cicero de Legib. Morrel 1557	Ditto	0–12– 0
[18]	Claudian Opera ven. 1495	Ditto	0–10– 0
[19]	Horatius Poet. ven 1576	Ditto	0– 9– 0
[20]	Vidae Poem Crem. 1535	Ditto	0– 9– 0
[21]	Claudianus ven 1500	Ditto	0– 9– 0
[22]	Orthogr. Graec. Ital. Aldi 150[?]	Ditto	0– 5– 0
[23]	Val. Flacc. Argan. Aldi	Ditto	0– 5– 0
[24]	Silius Ital. aldi 1523	Ditto	0– 5– 0
[25]	Virgilij Opera Seb. Gryph 1550	Ditto	0– 3– 6
[26]	P. Comestoe Scholst. Hist 1473	Ditto	1– 6– 0
[27]	Ptolomaei Cosmogr. Ulmae 1483	Ditto	1– 6– 0
[28]	Etomolog Magnum Graec. vent	Ditto	1– 6– 0
[29]	M.T. Ciceroni Ausc Quest vascos. 1533	Ditto	0–19– 0
[30]	Ptolomaei Geograph Ulmae 1486	Ditto	1– 6– 0
[31]	Petarca Verana 1476	Ditto	0–19– 0
[32]	Martial Epigram. ven 1482	Ditto	0–19– 0
[33]	Valerius Maximus ant: Editt	Ditto	0–19– 0
[34]	Isocrates Orationes Gr. 1485	Ditto	0–19– 0
[35]	Selsuss [sic for Celsus] de Re Med:Mediol. 1481		
		Ditto	0–19– 0
[36]	Ovidij Metamorph Pinerel 1480	Ditto	0–19– 0
[37]	Marcel de Propris Sermon Brix 1483	Ditto	0–19– 0
[38–91]	[Bound in calf]		
[92]	Tho Aquant. Secunda Mogunt 1467 fol Red Turk. Middle Piece and Side tools	}	1– 5– 0
[93]	Sentent Exscit Graecis Red Turk. 8°		0– 5– 0
			41–13–06

Nearly all these books can be identified with some certainty in the five volumes of Thomas Osborne's *Catalogus Bibliothecae Harleianae*, 1743, although it does not appear that the cataloguers were very good at distinguishing between turkey and morocco leathers:

[1] Osborne Cat.I.5419. *Tegm. Maurit. deaurat. Venet. ap.N.Jenson. 1476. fol.*

[2–5] I.5084 *Tegm. Maurit. deaurat. Venet.apud Juntas 1537. fol.*

*[6] I.3914. *Tegm. Maur. deaurat. Romae apud Sweynheim. & Pannartz. 1469. fol.*

[7] II.13694. *Tegm. Turc. deaurat. Bonon. 1494. fol.*

[8] V. 2340. *exemplar. nitidiss. literis initial. colorat. corio turcico deaurat. Venet. apud Aldum 1498. fol.*

HARLEIAN BINDINGS

[9] Not identified
[10] I.3936. *Tegm. Maurit. deaurat. Parmae* 1481. fol.
[11] I.5448. *Tegm. Maur. deaurat. Venet. per Nic. Jenson.* 1475. fol.
[12] I.*3560. *Tegm. Maurit. deaurat. Florent. ap. Giuntas* 1514. 8vo.
[13] I.4621. *Tegm. Maur. deaur. Venet. apud Aldum* 1519. 8vo.
[14] I.4067. *Tegm. Maurit. deaurat. Venet. apud Aldum* 1517. 8vo.
[15] I.4034. *Tegm. Turc. deaurat. Florent. apud Juntas* 1513. 8vo.
[16] I.4740. *Tegm. Maurit. deaurat. Mediolani apud Minitianum* 1502. fol.
[17] Not identified
[18] I.4054. *Tegm. Maurit. deaurat. Venet. per Joan. de Tridino* 1495. 4to.
[19] I.3780. *Tegm. Maur. deaurat. Venet. apud Aldum* 1576. 4to.
[20] I.4248. *Tegm. Maur. deaurat. Cremonae* 1535. 4to.
[21] I.4055. *Tegm. Turc. deaurat. Venet. per Christophorum Penis* 1500. 4to.
[22] Not identified.
[23] ?I.3960. *lineis rubris, foliis deauratis. Venet. apud Aldum* 1523. 8vo.
[24] ?I.3942. *foliis deauratis. Venet. apud Aldum* 1523. 8vo.
[25] I.3716. *foliis deauratis. Tegm. Maur. Lugd. apud Seb. Gryph.* 1550 8vo.
[26] I.759. *Ch. Max. Tegm. Turc. deaur.* 1473. fol.
[27] III.3255. *cor. Turc. deaur.* [*on vellum*] *Ulm* 1482. fol.
*[28] III.878. *Corio Turcico deaurat. Venet.* 1499. fol.
[29] Not identified.
[30] I.5467. *Tegm. Maur. deaur. Ulmae* 1486 fol.
[31] III.3484. *cor. Turc. deaur. Verona* 1476 fol.
[32] I.3969. *Tegm. Maurit. deaurat. Venet. per Tho. Alexandrinum* 1482 fol.
[33] ?III.767. *Cor. Turc. deaur. Edit. Antiq. sine Anno vel Loco.* fol.
'This book is fair, richly bound, and was printed towards the Close of the Fifteenth Century.'
*[34] III.745. *cor. Turc. deaur. Mediolani* 1493 fol.
*[35] III.1916. *cor. Turc. deaurat. Mediolani* 1481 fol.
[36] I.3852. *Tegm. Turc. deaurat. Pinerolii. Arte Jacobi de Rubeis* 1480 fol.
[37] I.5015. *Tegm. Turc. Brixiae, per Bonin.* 1483 fol.
[Items 38–91 are bound in calf]
[92] I.952. *Membran. Tegm. Maur. deaurat. Mogunt. per Petrum Schoiffher.* 1467 fol.
[93] Not identified.

* The books marked thus have been traced, as under:

[6] British Library (King's Library) 167.i.15. Osborne's price 8-8-0 is visible in pencil above the bibliographical references noted on the recto of the first free white endleaf. Illustrated in *The Book Collector*, Summer 1971, p. 226. '13-inch' (i.e. 13 inches or more tall, but less than 14 inches).

[28] Sold at Sotheby's 25 June 1969, lot 85A. Not illustrated in sale

catalogue. '16-inch'. It is the *Etymologicon magnum graecum*, printed at Venice in 1499.

[34] St. John's College, Cambridge. Ii.1.18. (Plate 2). Osborne's price 4-4-0 on a fly-leaf. '13-inch'. The date on the bill (1485) is an error. The book is the *editio princeps* of the Greek text of Isocrates, printed in 1493.

[35] Glasgow University, Hunterian Library. Be.3.27. Unpublished. '12-inch'.

TERRY BELANGER

Tonson, Wellington and the Shakespeare copyrights

Although the Copyright Act of Queen Anne (1710) limited the tenure of copyright already in existence to an additional twenty-one years, booksellers continued (until 1774) to maintain that there was a common-law basis for perpetual copyright unaffected by the Act. The most substantial profits in the eighteenth-century London bookselling world lay in the ownership of copyrights of this kind. Copyrights of a large number of the classics of English literature were jointly owned by varying groups of booksellers and there was constant communication between members of such groups to work out the arrangements for the publication and reprinting of their books. From time to time these copyrights were sold, sometimes in a private transaction, but more frequently by means of auctions attended by London booksellers, and it is in these records of trade sales of shares in a wide range of copyrights that one can study the detailed history of booksellers' investment in the continuing copyright of major writers. Of the booksellers concerned, one of the most important was Jacob Tonson I (who died in 1736) who strove to become the successor of Humphrey Moseley (d. 1661) as the chief publisher of notable works of English literature. A glance at the 1767 catalogue of the copyrights owned by the firm Jacob I founded shows how well he realised this goal.[1] In a sale which contained more than 600 lots, copyrights of works by Addison and Steele, Beaumont and Fletcher, Dryden, Ben Jonson, Milton, Spenser, and many other major writers were auctioned off, realising nearly £10,000.

Among the most valuable of the Tonsons' literary copyrights were those concerning the collected works and individual plays of William Shakespeare, and the 1767 catalogue shows that the firm claimed 2/3 of the copyright of Shakespeare's collected works, and varying rights to the plays when published individually—as follows:

[1] Notes begin on p. 206.

Tempest, 2/3	II Henry IV
Midsummer Night's Dream, 2/3	Henry V, 2/3
Two Gentlemen of Verona	I Henry VI
Merry Wives of Windsor, 2/3	II Henry VI
Measure for Measure	III Henry VI
Comedy of Errors	Richard III
Much Ado About Nothing, 2/3	Henry VIII, 2/3
Merchant of Venice, 2/3	Timon of Athens
Love's Labour's Lost	Coriolanus
As You Like It, 2/3	Julius Caesar, 2/3
Taming of the Shrew	Antony and Cleopatra
All's Well That Ends Well, 2/3	Titus Andronicus
Twelfth Night	Macbeth, 2/3
Winter's Tale, 2/3	Troilus and Cressida
King Lear	Cymbeline
King John, 2/3	Romeo and Juliet
Richard II	Hamlet, no share
I Henry IV, 2/3	Othello, no share

Directly under this list the following note is printed:

Mess. Tonson, *it is presumed have the whole Right, where there is no Share mentioned, of printing* Shakespear's *Plays separately, as it appears by his Impression Book, that he only delivered one 3d of such Plays as have the Words* two 3ds *added to the Title of each as above, when printed as single Plays.*

So we have here a list of the Tonson Shakespeare shares 'as it appears' by the impression book. Who owned the other parts of the Shakespeare copyrights?

Shakespeare shares not owned by the Tonsons begin appearing in the trade-sale catalogues in 1737, in lots 73-4 of the sale of William Feales:[2]

A Ninth of the following Copies. . . . Shakespear's *whole Works, third: And a Right of printing separately* Julius Caesar, *third*; Macbeth, *third*; Othello, *whole*; Hamlet, *whole*. [Plus] *Another Ninth of the above Copies.*

The Feales share of the collected works was 2/9 × 1/3; of *Othello*, 2/9 of the whole copyright, and so forth. No mention is made of the shares of any of the other individual plays.

The first 72 lots in the Feales sale consist of other 2/9 shares of more than 100 copyrights, and since this is a rather odd fraction, Feales presumably acquired his 2/9 × 1/3 right to the copyright of Shakespeare's collected works at the same time that he acquired his 2/9 right to the rest.

In the next decade or so there were about a dozen trade sales in which were listed various ninths, or fractions of ninths, of the same copyrights offered in the Feales sale. Looking at the imprints of early 18th-century editions of the books represented by these copyrights, it soon becomes evident that at least a great many of them had been formerly owned by Richard Wellington.

Richard Wellington died intestate in 1715,[3] and his estate was divided among his widow Mary and their three children, all minors: Richard, James, and Bethel. Under English common law, the estate would normally have been divided between the widow and the children at the rate of a third to the former and 2/3 to the latter. But there was a special 'Custom of London' which affected the estates of intestate London freemen like Richard Wellington. Because of the Custom of London, the actual division of the estate (and of the copyrights) was 4/9 to the widow and 5/9 in equal shares to the children.[4]

For a few years after the death of her husband, Mary Wellington administered the Richard Wellington copyrights, and her name appears on the imprints. But by the end of 1719 she was thinking about marrying John Poulson.[5] If she remarried, her 4/9 share of the copyrights would normally have become her husband's property. She wanted the whole estate of Richard Wellington to go to his children, however; and on 30 November 1719 she assigned both her personal 4/9 plus the 5/9 she held in trust for the children over to the booksellers John Darby, Arthur Bettesworth, and Francis Clay, in trust for the children until they came of age. The trustees could manage but not sell the copyrights; 4/9 of the income from them would be turned over to Mary Wellington until her death, after which it would be disposed of according to the terms of her will.[6]

In January 1721, Mary Wellington married John Poulson, first having had him sign an indenture by which he recognised and agreed to the provisions she had made for the disposal of her late husband's estate.[7] Mary Wellington Poulson died intestate in October 1726.[8] Her husband, disputing the terms of the indenture he had signed *before* his marriage, filed a Chancery bill in 1728 against the trustees Darby, Bettesworth, and Clay for his wife's 4/9 of 'Wellington's Copies'. In June 1729, the case was heard before the Lord High Chancellor, and the case was decided in favour of Poulson. Bethel Goodwin, the guardian of the three children, appealed this decision to the House of Lords, who upheld the Chancery decision in May 1730.[9]

As matters now stood, the copyrights were jointly held by Poulson and the three children, who were still minors and whose 5/9 share was therefore still held by the trustees Darby, Bettesworth, and Clay. Darby died in 1733, and the other two trustees continued alone until about 1734, when the children began coming of age.

The imprints of the books whose copyrights had been owned by Richard Wellington I reflect all of these events. Until the end of 1715, Richard Wellington's name appears alone.[10] Between 1716 and 1719 Mary Wellington's name replaces that of her husband.[11] After her assignment to Darby, Bettesworth, and Clay and her marriage to Poulson, the imprints sometimes give her married name, sometimes the names of the trustees.[12] In the latter case, the form was usually:

Printed for J. Darby, A. Bettesworth and F. Clay in Trust for R., J., and B. Wellington.

Poulson's name could have begun to appear on the imprints after the 1730 House of Lords decision, but the earliest I have seen his name is 1732.[13] In 1733, Darby's name disappears,[14] and soon afterwards the names of Richard and James Wellington begin to appear in their own right.[15] Bethel joins the others in his own right in 1735, and the trustees drop from the imprints.

From 1737 onwards, the trade-sale catalogues provide direct evidence about these copyrights. As we have seen, the Feales sale of that year offered a 2/9 share of the whole property. The catalogue does not directly state where Feales got his share, but two of the other lots (lots 79–80) are said to have been purchased from John Poulson, and I presume that the rest of them also came from him either directly or indirectly. Each of the children owned a 1/3 × 5/9 share; Poulson owned a 4/9 share: very elaborate arithmetic is necessary to support any hypothesis other than the one I suggest.

At the Feales sale, the Wellington copyrights were auctioned off in separate lots; the sale thus marked the beginning of the disintegration of this 2/9 share as a unit of the entire estate; a similar disintegration occurred at some, but not all, of the subsequent sales in which part or all of the whole constellation of copyrights came up.

In the same year as the Feales sale of 1737, Charles Corbett offered a 1/9 share of 'Wellington's Copies',[16] and in 1740, unsuccessfully, a further 1/9 share;[17] in the following year he listed still another 1/9 share.[18]

From these transactions it is clear that Corbett purchased, either directly or indirectly, the remaining 2/9 share of these copyrights held by John Poulson. He may have purchased them directly from Poulson (who disappears from 'Wellington's Copies' imprints in about 1734), or perhaps the Poulson 4/9 went in its entirety to Feales, who sold half of it to Corbett in a private transaction.

It will come as no surprise to students of the irrepressible Charles Corbett to find him trafficking extensively in shares of 'Wellington's Copies'—not only the Poulson share, but also various parts of the three Wellington sons' 5/9 share.[19] In 1738, Corbett offered a 1/6 × 5/9 share (that is, half of one son's share) which, the catalogue states specifically, was acquired from James Wellington.[20]

In 1741, Richard Wellington II listed a 1/3 × 5/9 share, which was bought in one lot by Daniel Browne.[21] In 1749 he offered another 1/3 × 5/9 share, again in a single lot.[22] This one was sold to the omnipresent Charles Corbett. Since young Richard started out with only one 1/3 × 5/9 share, he must have bought the share of one of his brothers. Since James had only half of his original 1/3 × 5/9 share left after 1738, Richard must have bought Bethel's share. This makes sense: both Richard and James were booksellers, but Bethel never seems to have entered the Trade.

At this point, the only share of 'Wellington's Copies' not accounted for is the 1/6 × 5/9 fraction still owned by James Wellington. I do not know what happened to it, but the share of this size that came up at the 1765 sale of Charles Hitch[23] may be it.

The history of 'Wellington's Copies' from Richard Wellington I's death in 1715 until the middle of the century may be summarised as follows:

1715	Richard Wellington I dies.
1719	Mary Wellington puts her 4/9 share and her children's 5/9 share in trust with Darby, Bettesworth, and Clay.
1721	Mary Wellington marries John Poulson.
1726	Mary Poulson dies.
1728	Poulson contests the ownership of his wife's 4/9 share,
1730	Poulson wins House of Lords decision.
1733	John Darby dies.
c. 1734	Poulson sells his 4/9 share, perhaps in equal parts to Feales and Corbett. Richard and James Wellington come of age.
c. 1735	Bethel Wellington comes of age.
1737	Feales 2/9 dispersed (sold largely to Richard Chandler, at whose

	sales in 1742 and 1745 the copyrights later come up). Charles Corbett begins trafficking in Wellington shares.
before 1738	James Wellington sells half his share to Corbett.
1741	Richard Wellington II sells a 1/3 × 5/9 share to Daniel Browne.
by 1748	Bethel Wellington sells his 1/3 × 5/9 share to Richard II, who sells it to Corbett.
before 1765	James sells half his share to Charles Hitch.

In the 1730s and afterwards there are a good many editions and reprints of the collected works of Shakespeare, and, as the Wellington shares were split up and sold and resold, the imprints of these editions become increasingly complex. In 1740, for example, the imprint of the second Theobald edition of the collected works has the names of H. Lintott, C. Hitch, J. and R. Tonson, C. Corbett, R. and B. Wellington, J. Brindley, and E. New. The imprint of the 1765 Samuel Johnson edition lists J. and R. Tonson, H. Woodfall, J. Rivington, R. Baldwin, L. Hawes, Clark and Collins, T. Longman, W. Johnston, T. Caslon, C. Corbett, T. Lowndes, and the executors of B. Dod. Confronted by an increasingly complex imprint, the proprietors of the Shakespeare copyrights sometimes took refuge in the formula: printed for J. and R. Tonson and the Rest of the Proprietors.

Between the trade-sale catalogue entries and the imprints we can explain practically all of the successive changes in ownership of the copyright of the collected works of Shakespeare—or nearly so. A systematic analysis of these imprints reveals certain anomalies. The edition of the collected works edited by Sir Thomas Hanmer and published in 1744 bears an Oxford imprint. This is easily explained. Hanmer and the University Press contested the right of Tonson and the other proprietors to the Shakespeare copyrights on the grounds that perpetual copyright had been abolished by the Act of Queen Anne—the point was, indeed, moot through this whole period. And though Tonson and his associates might use the courts to stop a pirate like Robert Walker, stopping Oxford was another matter. Unwilling to institute an action in Chancery, the proprietors compromised.[24]

Another anomaly in the Shakespeare imprints in the 1740s was the presence of the name of John Osborn (of Paternoster Row) alone on the imprint of an edition of the collected works published in 1747. It has been suggested that Osborn's edition 'was the result of an innocent error, and Tonson generously bought up the sheets and issued them with his own imprint';[25] what in fact happened is a good deal more entertaining.

In a series of pamphlets published in the late 1760s and early 1770s concerned with the question of perpetual copyright,[26] John Osborn is several times mentioned as an example of a bookseller who had been able to defy the London copyright monopolists' contention that common-law rights to literary property were prior to those vested in the 1710 Copyright Act: in about 1746 or 1747,

J. Osborn, a bookseller of property in Pater Noster Row, having quarrelled with his brethren, began printing very correct and cheap editions of some of their copies.[27]

In particular, he put out editions of Shakespeare and Milton. When threatened with a lawsuit, Osborn

... calmly answered, That, if they talked any more to him in that Style, he would print a Dozen of Books to which they had such pretended Rights.[28]

The outraged booksellers nevertheless

... found no resource but tempting him, by bribery, to quit his project. About the year 1750, they found means to induce him (it is said, by an annuity of 200 l.) to quit business.[29]

And Osborn, according to one of these pamphlets in 1774, 'enjoys [his pension] at this Hour.'[30] The booksellers were forced to buy up Osborn's edition of Shakespeare *at his price* (that is, what remained of it),[31] and Osborn happily left off trade.[32]

Richard Wellington I owned a large number of valuable copyrights —more than 200 of them are listed in the 1737 Feales trade-sale catalogue. The Wellington list included major copyrights of Milton, Dryden, Beaumont and Fletcher, Otway, Vanbrugh, Davenant, and many others, especially playwrights, and these copyrights were divided after his death in the same manner as those of the collected works of Shakespeare referred to above. Thus the Wellington 1/4 share of *Paradise Lost* (the other 3/4, inevitably, being owned by the Tonsons) was, beginning at the 1737 Feales trade sale, split up among an increasingly large number of London booksellers, and by 1739, when the exact fractions of ownership in the work were listed in connection with a lawsuit brought by Tonson and the other proprietors against Robert Walker, the division of the 1/4 part included the following:

John New, 1/9
Samuel Birt, $1/2 \times 1/9$
Richard Wellington II, $1/3 \times 5/9$
John Oswald, $1/4 \times 1/3 \times 5/9$

And so forth.[33] As with the copyright of the collected works of Shakespeare, the descent of ownership from Richard Wellington I to these later owners can be worked out by comparing imprints with relevant trade-sale catalogue entries—though one must remember that the Tonsons had a rather autocratic habit of putting their name, and their name alone, on the title pages of important literary works whether or not they owned quite all of the copyrights, and that imprint evidence thus sometimes obscures the multiple ownership of the copyrights of Wellington-*et-fils* and the Tonsons.[34]

The general lines of the ownership of the copyright of Shakespeare's collected works after 1737 are clear: a third of it was owned by Wellington, then by his heirs, and finally by an increasingly large number of London booksellers. The other 2/3 was owned by the Tonsons. But two questions remain to be answered: how did the 1/3–2/3 split between Wellington and Tonson come about; and why is it that the Tonsons owned all of the copyright of some of the individual plays, 2/3 of others, and no part of the rest? The two questions are closely connected.

Unfortunately, there are rather few editions—and therefore, imprints—of individual Shakespeare plays before the 1730s, at which time there begin to be a great many. There were a good number of earlier editions of *adaptations* of individual Shakespeare plays—Tate's *Lear*, for instance—but these are of no use, since the trade-sale catalogues make perfectly clear that the copyright of the original *Lear* and the one of the Tate adaptation were two separate items of literary property, without connection: the same was true of the original *Antony and Cleopatra* and Dryden's *All For Love*, the original *Macbeth* and the Davenant adaptation, and so forth. In seeking information about the copyright owners of the Shakespeare plays themselves we are restricted to plain text versions.

Wellington set up in business as a bookseller in about 1697. Many of his copyrights had previously been owned by Richard Bentley, who died in that year. In the months after Bentley's death the name K. Bentley appears on the imprints of some of his books; this was Bentley's widow, Katherine, who may have disposed of her husband's copyrights to Wellington.

Richard Bentley was in business by himself during the period 1688–97. For some years earlier (1683–7) he was in partnership with S. Magnes; before 1683, his partnership was with Mary Magnes (1677–82), and for a short time before that, with James Magnes. Presumably, therefore, Richard Bentley was in partnership first with James, then with James's widow Mary, and finally with their son, Samuel, before withdrawing from the partnership and going on by himself. The evidence for this succession of partnerships derives from the imprints of the books they published. For example, Wycherley's *Plain Dealer* was first published for James Magnes and Richard Bentley in 1677; the second edition has the same imprint. Another edition (1678) was published for Richard Bentley and Mary Magnes; another, in 1686, for Richard Bentley and S. Magnes; another, in 1691, for Bentley alone; another, in 1700, for Richard Wellington (and E. Rumball; Rumball was for a few years a partner of Wellington, but when this partnership was dissolved in about 1704, Rumball's share—if any—of their copyrights remained with Wellington). If one has the patience, one can make up lists of many of the previous owners of the copyrights of books eventually owned by Bentley, and after him by Wellington.

Such lists, together with what evidence the Stationers' Company registers provide, explain how Richard Wellington came to own the copyright of *Othello*. Imprint evidence is scarce, but the copyright seems to have belonged successively to Thomas Walkley (1622); Richard Hawkins (1630); Mead and Meredith (1638); William Leake (1639); Leake, Bentley and M. Magnes (1681), Bentley and S. Magnes (1687), Bentley alone (1695), Richard Wellington (1705).[35]

Similarly, the copyright of *Hamlet* was owned by John Smethwick (1607), Francis Smethwick (1642), Miles Flesher (1642), John Martyn and Henry Herringman (1676), Herringman and Richard Bentley (1683), Bentley alone (1695), Richard Wellington (1703).[36]

Another example is *Julius Caesar*, owned by Herringman and Bentley (1684), who still owned it in 1695.[37] The Tonsons claimed 2/3 of this copyright in 1767 and Richard Wellington I owned the other third, according to the 1737 Feales catalogue. Presumably, then, the Herringman share of *Julius Caesar* was 2/3, sold by him either directly or at one or more removes to Tonson. Similarly, *Macbeth* was owned jointly by Herringman and Bentley (1687) and later by Tonson and Wellington in a 2/3–1/3 proportion.[38]

Of the other 12 plays that the Tonsons owned 2/3 of in 1767, there are an insufficient number of editions before 1700 to be at all sure who owned the copyrights in the seventeenth century. Then there are the 20 plays in the 1767 list to which the Tonsons claimed entire ownership. Again, lack of editions defeats an attempt to determine precisely how the Tonsons acquired them. In order to get any idea of what happened, both to the 20 wholly-owned plays and the 14 partially-owned ones, we must rely on evidence from the Stationers' Company registers—very incomplete evidence, but at least less so for the seventeenth century than for the eighteenth.

Giles E. Dawson summarises, in so far as they are known, the arrangements made by Jaggard and Blount with the copyright owners of Shakespeare's plays in order to include 36 of them in the First Folio.[39] They registered 16 of the plays in their own names in 1623, and they had to negotiate for the rights to the other 20. The names of John Smethwick and William Aspley, who between them owned the copyrights of six of the plays, also appear on the title page of the First Folio, suggesting that they were joint undertakers in the venture with Jaggard and Blount.[40]

In 1627, Dorothy Jaggard assigned her deceased husband's share of the Shakespeare copyrights to Thomas and Richard Cotes—this would be a 1/2 share of the 16 plays owned by Jaggard and Blount as of 1623.[41] In 1630, Edward Blount assigned his share of the same property to Robert Allot.[42] The imprint of the Second Folio (1632) bears the names of Cotes and Allot, together with those of Smethwick, Aspley, and two new ones, Richard Hawkins and Richard Meighan. Hawkins by this time owned *Othello*, and Meighan owned four other Shakespeare plays—but why they should appear on the imprint of the Second Folio when the previous owners of their Shakespeare copyrights, Thomas Walkley and Arthur Johnson, did not on the First, I have no idea.[43]

In 1637, the Allot share of the Shakespeare copyrights was transferred by his widow to John Legate and Andrew Crooke,[44] but this was a forced sale caused by Mrs. Allot's desire to marry Philip Chetwynd, who was not a member of the Stationers' Company. Chetwynd later contested the sale, and by 1663, when the Third Folio appeared, he may have established his right to the Allot share—though, since his name appears alone on the imprint of the Third Folio, without any representation from the Jaggard–Cotes side of the original partnership, perhaps not.

In 1674, the Cotes share of the property was sold by E. Cotes, the widow of Richard, to John Martyn and Henry Herringman.[45] In 1683, the Martyn share went to Robert Scott,[46] and in 1709 it eventually came to Tonson[47]—that is, Martyn's half share of the Cotes half share of the 16 plays registered by Jaggard and Blount in 1623.

The imprint of the Fourth Folio (1685) lists the names of Henry Herringman, E. Brewster, R. Chiswell, and Richard Bentley. What relationship existed among them I cannot say. But Richard Bentley's copyrights went to Richard Wellington, and by 1737, 'Wellington's Copies' included a 1/3 interest in the collected works of Shakespeare. Bentley's share in the Fourth Folio, therefore, may have been 1/3. The Herringman-Brewster-Chiswell share would then have amounted to 2/3, and the Tonsons *eventually* acquired it. We know that Tonson bought the Herringman copyrights,[48] and Richard Chiswell may figure here simply as a distributor for Herringman, without a share in the copyright. But what about Brewster? There is some evidence that he bought at least some copyrights from Philip Chetwynd,[49] but though I have checked every Brewster entry in Wing, I cannot draw any relevant conclusions either to the way in which he acquired most of his copyrights, or what happened to them after he left off trade; nor am I as certain as Mr. Farr that the Chetwynd share of the copyright of Shakespeare passed to Brewster—there is too little evidence to tell. Mr. Dawson is, perhaps, overbold when he states that 'it may be said that no copyright in Shakespeare's Dramatic Works existed in the 17th century'; and that though 'separate plays and groups of plays passed from hand to hand by sale and bequest ... only the ownership of a large number of these entitled a man to initiate the publication of a collected edition.'[50] But I admit that I cannot present any concrete evidence to show that the copyright to the collected works was considered separately from the copyrights to the individual plays before 1737.

Leaving speculation behind for a moment, there is another piece of information to consider—the 1767 Tonson sale catalogue listing of the fractions of the individual plays claimed by that firm. This claim included a 2/3 right to fourteen plays and the whole right to twenty more, and no right in *Hamlet* and *Othello*. You would think that there would *have* to be some relationship between the original sixteen Jaggard and Blount plays and the Tonson percentages, as well as one between them and the plays owned in 1632 by Smethwick, Aspley, Hawkins, and Meighan, but there seems to be no such relationship. Tonson claimed a 2/3 right to the copyrights of seven of the original 16 Jaggard and Blount plays and a 100 per cent share of the other nine. He claimed a 2/3 right to *I Henry IV*, owned in 1639 by John Norton, and a 100 per cent right to *Richards II and III*, owned in 1634 by Norton. He claimed a 100 per cent right to *Love's Labour's Lost*, *Taming of the Shrew*, and *Romeo and Juliet*, which had been owned in the seventeenth century by the Smethwicks, and no right at all to *Hamlet*, which they had also owned. He claimed a 2/3 right to *Much Ado About Nothing*, owned in 1602 by Aspley, and a 100 per cent right to *II Henry IV*, also owned in 1602 by Aspley. There seems to be no relationship at all between the Tonson percentages and the seventeenth-century owners of the copyrights.

The order of the 1767 Tonson list follows that of the 1723–5 edition of Pope's Shakespeare, but there is no relationship evident to me between this order and the various percentages of the copyrights owned by Tonson: the first four plays on the list are *The Tempest*, *Midsummer Night's Dream*, *Two Gentlemen of Verona*, and *The Merry Wives of Windsor*; Tonson claimed 2/3 of the individual copyrights to all of these except *Two Gentlemen of Verona*, of which he claimed the whole. *The Tempest* and *Two Gentlemen of Verona* were among the original 16 Jaggard and Blount plays; *Midsummer Night's Dream* and *The Merry Wives of Windsor* were not.

The order of the Tonson list and of the Pope edition varies from that of the Rowe editions, which follow the order of the four Folios. The best I can suggest, then, is that the Tonson list was drawn up for the Impression Book sometime after the 1723 publication of the Pope edition of the collected works. An edition of *Macbeth* published in 1729 contains the imprint: Printed for J. Tonson, J. Darby, A. Bettesworth, and F. Clay in trust for R., J., and B. Wellington, and a variant of this formula also figures in some of the volumes of the 1728 Pope edition. By 1728, then, Tonson and the Wellington trustees seem to have come to some sort of agreement by which they settled the ownership of the copyright of the collected works and established shares of the copyrights of the individual plays, but I have so far been unable to determine the criteria used in reaching such a settlement.

NOTES

1. There are three extant collections of 18th-century booksellers' trade-sale catalogues, all with manuscript annotation giving the buyers' names and the prices paid. They are (1) the catalogues annotated by Aaron Ward and his son John, now in the John Johnson collection in the Bodleian Library, covering the period 1718–52 in 122 catalogues; (2) the catalogues of John Osborn and his successors the Longmans, now deposited in the British Library, covering the period 1718–68 in 168 catalogues (and including the 1767 Tonson one); and (3) the catalogues of John Murray and his successors, still in the possession of the firm, covering with gaps the period 1768–95.
2. No. 58 in the Ward collection; No. 27 in the Longman collection.
3. See *Admons.*, November 1715, in the probate records at the Public Record Office.
4. Control of the Wellington copyrights was disputed in a lawsuit which went to

the House of Lords in 1730. The House of Lords Library contains copies of the printed *Appellants Case* and *The Case of the Respondent John Poulson*, from which this information is drawn.

5. Poulson was almost certainly not concerned with the book trade, but I know nothing about him except where he is concerned with the Wellingtons.

6. *Appellants Case*, p. 1; *Respondent*, pp. 1–2.

7. *Appellants Case*, p. 2; *Respondent*, p. 2.

8. See *Admons.*, November 1726. Letters of administration were granted to Poulson.

9. *Journal of the House of Lords*, vol. 23, p. 569: Saturday, 9 May 1730.

10. That is, his name appeared alone on those books whose copyrights he owned all of. Many of the copyrights were owned jointly by Wellington and other booksellers.

11. See for example the 1719 edition of *Paradise Lost*, 'Printed for M. Wellington, over-against St. Clement's Church in the Strand.' Other issues of this volume have another title-page, with Tonson's name alone on the imprint. While it was more customary for there to be one title-page with a single imprint combining the names of all of the copyright owners, the practice of separate title-pages for each of the proprietors was not particularly uncommon (although one associates the practice more with the 17th than with the 18th century).

12. The trustees' names appear much more frequently than that of Mary Wellington Poulson, but for an example of the latter, see the 1722 edition of the novels of Aphra Behn. I have no idea why the trustees and Mrs. Poulson didn't simply stick to one form or the other (or use everybody's names, as they occasionally also did).

13. On the imprint of the 1732 edition of *Paradise Lost*.

14. His name is on the imprint of the 1732 edition of *Paradise Lost* but not on the 1734 edition of the works of Nathaniel Lee.

15. Richard and James are on the imprint of the 1734 edition of Lee. All three brothers are listed in their own right on the imprint of the 1735 edition of the works of Wycherley.

16. No. 61 in the Ward collection.

17. No. 81 in the Ward collection.

18. No. 87 in the Ward collection.

19. For a discussion of the variegated activities of Charles Corbett, see Chapter IV of my unpublished Columbia University dissertation, 'Booksellers' Sales of Copyright: Aspects of the London Book Trade 1718–1768' (New York, 1970).

20. No. 64 in the Ward collection; No. 29 in the Longman collection.

21. No. 86 in the Ward collection.

22. No. 113 in the Ward collection; No. 52 in the Longman collection.

23. No. 139 in the Longman collection.

24. Giles E. Dawson, 'Warburton, Hanmer, and the 1745 Edition of Shakespeare', *Studies in Bibliography*, II (1949–50), pp. 35–48.

25. Giles E. Dawson, 'Robert Walker's Editions of Shakespeare', in *Studies in the English Renaissance Drama in Memory of Karl Julius Holzknecht*, ed. Josephine W. Bennett, Oscar Cargill, and Vernon Hall, Jr. (New York, 1959), p. 58.

26. The most convenient list of these pamphlets is in the 'Book Production and Distribution' section of vol. 2 of the *New Cambridge Bibliography of English Literature* (Cambridge, 1971), cols. 286–8.

27. 'The Humble Petition of sundry Booksellers of London and Westminster', in

Petitions and Papers relating to The Bill of the Booksellers, now Before the House of Commons [London, 1774], p. 5.

28. *Considerations on the Nature and Origin of Literary Property* (Edinburgh, 1767), pp. 13–14. Here Osborn is mistakenly called Thomas Osborne.

29. 'The Humble Petition', in *Petitions and Papers*, p. 5.

30. *Observations on the Case of the Booksellers of London and Westminster* [London, 1774]. British Museum pressmark 215.i.4.(99).

31. *Considerations*, p. 14.

32. Osborn's trade-sale catalogues are Nos. 118 and 118* in the Ward collection and Nos. 55 and 56 in the Longman collection. The Folger and the Birmingham Shakespeare Library own copies of the Osborn edition of Shakespeare with the uncancelled title page.

33. R. C. Bald, 'Early Copyright Litigation and its Bibliographical Interest', *PBSA*, XXXVI (1942), p. 94.

34. See n. 11.

35. W. W. Greg, *A Bibliography of the English Printed Drama to the Restoration* (London, 1939–59), pp. 523–6; there is a copy of the 1705 Wellington edition at the New York Public Library.

36. Greg, pp. 311–5.

37. Ibid., 552–4.

38. See ibid., pp. 555–6; but there is some confusion here in the ownership of the copyright of the original version and of the Davenant adaptation which I have not yet sorted out. The Davenant version eventually ended up the entire property of Tonson; the genealogy of the original goes through Herringman, Bentley, and Wellington.

39. I am much indebted for what follows to his article, 'The Copyright of Shakespeare's Dramatic Works', in *Studies in Honor of A. H. R. Fairchild*, vol. xxi of *University of Missouri Studies* (Columbia, Missouri, 1946), pp. 11–35; for Jaggard and Blount, see pp. 15–17.

40. Ibid., p. 16.

41. Ibid., p. 17; Greg, p. 35.

42. Dawson, 'Copyright . . .', p. 18; Greg, p. 39.

43. The copyright of the collected works *may* by now have existed independently of that of the individual plays, but it probably did not. The Cotes and Allot variant imprint of the Second Folio appears on about 80 per cent of the copies of the edition, a reflection of their firm ownership of 16 plays plus, perhaps, a tenuous claim to about a dozen more whose copyrights by now may have been derelict. Smethwick, Aspley, Hawkins, and Meighan among them shared variant imprints on the other 20 per cent of the copies (see William B. Todd, 'The Issues and States of the Second Folio and Milton's Epitaph on Shakespeare', *Studies in Bibliography*, V (1952–3), pp. 96–7). The percentage of copies of the Second Folio allotted to the six undertakers thus seems to have been roughly proportional to the number of individual plays each one owned. But to assume that the ownership of any one of the 36 plays in the Second Folio created a 1/36 share in its collective copyright is to equate *I Henry IV* (half a dozen separately published editions before 1632) with *The Winter's Tale* (no separately published editions before 1735) and this seems illogical—though possible.

I take no credit for conclusions based on this analysis.

44. Dawson, p. 20; Greg, p. 46.
45. Dawson, p. 21; Greg, pp. 73–4.
46. Dawson, pp. 21–2; Greg, pp. 75–6.
47. Dawson, p. 25.
48. Ibid.
49. Harry Farr, 'Philip Chetwind and the Allott Copyrights', *The Library*, IV, xv, 1934, pp. 140, 158.
50. Dawson, p. 23; but see p. 27.

J. D. FLEEMAN

The revenue of a writer

Samuel Johnson's literary earnings

'No man but a blockhead ever wrote, except for money.' Johnson's dictum characteristically evades the complexities of an artist's motives, and offers only a simplified and defensive rationale. Yet it was the eighteenth century which saw the establishment of the self-supporting professional writer, and though Johnson was neither the first nor, financially, the most successful, his observation expresses the assurance of the 'author by profession' in a mercantile age.[1]

The evidence on which any account of an author's literary earnings can be based, is scanty. The following notes are an attempt to bring together the main details of Johnson's finances and to sketch the outlines of the rewards of his literature. As a diarist Johnson was irregular and as an accountant he was careless; the occasional survival of documents provides only accidental information; the evidence of payments made to him is concealed in largely uninvestigated records. A few new details have been taken from the bank records of the account of William Strahan the printer, in Gosling's bank, but their significance is still far from obvious and will have to wait for a thorough analysis of the account in conjunction with the surviving work-ledgers.[2]

The following tabular record is therefore little more than a series of rough guide-posts which may be followed only with caution in any future investigations.

1735
  1 Feb.   Lobo's *Voyage to Abyssinia* published (*Life*, i.87; *Johnsonian Gleanings*, v.97)[3]   £5– 5s.

1738
  13 May   *London, A Poem* published; copyright sold to Dodsley (*Life*, i.124)   £10–10s.

[1] Notes begin on p. 224.

	[Edward Cave sent Johnson 'a present' and printed part of the poem in the *Gentleman's Magazine*, May 1738, *Letters*, i.10, no. 6]	
2 Aug.	Began work on translation of Sarpi's *History of the Council of Trent*: 'Account between Edward Cave and Sam. Johnson, in relation to a version of Father Paul, &c. begun Aug. 2 1738; by which it appears that from that day to April 21. 1739, Johnson received for that work 49l. 7s. in sums of one, two, three, and sometimes four guineas at a time, most frequently two. . . .' (*Life*, i.135–6; *Lit. Anec.*, v. 27–28)	£49– 7s.
	Began editorial work on the *Gentleman's Magazine* at £100 p.a. (*Life*, i.115 'a regular coadjutor', also i.532, and A. Chalmers, *General Biographical Dictionary*, xix (1815) 53–6.)	£100
1739	Editorial work on the *Gentleman's Magazine*	£100
1740	Editorial work on the *Gentleman's Magazine*	£100
1741	Editorial work on the *Gentleman's Magazine*	£100
1742	Editorial work on the *Gentleman's Magazine*	£100
4 Feb.	No. 1 of Robert James's *Medicinal Dictionary* published; Johnson contributed and wrote the Dedication to Dr Mead (*Life*, i.159 n)	£5– 5s.
1743	Editorial work on the *Gentleman's Magazine*	£100
Autumn	Work on 'our Historical Design' (*Letters*, i. 20, no. 15)	£13– 2s.– 6d.
14 Dec.	Receipt for copyright of *Life of Savage* (*Life*, i.165 n; *MS. Handlist*, 34)	£15–15s.
1744	Editorial work on the *Gentleman's Magazine*[4]	£100
1745	Correction of S. Madden's *Boulter's Monument* (*Life*, i.318; *Johns. Misc.*, ii.212)	£10–10s.
1746		
18 June	Contract for *Dictionary* signed (Hawkins, *Life of Johnson*, 2nd ed. 1787, 345 n) *see* 1755.	
1749		
August	*Plan of a Dictionary* published; Lord Chesterfield made a present of £10 (*Life*, i.261 n)	£10
1748		
25 Nov	Receipt for copywright of *Vanity of Human Wishes* (*Life*, i.193 n; *Poems*, 110)	£15–15s.

1749		
Feb.	Receipts from performance of *Irene* (*Life*, i. 198 n, *Poems*, 276 n)	£195-17s.
8 Sept.	Receipt for copyright of *Irene* sold to Dodsley (*Life*, i.198 n; *MS. Handlist*, 44)	£100
1750		
20 March– 29 Dec.	*Ramblers* nos. 1–82 (two essays per week; parts of nos. 10 & 15, and nos. 30 and 44 not by Johnson; say 3 essays = 79 × 2 gns each).[5]	£165-18s.
1751		
1 Jan.– 31 Dec.	*Ramblers* nos. 83–187 (except part of no. 107 and nos. 97 and 100; say 3, = 102 × 2 gns)	£214- 4s.
18 April	Asks John Newbery for £2 (*Letters*, i.36, no. 32)[6]	£2
21 June	Strahan's bank account: 'To Mr Johnson'	£18-18s.
29 July	Asks Newbery for 1 gn 'for which I will account to you on some future production' (*Letters*, i.37, no. 33)	£1- 1s.
24 Aug.	Asks Newbery for another guinea (*Letters*, i.38, no. 34)	£1- 1s.
1752		
4 January– 14 March	*Ramblers* nos. 188–208 = 21 × 2 gns	£44- 2s.
17 March	Pays off a mortgage on the Lichfield house on the proceeds of the sale of 'a property' which was either a share or the copyright in the *Rambler*. (*Letters*, i.42–3, no. 40)[7]	£100
1753		
3 March– 29 Dec.	24 essays for Hawkesworth's *Adventurer* (*Life*, i.253: Yale ed. of *Johnson's Works*, ii. 1963, pp. 323 ff.), at 2 gns. per paper	£50- 8s.
1754		
19 Jan.– 2 March	5 essays for the *Adventurer*	£10-10s.
1755		
15 April	*A Dictionary of the English Language* published	£1575[8]
Dec.	Richard Rolt's *Dictionary of Trade & Commerce* published, with Preface by Johnson (*Life*, i. 358–9)	£3- 3s.[9]

1756
- 16 March — Samuel Richardson[10] sends 6 gns. to free Johnson from an arrest for a debt of £5–18s. (*Letters*, i.86, 89, nos. 90, 94) — £6– 6s.
- 2 June — Contract with Tonson for a new edition of Shakespeare (*Life*, i.545; *MS. Handlist*, 76) see 1765 below.

1757
- 1 January — No. 1 of the *London Chronicle* published; Johnson wrote the introductory article (*Life*, i.317) — £1– 1s.
- 8 June — Loan from Tonson (*MS. Handlist*, 77) — £100
- 6 Aug. — Receipt for 2 gns. from Andrew Millar (*MS. Handlist*, 78) — £2– 2s.
- 10 Sept. — Loan from Tonson (*MS. Handlist*, 77) — £26– 5s.

1758
- 10 Feb. — Loan from Tonson 'when you was arrested' (*Letters*, i.105, no. 112.1, *MS. Handlist*, 77) — £40
- 8 April–30 Dec. — 'Idler' essays in the weekly *Universal Chronicle*: 39 essays, less 3 written by others, = 36 × 3 gns. per paper.[11] — £113– 8s.

1759
- January–December — 'Idler' essays: 52 less 6, = 46 at 3 gns. — £144–18s.
- 19 March — Promissory note for £42–19s.–10d. to John Newbery (*Letters*, ed. Hill (1892), i.24 n.)[12]
- 19 April — *Prince of Abissinia* [= *Rasselas*] published (*Life*, i.341 n; *Johns. Misc.* i.415); copyright sold to Johnston and Dodsley[13] — £100
- 21 May & 22 June — Receipt for £25 for 2nd ed. of *Rasselas* paid in three instalments (*MS. Handlist*, 80). — £25

1760
- January–5 April — 'Idler' essays: 14 less 3, = 11 at 3 gns. — £34–13s.
- 20 March — Promissory note for £30 to Newbery (*Letters*, ed. Hill (1892), i.24 n)
- 21 April — Strahan's Sharebook (B.L. Add. MS. 48805) purchase of a third share in *Rasselas* from Johnson — £33– 6s.– 8d.[14]
- August — *Proceedings of the Committee for the Cloathing*

1761	*French Prisoners of War* published by Thomas Hollis, with Introduction by Johnson (*Life*, iv.491)[15]	£5– 5s.
	The Idler published by Newbery in 2 vols., 12°, Johnson paid for a 2/3 share (*Life*, i.335 n).	£84– 2s.– 4d.
1762		
19 July[16]	Civil list pension of £300 p.a. awarded to Johnson, payable quarterly (*Life*, i.376 n)	£150
1763	Pension	£300
April	Review of Graham's *Telemachus* in the *Critical Review* (*Life*, i.411)	10s.– 6d.[17]
1764	Pension	£300
October	Review of Grainger's *Sugar Cane* in the *Critical Review* (*Life*, i. 481–2 & n.)	
December	Notice of Goldsmith's *The Traveller* in *Critical Review* (*Life*, i.482).	£1–11s.– 6.
1765	Pension (the first and third quarterly payments are noted in Johnson's *Diaries* on 28 Jan. (p. 88), and 16 July (p. 96))	£300
10 Oct.	*The Dramatic Works of William Shakespeare* published, 8 vols. (1,000 copies); 2nd ed., 8 vols. (750 copies) published: 5 November. According to the contract with Tonson (2 June 1756, *above*), Johnson was to get 250 sets free for his subscribers. The subscription was 2 gns. Furthermore he was to have sets at 1 gn. each for subscribers in excess of 250. The first edition sold out in less than a month; Birch 'understood' that the subscribers numbered about 750. That number ought to have brought Johnson £1050, but no sources agree on such a figure, and instead record much smaller sums: £262–10s. and £375.[18]	£262–10s.
1766	Pension (the first quarterly payment is noted in Johnson's *Diaries* on 6 Jan (p. 101).)	£300
1767	Pension	£300
1768	Pension	£300[19]
1769	Pension	£300
28 Nov.	Strahan's bank account: 'To Mr Johnson'	£20
1770	Pension	£300

1771	Pension	£300
1772	Pension	£300
13 May	Strahan's bank account: 'To Sam¹ Johnson'	£51- 7s.
20 Oct.[20]	Strahan's bank account: 'To Dr Johnson'[21]	£15
22 Dec.	Strahan's bank account: 'To Dr Johnson'	£49-10s.
1773	Pension	£300
25 Jan.	Fourth edition (revised) of the folio *Dictionary* published. Johnson was paid for 'improvements' (*Life*, ii.498).	£300
1774	Pension	£300
8 Feb.	Strahan's bank account: 'To Sam Johnson'	£35- 7s.
18 May	Strahan's bank account: 'To S. Johnson'	£16- 2s.
27 Aug.[22]	Strahan's bank account: 'To Dr Johnson'	£10
3 Oct.	Strahan's bank account: 'To Dr Johnson'	£10-10s.
28 Dec.	Strahan's bank account: 'To Dr Johnson'	£5
1775	Pension	£300
3 Jan.	Strahan's bank account: 'To Dr Johnson'	£10-10s.
14 Feb.	Strahan's bank account: 'To Dr Johnson'	£100
	On this same date Strahan's sharebook (Brit. Mus. Add. MS. 48805) notes a payment for a third share in Johnson's 'Tour' [i.e. *Journey to the Western Islands of Scotland*], published on 18 January	£70[23]
24 Feb.	Strahan's bank account: 'To Dr Johnson'	£10-15s.
25 March	Strahan's bank account: 'To Dr Johnson'	£20
1 May	Strahan's bank account: 'To Dr Johnson'	£25
22 May[24]	Strahan's bank account: 'To Dr Johnson'	£61-19s.
1776	Pension	£300
1 Jan.	Strahan's ledger account 'Debts owing by William Strahan at the first of January 1776' (Brit. Mus. Add. MS. 48808): 'Dr Samuel Johnson'	£141-11s.
16 March	Receipt of payment by C. Rivington (*MS. Handlist*, 143)[25]	£100
1777	Pension	£300
15 July	Strahan's bank account: 'To Dr Johnson'	£61- 3s.[26]
4 Nov.	Johnson's *Diaries* (p. 281) list:	

'Mr Strahan owes me   110–0–0
  For Scotland
  For Pamplets
  For Edition of Polit.
  For Dictionary
  For in hand   81–0–0'[27]

SAMUEL JOHNSON'S EARNINGS

6 Nov.[28]	Received from Strahan (*Diaries*, p. 283)	£10
9 Nov.[29]	Received from Strahan (*Diaries*, p. 283)	£20
13 Nov.	Strahan's bank account: 'To Dr Johnson' £20.[30]	
8 Dec.	Received from Strahan (*Diaries*, p. 284)	£6– 6s.
10 Dec.	Received from Strahan (*Diaries*, p. 285)	£10
31 Dec.	Received from Strahan (*Diaries*, p. 286)	£3– 3s.
1778	Pension	£300
28 Jan.	Strahan's bank account: 'To Dr Johnson'	£15.
31 Jan.	Strahan's bank account: 'To Dr Johnson'	£74
12 Feb.	Strahan's bank account: 'To Dr Johnson'	£6
20 June	Strahan's bank account: 'To Dr Johnson'	£7– 7s.
5 Oct.	Strahan's bank account: 'To Dr Johnson'	£15
26 Nov.	Strahan's bank account: 'To Dr Johnson'	£18– 9s.– 8d.
1779	Pension	£300
19 April	Strahan's bank account 'To Dr Johnson'	£68–17s.–10d.
21 May[31]	Strahan's bank account: 'To Dr Johnson'	£30
23 June	Johnson deposited £100 with Henry Thrale (*Letters*, ii.296, no. 622)[32]	
3 Aug.	Strahan's bank account: 'To Dr Johnson'	£20
8 Sept.	Strahan's bank account: 'To Dr Johnson'	£10–18s.
20 Nov.	Strahan's bank account: 'To Dr Johnson'	£20
1780	Pension	£300
12 April	Strahan's bank account: 'To Dr Johnson'	£50
19 Oct.[33]	Strahan's bank account: 'To Dr Johnson'	£25
1781	Pension	£300
15 Feb.	Strahan's bank account: 'To Dr Johnson'	£18
2 March	Strahan's bank account: 'To Dr Johnson'	£7– 8s.
29 March	Strahan's bank account: 'To Dr Johnson'	£52–11s.
12 April[34]	Strahan's bank account: 'To Dr Johnson'	£20
11 May	Strahan's bank account: 'To Dr Johnson'	£10
15 May	Second and final instalment of *Prefaces to the Poets* published (first four vols. published 31 March 1779); John Nichols was chief proprietor (*Life*, iii.111, iv.35).	£315[35]
2 Oct.[36]	Strahan's bank account: 'To Dr Johnson'	£19– 2s.
1782	Pension	£300
20 March	Received from Strahan (*Diaries*, p. 315)	£50
25 March	Received from Strahan (*Diaries*, p. 317); Strahan's account on this date records the payment to Johnson of £78–14s.–6d.	
5 Aug.	Received from Strahan (*Diaries*, p. 322)	£5– 5s.
12 Aug.	Received from Strahan (*Diaries*, p. 323)	£3– 3s.

17 Aug.	Received from Strahan (*Diaries*, p. 324)	£4- 4s.
24 Aug.	Received from Strahan (*Diaries*, p. 326)	£4- 4s.
7 Sept.	Received from Strahan (*Diaries*, p. 330)	£5- 5s.
14 Sept.	Received from Strahan (*Diaries*, p. 331)	£4- 4s.
24 Sept.	Received from Strahan (*Diaries*, p. 334)	£4- 4s.
30 Sept.	Received from Strahan (*Diaries*, p. 335)	£4- 4s.
5 Oct.[37]	Received from Strahan (*Diaries*, p. 337)	£20
21 Nov.[38]	'Fund received from Mr Strahan for taxes &c. 3-3-0 of which remains 8-3½' (*Diaries*, p. 352)	£3- 3s.
8 Dec.	Received from Strahan (*Diaries*, p. 354)	£3- 5s.
14 Dec.	Received from Strahan (*Diaries*, p. 356) 'I think'[39]	£5- 5s.
21 Dec.	Received from Strahan (*Diaries*, p. 356) 'I think'	£5- 5s.
1783	Pension (Receipt for 27 March in *MS. Handlist*, 197)[40]	£300
29 Jan.	Strahan's bank account: 'To Dr Johnson'	£30
19 Feb.	Receipt for revising the text of the *Lives of the Poets* (*Life*, iv.35 n, 480; *MS. Handlist*, 195)	£100[41]
8 May	Strahan's bank account: 'To Dr Johnson'	£40
10 July[42]	Strahan's bank account: 'To Dr Johnson'	£30
27 Nov.	Strahan's bank account: 'To Dr Johnson'	£7-11s.
1784	Pension (Receipts for 3rd and 4th quarters: *MS. Handlist*, 229 and 231)	£300
22 Jan.	Receipt for copyright of *Journey* (*MS. Handlist*, 211)	£150
10 May	Strahan's bank account: 'To Dr Johnson'	£40
19 Oct.[43]	Strahan's bank account: 'To Dr Johnson'	£20
10 Dec.	Strahan's bank account: 'To Dr Johnson'	£88- 5s.[44]

It will be obvious that a great many of Johnson's works are not represented in the above list, and virtually none of the dozens of works by others which he furnished with Dedications or Prefaces.[45] There is no evidence to show what, if any, income Johnson may have received from the numerous reprints of his own works. He regularly retained the right to print one edition for himself, intending eventually to publish a collection of his works, but the plan came to nothing.[46] He seems to have parted with his copyrights soon after the first editions, and so may not have received anything more from them. The documents which survive are not easily seen in perspective: we do not yet know more than generalities about the profitability of firms like Bowyer's or Strahan's whose records still exist: we know even less about others who have left no records.[47] Professor Ransome's pioneering study suffered from the need to draw general inferences from limited instances.[48] Even with the information recorded in the foregoing list one is conscious of the 'crackling ice' and 'Gulphs profound' which beset this inquiry.

Johnson is known to have composed some forty sermons, but the dates of most of them are undiscovered and so they have not been included in the chronological list: he usually charged 2 guineas for a sermon, but his earnings from them were doubtless spread over many years.[49]

When Johnson came up to London to seek his fortune in March 1737, he had already had some slight dealings with Edward Cave of the *Gentleman's Magazine*, but he was also able to make use of the fact that he was the son of a bookseller. He had worked in Birmingham for Thomas Warren,[50] and he brought to London, according to Lucy Porter, a letter of introduction from Gilbert Walmesley to Henry Lintot. She added that 'Johnson wrote some things for him'.[51] Boswell was sceptical and adduced Johnson's own statement that 'Mr Cave was the first publisher by whom his pen was engaged in London'.[52] Yet in the early days Johnson approached Thomas Wilcox for assistance and was advised to 'buy a porter's knot' rather than think of a literary career.[53]

Johnson had written to Cave as early as 1734, but his use of a pseudonym, 'S. Smith', suggests that he was at that time relying less on personal influence than on intellectual merit.[54] Yet by July 1737 he was working for Cave on a translation of Sarpi's History, and receiving a fairly regular payment: the account quoted by Nichols shows that he received 47 guineas over a period of some 37 weeks, or on average a little over 26s. per week. This wage might have supported a prudent man, but Johnson was consorting with Henry Hervey Aston and Richard Savage, and he had a wife to support.[55]

This was the period of his poverty, yet by 1739, he had become a 'coadjutor' with Cave in the editing of the Magazine, at a stipend, according to Alexander Chalmers, of £100 a year. There are no records to show what he might have earned from the various pamphlets of this period, yet they are numerous enough. The special articles, reports of parliamentary debates, and various biographies published in the *Gentleman's Magazine* were no doubt considered as part of his editorial duties. There is no information to show what he might have earned for his work on the catalogue of the Harleian library in 1742–3, or for helping to arrange the materials published in the *Harleian Miscellany*, 1744–5. He may have knocked Osborne down with a Bible, but he was surely paid for his work, and at some stage Osborne gave him Theobald's copy of the second folio of Shakespeare.[56]

Though the early forties were busy for Johnson, and though 1740–1 was a year of high food prices and dearth,[57] he was probably earning more than £2 per week, and with careful management ought not to have had severe difficulties. The trouble was that Johnson almost certainly did not exercise careful management of his affairs: that he actually got through this difficult period in spite of his economic inefficiency, suggests that his earnings were sufficient to cover his and his wife's imprudence.

By 1745 he was feeling his way to larger enterprises. His proposals for a new edition of Shakespeare, supported in the year of rebellion with perceptive notes on *Macbeth*, were too enterprising for Tonson who felt his Shakespearian rights invaded.[58] Cave was not strong enough to resist and the project collapsed. In the following year Johnson committed himself to the major work of his life: on 30 April he signed and dated his manuscript 'A Short Scheme for Compiling a new Dictionary of the English Language'[59] and on 18 June he signed a contract for the compilation of the work itself.[60] The finances of this undertaking are sketchy. The contract was for 1500 guineas. Over nine years this produces an average of £175 p.a. or £3–10s. a week, from which Johnson had to pay his amanuenses.[61] It seems unlikely that the six assistants were all employed together or for the whole period of compilation. Sledd and Kolb suggest that the contracted sum ran out about the time when the first sheets were being printed,[62] and that Johnson, on being goaded to speed production, struck work on 1 November 1751;[63] they think that a revised agreement may have been made and that thereafter Johnson was paid on the delivery of copy.[64] There seems little doubt that Johnson received more money than was contracted for.[65]

During the period of compilation of the *Dictionary* Johnson engaged in other literary work: he wrote the *Rambler* twice a week for two years from March 1750 to 1752 and gained thereby a fairly regular 4 guineas a week. The death of his wife on 17 March 1752 left him responsible only for himself, though he seems to have found relief for his grief in paying off a debt of £100 on the mortgage on the Lichfield house.[66] The sale of a 'property' which produced this sum can only refer to some literary property, since Johnson had no other, and the most likely such property was the *Rambler*. From time to time he remitted money to his aged mother in Lichfield.[67]

After publication of the *Dictionary* in April 1755 Johnson cast about for some new undertaking. He toyed with the idea of a magazine of his own, but eventually became only the major contributor to the *Literary Magazine*, 1756–7, which provided an outlet for the occasional writings and reviews which he so much enjoyed.[68] The proposals for an edition of Shakespeare, issued on 1 June 1756, initiated the next phase of his major work, but there was no significant advance of money for it, and the incoming subscriptions were mismanaged.[69] He suffered the indignity of an arrest for debt in March 1756 and was released by Samuel Richardson, and again on 10 February 1758 he wrote to Tonson:

An accident has happened to me which Mr Strahan will tell you, and from which I must try to be extricated by your assistance. The affair is about forty pounds.[70]

Tonson sent the money and noted it was 'when you was arrested'. Tonson was the paymaster for the edition of Shakespeare. These incidents suggest that living alone had not improved Johnson's prudence, and that his private finances were not administered with much care. He was however able to earn a reasonably regular income of 3 guineas a week for the 'Idler' essays, the copyright of *Rasselas* brought £100 and helped to defray the expenses of his mother's funeral. Murphy, not the most reliable of witnesses, wrote:

Johnson now found it necessary to retrench his expences. He gave up his house in Gough-square. Mrs. Williams went into lodgings. He retired to Gray's-Inn, and soon removed to chambers in the Inner Temple-lane, where he lived in poverty, total idleness, and the pride of literature.[71]

This period was not for long however, for on 19 July 1762 he was awarded a Civil List pension of £300 per annum.[72]

From this time forward the pension meant that Johnson could not only remain solvent with little administrative effort, but could also save money. He seems not to have had his own bank account, but to have used Strahan as a personal banker.[73] Now that he had a substantial income Johnson could no longer operate on a simple day-to-day economy, and had to keep his money in a safe yet accessible place. Strahan's thriving business and their old acquaintance made him an easy choice.[74] Throughout the 1770s Strahan's bank account includes statements of payments to Johnson: it is possible there are earlier ones which have not been identified because Strahan, like most Scotchmen, didn't distinguish the spelling of Johnson's name from spellings like 'Johnston' or 'Johnstone' with which they were more familiar. Unfortunately the credit side of the account does not show the incoming payments of the quarterly pension. It seems that Johnson had to make his own arrangements about collecting the money from the Treasury,[75] and that he then conveyed the cash to Strahan who simply banked it together with other moneys of his own. The discrepancy between the dates of the receipt of sums noted in Johnson's diaries, and the dates of the payments from Strahan's account, suggest that Strahan sometimes supplied money from a cash float in his home or office, and then settled the account later on. The pension gave Johnson a workable figure within which to live, and it was in general beyond his expenses. Johnson rarely drew money in excess of £75 at any one time. He called on Strahan often enough for money to cover travelling expenses, or for general purposes, and no doubt Strahan kept him apprised of the state of his balance. The other credits which came from his writings, are similarly concealed in Strahan's account, and unluckily entries in Strahan's other records are left blank: we do not know what Johnson received for the political pamphlets of the early 1770s, or for the collected *Political Tracts* of 1776. Johnson did not perhaps know himself: on 5 March 1781 he wrote to Strahan:

Having now done my lives I shall have money to receive, and shall be glad to add to it, what remains due for the Hebrides, which you cannot charge me with grasping very rapaciously. The price was two hundred Guineas or pounds; I think first pounds then Guineas. I have had one hundred.

There is likewise something due for the political pamphlets, which I left without bargain to your liberality and Mr Cadel's. Of this you will likewise think that I may have all together.[76]

The final statement of Johnson's financial affairs is his will. The details are given by Boswell, and so the monetary element may be abstracted:[77]

In the hands of Bennet Langton	£750
In the hands of Mr Barclay & Mr Perkins	£300
In the hands of Dr Percy	£150
In 3% annuities 'in the publick funds'	£1000
In ready money	£100

It is curious that there is no mention of any possible credit with William Strahan, and that Langton and Percy are not otherwise known to have been involved in Johnson's finances.[78] Barclay and Perkins were the successor's of Thrale's brewery, and it has already been seen that Johnson deposited money with Henry Thrale. In addition Johnson owned his house in Lichfield, and directed that it should be sold by his executors: Hawkins recorded that it fetched £235.[79] There was also a sale of Johnson's books at Christie's from 16–19 February 1785 which brought a total of £320–9s.[80] The yield on Consols in 1784 was 5·4 per cent,[81] so that Johnson's assets at his death may be reckoned as:

Money in the hands of friends	£1200
3% annuities	1054
Ready money	100
Lichfield house	235
Library	320
	£2909.

In very rough terms it can be said that Johnson's income after 1762 was nominally in excess of £300 p.a., and it was perhaps as much as £400 for perhaps a quarter of that period. Over a 21-year period therefore the pension and his other earnings would have produced £6800, perhaps even £7000, and Johnson died worth little less than £3000. This means that he was able to save over 40 per cent of his income, despite his carelessness of money. Like many philosophers he had a clear view of the motes in the eyes of others. He reproved Langton:

I am a little angry at you for not keeping minutes of your own *acceptum et expensum*, and think a little time might be spared from Aristophanes, for the *res familiares*.[82]

Yet his diary for 1782 contains several instances of weak accounting: errors in simple addition,[83] misplacing of figures in the cash columns,[84] approximations,[85] and large omissions.[86] Johnson had a ready grasp of general economic principles in an age when the study was in its infancy.[87] He could summarise two centuries of rising living standards in a note on a Shakespearian allusion to a dowry:

Some light may be given to those who shall endeavour to calculate the encrease of *English* wealth, by observing, that *Latymer* in the time of *Edward* VI. mentions it as a proof of his father's prosperity, *That though but a yeoman, he gave his daughters five pounds each for her portion*. At the latter end of *Elizabeth*, seven hundred pounds were such a temptation to courtship, as made all other motives suspected. *Congreve* makes twelve thousand more than a counterballance to the affectation of *Belinda*. No poet would now fly his favourite character at less than fifty thousand.[88]

Yet his own economy was pure Micawber:

Make an impartial estimate of your revenue, and whatever it is, live upon less. Resolve never to be poor. Frugality is not only the basis of quiet, but of beneficence. No man can help others that wants help himself; we must have enough before we can have to spare.[89]

This advice to Boswell reveals a significant factor in Johnson's attitude towards money—charity. Dr. Maxwell told Boswell:

He frequently gave all the silver in his pockets to the poor, who watched him, between his house and the tavern where he dined.[90]

and Johnson admitted to Frances Rynolds that

as he return'd to his lodgings about one or two o'clock in the morning, he often saw poor children asleep on thresholds and stalls, and that he used to put pennies in their hands to buy them a breakfast.[91]

Such practices are not the road to riches, and it is clear that without the pension, awarded as Bute insisted 'as the reward of his literary merit'[92] and without the friendly control of William Strahan, he might have ended his days like any other Grub-Street writer.

NOTES

1. The dictum is reported in *Boswell's Life of Johnson*, ed. G. B. Hill, rev. L. F. Powell, Oxford 1934–64, iii. 19, hereafter cited as *Life*.

2. These accounts were first brought to my notice by Prof. J. L. Clifford of Columbia University. I am indebted to Miss K. Byron, the Archivist of Barclay's Bank, and to Mr. P. Philby of Gosling's Branch in Fleet Street, for permission to consult and quote from their records. As the bank was founded by Robert Gosling the bookseller, and established by his son Sir Francis, it is not surprising that many of his customers were members of the book trade. The names of Thomas Astley, William Bowyer, John Coles, William Innys, the Knaptons, Henry Lintot, Daniel Midwinter, John Nichols, Thomas Osborne, Samuel Richardson, Charles Rivington, Charles Say, the Tonsons, John Watts and Henry Woodfall, are all to be found in the ledgers, as well as the account of the Company of Stationers itself.

The entries are brief, consisting of credit and debit accounts, which simply list the dates, code numbers (presumably of notes of hand), names of persons, and finally the appropriate sum of money.

3. The following abbreviated references will be used throughout:

Diaries	*Diaries, Prayer & Annals*, vol. i. of Yale ed. of Johnson's Works, ed. D. & M. Hyde, & E. L. McAdam, 1958.
G.M.	*Gentleman's Magazine*
Gleanings	*Johnsonian Gleanings*, A. L. Reade, 11 vols., 1909–52.
Johns. Misc.	*Johnsonian Miscellanies*, ed. G. B. Hill, Oxford, 1897, 2 vols.
Letters	*The Letters of Samuel Johnson*, ed. R. W. Chapman, 3 vols., Oxford, 1952.
Lit. Anec.	J. Nichols, *Literary Anecdotes*, 9 vols., 1812–15.
MS. Handlist	*A Preliminary Handlist of Documents & MS of Samuel Johnson*, by J. D. Fleeman, Oxford, 1967.
Poems	*The Poems of Samuel Johnson*, ed. D. N. Smith & E. L. McAdam, 2nd ed., Oxford, 1973.

4. It is not certain when Johnson gave up this work, but it is unlikely that he continued after 1744.

5. Arthur Murphy in his Essay on Johnson, 1792 (*Johns. Misc.* i.393) recorded that Johnson got 4 gns. per week for the *Rambler*, so he may have been paid whether he was the author or not; but Murphy is too often unreliable for much weight to be given to his evidence. When Johnson invited Joseph Warton to contribute to the *Adventurer* (see 1753), a very similar work, he said the rate was 'two guineas a paper' (*Letters*, i.48, no. 46).

6. Johnson contributed the 'Life of Cheynel' to Newbery's *The Student*, in 1751.

7. The contract for the 2nd ed. of the *Rambler*, 1 Apr. 1751 (*MS. Handlist*, 48) mentions no payments; Johnson may not have parted with the copyright, for a revised and corrected edition was published in 1756. The payment of the sum was slow (see *Letters*, i.45, no. 42.2). For the mortgage, see *Gleanings*, iv. 2–38, esp. 8–11. Hawkins seems to have seen other evidence: 'By some papers now in my hands it seems that, notwithstanding Johnson was paid for writing the Rambler, he had a remaining interest in the copy-right of that paper, which about this time he sold' (*Life of Johnson*, 2nd ed. 1787, p. 326).

8. Hawkins wrote that Johnson received far more than the 1500 gns. contracted for, 'Of this, Johnson, who was no very accurate accountant, thought a great part would be coming to him on the conclusion of the work; but upon producing, at a tavern-meeting for the purpose of settling, receipts for sums advanced to him, which were indeed the chief means of his subsistence, it was found, not only that he had eaten his cake, but that the balance of the account was greatly against him.' (*Life of Johnson*, 1787, 2nd ed., p. 345).

9. Strahan's printing accounts (B.L. Add. MS. 48802 A, f. 16) record that Rolt was paid £65–0s.–6d. and Johnson received 3 guineas.

10. Richardson printed vol. IV of the second London edition of the *Rambler*, 6 vols., 12°, 1752. Johnson knew him certainly by 1753 (*Life*, i.145 n). Johnson's philosophy of debt is expressed in his undated letter to Joseph Simpson: 'Small debts are like small shot, they are ratling on every Side, & can scarcely be Escaped without a Wound. Great debts are like Cannon of loud noise but little danger. you must therefore be enabled to discharge petty debts that you may have leisure with security to struggle with the rest.' (*Letters*, i.126, no. 134).

11. This is the payment asserted by Thomas Birch in his letter of 25 October 1760 to Lord Hardwicke (B.L. Add. MSS. 35397–400). Hawkins claimed that Johnson also

had 'a share in the profits' of the *Universal Chronicle*, but there is no further evidence to show whether it was a profitable venture (*Life*, 1787, 2nd ed., p. 364).

12. This is an IOU presumably against an advance from Newbery against the contributions to the *Universal Chronicle*, of which he was, according to Hawkins (loc. cit.) one of the backers: his name stood alone in the imprint of the collected edition of 1761. The money involved in this note, as in that of 20 March 1760, is probably concealed in the payments for the 'Idler' essays.

13. Only Dodsley and Johnston are named in the Stationers' Register (1746–73, f. 192) as holding half-shares in the work. See 21 April 1760.

14. The original shares were halves between Johnston and Dodsley, but it seems that subsequently the plan was changed to thirds: or the entry in the Stationers' Register cannot be relied on for an accurate statement of proprietorship.

15. Hollis's own diary (MS. at Harvard) notes that the payment was made on 19 June (see J. L. Clifford, 'Johnson's Obscure Middle Years' in *Johnson, Boswell, and their Circle*, Oxford, 1965, pp. 102–3).

16. The following day Johnson wrote to Baretti without mentioning his pension, but remarking 'Mr Reynolds gets six thousand a year'. (*Letters*, i.139, no. 142).

17. The rate for contributions to the *Critical Review* was, according to Percival Stockdale, 2 gns. per sheet (*Life*, iv.214 n). Johnson's review of Graham occupies four pages, i.e. a quarter of a sheet; of Grainger, seven pages, and of Goldsmith, five pages: all three together add up to a whole sheet of sixteen pages.

18. Birch gave the information to Hardwicke in a letter of 5 Oct. 1756 (B.L. Add. MS. 35400 f. 316). The figure of £262–10s. is given in a note made by Tonson's servant, Somerset Draper, which was published by John Nichols in *G.M.* lvii (1787) p. 76 and *Lit. Anec.*, v (1812) p. 597; the original is in the Folger Shakespeare library (MS. Folger S.a.163, no. 4). The figure of £375 is printed as the value of the sets which Johnson received, in *An Account of the Expence of Correcting and Improving sundry Books*, n.d., p. 2, and repeated in the *Petition of the Booksellers for Relief from the Expenses of Correction and Improvement*, n.d. The case of the booksellers required the figure to be high, and accordingly the note made by Tonson's clerk deserves the most credence.

19. From 25 March 1768 pensions were taxed at 3s. in the £. (*Parliamentary History*, xvi, 417). That rate agreed with the Land tax rate (W. R. Ward, *The English Land Tax in the 18th Century*, Oxford, 1953, p. 101). When James Beattie received his pension of £200 p.a. in 1773 he was paid under the Scottish establishment and so escaped the tax at the Land tax rate on English pensions (*James Beattie's London Diary 1773*, ed. R. S. Walker, Aberdeen, 1946, p. 95). But see *post*, p. 229, n. 72; payments made under 'Secret service' were perhaps free from tax.

20. Johnson was in Lichfield on this date and did not return to London until 11 December. He had written to Strahan on 9 October, 'I shall desire you to help me to twenty pounds which I shall take with me, and shall leave a note of fifteen for you, to pay for me. You will receive the money while I am away. I shall leave you my letter for that purpose.' (*Letters*, i.282, no. 278.1)

21. Johnson was 'doctored' by Trinity College, Dublin, on 23 July 1765, and by Oxford on 30 March 1775. There is no conclusive evidence that he ignored the Dublin degree, preferring only the Oxford one; see *Life*, i.488 n.

22. On this date Johnson was travelling from Carnarvon to Bangor (*Life*, v. 452).

SAMUEL JOHNSON'S EARNINGS

He had written on 16 August to Robert Levet, 'I have sent you a bill upon Mr Strahan ... tell Frank [Barber] I hope he remembers my advice. When his money is out, let him have more.' (*Letters*, i.412, no. 359).

23. The sharebook notes that the share was bought from 'The Author' who should have received a total of £210. The £100 was perhaps part of that total for Johnson recorded the remainder, £110, as outstanding on 4 Nov. 1777 (*below*).

24. At this time Johnson was helping two of his former *Dictionary* amanuenses: 'Peyton and Macbean are both starving, and I cannot keep them' (*Letters*, ii.30, no. 393, and ii.31, no. 394); he was also about to set off for Lichfield (*Letters*, ii.34, no. 397.1).

25. Rivington published no work by Johnson, though he appears as an occasional partner, notably in the *Dictionary* and in the edition of Shakespeare. He is not known to have been concerned in the *Political Tracts*, published in 1776.

26. This withdrawal seems to have reduced Johnson's balance significantly. On 22 July he wrote to Boswell, 'I shall, perhaps, come to Carlisle another year; but my money has not held out so well as it used to do.' (*Life*, iii.127). He had been helping Isaac de Groot, a descendant of Hugo Grotius, whom he settled in the Charterhouse. (*Life*, iii.125).

27. This incomplete entry reflects the unevenness of Johnson's accounting. The £110 is the remainder from the sale of the copyright of the *Journey*; the other titles are presumably outstanding for settlement, but the sums involved are not known. Strahan's sharebook (B.M. Add. MS. 48805) records the purchase of a half share in *Political Tracts*, 1776, but leaves a blank for the amount paid.

28. On this date Johnson returned to London after his visit to Ashbourne and Lichfield (*Diaries*, p. 283); he had written on 20 Sept. to Mrs. Thrale asking for an advance of £10 from Henry Thrale 'by the next post' (*Letters*, ii.211, no. 549).

29. After a brief stay at home Johnson went on to Brighton on 14 November to join the Thrales (*Letters*, ii.233, no. 562).

30. This is presumably the sum which Johnson had received on 9 November, which was a Sunday. It may be inferred that Strahan gave him the money from his own ready cash, but later arranged for the sum to be deducted from his bank account as a payment to Johnson.

31. On this day Johnson left London and travelled to Daventry on his way to Lichfield (*Letters*, ii.288, no. 616).

32. R. W. Chapman speculated in *Letters* on the source of this sum, and was dissatisfied with the suggestion that it represented the proceeds of the sale of the copyright of the *Journey* (see 14 Feb. 1775 and note). The receipt dated 16 March 1776 (*above*) is the most likely source, but it is still not clear what the money came from, or where it had been in the meantime. It seems a large sum to keep to hand in the house.

33. Johnson was about to set off with the Thrales for Brighton (*Letters*, ii.405, no. 707.1).

34. Henry Thrale died on 4 April and was buried on 11th. Johnson was one of his executors and was left £200 in Thrale's will (*Life*, iv.86).

35. For a further *ex gratia* payment, see below, 19 February 1783.

36. Johnson set out for Lichfield on 15 October (*Diaries*, p. 310).

37. On 7 October Johnson went to Brighton with Mrs Thrale (*Diaries*, pp. 338-9).

38. Johnson came home on 20 November (*Diaries*, p. 351); Strahan seems to have looked after his affairs during his absence for Johnson wrote to him on 24 October and 14 November thanking him for his solicitude (*Letters*, ii.513, 515–6, nos. 811.2 and 814). Strahan apparently had written to Johnson, no doubt about business at home.

39. The curious remark 'I think' probably signifies nothing more than that Johnson was an inattentive accountant.

40. Johnson's *Diaries* (p. 360) noted on 15 July that he then signed the receipt for the 5 April instalment of £75. It was however not necessary for the receipt to be presented on the quarter day when the payment fell due.

41. Nichols in *Lit. Anec.* viii, 1815, p. 417, says 100 guineas, but the MS. is decisive.

42. On this date Johnson set out for a visit to Rochester (*Diaries*, p. 360).

43. On 16 October Johnson wrote to Strahan asking for 'two bank notes of ten pounds each' (*Letters*, iii.229, no. 1016.1). He was in Lichfield until 16 November.

44. On this day Johnson signed his printed pension receipt for £75 which was the Michaelmas quarterly payment (*MS. Handlist*, 229). He wrote to Strahan on the same day: 'I am very unwilling to take the pains of writing and therefore make use of another hand to desire that I may have whatever portion of my pension you can spare me with prudence and propriety' (*Letters*, iii.253–4, no. 1042.2).

45. A. T. Hazen, *Johnson's Prefaces and Dedications*, New Haven, 1937. Some payments may have been in kind: George Adams gave him 'a very curious meteorological instrument, of a new and ingenious construction' for dedicating to King George III his *Treatise describing and explaining the Construction and Use of new Celestial and Terrestrial Globes*, 1766.

46. *Life*, iii.321, iv.409.

47. Despite inferences derived from samples from Strahan's records in e.g. P. Hernlund, 'William Strahan's Ledgers: Standard Charges for Printing, 1738–85', *Studies in Bibliography*, xx (1967), 89–111.

48. H. Ransome, 'The Rewards of Authorship in the 18th century', *University of Texas Studies in English*, 8 July 1935, pp. 47–66.

49. *Life*, iii.507.

50. J. Hill, *Bookmakers of Old Birmingham*, 1907, pp. 39 ff., and *Life*, i.85 n.

51. *Life*, i.103.

52. Ibid.

53. Hawkins, *Life of Johnson*, 2nd ed. 1787, p. 43, and *Lit. Anec.* viii (1815), 416.

54. *Letters*, i.3–4, no. 3. It was probably fortuitous that Samuel Smith of St. Paul's Churchyard had been a partner with Michael Johnson in the publication of two books in 1696 and 1699.

55. Writing in 1743 Johnson described the sum of £50 a year as 'a Salary which though by no Means equal to the Demands of Vanity and Luxury, is yet found sufficient to support Families above Want, and was undoubtedly more than the Necessities of Life require.' (*Life of Savage*, 1744, ed. C. R. Tracy, Oxford, 1971, p. 96.)

56. The very Bible (Francfurt, 1597) was presented in 1598 to Erasmus Sidelmann by John Georg, Count Solms of Münzenberg, and passed into the Harleian collection. Johnson catalogued it in vol. i as no. 17. It is now in New College library, University of London (see *Times Literary Supplement*, 27 March 1959, p. 177). The Shakespeare folio passed from Johnson to Samuel Ireland, and was owned by Henry Irving before going to the Folger Shakespeare library.

57. T. S. Ashton, *An Economic History of England—The 18th Century*, 1972, pp. 53-4, 61-2.

58. G. Dawson, 'The Copyright of Shakespeare's Dramatic Works', *Studies in Honour of A. H. Fairchild*, Missouri, 1946, pp. 11-35. Tonson's minatory letter, dated 11 April 1745 is in the Folger Shakespeare library.

59. *MS. Handlist*, 36 (misdated '20 April').

60. Hawkins, *Life of Johnson*, 2nd ed. 1787, p. 345.

61. *Life*, i.187 lists the amanuenses. 'I pay three and twenty shillings a week to my assistants', he wrote to Strahan (*Letters*, i.41, no. 38). The figure was perhaps a total. On 18 June 1746 Francis Stuart signed a receipt for an advance of 3 gns. 'to be repaid out of twelve Shillings a week for which I contract to assist in compiling the Work' *MS. Handlist*, 35.

62. Strahan recorded printing 2000 copies of the first 70 sheets in December 1750 (B.L. Add. MS. 48800, f. 86).

63. *Letters*, i.38-9, no. 35.

64. J. H. Sledd & G. J. Kolb, *Dr Johnson's Dictionary. Essays in the Biography of a Book*, Chicago, 1955, pp. 227-30.

65. *Life*, i.183 n, and p. 4 n.1 *ante*; though Johnson later denied he had received more (*Life*, i.304 n).

66. There is some doubt about the exact date of the letter to Levett promising the payment. The question is canvassed by R. W. Chapman in *Letters*, i.42 n.

67. *Letters*, i.36-7, 45, 70, nos. 32.1, 42.2 and 69.

68. M. Waingrow, *The Correspondence . . . of James Boswell relating to the making of the 'Life of Johnson'*, New York, 1969, pp. 23-4, 59 and nn.

69. 'Sir, I have two very cogent reasons for not printing any list of subscribers;—one, that I have lost all the names, —the other, that I have spent all the money.' (*Life*, iv.111). More confusion is reflected in Johnson's letter to Tonson of 9 Oct. 1765 (*Letters*, i.178, no. 176.1).

70. *Letters*, i.105, no. 112.1.

71. *Essay*, 1792, in *Johns. Misc.*, i.416.

72. See p. 226, n. 19 and *Letters*, i.140 n where R. W. Chapman alleges that the pension was paid from secret service funds. If that was so it was perhaps exempt from tax, but with the reform of the Civil List in 1782 Johnson was paid at the Exchequer and might not have escaped taxation. I have not yet been able to resolve this question of the taxation of his pension.

73. *Life*, ii.137. As early as 1754 Strahan was helping with Johnson's financial affairs, and he paid some taxes for him (*Letters*, i.55-6, no. 52).

74. J. A. Cochrane, *Dr Johnson's Printer: the Life of William Strahan*, 1964, ch. 9-10.

75. See *Letters*, i.151, no. 152 of 2 July 1763 to George Grenville. Mr. Arthur G. Rippey of Denver, Colorado, who is the owner of the original, informs me that it bears a contemporary note recording the payment of the instalment to 'C. Lloyd' who was presumably the 'bearer'. This was perhaps Charles Lloyd (1735-73), Grenville's secretary (see *D.N.B.*).

76. *Letters*, ii.411-12, no. 713.

77. *Life*, iv.402-4 n, 440-45.

78. A. L. Reade showed that Johnson had invested in Langton's navigation on the

river Wey in Surrey (*Johns. Gleanings*, ii.58). Langton's papers relating to the canal are in the Record Office at Lincoln Castle.

79. Hawkins, *Life of Johnson*, 2nd ed. 1787, p. 599; Hawkins was one of the executors.

80. Various totals are given by Boswell and his editors (*Life*, iv. 444–5); the above sum is derived from a marked copy of the catalogue at Harvard, formerly owned by Sir Thomas Phillipps and perhaps the auctioneer's copy: Christie's file copy is missing.

81. B. R. Mitchell & P. Deane, *Abstract of British Historical Statistics*, 1962, p. 455.

82. *Letters*, iii.208, no. 999, dated 26 August 1784.

83. 25 Sept. 1782, *Diaries*, p. 334.

84. 8 Sept. 1782, *Diaries*, p. 330. Barber's weekly wage of 7s. is entered as 7 pence.

85. e.g. 13 Aug. 1782, *Diaries*, p. 323.

86. Barber's weekly wage, one of Johnson's few regular expenses, is irregularly recorded.

87. J. H. Middendorf, 'Johnson on Wealth and Commerce' in *Johnson, Boswell and their Circle*, Oxford, 1965, pp. 47–64.

88. *Shakespeare*, 1765, ii.514 n (*Merry Wives*, III.iv.13).

89. *Life*, iv.163.

90. *Life*, ii.119.

91. 'Recollections' in *Johns. Misc.*, ii.251.

92. *Life*, i.373.

GILES BARBER

Pendred abroad

A view of the late eighteenth-century book trade in Europe

In the early days of printing, when Latin was still the learned language of Europe, the book trade was predominantly international and many of the great publishers sent a large proportion of their edition abroad. The rise of the vernacular and the development of local markets reduced the international element and soon, in the days before copyright, the importation of even only a single copy of a successful work could allow a pirated edition to be produced profitably at home by local booksellers. Equally the historians of the book trade, with the exception of books on the initial development of printing or a few signal studies such as that of Graham Pollard and Albert Ehrman, *The distribution of books by catalogue* (1965), have tended to concentrate their work on a national basis. It was doubtless proper that information should first have been collected on a town or regional basis and indeed although historical surveys of printing and bookselling produced from the late seventeenth century onwards, can be found for various cities or countries, much information is still lacking. There is nevertheless a growing interest in the history of the international trade as such and for periods such as the Enlightenment, when French was the established language of civilised Europe, a certain amount of evidence exists.

The French national trade, centred on Paris, strictly controlled and forming therefore a recognised group, had at least a certain nominal unity. Annual lists, or *tableaux*, of the Paris booksellers existed from the early eighteenth century and A. M. Lottin's remarkable *Catalogue chronologique des libraires et libraires-imprimeurs de Paris* appeared in 1789. This work, based on a number of sources including even parochial tombstones subsequently destroyed by the Revolution, is highly genealogical and reflects the family atmosphere, and perhaps the static nature, of the trade in the French capital. Earlier C. M. Saugrin's *Code de la librairie et imprimerie de Paris* had been published in 1744, following the extension of these regulations to the whole country in March of that year. Such legal codes were available for a number of trades and in 1766, at a period when almanacs and similar small books were all the fashion, there was also a *Guide des corps des marchands*. It is therefore not surprising to find the same publisher, the widow Duchesne, producing in 1777 a *Manuel de l'auteur et du libraire*, a directory which, besides covering the Parisian and French provincial trade in some detail, has claims to be the first major European book trade directory.

This duodecimo booklet of one hundred and eighteen numbered pages provides: 1, the names of ministers and magistrates in charge of the French book trade together with those of the censors and inspectors; 2, advice on the formalities for obtaining permission to print, for importing books, etc.; 3, the names of the printers and publishers of Paris, present and retired, and their specialities; 4, similar information for the French provinces, and 5, a list of the most noteworthy ('accrédités') booksellers in the principal cities of Europe. The *Manuel* also contained a list of French papers advertising new books and a place index for all countries. The royal *privilège* (dated September 1766) is granted to 'le sieur [Antoine] Perrin' of whom nothing further seems to be known except that he does not appear to have been either a printer or a bookseller. An engraved title page and a following half-title are headed *Manuel de l'auteur et du libraire*, the former bearing the engraved arms of the Chancellor of France, the Marquis de Miromesnil, and the imprint 'A PARIS. Chez la Ve DUCHESNE Libraire rue St. Jacques au Temple du Gout.' Copies have also a letterpress title page which may either bear the same title and the imprints of four publishers (the *veuve* Duchesne, Le Jay, Valade, Ruault) or the title *Almanach de l'auteur et du libraire* and that of the *veuve* Duchesne alone. An introductory note looked forward to editions every year and the radical change in the French regulations certainly necessitated one in 1778. This was entitled simply *Almanach de la librairie*, published by Moutard, and gave additionally lists of Parisian engravers and music engravers (and music sellers), of book fairs, and the times of departure of stage coaches and other forms of conveyance. A further edition appeared in 1781 and, it has been suggested, another in 1784.[1]

Clearly the author of the *Manuel* is best informed, both quantitatively and qualitatively, about the trade in France and indeed his accuracy, both in name recording and in fact, will be seen to be defective in relation to other countries. Mr. Graham Pollard, in editing *The earliest*

[1] Note is on p. 265.

directory of the [English] *book trade, by John Pendred, 1785,* was seeking sources of information about the English trade and could say of international directories such as the *Manuel* and its successors that they were neither comprehensive nor reliable in their sections devoted to England. It is, however, now suggested that they do have evidential value as showing both some of the principal names known in the European trade and the importance of various towns at this time. Taken in conjunction with surviving trade account books such as those of the Cramers, the Luchtmans or those of the Société typographique de Neuchâtel, which, compared with each other, help to indicate the size of certain booksellers' trade, one can begin to identify the major international booksellers of late eighteenth-century Europe.

The *Manuel,* or, as it is more often entitled, the *Almanach,* gives in its original edition a list of 240 French towns with booksellers. Paris contains 146 active ones (including 14 widows) and a further 78 retired members. Of the provincial towns Lyons has 38 booksellers, Rouen 36, Bordeaux 25, Nancy 24, Toulouse 23, Marseilles 19, Caen, Nantes and Rennes 14 each, and Besançon and Strasbourg 13 each. Initials or full Christian names are usually given and accuracy is evidently high.

With regard to other European countries little editorial work is visible although comparison with the considerably enlarged 1781 edition shows that some work was done for the latter. Indeed the number of non-French entries rises from 500 in 1777 to 883 in 1781. It is also evident from this comparison that the nature of the notes used to compile the original copy must have been peculiar. In the first edition firms with three partners were sometimes given as three separate firms, the forenames of a bookseller were on occasion given as the surnames of different firms, scribal uncertainty (particularly in English and Dutch) leads to the reduplication of names with variant spellings, and notes are even transcribed as names, e.g. the 1777 Milan entry starts with the names 1. Jos. Richino, 2. Malacerta—probably a note meaning 'uncertain'—both of which are subsequently dropped. However, despite these errors, a very high proportion of the names appears to be basically correct, and initials, forenames or other corroborative information can be supplied from other sources.

For example, a brief glance at British and Irish coverage, verified against Plomer's *Dictionary of booksellers and printers, 1726–1775,* shows that of the ninety names given under eight towns, only five are duplicated by confusion, four are the names of authors or merchants not booksellers, four are deceased booksellers, and four appear to be inaccuracies. Of these last, however, at least one name, that of R. Blamire of the Strand, although not in Plomer, is in fact accurate as he is known to have published *Rhyme and reason: or, A fresh stating of the arguments against an opening through the wall of Queen's Square, Westminster, by a knight* in 1780. The remaining seventy-three names, or eighty-one per cent of the list, appear to be accurate although on occasion as little as one brief reference substantiates them in Plomer. Several British booksellers died in the year or two immediately preceding 1777 but this fact is not reflected in the 1781 edition which, on the British side, shows virtually no revision. This is far from being the case with continental towns and entries for towns such as Geneva, Naples, Rome and Stockholm show considerable changes between editions, amounting in the case of the last three to the almost total substitution of new names.

Coverage by country shows that, against the original 240 French towns, other nations are represented by the following numbers of towns: Germany 96, Italy 45, all the Low Countries 44, Switzerland 11, Great Britain and Ireland, Spain and Portugal 8 each, east European towns (including Russia) 7, and northern countries 6. Coming down to survey individual towns one finds that, taking entries in both editions together, London is well in the lead, having seventy-two booksellers listed, a remarkable figure considering that Paris, where one would expect a hundred per cent accuracy, is only almost exactly twice the size. Leipzig comes second with thirty entries, then Venice 22, Geneva 20, the Hague and Stockholm 19 each, Berlin 18, Madrid 17, Amsterdam 16, Naples and Nuremberg 15 each, Avignon, Brussels and Rome 14 each, and Frankfurt and Lisbon 11.

The compilers were presumably principally interested in foreign booksellers trading in French books, and indeed in London (but nowhere else) an asterisk explicitly shows that ten people dealt particularly in this field. The export aspect is further underlined in the *Almanach* by the notes to each town, giving the days of the week when the coach left Paris for it and whether prepayment of carriage was required. This bias towards the trade in French books might well increase the number of small German towns, represented on the strength of one small but general bookseller, while larger cities (e.g. Rome) are shown with the names of only a few, more specialised, agents. The London list is decidedly accurate in this respect identifying in particular Becket, De Hondt, Elmsley, Nourse, and Vaillant, all the principal contemporary importers of French and continental books.

Perusal of the list also shows that a number of firms operated in more than one town and even country. Alexander Donaldson is sited in both Edinburgh and London, Schreuder and the widow Merkus in Amsterdam and Leipzig, the Vasse firm in Antwerp and Brussels, Berger and Boedner in Butzaw, Rostock and Wismar, and the eventual move of Philibert from Geneva to Copenhagen is recorded with entries in both. The famous Waisenhaus, started in Halle in 1698, is also found in Brunswick, Salzburg and Zullicaw. The interesting Italo-Hispanic trade is revealed by the Pagliarini, established in both Rome and Lisbon, by the Bonnardel in Turin, Barcelona and Lisbon, and by the Reycends brothers in Milan, Turin and Lisbon. Most of these firms were engaged in bookselling and, while those also or mainly concerned with publishing (such as M. M. Rey in Amsterdam, Bourdeaux in Berlin, Walther in Dresden, the Cramers in Geneva, Neaulme at the Hague, Decker and Reich in Leipzig, Cotta in Stuttgart or Felice in Yverdon) have attained some fame, it has not yet been easy so far to identify those purely concerned with the more ephemeral (but not necessarily less profitable) business of merely handling books. Nevertheless from the study of several contemporary booksellers' account or letterbooks it is evident that certain names occur frequently and always in connection with large sums. A provisional list of such leading dealers would include the widow Merkus (Amsterdam and Leipzig), Haude and Spener (Berlin), Varrentrapp and Esslinger (both of Frankfurt), the Briançonnais Gravier and relatives (Genoa, Italy, Portugal), De Hondt (The Hague and London), Gosse (Geneva, The Hague and London), Moetjens (The Hague), Breitkopf and particularly Gleditsch (Leipzig), the Reycends brothers and Bonnardel already mentioned for the Italo-Hispanic trade, Trattner, 'chevalier du Saint Empire' (Vienna), and the mysterious Porcelli of Naples, possibly a successor there to Stefano Elia. In connection with the latter it is perhaps worth noting that much of the Italian trade seems to have lain in the hands of the French (including particularly the Briançonnais) or of persons apparently of Jewish descent (the Foa, Elia, Salmoni). Of course many of these booksellers travelled widely on business, both to the Leipzig fairs and elsewhere. The Luchtmans visited England, the Cramers and others Spain, and John Nourse of London was in The Hague and in Paris, to name but a few visits. Accounts were thus either settled at the fairs (predominantly in the Germanic world) or by 'traites' either drawn on some of these major booksellers with business in numerous centres or very often through Swiss Protestant bankers. In any case it is clear that trade was remarkably wide and active and that the names of the main dealers in the more far-flung towns such as Lisbon, Naples, Stockholm or Warsaw were well known to numerous other European booksellers.

Jaubert, discussing the book trade in his *Dictionnaire raisonné universel des arts et métiers* (1773) stresses (vol. 2, p. 582) that a knowledge of German, English and Italian is essential to a [French] bookseller, the two latter being indeed indispensable, since so many important works are published in those countries. The trade, he says, must engage in prompt and regular correspondence with foreign countries both to place their books and to import those suitable for their own country. The address book side of the *Almanach* would thus clearly have been of importance to French booksellers.

In the Germanic world greater emphasis still seems to have been placed on the traditional fair catalogues although Frankfurt, where the last fair was held in 1764, gradually yielded this role to Leipzig. For the first two-thirds of the eighteenth century the number of both publishers and publications present at the fairs remained fairly constant but there was a considerable increase towards 1780, the number of new titles rising from 624 in 1714 to 2115 in 1780 and even around 4000 by 1800. In particular foreign attendance rose and while Amsterdam is the one foreign centre constantly represented, having later two firms resident in Leipzig, it is soon joined by Copenhagen, Geneva, Stockholm and Leyden. Equally, whereas only five Amsterdam titles were recorded for 1710, the total had risen to sixty-seven by 1780, a year when London submitted fifteen works of which five were apparently in French.

The lists of names provided by the *Almanach* in the late 1770s and early 1780s reflect something of the state of the trade in the last years of the Ancien Régime. The more local printer-publisher-bookseller is about to specialise and distribution by fairs has given way to distribution by catalogue and by advertisement in the new periodical press. Increasing literacy and a far greater number of both circulating and private libraries have totally changed the nature of the market. Methods of production will soon have to be changed to keep pace with demand. Political and literary influences too have changed. The large Belgian trade in Spanish religious books, formerly centred on Liège, lapsed as printing and publishing developed in Spain. Censorship had completed the ruin of the formerly powerful Venetian press and Gasparo Gozzi's report of 1765 shows how Bologna, Parma, Milan, Florence, Lucca and

Leghorn had profited. Governmental censorship too held the French trade back from all except artistic development, and the Low Countries, already masters of the trade in the Classics in the seventeenth century, flourished during the struggle of the 'philosophes' with authority. Publishing, either free from censorship or openly piratical, was the basis of trade first in Holland, and later in Belgium which became in the early nineteenth century the main competitor of Paris as a centre of publishing in French.

By the later years of the eighteenth century however the over free re-printing of any work had gone so far that the debate on copyright, which was to last for at least eighty years, at last got under way simultaneously in England and in France in the 1770s. In Germany too the rise of a new and talented group of writers supported the movement and the creation of the Buchhandlung der Gelehrten in 1781 looks forward to the Prussian codification of the 1790s and, in a way, to the formal organisation of the trade represented by the foundation of the Börsenverein der deutschen Buchhändler in 1825. In date the *Almanach* is therefore on something of a watershed between two styles of trade and this adds to its interest we find in it both names already famous in the European book trade for over a hundred years, and other names which are still familiar today. The *Almanach* was produced in France and the bulk of it, ignored in this particular article, is of interest only for the French trade. Nevertheless, French civilisation being then much in vogue, the coverage given to Europe, while it cannot be used to give an accurate statistical picture of the trade, nevertheless gives a fascinating insight into an activity stretching from Moscow to Dublin and from Stockholm to Cadiz. A few famous names were known but one can now fill out the picture and it may be that this will enable further material to be traced.

Although the catalogue of the library of the Börsenverein lists one earlier item which appears to be some sort of directory (*Verzeichnis der meistlebenden Herren Buchhändler, welche die Leipziger und Franckfurther Messen insgemein zu besuchen pflegen*, 1741), the three successive editions of the *Almanach* really begin the era when general trade directories appear. Pendred's directory came out in 1785 but the disruptions of the following years prevented further progress on the continent until just after 1800. N. A. G. Debray's *Tableau des libraires, imprimeurs et éditeurs de livres des principales villes de l'Europe* (Paris 1804) and P. A. J. F. Pillet's *Annuaire de l'imprimerie et de la librairie de l'Empire français pour 1813* were among the first to continue the tradition, but thereafter the growing number of national directories began to replace the earlier international ones.

It is always interesting to see how one's own country fares in any international survey and it must be a particular conclusion of this one that the French compiler of the *Almanach* evidently possessed an outstanding knowledge of the London trade and that this knowledge is indicative, if not of England's general importance in the European trade, at least of its considerable standing as an importer of foreign books. Customs statistics show that in 1700 England received the vast majority of its foreign books through Holland and that by 1781 this had changed so that France, Holland and Germany ranked equal first, while Flanders and Italy could also make a good showing. Our few exports then went, in order, to Flanders, France, Holland and Germany with occasional sales to Italy, Russia, Spain and Portugal. This imbalance was of course heavily countered by British book exports to India and North America. The growth of English private libraries also stimulated our importation of antiquarian books and from early London sales of continental collections such as those of Loménie de Brienne (1724) or Esprit Fléchier (1725) to later ones such as Pinelli (1789/90) or Pâris d'Illins (1791) it is evident that English collectors were active.

The lists of European booksellers in the *Almanach* are not only an unrivalled and convenient listing of the trade at this time, highly informative of the cultural state of the continent, but also, by giving so broad a view of the trade at this time, allow for some consideration of the importance of England's role in that community.

TABLEAU DES LIBRAIRES

les plus accrédités des principales villes de l'Europe

The following list represents a conflation of those appearing under the heading 'Tableau des libraires les plus accrédités des principales villes de l'Europe' in both the 1777 and 1781 editions of the *Almanach*. Names occurring in 1777 appear in the left-hand column of personal names, those not reappearing in 1781 having after them the note '(Not 1781)'; those mentioned only in 1781 are indented to the right. Where booksellers have been identified from one of the authorities listed below the spelling of their names has been corrected, if necessary, and, where known, their initials have been given in square brackets. While the addition of initials, where they were not recorded, attests that the person named is known to have been a printer, publisher or bookseller, there are of course numerous other cases, both where the forenames were given and where it has not proved possible to trace them, where the persons listed certainly were members of the book trade.

Barber, Giles G. 'The Cramers of Geneva and their trade in Europe between 1755 and 1766'. *Studies on Voltaire*, XXX, 1964, pp. 377–413.
Brussels, Musée du livre. *Histoire du livre et de l'imprimerie en Belgique*, pts. 4, 5. Brussels, 1926, 29.
Kleinschmidt, J. R. *Les imprimeurs et libraires de la république de Genève 1700–1798*. Geneva, 1948.
Kossman, E. F. *De boekhandel te 's-Gravenhage tot het eind van de 18de eeuw.* The Hague, 1937.
Ledeboer, A. M. *Alfabetische lijst der boekdrukkers, boekverkoopers em uitgevers in Noord-Nederland*. Utrecht, 1876.
Parenti, M. *Dizionario dei luoghi di stampa falsi, inventati o supposti*. Florence, 1951.
Plomer, H. R. [and others], *A dictionary of the printers and book-sellers who were at work in England, Scotland, and Ireland from 1726 to 1775*. London, 1932.
Schmidt, R. *Deutsche Buchhändler, deutsche Buchdrucker*. 6 pts. Berlin, 1902–8.
Schwetschke, G. *Codex nundinarius Germaniae literatae bisecularis: Der Mess-Jahrbücher des deutschen Buchhandels Fortsetzung die Jahre 1766 bis einschl. 1846 umfassend*. Halle, 1877.

Tableau des libraires

Aix-la-Chapelle (Allemagne)
    Barchon
    Bougé
    Houben
Alcmaer (Provinces-Unies)
    Maag [J.]
Altona (Allemagne)
    Hellmann [J. H. S.]
Alexandrie (Italie)
    Jos. Delpian
Altenbourg (Allemagne)
    Richter [G. E.]

Altorf près Nuremberg
    Schüpfel [Lor.]
Amsterdam (Provinces-Unies)
  Boitte & Compagnie [J. F.] (Not 1781)
  De Bruyn [M.]
  Changuion [F. or D. J.]
  Chatelain [Z. et fils] (Not 1781)
  Veuve Merkus
  Meyer [A., J. or P.]
  Mortier [P.] (Not 1781)
  Reviol
  Rey [M. M.]   1781 Héritiers
  Schreuder [J.]
  Ulam [B.]
  Van-Harrwelt   1781 Héritiers
    De Groot [G.]
    Schneider [J. H.]
    Schouten [P.]
    Tartara [P. died 1773, widow continued]
Ancone (Italie)
    Nicol. Beletti
Anspach (Allemagne)
    Haueisen [Hof buchhandlung]
Anvers (Pays-Bas)
  Coligny
  Grange
  Marcour
  Michel Vasse
  Veuve Verdussen
    Cornelio Verdussen & Cie.
    Jérôme Verdussen
Arezzo (Italie)
    Michel Belotti
Arnheim (Pays-Bas)
  Nyhof [J.]
    Moelman [J. H.]
    Traast [J.]
Augsbourg (Allemagne)
    Lotter
    Mayer
    Muller
    Rieger fils [Matth. Rieger's Söhne]
    Stage [C. H.]

Veith
Wolff [J.]
Veuve [E.] Klet & Franck
Avignon (Comtat-Venaissin)
　Merande [F. B., bankrupt 1778]
　Chambaud [L.]
　Niel [J. J.]
　　　Aubert [J.]
　　　Bonnet frères
　　　Domergue [J. F.]
　　　Fabre [J.]
　　　Garrigan [J.]
　　　Guichard
　　　Journel
　　　Mereau [? Merande]
　　　Offray [P. and A.]
　　　Seguin [F.]
　　　Veuve Joly [A. G., died 1784]
Bamberg (Allemagne)
　　　Goebhard[t] [Tob.]
　　　Martin
Barcelone (Espagne)
　Bonnardel [J.] & Simon
Bareith (Allemagne)
　Vanden Kieboom [J. See also Breda]
　　　Lübeck [J. A.]
Basel (Suisse)
　Haerfler (Not 1781)
　Daniel Eckenstein (Not 1781)
　Imhof, Jean Rodolphe　1781 Imhof & fils
　Tourneisen, Emmanuel [J. J. jun.] (Not 1781)
　　　Flick [J. Jac.]
　　　Graben
　　　Schweighauser [J.]
　　　Serini [C. A.]
Bastia (Corse)
　Batini
　　　Mutel
Bautzen (Allemagne)
　　　Deinzer
　　　Drachstaedt
Bergame (Italie)
　　　Vincent Antoine Lancellotti

Berg-op-zoom (Pays-Bas Hollandais)
    Vanderlenden
Bergues [Pays-Bas]
    Legros (Not 1781)
Berlin (Brandebourg)
    Bourdeaux [E.] 'lib francois'
    Decker [G. J.]
    Haude & Spener [See Schmidt, pp. 389-95]
    Nicolaï [Fr.]
    Pitra [S.] 'lib francois'
    Birnstiel [F. W.] (Not 1781)
    Christ. Fred. Worff (Not 1781)
    Jasper (J.) 'lib. francois'
        Bosse
        Himbourg [Chr. Fr.]
        Lange [G. A.]
        Mylius [A.]
        Pauli [Joach.]
        Realschule
        Ringmacher [C. U.]
        Stahlbaum [Chr. Ludw.]
        Voss & fils
        Wever [Arn.]
        Winter [J. L.]
Berne (Suisse)
    Esman Haller [? Em. Haller]
    Kirchberger (Not 1781)
    Société typographique
        Nouvelle société typographique
Biene (Suisse)
        Heilmann [J. C.]
Bois le Duc (Pays-Bas Hollandois)
    Bresier [? Bresser, L. J.]
    Pailler [J. or H.]
Bologne (Italie)
        Lelio delle Volpe
        Taruffi frères
        Jos. Marie Viaggi
        Petrone Cagliari [? Petronio, patron saint of Bologna]
        J. B. Sarsi
        Jos. Lucchesini
        Franc. Smeraldi
        Louis Guidotti

            Charl. Trenti
Bommel (Provinces Unies)
            Salmons
Bouillon (Luxembourg)
    Rousseau [P.] (Not 1781)
    Société typographique
Brandebourg (Allemagne)
        Frères Halle
Breda (Brabant Hollandais)
    Van den Kieboom [J. See also Bareith]
Breme (Basse Saxe)
    Foerster [G. L.]
        Cramer [J. H.]
Breslau (Silesie)
    Gampert
        Gutsch [C. F.]
        Korn ainé, J. F.
        Korn jeune, G. Th.
        Loewe [Gottl.]
        Meyer [Joh. Ernst]
Bresse (Italie)
        Daniel Berlinde
        Charles Marie Rizzardi
Bristol (Angleterre)
    Pine [W.]
Bruges (Flandre Autrichienne)
    Stoover
    Van Praet
        Van Buscher
Brunswick (Allemagne)
        Maison des Orphelins [See Halle]
        Mayer
        Meissner
        Hérit. Schroeder
Bruxelles (Pays-Bas)
    Boubers [J. L.]
    Boucherie [J. J.] (Not 1781)
    Leclerc
    Flon, l'ainé
    Flon junior
    Lemay, Mademoiselle
    t'Serstevens [F.]
    Vanden Berghen [J.]

  Vasse, frères
  Veuve Vasse
    D'Ours [A.]
    Dujardin [H.]
    Lemmens [P. J.]
    Vleminckx [H.]
Butzau (Allemagne)
 Berger & Boedner
Cadix (Espagne)
 Caris [A.] & Bertrand [J. J.]
 Hermil, frères
 Ravet
Cagliari (Sardaigne)
  Bonav. Poro
  Terese Romero
Cambridge (Angleterre)
 T. Merril
 Merville [? Same as above]
Campen (Pays-Bas Hollandais)
  Clement [? S.]
Carlsrouhe (Allemagne)
  Macklot
  Schmieder
  Wirsm
Carpentras (Comtat-Venaissin)
 Guérin
 Vincent
Cassel (Allemagne)
 Hemmers
  Cramer [J. Jac.]
  Hemmerdé [J. F.]
Cavaillon (Comtat-Venaissin)
 Ducry
Chambery (Savoie)
 Dufour
Chemnitz (Allemagne)
  Stoessel [J. C.]
  Hérit. [D.] Stossel & Putscher
Cleves (Allemagne)
  Baerstecher
  Hoffmann
Coblentz (Allemagne)
  Huber

Cobourg (Allemagne)
   Ahl [R. A. W.]
   Findeisen [J. C.]
Coeten (Allemagne)
   Coerner
Cologne (Allemagne)
  Kratrang & Simonis 1781 Simonis
  Metternich [W.] 1781 Veuve Metternich
    Horst
    Putz
Coimbre (Portugal)
  Fr. Mallerne 1781 Maller
  Dubeux
Copenhague (Dannemarck)
  Chevalier
  Heineke & Faber (Not 1781)
  Philibert [C.]
  Moller
  Rothe [J. G.] 1781 Rothe, Theoph.
  Veuve Rak & Prost 1781 Prost [Chr. G.]
    Pelt [Fr. Chr.]
    Steinmann, P.
Dantzick (Pologne)
  Schmid
  Veuve Wareger (Not 1781)
    Florke [J. H. Flörken]
    Wedel [D. L.]
Delft (Hollande)
  H. Sterk
Dessau [Saxe]
    Librairie du Philantrope [Im Philanthropin]
Deux-Ponts (Allemagne)
  Le Tellier
Deventer (Pays-Bas Hollandais)
  Demoiselle Wanwick
Doesbourg (Provinces-Unies)
    Vorster
Dordreck (Pays-Bas Hollandais)
  Blussé [A.]
    Van Braam [P.]
Dresde (Saxe)
  G. Conrad Walter
  Heckel (Not 1781)

　　　　Groell [M. See also Warsaw]
　　　　Hilscher
　　　　Veuve [of J. N.] Gerlach
Dublin (Irlande)
　　　Ewing [T. Died 1776]
　　　Faulkner, T. E.
　　　J. Wilson
Dusseldorf (Allemagne)
　　　Fréd. Henri Jacobi
Eclang [really Erlangen]
　　　Walther [Wolfg.] (Not 1781)
Edimbourg (Ecosse)
　　　J. Balfour
　　　Creeck, W.
　　　Drummond [W.]
　　　Donaldson [A. or J.]
　　　Longmann [Not in Plomer]
Eisenach (Allemagne)
　　　Griesbach [M. G.]
　　　　Wittekind [J. G. E.]
Enchuise (Hollande)
　　　　Callenbach [R.]
　　　　Kieng
Erfourt (Allemagne)
　　　　Kayser [G. A.]
　　　　Weber [J. F.]
Erlangen (Allemagne) [See also Eclang]
　　　　Palm, J. J.
　　　　Schleich [F. A.]
Erseirth (Allemagne)
　　　Sauerlander
Faenza (Italie)
　　　　Jos. Ant. Archi
Ferrare (Italie)
　　　　Jos. Rinaldi
　　　　Fratelli Pormatelli
Flensbourg [Denmark]
　　　　Korte
Flessingue (Provinces-Unies)
　　　　Corbelin [T.]
　　　　Payenaar [P.]
Florence (Toscane)
　　　Albizzini

Bouchard [J.]
Bulle
Cambiagi [G.]
Marzi [A.]
Moücke [F.]
Bonducci [A.]
Papperini
P. Gaetan Viviani
  Allegrini [G.]
Franckfort-sur-Mein (Allemagne)
 Van Düren [frères]
 André [Andrea]
 Varrentrapp [Frz.]
 Bronner [H. L.]
 J. G. Esslinger Hérit.
 Fréd. Hillinghauser (Not 1781)
 Knoch (Not 1781)
  Reissenstein [J. Phil.]
  Fleischer [J. G.]
  Garbe [J. G.]
  Eichenberg hérit.
  Kaster
Franckfort sur l'Oder (Allemagne)
  Strauss [C. G.]
Fribourg (Suisse)
 Demoiselle Bosse (Not 1781)
 Jos. Bosse (Not 1781)
 Mademoiselle Eggendorffe [really Madame, the former Demoiselle Bosse. Shown as Madame in 1781]
 B. L. Piller (Not 1781)
Fribourg (Brisgovie)
  Wagner [Ant. Wagner & Sohn]
Fuglino (Italie)
  Casimire Gigucci
Gand (Flandres Autrichienne)
 Begyn
 Coquyt
 Gimblet
 Goessin
 J. Meyer
 M. Vasse (Not 1781)
Gênes (Italie)
 Yves Gravier

Schill (Not 1781)
　　　　　Jean Louis Bailleux
　　　　　Bernard Tarrigo
　　　　　Pierre Paul Pyzzorno
Genève (Suisse)
　　Bardin [I.]
　　Chirol [B.]
　　Cramer frères
　　De Tournes [J. & J. J.]
　　Duvillard Scherrer 1781 Duvillard fils & Nouffer
　　Mad. Holm [Not in Kleinschmidt] (Not 1781)
　　Jacoby [J. P.] (Not 1781)
　　Noblet [? G.] (Not 1781)
　　Pellet, J. L.
　　Prestre, J. E.
　　Philibert, Ant. (Not 1781)
　　Philibert & Chirol [also in Copenhagen] (Not 1781)
　　Teron l'ainé [J. B.]
　　　　J. P. Bonnant
　　　　Fremont dit Butini [P.]
　　　　L. A. Caille
　　　　J. S. Cailler
　　　　P. Gallay
　　　　G. Grasset
　　　　Société typographique
Giessen (Allemagne)
　　Braun
　　　　Krieger [? F. senior, or J. C., son]
Glasgow (Ecosse)
　　Rob. & André Foulis
Glogaw (Silesie)
　　　　Gunther [Chr. Fr.]
Goes ou Tergoes (Provinces-Unies)
　　　　Huismann [J.]
　　　　Overluys [F.]
Gorcum (Hollande)
　　　　Goetzée [N.]
Gorice (Allemagne)
　　Valeri
Gottingue (Allemagne)
　　Barmeier (Not 1781)
　　Dieterich [J. Chr.]
　　Veuve [A.] Vandenhoeck

Bossiegel [Vict.]
Kübler [D. F.]
Goude [Pays-Bas Hollandais]
Staal [J.]
Van der Clos
Greifswald [Allemagne]
Roese
Groningue (Hollande)
Barlinkoof [C.]
Haarlem (Hollande)
Bosch [J.]
Assendelft [P.]
Enschedé [J.]
Halle (Saxe)
    J. God. Trampe   1781 Veuve [Trampen]
    J. Jac. Curt
    J. Just. Gebauer   1781 Veuve Gebauer & Fils
    Hemmerde [C. H.]
    Renger   1781 Hérit. Renger
        Francke [C. P.]
        Hendel [J. C.]
        Kummel [C. C.]
        Maison des Orphelins [The famous Waisenhaus, founded 1698]
Halle (Souabe)
        Vester
Hambourg (Allemagne)
    Isaac Etienne & fils (Not 1781)
    Veuve Grund (Not 1781)
    Bohn [C. E.]
    S. Guerrin (Not 1781)
    Petit & fils (Not 1781)
    Westphal (Not 1781)
    Falginer (Not 1781)
    Héritiers Konig (Not 1781)
    Petit & Dumoutier (Not 1781)
        Gleditsch [F. L.]
        Virchaux [J. G.]
        Veuve [C.] Herold [N.B. also J. H. Herold, the publisher of the *Buchhändlerzeitung*, 1778–85]
Hanovre (Allemagne)
    Ebell (Not 1781)
    Foester (Not 1781)
    Schmidt [J. W.]

Helwing frères
Richter
Harlingue (Provinces-Unies)
Van der Plaats
Heidelberg (Allemagne)
Pfaehler le jeune
Heilbronn (Allemagne)
Eckebrecht [F. J.]
Helmstad (Allemagne)
Drymborne (Not 1781)
Weygand [J. F.]
Kühnlin [J. H.]
Hilpershausen (Allemagne)
Hanisch
Hirsfeld (Allemagne)
Hermstaedt
Hoof (Allemagne).
Vierling [J. G.]
Horn (Pays-Bas Autrichien)
Tallingius [T.]
Ingolstadt [Bavière]
Cratz
Jena (Allemagne)
Veuve Croker [J. R.]
Cuno [C. H.]
Fickelscheer [Fel.]
Fischer
Gollner [C. F.]
Guth [T. W. E.]
Hartung
Konigsberg (Prusse)
Kinter   1781 Kanter [J. J.]
Hartung [G. L.]
La Haye (Provinces-Unies)
P. Dehondt [See also London] (Not 1781)
Scheurleer [F. H.] (Not 1781)
D. Aillaud [Died 1765 but brother Pierre still in business]
Bernard [Kossmann records for 1741, 1743 only]
P. Van Os [Died 1769 but son Thomas still in business] (Not 1781)
H. Constapel [Specialist in French theatre] (Not 1781)
B. Gibert [Specialist in French books]
Gosse, P. Fréd. [son and grandson of famous booksellers, 1751-1826]
Et. de Groos [died 1770]

   Gosse junior & Pinet 1781 Gosse junior [P., 1718–94]
   Dehaan [E., 1706–80]
   Monterdam [? as below]
   Moetjens [Adriaen, son and grandson of famous booksellers, 1729–1802]
   Neaulme [Jean, 1694–1780]
   F. Gibert & Fréd. Staatman 1781 Staatman
   Vandaalen [N., 1716–87] (Not 1781)
   Vandieren [Johannes, 1719–94] (Not 1781)
   Veuve Vanthol & fils. [Pieter, 1707–94 and son, 1741–1822]
     De Tune
Langensalze (Allemagne)
     Martini [J. C.]
Lauban [Allemagne]
     Wirthgen [J. C.]
Lausanne (Suisse)
   Bousquet [M. M.]
   Marc Chapuis
   Grasset & Compagnie [F.]
   Verney (Not 1781)
   Jules Henri Pott
     Decombaz [G.]
     Lacombe [F.]
     Meliatt, Olivier
     Société typographique
Leeuwaerden (Provinces Unies)
   Chalmot [H. A. de]
Leipsick (Allemagne)
   Crusius [S. L.]
   Decker [? G. J.] (Not 1781)
   Casp. Fritsch
   Gebauer [? as below or see Nuremberg]
   Jacobaer & fils [F. G.]
   Weidmann & Reich 1781 Hérit. Weidmann & Reich
   Chret. Gotlieb. Hilscher
   J. Geoff. Dick 1718 Veuve Dick
   Peycaupp (Not 1781)
     Boehme [A. F.]
     Breitkopf [J. G. J., publisher of the *Magazin des Buc-hund*
      Kunsthandels, 1780–3]
     Buschel [J. G.]
     Georgi [G. T., son of the author of the *Allgemeines Europäisches*
      Bücher-Lexicon (1742–58)]
     Veuve Gleditsch [J. F.]

Heinsius [J. G.]
Hertel [Chr. Gottl.]
Holler ainé [? J. C. Gollner]
Junius [J. J.]
Kummer [P. G.]
Langenheim [J. C.]
Loewe [J. G.]
C. Muller
J. Godefroy Muller
Saalbach [U. C.]
Schneider [C. Fr.]
Schweikert [E. B.]
Sommer [W. G.]
Weigand [C. F., the publisher of Goethe's *Werther*]
Veuve Merkus d'Amsterdam
Schreuder d'Amsterdam

Lemgo (Allemagne)
    Meier

Leyde (Provinces-Unies)
    Haak [C. or D.]
    Luchtmans, frères [S. & J.]
    El. Luzac & Vandamn [D.]
    Murray
    Wetsteins [J.]
        De Dekker [C.]
        Douzzi [J.]
        Wischoff [J.]

Liege (Allemagne)
    Bassompierre, père & fils.   1781 Mademosielle C. Bassompierre
    Bonin
    Veuve Bourguignon
    Dessain   1781 Veuve Dessain
    Kints [E. ? retired by 1767]
    De Mazeau
    Plomteux [C.]
    De Soer [F. J.]
    Tutot [J. J.]

Liegnitz (Silesie)
    Siegart [D.]

Lindau (Allemagne)
    Otto [J.]

Lisbonne (Portugal)
    Jos. Bertrand

Borel, Martin & Compagnie
Colonig
Dubeux, frères [C. & J. J.]
Genioux, frères
Montuerde
Pagliarini [? See also Rome]
Georges Rey & Compagnie
J. B. Reycends
Rolland
Isidore de Vallée
Bonnardel [J. or L. A.]
P. Antoine

Liverpool (Angleterre)
    Williamson [R. ? Died 1776]

Livourne (Italie)
    Coltellini [M., publisher of the Leghorn *Encyclopédie*] (Not 1781)
        Jean Vincent Falorni
        Charles Giorgi
        Th. Masi & Comp.
        Franc. Natali

Londres (Angleterre)
    L'astérique désigne les Libraires qui vendent des Livres François
    Chrét. Albouche [Not in Plomer]
    Allen [? E. or G.]
    Almon [J.]
    P. Antoine & P. Barbier* [Not in Plomer]
    Baldwin [R.]
    Bathurst [C.]
    Becket* [C.]
    Bell [J.]
    Beunet, J. [? J. Bennet]
    Bew [J.]
    Bladon, S.
    Blamire, R. [Not in Plomer but published in 1780]
    Blythe [F.]
    Bowyer [W. Bowyer jr. died 1776]
    Brindley* [? J. 1726–58]
    Buckland [J.]
    Cadell [T.]
    Canam [? as below]
    Carnan, T.
    Caston, T. [? Caslon]
    Crowder [S.]

Davis* [T.]
Dehunt* [P. A. De Hondt]
Dilly [C. & E.]
Dodsley* [J.]
Donaldson [A. or J. And in Edinburgh]
Elmsly* [P.]
Evans [T.]
Flexney [W.]
Goldsmith [W.]
Hay [G. Not in Plomer, but published in 1780]
Heydinger [C.]
Hinton [J.]
Hooper [S.]
Johnson [J.]
Kearsley [G.]
Keith [G.]
Leacroft [S.]
de Letanville [? Thomas, author of *Child's guide to French tongue*, 1758 etc.]
de Lorme [Not in Plomer]
Lowndes, T.
Millar* [A. died 1768]
Murray [J.]
Newbery, Fr.
Nichols [J.]
Nicoll, W.
Nourse, J.*
Noble [F. & J.]
Overv [? as below]
Owen [W.]
Pame [? as below]
Payne [J. or T.]
Riley [G.]
Richardson [S. died 1761. ? R. and Urquhart]
Robinson [G.]
Robson [J.]
Roson [J. Not in Plomer, but published ca. 1773]
du Rouvray [J. P., Swiss merchant in London]
Sayer, R.
Setchell [? as below]
Shatwell [P.]
Strahan, W.
Suagg [? R. Snagg]

Thanc [? J. Thane. Not in Plomer but published in 1773]
Urquhart [See Richardson]
Vaillant* [P. 2nd]
Vilkie [J. Wilkie]
Walter [J.]
Wenman [J.]
Whiston [J.]
White [B.]
Wilson [D.]

Louvain (Pays-Bas Autrichiens)
    Van Overbeke
        Van der Haert

Lubeck (Allemagne)
    Iversen & Compagnie [? C. See also Altona]
    Jonas Schmidt
        Donatius [Chr. G.]
        Hellmann

Lucques (Italie)
    Rocchi (Not 1781)
        Jacques Giusti
        Jean Domin. Marescandoti
        Jean Ricomini

Lunebourg (Allemagne)
        Lemke [J. F. W.]

Macerate [Italie, Marche d'Ancone]
        Antoine Cortese

Madrid (Espagne)
    J. Gomes
    De la Higulva
    Samuel Pinto
    Barthelemi
    Corradi, [A.]
    Escribano
    Fernandez
    Franies [? B. Frances]
    Martin, Alphonse
    Orcel, frères
    Barth. Ulloa
    Joach. Jos. Barra
    Ant. Marin
    Simon Moreno
    Sanches
    Ant. Peres de Soto

Copin
Maestrict (Pays-Bas Hollandais)
  J. E. Dufour
  J. Le Kens
  Lanc. Meter
      Van Gulden
Magdebourg (Allemagne)
    Scheidhauer
        Creutz [J. Ad.]
        Seidel & Zapfe
Mainz (Allemagne)
        Hérit. Haeffner
Malines (Pays-Bas Autrichiens)
    C. Jeghers
        Van der Elst
Malte
  Nicolas Capaci
Manheim (Allemagne)
    Charles Fontaine
        Loeffler [T.]
        Schwan [C. F.]
Mantoue (Italie)
        André Bianchi
Marpurg (Allemagne)
        Hérit. Muller & Weldige
Masse-Carrare (Italie)
        Etienne Frediani
Memingen (Allemagne)
        Hanisch
Messine (Sicile)
        Franc. Caccia
Middlebourg (Hollande)
    P. Gilissen
Milan (Italie)
    Jos. Richino (Not 1781)
    Malacerta (Not 1781)
    Ant. Agnelli   1781 Fred. Agnelli
    J. J. Barelle
    Galeazzi, J.
    Hermille & Vincent (Not 1781)
    Marelli (Not 1781)
    Reycends, frères
        Ch. Cetti

Dom. Speranza
Mittau (Courlande) [= Lithuanie]
    Hinz [J. F.]
Modène (Italie)
    Soliani (Not 1781)
    Foa [? See also Reggio]   (Not 1781)
        Sylvest. Abboretti
Mons (Pays-Bas Autrichiens)
    Beautien   1781 Bottin
    Emman. H. J. Plon
    Fosset
    Hoyois
    Martin
    Vilmet
Moskou (Russie)
    Grandmaison
Moudon (Allemagne)
    Vincent [H. E.]
Munich (Allemagne)
    Richter [F. L.]
        Fritz Otto Cratz
Munster (Allemagne)
    Perrenon [Ph. H.]
Namur (Pays-Bas Autrichiens)
    Fontaine
Naples (Italie)
    Vincent Manfredy (Not 1781)
    Flauto [V.] (Not 1781)
    Raymond (Not 1781)
    J. Gravier (Not 1781)
    Hermill, père (Not 1781)
    Hermill, fils (Not 1781)
    Hernillet (Not 1781)
    De Malaspine (Not 1781)
    G. Roland (Not 1781)
    J. Domingues   1781 Dominique Terres
        Vincent Migliaccio
        Michel Stasi
        J. M. Porcelli
        Simoni frères
Neufchatel (Suisse)
    Fauche [S.]
    Société typographique

Sinnet [J.]
Nice (Italie)
    Ploteron
Nimègue (Holland)
    Heyman [? H.]
    Van Campen [Is.]
    Wolfzen [? H.]
Nordlingen (Allemagne)
    Beck [C. G.]
Nordhaussen (Allemagne)
    Gross [C. G.]
Novare (Italie)
    François Cavalli
Nuremberg (Allemagne)
    Homans (Not 1781)
    Gebauer [? G. Bauer, see also Leipzig] (Not 1781)
    Georg. Lochner
        Ammermuller [J. E.]
        Bauer [M. J.]
        Enders [J. A. Endter]
        Hausse [Chr. Gotth.]
        Monath [G. P.]
        Raspe [G. N.]
        Riegel [? C. Weigel]
        Schwarzkopf [Wolfg.]
        Hérit. Seligmann
        Wirsing
        Zeh [J. E.]
        Veuve Felsecker
Offembach (Allemagne)
    Weiss
Osimo (Italie, dans la Marche d'Ancone)
    Zuercetti [? Quercetti]
Oxford (Angleterre)
    Richard Clement[s] [Succeeded by Prince since 1750s]
    James Fletcher
    J. Newbury
    Jackson [W.] (Not 1781)
    Prince, D.
Padoue (Italie)
    Salomon
Palerme (Sicile)
        Jos. Orel

And. Rapetti
Parme (Italie)
    Faure, frères
        Phil. Carmignani
Perugia (Italie)
        Marc. Reginaldi
        Ant. Natali
Pesaro (Italie)
        Nicolas Gravelli
Pest (Hongrie)
        Weingand [J. M.] & Kopf
Pise (Italie, Toscane)
    P. Giovanelli & Compagnie (Not 1781)
    J. Pizzorni (Not 1781)
        Cath. Poleni
Pistoye (Toscane)
    Bracali
Plaisance (Italie)
    Phil. Jacob Pazzi (Not 1781)
        Mauro de Maine [? del Maino]
Porto (Portugal)
    Clamopin, Durand, Gronteau
Potsdam (Brandebourg)
        Horvath [C. C.]
Prague (Bohême)
    Clausec
    Fehereider
    Wolfgang Gerle
        Hochonberg
Presbourg [= Bratislava. Hongrie]
        Loewe [Ant.]
Purmerent (Bohême)
        Jordann
Queddlimbourg (Allemagne)
    Perrie
        Reussner [C. A.]
Ratisbonne (Allemagne)
    Veuve Sciffart
    Junckel
    Baden   1781 Veuve Baden
    Peez
        Montag
Reggio (Môdênois, Italie)

   Moyse Benjam. Foa [? See also Modène]
Riga (Livonie)
    Hartnoch [J. F.]
Rimini (Italie, Etat de l'Eglise)
  Albertini
Rinteln (Allemagne)
  Enard
    Muller
Rome (Italie)
  Pallas (Not 1781)
  Fulgoni (Not 1781)
  Zempel (Not 1781)
  Bouchard [? J. formerly of Florence] 1781 & Gravier
  Durand (Not 1781)
  Pagliarini frères [? See also Lisbon]
  Puccinelli (Not 1781)
  Settari [G.]
  Komarek (Not 1781)
  Generoso Salmoni
    Barbiellini, Natal.
    Giunchi [P.]
    Salvioni
    Salviucci, Franc.
Rostock (Allemagne)
  J. Ch. Kooppen 1781 Koppe
  Berger & Bodner
Rotterdam (Provinces-Unies)
  J. Daniel Bermann [Beman]
  Henri Beman
  Reynier Aremberg
  Bennet [L.] 1781 & Aak
  Veuve de Vuijk [F.]
  Aak [J. van]
    Bronkorst [J.]
Saint-Petersbourg (Russie)
  Clairval
  J. Vernander
  Weithbrecht [J. J.]
  Doulgoncki (Not 1781)
  Guill. Vyard
    Jean Zacharie Logan
Salamanque (Espagne)
  Alegria

Salzbourg (Allemagne)
    Mayers hérit. [J. J.]
    Maison des Orphelins [See Halle]
Sassari (Sardigne)
  Jos. Piattoli
Saxe-Gotha (Allemagne)
  Ettinger
  J. Chrét. Dieterich
Schaffouse (Suisse)
    Hurter & fils
Schillingsfurt (Allemagne)
  G. D. Lobegott
Schwerin [Allemagne, Mecklenbourg]
    Buchenröder
Seville (Espagne)
  Jos. Navarro
Sienne (Italie)
  Augustin Bindi 1781 frères Bindi
    François Rossi
    Char. Pazzini
Sneeck (Provinces-Unies)
    Olingius [M.]
Soraw (Allemagne)
    Hebold [G.]
Stetin (Allemagne)
    Draevenstaedt
Stockholm (Suède)
  Nypstromm & Skolpe (Not 1781)
  Chr. Askergren (Not 1781)
  Haldin (Not 1781)
  Heisselberg (Not 1781)
  Salvius [L.] (Not 1781)
  Ulf [C. C.] (Not 1781)
  Holmberg [J. C.] (Not 1781)
    Arboren
    Fought [E.]
    Fyrberg [A. A.]
    Giorwel [C. Christofferson, a librarian?]
    Lange
    Lochner
    Oerstroem
    Pfeiffer
    Runemarck

Segerdal
Sevederus [M. See also Uppsala]
Stutgard (Allemagne)
  J. B. Metzler
      Cotta [J. G.]
      Erhard [J. C.]
Thiel [Pays-Bas Hollandais]
      Repelius [T.]
Tournay (Pays-Bas Autrichiens)
  J. R. de Flinne
  Pingué
  Serré
  Varlé   1781 Veuve Varlé
      Joveneau
      Prevost
Trente (Italie)
      Michel Battrati
Tubingue (Allemagne)
  C. H. Berger
  J. G. Cotta
      Heerbrand
Turin (Piémont)
    Toussaint, Laurent (Not 1781)
    Bonnardel frères
    Bruscoli (Not 1781)
    Guibert & Orgeas
    Raby, Ant.
    Reycends frères
      Jean Michel Briolo
      Beltram, Re.
      Jos. Franc. Destasanis
Ulm (Souabe)
  J. Conrad Wohler
  Albert Fred. Bartholomei
  Gaum, J. F.
Upsal (Suède)
      Swederus [M. See also Stockholm]
Utrecht (Provinces-Unies)
    Cornel [? N. later at Rotterdam]
    Guillaume Le Fevre
    Sorly
    Van Paddenburg, frères
    Kroon [W. H.]

Kribber [C.]
Cl. Isaac Penet
Spruyt [H.]
    Bosh [J. C. or J. S.]
    Van Meyeré [R.]
    Van Poolsum [J. J.]
    Visch [M.]

Varsovie (Pologne)
  Rousseau
  Groll [M. See also Dresden]
  Poser [J. A.]

Venise (Italie)
  Remondini, Jos.
  Bassaglia [? P. and G. M.] (Not 1781)
  Colombani (Not 1781)
  Palesa [C.] (Not 1781)
  Pasquali, J. B.
  Zarta, Antoine
  Antoine de Castro, J. B. (Not 1781)
  Novelli, Pier
  Betinelli, Forest.
  Simon Occhi
  Ant. Bassaenza (Not 1781)
  Dougoni [Dorigoni]
  Angiola, Geremia (Not 1781)
  Caroboli & Pompeati (Not 1781)
  J. B. Indrich (Not 1781)
    Baglioni hérit.
    Bassegio, Laur.
    Gatti, Jean
    Pezzana, Franc.
    Pezzana, Ant.
    Pezzana, hérit. de Nic.
    Storti, Gasp.

Verceil [Italie]
    Jos. Panialis

Verone (Italie)
  Aug. Carrattoni
    Marc Moroni

Viceme [? Vicence = Vicenza]
    Ant. Veronese

Vienne (Autriche)
  Bernardi [Aug.]

        Veuve Deilhac
        Rodolphe Graesser
        Kraus, J. Paul
        Trattner, J. Thom.
            Bader
            Phelen
            Jean Pierre Kruechten
            Kurzboeck [J.]
            Veuve du fils de Trattner
Viterbe (Italie)
    Zenti
Weimar (Allemagne)
        Hoffmann [S. H.]
Wesel (Allemagne)
        Hoffmann
        Roeder [F. J.]
        Witzeki
Winterthur (Suisse)
        Steiner [J. H.] & Compagnie
Wismar (Allemagne)
        Berger & Bodner
Wittemberg (Allemagne)
    S. G. Zimmermann [? since 1713 in hands of Nicolai family]
        Ahlfeld [J. J.]
Wolfenbuttel [Saxe]
        Meissner [J. C.]
Wurzbourg (Allemagne)
        Stahel [J. J. or R.]
Ypres (Pays-Bas Autrichiens)
    A. J. Remy
    J. Remy frères (Not 1781)
    Walvein
        Le Clerc
Yverdon (Suisse)
    Felice [F. B.]
    Société typographique
        Prof. Lex [J. F., also Recteur du collège]
        Du Puget fils
Zell (Allemagne)
        Gsellius
        Runge
        Schuez
Zittaw (Allemagne)

   Spickermann
Zullicaw (Silesie)
   Fromann [N. S.]
   Maison des Orphelins.
Zurich (Suisse)
 Fueslin (1781 as below)
 Gesner (1781 as below)
 Heidegger & Compagnie [H.]
 Hoffmeister
 Orel 1781 Orell, Gesner, Fusslin & Co.
Zutphen (Provinces-Unies)
 Van Hoorn [A. J.]
 Van-Bulderen [H.]
Zwol (Pays-Bas Hollandois)
 Vanzantem [? J. later at Rotterdam]

NOTE

1. For the 1784 edition see J. Grand Carteret, *Les almanacs français* (Paris, 1896), p. 147. The copies of the other editions of the *Almanach* known to me include: 1777 Bibliothèque nationale and Cercle de la librairie, Paris, Bibliothèque publique et universitaire, Geneva; 1778 Cercle de la librairie; 1781 Cercle de la librairie, British Library, St. Bride Printing Library, Bodleian Library (red morocco and with the arms of the Chancellor, the marquis de Miromesnil), Bibliothèque historique de la ville de Paris (red morocco with the arms of Le Camus de Néville, the Directeur général).

APPENDIX

A contemporary German survey of the European book trade was contributed to the *Oeconomische Encyclopaedie* (Berlin, Leipzig, pt. 7, 1776, pp. 190–210) by J. G. Krünitz. I am greatly indebted to Georgina Warrilow for the following translation. The notes at the end are Krünitz's own.

The book trade is an important branch of commerce and can be divided into different classes. The true book trade consists not only in the buying and selling of existing books but also in the publication of new ones. A bookseller [Buchhändler], in earlier days called a Buchführer, L. Bibliopola, Fr. Libraire or Marchand libraire sells his own publications for ready money, selling sometimes all his available volumes, sometimes only a proportion of them, but in any case engaging in cash [Contant] dealing; or he may trade with the producers of other publications, with whom he can barter and exchange goods, thus providing himself with a retail stock [Sortiment]. The term bookseller is also applied to those who, although they themselves publish only hymn and prayer books, almanacs, calendars and other small items, deal also with the published work of the first mentioned type of bookseller. Finally there are other booksellers (who may be distinguished by the name Bücherhändler) who collect, by various means, both old and new bound books, and resell them singly, or by lot at auction, even also lending out the volumes for a fee. These may be described as antiquarian bookdealers [Antiquarii]. I shall be dealing in this article with the first-mentioned type of bookseller.

Before the invention of printing there existed a trade in manuscripts; but since the invention of printing in the fifteenth century the book trade has reached its present peak. At first even the greatest scholars engaged in printing and the book trade. Today however booksellers exist in such sufficient numbers, especially in large cities, that the learned would scruple to compete against them, for the bookseller, to maintain a livelihood, must put himself to considerable expense in printing, publishing and selling books. Herr Klopstock has recently proposed a 'learned republic' whose members would engage in trading the scholarly writings and products of their own association without the intervention of booksellers, procuring through their own endeavours a greater profit; but —— [sic] I leave this proposal to the critical judgment of each scholar and writer.[1]

For the establishment of the book trade the same economic requirements are necessary as those which ensure success in any other branch of commerce. These are—that the trade promotes the good of the country, that the goods traded are sound and reliable, and the prices competitive. It is essential therefore that a sufficient number of books is printed and published in any given country to be traded abroad against foreign books and to bring foreign money into the country. The law enjoining that books published in a country should also be printed there is no more unfair than the law prohibiting merchants from importing from abroad the same goods as are manufactured at home. It follows that a country's printing offices must be well organised and must operate as efficiently and economically as their foreign

[1] Notes begin on p. 276.

counterparts. A slight difference in price between available goods will have little effect but a high price for a book combined with bad printing has undesirable results.

The quality of the book is as essential to the prosperity of the book trade as the standard of goods in any other branch of commerce. The way in which the value of a book is related to the attitude of the buyer must be understood; to the bookseller a book is good when it finds a ready sale, however slight or mediocre its true worth. Important factors are public taste, the content of the book and the language in which it is written. Those works whose content and language appeal only to a minority of readers clearly never command such a universal market as those appealing to a greater proportion of the reading public.

Finally, prices sufficiently attractive to encourage purchasers are a further essential. Very large works commanding extremely high prices are suitable only for the great libraries and this market is not the most significant. Moreover even moderately-sized books find far less sale [Debit] when their price is high in relation to their size. A reader is more inclined to debate the purchase of such a work and to decide not to buy it if his need of it is not imperative. But a scholar will buy a book at a low price out of sheer curiosity, or on account of some particular passages in it, or to enrich his library, even though he could perfectly well do without it.[2]

The observance of these basic economic rules goes far to establish a prosperous book trade but they are not enough in themselves to ensure universal success. Certain other measures must be taken to achieve this for there are some obstacles to the trade which can only be overcome by appropriate police regulations. Some consideration must be given as to where the book trade should be carried on as not all places are equally suitable. If successful trade needs the efficient production of worthwhile books, then it is also true that the place of production is important, being directly related to the availability of a ready market. It is well known that the greatest sale of books occurs at the book fairs where there is trade with foreign dealers. Those cities where the greatest book fairs are held are Leipzig and Frankfurt, and of these I will later give an account.

In capital cities and large towns with universities a good and ready market exists, but goods destined for foreign markets must reach them either through the book fairs or by direct dispatch abroad, and this second alternative involves a freight charge which increases the final cost of the book.

Care must be taken to ensure that booksellers do not compete too ruinously against each other, as for example when one man secretly prints a work for which another holds the privilege.³

It is equally disadvantageous to the trade as a whole if one dealer institutes an auction or lottery of his entire stock, or a portion of it, for by this means books may well be sold below the current price to the detriment of other dealers. For this reason, some codes of law, that of Saxony for instance, forbid the auctioning of unbound books.

A third disadvantage to the trade results from too high a tax being levied on paper, directly resulting in increased costs of printed books.

In the Prussian royal domains all printed books whether bound or unbound are free of excise, and paper carries a very light tax, for example in Silesia only one halfpenny in the crown.

Satisfactory market prices for books can also be adversely affected if the bookseller has to pay too much for his privilege. The sale of privileges is an easy way of increasing royal revenues and the urge to abuse this should be resisted. The dealer will immediately add his increased cost to the book price. If moderation is exercised in this field and a reasonable liberality shown in the setting of charges, publication of books will be encouraged.

The book trade is a free and open profession unhindered by many guild and union regulations, except that those who wish to follow it must complete an apprenticeship of five or six years and then be declared proficient by their masters.

Outside Germany it is customary for most booksellers in Holland, England, France and Italy to deal only in their own publications; they do not trade through book fairs but either sell their editions for cash, or deal on account with other booksellers, usually with a rebate [Rabatt] of a fixed percentage, only the remainder of the current account after such dealings being paid in cash. In such countries the prospective buyer must first discover where the book is published and then either buy direct for cash from the specific bookseller, or persuade another dealer to order the volume for him. This system gives the would-be purchaser so much inconvenience that many books which he would like to acquire no doubt remain unsold.

In Germany there has long been a flourishing trade in books based on the two fairs held at Frankfurt-on-Main and Leipzig, at Easter and in the autumn of each year. Very many booksellers from all parts of Germany congregate there as well as some Dutch and Swiss dealers and others from Strasbourg, Breslau, Glogau, Liegnitz, Pressburg,

Danzig, Königsberg, Mietau, Riga, Stockholm, Flensburg and Copenhagen; and for some years past occasionally a bookseller from Lyons and one from London. A dealer who cannot visit the fair in person or is unable to send his assistant will pay a commission to one of his colleagues to carry out his commitments and deal with his business. The Leipzig Easter fair attracts a greater number of dealers than the autumn fair, greater business being transacted then because all yearly accounts are settled in the spring.

The following lists and figures give some indication of the leading position which the Leipzig fair has attained in the book trade. (1) Leipzig alone has 26 bookshops of which 19 are bookshops proper and 7 are printing offices which at the same time sell their own publications. (2) In Berlin there are 10 bookshops and 3 printing offices selling their own works. (3) In Nuremberg, 12 bookshops. (4) In Halle, 5 bookshops and 6 printing offices which also sell books. (5) In Frankfurt-on-Main, 10 bookshops. (6) In Hamburg, 7 bookshops and additionally 1 printing office. (7) In Vienna, 8 bookshops. (8) In Jena, 5 bookshops and one printing office. (9) In Augsburg, 4 bookshops. (10) In Brunswick, 4. (11) In Göttingen, 4. (12) In Dresden, 3. (13) In Hanover, 3. (14) In Ulm, 3. (15) In Zell, 3. (16) In Bautzen, 2. (17) In Bremen, 2. (18) In Cassel, 2. (19) In Chemnitz, 2. (20) In Erfurt, 2. (21) In Gotha, 2. (22) In Lübeck, 2. (23) In Magdeburg, 2. (24) In Mannheim, 2. (25) In Prague, 2. (26) In Regensburg, 2. (27) In Stuttgart, 2. (28) In Tübingen, 2. (29) In Wittenberg, 2.

Those towns possessing only one bookshop are (30) Altenberg, (31) Altona, (32) Ansbach, (33) Bamberg, (34) Bayreuth, (35) Brandenburg, (36) Karlsruhe, (37) Cleve, (38) Coburg, (39) Cologne, (40) Köthen, (41) Eisenach, (42) Erlangen, (43) Frankfurt on the Oder, (44) Giessen, (45) Greifswald, (46) Halberstadt, (47) Hanau, (48) Heilbronn, (49) Helmstadt, (50) Hildburghausen, (51) Hirschfeld, (52) Hof, (53) Langensalze, (54) Lauban, (55) Lemgo, (56) Lindau, (57) Lüneburg, (58) Marburg, (59) Münster, (60) Nördlingen, (61) Nordhausen, (62) Quedlinburg, (63) Rintenl, (64) Rostock, (65) Sorau, (66) Stettin, (67) Weimar, (68) Wismar, (69) Würzburg, (70) Zittau, (71) Züllichau.

These 71 German towns contain altogether 188 bookshops including those printing offices also engaged in bookselling and these are the traders who hold the Leipzig fair; with these should also be reckoned the booksellers of the Austrian Netherlands and others who do not attend the fair.

Foreign booksellers visiting Leipzig are as follows: (a) from Holland, besides the two Amsterdam booksellers permanently established in Leipzig, there are also (72) from Leiden 3; (b) from Switzerland (73) from Basle 3, (74) from Berne 2, (75) from Geneva 1, (76) Lausanne 1, (77) Zürich 1; (c) from Alsace (78) from Strasbourg 2; (d) from Silesia (79), from Breslau 5, (80) from Glogau 1, (81) from Liegnitz 1; (e) from the kingdom of Prussia, (82) from Königsberg 2; (f) from formerly Polish Prussia, (83) from Danzig 2; (g) from Courland (84) from Mietau 1; (h) from Livonia, (85) from Riga 1; (i) from Sweden, (86) from Stockholm 1; (k) from Denmark and Schleswig, (87) from Copenhagen 4, (88) from Flensburg 1; (l) from Hungary, (89) from Bratislava 1. For some time now every few years (m) from France, (90) from Lyons 1; and (n) from England (91) from London 1. This totals 34 foreign booksellers visiting the fair and this number added to the already listed German traders, makes altogether 222 merchants whose trade is concentrated on the Leipzig fair.

Each of these booksellers sends to the fair as many copies of each of his available publications as he believes he may reasonably sell or barter. If he expects to find enough cash buyers he may offer his publications for sale with a rebate of up to 33 per cent and this is the manner in which the printers in our list deal with their own works. However most booksellers also engage in a permanent mutual trade of exchanging their own books with those of other dealers, in which case only the balance [Saldo] need then be paid in cash with a rebate of up to 25 per cent, usually only 16 per cent. Each bookseller takes as many other publications as he can balance by this method of exchange and the cash balances may run for settlement from one Easter fair to the next, a half year's credit being extended for items traded at the autumn fair.

After the fair, cheap return freight charges usually operate from Leipzig to those other places where bookshops are situated. By this means each German bookseller can procure from another whatever stock he wishes, and send it home with the greatest convenience, ease, and uniformity of transport costs. Even outside the fair-times similar convenient opportunities exist in Leipzig and other large cities. Book packets are relatively lightly rated in the post, and new books appearing between the fair-times can be cheaply exchanged between booksellers, who are thus enabled to build up a stock of their own and other dealers' publications.

Another advantage existing for some years past is that booksellers have been able to send to Leipzig, some weeks before the fair occurs, the titles of those new books which they intend to take to the fair. The titles are then included in the alphabetically arranged list from which the Fair Catalogue is formulated. This is printed and circulated to all bookshops enabling booklovers and intending purchasers to give their orders in advance of the fair, being thereby more certain of obtaining what they want. Moreover, after each fair the bookseller takes care to circulate amongst his customers a catalogue showing his own new publications and such retail stock as he has brought back from the fair, the prices of all items being indicated.

The German book trade operates with a convenience to the general public not known in any other country. The customer is saved the trouble of first discovering the printer of each work, and having discovered his name, of writing to him or to some other bookseller for a copy of the book, being subsequently obliged to buy the volume after he has written for it. In Germany a customer sees in any bookshop a variety of works, published in many different places and he may study the volumes before deciding to buy one. Should a particular volume not be in stock it can quickly and without further cost be sought from a neighbouring bookseller. One should consider too the advantages of that encouragement of German literature which results from the fact that any book, once it has been carried to the Leipzig fair, can be made known in a few weeks throughout Germany, and can be offered for sale in a hundred different catalogues. The wide variety of monthly and weekly periodicals and newspapers, both scholarly and political, offers many opportunities for the review of new books. A scholar or writer in Germany need make little effort to advertise his works or call attention to his first appearance in print, as in a short time his writings can be known by name in catalogues throughout the country, and copies of his works can be seen and examined by any reader who is interested in them, without the expense of ordering.

The bookseller has the benefit of knowing that he may be able to deposit a certain percentage of his own publications profitably at each single fair and that he will be able to sell for cash such retail stock as he has acquired there.

It can however happen that retail stock obtained through the fairs may become dead stock [Ladenhütern], whose sale is difficult or unlikely. Nevertheless if a bookseller is not to disregard his customers' tastes and inclinations he is bound to invest a good deal of capital in large stocks of books, some of which may not be sold for a long time, if ever. He must exercise great skill and care in the composition of his stock and in ensuring that he does not acquire by exchange too many works not in accordance with his particular market. It can easily happen that, having put his cash into his own published stock, which may be good material, he loses by exchanges of it for other unsaleable volumes. Such experiences teach him the precautions essential to the German bookseller if he is to survive in trade.

It is clear that the book trade represents an important branch of commerce and a considerable source of livelihood to many, from papermakers to bookbinders; that it contributes to a variety of economic undertakings in transport, freight and the postal systems, and wherever it exists in Germany has the economic benefit that the bookseller brings foreign goods into the land mainly through exchange and not through outgoing currency, and that the flow of cash from customers is retained in the country. On these grounds any state with a flourishing book trade should take a serious interest in maintaining its prosperity.

The greatest centre of the German book trade being Leipzig it is not surprising that it is in Saxony that the most effective legal measures have been devised for the protection and furtherance of the trade. I will set out these measures as they appear in Herr Schmieder's *Sächsische Polizeiverfassung*, p. 513.

> Booksellers shall not act to the prejudice of bookbinders, auctioneers, book-pedlars and ballad-mongers, and booksellers shall maintain fairness in their dealings with each other; the auctioneer shall not deal in unbound books, and the book-pedlar and ballad-monger shall trade only in almanacs, calendars and pamphlets of not more than 10 to 12 sheets, under pain of forfeiture of their goods.
>
> The privilege is accorded to the booksellers of Dresden that they may carry on their trade in publishing and selling books on all subjects, to the exclusion of all neighbouring booksellers, who may not establish a similar trade in the city; for in their monopoly the Dresden merchants are granted full protection.
>
> The booksellers are also protected against unauthorised reprinting of their works throughout the kingdom of Saxony and against the importation of such unauthorised volumes into the kingdom. Should such illegal activity be detected the sale of the unauthorised volumes may, with summary justice, be forbidden and the offending trader compelled to make compensation to the injured bookseller. However, the complainant bookseller must show that he has the legal privilege to the book or translation vested in him by the author, or, if he is a foreigner, he must show that in his own land there is reciprocal legislation as regards Saxon subjects.
>
> Such proofs may be difficult and sometimes impossible for booksellers to

show conclusively. They have sought to avoid these problems and to assure themselves of a fuller protection against piracies either by obtaining a privilege sanctioned by the Elector, or by entering their own printed works in one of the Protocols of the Leipzig Book Commission. Such registration has the force and effect of a privilege—no unauthorised printings may be made, exchanged or imported into Saxon lands during the time of the Fair or at any other period. Those found trading in such copies shall have all such goods confiscated or, if the goods cannot be impounded, then the offender must pay a fine of their total value, with additionally, the sum of 50 crowns of which half goes to the Procurator-Fiscal and half to the complainant bookseller. To obtain justice in such cases from the Electoral Book Commission in Leipzig, or from the ordinary magistracy in other places, it is necessary that the bookseller supply either the privilege or the form obtained on registering his works in the Protocol. The pretext that the offending volumes are only in transit through Saxony cannot be justified if the volumes are unpacked. Those who become involved as middlemen in any sales of piracies, or who knowingly conceal such sales, can suffer a substantial fine.

In exchange for such protection the booksellers are obliged to ensure that a sufficient number of books, well printed on good paper, is available to the public at reasonable prices. On the other hand if a bookseller abuses his privileged warrant by producing a poor edition or a bad translation, thereby preventing publication of a better one, or by charging an unnecessarily high price for a book, particularly one useful for religious or educational purposes, then his privilege may be withdrawn and the work transferred to another who can produce it at a cheaper price.

It has been stated earlier that books registered with the Protocols of the Leipzig Book Commission, either by foreign or domestic booksellers, have the same protection as otherwise privileged books. The Book Commission enacts as follows—

'I. Each bookseller is free to seek privilege for his books from the sovereign authority whose warrant must be printed verbatim in the volume.

II. Those not desiring to obtain a privilege in the above manner, whether they are domestic or foreign booksellers, may, if they participate in the Leipzig Book Fair, submit the titles of those books for which they claim a privilege to an Inspector of the Commission's Protocol for inclusion in the Commission's list, which inclusion has the force of a privilege and guarantees equal legal protection.

III. All booksellers participating in the Leipzig Book Fair may so register their newly printed books provided that
   1. They provide substantial claims to be the legitimate publishers of such

works and while the Commission will not necessarily examine such claims, in doubtful cases the evidence may be investigated by the Electoral Church Commission.

2. The publisher must show the complete title of his work and undertake to print it, clearly and well, on good paper, under his own imprint. The general expression 'under the imprint of the Company of booksellers' cannot be allowed. The publisher must arrange for the whole work to be ready within a year, or, in the case of a very large work, at least a portion of it must be completed in that time, or good reason shown for failure to do so. If the work is not completed the bookseller may forfeit the right of registration.

3. Each trader is at liberty to have registered all those existing volumes which he has ready in stock which are not yet privileged, but the conditions of 2. above must be observed.

4. In the case of translations, the publisher first registered in the Protocol is given preference. He must supply a complete translation within a year, or a portion of the total if the work is large. Under the above-mentioned caution he must produce a good and efficient translation, and if after investigation it is found to be faulty, another publisher will be allowed to supply an improved text.

IV. A Protocol registered book enjoys the same protection as one with a royal privilege, that is, the protection has force and effect for 10 years; but shortly before the expiry of that time the publisher may apply to re-register the book for a further period and retains the privilege against other applicants.

V. The bookseller must deliver to the Commission 20 copies of each registered work or 15 copies if the work costs more than 3 crowns, and he must present the same number of copies of each new edition, with not less than 1 crown for stamp duty. A fee of 4 pence is also necessary for the Clerk to the Protocols, for each book registered.

VI. The Book Commission must deliver every three months to the Church Commission a specification of all registered books, and must, if required, supply to the bookseller (for a charge) any desired extracts from the Protocols.

VII. For the further encouragement and protection of the trade the booksellers congregating at the Leipzig Fair may elect as representatives or deputies

(1) 3 Saxon booksellers, 2 from Leipzig and 1 from some other city in the kingdom

(2) 6 representatives of other visiting foreign booksellers, all nine to decide on such things as best serve the common good of the book trade and to inform the Book Commission of their findings. These deputies can, when doubtful cases come before the Commission, give their advice verbally or in

writing, without loss of time, or legal complications, reporting directly to the Saxon Church Commission.4

A recently established institution relating to the book trade is the so-called *Hanauer neuer Bücher-Umschlag*, founded on 26th June 1775. The founder members, both foreign and domestic booksellers (according to private information), numbering only 8, held their first deliberations in the great hall of the Town Hall in the New Town, and at this meeting several regulations governing the new body were formulated and agreed. In future the annual meeting of the *Hanauer neuer Bücher-Umschlag* will be held on August 1st. On the 7th of July a decree from Vienna was published which expressly forbade some of the liberties and agreements granted by the Bücher-Umschlag. Whether this new body will be of any future force and influence, whether it will bring system and order into the Austrian book trade, which has been in decay for the past 20 years, time alone will tell.5

In conclusion there follow some observations on the book trade in the remaining European states and kingdoms. The English nation appears unique in that books of considerable importance are in their country printed by subscription, a system by which a number of individuals join to defray the cost of printing and to assure the author of adequate remuneration.

The English and French book trades have in common with each other, and with certain other European states, the advantage that the publisher of any saleable book can count on selling a complete edition of it, and indeed, in a short time, the certainty of selling further editions. This is true in both capital cities London and Paris, and nowhere else in Europe is it so likely that a considerable edition of a new work will find a complete sale in a few days.

For instance in February, 1774, it was reported from Paris that 14,000 copies of a *Mémoire* by Beaumarchais were bought up in two days and the printer was forced to ask for a guard to be set on his house against the crowds of people who flocked to obtain copies. Such incidents are not likely to happen outside Paris or London.

A bookseller may employ correspondents or commission agents outside the capital to promote his sales and to save making efforts himself to further his trade, although English and French booksellers have no particular reason to seek such outside custom.

However the foreign trade of both England and France is so vast and prosperous in so many different fields that they have little need to regard the book trade as forming a vital component in their foreign commerce. But for the Dutch on the other hand, the book trade is a profitable commercial activity; not only do they seek to sell their own publications abroad, but they are zealous reprinters of English and French works, selling them not only at home in the Netherlands but also abroad, more particularly the English reprints in France, and the French reprints in England, with considerable profit.

In England an act of the eighth year of Queen Anne confirms to the publisher of any work the right of forbidding its reprint by others for 14 years. At the end of this time the right reverts to the author who may offer it to another printer for a further 14 years. But at the expiry of the second period the right to print the text is open to all.

In France the fact that foreign reprints are so heavily imported imposes a certain handicap on French booksellers; this is accentuated by the fact that a severe censorship forbids the publication of many original works, which would certainly be printed in other countries. As a result many French books are secretly printed in France with foreign imprints, or they are in fact printed abroad and, despite the censorship, imported into the country and distributed. To counteract this a heavy import duty is levied on foreign books, with little advantage to scholarship or entertainment and little is ultimately achieved, since either the duty is paid or a flourishing trade results in contraband books.[6] Once this kind of contraband smuggling exists it is small wonder that valuable foreign reprints find their way into the country.[7]

The French censorship however is nothing like so severe as the Spanish. A Spanish reprint is not likely to harm a foreign bookseller and a foreign reprint as little likely to harm a Spanish bookseller. This is also the case in Portugal, Poland and Hungary. The numerous Italian states trade in books mainly with each other or with Switzerland, France, Spain or Portugal.

As for the book trade in Sweden, that is the subject of a report by Herr Menander set out in detail in the *Göttinger Anzeiger*, 1757, p. 744.[8]

NOTES

1. *Zufällige Gedanken eines Buchhändlers* (Herr Reich of Leipzig) *über Herrn Klopstocks Anzeige einer gelehrten Republik*. 1773.

2. *Eine Untersuchung, ob auch die Bücher von der Policey taxirt werden können*. Taken from Herr President Philippi's instructive *Briefe über verschiedene Gegenstände der Staatswirthschaft, Policei und Moral*. Berlin, 1770, pp. 326–59.

3. *Der Bücher-Nachdruck, nach achten Grundsätzen des Rechts geprüfet,* by J. S. Pütter. Göttingen, 1774. *Der gerechtfertigte Nachdrucker, oder Jo. Tho. v. Trattners erwiesene Rechtmässigkeit seiner veranstalteten Nachdrucke als eine Beleuchtung der auf ihn gedruckten Leipziger Pasquille.* Vienna, Leipzig, 1774.

4. *Gnädigstes Mandat, den Buchhandel betreffend, d. d. Dresden, d. 18 Dec. 1773,* in No. 3 of the *Leipziger Intelligenz Blatt,* 1774, pp. 21-4.

5. *Hanauer neuer Bücher-Umschlag, erstes Jahr mdcclxxv. Worinnen die von Ihr Hochfürstl. Durchlaucht gnädigst verliehene Freiheiten, ein Vorbericht und die vollständige Anzeige von denen Büchern und Schriften enthalten ist* [&c.]. Hanau, Frankfurt-on-Main

6. News of December 1773 indicated that the tax on foreign French and Latin books of 20 pounds sterling per hundredweight which had hitherto to be paid is now reduced, following the remonstrances of the booksellers, to just over 6 pounds sterling.

7. Most reprints of French books are produced either in Holland or, more recently and persistently, in Brussels, Liège, Geneva, Yverdon and Avignon.

8. *Unpartheyische Gedanken über einige Quellen und Wirkungen des Verfalls der jetzigen Buchhandlung.* Schweinfurt, 1733.

Betrachtungen über die Buchhandlung in *pt. 1, Vortheile der Völker durch die Handlung.* Liepzig 1766, p. 733.

Vom Buchhandel in *Jo. Joach. Bechers polit. Discurs von den eigentl. Ursachen des Auf- und Abnehmens der Städte und Länder,* Frankfurt, Leipzig 1754, pp. 1389-1406.

Vom Buchhandel, in Hrn. Bergius *Magazin,* Vol. 1, p. 362 and his *Neues Magazin,* Vol. 1, pp. 347-352.

Mirmidons Abhandlung von der heutigen Buchhandlung, und derselben Verbesserung. Frankfurt, Leipzig 1756.

Christ. Schoettgen diss. de librariis & bibliopolis antiquorum. Leipzig 1710.

Another revised edition in German, with the title *Historie der Buchhändler, wie solche in alten und mittlern Zeiten gewesen, aus tüchtigen Nachrichten zusammengetragen von Christ. Schöttgen.* Nüremberg, Altdorf, 1722.

Adr. Deodat Steger diss. de publica rei librariæ tutela. Leipzig 1740.

A. N. L. MUNBY

Dibdin's reference library

The Sale of 26–28 June 1817

Mr. Graham Pollard, whose friendship I have enjoyed for close on forty years, may well ask why his seventieth birthday should be celebrated with an article on T. F. Dibdin. The two bibliographers have indeed striking dissimilarities. One, for example, habitually rushed into print, whereas the other . . .

The quality of Mr. Pollard which I have most envied and admired is his mastery of the whole range of bibliographical reference material, however obscure, exemplified in his sections on Book Production and Distribution in the first edition of *C.B.E.L.* and especially in the noble volume which the late Albert Ehrman presented to the Roxburghe Club in 1965, *The Distribution of Books by Catalogue*. Catalogues of bibliographical libraries have always been my favourite reading and I have long marvelled at the range and quality of T. F. Dibdin's reference books, dispersed under duress in 1817. The sale catalogue of 'the library of an eminent bibliographer' is very uncommon. In the course of many years of recording locations of auction catalogues only four copies have come my way, in the British Library, the Bodleian, Harvard University Library and at the Grolier Club, New York. It therefore seemed to me appropriate in a volume produced in a bibliographer's honour to provide an edition of this catalogue of a library so rich in the tools of a bibliographer's trade.

It is customary to decry the abilities of Thomas Frognall Dibdin, and certainly his snobbery, prolixity, facetiousness and inaccuracy invite ridicule. Nevertheless his enthusiasm infected a whole generation of collectors with bibliomania; the Roxburghe Club, in the foundation of which he was deeply implicated, survives even to this day; and in the words of the late William A. Jackson, no mean judge, 'the typographic merits of many of his publications, particularly in the fine paper copies, can hardly be exaggerated. Some of them are among the finest productions of M'Creery, Bensley, Bulmer, and Nichols, and those printers must have been driven nearly distracted by his demands for still more proofs, more India paper vignettes, and more color insertions.' It was doubtless to the lavishness and extravagance of his printing operations that we owe the existence of the auction catalogue here reproduced.

I have indeed no explicit evidence on this point. Dibdin was by no means a reticent man and it is odd that in his *Reminiscences of a Literary Life*, 1836, he gives no account of the circumstances under which his reference library came under the hammer. It is possible that the anguish which this sacrifice must have entailed precluded any further reference to it. We know that Dibdin's financial resources were stretched by the production of the second edition of his *Bibliomania* in 1811. When this finally shewed a profit he embarked on the preparation of his most elaborate work, *The Bibliographical Decameron*, 3 vols., 1817. Over £4500 were laid out on its production, £2000 of which, according to a prospectus, were disbursed to the illustrators and block-makers before publication, as well as £600 to the paper-maker in 1817. Despite the receipts at this time of some profits from the second volume of his *Typographical Antiquities*, 1812, these were sums which Dibdin could hardly command, and we can envisage the pressures which forced him to raise money by the sale of the tools of his bibliographical trade.

The Bodleian copy of the catalogue (Douce cc. 298 (3)) is here reproduced by kind permission, together with the prices and buyers and some significant annotations from the auctioneer's copy in the British Library (S.C.E.7(10)), the occasional illegibility of which renders it unsuitable for reproduction as a whole. Characteristically, Dibdin arranged for twenty-four special copies to have the heading 'Bibliotheca Rosicrusiana' added to the title-page, and one of these, formerly Dawson Turner's, is at Harvard. Dibdin owned a bibliographical reference library of great distinction. Hardly any major work appears to be lacking and the proportion of copies on Large Paper or in some other way remarkable is very high. His series of the earliest works is notable; Gesner's *Bibliotheca Universalis*, 1545, in stamped vellum (419), the 1559 Bale on Large Paper (201), Maunsell's *Catalogue of English Books*, 1595 (82), runs of the Term Catalogues (27–8)—these were not books much collected at this date, and he owned many of the great rarities of later periods, two French books, for example, both printed in twelve copies only, the folio De Boze catalogue of 1745 (256) and Debure's *Musæum Typographicum*, 1755 (505). His sale catalogues were especially enviable. He possessed the first English example, that of the library of Lazarus Seaman (1676), sold in lot 30 with numerous others bound in six quarto volumes, which Richard Heber did well to secure for £8 2s. 6d. Many of the greatest auction catalogues—Farmer, Mead, Roxburghe, Steevens, Girardot de Préfond, La Vallière, Crevenna—he owned on Large Paper. The last of these (261) fetched £8 8s. 0d., the highest priced catalogue in the collection, and the present writer counted himself fortunate to secure for £5 10s. 0d. one hundred and thirty years later the identical copy with Dibdin's mock-heraldic bookplate bearing Caxton's device among its quarterings. Among other rarities may be noted the first edition of John Dunton's *Life and Errors*, 1705 (474), a long run of Thomas Osborne's catalogues (95), and the purchaser's copy, with prices in manuscript, of Bryan Fairfax's library, 1756 (47) withdrawn from public sale when it was acquired by private treaty for Francis Child. It is said that all except twenty copies of this catalogue were destroyed and it is no surprise to see that Richard Heber once again was the purchaser. Heber indeed supported his friend Dibdin's auction nobly, buying one hundred and fifty-two lots, or a fifth of the whole sale. He attended throughout all three days and his purchases far outstripped those of any other private individual. Two other Roxburghers bought in person, William Bentham, F.S.A. (1757–1837), and James Heywood Markland, F.R.S. (1788–1864). Their purchases were however very small; after Heber the greatest number of lots bought privately fell to Dibdin's friend John North, who had been the underbidder for the Bedford 'Missal' in 1815 and three of those manuscripts are reproduced in the first volume of Dibdin's *The Bibliographical Decameron*. North bought twenty-four lots for £62 14s. 6d., nearly all Large Paper copies of sale catalogues, including a 'matchless copy', bound in blue morocco by Lewis, of the Roxburghe catalogue, which cost him £8 8s. 0d. Francis Douce made one purchase in the rooms (lot 355) and James Bindley two (690 and 713); a lesser-known collector who competed was William Simonds Higgs, F.S.A., whose library was in its turn dispersed by Sotheby on 26 April 1830. Three names are too common to admit of wholly certain identification. It would be tempting but probably erroneous to equate 'Miller' with the founder of the Britwell Library, whose collecting career De Ricci does not trace back beyond the Sykes sale of 1824: 'Lloyd' on the other hand may well have been that very interesting collector, Thomas Lloyd (see my *Phillipps Studies*, III, p. 152) and 'Wilson' William Wilson, F.S.A., of the Minories, owner of the Douce Apocalypse. The London trade, as might have been expected, shared with Heber the domination of the sale and the names of Arch,

Boone, Clarke, Evans, Lawford, Lepard, Longman, Nicol, Payne, Rodd and Triphook will be familiar to all students of Dibdin's works.

Dibdin bought and sold books on quite a large scale. His most spectacular operation in this line was of course his purchase in 1811 from the Dean and Chapter of Lincoln Cathedral of the group of rarities, including four Caxtons, which he advertised for sale in his pamphlet, *The Lincoln Nosegay*. His search for early printed books for his patron, Earl Spencer, must occasionally have left him with duplicates or imperfect copies from which Spencer's examples had been 'improved', and in this category perhaps are his two Caxtons in this sale, lot 738, *Eneydos*, and 739 *Lyf of saynt Katherin of senis* the latter printed by Wynkyn de Worde in Caxton's types. These fetched £21 and £34 13s. od. respectively, a significant fraction of the sum of £726 11s. 6d. realised by the whole library. Many of the books had been lavishly rebound for Dibdin by Charles Lewis, and it may be doubted whether he recovered the money which he had laid out on the collection. Increasingly severe pecuniary difficulties dogged him until his death in 1847, and he certainly never formed a second library on this scale. Such books as he retained in 1817 or acquired later were sold off piecemeal. On 15 February 1822 Evans sold all the drawings by George Lewis and others which Dibdin had commissioned for his *Bibliographical Tour in France and Germany*: dispersed in 137 lots, they realised the substantial sum of £568 1s. 6d., and many of them are to be found today in extra-illustrated copies of that work. Two other sales can only have been made under duress. The bookseller, John Thomas Payne, acquired Dibdin's own set of Roxburghe Club publications up to 1837, perhaps the date of the transaction. They appeared in Sotheby's catalogue of Payne's books sold on 28 April 1857 on his retirement from business. On 2 August 1838 Dibdin reported to Dawson Turner that he had sent books worth £30 to Evans, the auctioneer, 'the very last books I possess'd'. Turner, the Yarmouth banker who collected autographs, involved himself in Dibdin's financial problems and in 1839 he made several purchases of the bibliographer's correspondence. Dibdin had scruples about selling the letters of his friends, but necessity compelled him to do so, and in October 1839 he sent Turner 'a precious epistolographical cargo' of letters from Richard Heber and from his patron Earl Spencer. These transactions were the source of the extensive files of Dibdin's papers which are to be found in the sale catalogue of Dawson Turner's manuscripts held by Puttick and Simpson on 6 June 1859 and the four following days (lots 134–43 and 446). Of these I have noted the following locations: lot 134 (biographical material) Harvard, Houghton ms. Eng. 1177.2*; lot 136 (*Bibliomania* file) B. L. Egerton ms. 2974; lot 137 (*Bibliographical Decameron* file) Harvard, Houghton ms. Eng. 1177*; 138 (*Bibliographical Tour* file) Mr. Robert S. Pirie, Aquila Farm, Hamilton, Mass., U.S.A.; lot 142 (*Northern Tour* file) Henry E. Huntington ms. D1; lot 143 (*Reminiscences* file) Bodleian ms. Eng. Misc. d. 85-6. These files provide ample documentation for the study of the production and marketing of books by subscription.

A small engraving of Dibdin's book-lined study is to be found on p. 469 of Vol. III of *The Bibliographical Decameron*, entitled 'View of a late bibliomaniacal Interior'.

Only one writer, so far as I know, has studied Dibdin's library in any detail. On 19 May 1960, Mr. Ronald Hall, Acting Librarian of The John Rylands Library, Manchester, addressed the Manchester Society of Book Collectors on the subject of Dibdin, and his address was printed in the *Manchester Review*, vol. IX, 1961, pp. 193–210. This is far the best account in print of Dibdin's activites as a book collector, and on pp. 196–201 will be found some valuable notes on the contents of the sale catalogue of 1817. We still lack a full-dress life of Dibdin, for which ample, perhaps even over-ample, sources exist in widely scattered collections. Mr. Anthony Lister, of Alsager College of Education, Cheshire, has for some years assembled materials for a biography, which would be assured of a wide circle of interested readers: and I am especially grateful to Mr. Lister for having supplied me with a number of quotations from letters in this introduction and for other advice.

A

CATALOGUE

OF THE LIBRARY

OF

AN EMINENT BIBLIOGRAPHER,

T. F. Dibdin.

CONTAINING

A MOST INTERESTING AND CURIOUS COLLECTION

OF

BIBLIOGRAPHY AND LITERARY HISTORY.

ALSO,

The Boke of Eneydos, compyled by Vyrgyle, reduced into Englysse, and imprynted by Caxton,

AND

The Lyf of Saint Katherin of Senis, with the Revelacions of Saynt Elyzabeth, the Kynges doughter of Hungarye. Imprynted by Caxton.

The Books are all in fine condition, and principally bound by Lewis, and other eminent binders.

THEY WILL BE

SOLD BY AUCTION,

BY MR. EVANS,

AT HIS HOUSE, No. 26, PALL-MALL,

On Thursday, June 26, and Two following Days.

1817.

CATALOGUE

OF THE LIBRARY

OF AN EMINENT BIBLIOGRAPHER.

FIRST DAY'S SALE.

The Sale will commence PUNCTUALLY AT HALF PAST TWELVE.

1 Ames's Catalogue of English Heads,   1748
2 Catalogue of the Duke of Argyle's Library, 4to. privately printed,   *Glasg.* 1758
3 —— Askew's Library, LARGE PAPER, *with prices and names,*   1775
4 —— of Askew's MSS.   1785
5 —— Allen's Library, LARGE PAPER, *prices and names,*   1795
6 —— Alchorne's Library, LARGE PAPER, *with prices and names.*
7 —— Bridges's Library, LARGE PAPER, *with prices, blue morocco,* 8vo.   1725
8 —— Bridges's Library, *with prices,*   1725
9 —— Bishop Burnet's Library,   1715
10 —— C. Bernard's Library, *priced,*   1710
11 —— Dr. F. Bernard's Library,   1698
12 —— Bibliotheca Universalis Selecta, *priced,* 8vo. *russia,*   1786
13 —— Bibliothecæ Bodleianæ, folio, first edition, 1674
14 ——   2 vol. folio,   1737
15 —— Beauclerk's Library, *with the prices,* 8vo. *gilt, extra,*   1781
16 —— Lord Bute's Prints, 1794, and Catalogue of English and Foreign Prints,   1799

B

CONDITIONS OF SALE.

I. THE highest Bidder to be the Buyer; and if any Dispute arises between two or more Bidders, the Lot so disputed shall be immediately put up again and re-sold.

II. No Person to advance less than 1*s.*; **above** Five Pounds 2*s.* 6*d.* and so in Proportion.

III. The Purchasers to give in their Names and Places of Abode, and to pay down 5*s.* in the Pound in Part Payment of the Purchase-money; in Default of which the Lot or Lots so purchased to be immediately put up again and re-sold.

IV. The Lots to be taken away, at the Buyer's Expence, within Three Days after the Conclusion of the Sale; and the remainder of the Purchase-money to be absolutely paid on or before Delivery.

V. The Books are presumed to be perfect, unless otherwise expressed; but if, upon collating, AT THE PLACE OF SALE, any should prove defective, the Purchasers will be at Liberty to take or reject them.

VI. Upon failure of complying with the above Conditions, the Money deposited in Part of Payment shall be forfeited, and all Lots uncleared within the Time aforesaid, shall be re-sold by public or private Sale, and the Deficiency (if any, attending such Re-sale, shall be made good by the Defaulters at this Sale.

☞ No Books will be delivered during the time of Sale.

Gentlemen who cannot attend the Sale may have their Commissions faithfully executed by their humble Servant,

R. H. EVANS,
26, *Pall-Mall*

Printed by W. Bulmer and Co. Cleveland-row, St. James's

[2]

17 Catalogue of Portraits in the Basiloologia, FINE PAPER, prices and names, 8vo. - - 1811
18 ———— Browne's Library, prices and names, 8vo. 1791
19 ———— Barnard's Prints and Books of Prints, prices, uncut, - - - 1798
20 Sir J. Bankes's Library, 5 vol. 8vo. rare, 1798
21 Duplicates of British Museum, 8vo. 1805
22 Boucher's Library, 8vo. 1806
23 Brande's Library, LARGE PAPER, the greater part priced, 8vo. - - 1807
24 ———— Brande's Library, part 2, - 1808
25 Catalogus Librorum, MSS. Bib. Cottonianae, folio, Oxon. 1696
26 Catalogue of the Manuscripts in the Cottonian Library, folio, - - 1802
27 Clavel's Catalogues, 1675-90, folio.
28 ———— 1680, folio, uncut, rare.
29 Catalogue of the most Vendible Books, 4to. - 1658
30 Curious Collection of Catalogues of the Libraries of Whateley. and S. Rutland, 1683. J. Lloyd, 1683. C. Adams, 1683. D. Rogers, 1683. Anonymous, 1683. Chaucer, Tonstall, Bathurst and Gunter in 1683 and 1684. Owen, Smallwood, More in 1684. Jacomb and Millington, 1687. Gore de Re Heraldica, 1674. Langbaine's English Plays, 1688. Seyman, 1676. Pulleyn, 1657. Sargar, 1678. Gataker, 1681. Rea, 1682. Humphry, 1682. Walford, 1688. Bp. Gulston, 1688. Manton, 1678. Worsley, 1678. Dunton, 1680. Stubb, 1680, &c. &c. in 6 vol. 4to. A VERY RARE AND CURIOUS COLLECTION.
31 Catalogue of the Libraries of Wm. and H. Cavendish and J. Hollis, Dukes of Newcastle, LARGE PAPER, morocco, 8vo. - - - 1718
32 ———— A. Collins's Library, 8vo. both parts, 1730
33 ———— A. Collins's Lib. both parts, part 1, priced, 1730
34 ———— Crofts's Library, LARGE PAPER, prices and names, - - - 1783
35 ———— Concanon's Library, priced, of Mills's, &c.
36 ———— Chymical Books, - - 1675

287

[3]

37 Catalogue of Daly's Library, prices and names, 1792
38 ———— Dorville's Library, - 1804
39 ———— of a distinguished Collector, - 1799
40 ———— De Missy's Library, partly priced, 1776. of Consul Smith's Books, priced, 1773.
41 ———— the Libraries of Ewer, Woodford, Maddison, Boucher, &c.
42 ———— Editionum Sæculi XV. in Bib. Bodleiana, 8vo. 1795
43 ———— Edwards's Library, LARGE PAPER, morocco, prices and names, - - 1815
44 ———— Friends Books written by Quakers, 1708
45 ———— Folkes's Library, LARGE PAPER, uncut, 1756
46 ———— Library of the Faculty of Advocates, Edinburgh, 2 vol. folio. - - 1742
47 ———— Bryan Fairfax's Library, with the prices at which they were estimated. MS. Memorandum, 1756
•.• This Library was sold to Francis Child, Esq. for 2000l. and all the Catalogues destroyed except 20. And what renders this one more valuable than any of the rest, it has the Taxation Prices by Mr. Child (before he made the purchase) affixed to each number.
48 ———— Sir C. Frederick's Books, and MSS. with prices and names, - - 1786
49 ———— Fagel's Library, both parts.
50 ———— Farmer's Library, LARGE PAPER, only 12 copies printed, with prices and purchaser's names, morocco, 1798
51 ———— Fillingham's Books, - - 1805
52 ———— Ford's Books for 1810, LARGE PAPER, in russia.
53 ———— Ford's Books for 1811, LARGE PAPER, morocco.
54 ———— the Gough Collection in the Bodleian, 4to. extra, 1814
55 ———— Gough's Library, - - 1810
56 ———— Gordon of Gordonstoune's Library, FINE PAPER, 1816
57 ———— the Duke of Grafton's Library, LARGE PAPER, with prices and names, extra, - 1815

[4]

58 Catalogue of Goldsmid's Library, *with prices.*
59 ——— Orator Henley's Library, - 1759
60 ——— the Harleian Library, 5 vol. 8vo. - 1743
61 ——— of the Harleian Manuscripts, 3 vol. fol. 1808
62 ——— Hoblyn's Library, LARGE PAPER, *russia,* 1769
63 ——— Hoblyn's Library, *priced,* 1778
64 ——— Haslewood's Library, - 1708
65 ——— Hearne's Do. *in russia,* 1735
66 ——— Hutton's Do. *priced,* wants title.
67 ——— Herbert's Do. - 1796
68 ——— Heathcote's Duplicates, 1803
69 ——— J. Hunter's Books, - 1805
70 ——— Heath's Books, LARGE PAPER, *with prices,* 1810
71 ——— Henderson, the Comedian's Library, 1786
72 ——— Junot's Library, *prices and names, vellum,* 1816
73 ——— the Lansdowne Books and MS. 2 vol. 1807
74 ——— Longman's Bibliotheca Anglo-Poetica, LARGE PAPER, *in russia by Lewis,* 1815
75 ——— Librorum ad Rem Medicam spectantium in Bibliotheca-Academica Edinburgensi, 8vo. 1773
76 ——— Universalis Librorum, 2 vol. 8vo. *Lond.* 1699
77 ——— Librorum MS. in Bib. C. Christi Cantab. first edition, folio, 1722
78 ——— MSS. in Bennet College, by Nasmith, *uncut,* 4to. 1777
79 ——— Librorum Novorum, 2 vol. 8vo. 1697
80 ——— Lloyd (of Wygfair)'s books, *with prices,* 1816
81 ——— Laskey's Account of the Hunterian Museum, Glasgow, 1813
82 ——— Maunsell's Catalogue of English Printed Bookes, both parts, 1595, folio, *Rare.*
83 ——— Catalogue of More's Books, *with prices, extra,* 1779
84 ——— Sir W. Musgrave's Portraits, *prices and names.*
85 ——— Monro's Library, - 1792
86 ——— Ebenezer Mussel's Books, - 1766
87 ——— Maittaire's Books, *with prices,* 1748
88 ——— Mead's Museum, *partly priced.*
89 ——— Meul's Books, LARGE PAPER, *uncut, priced, with a few purchaser's names,* - 1754

[5]

90 Catalogus Bibliothecæ Monastico-Fletewodianæ, *morocco, priced,* 1774
91 Catalogue of G. Mason's Books, 4 parts, *prices and names,* 1798
92 ——— G. Mills's Books, *fine paper,* - 1800
93 ——— Bibliothecæ Norfolcianæ, 4to. - 1681
94 ——— Sir H. Newlon's Books, - 1716
95 ——— Collection of Osborne (the Bookseller)'s Catalogues between 1738 and 1766, 9 vol.
96 ——— Osborne's Catalogue, containing N. Boothe's Library.
97 ——— Catalogue of the Paitoni Library, - 1790
98 ——— the Paris Library, *priced,* 1790
99 ——— the Paris Library, *with prices and names,* 1791
100 ——— Major Pearson's Library, LARGE PAPER, *with prices, morocco,* 1788
101 ——— Pinelli's Library, *priced,* 1789
102 ——— Bibliothecæ Pinellianæ, a Morellio, 6 vol. in 3, extra, - *Ven.* 1787
103 ——— Ratcliffe's Library, *prices and names, morocco.*
104 ——— Rawlinson's Books, *priced,* 1756
105 ——— Ritson's Books, - 1803
106 ——— Reed's Books, LARGE PAPER, *priced, green morocco,* 1807
107 ——— the Library of the Royal Institution, LARGE PAPER, *morocco,* 1809
108 ——— Roscoe's Library, - 1816
109 ——— Roscoe's Drawings and Engravings, 1816
110 ——— Roxburghe Library, - 1812
111 ——— Catalogue of the Roxburghe Library, 1812, LARGE PAPER, *with prices and names of purchasers.* Beautifully bound in blue morocco by Lewis. A matchless Copy.
112 ——— Catalogue of Southgate's Books, Coins and Medals, 1795
113 ——— G. Smyth's Books, *partly priced.*
114 ——— Stukeley's Coins, 1766, of Bishop Pococke's Coins, 1766.
115 ——— Stace's Books, - 1808
116 ——— Duke of St. Alban's books, *partly priced,* 1796

288

117	Catalogue of Sion College Library, 4to.	1630
118	——— Strange's descriptive Catalogue of Pictures, 1769	
119	——— G. Steevens's Library, LARGE PAPER, with purchaser's names to the leading articles,	1800
120	——— Colonel Stanley's Books, LARGE PAPER, *prices and names, morocco,*	1813
121	——— Strange's Library,	1801
122	——— Sir J. Sebright's, Meyrick's, Foster's, &c.	
123	——— Swedenborg's Works,	1785
124	——— Smith's Books, *with prices,*	1682
125	——— J. Scott, Bookseller,	1804
126	——— Stace,	1807
127	——— Bibliotheca Salmonianæ, interleaved, *with prices,*	1744
128	——— Talleyrand's Library, FINE PAPER,	1816
129	——— Ralph Thoresby's Books.	
130	——— Lord Thurlow's Books, &c. *priced,*	1804
131	——— Horne Tooke's Library, LARGE PAPER, only 12 printed, *with prices and names, russia,*	1813
132	——— Towneley Library, 2 parts, LARGE PAPER, *with prices and names, morocco,*	1814
133	——— Archbp. Tillotson's Library, *priced,* 1695. Sir C. Scarburgh's books.	
134	——— Libr. MS. in Bibliothecis Tenisonianis, et Dugdalianis,	1692
135	——— Tyson's Books,	1781
136	Universal Catalogue, 2 vol.	1772
137	Catalogue of Willett's Library, FINE PAPER, *prices and names,*	1813
138	——— Williams's Books left to Red-Cross-Street Library,	1727
139	——— E. Wynne's Books, *with prices, morocco,*	1786
140	——— West's Library, interleaved, *with prices and names,*	1773
141	——— Anthony Wood's MSS.	1761
142	——— Wright's Books, FINE PAPER, *rare, with prices,*	1787

143	Catalogue of Dr. Woodward's Books,	1728
144	——— P. Carteret Webb's Books,	1771
145	——— J. Wilkes's Books,	1802
146	——— Woodhull's Duplicates,	1803
147	——— Woodhouse's Books, *with prices and names,* 1803	
148	——— Woodhouse's Prints, FINE PAPER, *partly priced,* 1801. of Woodhouse's Books, *priced,* 1803.	
149	Casley's Catalogue of the MS. in the Royal Library, 4to. LARGE PAPER, *in russia,*	1739
150	Brooke's Bibliotheca Legum Angliæ, 2 vol. 8vo.	1788
151	Catalogo de la Libreria Capponi, 4to.	1747
152	Catalogus Bibliographicus Librorum in Bibliotheca Cæs. Reg. Acad. Theresianæ Extantium,1801, 4to. (69th copy).	
153	Abranielis Comment. in Isaiam,	*Elz.* 1631
154	Admonition to be redde in the Churches of the Citie and suburbes of London, by the pastours and ministers of the same. *Imprinted by Wyllyam Seres,* 1561, 4to. black letter, 4 leaves.	
155	Adam out of Eden, 12mo.	1659
156	Aschami Epistolæ, 12mo.	*Lond.* 1578
157	Ashmoles' Order of the Garter, 1672, folio, wanting the plates.	
158	Arguments relating to a Restraint upon the Press, 1712, 8vo.	
159	Aristote du Monde, &c. Songe de Scipion, *Lyon.* 1542, 12mo.	
160	Æginetæ Præcepta Salubria. Parisiis ap. H. Stephanum, 1516, 4to. This is the only work which has come to my knowledge containing the device of old Henry Stephens, of which Maittaire appears to have been ignorant, D.	
161	Almeloveen de Vitis Stephanorum, 12mo.	1683
162	Almeloveen Bibliotheca Promissa et Latens, 1688, 12mo.	
163	Audifredi Editiones Romanæ Sæculi, XV. 4to.	1783
164	——— Editiones Italicæ Sæculi, XV. 4to.	1794
165	Affo, Tipografia Parmense, 1791, 4to.	
166	Antonii Bibliotheca Hispana, 4 vol. *best edition,*	1788
167	Arcana Bibliothecæ Synodalis et Typographicæ Moscuensis Sacra, &c. *Lips.* 1726, 12mo. *calf, gilt leaves, rare.*	

[8]

168 Achard, Cours Elémentaire de Bibliographie, 1806, 3 vol. in 1.
169 Account and Extracts of the Manuscripts in the Library of the King of France, 1789, 8vo, 2 vol.
170 Ayscough's Catalogue of the Manuscripts preserved in the British Museum, hitherto undescribed, 1772, 4to.
171 Brunet, Manuel du Libraire, 1810, 8vo. 3 vol. FINE PAPER, *morocco, gilt leaves.*
172 Barbier Dictionnaire des Ouvrages Anonymes et Pseudonymes, 1806, 4 vol. 8vo. *calf, extra.*
173 Beughem Bibliographia Eruditorum Critico-Curiosa, 1694, 12mo.
174 Bandini Annales Typographiæ Juntarum, 1791, 8vo. 2 vol. in 1.
175 Bibliotheca Arabico-Hispana Escurialensis, 4to. 1760
176 Bibliotheca Renati, folio, *uncut, wants title.* Ruddiman's Copy.
177 Biblioteca de' Scrittori Vicentini del Angiolgabriello, 1772, 4to. 6 vol. in 3. *calf extra.* A work of considerable rarity in this country.
178 Bibliotheca Anti-Trinitariorum, 1684, 8vo. Harwood's copy, and has his autograph.
179 Bibliotheca Politico-Heraldica Selecta, 8vo. 1705
180 Bibliotheca Magna et Elegantissima Zuylichemiana Rarissimorum Exquisitissimorumque Librorum, 1701, 8vo. These books were sold by auction by the well-known Vander Aa, and has a curious prefix 'to the Buyers.'
181 Bibliotheca Benedictino-Mauriana, 1716, 8vo.
182 Beughem, Bibliographia Crit. Curiosa, 1689, 12mo.
183 Beughem, Bibliographia Mathematica, 1688, 12mo.
184 Beyer, Memoria Hist-Critica Librorum Rariorum, 1736, 8vo.
185 Bruggemann's View of the English Editions, Translations, and Illustrations of the Ancient Greek and Latin Authors, 1797, 8vo.
186 Bridgeman's Legal Bibliography, 1807, 8vo. *gilt leaves.*
187 Bauer: Bibliotheca Librorum Rariorum Universalis, 1770, 8vo. with all the parts, in 3 vol. *russia, a fine copy.*

[9]

188 Barbier, sur 60 Traductions Françoises de l'Imitation de Jésus Christ, 1812, 8vo. 'LARGE PAPER, *morocco,* by Lewis.
189 Braun, Notitia Historico-Literaria De Libris—usque ad Ann. 1479. Impress. In Bibl. Monast. SS. Vdalric. et Afræ August. extant, 1788, 4to. 2 parts in 1 volume.
190 —— De Codicibus Manuscriptis in Bibl. Eadem, 1791, 4to. 6 vol. in 1, *russia, marbled leaves,* RARE.
191 Biographia Dramatica, 4 vol. in 2, *russia, gilt leaves,* 8vo.
192 Sir E. Brydges's Censura Literaria, 1805, 10 vol. 8vo.
193 ——————— Restituta, 4 vol. 8vo. - 1814
194 British Bibliographer, 4 vol. fine copy, - 1810
195 Boni et Gamba, Biblioteca Portatile, 1793, 8vo. 2 vol. *morocco, gilt leaves.*
196 Boni, Libri Primi a Stampa, &c. dall' Italia Superiore, 1794, folio, *extra, gilt leaves.*
197 Bibliotheca Historica de Portugal, e do Ultramar. *Lisboa.* 1797, 8vo. *morocco.*
198 Bibliotheca Literaria, 10 parts, complete, *morocco,* 4to.
199 Bibliotheca Carmelitana, 1591, 4to. RARE, *russia, gilt leaves.* Sir Roger Twysden's Copy.
200 Bale, Summarium Illustrium Maioris Britanniæ Scriptorum, printed at Ipswich, 1548, 4to. *russia, fine copy.*
201 —— Idem Opus. *Basil.* 1559. folio. Edit. Opt. *very fine copy,* LARGE PAPER.
202 Bibliotheca Scriptorum Societatis Jesu, A. Alegambe, 1643, folio.
203 Bibliotheca Historica Struvii, Buderi, A. Meuselii, 1782, 8vo. 11 vol. *a beautiful copy.*
204 Burckhard, Historia Bibliothecæ Augustæ quæ Wolffenbutelli est 1740, 4to. A very interesting Work.
205 Bullart, Academie des Sciences et des Arts, 1682, folio, 2 vol. *fine impressions of the plates.*
206 Breitkopf's Work on Printing in the German language, 1779, 4to.
207 Bassan, Dictionnaire des Graveurs, 1809, 8vo. 2 vol. in 1. *morocco, gilt leaves.*
208 Bibliotheca sive Antiquitates Urbis Constantinopolitanæ,

C

[10]

Argent. 1578. 4to. *morocco, gilt leaves.* The Roxburghe copy: a volume of excessive rarity, and in which are found catalogued ' the entire 24 Comedies of Menander, with the explications of Michael Psellus.'

209 Bibliothèque des Auteurs de Bourgogne par feu M. l'Abbé Papillon, 1745, folio, 2 vol. *uncut.*
210 Bellum Papale, Auctore Thoma James, 1678. 12mo.
211 Baillet: Jugemens des Savans, 1725, 8vo. compleat in 11 vol. *white calf, gilt leaves.*
212 Bonasus Vapulans, or Some Castigation given to Mr. John Durell, for fouling himself and others in his English and Latin Book. By a Country Scholar, 1672, 12mo.
213 Bachaumont, Mémoires Secrets pour servir à l'Histoire de la Republique des Lettres en France, depuis MDCCLXII, jusqu'à nos jours, 1777, 8vo. 16 vol. in 8. *very neat set.*
214 Burnet's History of his own Time, 1725, 8vo. 6 vol.
215 Burnet's History of the Reformation, 1681, folio, 3 vol. *portraits.*
216 Barret's theorike and practicke of warre, *wants 1 leaf*, folio, 1598.
217 Baliverneries, ou Contes Nouveaux d'Eutrapel, 1548, 12mo. (a reprint limited to 30 copies), *morocco by Lewis.*
218 Bayle, Dictionnaire Historique et Oeuvres mêlées, 8 vol. folio, 1730.
219 Budæi Epistolæ, - - Basil. 1521
220 Bowyer's Miscellaneous Tracts, 1785, 4to.
221 Blount's Censura Authorum, 1690, folio.
222 Bacon's Life of Henry VII, 8vo. - 1786
223 ——— Essays, 2 vol. LARGE PAPER, 8vo. 1720
224 Beveridge's Private Thoughts upon Religion, 1709, 8vo.
225 Bezæ Poemata Juvenilia, 1569. Ludus Arithmomachiæ, 1556, 8vo. *imperfect, &c.*
226 Bembo, gli Asolani, (Mr. Fox's copy), Aldus. 1531
227 Brief Memorial of Dr. J. Spotiswode, 4to. 1811
228 Bates, Vitæ Doctorum Virorum, 4to. - 1681
229 Comenii Janua Linguæ Latinæ, *portrait,* 8vo. 1656
230 Canones et Decreta Concilii Œcumenii et Concilii generalis, folio, 1564

291

[11]

231 Cailleau, Dictionnaire Bibliographique, 4 vol. 8vo. 1790
232 Chevillier, Origine de l'Imprimerie de Paris, 1694, 4to. *morocco,* FINE PAPER.
233 Caille, (La) Histoire de l'Imprimerie et de la Librairie, 1689, 4to. *morocco,* FINE PAPER.

*** These are presumed to have been presentation copies, by their respective authors; and have, exclusively of their extreme beauty of condition, some little varieties from the generality of copies.

234 Clement, Bibliothèque curieuse, Historique et Critique, 1750, 9 vol. 4to. *beautiful copy.*
235 Caslon's Specimens of printing Types, 1766, 8vo. *morocco.*
236 Camus, Mémoires sur les Collections de Voyages de Debry, et Thevenot, 1802, 4to.
237 Catalogus Bibliothecæ Mus. Britannici, 1813, 5 vol. All yet published. *Only 250 copies of this catalogue are printed.*
238 Catalogus Auctorum qui Librorum Catalogos, Indices, Bibliothecas, &c. scriptis consignârunt. Ab Antonio Teisserio, 1686, 4to.
239 Clarke's Bibliographical Dictionary and Bibliographical Miscellany, 8 vol. in 4, 8vo. - 1802
240 Cabinet de la Bibliothèque de Sainte Geneviève, 1692, LARGE PAPER, *fine copy.*
241 Clarke's Bibliotheca Legum, - - 1810
242 Cinelli Biblioteca Volante, 1736, 4to. 4 vol. *calf extra.*
243 Colomiès Bibliothèque Choisie, 1682, 8vo. *first edition.*
244 Catalogue of all the Books relating to the Popish Plot, 1680, 4to.
245 Commercii Epistolaris Uffenbachiani Selecta Vitamque Ulfenbachii præmisit J. G. Schelhornius, *Ulm.* 1753, 8vo. 4 vol. A very curious collection of Epistles, with anecdotes of many eminent distinguished characters in our own country towards the beginning of the 18th century
246 Clarorum Venetorum Epistolæ ad Magliabechium.
247 ——— Belgarum Epistolæ ad Eundem, 1745, 12mo. 6 vol.

[12]

248 Child-Birth, or the Happy Delivery of Women, 1635, 4to. *wood cuts, scarce.* With the Nursing of Children, 1635, 4to.
249 Cicero's Epistles to Brutus, by Markland, 8vo.
250 Ciacconius de Triclinio, 1689, 12mo. *plates.* 1765

SECOND DAY'S SALE.

The Sale will commence PRECISELY AT HALF PAST TWELVE.

251 Catalogue of the valuable and curious Collection, late the property of Mr. Thomas Keigate, 1810, 8vo. 1772
252 Catalogue of Cobenzel's Books, - 1772
253 Catalogue of the Library of the Company of Philadelphia, Philadelph. 1789
254 Catalogue des Livres de la Bibliothèque d'Avignon, 8vo. 1806.
255 ——— de Boze, *with prices,* - Par. 1753
256 ——— des Livres de Boze, (folia), LARGE PAPER, *only 12 copies printed,* Par. 1745
257 ——— de Boutourlin, *fine paper,* - Par. 1805
258 ——— de la Bibliothèque de feu M. Benette, *Paris 1748, avec les pris,* 3 vols.
259 ——— d'une Bibliothèque de Littérature, 1776
260 Catalogue Raisonné des Livres de Crevenna, 6 vol. in 3, 4to. first edition, containing notes not found in the subsequent; extra by Lewis, - - 1775
261 Catalogue Raisonné des Livres de Crevenna, 5 vol. 4to. LARGE PAPER, *with the prices,* extra by Lewis, *Amst.* 1789
262 Another copy, 5 vol. 8vo. This was formerly Mr. Edwards's copy, who has marked the condition of each article in pencil on the margin.
263 Catalogue de Crozat, - - Par. 1751
264 Another copy, *with prices,* - - *ibid.* 1751

[18]

265 Catalogue des Livres de Caillard, *only 25 copies printed:* a presentation copy from Mr. Caillard to Larcher, *blue morocco,* 1805
266 ——— Caillard, LARGE PAPER, *with the prices, splendidly bound in blue morocco,* by Lewis, Par. 1810
267 ——— du College de Clermont, *prices,* Par. 1764
268 ——— de Couvay, - - *ib.* 1755
269 ——— de Cotte, FINE PAPER, - *ib.* 1804
270 ——— des Livres de Cotte, *with prices,* 1804, de Patu de Mello, *with prices.*
271 ——— des Livres de d'Ourches, par Brunet, LARGE PAPER, *only twenty printed; with the prices,* Par. 1811
272 ——— de l'Abbé Delan, *with prices,* Par. 1755
273 ——— de Didot, - - Par. 1810
274 ——— des Pierres Gravées du Duc d'Orléans, Par. 1786. Des Livres d'Ennery, 1786, and others in the volume.
275 ——— de D'Aumont, *with prices,* - Par. 1782
276 ——— Dufrnense, *with portrait,* - Par. 1662
277 ——— de D'Aguessau, *with prices,* Par. 1785
278 ——— de Delatour, Soulavie, &c.
279 ——— du Duc d'Estrées, 2 vol. *with prices,* Par. 1740
280 ——— de Falconet, 2 vol. *with prices,* Par. 1763
281 ——— de Goutard, *priced,* Par. 1780. Catalogue de Loménie, 1797. Catalogue de Limare.
282 ——— de Gaignat, 2 vol. LARGE PAPER, *with prices in the margin, yellow morocco,* - Par. 1769
283 ——— de Goutard, LARGE PAPER, *with prices,* Par. 1780
284 ——— de Gerard de Préfond, LARGE PAPER, *only 6 copies printed,* with the prices, - Par. 1757
285 ——— des MSS. de la Bib. de Geneve, Gen. 1779
286 ——— de Guyon, Par. 1759 ; de Macarty, 1779 ; de Boissy, 1792.
287 ——— de d'Hangard, *with prices,* Par. 1812
288 ——— de la Bibliothèque de la Maison des Jesuites, *prices, ussia,* - - Par. 1763
288* ——— , *prices,* - Par. 1764
289 Bibliotheca Havardiana Cantabrigiæ Nov.-Anglorum, Boston, 1790

[14]

290 Catalogue de Larcher; - Par. 1813
291 ——— des Livres rares, Par. 1801. Catalogue de Barthelemy, Par. 1800.
292 ——— des Livres du Cardinal de Loménie, with prices, 1797
293 ——— des Livres du Cardinal de Loménie, 2 vol. with prices, - - - 1792
294 ——— of the Library of Count Louis Henry de Loménie, - - - - 1724
295 ——— de Livres choisis, priced, - ib. 1789
296 ——— des Livres de Limare, - 1786
297 ——— des Livres rares de Limare, with prices, Par. 1786; de d'Ennery, with prices, 1786.
298 ——— des Livres de Lambert, - Par. 1780
299 ——— de Lemarié, - - 1776
300 ——— des Livres de Macarthy, 2 vol. with prices, Par. 1779
301 ——— des Livres de Macarthy, 3 vol. LARGE PAPER, 1816
302 ——— de Mirabeau, with prices, - Par. 1791
303 ——— Merigot, - - ib. 1800
304 ——— de Monnier, priced, 1803; de Trudaine, wants title, priced.
305 ——— de Noailles, with prices, - Par. 1740
306 ——— de Pompadour, with prices, Par. 1765
307 ——— de Pont-de-Vesle, - Par. 1774
308 ——— de Prault, de Fourcroy, Declos, &c.
309 ——— de Proli, - - 1785
310 ——— des Livres précieux de M. R. 8vo. LARGE PAPER, extra by Lewis, 1809.
311 ——— de Randon de Boisset, with prices, Par. 1777
312 ——— de Rothelin, portrait, with prices, Par. 1746
313 ——— de Reviczky, fine paper, morocco, Ber. 1794
313* ———, original edition: with all the Supplements, green morocco.
314 ——— of Rotsgard, 1727; of Ileinson, 1728, &c. &c.
315 ——— de Secousse, with prices, - Par. 1755
316 ——— de Siméon, 1801. Catalogue de Bailly, 1800.

293

[15]

317 Catalogue de Semonville, with prices, Par. 1732
318 ——— des Livres de Serna Santander, 5 vol. Brux. 1803
319 ——— Saint-Ceran, FINE PAPER, with prices, in russia, - - Par. 1791
320 ——— St. Martin, Tourneisen, &c. 1798
321 ——— du Prince de Soubise, priced, 1798
322 ——— du Prince de Soubise, partly priced, Par. 1806
323 ——— de Villoison, - Par. 1806
324 ——— des Livres du Duc de La Valliere, 1772. Catalogue des Livres de La Valliere, 1785, &c. &c. in 2 vol. Par. 1767
325 ——— La Valliere, LARGE PAPER, priced, Par. 1767
326 ——— La Valliere, 3 vol. in 6, LARGE PAPER, with the prices annexed to each article, extra gt. leaves, Par. 1783
327 ——— La Valliere, 6 vol. (the collection sold to Count D'Artois), LARGE PAPER, - Par. 1784
⁂ The three preceding articles are uniformly bound by Lewis.
328 Catechismus, Gr. et Lat. 8vo. - Lond. 1573
329 Coppie of the Ressoning which was betwix the Abbote of Crossagnell and John Knox, 1563, 4to. reprint, bds.
330 Libellus S. J. Chrysostomi, quid nemo læditur nisi a se ipso, Colinæus, 1530.
331 Cave, Historia Literaria Scriptorum Ecclesiasticorum, 1740, folio, 2 vols. Edit. Opt.
332 Chaufepié, Supplement au Dictionnaire de Bayle, 1750, folio, 4 vol.
333 Chaufepié's Life of Servetus, 1771, 8vo.
334 Chronicon Insigne Monasterii Hirsangiensis cura Trithemii, 1559, folio.
335 Chronique d'Einsidlien, ou L'Historie de l'Abbaye Princiere de la Sainte Chapelle et du Peléninage de Notre Dame des Hounites, 1787, 8vo. frontispiece. A curious and rather uncommon book.
336 Considerations and Proposals in order to the Regulation of the Press, 1663, 4to.

[16]

337 Common Prayer Book, folio, *blue morocco*, - 1776
338 The Classical Journal, 1816 .8vo. vol. 1 and 2, calf extra.
339 Chalmers's Biographical Dictionary, 5 first volumes.
340 G. Chalmers's Apology for the Believers in Ireland's Shakspeare, 2 vol. - - - 1797
341 Chalmers's (G.) Life of Ruddiman, 1794, 8vo. morocco, portrait.
342 Correspondence of Wakefield and Fox, 1813, 8vo.
343 Ciceron, Lettres à Atticus, par Mongault, 4 vol. 12mo. 1787.
344 Clapham's Bibliotheca Theologica, *plates*, 1597, 4to. Clapham on the Syne against the Holy Ghost, 1598.
345 Du Pin, Bibliothèque des Auteurs Ecclesiastiques, *Paris*, 1690, 4to. 16 vols.
346 Du Pin's Universal Library of Historians, 1709, 8vo. 2 vols.
347 Dictionnaire de Bibliographie Françoise, 1812, 8vo. vol. 1 and 2: all yet published.
348 Declaracyon and Power of the Chrysten Fayth, *imprynted by me, Robert Wyer*, 12mo. no date.
349 De Virgilii Editionibus (from Heyne's Virgil.)
350 Dictionnaire Universel, Historique, Critique et Bibliographique, 1810, 8vo. 22. vol. sewed.
351 Deux Livres des Venins, 1568, 4to. *calf, extra gilt leaves*. A curious work, *wood cuts*.
352 Le Discours demonstrant sans feincte
Comme maints Pions font leur plainte
Et les Tauernes desbauchez
Pourquoi Tauerniers sont faschez.
A Rouen, Au portail des Librariers, par Jehan du Golt, &c. 12mo. *wood cut.* A rare piece of early French poetry, *in morocco, gilt leaves*.
353 De Dissectione Partuum Corporis, 1545, *Paris*, folio.
354 Description des Catacombes de Paris, - 1815
355 Druckstucke aus dem XV. Jahrhunderte, &c. By Paul Hupfaner, 1794, 8vo. *wood cuts*.
356 Description of the Merly Library in the County of Dorset, 1785, folio, *plates*.
357 Doni, la Libreria, 1580, 12mo. *morocco*.

294

[17]

358 De Confusione Calvinianae Sectae apud Scotos : Smetonio Scoto Auctore, *Edinb.* 1571, 4to.
359 Dictionnaire de la Chasse et de Pêche, *Paris*. 1767, 12mo. 2 vol.
360 De Antiquiss. Turicensis Bibliothecæ Libro in Membrana Purpurea Titulis aureis ac Litteris argenteis exarat. Auctore Breitingero, 1758, 4to.
361 Desessarts, Les Siecles Littéraires, 1800, 8vo. 6 vol.
362 Davies' Dramatic Miscellanies, 1785, 8vo. 3 vol.
363 De La Croix, Bibliothèque Française, par Juvigny, 6 vol. 4to. LARGE PAPER, - 1772
364 De Bure Bibliographie Instructive, 1763, 4to. 8 vol. in 7, LARGE PAPER, *white calf, gilt leaves, bound by Lewis*.
365 Dictionnaire Bibliographique par Dessessarts, 1804, 8vo.
366 Delandine, Manuscrits de la Bibliothèque de Lyon, 1812, 8vo. 3 vol.
367 Denis, Suffragium pro Johanne de Spira, 1794. This is a curious and rare tract.
368 —— Supplementum Annal. Typog. Maittairii, 1789. 2 parts in one volume, LARGE PAPER.
369 —— Codices Manuscripti Theologici Bibl. Palat. Vindobon. Latini, &c. 1793, folio, 3 vol. 4to.
370 —— Bibliotheca Typographica Vindobonensis, 1782, 4to.
371 Della Libreria Vaticana de Mutio Pansa, 4to.
372 Directions to form a Library, 1766. Johnson's Logography, 1783
373 Dissertation sur les Bibliothèques, 1758, 8vo. *beautiful copy, bound by Lewis*.
374 De Initiis Typographiae Physiologicis, 1740, 4to.
375 Disquisito in Notas Characteristicas Librorum, 1740, 4to. Autore Jungendires. These are two rare typographical tracts, *bound in one volume*.
376 Dominica, 1560, 8vo. *wants title, wood cuts, calf extra*.
377 Engel, Catalogus Librorum Rarissimorum, 1743, 8vo· To which are added.—The Spicilegium Libror. Rarior.—The Catalogus Bibl. Selectae Cod. MSS. et Edit. Rarior. T. Boendermakeri, 1722, 8vo.—and the 'Atlas de feu Mr.

D

[18]

Boendermaker, contenu dans cent trois gros volumes. A very extraordinary collection relating to Geography.
378 Essai Historique sur La Bibliothèque du Roi, 1782, 8vo.
379 Erasmi Opera ; Basiliæ, 1540, folio, 10 vol. *portrait of Erasmus.*
380 Erasmi Nov. Test. Græc. Lat. 1522, folio.
381 Erasmus's Colloquies by Bailey, 8vo. - 1733
382 Erasmus de Ratione Concionandi, - 1535
383 Eusebii Præparatio Evangelica, Lutet. 1544, folio, Edit. Prin.
384 Epistolarum conscribendi methodus, 8vo. - 1597
385 Eutropius, 1539, 12mo, Ex officina Colinæi.
386 Epreuve du Premier Alphabet, &c. pour L'Imprimerie Royale, 1743, 18mo. A specimen of the smallest types that exist. Several heads are introduced, and among them are proof impressions of the portraits of Fontaine and Moliere, *red morocco, gilt leaves.*
387 Edinburgh and Quarterly Reviews, 2 odd numbers of each, and Poems of Lord Byron.
388 Enderbies' Cambria Triumphaus, 1810, folio.
389 Foscarini Letteratura Veneziana, 1752, folio.
390 Foppens Bibliotheca Belgica, 1739, 4to. 2 vol.
391 La France Littéraire, 1769, 3 vol. 8vo.
392 —— Nouveau Supplement à la, 1784, 8vo. 2 vol.
393 Fabricii I. Alberti Bibliotheca Latina, 1697, 8vo. First Edition.
394 Fabricii Bibliotheca Latina, 1703, 8vo. *uncut.*
395 Fabricii Bibliotheca Latina, Ernesti, 1773, 8vo. 3 vol.
396 —— Bibliotheca Græca Cura Harles, 1790, 4to. 10 vol.
397 —— Alberti Opusculorum Historico-Critico-Literarium Sylloge, 1738, 4to. Portrait added. An interesting and uncommon work.
398 —— Joannis Bibliotheca, 1722, 6 vol. in 3, *vellum.*
399 Fabricii Bibliotheca Mediæ et Infimæ Latinitatis, 1754, 4to. 6 vol. *vellum.* This Edition has now become of rare occurrence.
400 —— Idem Opus. 1733, 6 vol. 12mo.

[19]

401 Fabricii Bibliographia Antiquaria, 1760, 4to. Edit. Opt.
402 Freytag, Analecta Litteraria de Libris Rarioribus, 1750, 8vo. 2 vol. in 1.
403 —— Adparatus Literarius, *Lips.* 1752, 8vo. 3 vol. *neat.*
404 Formey, Conseils pour former une Bibliothèque, 1755, 8vo.
405 Fournier le Jeune. Manuel Typographique, 1764, 8vo. 2 vol. *beautiful copy.*
406 Fournier Methode pour Etudier l'Histoire, 1772, 8vo. 15 vol. *best edition.*
407 Fournier Le Jeune. This volume comprehends the entire *Six Tracts* relating to the Dissertation sur l'Origine et les Progres de l'Art de graver en Bois, 1758, and De L'imprimerie Primitive en taille de Bois, 1759. It is a fine copy, and this Collection is rarely found in such condition.
408 Flores Legum. Printed by Petit. bl. letter. Old stamped binding.
409 Florilegium Historico-Criticum Librorum Rariorum, 1747, 8vo.
410 Fischer sur les Monumens Typographiques de Jean Gutenberg, 1802, 4to.
411 Fuller's Good Thoughts in Bad Times, together with Good Thoughts in Worse Times, 1680, 12mo.
412 Fuchsii Historia Plantarum, *Lugd.* 1561, 12mo. *wood cuts.*
413 Figure del Vecchio Testamento con versi per Maraffi Lione, 1554, 8vo. *russia.* The wood cuts are by the famous Salamon, or the Petit Bernard, *beautiful copy.*
414 Frankenau, Bibliotheca Hispanica, 4to. *Lips.* 1724.
415 Fontanini dell' Eloquenza Italiana, del Zeno, 2 vol. 4to. 1753.
416 Goujet, Bibliothèque Françoise, 1741, 8vo. 18 vol. *rare.*
417 Gallois, des Plus Belles Bibliothèques de l'Europe, 1685, 12mo.
418 Another Copy, - - - 1697
419 Gesneri Bibliotheca Universalis, 1545, folio. *Stamped vellum binding.*
419* —— Cura Fusii, 1583, folio.

[20]

420 Gough's British Topography, 1780, 4to. 2 vol.
421 Gutch's Collectanea Curiosa, 1781, 8vo. 2 vol.
422 Godwin, De Præsulibus Angliæ, 1743, folio, *portrait, fine copy.*
423 The Guardian of Instruction, or the Gentleman's Romance, 1688, 12mo.
424 Gerdes, Florilegium Librorum Rariorum, 1763, 8vo.
425 The Grounde of Artes, &c. made by R. Recorde, and emprented by M. John Dee, 1582, 12mo. *cuts.*
426 Gursleviani Scrittori Legari, 1667, 4to.
427 Geret, Vita Alii Pii Manutii, 1753, 4to. *plates.*
428 Gerson de Remediis contra Pusillanimitatem, &c. Printed apparently at Cologne, *russia, fine copy.*
429 Haslewood's Bibliographical Introduction to the Book of Hawking, 1810, folio, *calf.*
430 Historia Litteraria, *Lond.* 1731, 8vo. 4 vol.
431 Heinecken, Idée d'une Collection complette D'Estampes, 1771, 8vo. *russia.*
432 ——— The same work, as originally published in German, *russia, gilt,* 1768, 8vo. *rare.*
433 Haym, Notizia de' Libri Rari, 1726, 8vo. in Londra, *first edition.*
434 Haym, Biblioteca Italiana, *Milan.* 1803. 8vo. 4 parts in 2 vol.
435 Hyll's briefe and pleasaunt treatyse, teachinge howe to dresse, sowe, and set a Garden, &c. 1563, 12mo.
436 Hereafter folowe X certayne Places of Scrypture, &c. Imprynted by me *Robert Wyer, without date,* 12mo. With the Royal Arms, and Device of Wyer at the end.
437 Harles Introd. in Not. Lit. Rom. cum Supplemento, 5 vol. 8vo. - - - - - 1794
438 ——— Introd. In Hist. Ling. Græc. cum Supplemento 1792, 8vo. 5 vol.
439 Howell's Familiar Letters, 1705, 8vo.
440 Hartwood's Biographia Classica, 1778, 8vo.
441 Hoogeven Doctrina Particularum Linguæ Græcæ. Glas. 1813, 8vo.

[21]

442 Hugonis Pia desideria, *plates, gilt leaves,* 8vo.' 1624
443 Heylyn's Life of Archbishop Laud, 1668, folio.
444 Harpsfield Historia Anglicana Ecclesiastica, 1622. folio.
445 Hammond on the New Testament, 1653, folio.
446 Histoire de la Compagnie de Jesus, 1761, 8vo. 4 vol. in 2.
447 Histoire du Cardinal Ximenes, 1693, 8vo. 2 vol. *portrait.*
448 Histoire des Egliscs de Piemont, ou Vaudoises, 1669, folio.
449 Histoire des Comtes de Tolose, 1623, folio, *curious plates.*
450 Hecatongraphie, les descriptions de cent figures et hystoires, *beautiful wood cuts,* 1543, 8vo. *yellow morocco.*
451 The Haven of Health, London, 1636, 4to.
452 Histoire de la Littérature Grecque, par Schoell, 1813, 2 vol. 8vo.
453 Historia Bibliothecæ Reiss. Noribergensis Auctore Sanberto Norib. 1643, 18mo. *frontispiece, a rare book, red morocco, gilt leaves.*
454 G. Hornii Rerum Britannicarum Libri Septem, 1648, 8vo.
455 Horatii Vita a Masson, 1707, 8vo. *frontispiece.*
456 Horatii Ars Poetica, ap. R. Stephanum, 1533, 4to.
457 Hawkins' Two Sermons upon the Iniquity of Witchcraft, 1808, 8vo.
458 Harris's Life of James I. 1772, 8vo. *uncut.*
459 Introduction to the Literary History of the XIVth and XVth Centuries, 1798, *boards.*
460 A just and modest Reproof of a Pamphlet called Scotch Presbyterian Eloquence, 1693, 4to.
461 Icones Veteris Testamenti. *Lugduni, apud J. Frellonium, 1547,* 4to. *wood cuts, from the designs of Holbein, morocco.*
462 Illustrium Ymagines, *Lugduni in Ædibus A. Blanchardii Calcographi, impensis honestorum Virorum S. Mousnier et Juste,* 1524, 12mo. *Curious wood cuts of portraits, with the device of Juste.*
463 Jansen, Origine de la Gravure en Bois et en Taille-Douce, &c. 1808, 8vo. LARGE PAPER, *morocco.*
464 Jansen, De L'Invention de l'Imprimerie, 1809, 8vo.
465 Juvenalis et Persii Satyræ, *Dublin.* 1728, 12mo. *morocco.*
466 Juelli Apologia Ecclesiæ Anglieanæ, *Londini,* 1599, 12mo.

467 Indice Manuale tratto dal Libro, *Milano*, 1812, 12mo.
468 Jacob, Traicté des Bibliothèques, 1694, Naudé, Avis sur les Bibliothèques, 1694, 8vo. *russia, gilt leaves*. These two Tracts, which are usually in very soiled condition, are here in a fine state of preservation.
469 Kennet's Sermon at the Funeral of the Duke of Devonshire, 8vo. 1708.
470 Koeglerus, Notitiæ SS. Bibliorum Judæorum in Imperio Sinensi, 1805, 8vo.
471 Peter Langtoft's Chronicle, 2 vol. in 1. Bagster's Edition, *in russia.*
472 Robert of Gloucester's Chronicle, 2 vol. in 1. Bagster's Edition, *in russia.*
473 Lloyd's Memoirs, 1668, folio.
474 The Life and Errors of John Dunton, 1705, 8vo. RARE, *in russia.*
475 Lightfoot's Miscellanies, Christian and Judaical, 8vo. 1623
476 Lelong, Bibliotheca Sacra Cura Boernei at Maschii, 1778, 4to. 4 vol.
477 ——— Bibliothèque Historique de la France, par M. Fevret de Fontelle, 1768, 5 vol. *fine copy.*
478 Lichtenberger Initia Typographica, 1811, 4to. *russia.*
479 Lunze, Monumentorum Typographicorum Decas, 1799, 8vo.
480 Lives of Leland, Hearne and Wood, 1772, 8vo. 2 vol. *russia.*
481 Lambinet Origine de l'Imprimerie, 1810, 8vo. 2 vol.
482 L'Academia Peregrina del Doni, 1551, 4to. *imperfect.*
483 Latimer's Sermons, 1581, 4to.
484 Martin Luther's Sermons, 1581, 4to.
485 Liber Confessionum Sancti Augustini, folio, *printed by Mentelin, without date.*
486 Liber Precum, &c. Printed by Vauhollur, 1574, 8vo. *russia.* The frontispiece of this rare book has been copied by Ames and Herbert, forming the central compartment of their respective works.
487 Lettera di Bandini sopra la Biblioteca Laurenziana, 1773, 12mo. *gilt leaves, an uncommon tract.*

488 Lettera Pastorale, &c. Stampata per Bodoni, 12mo. an exquisite specimen of Bodoni's smaller types, *morocco, privately printed.*
489 Lyræ Comment. in S. Scripturam, (last **volume**) *Venet.* 1489, folio. With the large device of Scot.
490 Laire, Specimen Historicum Typographiæ Romanæ, 1778, 4to. *morocco.*
491 Lomeier de Bibliothecis, 1680, 8vo.
492 Les Trois Siecles de notre Literature, 1773, 8vo. 2 vol.
493 Livre de la Fontaine périlleuse, avec la Chartre d'Amours, 1572, 12mo. Rare poetical tract, *morocco, gilt leaves.*
494 Leichius de Origine Typographiæ Lipsiensis Anno Typog. Seculari III. 4to.
495 Lives of Lely and Ashmole, 1774, 8vo.
496 Lemoine's Art of Printing, 1797, 8vo.
497 Lipsii Opera, 1675, 8vo. 5 vol.
498 Lavaterus de Spectris, 1687, 12mo. *frontispiece.*
499 Leon Hébrieu de l'Amour, 2 vol. in 1. Lyon, Jean de Tournes, 1551, 8vo. *beautiful device.*
500 Maittaire Annales Typographici, 5 vol. 1709, 1733, &c. 4to.
501 ——— Hist. Typog. Stephanorum, 1709, LARGE PAPER, *morocco.*
502 ——— Hist. Typog. Insig. Parisiensium, 1718, LARGE PAPER, *morocco.* These two latter volumes are uniformly and splendidly bound by C. Lewis.
503 Meermanni Origines Typographia, 1765, 4to. 2 vol. LARGE PAPER, *morocco, very fine copy.*
504 Meerman, &c. De Chartæ Vulgaris Origine, 1767, 12mo. *an uncommon tract.*
505 Museum Typographicum, in qua omnes ferè Libri rarissimi notatǫue dignissimi accuratè recensentur, a Guillelmo-Francisco REBUDE, juniore Bibliopola Parisiensi, Anno 1755, 8vo.

⁎⁎ This was the first Tract which De Bure ever published under the anagram of Rebude : it was privately printed for his friends, and only 12 copies are said to have been struck off. The present is bound in red

[24]

morocco, and has a double Set of prices in the margin: one, of the supposed value of books at the time of the publication, the other of that in the year 1786. It may with propriety, therefore, be considered an unique copy.

506 Montfaucon, Palæographia Græca, 1708, folio.
507 ———— Diarium Italicum, 1702, 4to.

THIRD DAY'S SALE.

The Sale will commence PRECISELY AT HALF PAST TWELVE.

508 Lot of Bookseller's Catalogues.
509 Another Lot of Bookseller's Catalogues.
510 Catalogues of Commelin, Elsevir, Janson, Orlers, &c. 4to.
510* Catalogue of the Portland Museum, *with the prices*, 1786
511 Basan, Catalogue Raisonné des objets de curiosités de Marietta, *with prices*, — — — *Par.* 1775
512 Huber, Catalogue raisonné d'Estampes de Winckler, 2 vol.
513 Catalogo della Libreria Floncel, 2 vol. in 1, *with prices*, *Par.* 1774
514 Catalogus Librorum Impressorum J. Smithii ante annum, 1500
515 Catalogus Librorum Bibliopolii Elzeviriani, 1674, *morocco, uncut*, 12mo.
516 Catalogus Librorum ex Variis Partibus Europæ advectorum per Scott, — — — 1674
517 Bibliotheca Solgeriana, 3 vol. — *Nor.* 1760
518 ———— Collegii Sionensis, — *Lond.* 1724
519 ———— Thuana, — — *Par.* 1679
520 ———— Thomasiana, 2 vol. — *Norimb.* 1765
521 ———— Telleriana, *portrait*, — *Par.* 1693
522 ———— Vander Aa, *fine copy in green morocco*, 1729
523 ———— Vilenbroekii, *in russia*, — *Amst.* 1729

[25]

524 Vogel, Specimen Bibliothecæ Germaniæ Austriacæ, 3 vol. FINE PAPER, — — *Vien.* 1779
525 Bibliotheca Fayana, FINE PAPER, *with prices*, *Par.* 1725
526 ———— Rousseau, — — *Davent.* 1728
527 Celsii Historia Bibliothecæ Upsaliensis, — *Upsal.* 1745
528 Bibliotheca Codicum MSS. Græcorum Bibliothecæ Regiæ Bavaricæ, 5 vol. — — *Monach.* 1706
529 ———— Josephi Smithii, — *Ven.* 1755
530 ———— Comitis de Hoym, *with prices, morocco by Lewis*, — — — *Paris.* 1738
531 Anderson, Catalogus Librorum de Rebus Britannicis. 1713
532 Bibliothecæ Americanæ primordia. — *Par.* 1706
533 Bibliotheca Bigotiana, 8vo. *morocco*, — *Par.* 1711
534 ———— Bultelliana, 8vo. 4to. *with prices*, *Par.* 1700
535 ———— Baluziana, 2 vol. 8vo. — *Hamb.* 1716
536 Bartholini Bibliotheca Danica, 8vo.
537 Bibliotheca Bentesiana, — — *Amst.* 1702
538 Bandinii Catalogus Codicum Latinorum Bibliothecæ Mediceæ Laurentianæ, 5 vol. folio, — *Flor.* 1774
539 Bibliotheca Heilsbronnensis, *Norib.* 1731, with the Antiquities of Heilbron, 18 plates, folio.
540 Biscii Catalogus, Bibliothecæ Mediceo-Laurentianæ, folio, *Flor.* 1752
541 Bibliotheca Aprosiana, *original edition*, 12mo. 1673
542 Bibliotheca Aprosiana, cura Wolfii, 8vo. 1734
543 Bibliotheca Colbertina, 3 vol. *with prices*, *Par.* 1728
544 ———— Cordesiana, *very fine copy, in russia*, *Par.* 1643
545 ———— Duboisiana, 4 vol. *with prices*, *Haye.* 1725
546 ———— Dalmanniana. — *ib.* 1723
547 Denis, Codices MSS. Theologici Bib. Palatinæ Vindobonensis, 3 vol. folio, — — *Vindob.* 1793
548 Fossii Catalogus Codicum Saeculi XV. Impressorum Bibliothecæ Magliabechianæ, 2 vol. in 1, *Flor.* 1793
549 Bibliotheca Hohendorfiana, 3 vol. in 1, *in russia*, *Haye.* 1720
550 ———— Ilulsiana, 3 vol. in 6, interleaved, *Hagæ Com.* 1730
551 ———— Krohniana, — *Hamb.* 1796
552 ———— Lamouiana, 3 vol. in 1, *in russia*, *Par.* 1791

E

[27]

553 Laire Index Libiorum ad annum 1500, (Lomenie's Collection), 2 vol. FINE PAPER, partly priced, *Senon.* 1791
554 Laire, Index Librorum ad annum 1500, 2 vol. in 1, 1791, partly priced, in russia, and vol. 3, in calf, 1792.
555 Lambecii Prodromus Literarius, 1659, folio.
556 —— Recensio, Cod. MSS. seu Bibliotheca Accoamatica Auctore Reimanno, 1712, 8vo. A curious and somewhat scarce volume.
557 Lambecii Commentarii de Bibliothecæ Cæsarea Vindobonensi, edidit Kollarius, 8 vol. *with all the plates*, VERY SCARCE, folio, - - *Vind.* 1766
558 Bibliotheca Maarseveniana, - - *Amst.* 1704
559 —— Menarsiana, *with prices*, . *Hagæ.* 1720
560 —— Marckiana, *with prices*, *Hagæ Com.* 1712
561 —— Menckeniana, - - *Lips.* 1723
562 Montfaucon, Bibliotheca Coisliniana, folio, *Par.* 1715
563 —— Bibliotheca Bibliothecarum Manuscriptorum, 2 vol. folio, - - *Par.* 1739
564 Mittarelli, Bibliotheca Codd. MSS. Monasterii S. Michaelis Venetiarum, LARGE PAPER, Pope Pius VI. copy, folio, 1779
565 Morelli, Bibliotheca MSS. Divi Marci Venetiarum, 1802
566 Nessel, Catalogus Cod. MSS. Græcorum Bibliothecæ Vindobonensis, folio, - - *Vind.* 1690
567 Bibliotheca Nicolaiana, *with prices*, - *Amst.* 1698
568 —— Oizeliana, *with prices*, - 1687
569 —— Roveriana, - - *L. Bat.* 1806
570 —— Slusiana, - - *Romæ.* 1690
571 —— Sarraziana, *with prices*, *Hagæ. Com.* 1715
572 Memorie Trevigiane sulla Tipografia del Secolo XV. *Venez.* 1805, 4to.
573 Mercier, Supplement à l'Histoire de l'Imprimerie de P. Marchand, 1773, 4to. russia, fifth edition.
574 —— ——, 1775, 4to. russia, gilt leaves, second edition, rare.
575 Morelli Notizia d'Opere di Disegno, &c. 1800, 8vo.
576 Marchand Histoire, de l'Imprimerie, 1740, 4to. russia, with the second Supplement of Mercier to the same work.

577 Marchand, Dictionnaire Historique, 2 vol. in 1, *scarce*, folio, 1758
578 Morhofii Polyhistor Literarius, 1747, 4to. 2 vol. Edit. Opt.
579 Memoirs of Literature, 1722, 8vo. second edition, 9 vols.
580 Mémoires de l'Institut National des Sciences et Arts, An. VI. 4to. 3 vols.
581 Mabillon, De Re Diplomatica cum Supplemento, 1681, 2 vol. folio.
582 —— Diarium Italicum, 1687, 4to. 2 vols. vellum.
583 H. Mercurialis Foroliviensis Opuscula, *Venel.* 1644, folio.
584 Manutii (Pauli) Bunelli, &c. Epistolæ, 1581, 8vo.
585 —— (Pauli) Epistolæ, 1720, 8vo. portrait.
586 Moxon's Mechanical Exercises (the Art of Printing only).
587 Miscellanea Antiqua Anglicana, extra by Lewis.
588 Manuale ad Usum Sarum. *Rothomagi*, 1554, 4to.
589 Morgan's Phœnix Britannicus, 4to. 1732.
590 Millot, Histoire Litéraire des Troubadours, 1802, 12mo. 3 vols.
591 Menagiana, *Amst.* 1713, 12mo. 4 vol.
592 Morhof, De Rat. Conscrib. Epist. 1716, 8vo.
593 Morhofii Dissertationes Academicæ, 4to. 1699.
594 Maichelii Introd. ad Hist. Litter. de Præcipuis Bibliothecis Parisiensibus, 1721, 8vo. vellum.
595 Michaelis Hospitalii, (Cancell.) Epistolæ, *portrait*, 1592, 8vo.
596 Memoirs of the Renowned Peiresc, 8vo. portrait by Gaywood, 1657
597 Meursii Glossarium Græco Barbarum, 1614, 4to.
598 Montfaucon, Antiquité Expliquée, avec le Supplement, 15 vol. *best edition*, folio, - - *Par.* 1719
599 Metamorphosis of Ajax, by Sir J. Harrington, 8vo. 1814
600 Neustria Pia, 1663, folio.
601 Nicolson's Historical Libraries, 1736, folio.
602 Nicolson's Epistolary Correspondence, 1809, 8vo. 2 vol. in 1.
603 Notices et Extraits des MSS. de la Bibliothèque du Roi, 1787, 6 vol.
604 Nichols' Literary Anecdotes, 1812, &c. 8vo. 8 vols. (with Index,) *extra, by Lewis*. Vol. IXth and Index, *boards*.

605 Niceron, Mémoires des Hommes Illustres, 1729, 8vo. 40 vols. *rare.*
606 Nouveau Traité de Diplomatique, 1750, 4to. 7 vols.
607 Notice d'un Livre imprimé à Bamberg en MCCCCLXII, An. VII. Folio, of which size only twelve copies were printed.
608 Novelle Scelte rarissimi stampate a spese di XL Amatori, 1814, 8vo.
609 Notizie intorno a due rarissime. Edizioni del Secolo XV. di Pezzana, *Parma.* 1808, 8vo. LARGE PAPER, *of which only 6 copies are said to have been printed. Bound by Lewis.*
610 Née de la Rochelle, Eloge de Gutenberg, 8vo. LARGE PAPER, *morocco, by Lewis.*
611 Notitia Bibliothecæ Principalis Vinarientis (Wittemberg), 1712, 4to.
612 Orlandi Abecedario Pittorico, 1753, 4to.
613 ———— Notizie degli Scrittori Bolognesi, 1714, 4to.
614 ———— Origine e Progresse de la Stampa, 1722, 4to.
615 Oldys's British Librarian, 1738, 8vo. *russia.*
616 Lord Orford's Works, vol. 3, 4, and 5 relating to Engravers and Painters, 4to.
617 Osmont, Dictionnaire Typographique, 1768, 8vo. 2 vol. *in russia.*
618 Opera Rariora in Bibliotheca Rebdorfiana Eichstad, 1790, *rare.*
619 Osiandri Harmonia Evangelica, *wood cuts, wants the last leaf.*
620 Opusculum Tripartitum de Præceptis Decalogi, &c. (Printed by Ulric Zel,) *without date,* 4to. Harleian Copy, *morocco.*
621 Oratio de Vita Oporini (Typographi) 1569, *scarce.*
622 Pappe with an hatchet, Alias, a Figge for my God sonne. Or Cracke me this nut, &c. *without date,* 4to.
623 Parker, de Antiquitate Britannicæ Ecclesiæ curâ Drake, 1729, *folio, portrait.*
624 Placcii Theatrum Anonymorum et Pseudonymorum, 1708, 2 vols. in 1, *folio.*
625 Papillon, de la Gravure en Bois, 3 vols. in 2. 1766, 8vo.
626 Pancirollus de Rebus Memorabilibus, 4to.
627 Poiret de Deo, Anima, et Malo, 1685, 4to.
628 ———— de Eruditione Solida, 1707, 4to.
629 ———— de Eruditione Triplici, 1707, 4to.
630 Pauli Jovii Historia sui Temporis, *Venet.* 1559, 12mo. 3 vol. *red morocco.*
631 Politiani Opera, *Lugd.* 1528, 12mo. 2 vols. with MS. notes of Thomas Rudd, Librarian of Durham Cathedral Library.
632 Polydorus Virgilius de Inventoribus Rerum, 1498, 4to. EDITIO PRINCEPS.
633 ———— 8vo. - *Elz.* 1671
634 Panzer, Annales Typographici, 1793, 4to. 11 vols.
635 Panzer's Annals of German Typography, 4to. 1788.
636 Peignot Repertoire Bibliographique Universel, 1812, 8vo. LARGE PAPER, *extra in russia, by Lewis, gilt leaves. Only 4* LARGE PAPER *copies printed, and the present presumed to be the only one in this country.*
637 Peignot, Repertoire de Bibliographies Spéciales, &c. 1810, 8vo.
638 ———— Curiosités Bibliographiques, 1804, 8vo.
639 ———— Dictionnaire Raisonné de Bibliologie, 1802, 8vo. 3 vols.
640 ———— Dictionnaire des Livres condamnés au feu, 1806, 2 vol. in 1, 8vo.
641 ———— Essai sur l'Histoire du Parchemin et du Vélin, 1812, 8vo. LARGE PAPER, only 12 copies printed, *morocco, gilt leaves, bound by Lewis.*
642 Philobiblon Richartii Dvnelmensis. *Oxoniæ,* 1599, 4to. *morocco, uncut, first edition in this country.*
643 Plan du Traité des Origines Typographiques, par M. Meerman, 1762, 8vo. *calf, gilt leaves.* A very scarce tract, of which the Abbé Goujet is the reputed author. It contains notices of books not afterwards inserted in Meerman's larger work.
644 Pitseus, de Scriptoribus Britanniæ, 1619, 4to. *rare.*
645 Palmer's History of Printing, 1733, 4to.
646 Première Epreuve d'une Nouvelle Presse pour le Service de l'Imprimerie Royale et approuvée, 1783, 8vo. *calf gilt.*

[31]

647 Photii Bibliotheca. Paul. Stephanus, 1589, folio.
648 Phenix, a Revival of Scarce and Valuable Tracts, 1707, 2 vols.
649 Pater, de Germaniæ Miraculo Optimo Maximo Typis Literariun, &c. 1710, 4to.
650 Prospetto di Varie Edizioni degli Autori Classici del Eduardo Arwood, *Ven.* 1780, 8vo. *yellow morocco.*
651 Promptuariun Iconum Insigniorum, &c. 1578, 4to. *fine copy in russia.*
652 Paradini Symbola Heroica, 1567, 12mo. *clean copy.*
653 Pystels and Gospels of every Sonday and holy Daye in the yere. Black letter. Fine device of St. John, 12mo.
654 Percel (Dufresnoy) de l'Usage des Romains, 1734, 2 vols. 12mo.
655 Pignorius de Lewis, 1656, 4to. *portrait.*
656 Pinkerton's Essay on Medals, 1789, 2 vol.
657 Peiresci Vita, Authore Gassando, *portrait*, 1655, 4to.
658 Pauli 2 P. M. Gesta, 4to. - - - 1740
659 Neve's Animadversions on Phillips's Life of Cardinal Pole, 8vo. - - - - 1766
660 Quirini Specimen Literature Brixianæ Sæculi XV. **LARGE PAPER**, 4to.
661 Quirini de Optimorum Scriptorum Editionibus, 1761, 4to.
662 Repertoire de Littérature Ancienne, ou Choix d'Auteurs Grecs et Latins, 1808, 8vo. 2 vols. in 1.
663 Rive, la Chasse aux Bibliographes, 1789, 8vo. *morocco, gilt.*
664 Rive, Prospectus d'un Ouvrage proposé par Souscription par M. L'Abbé Rive, 12mo, never published. This was the Prospectus of the projected work respecting illuminated MSS.
Etrennes aux Joueurs de Cartes, 1780, 12mo. These two Tracts are bound in one Volume; *morocco.*
665 Richarderie, Bibliotheque des Voyages, 6 vol. in 3, *gilt leaves.*
666 Renouard, Imprimerie des Aldes, 1803, 8vo. 2 vols. *morocco.*
667 Rawlinson's Method of Studying History, 1730, 8vo. 2 vols.
668 Rossi, de Bibliotheca Judaica Anti-Christiana, 1800, 8vo.
669 —— de Typographia Hebræo-Ferrariensi, 1780, 8vo.
670 Rossi, Annales Hebræo-Typographici, 1795-9, 4to. 2 vols. in 1, *extra.*
671 —— Dizionario Storico degli Autori Ebrei, 1802, 8vo.
672 Relationes de Libris Novis Gottingæ,1752, &c. 8vo. 9 vols.
673 Roccha Bibliotheca Vaticana, 1591, 4to. *rare.*
674 Ross's View of all Religions, 1672, 8vo. *portrait.*
675 Ritsons' Bibliographia Poetica, 1802, 8vo.
676 Ritson's Robin Hood, 1795, 8vo. 2 vols. *russia.*
677 Reimanni Cat. Bibl. Theolog. with the Accessiones Uberiores, 1731, 8vo. 4 vols. *rare.*
678 Ringelbergii Elegantiæ, 1529, 12mo. *morocco, gilt leaves.* The portrait of Ringelbergius, at the end of this scarce tract, is that from which Faithorne drew and Ames published, the spurious head of Wynkyn de Worde. This portrait will be republished in the Bibliographical Decameron.
679 Religio Bibliopolæ, 12mo. - - 1691
680 Rituale Græcorum complectens Ritus et Ordines, 8vo. 1647, folio.
681 Reading Races, or the Berkshire Beauties, a Poem, 1777, 4to.
682 Rerum Sicularum Scriptores. Francof. ad Mœn. 1579, folio.
683 Reason and Judgement, or Special Remarks of the Life of the late renowned Bp. Sanderson, 1663, kto.
684 Schoenman, Bibliotheca Patrum Latinorum, 1792, 2 vols. 8vo. *russia.*
685 Saxii Onomasticon Literarium, 1775, 8vo. 8 vols. *extra.*
686 Saxii, Historia Literaria Typographica Mediolanensis, 1745, folio, *rare.*
687 Schelhorn, Amœnitates Historiæ Ecclesiasticæ et Literariæ, 1737, 8vo. 2 vols.
688 —— Amœnitates Literariæ, 1730, 8vo. 14 vols. in 7.
689 Schmidius de Bibliothecis, 1703, 4to. 3 vols. A very useful and uncommon collection of bibliographical tracts.
690 Schwandnerus de Charta Linea Antiquissima, 1788, 4to. A curious tract.
691 Saxius, de Studiis Literariis, 1729, 8vo.

301

[32]

692 Santander, Dictionnaire Bibliographique Choisi du XVeme. Siècle, 1805, 8vo. 3 vols. *morocco.*
693 —— sur la Bibliothèque du Bourgogne, 1809, 8vo.
694 Specimen Bibliothecæ Hispano-Majansianæ ex Museo Davidis Clementis, 1753, 4to. *rare.*
695 Summario de Bibliotheca Luziana. Lisbon, 1785, 8vo. 3 vols.
696 Struvii Notitia Rei Litterar. Cura Fischeri, 1754, 8vo. *vellum.*
697 Seiz, Annus Festivus Sæcularis Inventæ Artis Typographicæ, &c. 1741, 8vo. *with all the plates.*
698 Seemiller Incunabula Typographica. Ingolst. 1787, 4to. 4 parts in one volume.
699 Serie dell' Edizioni Aldine, 1803, 8vo. *russia, gilt.*
700 Schoepflini Vindiciæ Typographicæ, 1760, 4to.
701 Spoerlini Introductio in Notitiam Insignium Typographicorum, 1730, 4to.
702 Struvii Notitia Rei Litterariæ, 1715, 8vo. *first edition.*
703 Singer's Researches into the History of Playing Cards, &c. 1816, 4to. *extra, gilt leaves.*
704 Schwarz, de Origine Typographiæ, 1740, 4to. Three Parts, *rare.*
705 Spizelii Infelix Literatus, 1680, 8vo. A very curious performance.
706 Sacra Bibliothecarum Illustrium Arcana relecta, 1668, 8vo.
707 Savage's Librarian, vol. 1 and 2, 1808, 8vo.
708 Seelen, Selecta Litteraria, 1726, 8vo. bound by Lewis.
709 Strutt's Manners and Customs, 1774, 4to. 3 vols. in 1. *without the plates.*
710 Saldenus, de Libris Varioque eorum Usu et Abusu Libri Duo, 1688, 8vo. *frontispiece.*
711 Southey's Curse of Kehama, 1810, 4to. *russia, marbled leaves.*
712 —— Madoc, 1805, 4to. *russia, extra.*
713 Scott's Minstrelsy of the Scottish Border, 2 vol. Presentation Copy to the Duke of Roxburghe, - 1802
714 Old Ballads, 3 vol. *cuts, fine copy,* - 1727
715 Suetone, par Langelier, Par. 1540, *morocco.*

[33]

716 H. Stephani Querimonia Artis Typographicæ, *original edition, rare,* 4to. 1569.
717 H. Stephani Pseudo-Cicero et de suæ Typogr. Statu et Art. Typog. Querim. &c. 1737, 8vo. *rare.*
718 Sallengre Mémoires de Litterature, 1715, 8vo. 14 vols.
719 Les Saisons, Poeme, *Amst.* 1771, 8vo.
720 Summa Theologiæ S. T. Aquinatis, Pars Prima, 1624, 8vo. 6 vols.
721 St. Palaye, Mémoires de Chevalerie, 3 vol. 12mo. 1781.
722 Schotti Technica Curiosa, sive Magica Curiosa, 1664, 4to. 3 vol. *plates.*
723 Tracts on Printing, 1669, 4to.
724 Tracts on Printing: Rowe Mores, (only 80 copies printed,) Supplement to the same by Nichols. Bowyer and Nichol's Origin of Printing, Supplement to the same. Biographical Memoirs of Wm. Ged. Enquiry into the Origin of Printing in Europe, *uncut. Reed's copy.*
725 Tauner, Bibliotheca Britannico-Hibernica, &c. 1748, folio.
726 Toderini Letteratura Turchesa, 1787, 8vo. 3 vols.
727 —— the same work in French, 3 vols. 8vo.
728 Tenhove's Memoirs of the Medici Family, by Clayton, 2 vol. 4to. - 1797
729 Toppi Bibliotheca Napoletana, 1678, folio, *frontispiece.*
730 —— Another Copy.
731 Tractatus Varii Latinia Crevier, Brotier, &c. *Lond.* 1788, 8vo.
732 Tractatus de Sphera J. de Sacrobosco, ap H. Steph. 1567, folio.
733 Translations from Xenophon, &c. on Rural Œconomy, 1767, 8vo.
734 Trithemii Epistole, 1536, 4to. Edit. Prin. *rare.*
735 Triga Libellorum Rarissimorum, 1727, 4to.
736 Thomson's Seasons, 1730, 8vo.
737 Thomson's Winter, 1726, 8vo. *first edition.*
738 The Boke of Eneydos compyled by Vyrgyle, and reduced into Englysshe by me William Caxton, *wants 4 leaves of Preface.* EXTREMELY RARE, and a very interesting book, MCCCCLXXX.

F

[34]

739 LYF OF ST. KATHERIN OF SENIS, with the Reuelacions of Saynt Elysabeth the Kynges doughter of Hungarye, *a fine copy*, and perfect, with the exception of one leaf (Sign. p. 3.) bound *in morocco by Lewis*, IMPRYNTED BY CAXTON.
740 Vallois Discours sur les Bibliothèques Publiques, a copy presented by Cardinal Quirini to Capelius, 1751, 8vo. *extra, gilt leaves, scarce*.
741 Virgil's Georgics by Sotheby, - 1800
742 The Universal Historical Bibliotheque, or an Account of most of the Considerable Books printed in all Languages in the Month of January 1686, 1687, 4to.
743 The Universal Librarian, 1751, 8vo.
744 Vie d'Etienne Dolet, Imprimeur à Lyon, 1779, *uncut, russia, half bound*.
745 Vogt, Catalogus Hist. Crit. Librorum Rariorum, 1793, 8vo. *neat copy*.
746 Vossius de Historicis Latinis, 1651, 4to.
747 Volpi Cominiana Annali della Typografia, Padoua, 1809, 8vo. *portrait*.
748 Vigneul Marville, Mélanges de Litterature, 1700, 8vo. 3 vols.
749 Voyage autour de ma Bibliothèque, Roman Bibliographique, 3 vols. in 1, 1809, 8vo.
750 Vindication of Richard Atkyns, 1669, 4to.
751 Vie et Actions Heroiques et Plaisantes de Charles V. 1699, 12mo. 4 vols.
752 Vita Lutheri Heornschmidii, 1742, 8vo. *fine portrait*.
753 Wolfi Monumenta Typographica, 1740, 8vo. *half bound in russia*, in 11 volumes.
754 Wolfi Bibliotheca Ebraea, 1714, 4to. 3 vols.
755 Warton's History of English Poetry, and Ritson's Observations upon, 1782, 4 vol. 4to.
756 Weekly Memorials, or an Account of Books lately set forth, 1683, 4to.
757 Watson's History of Printing, 1713, 8vo. LARGE PAPER, *morocco, gilt leaves, rare*.

303

[35]

758 Wurdtwein, Bibliotheca Moguntina, 1787, 4to.
759 Walker's Sufferings of the Clergy, 1714, folio.
760 Who wrote Cavendish's Life of Wolsey? 4to. 1814
761 Xenophontis Cyri Institutio, Gr. Lat. *Glasg.* 1812, 8vo. *boards*.
762 Zani dell' Origine e de' Progressi dell' Incisione in Rame e in Legno, &c. 1802, 8vo.
763 Zapf, Annales Typographiæ Augustanæ, 1778, 4to.
764 Zapf Augsburgs Buchduckergeschichte, 1786, 4to. 2 vols. in 1.
765 Marsh's Illustration of the Hypothesis, 1803, 8vo.
766 Hadrianus Barlandus de Hollandiæ Principibus, *Antverpiæ. apud J. Theobaldum*, 1519, 4to. With the device of Thibaut, *a rare book*.
767 De Emendatione Ecclesiæ, A Pedro de . A beautiful specimen of Basil printing, of the XVIth century, *without date, calf extra*.
768 The Examination of Tilenus in Utopia, 1658, 8vo.
769 Persii Satyræ cum Comment. Britannici, Lugd. 1510, 4to. title damaged.

770 Le Remede damour Cõpose par Eneas Siluius. Autremẽt dit Pape pic second translate de latin en francoys, par Maistre Albin des auenelles chanoine de leglise de soissons avec aucunes additions de Baptiste Mantuē. *On les vẽd a Paris en la rue neufue nostre Dame, a lenseigne de lescu de France*, 4to. bl. letter, *without date*, wood cut frontispiece. A very rare and early French metrical version of a work of the most distinguished popularity in the XVth century.

A. N. L. MUNBY

Annotations in the auctioneer's copy in the British Library [S.C.E.7(10)]

Lot
- 56 deleted and 'Dr Peirson's Cat.' substituted.
- 108 deleted and 'Tutet &c.' substituted.
- 110 deleted and 'Crozat Tugny' substituted.
- 134 deleted and 'Caillard' substituted.
- 137 'Merly' added to description.
- 153 'L.P.' added to description.
- 224 deleted and 'Catalogue de d'Ourches' substituted.
- 246 'Coplestone's Prael', added.
- 247 'Astle on Origin' added.
- 263 'Borromeo 1794' added.
- 267 'Magliabechi. 4 vol.' added.
- 293 'Lort's Catalogue' added.
- 300 'de Macarthy' deleted and 'precieux' substituted.
- 306 '1 leaf mss.' added.
- 310 'M.R.' identified as M. Renouard.
- 324 First item, 1772 La Vallière catalogue, deleted.
- 347 'and 2' deleted.
- 350 '22 vol.' altered to '29 vol.'.
- 400 'Fischer's Printing in German. 1800' added.
- 406 'Fournier' deleted and 'Dufresnoy' substituted.
- 430 'By Bower' added.
- 439 'Clement's Annals 4 vol. in 2' added.
- 445 'Smith's Grammar.' added.
- 447 'Ray's Proverbs.' added.
- 454 'Byng's Cat.' added.
- 460 'Dibdin on the Classics' added.
- 463 '2 vol.' added.
- 469 'Porson's Catalogue with prices' added.
- 477 'Fontelle' altered to 'Fontet'.
- 480 'Hunter's Catalogue' added.
- 483 'Erasmi Vita & Aesopus' added.
- 547 'Cat. Lugduno-Bat.' added.
- 560* 'Marckiana', inserted lot.
- 573 'fifth edition' altered to 'first edition'.
- 574 'Fell's specimens of Oxford Types' added.
- 576 'second Supplement' altered to 'second Edition of Supplement'.
- 579 '8 vol.' added.

582 'Diarium' altered to 'Museum'.
614* 'another', inserted lot.
622 'Steevens's Cat.' added.
664 664* inserted before second tract.
672 '9 vols.' altered to '8 vol.'.
681 'Griffin's Fidessa' added.
701 'S. Ireland's Cat. priced' added.
719 '& others' added.
720 'Foscarini Veneria' added.
726 'Lake's Catal.' added.
737 'first edition' altered to '3rd edition'.
739* 'Bp. Fysher—1529', inserted lot.
746 'Dormer's Catalogue' added.
751 '4 vols.' altered to '2 vol.'.
755 'Vol. 2, 3, & 4' added.
759 'Dodd's Catalogue' added.
760 'Loft of Catalogues' added.
770 This lot is printed on a separate slip and inserted.

1	Payne		5		24	Lepard		6
2	Higgs		11		25	Jacobs		1
3	Heber	2			26	Triphook		2
4	Payne		2		27	Payne		18
5	Payne	1	12		28	Payne		6
6	North	1	10		29	Payne		5
7	Higgs		16		30	Heber	8	2 6
8	North		4		31	North	2	12 6
9	Heber		15		32	Heber		11
10	Higgs		16		33	Heber		15
11	Payne		5		34	Heber	1	
12	Higgs	1	9		35	Payne		1
13	Jacobs		5		36	Payne		5
14	Heber	1	2		37	Payne	1	1
15	Triphook		11		38	Clarke		1
16	Clarke		2		39	Bentham		1
17	North	1	7		40	Heber		7
18	Payne		7		41	Triphook		1
19	Payne		7		42	Heber		2
20	Arch	5	12 6		43	Payne	2	3
21	Triphook		3		44	Payne		8
22	Triphook		1		45	North		15
23	Higgs		13		46	Heber		11

47	Heber	4	1		90	Payne	1	12
48	Payne		11		90*	Heber		11
49	Heber		5		91	Heber		9
50	North	3	16		92	Higgs		4
51	Nicol		6		93	Clarke		2
52	Arch		9		94	Heber		7
53	Arch		13		95	Payne		1
54	Triphook	1	12		96	Heber		2
55	Higgs		7		97	Bourn		1
56	Longman		11		98	Longman		5
57	North	1	11 6		99	Arch		6
58	North	1	1		100	North	2	7
59	Payne		15		101	Heber		4
60	Ewen	1	7		102	Miller	1	16
61	Arch	2	3		103	North	2	8
62	North		19		104	Heber		13
63	Heber		6		105	Longman		10
64	Heber	1	3		106	Heber	2	19
65	Nicol	1	5		107	Corrie	1	10
66	Clarke		2		108	Heber		7
67	Nicol		3		109	Heber		1
68	Payne		5		110	Heber		7
69	Nicol		5		111	North	8	8
70	North	1	10		112	Arch		2
71	North		14		113	Clarke		1
72	Triphook		19		114	Nicol		12
73	Longman		15		115	Jacobs		2
74	Corrie	3	6		116	Nicol		2
75	Nicol		12		117	Bramstone		2
76	Payne		6		118	John		2
77	Payne		4		119	Markland		18
78	Payne		7		120	Heber	1	3
79	Evans		1		121	Miller		1
80	Heber		17		122	Nicol		1
81	Heber		9		123	Payne		3
82	Payne	2	8		124	Bramstone	1	1
83	Higgs	1	1		125	Miller		1
84	Heber		18		126	Lepard		2
85	Clarke		1		127	Heber		15
86	Nicol		4		128	Jacobs		3
87	Clarke		17		129	Nicol		5
88	Miller		1		130	Nicol		6
89	Higgs	1	17		131	Payne	1	11 6

132	North	3	8		174	Goodenough		8
133	Heber	1	8		175	Triphook		2
134	Triphook		4		176	Payne		3
135	Nicol		1		177	Nicol	5	
136	Payne		9		178	Payne		6
137	Triphook	1	16		179	Payne		4
137*	Triphook		3		180	Clarke		2
138	Corrie		5		181	Payne		8
139	Payne		18		182	} Payne		1
140	Payne	2			183			
141	Payne	1	1		184	Heber		1
142	North	2			185	Meredith	1	2
143	Payne		3		186	Heber		5
144	Payne		1		187	Payne	2	9
145	Bentham		2		188	Triphook		10 6
146	Clarke		1		189	Heber	1	1
147	North		15		190	Triphook	2	12 6
148	Heber		16		191	Triphook	2	6
149	North	2	10		192	Arch	3	15
150	Payne		8		193	North	1	16
151					194	North	5	15 6
152	Heber		15		195	Nicol		19
153	Nicol		15		196	Nicol	1	17
154	Heber		7		197	Payne	1	5
155	Fazakerly		2 6		198	Payne		8
156	Bourne		1		199	Nicol	1	10
157	Triphook		7		200	Arch	1	9
158	Nicol		7		201	Payne	4	5
159	Payne	1			202	Heber		1
160	Payne	1	11		203	Heber	3	10
161	Nicol		2		204	Clarke		6
162	Fazakerley		1		205	Payne	2	18
163	Triphook	1	1		206	Nicol		16
164	Triphook		19		207	Symonds	2	3
165	Heber		10		208	Triphook	3	10
166	Wellesley	5	12 6		209	Heber	1	2
167	Payne	1	4		210	Payne		7
168	Payne		15		211	Triphook	2	
169	Payne		5		212	Heber		1
170	Triphook		9		213	Heber	1	19
171	Triphook	1	11 6		214	Arch		5
172	Lepard	2	5		215	Corrie	4	17
173	Hare		1		216	Payne		3

217	Evans		19		260	Clarke	2	11
218	Wilson	4	19		261	North	8	8
219	Heber		1		262	Heber	3	10
220	Arch		7		263	Clarke		7
221	Blair		3		264	Payne		16
222	Arch		1		265	North	3	10
223	Arch		10		266	Clarke	2	13
224	Heber		2		267	Heber	1	2
225	Payne		1		268	Payne		1
226	Lepard		9		269	Payne		11
227	Payne		6		270	Heber		15
228	Arch		1		271	North	2	8
229	Triphook		3		272	Heber		1
230	Triphook		1		273	Clarke		4
231	Hayes		11		274	Heber		7
232	Triphook	1	1		275	Payne		8
233	Triphook		19		276	Payne		11
234	Heber	4	19		277	Heber		2
235	Payne		8		278	Payne		10
236	Triphook		1		279	Heber		12
237	Arch		4		280	Heber		4
238	Wellesley		1		281	Heber		10
239	Arch	1	13		282	Clarke	2	11
240	Lepard	1	5		283	North		17
241	Heber		2		284	North	1	18
242	Heber	3	5		285	Clarke		2
243	Triphook		1		286	Heber		5
244	Payne		8		287	Heber		9
245	Heber		4		288	Lepard		16
246	Wellesley		10		288*	Heber		3
247	Symonds	1	13		289	Clarke		10
248	Clarke		4		290	Triphook		2
249	Evans		1		291	Heber		3
250	Clarke		1		292	Heber		9
251	Clarke		1		293	Miller	1	3
252	Heber		6		294	Payne		8
253	Payne		14		295	Triphook		10
254	Payne		9		296	Heber		2
255	Clarke		12		297	Heber		10
256	Clarke	2	19		298	Heber		1
257	Nicol		10		299	Heber		1
258	Heber		11		300	Heber		8
259	Payne		6		301	Wilson	2	15

302	Lepard		5	344	Rodd	1 10
303	Heber		2	345		
304	Heber		13	346	Clarke	2
305	Heber		3	347	Money	1
306	Payne		10	348	Rodd	11
307	Heber		9	349	Heber	5
308	Payne		16	350	Clarke	3 15
309	Payne		5	351	Payne	1 1
310	Nicol		16	352	Lepard	2 11
311	Payne		6	353	Payne	5
312	Clarke		9	354	Payne	3
313	Clarke	1	10	355	Douce	15
313*	Lepard	1	13	356	Jacobs	5
314	Payne		2	357	Payne	13
315	Payne		2	358	Rodd	9
316	Payne		4	359	Payne	6
317	Payne		8	360	Payne	10
318	Clarke	1	7	361	Heber	9
319	Lepard		11	362	Rodd	5
320	Triphook		9	363	Lepard	4 19
321	Lepard		6	364	Clarke	7
322	Heber		4	365	Heber	6
323	Money		2	366	Clarke	1
324	Clarke		6	367	Lepard	14
325	Clarke	1	1	368	Lepard	1 16
326	Clarke	4	5	369	Heber	1 1
327	Clarke	2	15	370	Heber	5
328	Rodd		8	371	Clarke	3
329	Rodd		8	372	Payne	7
330	Heber		2	373	Clarke	12
331	Heber	1	2	374, 375	Payne	1
332	Wilson	2	12			
333	Payne		2	376	John	6
334	Payne		5	377	Payne	1 4
335	Payne		19	378	Heber	3
336	Payne		4	379	Triphook	2 4
337	Clarke		13	380	Evans	3
338	Clarke		4	381	Ewen	7
339	Lepard		19	382	Payne	2
340	Rodd		7	383	Triphook	1
341	Payne		12	384		
342	Bourne		1	385	Payne	2
343	Triphook		6	386	North	2 2

387	Triphook		10		429	Lepard		16
388	Taylor		13		430	Heber		5
389	Triphook	1	1		431	Bourne	1	13
390	Clarke	1	1		432	Triphook	1	2
391	Heber		3		433	Bourne		1
392					434	Evans		8
393	Bourne		1		435	Taylor		2
394	Evans		8		436	Rodd		12
395					437	Heber		10
396	Heber		6		438	Heber	1	
397	Payne		5		439	Miller		8
398	Payne	1	1		440	Lawford		3
399	Heber	1	12		441	Evans		2
400	Clarke		1		442	Clarke		5
401	Triphook		4		443	Bourne		1
402	Payne		6		444	Goodenough	1	
403	Triphook		15		445	Taylor		3
404	Clarke		2		446	Payne		2
405	Clarke		16		447	Taylor		3
406	Payne	1	15		448	Payne		8
407	Heber		14		449	Payne		12
408	Bramstone		2		450	Heber	3	6
409	Wellesley		2		451	Bourne		1
410	Triphook		9		452	Heber	1	
411	Rodd		2		453	Clarke	2	10
412	Clarke		4		454	Bentham		1 6
413	Clarke	1	11		455	Bourne		1
414	Payne		11		456	Taylor		1
415	Clarke		8		457	Taylor		1
416	R. Neville	1	6		458	Taylor		2
417	Clarke		1		459	Payne		1
418	Clarke		1		460	Wellesley		3
419	Triphook		3		461	Payne	1	1
419*	Bramstone		5		462	Clarke		14
420	Boone	3	13 6		463	Clarke	2	10
421	Taylor		7		464	Clarke		5
422	Goodenough		13		465	Clarke		2
423	Bourne		1		466	Heber		1
424					467	Heber		9
425	Rodd		5		468	Clarke	1	17
426	Heber		1		469	Wellesley		7
427	Clarke		4		470	Nicol		17
428	Heber		7		471	Boone	1	3

DIBDIN'S REFERENCE LIBRARY

472	Boone	1	3	514	Payne			8
473	Taylor		3	515	Lloyd		3	3
474	North	2	2	516	Payne			6
475	Payne		2	517	Heber		1	
476	Goodenough	1	17	518	Miller			3
477	Triphook	3	15	519	Clarke			2
478	Triphook		17	520	Clarke			2
479	Payne		9	521	Triphook			4
480	Payne		2	522	Miller			6
481	Heber	1	1	523	Heber			6
482	Clarke		2	524	Nicol		1	16
483	Bourne		3	525	Payne			8
484	Corne	2		526	Payne			8
485	Heber		2	527	Heber			1
486	Bramstone		9	528	Heber		6	5
487	Nicol		14	529	Clarke			15
488	Payne		12	530	Triphook		1	6
489	Clarke		2	531	Triphook			18
490	Lepard		12	532	Miller			1
491	Payne		1	533	Triphook			2
492	Bourne		1	534	Heber			2
493	Heber	2		535	Heber			6
494	Lepard		10	536	Heber			2
495	Holland		8	537	Bourn			3
496	Clarke		2	538	Payne		4	13
497	Taylor		5	539	Heber		1	13
498	Bourne		1	540	Clarke			10
499	Heber		2	541	Triphook			14
500	Heber	2	12 6	542	Hayes			2
501	Goodenough	4	14 6	543	Lepard			7
502	Clarke	3	15	544	Payne			15
503	Triphook	2	4	545	Payne			2
504	Heber		3	546	Payne			9
505	Clarke	2	15	547	Heber			4
506	Lloyd	1		548	Triphook			19
507	Taylor		1	549	Payne			6
508	Triphook		9	550	Triphook			4
509	Triphook		12	551	Heber			1
510	Wellesley	1	11 6	552	Triphook			15
510*	Ewen		5	553	Triphook			17
511	Clarke		9	554	Heber		1	1
512	Heber		11	555	Bourn			1
513	Heber		18	556	Evans			2

311

No.	Name	£	s.	d.
557	Heber		4	12
558	Heber			1
559	Heber			1
560	Heber			1
560*	Burn			1
561	Clarke			2
562	Triphook			17
563	Payne		1	2
564	Payne		1	10
565	Heber			2
566	Heber	1	11	6
567	Triphook			3
568	Heber			2
569	Jacobs			2
570	Heber			1
571	Heber			2
572	Payne		1	3
573	Heber			6
574	Wellesley			5
575	Heber			5
576	Lepard		1	19
577	Triphook			17
578	Triphook		1	1
579	Bourn			6
580	Triphook			17
581	Hayes		1	19
582	Clarke			14
583	Bourn			1
584	Hayes			1
585	Hayes			1
586	Triphook			2
587	Ewen		1	2
588	Bourn			1
589	Rodd			10
590	Nicol			16
591	Miller			9
592	Hayes			1
593	Hayes			2
594	Hayes			1
595	Clarke			2
596	Rodd			5
597	Hayes			6
598	Triphook		17	17
599	Meredith		1	2
600	Hayes			11
601	Arch		1	13
602	Bentham			12
603	Heber		1	19
604	Ponton		9	10
605	Miller		6	6
606	Heber		4	5
607	Lepard			5
608	Triphook		1	15
609	Triphook		1	19
610	Clarke		1	4
611	Tray			2
612	Triphook			7
613	Heber			7
614	Triphook			7
614*	Triphook			7
615	Major		1	1
616	Triphook		1	5
617	Triphook			10
618	Payne		1	1
619	Triphook			1
620	Heber			7
621	Heber			3
622	Wellesley			6
623	Bourn			4
624	Payne			16
625	Lepard		1	6
626	Triphook			5
627	} Bourn			2
628				
629				
630	Bourn			1
631	Bentham			2
632	Heber			3
633	Payne			4
634	Hayes	6	8	6
635	Holland			3
636	Triphook		2	5
637	Triphook			6
638	Money			5
639	Lepard			15
640	Triphook			8

641	Triphook		15		683	Rodd		4
642	Clarke	2	11		684	Triphook	1 11	6
643	Lepard		16		685	Hayes	2	19
644	Amyott	1	3		686	Triphook		12
645	Miller		6		687	Hayes		8
646	Payne		4		688	Hayes	1 11	6
647	Hayes		4		689	Heber		15
648	Corrie		8		690	Bindley		15
649	Heber		8		691	Heber		15
650	Clarke		7		692	Triphook	1	14
651	Triphook		17		693	Triphook		3
652	Hayes		4		694	Heber		5
653	Rodd		11		695	Clarke		8
654	Evans		7		696	Hayes		3
655	Bourn		1		697	Triphook		7
656	Boone		9		698	Heber		14
657	Bourn		1		699	Lloyd		7
658	C. Sumner		4		700	Hayes		4
659	Ewen		6		701	Heber		8
660	Triphook		10 6		702	Hayes		1
661	Heber		10		703	Lloyd	3	10
662	Heber		5		704	Heber		5
663	Clarke	2	7		705	Payne		6
664	Clarke	1	4		706	Heber		1
664*	Heber		9		707	Higgs		8
665	Payne	2	4		708	Triphook		8
666	Goodenough		13		709	Triphook		5
667	Bentham		2		710	Hayes		8
668	Nicol		4		711	Lawford		17
669	Heber		4		712	Knox	1	4
670	Nicol	1	5		713	Bindley	1	2
671	Heber		16		714	Wellesley	5	10
672	Evans		4		715	Clarke	1	3
673	Clarke		6		716	Nicol		16
674	Bourn		1		717	Goodenough		10
675	Lawford		7		718	Heber	1	
676	Conie	1	6		719	Bourn		1
677	Heber		7		720	Heber		6
678	Heber		10		721	Nicol		12
679	Rodd		2		722	Triphook		9
680	Heber		5		723	Heber		19
681	Nicol		5		724	Heber	1	
682	Payne		3		725	Payne	1	19

726	Arch		6	749	Lepard		7
727	Arch		6	750	Triphook		4
728	Triphook		15	751	Lepard		13
729	Heber		1	752	Heber		5
730	Bourn		1	753	Triphook	1	1
731	Arch		1	754	Hayes		6
732	Arch		2	755	Triphook	2	8
733	Burn		1	756	Heber		1
734	Heber		1	757	Rodd	1	15
735	Hayes		2	758	Heber	1	
736	Bourn		1	759	Arch		2
737	Wellesley		3	760	Heber		3
738	Triphook	21		761	Arch		5
739	Triphook	34	13	762	Triphook		19
739*	Lawford	3	3	763	Fazakerley		4
740	Heber		6	764	Heber		7
741	Field		3	765			
742	Triphook		1	766	Heber		3
743	Bentham		2	767	Triphook		4
744	Triphook		4	768	Fazakerley		2
745	Fazakerley		19	769	Bourn		1
746	Fazakerley		2	770	Triphook	2	9
747	Triphook		15	Total		726 11	6
748	Hayes		9				

DAVID ROGERS

Francis Douce's manuscripts
Some hitherto unrecognised provenances

It carries no reflection on the prowess of Falconer Madan in publishing, within the span of a single decade, summary descriptions of nearly thirty thousand Bodleian manuscripts, to point out that here and there over the vast range of materials he described there are corrections of fact and supplementary details to be gleaned. His great achievement, which is far from being his only claim to be remembered and respected (though to its shame none of this has brought him a place in the *Dictionary of National Biography*), stands secure on its own merits. To complete his task of catching up on the backlog of centuries he had resolutely to avoid any temptation to spend time pursuing minor enquiries down the alleys of research. It is remarkable that so little of importance escaped his eye, even with Nicholson constantly peering over his shoulder with eager hostility to catch him out.

What follows here is no more than a series of disjointed footnotes to one small section of Madan's *Summary Catalogue*, gathered as a result of browsing for many years in and around a single collection, and bearing chiefly on provenance, with occasional remarks on bindings. That one collection has rightly been described by Dr. A. N. L. Munby in his *Connoisseurs and Mediaeval Miniatures, 1750–1850* (p. 43) as 'the most valuable single accession of manuscripts, books, prints and drawings ever to be received by the Bodleian'. In Chapter III of that book, written with all Dr. Munby's accustomed blend of learning, wit, charm and sound judgement, he has given the best account yet penned of Francis Douce himself, of his friends and foes, and of the formation of his vast collection. He has also drawn attention to the rich documentation available by the fact that the Bodleian now also possesses Douce's correspondence and a series of notebooks kept by him for most of the later and richer half of his collecting life. Among these, what I refer to below as his accession notebooks are invaluable, though they are also, Dr. Munby ruefully complains (p. 50) 'scrappy, incomplete and tantalising, because often the entries are too cryptic to admit of exact identification'. After systematic attempts to make such identifications I can echo Dr. Munby's complaint. But the notebooks can be supplemented, as Dr. Munby shows, by a study of the many copies, preserved in the collection, of sale catalogues (and at least one bookseller's catalogue—see under MS. Douce 91), marked with the collector's own notes of his purchases and the prices he paid. Here again I have tried to make a comprehensive search through all these catalogues. Dr. Munby's chapter on Douce gives a survey of the formation of the whole collection of some 400 manuscripts, and understandably highlights some of its principal treasures. The notes which follow here use mainly the same sources to document the provenance of almost one hundred of Douce's manuscripts, many of them admittedly of minor importance or beauty, yet all manifesting in some way the extraordinarily wide range which Douce's interests embraced. I have not repeated identifications already made in Dr. Munby's book unless there has been some further fact or detail to add. Here and there a lucky discovery has enabled me to develop more fully the scope of Douce's activities in relation to some particular sale, for example that of his friend Robert Lang (see MS. Douce 81).

If any people have the patience to sift through this ragbag of miscellaneous scraps, I trust it may add an occasional clue to someone's search for an elusive piece of information, or afford some sidelights on a great lover of books and his multifarious collecting activities. One who I dare hope will even enjoy the perusal of this essay in sale-room gossip is the friend who, in addition to all his other contributions to the history of manuscripts and printing, has himself described with so much learning and authority, *The distribution of books by catalogue*. He will discern in it a tribute of admiration and affection.

NOTE

In an attempt to make the information contained here at all findable, the Douce manuscripts on which I have anything to say are arranged in their shelfmark order, with only a skeleton description of the content and date. I have presupposed that the *Summary Catalogue* itself is always at the reader's elbow. Each entry is, however, designed to be read on its own, the source of my information being explicitly stated each time, so that it can be consulted piecemeal, if need be, as a supplement to the *Summary Catalogue*. But to make the lines of Douce's collecting clearer, I have tried to cross-refer between manuscripts derived from common sources. Finally, to avoid endless tedious repetitions. I have employed the following abbreviations throughout—

FD is Douce himself.

SC is the *Summary Catalogue*, the numbers of which are not quoted, to avoid confusion, since they run in one sequence following the shelfmark order of the collection.

ANLM is Dr. Munby, who has died since this article was sent to press. I desire to pay tribute to his unfailing kindness and to the inspiration I have derived from his work. Page references are to his book *Connoisseurs and Mediaeval Miniatures, 1750–1850*, Oxford, Clarendon Press, 1972, unless stated otherwise.

MS. Douce 2: Medical treatises. 14th cent.

This is no doubt the item bought from the bookseller John Cochran and noted in FD's accession notebook (MS. Douce e.68, fol. 6 verso) under October 1826 as 'MS. of Arist. secreta secretorum &c. Cochran'. For other purchases from Cochran, see below under MSS. 91, 294 and 365.

MS Douce 8: Prayers in Latin and Italian. 15th cent.

An ownership monogram (query ZG?) 18 mm in height, is stamped on the second blank leaf with a hand stamp. This MS. was lot 301 in the Duc de La Vallière's sale, Paris, 1783, and was there bought by P. A. Bolongaro-Crevenna, at whose sale in Amsterdam in 1790 it was lot 360. This was not, however, one of FD's own purchases at the Crevenna sale, for which see below, under MS. Douce 111.

MS. Douce 9: Officium Beatae Maria Virginis, Italian, 1507.

As recorded by the SC, this was lot 2556 in the second Hanrott sale, in August 1833. On that occasion it went to the bookseller William Pickering for £11/15/–, and is probably among the unspecified purchases noted in FD's accession notebook for that month and year (MS. Douce e.68, fol. 24 verso) under the entry: 'Several fine articles from Hanrott's sale at Evans's'. The MS. is in an Italian binding of eighteenth-century green morocco, and has prefixed a typical note in Hanrott's characteristic handwriting.

MS. Douce 13: English treatises. 14th cent.

Acquired in November 1808, according to FD's accession notebook (MS.

Douce e.66, fol. 33 verso): 'From Simco's catalogue—Warners Albions England—Teagues looking glass a MS. play—Ms. Charter of heaven.' Of these three purchases, the first should be one of the three printed editions now in the Douce collection, the second is not to be found among the present Douce MSS., and the third is the title of the first item in MS. Douce 13. John Simco was a book and print seller in business at No. 2, Air Street, Piccadilly, from whom FD made numerous purchases.

MS. Douce 15: Stories from Genesis and Exodus. England. 15th cent.

Under April 1807 in his accession notebook (MS. Douce e.66, fol. 20 recto) FD recorded: 'Seven MSS. at Sebright's sale viz. Life of Adam. Chronicle Norman French. Avesbury. Vita Thomae Becket &c. See Catalogue.' The latter reference is no doubt to FD's own copy (Douce CC 392(1)) of *A catalogue of the duplicates and a considerable portion of the Library of Sir John Sebright, Bart. . . . also the very curious collection of manuscripts, . . . collected by Sir Roger Twysden and Mr. E. Lhwyd*, which was auctioned by Leigh and Sotheby in a seven-day sale, beginning 6 April 1807. FD's own copy clearly marks five MSS. as bought by himself:

lot 1105 for 2/6. Described as 'Officium Beatae Mariae Virginis, *in membranis*, 12mo'; not identified among the Douce MSS.
lot 1130 for £2/5/–   Now MS. Douce 128.
lot 1139 for 7/6.   Now MS. Douce 287.
lot 1141 for 13/6.   Now MS. Douce 136.
lot 1216 for 10/6.   Now MS. Douce 330.

Another Bodleian copy of the auction catalogue (2591 d. 84(2)), which belonged to William Upcott, shows FD as the purchaser of two further MSS., thus bringing his total to seven, as stated in his own notebook:

lot 1101 for 4/6.   Now MS. Douce 15 (the present MS.), described in the sale as 'A Discourse of the Creation of the World, with the Life of Adam, on vellum. 12mo'; this corresponds to the first entry in FD's notebook.
lot 1115 for 6d.   Described as 'Part of the Apocalypse in Greek and Latin, and the first Chapter of Malachi in Hebrew, Greek and Latin'; not to be found among the present Douce MSS.

MS. Douce 17: Legal pieces. Early 14th cent.

The SC records separately both the ownership of Gustavus Brander and FD's acquisition inscription dated 1790. These are linked by the fact that the library, prints and manuscripts of Gustavus Brander, himself a former curator at the British Museum, who lived from 1720 to 1787, were auctioned by Leigh and Sotheby on 8 February 1790. FD's copy of the sale catalogue (Douce CC 297(3)) records his own purchase of some dozen manuscripts, among which at least four are easily identifiable in his collection today. The present MS. was lot 1083 and cost FD 1/6; for three others, see below, MSS. Douce 27, 36, 265; see also no. 368.

MS Douce 27: Statutes of Edward III, late 14th cent.

This was lot 1088, and cost FD 1/6, at the Brander sale in 1790, on the evidence quoted above under MS. Douce 17.

MS. Douce 28:

A pen-facsimile copy of the 1511 Paris edition of Pierre Gringore's *Le ieu du prince des sotz* was lot 1004 in the sale of Robert Lang's library by Evans on 17 November 1828. The lot was described as bound in red morocco with gilt leaves, and all this agrees with the present MS. Lot 1004 was not, however, one of the 81 lots on which FD marked bids before the sale (see below, MS. Douce 81). It went to Techener, his principal rival for the early printed books in this sale, for 12/-. If this identification is correct, the purchase represents an afterthought in FD's mind when the sale was over.

MS. Douce 36: The Book of Tobit, English. 15th cent.

Of the three later owners recorded in SC, Joseph Ames is, of course, the bibliographer (1689–1759) at whose sale on 5 May 1760 this MS. was lot 825 and presumably went to Mark Cephas Tutet. At Tutet's sale on 15 February 1786 it was lot 500 and was bought for £1/12/- by Gustavus Brander. For Brander, see above under MS. Douce 17. FD paid 16/- for this MS. in 1790 at Brander's sale, in which it was lot 1085. Another MS. which belonged successively to Ames and Tutet is MS. Douce 140, see below.

MS. Douce 39: Hours of the use of Metz. 14th cent.

One of the lots purchased by FD at the Higgs sale, 20 April 1830 (see below, under MSS. Douce 336–7). On the first leaf of the volume is written in a later hand 'office diuin Mcccviii'; the entry in the Higgs sale catalogue, lot 712, begins 'Officium, Lat. (1308) 12mo, with seven Miniatures ...' and mentions the velvet binding. It cost FD £4. See also MS. Douce 336–7, below.

MS. Douce 40: Hours of Bona Sforza, 1527–8.

In April 1824 FD's accession notebook (MS. Douce e.68, fol. 1 verso) contains the short entry 'Milan horae Woodburne'. One of the treasures of his great assemblage of fine illuminated MSS. is the Horae painted for the Sforza princess who married Sigismund I of Poland. Though now known to be illuminated by the Polish Cistercian painter Stanislas of Mogila (Stanislaus

Claratumbensis), the Milanese connections of the MS. are proclaimed by the Sforza-Visconti arms frequently worked into the borders. FD might well have described the volume briefly for his own purposes as his 'Milan horae'. If this identification holds good, the dealer through whom he acquired this book was either Samuel or Henry Woodburn. Both were principally interested in paintings, but also dealt in illuminated MSS. where these were held to show high artistic quality.

It should be noted that a companion volume (British Library, Add. MS. 15281), illuminated by the same artist for Bona's husband, came from the Polish Treasury into the possession of the Polish princess Maria Clementina Sobieska, wife of the Old Pretender. From her son, the Cardinal of York, it passed to his friend the Duke of Sussex, a younger brother of George IV (to whom the Cardinal bequeathed the Stuart regalia), and an ardent book collector. Did the Queen's prayerbook also find its way to Italy with the Stuarts, and did it come on the market after the Cardinal's death in 1807?

MS. Douce 46: John Stubbs, The descoverie of a gaping gulf, 16th cent.

The autograph of an eighteenth century 'Wm. Herbert' recorded by SC is that of the bibliographer (1718–95), at whose sale on 21 November 1798 this was lot 908. FD did not, however, acquire it then. The volume bears a later item number pencilled inside the front cover, with the price £1/1/-, which probably are marks by the bookseller Thomas Thorpe.

MS. Douce 47: 17th cent. Latin comedy, featuring Nottola.

SC mentions 'the armorial bookplate of Peter Hall (19th cent.)'. This was Rev. Peter Hall (1802–49), of Brasenose College. Later to prove a prolific editor and topographer, he must have started book collecting early or inherited a collection, for a sale by Evans on 20 March 1826 under the title *Catalogue of a choice and select portion of the Library of a collector* proves to be his, and another sale, held the following year by Sotheby on 25 June and equally anonymous, is described as the 'third and principal portion of a collector's Library' (the second has not yet been identified). He continued collecting, for another sale was held in 1846 and a final one after his death. The Stubbs MS. was lot 909 in his 1827 sale, and went to the bookseller Burn for 4/-. It was therefore probably one item in that 'Parcel of books from Burn' which is entered for the same month, June 1827, in FD's accession notebook (MS. Douce e.68, fol. 9 recto).

MS. Douce 61: Hyeronimi Morlini Novellarum opus. 18th cent.

Noted in FD's accession notebook as 'Morlini MS.', one of several items bought in February 1830 from Payne's Catalogue (see MS. Douce e.68, fol. 14 verso).

DOUCE MANUSCRIPT PROVENANCES

MS. Douce 65: 'Ywain & Gawin', a transcript made in 1777.

The library of John Watson Reed, who made this transcript, was sold by Egerton on 1 March 1790. According to FD's own copy of the sale catalogue (Douce CC 301 (3)), he bought four items, this MS. being lot 358 and costing him 8/6.

MS. Douce 68: Album Amicorum of Emanuel de Meteren, 1575-1609.

The SC is mistaken in stating that FD bought this at the John Henderson sale, 1786. That was the sale of the library of John Henderson, the noted Shakespearean actor, who died in 1785. FD's own copy (Douce HH 24(2)) of the sale catalogue of another John Henderson, described as 'of Charlotte St., Fitzroy square', whose books were sold on 18 Feb. 1830, shows that this MS. was lot 347 and was bought by FD for £16/10/-.

MS. Douce 71: Strip almanac, written in 1432.

According to his accession notebook (MS. Douce e.68, fol. 15 recto) FD acquired in April 1830 this 'Ancient Almanac. Of Thorpe, formerly Jadis's'. Thorpe, whose price '3/13/6' is pencilled inside the front cover, had himself purchased it three months previously for £1/14/-, when it was lot 735 in a sale held by Evans on 25 January 1830, described as 'bound in velvet by Lewis'. In that sale, entered in the British Museum's *List of Catalogues of English Book Sales* as the auction of Craven Ord's manuscripts, the latter (including his Suffolk collections which went to the inevitable Sir Thomas Phillipps) appear to extend only from about lot 971 to lot 1107, the last lot in the sale. The earlier section is described on the title page as '*Catalogue of a valuable collection of books of a gentleman gone abroad; . . .*' and it proves to contain many items, including the almanac lot 735, which had already appeared in *A Catalogue of some books, in the possession of H. Jadis, Esq. in Bryanstone Square*. London: Printed at The Temple Printing Office, by J. Moyes, Bouverie Street. M.DCCC.XXVI.

It seems, then, that the anonymity of that 1830 sale conceals once again the shadowy figure of Henry Jadis, a collector whose library, especially strong in Shakespeareana, early voyages and sea warfare, had already been partly dispersed by the auctioneer Evans in two earlier sales, both likewise anonymous. The first of these was on 19 May 1826, *Catalogue of rare, curious and valuable books, forming a portion of the Library of an eminent collector*, who is identified as Jadis in a Bodleian copy (Mus. Bibl. III 8°. 147(4)). The second sale, the *Library of an eminent collector*, auctioned on 3 March 1828, is once again that of Jadis, according to a note by FD himself at the back of one of his bound volumes of sale catalogues (Douce CC 299). It now seems that to these should be added the earlier and larger part of the 1830 Craven Ord catalogue.

MS. Douce 81: Pen-facsimile of a printed edition of the 'Mistère du martir sainct Christoffe'. 18th cent.

When, at an auction beginning on 17 November 1828 and lasting eleven days, R. H. Evans sold the library of French literature formed by Robert Lang of Portland Place, FD was naturally very interested. Lang, who was a friend of FD, and Dibdin's 'Meliadus', owned many choice examples of early French poetry, romance and drama, both in manuscript and print, of exactly the kinds which were the objects of FD's own special knowledge and attention. Although his notebook merely refers to 'Several books from Lang's sale' (MS. Douce e.68, fol. 11*), we are more fully informed about this than about any other auction in which he made bids. By a happy chance, one of the Bodleian copies of the sale catalogue (Mus. Bibl. III 8° 478(8)) though not one of FD's own copies, of which there are two, preserves, bound in with it, several papers of considerable interest. First comes a list entirely drawn up in FD's own hand and extending to four quarto pages, detailing no less than eighty-one lots in which FD was interested. Against each is marked his maximum bid; for all save three lots there is an exact figure, and even for lot 1910 (a collection of thirty-eight newsbooks of the reign of the Emperor Charles V) he specifies firmly '10/10/- (not more)'—it went to Thorpe for £54. For three lots he was prepared to go beyond the figure stated, and two of these he secured comfortably while the third, a fourteenth-century French Lives of Saints written by Walter of Verdun, for which he was prepared to go to twelve guineas 'or more', was lost to Payne at £19-10-0.

Obviously FD could not expect to be successful in all or even many of the lots for which he was prepared to bid; most of his bids were modest, and only eight of the eighty-one exceeded £10. In fact he was repeatedly outbidden, for example by Techener the Paris bookseller, for early black-letter volumes, though he often lost them only by narrow margins of a shilling or two. With his bids on MSS. he was much less successful. By 1828 FD was already seventy-one, and he had been collecting manuscripts for more than fifty years. It would not be surprising if, like other men in old age, he was slow to adjust to the rise in the prices that good manuscripts were fetching, compared with what he paid when he was a younger man. But it would be unfair to blame FD too much for the unrealistic level of his bids. He was not the only bidder taken by surprise by the high prices achieved by the MSS. in this sale. ANLM has printed in *Phillipps Studies* (iii, 55) part of an aggrieved letter from the bookseller Thorpe to Sir Thomas Phillipps, written after he had learned that it was really Phillipps who had paid such high prices at the Lang Sale, prices which Thorpe stigmatised as ten times more than they need have been. At that time Thorpe and that irascible baronet were in one of their periodic quarrels, and Thorpe, unaware (so he protested) that Sir Thomas had transferred his custom to the firm of Payne and Foss, had bid up many lots against them. The result was disastrous from FD's point of view. Payne, on behalf of Phillipps, secured, but at enhanced prices, all the early French MSS., including eleven splendid items on which FD had entered bids. How far apart were the horizons of these two contestants can be judged from a couple of examples. Lot 1962, a thirteenth-century collection of *Contes Devots*, on which FD set his limit at 11 guineas, was bought for Phillipps at £69, and lot 2337, a rare romance of Theseus of Cologne, went to the same collector for £45/3/-, where FD's bid was only £2/10/-.

The autograph list of FD's bids has been marked with the price actually fetched by each lot, and his successful bids are ticked. After this list follows another, headed 'Mr. Singer Bought at Evans's Nov. 17. [18]28 Lang's Library'. This is the auctioneer's clerk's own list and bill for the many lots at this sale bought by FD's great friend and fellow-collector Samuel Weller Singer (1783-1858). Now all the items ticked as bought on FD's own list (and these can be identified today in the Douce collection) are to be found among Singer's purchases and are ticked there in red ink. From this it follows that FD's bids were executed for him by his friend bidding in his own name, possibly for reasons of discretion to avoid arousing unnecessary competition. Ironically, at the Theodore Williams sale eighteen months previously Singer had performed the same service on behalf of Sir Thomas Phillipps. Not all Singer's purchases at the Lang sale were for FD; a few were bought by him beyond FD's maxima, and these and other lots were acquired no doubt for Singer's own collection or for other friends. But out of a total of £26/8/6 which Singer paid for sixty lots, FD finally paid him £52/17/6 for twenty-six of them. This is confirmed by the third MS. list preserved, a list of twenty-five lots with prices totalling £51/3/6, at the top of which FD has added in red ink in his own hand the single word 'Mine'. These twenty-five lots include two items on which FD had made no bid, and one on which his bid had been exceeded. His twenty-sixth purchase, not in this third list, was a lot he did not bid for. The 1488 Lyons edition of *Le miroir de la redemption humaine*, lot 1733, went to Techener for £2/12/6 but was returned as imperfect and resold to Singer for £1/14/-. FD agreed to take it from him at that price, and it is now shelfmarked Douce 288.

Only two out of FD's twenty-six purchases were manuscripts, and both were eighteenth century, lots 614 and 1542. On lot 614, the present MS., FD's limit was 5 guineas and Singer secured it for £4/18/-, with Techener as the underbidder. The 'M. Meon' whom FD named as the owner of this MS. before it was Lang's, is evidently Dominique Martin Meon, who published various collections of medieval French poetry. His library was dispersed in three anonymous sales at Paris in 1803, 1815 and 1818. On FD's other MS. from Lang's sale, see MS. Douce 230, below.

MS. Douce 84: English and Latin treatises. 15 cent.

Presented to FD in March 1804, according to the accession notebook (MS. Douce e.66, fol. 4 verso): 'MS of medicine and poetry, temp. H[enry] 6. given me by Mr. Combe'. This was Taylor Combe (1774–1826), the numismatist. Though ANLM has identified the donor (p. 50), he does not mention which manuscript in the Douce collection is referred to by FD's note.

MS. Douce 90: Collections on the Troubadours.

The 1840 printed catalogue of the Douce collection, followed tentatively by the SC, attributes the handwriting of this MS. to the abbé Gervais De La Rue, a friend of FD who was Professor of History at Caen University and Canon of Bayeux. But the writing does not resemble that of the abbé, whose hand is to be found *in extenso* in MS. Douce 377 and elsewhere in the Douce collection. The true identity of the writer is revealed in an accession notebook (MS. Douce e.67, fol. 30 verso) under May 1818, where FD records four purchases, one described as 'MS. Provençal collections', made by him 'At Plumptre's sale'. This auction, not recorded in the British Museum's printed catalogue of auction sales, was held in London by Thomas King, Junior, on 19 May 1818, and FD's own copy of it (Douce CC 298(5)) marks his four purchases, namely lots 316, 329, 339 and 350, among which lot 316 (for which he paid £1/2/0, with lot 313 included) is the present MS., described by the cataloguer as 'Particulars relevant to the Troubadours, &c.' The owner of the library from which these items came was Mrs. Anne Plumptre, born in 1760, who died at Norwich on 20 Oct. 1818, a few months after the auction of her 'Library of books, shells, minerals, and other valuable effects,' which included 2 telescopes and a harp. FD was a friend of this literary lady, the first English translator of Kotzebue, and of her sister Annabella, and an autograph letter to him from Anne (MS. Douce d.31, fol. 65–7) shows that these Provençal collections were written out by her. She had spent the years 1802–5 in the South of France, and described it in her book, *A Narrative of a Three Years' Residence in France*, published in 1810. FD's three other purchases at her sale were of printed books all concerned with Provence, and he owned three other short MSS. on Provençal history which had belonged to her, though not derived from her sale; see MSS. Douce 342–4 below.

MS. Douce 91: Marguerite de Valois, 'Le Débat d'Amour'. 16th cent.

A pencil note inside the front cover, 'Hohendorf 4° 80', evidently refers to the *Catalogue de la Bibliothèque de George Guillaume Baron de Hohendorf*, A La Haye, 1720. Later it was lot 967 in the sale of the library of Rev. Henry Drury, 19 Feb. 1827 and became item 353 in John Cochran's *Catalogue of manuscripts ... now selling*, 1829, where it is illustrated with a full-page plate opposite page 108. FD's copy of this catalogue (Douce C 627) records his purchase of this for 15 guineas, which is noted also in his accession notebook under June 1829 (MS. Douce e.68, fol. 13 verso). Other purchases from Cochran's 1829 catalogue are MSS. Douce 2, 294 and 365.

MS. Douce 97: James I's Basilicon Doron. 17th cent.

The date at which this manuscript was given by John White Esq. to FD is the year 1801, according to MS. Douce e.69, fol. 5 verso.

MS. Douce 107: Richard Rolle, &c., Latin and English. 15th cent.

Bought in January 1834 from the bookseller Pickering; on folio 25 verso of the accession notebook for that year (MS. Douce e.68) is the entry: 'MS. Hampoles varia ... of Pickering'.

MS. Douce 111: Romance 'La Robe d'ecarlate'. 15th cent.

After passing, as FD himself noted, through the sales of the libraries of Louis Jean Gaignat (lot 1790) and the Duc de La Vallière (lot 2843; bought by Pietro Antonio Bolognaro-Crevenna) this MS. was bought by FD at the Crevenna sale in Amsterdam in 1790. On folio 43 verso of MS. Douce e.83 is FD's own autograph list of 'Books bought at the Crevenna sale'. Among its nine items are six manuscripts. The fifth entry—'4921 Genin. MS. from La Vallière 2843—describes the present MS.; it cost FD 12 florins. The sides of the early sixteenth-century French blind-tooled calf binding were mounted in the present morocco binding, evidently for the Duc de La Vallière.

For the other five MSS. from the same sale, see MSS. Douce 152, 215, 278, 300 and 303 below.

MS. Douce 113: Biblia Latina. French late 13th cent.

It is a note on the title page of FD's own copy of the sale catalogue (Douce CC 301(1)) which is our authority for identifying the anonymous owner of 'a very elegant and curious Cabinet of Books lately imported from France ... together with a considerable number of manuscripts ...' which Leigh and Sotheby began to sell by auction on 18 May 1789. The owner was Count Justin MacCarthy Reagh, descendant of an Irish exile family living near Toulouse who became, then or perhaps later, a close friend of FD. The latter's shelves still hold many splendid former MacCarthy books, both manuscript and printed, acquired from the Count's sales before and after his death in 1811, or sometimes by other means during the lifetime of the two friends. In 1791, for example, FD records against lot 353 in his copy (Douce C 167)

325

of the sale catalogue of the *Bibliotheca Parisiana*, 'I bought this article to exchange with Count MacCarthy. F.D.'

From his own annotations in the 1789 sale catalogue it is revealed that FD bought fifteen printed books and no less than eighteen MSS., and ANLM pays tribute (p. 22) to the percipience of the young collector in buying high quality MSS. at very moderate prices. Not all the purchases which FD marked in his catalogue (and these are confirmed in the official auction room copy) can be identified today in the Douce collection, but the present volume, MS. Douce 113, was undoubtedly lot 1584; the binding by Derome, mentioned in the sale catalogue, adds confirmation. It cost FD £1/6/-. For other purchases at the 1789 MacCarthy sale, see below, MSS. Douce 129, 211–12, 213, 226, 318, 327 and 368.

MS Douce 117: Ovid's Metamorphoses Book I, translated into French by Clement Marot. 16th cent.

In the accession notebook (MS. Douce e.68, fol. 10 verso) under May 1828 is recorded the purchase of this MS. from the bookseller Triphook: 'MS. Ovid Marot illumin^d. Triphook'.

MS. Douce 120: Chronicle in French. England, early 14th cent.

FD's own note: 'Bought at Dr. Campbell's sale, May 1776'. Probably this was lot 13 among the MSS. on p. 114 of the sale catalogue of John Campbell's Library, starting 24 April 1776. In the official auction room copy of the catalogue no buyer's name is recorded, only the letter 'm'—standing probably for 'money', i.e. cash down. The lot fetched 1/6.

MS Douce 121: The Romance of Renault de Montauban. French, early 13th cent.

SC states, 'The binding (about A.D. 1800?) bears the arms of the family of Goldsmid of Palmeira'. On 11 December 1815 Evans began the auction of the library of John Louis Goldsmid, whose collection included the famous Towneley Mysteries. The present romance was lot 699 in that sale and went to Triphook for £4/10/-. For another lot from the Goldsmid sale see MS. Douce 387.

MS. Douce 123: Nicolai Caputi tractatus de tarantula. 1734.

'The volume', says SC, 'bears the armorial bookplate of Frederick North earl of Guilford (*d.* 1827)'. It formed part of lot 311 of the sale of 'Manuscripts (removed from Corfu)' auctioned, after the earl's death, by Evans on 8 December 1830. FD's accession notebook (MS. Douce e.68, fol. 16 verso) records under November–December 1830 his purchase of: 'Tarantula ms. of Bohn'.

MS. Douce 128: Latin and French treatises. 14th and 15th cent.

This is the fourth of the seven MSS. acquired by FD at Sir John Sebright's sale (see above, under MS. Douce 15) on 6 April 1807. It was lot 1130 and cost £2/5/0. This volume includes the items mentioned in his accession notebook (MS. Douce e.66, fol. 20 verso) as 'Chronicle Norman French' (item 3 in the SC), and 'Avesbury' (item 4), the latter the Chronicle of Robert of Avesbury printed by Hearne in 1720 from this MS. when it was in the possession of Sir Thomas Sebright, the ancestor of the 1807 owner. Although this MS., which once belonged to the Kentish antiquary William Lambarde (1536–1601), does not contain the autograph of Sir Roger Twysden (1597–1672), another Kentish antiquary, the latter's collections did come into the possession of Sir Thomas Sebright, so Hearne's statement that it once belonged to Twysden is probably correct.

MS. Douce 129: Mathematical and historical pieces. Early 15th cent.

SC records the 1789 MacCarthy provenance (see above, MS. Douce 113) of this collection. It was lot 1609 and cost FD 3/6.

MS. Douce 136: Statutes of the Gilbertine Order. s. xiii

The autograph of Sir Roger Twysden (see MS. Douce 128) shows that this MS. passed with his collections into the possession of Sir Thomas Sebright, and was one of the seven MSS. which FD acquired in April 1807 at Sir John Sebright's sale (see above, under MS. Douce 15). It was lot 1141 and cost 13/6. In Madan's 'Corrections' printed in vol. V of SC, the Sir John Sebright provenance is given on 'information from W. H. St. J. Hope'.

MS. Douce 138: Higden's Polychronicon. 15th cent.

Acquired from an unnamed source in August 1826, according to the entry 'Ms. Higdens polychronicon' in MS. Douce e.68, fol. 6 verso.

MS. Douce 140: Primasius in Apocalypsim. Hiberno-Saxon, 7th–8th cent.

The later ownerships of this, FD's most ancient MS., which he was justly proud of obtaining at the Tyssen sale in 1801 for the trifling sum of £2/9/-, is outlined in SC and has been summarised by ANLM, p. 52. A few additions and corrections of detail are all that need be added. Its sometime owner Walter Clavell is not 'of the late seventeenth century' as ANLM suggests; the certificate dated 13 June 1700 which is tipped in at the front of the MS. is his receipt for his fee on entering the Inner Temple, and shows that he was the Walter Clavell of the Inner Temple who became F.R.S. and whose library was auctioned by John Heath on 29 March 1742. The Primasius was lot 27 among the 'Codices Manuscripti in Quarto' on p. 85 of the sale catalogue, and according to a note by Richard Rawlinson written into one of the Bodleian copies of that catalogue (Mus. Bibl. III 8°. 51) it 'Cost 27/17/6.' In the entry describing the Primasius in the catalogue of the Ames sale, 5 May 1760, lot 1350, it is stated that it was Ames himself who bought it for this price at the Clavell sale. If this statement is true (and Rawlinson's note seems to give independent confirmation that it is), the price £27/17/6 (note the final 6d.) found on the manuscript catalogue leaf prefixed, refers to the Clavell sale in 1742 and not earlier, as SC and ANLM suggest. At Tutet's sale on 15 February 1786 it was lot 511.

MS. Douce 141: Prick of Conscience. Early 15th cent.

'Owned' says SC 'by Joseph Haslewood . . .'; this was lot 1319 at the Haslewood sale by Evans, 16 December 1833. FD, on the verso of the last leaf covered by his list of accessions (MS. Douce e.68, fol. 25 verso), written in 1834 only a couple of months before his death in March, entered this as the first acquisition of the new year: 'Hampoles P[rick] of Conscience Singer = Haslewood', showing that he acquired it after the sale from his friend S. W. Singer, for whom see above, under MS. Douce 81.

MS. Douce 145: Commentaries on the Song of Songs. 12th cent.

An entry in FD's accession notebook (MS. Douce e.67, fol. 28 recto) under June 1817 runs 'Ms Cantica = Johnson sale Evans'. This leads back to the sale held by Evans on 2 June 1817 of the collection of John Mordaunt Johnson (1776?–1815), a British diplomat abroad who died in Florence; this MS. was lot 162 in that sale.

MS. Douce 147: Vegetius, &c. 15th cent.

Bought, like MS. Douce 120 above, by FD at the Campbell sale, 1776. This was probably lot 12 and fetched 4/–. Again, no buyer is named in the auctioneer's own copy of the catalogue, but it was probably FD himself.

MS. Douce 152: Hours of the use of Amiens. 15th cent.

One of the six MSS. bought by FD at the Crevenna sale in 1790, in which it was lot 334 and cost him 43 florins. In his own list of purchases (see under MS. Douce 111) the last entry describes this MS.: '334. Heures (Je me plains) Ms. folio, with singular grotesques executed "par penitence" says the best edit. of the Crevenna catalogue, which seems a very silly conjecture'.

MS. Douce 161: Rondes de tables. 18th cent.

FD's marked copy (Douce TT 147(4)) shows that he paid 3/- for this at the Samuel Tyssen sale, 7 December 1801, in which it was lot 2520.

MS. Douce 166: Two numismatical treatises by Bonnet c. 1700.

The note by Dr. John Calder (1733–1815), Librarian of Dr. Williams's Library, mentioned by SC as occupying folio 1, suggests that this is possibly the 'Treatise on Coins in folio' which was part of lot 905 in the Calder sale, 12 March 1816.

MS. Douce 168: Olivier de la Marche, Le Chevalier deliberé. 16th cent.

In November–December 1830 FD records in his accession notebook (MS. Douce e.68, fol. 16 verso) 'Ms. illum^d. chevalier deliberé Thorpe'.

MS. Douce 177: Petrus Berchorii, Reduction morale. 15th cent.

In a notebook recording gifts made to him (MS. Douce e.69) FD records under the year 1802 (fol. 5 verso) 'Five ancient Mss. on vellum Wilbraham'. This generous donor was FD's close friend and correspondent Roger Wilbraham (1743–1829), and the present MS. might well be one of those five.

MS. Douce 189: Part of the Roman de Lancelot du Lac. 14th cent.

Given, according to the SC, to the prince de Soubise in 1774. It is therefore presumably lot 5351 in the Soubise sale, 1789. The watermarks in the endpapers indicate that the volume was rebound in England; this would explain the absence of the characteristically elaborate Soubise shelfmark, written in ink inside the front cover (or on the front cover), as found in most Soubise books, including the great de Thou family library which formed part of that collection. For an example of the Soubise shelfmark, cf. MS. Douce b.2 below.

MS. Douce 194: Papers on ceremonies concerning the English royal family, 1500–1736.

SC identifies this with lot 4217 in the Richard Gough sale, 1810. True, the auctioneer's official copy of the sale catalogue records the buyer of lot 4217 as Douce, for 2 guineas. But FD's own copy (Douce CC 392(3)) is marked 'Museum 2/2/-,' and as FD was at that date head of the Department of Manuscripts at the British Museum, he is likely to be correct. Among his own many purchases at the Gough Sale FD may well have bid for some items on behalf of the Museum but under his own name, or he may have yielded some of his own lots to the Museum after the sale. At all events, the

Gough catalogue describes lot 4217 as 'A large volume lettered "Christening of Princes, Creations &c"'. But MS. Douce 194 is lettered 'Marrages [sic] & Christening of Princes', and is surely the item recorded in FD's accession notebook (MS. Douce e.67, fol. 32 verso) as 'MS Marriage & Christ^g', which he bought from Triphook in December 1818.

MS. Douce 196: Histoire de Troie, 1323.

FD's marked copy (Douce C 167) shows that he bought this MS. at the sale of the *Bibliotheca Parisiana*, London, 26 Mar. 1791, as lot 370 for 5 guineas. Note that a metal armorial stamp has been removed from the centre of both covers, and a title label from the upper cover. See also MS. Douce 331.

MS. Douce 202-3: Valerius Maximus. French translation. 15th cent.

This had been lot 890 in the sale of Part I of the Library of John Towneley (whose bookplate it bears) on 8 June 1814, when it went to Longman for £32/11/-. As ANLM points out (p. 54), FD acquired it out of George Hibbert's collection, sold from 16 March 1829 for a period of 42 days. It was lot 8242 and was bought by Payne for £17/10/-. Though Payne acted for FD at this sale, the wording of the entry in the accession notebook (MS. Douce e.68, fol. 13 verso) 'Ms. Valerius Maximus Hibberts from Payne' rather suggests that the decision to buy it came after the sale, when it was in Payne's stock.

MS. Douce 204: Speculum humanae salvationis. Early 15th cent.

Bought, as SC states, at the Chauncy sale in 1790. FD's marked copy (Douce CC 301(5)) of the catalogue of this sale, held on 15 April 1790, shows that among a dozen purchases was this MS. which, as lot 3951, cost him £4/14/6. See also MS. Douce 335.

MS. Douce 206: Four specimens of pen facsimile of printed books. 18th cent.

SC says FD 'seems to be wrong in identifying it with no. 465 of the *Bibliotheca Parisiana*', FD's note inside is quite specific: 'This Ms came from the Bibliotheca Parisiana See No. 465 where it was sold for 7.7.0. I bought it afterwards of J.S. [? = John Simco. SC misreads "J.P."] for three', and it is difficult to believe he could be mistaken, especially since items 2, 3 and 4 agree *exactly* with the description of lot 465 in that sale. Is the explanation that FD subsequently added item (1), which alone of the four is not signed by Leselabart, and rebound the collection in crushed blue morocco? His accession notebook records (MS. Douce e.68, fol. 23 recto) in February 1833 that he acquired from the Parisian bookseller Treuttel 'Another modern copy of the Lyons Dance of Death' which could be a description of the first item.

MS. Douce 211-12: French Bible, translated by Guyart Desmoulins. Early 14th cent.

Bought by FD at the 1789 MacCarthy sale, lot 1581, for £7. See above, MS. Douce 113.

MS. Douce 213: Boccaccio, Decameron. French translation by Laurent de Premierfait. Mid 15th cent.

The unidentified arms on the covers are those of the Marquis de Paulmy (1722–87) but it is not clear whether he or another owner wrote the inscription which describes the writer as also owning a finer MS. of the same text on vellum with 100 miniatures. True, Paulmy did own such a MS. (now Bibliothèque de l'Arsenal, ms. 5070), but it is not dated 1408, any more than the present MS. is dated 1418, as the inscription maintains. Certainly the hand is not that of Count MacCarthy, at whose anonymous sale in 1789 FD bought the volume as lot 1646 for £2. See above, MS. Douce 113.

MS. Douce 215: Romance of 'Lancelot'. 14th cent.

One of the 6 MSS. bought by FD at the Crevenna sale in 1790, in which it was lot 5138 and cost him 15 florins 10 sols. Described in his own list (see under MS. Douce 111) as the eighth of his purchases: 'Partie de Lancelot du lac. Ms from La Vallière 4006.'

MS. Douce 221: Album Amicorum of Theodora van Wassenaer. 1595–1603.

Although containing the ownership inscription of 'Gustavus Brander 1785', for whom see above, MS. Douce 17, it is not to be found in his sale catalogue in 1790. Dr. Charles Combe gave it to FD in 1801, the year in which it is entered in the notebook of gifts (MS. Douce e.69, fol. 5 recto) as 'A very curious 4to album Dr. Combe'.

MS. Douce 225: John Stowe, Chronicles (autograph). Before 1568.

On the authority of FD's own marked copy (Douce CC 392 (3)), he bought this at the Gough sale, 5 April 1810, lot 4143 for 6/-. See MS. Douce 251, above.

MS. Douce 226: Life of St. Hilary. Early 12th cent.

Bought by FD at the 1789 MacCarthy sale, lot 1659 for 1/6. See above, MS. Douce 113.

MS. Douce 230: Jehan d'Abondance, Le joyeulx mistère des Trois Rois. 18th cent.

This was lot 3387 in the Duc de la Vallière's sale in 1783, and is in a red morocco binding typical of that Library. The SC date "written in about A.D. 1800' is therefore too late, by some fifty years probably. At Robert Lang's sale in 1828 (see above, under MS. 81) this was lot 1542 and still bears its numbered ticket. FD put 15/- on it, and Singer secured it for 16/-, which FD paid him for it.

MS. Douce 242: Aesop. Late 13th cent.

'F. Douce. The gift of Mr Singer' is the inscription quoted by SC. The year was 1826, when, under November, occurs this entry in FD's accession notebook (MS. Douce e.68, fol. 7 recto): 'Singer gave me an imp[erfect] MS. Aesop temp[oris] E[duardi] I.'

MS. Douce 251: Sir Henry Spelman, Archaismus graphicus. 1698.

FD owned another MS. also, MS. Douce 289, of the same work, but it is the wording of the title of this which exactly agrees with that of lot 4154 for which FD paid 2/6 at the Gough sale, 1810, on the testimony of his own marked copy (Douce CC 392 (3)) of the sale catalogue. Other former Gough Mss. are MS. Douce 225, 316, 317, 350, and e.3.

MS. Douce 255: Rules for games, in Italian. 17th cent.

Acquired in January 1822, according to the following entry in FD's accession notebook (MS. Douce e.67, fol. 42 recto): 'Italian games Ms. (Rodd jun^r).'

MS. Douce 262: 'The Cloud of Unknowing', &c. 15th and 16th cent.

The Edward Jacob mentioned by the SC as owning this MS. in 1770, was the antiquary and naturalist (1710?-88), whose library was sold at auction on 13 Feb. 1789. This MS. was lot 1671 and went to King for 4/6; it is not known whether FD acquired it then or later.

MS Douce 278: French treatise on heraldry. 15th cent.

Bought at the La Vallière sale by Paul Bolongaro Crevenna, at whose sale in 1790 this was lot 6550 and fetched 1 florin. It was one of the six MSS. bought by FD and in his own list (see under MS. Douce 111) it is the third item, described as 'Traité du Blason Champ clos 4°. MS.'

MS. Douce 279: 'The Apprentices', a mock tragedy, 1770.

The attribution to the draughtsman and architect John Carter (1748–1817) is strengthened when we find in FD's accession notebook (MS. Douce e.67, fol. 30 recto) that in March 1818 he acquired 'Carter's the play of the

DOUCE MANUSCRIPT PROVENANCES

Apprentices'. In the sale of Carter's books, which took place on 23 Feb. 1818, this MS. was lot 129 and went for 4/- to the bookseller Rodd.

MS. Douce 285: Treatise on mead. 17th cent.

This is evidently the 'Old Ms. on Mead. Triphook' entered in FD's accession notebook (MS. Douce e.67, fol. 31 verso) as acquired in July 1818.

MS. Douce 287: William Fitz-Stephen's Latin Life of Becket. 13th cent.

Owned originally by the Kentish Abbey of Lessness, the patron of which was St. Thomas of Canterbury, this MS. was given to Edward Lhuyd (1660–1709), keeper of the Ashmolean Museum, in 1699. After Lhuyd's death, part of his collection was acquired by Sir Thomas Sebright and this is one of the seven MSS. bought at Sir John Sebright's sale (see above, under MS. Douce 15) on 6 April 1807. As lot 1139 it went to FD for 7/6 and is described in his accession notebook as 'Vita Thomae Becket'. For another Lessness MS. from the Sebright sale see below, MS. Douce 330,

MS. Douce 294: Johannes Burchardus, Diarium pontificatus Papae Alexandri VI. 17th cent.

The Library of Giuseppe Renato, Cardinal Imperiali (1651–1737) was described in a printed catalogue in folio, issued in Rome in 1711, but this does not seem to include his MSS., of which the present volume was one. After the death of the Earl of Guilford in 1827 it was sold as lot 185 in Part 3 of his library, 28 February 1829, and evidently went to the bookseller John Cochran, for it was purchased from his 1829 *Catalogue* (see MS. Douce 91) by FD as item 206 for 2 guineas. See also MSS. Douce 2, 91 and 365.

MS. Douce 295: Dives et pauper. English. 15th cent.

One of FD's last acquisitions, entered on the final page of his accession notebook (MS. Douce e.68, fol. 25 verso) in January 1834 as bought from Pickering together with MS. Douce 141 (see above). This was two months before his death.

MS. Douce 300: Guillaume de Deguileville, 'Le pelerinage de la vie humaine' 15th cent.

Bought at the La Vallière sale by Paul Bolongaro Crevenna, at whose sale in 1790 this MS. was lot 4918. It is the sixth item in FD's list of his purchases at this sale (see under MS. Douce 111) and cost him 18 florins. He describes it as 'Guillevile pelerinage Ms. from La Vallière 2763'. The binding, not mentioned in the SC, is of French red morocco and is a typical example of the elegantly austere bindings made for the Duc de La Vallière.

MS. Douce 303: Romance of 'San Graal'. 13th cent.

Bought at the La Vallière sale by Paul Bolongaro Crevenna, at whose sale in 1790. this MS. was lot 5133. It is the seventh item in FD's list of his purchases at the Crevenna sale (see under MS. Douce 111) and cost him 3 florins. He lists it as 'S. Graal Ms. from La Vallière 3993'. The binding is similar to MS. Douce 300, above.

MS. Douce 305: Guillaume de Deguileville, 'Le pelerinage de l'âme,' 1435 &c.

The SC records the ownership of 'W. Hone 1820', which is written on a front flyleaf, and 'W. Hone Par: Coll: N°. 743' which is written in the same hand on the first page of text. This is the autograph of William Hone (1780–1842), the radical bookseller, antiquarian and political pamphleteer, and the MS. was lot 639 in a *Catalogue of Books, Books of Prints, &c. collected for a History of Parody by Mr. William Hone . . . every article signed with Mr. Hone's autograph* which was auctioned by Southgate on 22 Feb. 1827. It is recorded in FD's accession notebook (MS. Douce e.68, fol. 7 verso) under February 1827 with other purchases he made at this sale; these also bear Hone's autograph and a reference to his parody collection.

MS. Douce 311: Hours of the use of Rome. *c.* 1488.

The presence of the date 1488 confirms that this was lot 1030 in the Theodore Williams sale on 5 April 1827, when it went to Hurd for £143/17/–. The identification is important, for the Williams sale catalogue reveals that this book had formerly belonged to Baron Denon, i.e. Dominique Vivant (1747–1825), Baron de Denon, painter, archaeologist and Napoleon's adviser on art plunder, whose own collections were sold in 1826. The Williams catalogue also says that it was acquired from him by Robert Heathcote, a very considerable collector in his own right. The MS. appears to have changed hands several times in quick succession, if Heathcote did not obtain it until after the Baron's death. If so, he must have sold it almost at once for it to have passed into the Williams collection in time to be rebound in its present sumptuous binding by Charles Lewis and sold with Williams's splendid library early in April 1827. A 'Mr. Farmer' is introduced into the plot by an annotation in one of the Bodleian copies of the Williams sale catalogue (Mus. Bibl. III 8° 611) where the lot is said in a MS. note to have 'Cost 150 gns. of Mr. Farmer'. This was probably the price paid by Williams for the book, and Farmer an intermediary between him and Heathcote. It was certainly Williams who commissioned the present binding; on this see G. G. Barber and D. M. Rogers, 'A "Duodo" pastiche binding by Charles Lewis', *Bodleian Library Record* VIII (1969), no. 3, 138–144. FD does not record the acquisition of this MS. in his accession notebook, though he does enter in April 1827 'Part of an Egyptian papyrus roll, & a large sycamore Idol of Osiris . . . From Denon's coll^n.'

MS. Douce 315: W. Hawkesworth, Labyrinthus, a Latin comedy. *c.* 1625.

As happened not infrequently at this stage of his life, FD has made two entries for the same item in his accession notebook (MS. Douce e.68, fol. 17 recto) both under March 1831. The second entry mentions that he bought it from Thorpe the bookseller.

MS. Douce 316: Latin account of Queen Anne's coronation, 1702.

FD's copy of the sale catalogue (Douce CC 392(3)) shows that he was the purchaser at the Gough sale, 5 April 1810, who paid 5/6 for this MS. when it was lot 4319. See MS. Douce 251 above.

MS. Douce 317: Dr. John Taylor, Commonplace book. 18th cent.

Probably this is one of the three lots 365–7 in Dr. Anthony Askew's collection of MSS., auctioned by Leigh and Sotheby on 7 March 1785. Certainly it was lot 4195 in the Gough sale, 5 April 1810, when FD bought it for 10/6, as his copy of the sale catalogue reveals (Douce CC 392(3)). See MS. Douce 251 above.

MS. Douce 318: Life of Alexander the Great, translated into French. 15th cent.

SC only states, on the basis of the autograph signature it contains, that this volume was 'Owned by "Guyon de Sardière" in the 16th cent.' But Jean Baptiste Denis Guyon, seigneur de Sardière, was a great-nephew of Madame de Guyon. He was probably dead by 1759, for in that year his library, rich in early French literature, was catalogued for sale in Paris. Before the sale, however, it was bought *en bloc* by the Duc de La Vallière. The present volume is not to be found in the Duc's final sale in 1783, but must have been earlier discarded when the Duc obtained the translator's own copy of this text, which was lot 4844. The discarded MS. passed to Count MacCarthy, at whose anonymous sale in 1789 it was bought by FD, lot 1656, for 16/-. See above, MS. Douce 113.

MS. Douce 320: Rule of St. Benet and Psalter, in French. 12th–13th cent.

The 'H. Powle' whose autograph and pressmark, 'E.13', are mentioned by SC, is Henry Powle (1630–92). Master of the Rolls and Speaker of the

Convention Parliament. He also owned Bodleian MS. Add. C 40 (SC 27837) which was no. 'A.1' in his collection, and MS. Rawl. statutes 34 (SC 15889). According to SC 27837, his books passed after his death to Lord Halifax, and were sold when the Library of Charles Montague, 3rd Earl of Halifax, was auctioned by Cox on 11 March 1740.

MS. Douce 324: The Romance of Gawain and Galeron. 15th cent.

FD's own note inside says he bought this at Ritson's sale, [5] December 1803; it is therefore lot 975, which cost him 15/-. See also MSS. Douce 340 and 354.

MS. Douce 327: Vulgate New Testament. Late 13th cent.

ANLM remarks (p. 21) that Count MacCarthy was among the buyers at the sale of the Rev. Caesar De Missy's library on 18 March 1776, 'who had spent his life gathering materials for an edition of the New Testament'. This was one of his codices, and was lot 1623 in the sale, when it was bought by MacCarthy for 9/6. At the anonymous MacCarthy sale in 1789 (see above, MS. Douce 113) it was lot 1580 and was bought by FD for 7/-.

MS Douce 330: Berengaudus on the Apocalypse. 12th cent.

This MS., like MS. Douce 287, came originally from the Kentish abbey of Lessness. It passed into the possession of Sir Thomas Sebright with the collections of Sir Roger Twysden (see MS. Douce 136, above), who owned it in 1635, and was the last of the seven MSS. bought by FD at Sir John Sebright's sale (see above, under MS. Douce 15) on 6 April 1807. It was then lot 1216 and FD paid 10/6 for it. Concealed beneath FD's livery of green sheepskin over the spine and flowered paper over the boards, is the manuscript's original twelfth-century binding.

MS. Douce 331: Boccaccio, 'Le Roman de Troyle' 13th cent.

Besides the note on the Gaignat provenance, there is another by FD referring to lot 3617 in the La Vallière sale, 1783. That however, seems to have been a different MS. of the same text. The present MS. was lot 369 in the sale of the *Bibliotheca Parisiana*, 26 March 1791, and FD's own copy of the auction catalogue (Douce C 167) shows that he bought it then for 11/6. See also MS. Douce 196.

MS. Douce 335: The Master of Game. Early 15th cent.

'With the armorial bookplate of Charles Chauncy M.D.', says SC. From the evidence of FD's marked copy (Douce CC 301(5)), this MS was bought by FD at the Chauncy sale in 1790, like MS. Douce 204 above. It was lot 3145 and cost him 5 guineas.

MSS. Douce 336–7: 'Le Miroir du Monde'. 15th cent.

FD's accession notebook (MS. Douce e.68, fol. 15 recto) shows that in April 1830 he acquired '4 fine ill^d MSS.' from 'Higgs sale'. This was the auction of the small but choice library of William Simonds Higgs, F.A.S., held by Sotheby on 20 April 1830. Douce's copy of the catalogue is not preserved in his collection, but a Bodleian priced copy with buyer's names (Mus. Bibl. III 8°. 639(1)) shows that among other purchases FD bought four lots from the sections at the end of the sale headed 'Missals, Printed and Manuscript' and 'Miscellaneous Manuscripts'; these were lot 707, an *Horae Romanae* on vellum, printed at Paris in 1526 (now Douce BB 114, with the Higgs book-plate); lot 709, another Paris printed Book of Hours; lot 712 (now MS. Douce 39, see above) and lot 715 the present MS., for which he paid 31 guineas. It is bound in 2 volumes in seventeenth-century French olive morocco with doublures.

MS. Douce 340: A list of river-names in Great Britain.

Written by Joseph Ritson, it was lot 977 in the Ritson sale of 5 December 1803 and on the testimony of FD's copy of the sale catalogue (Douce CC 393 (14)), was bought by him for 4/–. See also MSS. Douce 324 and 354.

MSS. Douce 342–4: Papers on Provençal history. Early 19th cent.

After the death of his friend Anne Plumptre in October 1818 (see above, under MS. Douce 90), FD records in his accession notebook (MS. Douce e.67, fol. 35 recto) under Oct. 1819 'Miss Plumptre's present of her sister's MS. coll. of Provençal matters by the hand of Mr. Goddard.' The sister was Annabella, whose *floruit* in DNB ends in 1812, but who evidently survived Anne and made this gift to an old friend who had already shown his interest in these collections. Anne had perhaps taken these MSS. with her to Norwich, where she died, since the Mr. Goddard who passed them to FD was a Norwich bookseller. By the evidence already quoted, MS. Douce 342 is in the hand of Anne Plumptre, not of the abbé de La Rue, and so is MS. 344. MS. 343 is not in her hand but clearly forms part of the same gift. These MSS. are likely to date from her residence in Provence, 1802–5, or thereafter.

MS. Douce 350: Coronation of King George II. 1727.

Given to Gough in 1786 (SC), it was lot 4318 in the Gough sale in 1810, and is shown in FD's marked copy (Douce CC 392 (3)) as bought by him for 5/6. See MS. Douce 251, above.

MS. Douce 354. Iliad Book I, translated by J. Baynes. 1784.

Bought by FD at Ritson's sale (SC). This was lot 966 and cost him 7/–. See also MSS. Douce 324 and 340.

MS. Douce 358. Extracts from a volume of French fables 18th cent.

The accession notebook which covers April 1830 (MS. Douce e.68, fol. 15 recto) contains this entry: 'MS of fabliaux. Caylus. Renouard's sale'. The attribution to the Comte de Caylus derives from the sale catalogue of Antoine Augustin Renouard, the bibliographer, a portion of whose library was auctioned by Evans, 26 April 1830. The catalogue entry for lot 645, which is the present MS., has the following note: 'This interesting collection is said to have been made by the celebrated Count Caylus.' When FD had acquired the volume he wrote inside it: 'This volume of fabliaux belonged to M. de S^t. Palaye (i.e. Jean Baptiste La Curne de Sainte-Palaye, 1697–1781, the French medievalist), being a part of his large MS. collections', which is not to say, as SC does, that it was expressly written for him.

MS. Douce 363: English miscellanea, written out by Stephen Batman and John Dee. Late 16th cent.

In the accession notebook under February 1807 (MS. Douce e.66, fol. 19 recto) FD wrote: 'I purchased Mrs. Comers Ms. of Dee, Cavendish's life of Wolsey, account of Morton &c. &c.', which describes some of the items which go to make up the present volume.

MS. Douce 365: Moral and religious treatises in French, written in 1475 for Margaret, Duchess of Burgundy.

In FD's copy of the *Catalogue of a singularly curious and valuable selection from the Library of a Gentleman* [John Bellingham Inglis], sold by Sotheby on 9 June 1826 (Douce II 7) he has written against lot 1650 '[£]30.10 Cochran. See his catalogue No. 73. It is now mine F.D.' In his copy (Douce C 627) of John Cochran's *A catalogue of manuscripts in different languages, ... now selling ...* London, 1829, against item 73, which is illustrated with a full-page plate in the catalogue, he has written in pencil 'D' and 'From Mr. Inglis's library. See no. 1650'. In 1829 this cost him 45 guineas. It is also recorded under June 1829 in his accessions notebook (MS. Douce e.68, fol. 13 verso), as 'MSS Duchess of Burgundy, Roman en vers &c. Cochran'. The latter is now MS. Douce 91 (see above). The binding, correctly described by SC as 'Contemporary Flemish work', has been shown by Mr. Graham Pollard in *The Library* (5th ser. XXV (1970) 205–6) to be by the binder who worked for Caxton, first at Bruges and later in Westminster, and whose name was probably Jacobus Bokebynder.

MS. Douce 368: Bede, Historia ecclesiastica. Late 12th cent.

There is some difficulty about identifying this, the only MS. of Bede now in the Douce collection. Despite the bookplate of Philip Carteret Webb, whose library was auctioned on 25 February 1771, and despite FD's own note inside saying that he bought it at the Brander sale (8 February 1790, see MS. Douce 17, above), it is not apparently to be found in either sale catalogue. But on the other hand FD certainly bought a MS. of this history at the anonymous MacCarthy sale in 1789 (see MS. Douce 113), paying £1/2/- for lot 1633.

MS. Douce 369: Parts of 2 Wycliffite Bibles. Late 14th cent.

Recorded in FD's accession notebook (MS. Douce e.67, fol. 32 recto) under November 1818: 'Wicliffe's Testament MS ... Triphook'.

MS. Douce 371: Le Roman de la Rose. 15th cent.

In the catalogue of the sale of the collection of Charles-Gilbert, Vicomte de Morel-Vindé, held in Paris on 17 March 1823 (the sale in which MS. Douce 360, the Roman de Renart, also occurs), lot 1380 was a MS. of the Roman de la Rose described as having 143 leaves, written in the XVth century, with miniatures, and bound in green morocco. MS. Douce 371 is foliated i–cxlii in an old hand, and the other particulars agree.

MS. Douce 376: A copy of 'Otuel a Knight.' c. 1800.

The year of this gift by G. Ellis is given in a notebook recording donations (MS. Douce e.69, fol. 5 recto) as 1801.

MS. Douce 387: J. Bochius, descriptio spectaculorum in adventu Ernesti archiducis. Antuerpiae, 1594.

This was lot 723 in the Goldsmid sale (see MS. Douce 121), 11 December 1815, and went to Triphook for £6/8/6.

MS. Douce a.1: Fragments from an Antiphoner. 15th cent.

Possibly this was originally the MS. recorded in the accession notebook (MS. Douce e.67, fol. 24 verso) under July 1816 as 'A large antiphoner ... of Rodd.'

MS. Douce b.2: Machines et Ustenciles de guerre. c. 1590.

The elaborate stressmark 'I Cab. T.1.A.2', quoted by SC, is typical of the Soubise library, and this MS. was in fact lot 3993 in the 1788 Soubise sale. See also MS. Douce 189.

MS. Douce e.3: Francis Carter, Weights and coins of all nations. 1775.

On the testimony of his marked copy (Douce CC 392(3)) of the sale catalogue, FD bought this as lot 4295 in the Gough Sale, 5 April 1810, for £1/14/. See MS. Douce 251, above.

MS. Douce e.4: E. Marmion, Illustrations for Quarles's *Argalus and Parthenia*. c. 1653.

Acquired in May 1807, according to an entry in the accession notebook, MS. Douce e.66, fol. 21 verso.

JOHN DREYFUS AND PETER C. G. ISAAC

William Bulmer's will

INTRODUCTORY NOTE BY JOHN DREYFUS

When Mr. Charles Ryskamp invited me to lecture in 1973 at the Pierpont Morgan Library on 'Baskerville, Bell, Bulmer and Bensley', I was surprised to find that only two of their wills had been published—those of Baskerville and Bell.

I located a transcript of Bulmer's will in the Public Record Office and immediately sent a xerox copy to Professor Isaac, whose paper on William Bulmer (1757–1830) had been of particular value to me in preparing my lecture.[1] With the xerox copy I sent my rough typescript of part of the text which I transcribed with some difficulty from the scrivener's rather ornate hand. The text printed below has been carefully corrected and completed by Professor Isaac, who has also supplied most of the footnotes.

The provisions of Bulmer's will increase our knowledge of his friends and relations, of his character and style of living, and also of the particular pride which he took in some of the books he had printed. That Bulmer had an orderly mind was already apparent from his lucid and consistent typographical style; what is now clear is that he chose to have his will drafted by an extremely orderly lawyer who anticipated so many eventualities that the document is exceptionally long and sometimes repetitious. Consequently one long and tedious passage has been omitted, but the nature of the excision is amply explained by Professor Isaac in his note at the point where the break occurs.

The transcript has been made from a volume of Prerogative Court of Canterbury Register Copy Wills P.R.O. Prob. 11/1775 in the Public Record Office, to whom acknowledgement is made for friendly and efficient assistance. While the spelling and capitalisation of the original transcript has been preserved, the long f has been here transcribed as s, and the initial use of ff in names has been rendered as F.

[1] Notes begin on p. 347.

JOHN DREYFUS AND PETER C. G. ISAAC

TRANSCRIPT OF WILLIAM BULMER'S WILL

This is the last Will and Testament of me William Bulmer of Clapham Rise in the County of Surrey Esquire   I direct all my just debts funeral and testamentary expenses to be paid and satisfied as soon as conveniently may be after my decease   I give and bequeath unto my brother Ralph Bulmer the sum of five hundred pounds to be paid to him within six months next after my decease and I give and bequeath unto my Executors hereinafter named the sum of five hundred pounds upon trust to invest the same within six months after my decease in the purchase of a Government life annuity in the name and on the life of my said Brother Ralph Bulmer which annuity I direct shall be received by my said brother for his own absolute use and benefit during his life and I give and bequeath unto my said brother Ralph Bulmer my two Leasehold houses and other premises situate in Broom house Lane near Parsons Green Fulham and also my other Leasehold house and premises situate and being No. 12 Park Street Islington to hold the same Leasehold premises respectively with their respective appurtenances unto my said brother Ralph Bulmer his executors administrators and assigns for all the residue of the respective terms of years and interest I have therein subject nevertheless to the payment of the respective yearly rents and to the full performance of the several covenants in the Leases of the same premises respectively reserved and contained on the part of the lessee or asignee   Thereof I give and bequeath the sum of five hundred pounds to Frederick Maitland son of my late sister (Mrs. Ann Maitland[2] of Dublin) who some years ago assumed the name of Samuel Ellwood and was I understand is or was serving in the East Indies in His Majestys 13th. Regiment of Light Dragoons which Legacy I direct my Executors hereinafter named to invest in the three pounds per Cent Consolidated Bank Annuities at the end of twelve months next after my decease if any difficulty should occur in discovering the said Frederick Maitland or in ascertaining whether he is living and if he be found to be dead at the time of my decease then my will is that the said five hundred pounds fall into and become part of my personal estate   I give and bequeath to my brother in law Mr. Thomas Graham of Newcastle upon Tyne the sum of one hundred pounds   I give and bequeath unto Mrs. Eliza Bulmer of Portsmouth widow of my late Nephew William Kirsop Bulmer[3] the sum of two hundred and fifty pounds   I give and bequeath unto my said executors hereinafter named the sum of one thousand pounds sterling upon trust to invest the same in the purchase of three pounds per cent consolidated Bank annuities in their joint names and to stand possessed thereof when so invested upon trust for William Frederick Bulmer and Charles Bulmer the two Children of the said Eliza Bulmer by my said late Nephew William Kirsop Bulmer in equal shares and to pay or transfer one moiety or equal half part of the said Bank annuities unto each of them my said Nephews when and as they respectively attain the age of twenty one years and in the mean time I direct my executors to receive the dividends on the said Bank Annuities half yearly and forthwith apply the share of each in for and towards his maintenance education and support and in the event of the death of either or both of them the said William Frederick Bulmer and Charles Bulmer under the age of twenty one years then the moiety or share of either of them the said William Frederick Bulmer and Charles Bulmer so dying shall sink into and become part of the residue of my personal Estate from the time of the respective deceases of either of them and shall be disposed of accordingly   I give and bequeath unto each of the two Daughters of my late Cousin Joseph Bulmer[4] of Newcastle upon Tyne Builder videlicet Mrs. Mary Hedley and Mrs. Ann Richardson the sum of one hundred pounds for their own separate and absolute use and benefit independant (sic) of any husband they may respectively have and I direct that their several receipts alone notwithstanding coverture[5] shall be a sufficient discharge to my Executors for the said legacies respectively   to each of the four daughters of Robert Borrodale Dodd[6] Engineer of Newcastle I give and bequeath the sum of fifty pounds to be entirely at the disposal of my dear wife to be distributed and applied by her for the separate use of those children as to her shall appear most desirable   I give and bequeath to my said executors hereinafter named the further sum of two hundred pounds sterling upon trust to invest the same in the purchase of three pounds per cent consolidated annuities in their joint names as aforesaid and when so purchased to stand possessed thereof upon trust for and to transfer or pay the same unto Anna Hedley the Daughter of the said Mrs. Mary Hedley when and as soon as she shall attain the age of twenty one years and in the mean time I direct my Executors to receive the dividends on the said Bank annuities half yearly and forthwith apply the same in for and towards the maintenance education and support of the said Anna Hedley and in case the said Anna Hedley shall die under the age of twenty one years then I direct that the said last mentioned Bank annuities shall also fall in and become part of the residue of my personal estate and to be disposed of accordingly   I give and bequeath to Mary Hedley the eldest Daughter of the aforesaid Mrs. Mary Hedley the sum of fifty pounds   I give and bequeath unto The Reverend Isaac Jackman[7] of Union place Lambeth the sum of one hundred pounds and to his wife Mrs. Jackman a mourning ring and to his son the Reverend William Jackman[8] a mourning ring   I give and bequeath unto Miss Susan Jackman[9] Daughter of the said Isaac Jackman the sum of one hundred pounds together with my set of large proof prints of Boydells Shakespeare[10] and a copy of the etchings of the said prints   I give and bequeath unto Miss Harriet Nicol and to her brother William Bulmer Nicol Son and Daughter of Mr. William Nicol[11] of the Shakespeare Printing Office the sum of one hundred pounds each   I give and bequeath unto Doctor Peter de Sales La Ferier[12] my Copy of the transactions of the Royal Society of London[13] bound in twenty eight volumes quarto and likewise my Copy of Chalmers Biographical Dictionary bound in thirty two volumes octavo[14] and to my Niece Mrs. Mary Anne Adams La Ferier[15] wife of the aforesaid Dr. La Ferier I bequeath my Copy of Boydells Shakespeare[16] together with a volume of the Etchings of the Copper Plates belonging to the work printed by me at the Shakespeare press bound in ten volumes red Morocco as likewise my copy of the edition of the poetical works of Milton[17] bound in three volumes blue morocco both which works it is my particular desire she will preserve in her family

To Mr. William Nicol of the Shakespeare printing office I will and bequeath the proof sheet edition of Boydells Shakespeare half bound in nine volumes containing the marginal observations of the late Mr. Steevens[18] Dr. Farmer and Mr. Isaac Reed the plays of which edition are bound up in the manner they were actually printed   I likewise bequeath to the aforesaid Mr. William Nicol my office copies of the tracts printed by me at the Shakespeare press for the Roxburgh [sic] Club[19] making about seventeen volumes both of which works it is my particular request may remain in the family of Mr. Nicol   I give and bequeath unto Richard Batsford of the Shakespeare Printing Office the sum of fifty pounds   I give and bequeath unto Dorothy Drummond Daughter of the late James Drummond of Gateshead Fell near Newcastle upon Tyne the sum of fifty pounds   I give and bequeath unto my early acquaintance Mr. Robert Pollard[20] of Holloway the sum of twenty five pounds and I give five pounds to my late female servant Jane Precious   I give and bequeath to my present female servant Mary Horey five pounds and to (word missing) Drake Gardener I bequeath five pounds   I give and bequeath unto the Treasurer or other authorized officer of the Literary Fund Society established in the year one thousand seven hundred and ninety the sum of fifty pounds to be applied in furtherance of the benevolent purposes of that Society

I give and bequeath unto my friend Mr. John Brettell[21] late of Rupert Street Printer and to my friend Mr. John Walter[22] of Ebury Street Pimlico my Executors hereinafter named the sum of one hundred pounds each in consideration of the trouble they will have in the execution of the trusts and executorship of this my Will and I also give unto the said John Brettell and John Walter a ring each and I also give a ring unto each respectively of the following persons videlicit [sic] The Reverend Isaac Jackman and Miss Susan Jackman Mrs. Nicol of Pall Mall Mrs. Brettell Mr. and Mrs. La Feriere Mr. Thomas Graham Miss Anna Hedley Mr. Leigh Thomas of Leicester place Reverend Dr. Dibden[23] [sic] Mr. Robert Pollard and Mr. William Miller of Albourn Green and I direct that each of the rings hereby bequeathed shall be of the value of three Guineas   And as to all the rest residue and remainder of my Real and Personal Estate whatsoever and wheresoever and of whatever nature or description and over which I have any right or power of disposition (excepting only the share in Fulham Bridge and the Leasehold Premises hereinafter respectively appointed and disposed of) subject to the payment of my just debts funeral and testamentary expenses and the several Legacies by this my will or any Codicil or Codicils thereto given or bequeathed or by me hereafter given or bequeathed I give devise and bequeath the same and every part thereof unto my dear wife Elizabeth Bulmer her heirs executors administrators and assigns for ever according to the respective natures and qualities thereof to and for her and their own absolute use and benefit and it is my desire that all monies lent by me on Bonds Promissory notes or other securities whatever outstanding may be got in by my executors as soon as they conveniently can after my decease ...

A long passage is omitted here in which WB disposes of a one-thirtieth share in Fulham Bridge and related leasehold property on the south side of the Strand. This was originally secured for himself and his wife by an agreement with his elder brother Sir Fenwick Bulmer (baptised at St. John's, Newcastle, 30 September 1745), a druggist in the Strand, who was knighted, as senior member of the Honourable Band of Gentlemen Pensioners, at the coronation of George IV. The other two parties to the agreement were the Rev. Isaac Jackman and Charles Smith, a mapseller in the Strand. The agreement conveyed this share and leasehold property, after the death of Bulmer and his wife, to the illegitimate children of Sir Fenwick Bulmer, Henry Morgan Bulmer and Mary Anne Adams de Sales la Terrière, and to their children. This bequest is given force by naming, in order of preference, the minors who are to inherit if they survive to twenty-one or if, in the case of Mary Ann de Sales la Terrière, she marries before twenty-one. In order of preference these minors are Mary Ann de Sales la Terrière, daughter of Mary Anne Adams de Sales la Terrière (wife of Dr. Peter), Fenwick Bulmer de Sales la Terrière, her third son, William James Bulmer de Sales la Terrière, her fourth son, Peter Philip de Sales la Terrière, her eldest son. If none of these survive to inherit the share and property pass to Mrs. Mary Anne Adams de Sales la Terrière.

... And I hereby nominate and appoint my said dear wife Elizabeth Bulmer and my friends the said John Brettell and John Walter Esquires to be Executrix and Executors of this my Will and my will further is that if any of my said Executors and Trustees hereby nominated and appointed or either of them or any future trustee or trustees to be appointed as hereinafter mentioned shall happen to die or desire to be discharged from or refuse or decline or become incapable to act in the trusts of this my Will before the same shall be fully performed it shall and may be lawful for the surviving trustee or trustees in case of the death of the other or others of them and the continuing trustees or trustee for the time being in case of any trustee or trustees desiring to be discharged or refusing or declining or becoming incapable to act as aforesaid or in case there shall be no surviving or continuing trustees or trustee then for the executors or administrators of the last surviving or last acting trustee by any writing or writings under their his or her hands and seals or hand and seal from time to time to nominate and appoint some other proper person or persons to be a trustee or trustees in the stead or place of the trustee or trustees so dying or desiring to be discharged or refusing or declining or becoming incapable to act as aforesaid and that when and so often as any new trustee or trustees shall be nominated and appointed as aforesaid all the said trust estates monies and premises shall be thereupon assigned and transferred in such manner and form so that the same shall and may effectually vest in the surviving or continuing trustee or trustees if any thereof and the new trustee or trustees or if there shall be no continuing trustee or trustees then in such new trustees wholly upon such and the same trusts and with and subject to the same powers and provisoes as are hereinbefore declared and expressed of and concerning the same trust premises respectively and I direct that my said executors shall be answerable only for so much of the trust monies and premises as they shall actually receive or shall come into their possession or power and that neither of them shall be answerable for the acts receipts neglects or defaults of the other of them or for any loss which may happen to the trust property so as the same happen without their neglect or wilful default and I declare that it shall be lawful for my said Executrix and Executors to deduct and retain to themselves all costs damages and expenses which they may incur or be put unto in the execution of the trusts of this my Will and hereby revoking all other wills by me at any time heretofore made I do declare this only to contain my last Will and Testament   In Witness whereof I the said William Bulmer have to this my last Will and Testament contained in eleven sheets of paper set my hand and seal in manner following that is to say my hand to the first ten sheets and my hand and seal to this eleventh and last sheet thereof this twenty first day of August in the year of our Lord one thousand eight hundred and thirty   William Bulmer (*signature and seal*)   Signed sealed published and declared by the said William Bulmer the Testator as and for his last Will and Testament in the presence of us who in his presence at his request and in the presence of each other have hereunto subscribed our names as witnesses   Henry Young Essex Street Strand   James Hyde same place   George Frederick Smith same place. *Proved* at London 24th. September 1830 before the Worshipful Jesse Addams Doctor of Laws and Surrogate by the oaths of Elizabeth Bulmer Widow the Relict John Bretell Esquire and John Walter Esquire the Executors to whom administration was granted having been first sworn duly to administer.

NOTES

1. Notably his 'William Bulmer, 1757–1830: an introductory essay' in *The Library*, 5th series, vol. 13, pp. 37–50, and his *Second Checklist of Books, Pamphlets & Periodicals printed by William Bulmer* (Allenholme Press, 1973).

2. Baptised at St. John's Church, Newcastle, 18 February 1750/1.

3. Presumably the son of his elder brother Blackett (baptised at St. John's, 11 April 1748) who married Margaret Kirsopp at All Saints' Church, Newcastle, on 19 May 1773.

4. Possibly the son of John Bulmer, brother of William's father Thomas, who was baptised at St. John's, 12 September 1748.

5. Coverture refers to the status of a married woman as a *feme covert* having a legal status indistinguishable from that of her husband. She could not own property and could, therefore, not enter any agreement on her own. The earliest removal of these disabilities was the *Married Women's Property Act*, 1881, and it was not until the coming into effect of the *Law Reform (Married Women and Tortfeasors) Act*, 1935, that these legal disabilities were substantially removed. The agreement mentioned in the passage omitted later had WB as the party of the second part and WB and his wife as the party of the third part. Only in this way could she be brought into an agreement involving property.

6. Of St. Andrew's, Newcastle, who married Eleanor Bulmer, daughter of Joseph Bulmer, of Northumberland Street, Newcastle, on 27 October 1807. Dodd practised as a civil engineer in London at one time (*Newcastle Courant*).

7. St. Catherine's College, Cambridge, 1799. Ordained deacon at Ely, 1801; curate, Chatteris, Cambs., 1801. Rector of Ashley cum Silvering and vicar of Kirtling, Cambs., 1812–31. For 25 years he was Preacher at the Chapel of the Philanthropic Society, Lecturer at St. Clement Danes, Chaplain to the Asylum for the Indigent Blind and to the Royal Humane Society.

He lived from 1804, or earlier, to 1831 at Union Place in the Lambeth Road, almost next door to Lambeth Palace, and, in view of all his London appointments cannot have taken his Cambridge parishes very seriously. He died at Lambeth 5 May 1831.

The *Gentleman's Magazine*, ci, part 1 (1831), 647, says, 'It is proposed to publish for the benefit of his family, "Lectures on the Evidences of Christianity and on the Catechism and Liturgy of the Church of England, preached at the Philanthropic Society's Chapel".' (E. E. F. Smith, Hon. Secretary, Clapham Antiquarian Society.)

8. Second son of the Rev. Isaac Jackman, born in Lambeth 6 October 1804. Trinity Hall, Cambridge, 1821; matriculation 1821, Ll.B. 1827. Ordained deacon, 1828; priest 22 December 1833. Vicar of Fakenham, Suffolk, 1842–78. Hon. Canon of Norwich, 1854. Diocesan Inspector of Schools for Deanery of Ipswich, 1870. Died 1878? Lived at Brooke House, South Side, Clapham Common from 1835, or earlier, until 1842; he kept a school there. (E. E. F. Smith.)

9. Married at Holy Trinity, Clapham, 12 March 1835 to the Rev. Henry Dawson, widower, vicar of Hopton, Suffolk. Married by the Rev. Philip S. Dodd, Rector of Penshurst, Kent. (E. E. F. Smith.)

10. These large prints (27 × 20 in.) were published in two broadside volumes in 1803. They were engraved from paintings in the Shakespeare gallery formed by John and Josiah Boydell. The publication is mentioned by Dibdin in his *Bibliographical Decameron*.

11. Son of George Nicol (bookseller to George III), who, with Boydell, helped William Bulmer to set up the Shakspeare Printing-Office in Cleveland-Row, St. James's, in 1790.

12. The surname is actually Terrière; presumably the scrivener had misread the capital T for a capital F. Dr. de Sales (later sometimes Salis) la Terrière married Mary Anne, the illegitimate daughter of WB's elder brother Sir Fenwick Bulmer.

13. Bulmer printed these from vol. 82 (1793) to vol. 111 (1821). Nichols *Illustrations of the Literary History of the Eighteenth Century*, vol. 3, p. 697, has a very circumstantial tale of the transfer of the printing from his firm to that of WB.

14. Alexander Chalmers, *The General Biographical Dictionary*, 32 vols., 8vo, 1812–17

(expanded by Chalmers from *A New and General Biographical Dictionary* revised by W. Tooke, R. Nares and W. Beloe, 15 vols., 1798–1810).

15. See note 12 above.

16. Published in parts, folio, between 1791 and 1801; it was edited by Steevens and Reed. There were further (smaller) plates in this edition.

17. Published 1794/5/7 and with a portrait and 30 plates, and originally issued in parts. This and the Shakespeare were both mentioned by Dibdin. H. V. Marrot in *William Bulmer: Thomas Bensley—A Study in Transition* declared that Bulmer's edition of Milton was 'as good as poetry can be in typography' (p. 48).

18. See note 16 above.

19. See Nicolas Barker, *The Publications of the Roxburghe Club 1814–1962* (printed for the Roxburghe Club, 1964). His bibliographical table of the Club's publications on pp. 66–9 attributes sixteen to Bulmer, but no printer is assigned to one of the Club's publications in 1820.

20. A copper engraver, baptised in St. John's Church, Newcastle, on 2 May 1757. He was apprenticed to John Kirkup in Newcastle and later learnt engraving with Isaac Taylor, of Holborn. WB, Pollard and Thomas Bewick were apprentices in Newcastle at about the same time, and maintained a close friendship for the rest of their lives (see 'Robert Pollard's Three Newcastle Apprentices' in *Bulmer Papers*, vol. i, pp. 3–8). The end of his life was spent in poverty and obscurity and he died on 23 May 1838. (See *DNB*, which wrongly gives his date of birth as 1755.)

21. John Brettell was active in London as a master printer from 1801 to 1832 (see William B. Todd *A Directory of Printers and Others in Allied Trades, London and Vicinity 1800–1840* (1972), p. 24).

22. Presumably John Walter, Jr., of Printing House Square, who in 1803 assumed charge of printing *The Times*, and who died 28 July 1847 (see Todd op. cit., p. 203).

23. The Rev. Dr. T. F. Dibdin, the bibliophile and author of the *Bibliographical Decameron*, etc.

MICHAEL L. TURNER

Tillotson's Fiction Bureau

Agreements with authors

One of the persistent themes of nineteenth-century publishing was the attempt of the more 'respectable' authors to reach the ever increasing reading public of the lower classes. It is now recognised that this public appeared earlier and was larger than has sometimes been supposed, and that it had its own distinct literature. As Dr. Louis James has shown, in the earlier part of the century, it was to such writers as M. J. Errym, T. P. Prest, G. W. M. Reynolds and the two Pierce Egans that these readers turned, rather than to Dickens and Thackeray, or even Ainsworth and Marryat.[1] In spite of the enormous circulations achieved by some of the better authors through part publication during the eighteen-forties, it was only in the fifties that they began to realise that there was still an 'unknown public' in the buyers of penny periodical literature, which promised 'a great, an unparalleled prospect' for 'the coming generation of English novelists'.[2]

The economic advantages of a larger audience naturally appealed to the authors. This was the period when the respectability and professionalism of authorship were being firmly established. It is true that the best authors were able to make hitherto unheard of amounts of money, but the great majority of writers had to work hard for their livelihood;[3] and, with an ever increasing awareness of the nature of the property which they were creating for themselves, they were continually on the look out for new ways of marketing this property and thus increasing their returns.

By the eighteen sixties it was clear that the real secret of reaching the masses lay in cheapness, as Edward Lloyd and G. W. M. Reynolds had shown with their penny periodicals and part publications. Consequently it was through the ever increasing number of penny and halfpenny provincial newspapers that the better authors at last began to reach the limits of the nineteenth-century fiction market.

[1] Notes begin on p. 371.

One such paper, for long claiming to be the first halfpenny daily evening paper in England, was W. F. Tillotson's *Bolton Evening News*, which first appeared on 19 March 1867. It was this same firm of Tillotson, through its 'Fiction Bureau', which was to be one of the largest suppliers of syndicated fiction to the provincial and colonial newspaper press throughout the following sixty years.

In 1934, Graham Pollard wrote an essay entitled 'Serial Fiction'[4] in which he traced the history and development of publishing fiction in serialised form down to the point of the 'Fiction Bureau', ending his account with a brief example of their method of distribution. In the early nineteen sixties he encouraged me to take a closer look into the workings of the Tillotson enterprise, and gradually over the next few years—with regular prods and a great deal of advice from H.G.P.— this was done. This study of the agreements between Tillotsons and their authors was part of that work, and it is, therefore, with great pleasure and a deep sense of gratitude for all his many kindnesses that I offer it to Graham on this occasion.[5]

The surviving records of the Tillotson 'Fiction Bureau'

With the exception of the first two volumes of agreements listed below, all the records of the Bureau which I saw were lent to me by Mr. Taylor of Newspaper Features Ltd., to whom Tillotsons sold the business in 1935. Nothing was to be found in Bolton in the early sixties, not even the volume of letters used by Mr. Singleton in 1950. It is probable that there may have been other items in Mr. Taylor's possession at one time, for the work done by R. L. Purdy on Thomas Hardy seems to refer to records other than those seen.

Notebooks. There are four pocket notebooks, which contain details of the amounts paid for serials and short stories. I have lettered them 'A'–'D' for convenience.

'A' This is the earliest, and seems to contain entries from the beginning of the Bureau's existence.

'B' Contains the same information as 'A', but in a more orderly fashion.

'C' Repeats some of the information in 'A' and 'B', but also contains some later material bringing in details from just after the turn of the century.

'D' This notebook sets out all the short story and storyette series from

1904 through until 1939 in date order of publication, giving details of the purchase price and the rights acquired. A few of the earlier items had already appeared in notebook 'C'.

Ledgers. There are two ledgers, which contain details of the sales of the short story, storyette, and feature series. I have lettered them 'A' and 'B'.

'A' This contains details of the short story and storyette series from 1908 through to 1926. Also feature and special material for the same period and slightly later.

'B' This contains details of Christmas stories and special material from 1908 through to 1934.

Agreement books. Ten volumes, containing Tillotson's copies of their agreements with the authors, exist for the years cited. Odd letters are bound into these volumes.

1885–7 [Bodl. MS.Eng.Misc.f.395/1]	1907–8
1890–4 [Bodl. MS.Eng.Misc.f.395/2]	1917–19
1890–1	1920–2
1899–1900	1923–5
1905–6	1926–8

Programmes. Printed programmes, sent out to customers listing the following year's material, have been seen for

1894	1907
1905	1909–32

Christmas programmes have been seen for

1905	1931–2
1913	

The background to the agreements

The legal basis of the question of copyright has always been most complex. The situation in this country, prior to the act of 1911, is best described in the words of the *Report of the Royal Commissioners* in 1878—[6]

5. The law of England, as to copyright . . ., consists partly of the provisions of fourteen Acts of Parliament, which relate in whole or in part to different branches of the subject, and partly of common law principles, nowhere stated in any definite or authoritative way, but implied in a considerable number of reported cases scattered over the law reports.

6. ...

7. The first observation which a study of the existing law suggests is that its form, as distinguished from its substance, seems to us bad. The law is wholly destitute of any sort of arrangement, incomplete, often obscure, and even when it is intelligible upon long study, it is in many parts so ill-expressed that no one who does not give such study to it can expect to understand it.

8. The common law principles which lie at the root of the law have never been settled. ...

9. The fourteen Acts of Parliament which deal with the subject were passed at different times between 1735 and 1875. They are drawn in different styles, and some are drawn so as to be hardly intelligible. Obscurity of style, however, is only one of the defects of these Acts. Their arrangement is often worse than their style. Of this the Copyright Act of 1842 is a conspicuous instance.

In repealing seventeen entire Acts, and portions of four others, the Copyright Act of 1911 went a considerable way in simplifying the situation.

International copyright was equally complicated. The position before 1886, was that protection abroad had been dependent upon a series of individual conventions made on the basis of an act of 1844. The Convention held at Berne in September 1886 gave rise to the foundation, on 5 December 1887, of an 'International Union for the Protection of Literary and Artistic Works'. This act of foundation was amended by the 'Acts of Paris' in May 1896, and entirely recast in Berlin in November 1908—the Convention coming into force on 9 September 1910. An additional Protocol was added in 1914 at Berne, and the whole Act was again revised in Rome in June 1928—taking effect from 1 August 1931. Great Britain was a member of the Union from the beginning, and though many other nations ratified the various agreements, they did so at widely different times, and—like Great Britain—with individual reservations.

For the English-speaking world, the position was further complicated by the persistent refusal of the United States of America to become a member of the International Union. The American author gained protection abroad through a series of bi-lateral treaties; one or other of the inter-American agreements; or, by publishing in a country which was a member of the International Union. For the foreign author there was no statutory protection in the United States prior to 1 July 1891; after that date, providing a number of requirements were fulfilled protection could be obtained. The most significant requirement for the

English author was that English language books must be manufactured in the United States. Thus, although many ingenious publishing arrangements were devised during the period, the most practical method that had evolved by the end of it for the English author to obtain the maximum overseas protection, was for him to publish in Great Britain —thus covering all the countries signatory to the Rome Revision—and simultaneously to publish and copyright in the United States, making a statement in the American copyright notice reserving rights in the Pan-American countries.[7]

Against this complicated legal background, there took place a remarkable proliferation in the number of ancillary rights. In the early years of the nineteenth century, in disposing of the volume rights of a novel, an author had in effect been disposing of the entire rights. In truth, he would not have thought in terms of volume rights—merely, how much he could get for his manuscript. By the eighteen seventies the introduction of new methods of production and publication, such as part issues and magazine serialisation, had led the more astute authors to sell volume, magazine, and number rights separately or in combination. Through the growth of new media; increased copyright legislation throughout the world; and, with the assistance of the newly emergent literary agent, this process progressed much further during the next sixty years. It became possible to protect material in almost any combination of form, language or country. The results of this may be seen in an instance quoted by the literary agent Curtis Brown to the Society of Women Journalists in 1924—[8]

> Few writers know how many such markets there are, and no author living can deal with them all, aside from such occasional offers as happen to come in unsought, without giving more time to barter than he does to production. Let us take, for example, a certain novel of universal interest managed by our firm, of which the sales were: (1) American serial rights; (2) English serial rights; (3) Australian serial rights; (4) American and Canadian book rights; (5) English and Australian book rights; (6) Swedish book rights; (7) Danish and Norwegian rights, book and serial; (8) Continental rights in the English language; (9) French book and serial rights; (10) Italian book rights; (11) Spanish book rights; (12) Russian rights (yes, even Russian rights, although there is no copyright in Russia, and the sale amounted to £5); (13) Dutch rights; (14-19) Dramatic rights in six of the countries named; (20) World film rights; (21-3) second serial rights in three countries; (24) Polish rights (this was a surprise); (25) cheap rights in Great Britain; (26) separate cheap rights in America; (27) — but why go on? We are still dealing with rights in that novel and hope to get up to thirty.

This may be special pleading and an exceptional instance, but it does illustrate the possibilities and the increasingly professional attitude amongst writers and their agents. Curtis Brown was right—for better or worse the literary agent had become a necessity.

Alongside this growth in the number of ancillary rights, there took place changes in the methods available for disposing of those rights. It has just been shown how the oldest and simplest method—outright sale of all rights—attained a certain degree of sophistication through fragmentation by form, language and country, and by combinations of these facets. Two other limiting factors were introduced—the sale of rights for a limited period of time; and, the sale of rights for a limited number of copies or appearances. Of the new systems which were being tried out, the half-profit system gained a fair amount of popularity amongst authors. The publisher might shoulder all the costs, or ask the author to share in them, the authors reward being a share in the profits, if any! However, the system entailed—like the older one—the abandonment by the author of his copyright to the publisher, and by the eighteen-nineties many authors were becoming less willing to do this completely, so the system fell into disfavour. Greater and more lasting success was accorded to the royalty, in which the publisher undertook the costs of the book and agreed to pay the author a fixed royalty on every copy sold; every copy sold beyond a certain number; or, on every copy sold after the costs had been defrayed—depending on the bargaining power of the author. Finally, the author might publish on commission, that is, bear the whole cost of production and marketing himself and pay the publisher a fee for his services as an agent between himself and the public. Although very often found to be one of the fairest methods of publishing, it obviously entailed the outlay of a good deal of money, time and energy, which not all authors either could or were willing to meet.

It is against this legal background and in the context of the rapidly changing nature of literary property that the Tillotson agreements must be seen. Although only dealing with a small section of the market, it is through them that the closest picture of that section can be obtained. Apart from an early group—the subject matter and form of the agreements remains remarkably consistent throughout the whole period, though the mode of expression becomes much more succinct in later years. The agreements show the sort of rights which Tillotsons were acquiring in the material that they were buying; how much they were paying for those rights; the various methods of payment; something of the preparation of the copy for the press; and, the bounds of freedom within which both parties were allowed to work as a result of the agreement.

The early group of agreements

The early group date from 1880, 1885–7, and 1890–3. They are of two types, each consisting of a single leaf proforma. The first is in the form of a memorandum—[9]

[Down the side of the form] Transfer to W. F. TILLOTSON of Copyright. No. . . .

Memorandum
[Date.]

In consideration of the Sum of . . . paid by him to me, I hereby assign to Mr. W. F. TILLOTSON, West Bank, 28, Chorley New Road, Bolton, publisher, the . . . Copyright, and all my Interest in the Book entitled . . . written by . . .

[Signature & Address.]

[Witness.]

After William Frederic's death in 1889, the transfer is made to 'TILLOTSON & SON', and done in the names of 'MARY TILLOTSON AND WILLIAM BRIMELOW, both of Bolton'. The second type, all from the 1891–3 period, are in the form of receipts—[10]

[Down the side of the form] Cession to TILLOTSON & SON of Copyright. No. . . . [Date.]

Received from TILLOTSON AND SON (Mary Tillotson and William Brimelow), of Bolton by payment of . . . the sum of . . . for the Copy and Copyright of a Manuscript, entitled . . . and of which I am the Author.

[Signature.]

Though both groups appear to be designed for the complete surrender of all rights, the first does allow for the insertion of certain limitations. Apart from pluralisation, when more than one manuscript was concerned, there are only two instances of amendments in the second group. Henry Herman sells 'the [print] Copy and [remaining] Copyright of a [Series of Stories],'[11] and J. R. Hutchinson sells 'the Copy and Copyright [*subject to condition stated] of Manuscripts . . .', the condition being that '[*Author reserves right of subsequent English volume publication.].'[12]

The first group are sometimes used for the surrender of all rights,[13] but most are limited in one or other of the following ways—'Serial',[14] 'Serial right outside America',[15] 'Serial, American & Continental',[16] 'Serial & translation rights',[17] 'Serial Publication ... such story not to be published by me in volume form for six months after Serial publication has first taken place',[18] 'Newspaper',[19] even 'Newspaper publication in both Hemispheres',[20] '[remaining right]',[21] 'except bookrights',[22] 'excepting the right of subsequent volume Publication in this country',[23] 'except the right of Dramatisation',[24] and 'the privilege ... of publishing this Story in any collected Edition of his works'.[25] These limitations also occur in combinations. Very often the right to exclude subsequent book rights is associated with the sale of serial rights in one form or other.

The later agreements

The remaining agreements are much fuller. Each part or clause of the agreement occupies a single oblong leaf. In the earliest ones these again take the form of a printed proforma, but by the mid eighteen nineties they were on the whole individually typed, the later printed agreements often being a mass of alterations and emendations. This is an indication of the growing strength of the author in his bargaining position, in that he was less willing to have ready-made standard agreements foisted upon him. Each leaf was numbered and initialled by the parties. An agreement consisted of a combination of such clauses as:

Statement of the parties

The first clause was simply a statement as to the parties to the agreement—

'Memorandum of an Agreement made this ... day of ... on this and the following ... sheets of paper, partly printed and partly written, Between ... of ... hereinafter called "the said Author", of the one part, and WILLIAM FREDERIC TILLOTSON, of Bolton, in the County of Lancaster, Proprietor of the "Bolton Weekly Journal", hereinafter called "the said Publisher", of the other part.'

The necessary adjustments were made in the description of the Tillotson party after the death of William Frederic, when the business was incorporated under the Joint Stock Companies Acts of 1862 and 1893, and again after the new Acts of 1908 and 1917.

The vast majority of transactions are with individual authors, and the authors usually signed their own agreements. Those who wrote under pseudonyms would normally use their own names on the contract,[26] for instance—'Ouida' = Marie Louise de la Ramée,[27] 'John Strange Winter' = Mrs. Arthur Stannard,[28] 'L. T. Meade' = Mrs. L. T. Toulmin Smith,[29] and, 'Rita' = Mrs. Desmond Humphreys.[30] Occasionally, an agent would make the contract on the author's behalf, in which case he was referred to subsequently as 'the said agent' or 'the said author's Agent'. In 1886, A. P. Watt acted on behalf of 'Sarah Tytler',[31] and a year later for Robert Buchanan.[32] In 1918, J. B. Pinker acted on behalf of Louis Joseph Vance,[33] whilst in 1921 one of Vance's tales was bought from Curtis Brown Ltd.[34] Some authors, although making the agreements in their own name, used their agent as an address. Victor Waite[35] and Tom Gallon[36] used A. P. Watt in this fashion, whilst Thomas Cobb used J. B. Pinker.[37]

Tillotson bought some of his material 'second-hand' from other newspaper proprietors, publishers and syndicates—as for example, in two agreements with Sir W. C. Leng & Co. ('Sheffield Telegraph'), Ltd., by which they acquired rights in a number of serial stories by E. P. Oppenheim,[38] whilst further rights in a story by Oppenheim were acquired from George Newnes Ltd.;[39] in an agreement with the Bradford & District Newspaper Company Ltd., for partial rights in a story by J. S. Fletcher;[40] in another with the Authors' Syndicate for certain serial rights in a Marion Crawford novel;[41] in one with W. E. Adams, of *The Newcastle Weekly Chronicle* for the remaining serial rights in stories by 'Morice Gerard' and Mark Eastwood;[42] for several years Tillotsons bought the serial use of the contents of *Vanity Fair* in those cases where the copyright was owned by the magazine;[43] and finally, photographic copy was bought from the Press Photographic Agency Ltd.[44]

On the other hand, when they had used such rights in a story that they wished to use, and yet still controlled further rights which they did not wish to use, they would dispose of them to other publishers such as R. E. King & Company Ltd.,[45] Odhams Press Ltd.,[46] Digby, Long & Co.,[47] and Chatto & Windus.[48] On one occasion the film rights in a novel by Lady Troubridge were sold to the Agenzia Letteraria Internazionale in Milan for £75, when exactly the same rights had been bought from the author only twelve days previously for £63.[49] Whilst on another occasion Tillotsons acted as agent, on a 10 per cent commission, for the sale of one serial use of Mary Cholmondeley's 'The

Prisoners' in the *Morning Leader* and its associate paper the *Northern Echo* of Darlington, on behalf of Hutchinson & Co. who owned the rights.[50] So far as can be judged from the available evidence, these two cases would appear to be exceptions.

Authors were sometimes warned against making contracts with other parties and 'their administrators, executors, and assigns, or successors, as the case may be'.[51] This form is very rare in these proformas. The first was an agreement with Wilkie Collins for the 'Consecutive serial publication in newspapers published in the English Tongue' of a new unnamed story, but the form was made pointless by a later clause in the contract which stated 'Tillotson & Son shall not be at liberty to assign to any other person or persons or to dispose in any way of any of the rights to which they are entitled by this Agreement without first obtaining the Author's consent.'[52] The second was in the agreement with Lady Troubridge for the film rights in 'Love the Locksmith', which was bought with the specific intention of resale.[53] Nevertheless, the continuity of the agreements does not seem to have been affected by either the death of William Frederic, or the sale of the business to Newspaper Features Ltd. in 1935. Indeed the letter announcing the sale, specifically stated 'we . . . have transferred to them [i.e. Newspaper Features Ltd.] all copyrights we possess in serials, short stories, articles, &c.'.

The consideration

The second clause contains the nucleus of the Agreement. In it a statement is made as to exactly what is being bought and sold and for how much. There are three versions of the printed proforma for this clause—

'In consideration of the sum of . . . to be paid by the said Publisher, the said Author agrees to sell, and the said Publisher agrees to purchase, the exclusive . . . Copyright of and in the said Author's original Novel or Story called . . .'

or—

'In consideration of the sum of . . . to be paid as hereinafter provided, the said Author agrees to sell, and the said Publisher agrees to purchase, the exclusive . . . Copyright—together with the right of supply to America of Advance Sheets—of and in the said Author's original Novel or Story called . . .'

or—

'In consideration of the sum of . . . to be paid as hereinafter provided, the said Author agrees to sell, and the said Publishers agree to purchase, the absolute . . . Copyright—together with the sole right to translate and reprint as stated—of and in the said Author's original Novel or Story called . . .'

These formed the basis on which many variations occurred, through annotation and emendation. The typed equivalents, from the late eighteen nineties onwards, followed much the same pattern, though as will be seen there were fewer variations.

The consideration was invariably a sum of money. The methods by which payments were made was given later. Occasionally, besides the monetary consideration, Tillotsons would return various rights in other stories, which they had previously acquired, but for which they no longer had any use. An example of this has already been noted in the purchase of 'The Mystery of Thorncliffe Hall' from Edgar Pickering on 5 October 1918;[54] a much earlier example was the purchase of 'Sweet is Revenge' from Fitzgerald Molloy on 6 June 1890.[55]

Some indication of the variety of rights acquired will have been noted from the examples already cited, and indeed all of those mentioned with regard to the early group of simple agreements may be found in the fuller forms.[56] The earlier years saw the greatest variety; after the turn of the century the formula was generally for serial and translation rights; and, after the First World War, it was invariably for no more than British and Colonial Serial Rights (excepting the North American Continent).

The author did not always make an outright sale of his rights; sometimes he merely leased them,[57] or allowed Tillotsons to use them for a limited period of time,[58] or even for a particular occasion.[59]

As has been pointed out, before the United States Copyright Act of 1891, there was no way for an Englishman to secure protection for his work in that country, other than by becoming an American citizen or by taking an oath of intention to do so. One of the devices which British authors used in an attempt to overcome this difficulty, was to supply advance sheets to some American publisher—for a price. The publisher hoped, that with this advantage, he would thereby anticipate the 'pirates' and secure a large portion of the market before the unauthorised reprints appeared.[60] The second of the printed proformas quoted shows that Tillotson made quite a business out of this practice, and we know that he established a New York office on his visit to the

United States shortly before his death in 1889. Before 1891 most of the fuller agreements are based on this formula. An additional clause was sometimes incorporated into the agreement, which stated the restrictions within which Tillotsons had to work but which clearly gave them freedom within the United States—

'That the said Publisher's rights shall be confined to Serial Publication of the said Novel or Story, and the supply of Advance Sheets to the United States of America. That all other Home and Foreign rights of Publication shall be reserved to the said Author.'

This particular form has the caption 'Publisher confined to serial issue except in the United States'. That American volume rights were included in this right to supply advance sheets appears to be confirmed by the fact that on purchasing 'The Mahdi' from Hall Caine, the deal included the return of the American volume rights of 'The Prophet', the agreement for which had been for the lease of the serial rights 'together with the right of supply to America of Advance Sheets.'[61] In the late eighteen eighties there was growing pressure on the American government to afford some sort of protection for foreign authors. Prolonged discussions took place, and representations were made by several groups of British authors. Hopes for a settlement are reflected in an agreement between Thomas Hardy and Tillotson made on 29 June 1887. Folio seven of this agreement is the printed proforma just quoted; it has been continued in ink: '. . . the said Author; and in the event of there existing at the date referred to in Folio 6 of this Agreement international Copyright between Great Britain and the United States of America, the Book form of Publication in the United States shall be held to belong to the said Author, who undertakes in such event to pay to the said Publisher the sum of Fifty Pounds'.[62] The practice of supplying advance sheets became unnecessary after 1891, for protection could be gained provided certain formalities were adhered to and manufacture took place within the United States. After this date Tillotsons had fewer dealings in American rights, though they did still buy them occasionally.[63]

The general practice after the First World War was to exclude all North American rights. Canada presented a special problem. Though a signatory of the Berne Convention, she was in some respects at odds with it and with the 1911 British Act which applied throughout the Dominions. Because of the virtual control of the Canadian market by

American publishers, provision had been made to allow the supply of literature which otherwise might not have been available. Thus the Canadian Act of 1921, for example, granted the right to licence the printing of a book and the publishing of a serial in Canada to persons other than the owners of the Copyright.[64] In practice this meant that authors reserved the Canadian rights and made special arrangements for them, usually by means of American publication followed by Canadian registration.[65]

Very occasionally, Tillotsons bought English language Continental rights. In a letter of 6 November 1892, W. E. Norris writes—'I am willing to accept your offer of £25 for the Continental rights of "St. Ann's", making the sum of £225 for the entire book rights'. The original contract, for 'A Story of English Life' had been £200 for the 'absolute Serial Copyright—together with the sole right to translate'.[66] Long before Tillotson entered the market, however, English language rights for the continent of Europe had been practically a monopoly of the Firma Tauchnitz of Leipzig, whose 'Collection of British Authors' was familiar to continental travellers from 1841 up to the beginning of the Second World War.[67] Where rights for the publication in the English language were concerned, therefore, some formula along the lines of 'Tauchnitz Edn. excepted' was fairly common.[68]

After the American copyright act of 1891, and what might be regarded as the collapse of the American market for Tillotsons, translation rights became one of the main lines of business.[69] The third version of the proforma was the basis for these agreements. This was, of course, the right to translate from the original English into a foreign language; sometimes English language rights were bought from foreign authors.[70]

One or two authors may be regarded as having been under contract to Tillotsons, and their agreements of necessity took a somewhat different form. On 9 March 1891 J. Monk Foster undertook to sell 'exclusive copyrights of and in all literary and fictional contributions which the said Author shall produce from April 1st 1891 to March 31st 1894'; and again on 13 January 1899 he further agreed to 'write for and deliver to the said Company, within a period of three years (commencing April 1st 1899 and concluding March 31st 1902), four serial stories of not less than 100,000 words each, and three Christmas stories of 5,000 to 6,000 words each—an aggregate of 420,000 words.'[71] Other authors committed themselves to giving Tillotsons the first refusal of future works, but more of that later.

Methods of payment

The two agreements made by Foster led to an unusual method of payment. In the first case—

'For such copyrights the said Publishers agree to pay the said Author the sum of £2 weekly from March 1st 1891 to March 31st 1891; £2.5s. weekly from April 1st 1891 to March 31st 1892; £2.7.6d. weekly from April 1st 1892 to March 31st 1893; and £2.10s. weekly from April 1st 1893 to March 31st 1894. The said Author further agrees to deliver the complet on of any manuscript not completely delivered or due to be delivered at the time of the expiration of this Agreement, on receiving from the said Publishers a further sum of £2.10s. per 3,100 words contained in such concluding portion of manuscript.'

and, in the second—

'For the entire Copyright of such Serials and Short Stories, the said Company agree to pay the said Author the sum of £10.10s. per Calendar month.'

Normally, payment was made by cash or bill on one, two, three, or even four dates, which were either specifically stated, or bore some relation to the signing of the agreement, the delivery of the manuscript, the publication of the first instalment, the publication of another-stated instalment, and the publication of the last instalment. There are five printed versions of the proforma covering this part of the agreement—

'That for such Copyright, the said Publisher has paid the said Author the said sum of . . . the payment of which said sum the said Author hereby acknowledges to have received; the completed MSS. of the said Novel or Story having been delivered to and received by the said Publisher.'

or—

'That for such Copyright, the said Publisher shall pay the said Author the said sum of . . . by Two Bills of . . . [drawn at] . . . Months, the first of date on which the Opening Chapters of Instalment shall first be published; and, the Second of date on which the . . . Instalment shall first be published, provided the completed MSS. of the said Novel or Story shall have been delivered.'

or—

'That for such Copyright, the said Publisher shall pay the said Author the said sum of . . . by Two Payments in Cash of . . ., the First on the day on which the Opening Chapters or Instalment shall first be published; and the

Second on the day on which the ... instalment shall first be published, provided the completed MSS. of the said Novel or Story shall have been delivered.'

or—

'That for such Copyright, the said Publisher shall pay the said Author the said sum of ... by Three Payments in Cash of ... the First on the day on which the Opening Chapters or Instalment shall first be published; the Second on the day on which the ... Instalment shall first be published; and the Third on the date of delivery of the completed MSS. of the said Novel or Story.'

or—

'That for such Copyright, the said Publishers shall pay the said Author the said sum of ... by Three equal Payments in Cash; the First on the day on which the Opening Chapters or Instalment shall first be published; the Second on the day on which the ... Instalment shall first be published; and the Third on the date of the completed first publication of the said Novel or Story.'

There is hardly an instance, in the use of these printed forms, where some alteration has not been made. The first payment is very often the date of delivery of the MS., whilst the second becomes the date of publication of the first instalment, and so on. Specific dates are given instead of days relating to the publication. Very often the words 'but not later than ...' are added to the end of the clause. An agreement with Fergus Hume on 7 January 1899, contains a slightly more unusual arrangement—[72]

'That for such Copyright, the said Company shall pay the said Author the said sum of £120 as follow[s]: Ten pounds in cash on receipt of the first instalment; £10 on receipt of each alternate instalment succeeding; £50 when the story has been completely delivered; and £10 on publication of the first serial instalment.'

Besant arranged for four payments of £325 each in return for 'Herr Paulus', by payments on the day of publication of the first, thirteenth and twenty-sixth instalments, 'and on the said latter date payment by Bill at six months for the fourth & last payment.'[73] On 3 February 1899 Frankfort Moore signed an agreement which provided for the payment of an additional £50 'in the event of the said Company securing a London illustrated Weekly or Magazine as subscriber for the story ... on the date of commencing publication.'[74] After the First World War, it became much more common for the payment to be made to the author's agent, and in these same years the statement regarding the method of payment was more often than not reduced to a mere phrase in the 'Consideration Clause'—'In consideration of the sum of . . ., to be paid by cheque on the next monthly settling day following complete delivery of copy, the said Author agrees to sell and the said Company agrees to purchase, . . .'[75] At least from 1904, settling day for Tillotsons would seem to have been the fifteenth of the month, unless it happened to be a Sunday or holiday.[76]

As the business was predominantly concerned with serial rights rather than volume rights, royalty agreements are rare. The purchase of volume rights did occasionally lead to such an arrangement, as when Richard Marsh sold the English and Colonial Volume rights of 'The Joss' on the following terms and conditions—[77]

'Seventy guineas (£73.10s.) for the first 2,000 copies sold; 15% royalty on the third thousand; 20% on the fourth and fifth thousands; 25% on all copies sold after the first 5,000. A royalty of 3d. per copy on all copies sold in the special Colonial edition. . . . the book to be issued at Six Shillings; . . . the American Volume Rights of the same story, for the sum of Thirty guineas on account, and 10% royalty on all copies sold. That all moneys due to the said author under this Agreement on account, shall be paid by Bill at six months, or cash down less 2½%, as the said Author may desire, on completion of this Agreement.'

Such agreements must be regarded as unusual for Tillotsons.

Nature, preparation and delivery of the copy

A group of the printed proformas may be taken under this general heading; as in other respects the same matter is compressed into a much simpler form in the later typed agreements.

The first of these governs the length of the story or novel—

'That such Novel or Story shall consist of matter equal in length to . . .; that is to say, the total number of Instalments shall not be fewer than . . .; the average length of Instalment to be . . . words.'

The total length is often described as 'The Author's average three [or two] volume novel', or more simply as so many thousand words. This form is also used, with suitable emendations, as the basis for selling a number of short stories.

There may then follow a guarantee of originality, together with a safeguard against any possible legal proceedings that may result from publication—

'The said Author guarantees that the Work will be original, and in no way whatever an infringement of any copyright belonging to any other person, and that it will contain nothing of a scandalous or libellous character, and the said Author, and his Executors and Administrators, shall and will hold harmless the said Publishers from all manner of claims and proceedings which may be made and taken against them on the ground that the said Work is such infringement, or contains anything scandalous or libellous.'

The method of delivery is usually laid down—

'That the said Author shall fully prepare for the Press the whole of the said Novel or Story, no portion of which he declares has been previously published; and that he will Correct the Proof Sheets, and shall deliver the copy in the following order and speed:— . . . Instalments, on or before the . . . day of . . .; and the remainder by Weekly Instalments, until completed.'

Occasionally, the method of payment makes it quite clear that serialisation may have begun before the complete copy was delivered,[78] and this is likely to be borne out by this clause in relation to a later one in which the date of first publication is given.[79] Sometimes, rather than being expressed as a duty of the author, the correction of proofs is seen as a right—

'That the said Publisher shall send, for the said Author's revision and correction, the usual Proofs with the MSS. of the said Novel or Story, together with not less than . . . Advance Copies of each Instalment in time for Foreign simultaneous publication.'

The advance copies might also serve the needs of a translator.[80]

Where the story remains to be written, the general locale and period may be stipulated.[81] A synopsis of the story might already have been approved,[82] or one might be called for.[83] In later years it was a commonplace for the agreement to contain some such sentence as—'The said Company shall also be at liberty to make such alterations in the story as the exigencies of serial publication in their judgement require'. Though in earlier years, Wilkie Collins for one, in an agreement already identified with 'The Legacy of Cain', specifically stated, 'That no alteration of any sort shall be made in the proofs revised for press by Wilkie Collins without first obtaining his permission'.[84] A similar freedom was often allowed to Tillotsons in the matter of the title. It will have been noted that the title given in the agreements was often tentative, and in a clause—yet to be discussed—in which Tillotsons state their method of publication, the words 'under its present title or some other which they may select' are often added. Here again, there was sometimes some slight resistance. The agents A. M. Heath & Co. Ltd. writing on behalf of Louis Vance had pleasure 'in sending you the enclosed signed paper which follows exactly the formal contract you sent us except that Mr. Vance has deleted the words "under any title". He says that he would be very willing to meet you in respect of alteration of the title but feels that he ought not to give unlimited freedom in this direction.'[85]

The rights and limitations of the publisher

In the discussion of the right to supply advance sheets for the American market, a clause was quoted which was sometimes used to clarify the area within which the publisher could work.[86] Another such clause, for use under less limited agreements, was—

'That the said Publishers shall be confined in Great Britain and Ireland and the British Dominions to the Serial Form of Publication, plus all Rights of Translation and Authorised Publication on the Continent of Europe and in the United States of America, of the said Novel or Story.'

In those cases where the original agreement had been for a limited number of rights, provision was sometimes included for the publisher to purchase the remaining rights at some time in the future—

'That the said Publishers shall have the liberty or option to acquire by purchase, and the said Author will offer to the said Publishers, all the Copyright—absolute, entire and unrestricted—of the said Novel, at the total price of . . . the sum remaining unprovided for by Folio . . . to be paid . . .; but such option or acceptance shall be determined within . . . from the date hereof.'

When the rights involved in the agreement had been purchased or leased for a limited period only, an additional clause was added to make the position quite clear—

'That all Rights of Publication or Sale hereby granted to the said Publishers, shall absolutely cease and determine on the . . . day of . . ., save and except in such cases where the said Publishers have at that date contracted with another Publisher, whose Publication of the said Novel or Story has actually commenced.'

Invariably Tillotsons gave an indication of how and when they intended to publish—

'That the said Publishers may Print, and Publish the said Novel or Story in the "Bolton Weekly Journal," and in such other Publication or Publications as they may elect; but that the earliest publication shall commence not later than the . . . day of . . . .'

A penalty was often added to this clause—

'. . . In absolute default of publication, the said Publishers shall pay to the said Author the sum of . . .',

and authors usually added after this '. . . and return to him the MS. and Copyright.'[87]

The author might ask for notice of the dates arranged for the commencement of the first serial issue,[88] presumably so that the American publication could be arranged accordingly. In fact such a request was often met by another on the part of the publishers 'that serial publication in America shall neither begin nor conclude in advance of the dates arranged by the said Company for their first usor'.[89]

London papers and publications were more often than not excluded from Tillotson's arrangements, and if an author had already sold some material to another publisher for the period in question, that publisher's publications would also be excluded.[90] Sometimes, other publications were specifically excluded for no immediately apparent reason, though it was probably to prevent a clash with other matter already disposed of.[91]

The rights and limitations of the author

Some of the author's rights have been outlined incidentally in dealing with those clauses which defined the limitations upon the publisher.

The author himself gave assurances that he would not allow other forms of publication of the story, particularly volume publication, to interfere with the newspaper serialisation—

'That the said Author shall not Publish, or allow to be Published or Printed otherwise than as herein agreed, the said Novel or Story in any form whatever, before the . . . day of . . .'

or,

'That the said Author shall not Publish or consent to the Publication of the said Novel or Story in Volume form before the . . . day of . . .'

The date was fixed for some time after the completion of the first serial issue, usually some months, but the cheaper the volume envisaged, the longer would be the time between serial issue and volume publication.[92]

Not only had these assurances to be given, but the author could not publish any other story in the same way during the same period—

'That the said Author shall not Publish, or allow to be Published or Printed in Serial Form, any other Novel or Story written by the said Author in any Newspaper or Weekly Magazine Published outside London before the ... day of ...'

As with the Publisher's guarantee to publish, there was often a penalty clause added—

'...; under penalty of paying to the said Publishers on demand the sum of Two Hundred Pounds.'

This sum was brought into line with the sum for which the publisher was liable if he did not fulfil his side of the contract—usually about £50. This clause might only be for stories written under a particular pen-name, leaving the author free to publish during the same period under a different name.[93] Of course, if an author had already sold material to another publisher, which was likely to clash, then that had to be excluded from this clause.[94] Also matter over which the author no longer had any control might be mentioned.[95]

Agreement as to future stories

It has already been noted that some authors were in effect under contract to write for Tillotsons for a number of years;[96] in many other instances the following clause was inserted at the end of the agreement—

'That the said Author shall during the ensuing five years from the completed Serial Publication of the present Novel or Story give to the said Publishers the offer or refusal of any further Novel or Story he may write for ... Publication, at the lowest price the said Author will accept for the same from any other person for ... Publication.'

This type of clause was always opposed by spokesmen of such bodies as the Society of Authors, although it appears to have been very common, and judging from the Tillotson agreements to have been agreed to by very many authors.[97] A letter from Arthur Marchmont states the authors' objections fairly—[98]

'...: and have cancelled the last clause. Of course I shall always be willing to continue business relations with your firm, but as the clause stood, it would have precluded my making any separate arrangement without your being parties to it. I could not agree to this unless a fairly substantial sum were the consideration in the present transaction. I shall however always be glad to make you the first offer of such stories as I write for serial publication, and this I take to be the object you have in view.'

It might seem that Marchmont is in the end agreeing to all that Tillotsons asked, but the distinction of not including such a clause in the Agreement is a valid one. Emily Cameron, though not removing the clause, inserted 'not as a binding Agreement, but as a matter of courtesy',[99] a formula adopted by several authors. Lily Tinsley reduced the period from five to two years,[100] but the majority accepted the clause as it stood.

Attestation

Finally, came the signatures—

'Signed in Duplicate by the said WILLIAM FREDERIC TILLOTSON ... in the presence of ... and also by the said ... in the presence of ...'

NOTES

1. L. James: *Fiction for the Working Man*, 1963.
2. W. Collins: 'The Unknown Public', in *Household Words*, xviii (1858), pp. 217-22.
3. C. E. Tanzy: *Publishing the Victorian Novel; a study of the economic relationships of novelists and publishers in England 1830–1880*, Ann Arbor, University Microfilms, 1961. A dissertation in partial fulfilment of the requirements for the degree of Doctor of Philosophy at The Ohio State University.
4. G. Pollard: 'Serial Fiction', in John Carter ed., *New Paths in Bookcollecting*, 1934.
5. For a general account of the various Tillotson enterprises see F. Singleton, *Tillotsons, 1850–1950, centenary of a family business*, Bolton &c., 1950. At the time of my original work on Tillotsons, for a B.Litt. thesis at Oxford in 1968, both Mr. Taylor, of Newspaper Features, and Mr. Singleton were extremely helpful to me, and I would like to record my thanks.
6. Copyright Commission. *The Royal Commissions and the Report of the Royal Commissioners*, C.2036, 1878.
7. There are many books on copyright and the marketing of literary property. I have relied chiefly on L. C. F. Oldfield: *The Law of Copyright ...*, 1912; G. H. Thring, *The Marketing of Literary Property, Book and Serial Rights*, 1933; and, P. Wittenberg: *The Protection and Marketing of Literary Property*, New York, 1937. Since my original work on the agreements we have had the benefit of Mr. Nowell-Smith's

Lyell Lectures—*International Copyright Law and the Publisher in the Reign of Queen Victoria*, Oxford, 1968.

8. C. Brown: 'On Marketing for Authors', in *The Woman Journalist* (September 1924), pp. 11–12.

9. The 1880, 1885–7 agreements of this type are in Bodleian MS.Eng.Misc.f. 395/1; those for 1890–3 in Bodleian MS.Eng.Misc.f.395/2.

10. Bodleian MS.Eng.Misc.f.395/2, ff. 56–81 and 88.

11. Henry Herman: 'Lamplight Stories'. A series of thirteen stories: 'A Dead Man's Story', 'Abashed the Devil Stood', 'A Tragedy of Error', 'A Marriage in Heaven', 'Dandy's Licence', 'The Postman's Daughter', 'The Grey Friar of St. Drome', 'Found', 'From Lethe's Banks', 'Two Strokes of the Pen', 'The Night of the Blizzard', 'The Latest Marriage à la Mode', and 'The King of the Gnomes'. 80,000 words. £50 on 9 Mar. 1892. [Bodl.MS.Eng.Misc.f.395/2, f. 63; Notebooks 'A', p. 86; &, 'B', p. 106.]

12. J. R. Hutchinson: 'Booked Through', 'The Wrong Boot', 'Last of the Thugs', 'Caught with Chaff', and 'Shot thro' Jalousies'. 2,000 words each. £5. 5s. Not dated. [Bodl.MS.Eng.Misc.f.395/2, f.75; Notebooks 'A', p. 10; &, 'B', p. 118.]

13. Ina L. Cassilis: 'The Pale Lady of Treherne'. 6000 words. 15s. on 27 Sep. 1880. [Bodl.MS.Eng.Misc.f.395/1, f. 163; Notebooks 'A', p. 5; &, 'B', p. 42.] In the cases of the surrender of all rights, sometimes the form is merely left unamended, sometimes the words 'absolute', 'entire' and 'sole' are inserted. There appears to be no distinction between these usages. Of this and the following amendments I have quoted only one example.

14. William Black: 'The Wise Women of Inverness'. 24,000 words. £200 on 27 Feb. 1885. [Bodl.MS.Eng.Misc.f.395/1, f. 169; Notebooks 'A', p. 1; &, 'B', p. 18.]

The copyright acts do not appear to define 'serial rights'. In the case of Heinemann v. Smart Set Publishing Co., in 1909, the meaning of 'magazine rights' and 'serial rights' was discussed. In the case of 'serial rights' evidence was given that it meant publication of a novel by instalments in a periodical, and that there must be two parts at least. 'Magazine rights' had no definite trade meaning, though it appears to have been applied in the United States to the better class magazines. As the majority of the short stories—single appearance—were bought on the basis of 'serial copyright' [Notebook 'D' passim], Tillotsons' usage of the term, would appear to mean 'newspaper publication' generally. For Heinemann v. Smart Set Publishing Co., see *The Times*, 15 Jul. 1909, p. 3.

15. Amelia E. Barr: 'A Sister to Esau'. 70,000 words. £50 on 15 May 1891. [Bodl.MS.Eng.Misc.f.395/2, f. 21; Notebooks 'A', p. 73; & 'B', p. 22.]

16. George Augustus Sala: 'The Potter of Pfeffer Kuchenstein'. 16,000 words. £75 on 27 Jun. 1891. [Bodl. MS.Eng.Misc.f.395/2, f. 32; Notebooks 'A', p. 126; &, 'B', p. 222.]

17. Helen [Mathers] Reeves: 'My Other Self'. 8,000 words. £20 on 12 Jul. 1892. [Bodl.MS.Eng.Misc.f.395/2, f. 53; Notebooks 'A', p. 54; &, 'B', p. 154.]

18. Marie Corelli: 'Song of Miriam'. 6,000 words. £10.10s. on 7 Oct. 1892. [Bodl.MS.Eng.Misc.f.395/2, f. 55; Notebook 'A', p. 120; &, 'B', p. 52].

19. Dutton Cook: 'The Key of the Iron Safe'. 10,000 words. £12.12s. on 5 Nov. 1880. [Bodl.MS.Eng.Misc.f.395/1, f. 166; Notebooks 'A', p. 5; &, 'B', p. 48.]

20. Thomas Hardy: 'A Mere Interlude'. 12,000 words. £80 on 24 Sep. 1885. [Bodl.MS.Eng.Misc.f.395/1, f. 176; Notebooks 'A', p. 9; &, 'B', p. 108.]

21. Annie S. Swann: 'Twice Tried'. 80,000 words. First published in *The People's Friend*. £20 on 26 Aug. 1886. [Bodl.MS.Eng.Misc.f.395/1, f. 181; Notebooks 'A', p. 21; &, 'B', p. 218.]

22. Henry Herman: 'Punch the Postman', 5,000 words. £6 on 27 Feb. 1891. [Bodl.MS.Eng.Misc.f.395/2, f. 7; Notebooks 'A', p. 86; &, 'B', p. 106.]

23. Bessie Temple: 'Liz, A Transvaal Heroine'. 80,000 words. £15 on 8 Mar. 1891. [Bodl.MS.Eng.Misc.f.395/2, f. 11; Notebooks 'A', p. 66; &, 'B', p. 238.]

24. Frederick Boyle: 'The Higher Training, or the Lovely Monomaniac'. 15,000 words. £31.10s. on 6 Mar. 1891. [Bodl.MS.Eng.Misc.f.395/2, f. 12; Notebooks 'A', p. 102; &, 'B', p. 16.]

25. David Christie Murray: 'The Queen's Scarf'. 22,000 words. £150 on 19 Feb. 1885. [Bodl.MS.Eng.Misc.f.395/1, f. 168; Notebooks 'A', p. 13; &, 'B', p. 158.]

26. However, cf. below, p. 378, n.93.

27. 'Ouida': 'Don Gesualdo'. 24,000 words. £340 for 'exclusive Right of Publication in the English Tongue, Tauchnitz Edition excepted' on 10 Sep. 1885. [Bodl.MS.Eng.Misc.f.395/1; ff. 19–22; Notebooks 'A', p. 15; &, 'B', p. 184.]

28. 'John Strange Winter': 'Beautiful Jim'. 72,000 words. £315 for 'Serial Copyright—together with the right of supply to America of Advance Sheets' on 1 Jun. 1887. [Bodl.MS.Eng.Misc.f.395/1, ff. 136–44; Notebooks 'A', p. 22; &, 'B', p. 252.]

29. 'L. T. Meade': 'The Husband of Agnes Haye'. 120,000 words. £200 for 'absolute Copyright' on 25 Feb. 1891. [Agreement book 1890-1, ff. 238–45; may be either 'A Dark Conspiracy' or 'A Soldier of Fortune', Notebooks 'A', p. 35; &, 'B', p. 156.]

30. 'Rita': 'A Craven Heart'. 80,000 words. £180 for 'Absolute Serial, American Volume and translation Copyright' on 26 Mar. 1900. [Agreement book 1899-1900, ff. 129–34; Notebook 'C', p. 69.]

31. 'Sarah Tytler': 'Logie Town'. 150,000 words. £120 for 'Serial Copyright together with the right of supply of Advance Sheets to America' on 10 Jun. 1886. [Bodl.MS.Eng.Misc.f.395/1, ff. 46–9; Notebooks 'A', p. 17; &, 'B', p. 236.]

32. Robert Buchanan: 'The Heir of Linne'. 60,000 words. £100 for 'Serial Copyright' on 17 Feb. 1887. [Bodl.MS.Eng.Misc.f.395/1, ff. 103–6; Notebooks 'A', p. 4; &, 'B', p. 18.]

33. Louis Joseph Vance: 'The False Faces'. 13 instalments. £50 for 'entire British and Colonial Serial Rights (outside America and outside its publication in the 1917 issues of the "Philadelphia Saturday Evening Post")' on 23 Mar. 1918. Began serialisation 5 Jul. 1919. [Agreement book 1917-19, ff. 36–40; Programme, 1919.]

34. ——: 'The Face of his Dreams'. 13 instalments. £100 for 'British & Colonial Serial Rights (outside Canada)', on 3 Aug. 1921. Began serialisation 7 Jan. 1922. [Agreement book 1920-2, ff. 110–5; Programme 1922.]

35. Victor Waite: 'The Moor End Mystery'. 40,000 words. £31.10s. for 'serial rights in the English Language' on 6 Dec. 1899. [Agreement book 1899-1900, ff. 97–9; Notebook 'C', p. 154.]

36. Tom Gallon: 'The Shadow of Mr. Lamont'. 70,000 words. £140 for 'British and Colonial Serial Rights' on 11 Apr. 1905. [Agreement book 1905-6, ff. 46–51.]

37. Thomas Cobb: 'A Pretty Conspirator' [or 'Jeremy']. 52,000 words. £80 for 'Serial Copyright' on 18 Mar. 1905. [Agreement book 1905-6, ff. 26–32.]

38. E. P. Oppenheim: 'The Sufferers'. 80,000 words. £300 for 'entire British and

Colonial Serial Rights ... not to sell the story for publication, nor allow it to be published, within sixty miles of Sheffield, the City of Hull excepted' on 17 Nov. 1905. [Agreement book 1905-6, f. 133.] The second agreement was for the transfer of three out of six stories bought by Leng 'for first publication commencing in the Spring of 1909, 1910, and 1911'. Tillostons did not offer a full length serial by Oppenheim in 1909; in 1910, 'Sons of Pride', 20 instalments commencing on 30 Apr.; and, in 1911, 'The Tempting of Tavernake', 20 instalments commencing on 6 May. For the three stories they paid £350 each for 'British and Colonial Serial Rights'. [Agreement book 1907-8, ff. 68-9; Programmes, 1910 & 1911.]

39. ——: 'The Wrath to Come'. 17 instalments. £250 for 'British and Colonial Serial rights' on 22 May 1924. Began serialisation 3 Jan. 1925. [Agreement book 1923-5, f. 104; Programme, 1925.]

40. J. S. Fletcher: 'The Root of All Evil'. £50 for 'British Serial Rights ... except the right of its first appearance in the "Yorkshire Observer Budget" ' on 1 Dec. 1919. [Agreement book 1917-19, f. 124.]

41. F. Marion Crawford: 'The Diva's Rubies'. £150 for 'all serial rights in the British Empire, excepting Canada, and subject to the sale of the British serial rights to the Proprietors of "The Gentlewoman", exclusively to May 1st, 1908' on 5 Dec. 1907. [Agreement book 1907-8, f. 106.]

42. 'Morice Gerard': 'The Crowning of Esther'; and, Mark Eastwood: 'Under the Shadow of the Fortress'. 90,000 words. £35 for 'Remaining Serial Rights' on 7 Nov. 1899. [Agreement book 1899-1900, f. 65; Notebook 'C', p. 39 & p. 54.]

43. Agreement books 1905-6, f. 25; 1907-8, f. 8.

44. Agreement book 1907-8, f. 147.

45. Dora Russell: 'Footprints in the Snow'. 150,000 words. £15 for 'sole right ... to print and publish in volume form ... save and except the right to publish a threepenny edition, Messrs W. C. Leng & Company having exclusive right to publish and sell the story as a threepenny book' on 27 Apr. 1908. [Agreement book 1907-8, f. 146.] Tillotsons originally paid £250 for [?absolute] copyright. [Notebooks 'A', p. 18; &, 'B', p. 200.]

46. Edgar Pickering: 'The Mystery of Thorncliffe Hall'; &, J. K. Prothero: 'A Prince of Vagabonds'. 13 instalments each. £25 for 'sole right licence and authority to print and publish ... in abridged volume form at a nominal selling price of 4d. ... in the United Kingdom of Great Britain and Ireland its Colonies and Dependencies for a Period of three years from the dates of publication which dates shall not be later than June 30th 1921, after which period all rights shall revert to the Proprietors' on 16 Mar. 1921. [Agreement book 1920-2, f. 75.] 'The Mystery of Thorncliffe Hall' began serialisation on 5 Oct. 1918, the 'absolute copyright' having been acquired for the 're-transfer ... of all rights held ... in ... 'A Bid for a Crown', 'The Castle in the Wood', and 'Averal', plus ... £15' on 13 Aug. 1917. [Agreement book 1917-19 ff. 16-19; Programme, 1918.] 'A Prince of Vagabonds' began serialisation on 6 Jul. 1912. [Programme, 1912.]

47. Digby, Long & Co. were in the habit of buying the volume rights of large numbers of short stories at a time. [Agreement book 1905-6, f. 75.]

48. Bret Harte: 'The Argonauts of North Liberty'. 31,000 words. £5.5s. for 'remaining British and Colonial Volume Rights' on 3 Oct. 1906. [Agreement

book 1905–6, f. 224.] Tillotsons had paid £455 for 'excl. Eng. Copyright (Tauch. Series ex.) & American Serial Usor'. [Notebooks 'A', pp. 9–10; &, 'B', p. 110.]

49. Lady Troubridge: 'Love the Locksmith'. [Agreement book 1917–19, ff. 73–4.] Tillotson must have owned serial rights previously, 13 instalments began publication on 7 Jan. 1911. [Programme, 1911.]

50. Agreement book 1917–19, f. 73.

51. 'It is the greatest mistake for an author to contract with the executors, administrators, and assigns, or successors of a publisher. The contract is between principal and agent, and is a personal contract. Supposing an author were dealing with one of the best publishing houses in England, and the partners of that publishing house, for some reason or other, desired to retire from the business; to clear up matters they might put up the contracts for sale by auction or otherwise. Under those circumstances an author might find the right to publish his work purchased by some enterprising tradesman, who would bring it out in a manner and form which would be utterly repulsive to the author, and he would have no means of stopping him; and the same thing might occur should the firm go bankrupt. It is, therefore, a most dangerous thing to allow the agent who is dealing with the property to have a right to assign his agency.'—G. H. Thring: *Forms of Agreement issued by the Publishers' Association: with comments* [1903], p. 1.

52. Tillotsons paid Collins £1000 for the rights mentioned above, which were limited to a two-year period, plus the right 'solely to supply advance sheets of the story to the United States of America', on 29 Dec. 1886. The agreement also stated that 'the first serial instalment of the story shall be published in Great Britain on a day not later than the 21st day of February 1888'. 'The Legacy of Cain' began to appear in the *Bolton Weekly Journal* on 18 Feb. 1888. A pencil addition to the agreement noted that the 'German rights of trans. & publⁿ.', had been acquired for a further £80. The Notebook entries of 'The Legacy of Cain' agree in all respects with these facts. [Bodl.MS.Eng.Misc.f.395/1, ff. 85–6; Notebooks 'A', p. 5; &, 'B', p. 40.]

53. See above n. 49.

54. See above n. 46.

55. '16 or 18 instalments of not more than six thousand words each'. £50 'and the surrender forthwith by them to the said Author of the English Volume Copyright in the story "How Came He Dead?" ' for 'absolute serial copyright ... together with the right of authorised publication in America and on the Continent of Europe ... dramatisation rights ... reserved to the said Author'. [Agreement book 1890–1, f. 112; Notebooks 'A', p. 32; &, 'B', p. 160 give the price as £150.] 'How Came He Dead?' 70,000 words. £200 for 'absolute copyright (dramatisation rights alone being reserved by the author)'. [Notebooks 'A', p. 32; &, 'B', p. 160.]

56. See above pp. 357–8.

57. Sir Thomas Hall Caine: ['The Prophet']. 150,000 words. £1000 'said Author agrees to lease to and the said Publishers agree to accept the lease of the exclusive Right to publish in Serials only—together with the right of supply to America of Advance Sheets' on 28 May 1890. The American rights were later returned as part payment for 'The Mahdi'. [Agreement book 1890–1, ff. 101–11; Notebooks 'A', p. 57; &, 'B', p. 46.]

58. Nat Gould: 'A Dead Certainty'. 75,000 words. £50 for serial and translation

rights 'the agreement being that you are to have exclusive serial rights for seven years,'—letter from Routledge & Sons, Ltd., on 13 Nov. 1899. [Agreement book 1899–1900, f. 82; Notebook 'C', p. 55.]

59. Gertrude Page: 'Love in the Wilderness'. £150 for 'the right of one serial use in one publication' on 5 Apr. 1921. [Agreement book 1920–2, ff. 76–8.]

60. Mr. Pollard's introduction to I. R. Brussel: *Anglo-American First Editions*, 1935, gave a clear account of the position during this period, but since then we have had Mr. Nowell-Smith's Lyell Lectures (see n. 7 above).

61. See above n. 57.

62. The title of the novel to which this agreement refers is not given, but it seems certain that it is the original agreement for what became 'Tess of the D'Urbervilles'. Hardy was to be paid £1050 for the serial rights together with the right to supply advance sheets to America. The Agreement was cancelled on 24 Sept. 1889, because of difficulties over certain passages in the text. [Bodl.MS.Eng.Misc.f.395/1, ff. 152–61.]

63. See above n. 30.

64. G. H. Thring: op. cit. pp. 13–15.

65. Arthur Applin: 'His Final Choice'. 13 instalments. £125 for 'entire British & Colonial Serial Rights (outside North America)' on 26 February 1923. Began serialisation 4 Oct. 1924. [Agreement book 1923–5, ff. 1–6; Programme, 1924.] The vast majority of the agreements from 1920 onwards adopt this form.

66. Agreement book 1890–1, ff. 283–93; Notebooks 'A', p. 70; &, 'B', p. 176.

67. S. Nowell-Smith: 'Firma Tauchnitz 1837–1900', in *Book Collector*, xv, 4 (Winter 1966), pp. 423–36.

68. 'Ouida': 'A House Party'. 55,000 words. £500 for 'right of publication in the English tongue, Tauchnitz Edn. excepted, and of translation excepting French and German.' on 6 Apr. 1886. [Bodl.MS.Eng.Misc.f.395/1, ff. 27–30; Notebooks 'A', p. 15; &, 'B', p. 184.]

69. Evelyn Everett-Green: 'Married in Haste'. 60,000 words. £63 for 'Absolute Serial Copyright, together with the sole right to translate and print in foreign languages' on 31 Jan. 1905. [Agreement book 1905–6, ff. 6–11; presumably 'The Marriage of Marcia' in Notebook 'C', p. 57.]

70. E. Zola: 'The Dream'. 80,000 words. £200 for 'right of Eng. Pub^n.' plus £10 for 'cost of transl.' [Notebooks 'A', p. 119; &, 'B', p. 266.]

71. Agreement books 1890–1, ff. 263–9; &, 1899–1900, ff. 7–12.

72. Fergus Hume: 'The Vanishing of Tera'. 65,000 words. £120 for 'absolute Copyright'. [Agreement book 1899–1900, ff. 1–6; Notebooks 'A', p. 141; &, 'B', p. 114.]

73. Sir Walter Besant: 'Herr Paulus'. 156,000 words. £1300 for 'exclusive Serial Copyright—together with the right of supply to America of Advance Sheets' plus 'All rights of Translation and Authorised Publication on the Continent of Europe (save and except in the Tauchnitz Series of English Authors)' on 22 Jul. 1885. [Bodl. MS.Eng.Misc.f.395/1, ff. 10–18; Notebooks 'A', p. 1; &, 'B', p. 22.]

74. F. Frankfort Moore: 'The Girls of the House'. 75,000 words. £300 for 'absolute Serial Copyright—together with the sole right to translate and print in foreign languages' on 3 Feb. 1899. [Agreement book 1899–1900, ff. 13–21; Notebook 'C', p. 102.]

75. J. B. Harris-Burland: 'The Half Closed Door'. 13 instalments. £125 for 'the

British & Colonial Serial Rights' on 5 May 1920. Began serialisation on 2 Apr. 1921. [Agreement book 1920-2, ff. 19-24; Programme, 1921.]

76. See 'date of payment' column in Notebook 'D'; &, Agreement book 1923-5, f. 113.

77. 85,000. £102.7s.6d.—the one hundred guineas less $2\frac{1}{2}\%$ for the money on account. At some time previously Tillotsons had bought the serial and translation rights for £315. [Agreement book 1899-1900, f. 50; Notebooks 'A', p. 273; 'B', p. 174; &, 'C', p. 95.]

78. Sir Gilbert Campbell: 'The Avenging Hand', a series of 20 detective stories. 100,000 words. £105 for 'absolute, entire & unrestricted Copyright' on 22 Jan. 1890. First payment to be made 'On delivery of Completed Manuscript or on the day on which the Opening Chapters or Instalment shall first be published whichever is earlier'. [Agreement book 1890-1, ff. 1-12; Notebooks 'A', p. 47; &, 'B', p. 46.]

79. Joseph Hatton: 'London Livery'. 156,000 words. £400 for 'exclusive Serial Copyright—together with the right of supply to America of Advance Sheets' on 25 Apr. 1887. 26 instalments 'delivered Weekly, commencing not later than the Third day of November, 1888', earliest publication 'not later than the Twenty Eight day of February 1889'. [Bodl.MS.Eng.Misc.f.395/1, ff. 127-35; may be 'The Great World' of Notebooks 'A', p. 10; &, 'B', p. 100.]

80. Bret Harte: 'Colonel Starbottle's Client'. 15,000 words. £210 for 'Serial use in the English Language for the space of two years' on 20 May 1890. [Agreement book 1890-1, ff. 91-100; Notebooks 'A', p. 65; &, 'B', p. 110.]

81. Carlton Dawe: An unnamed story. £78 for 'British and Colonial Serial Rights' on 28 Nov. 1907. 'The story to deal with present-day life, and the scenes to be laid in England'. [Agreement book 1907-8, ff. 98-105.]

82. Rev. Ottwell Binns: 'Linked by Peril'. 13 instalments. £48 for 'serial copyright' on 27 June 1917. Serialisation began 5 Jan. 1918. [Agreement book, 1917-19, ff. 6-11; Programme, 1918.]

83. 'Headon Hill': 'The Sentence of the Court'. 65,000 words. £150 for 'absolute Serial Copyright—together with the sole right to translate and print such translation' on 22 Mar. 1899. [Agreement book 1899-1900, ff. 31-8; Notebook 'C', p. 66.]

84. See above n. 52.

85. Louis Joseph Vance: 'When Woman Loves'. 13 instalments. £100 for 'British & Colonial Serial Rights (outside Canada),' on 14 Nov. 1923. Serialisation began 5 Jul. 1924. [Agreement book 1923-5, ff. 43-4; Programme, 1924.]

86. See above p. 362.

87. Sir Gilbert Campbell: see above n. 78.

88. Arthur W. Marchmont: 'Lord Almanthorpe's Dilemma'. 15 instalments. £140 for 'British and Colonial Serial Rights' on 29 Oct. 1907. [Agreement book 1907-8, ff. 85-91.]

89. Carlton Dawe: see above n. 81.

90. Esther Miller: 'The Secret of the Sea'. 13 instalments. £130 for 'exclusive Serial Rights outside America' on 20 Oct. 1908. Serialisation began 1 Oct. 1910. 'The said Company agrees not to sell the said story, or allow it to be sold, for first or simultaneous first publication in any of Messrs. Harmsworths' papers', a later clause make it apparent that Miss Miller had already sold some stories to Messrs. Harmsworth. [Agreement book 1907-8, ff. 183-8; Programme, 1910.]

91. 'Ralph Rodd': Three unnamed novels. £100, £110, and £120 respectively for 'entire serial copyright' on 2 Nov. 1908. 'The said Company agrees not to sell to the "Sheffield Weekly Telegraph", the "Sunday Chronicle", "Ideas", or "The Umpire", any one of the three serials it acquires by this agreement.' [Agreement book 1907-8, ff. 189-96.]

92. 'Mary Drewe Tempest': 'The Second Mrs. Fairfax'. 13 instalments. £50 for 'serial copyright' on 14 Apr. 1923. Began serialisation 5 Apr. 1924. 'Also not to issue the volume or allow its issue in a fourpenny or sixpenny edition within two years after completion of first serial issue.' [Agreement book 1923-5, ff. 32-6; Programme, 1924.]

93. 'Anthony Partridge' invariably entered into this clause the phrase 'under his pen-name of "Anthony Partridge".' It seems evident that this was a pseudonym, though the agreements are always made out under it, and so signed. [E.g. Agreement book 1907-8, ff. 54-61.]

94. Cf. above n. 90.

95. George Griffith: 'A Woman's Trust'. 15 instalments. £125 for 'Serial Copyright and sole right to translate and print such translation' on 10 Feb. 1905 [Agreement book 1905-6, ff. 12-18.]

96. See above p. 363.

97. G. H. Thring: op. cit., chap. iv, 'Future Book Clauses', pp. 111-19.

98. Arthur Marchmont: 'Miser Hoadley's Secret'. 70,000 words. £20 '... plus a further sum of £12 on receipt of the same from the "Weekly Times & Echo", London,' for 'all rights' on 30 Dec. 1890. [Agreement book 1890-1, ff. 233-7; Notebooks 'A', p. 67; &, 'B', p. 162.]

99. Emily Lovett Cameron: 'A Hard Lesson'. 100,000 words. £150 for 'Serial & American Copyright—together with the sole right to translate and reprint', and later Continental rights excluding Tauchnitz edition, on 25 Jan. 1890. [Agreement book 1890-1, ff. 13-23; Notebooks 'A', p. 48; &, 'B', p. 42.]

100. Lily Tinsley: 'A Living Lie'. 170,000 words. £75 for 'absolute serial & American Copyright—together with the sole right to translate' plus £10 for re-writing a portion, on 8 Sept. 1890. [Agreement book 1890-1; ff. 188-99, & 294; Notebooks 'A', p. 62; &, 'B', p. 236.]

Writings of Graham Pollard

All books and articles carry the author's name unless noted to the contrary
HGP = (Henry) Graham Pollard

SCHOOLBOY VERSE

'And a highway shall be there...' (Kitson Clark prize poem). *Salopian* xxxviii, 15 (26 July 1919), 363–4. Four shorter pieces in *Salopian* 7 February '1919' (*sic* for 1920), and two 21 February and 6 April 1920.

'Life' and 'Love must be good...'. *Public School Verse 1919–1920*, introduction by John Masefield, edd. Martin Gilkes, Richard Hughes, P.H.B. Lyon, 1920, 53–4. HGP suggested the anthology to P.H.B. Lyon, headmaster of Rugby School, who organised it.

UNIVERSITY JOURNALISM

The New Oxford, 1 (January 1920)–21 (1 June 1923). Started by Kenneth Lindsay as the organ of the Oxford University Labour Club. 14–17 ed. Malcolm Macdonald, 18–19 Richard Pares, 20–21 HGP, who contributed:
'James Elroy Flecker', 14 (28 October 1922), 8–10.
'Bibliographical Notes' (unsigned), 15 (11 November 1922), 10–11.
'A Note on the Assumptions of Cubism' (unsigned), 17 (5 December 1922), 6–8.
'A Defence of Viscount Milner' (signed H.G.P.), 18 (3 February 1923), 4–5.
'Georgian Poetry' (signed X), 18 (3 February 1923), 8–11.
'The OUDS' (signed X), 19 (17 February 1923), 10–11.
'The Annals of Sedition' (signed G), 20 (3 March 1923), 8–10.
Review of R.W. Postgate, *Out of the Past* (signed H.G.P.), 20 (3 March 1923), 11.
'The Scope for Reprinting' (unsigned), 21 (1 June 1923), 7–8.
Review of Harold Acton, *Aquarium* (unsigned), 21 (1 June 1923), 8–11.
'De diaboli lapsi oeconomica interpretatione' (signed X). *The Oxford Broom*,

edd. Harold Acton and Alfred Nicholson, cover design by Evelyn Waugh, i, 3 (June 1923), 5–10.

POLITICS

The Distributive Worker, 1 (June 1927)–5 (March 1928), ed. HGP (roneoed). Imprint to no. 1, 'Issued by the Communist Group in the Distributive Trade Unions', changed in the later numbers to 'The Distributive Workers Advisory Committee'.

'The Role of the Censorship'. *Labour Monthly* xi (1929), 433–8.

TYPE DESIGN

Catalogue of I *Typefounders' specimens,* II *Books Printed in Founts of Historic Importance,* III *Works on Typefounding Printing and Bibliography, offered for sale,* Birrell & Garnett, 1928. Quarto, 75 copies on special paper, 1750 on ordinary paper. Authorised facsimile reprint published by Tony Appleton 1972, 500 copies.

'Baskerville's Jobbing Work'. *Fleuron* vii (1930), 155–6.

'The History of Type Design' (unsigned review of A.F. Johnson, *Type Designs, their history and development*). *TLS* 28 March 1935.

'Type Design in England' (unsigned review of W. Turner Berry and A.F. Johnson, *Catalogue of Specimens of Printing Types by English and Scottish Printers and Founders 1665–1830*). *TLS* 22 August 1935.

'A List of Type Specimens'. *Library* 4 ser., xxii (1942), 185–204. Signed by Harry Carter, Ellic Howe, A.F. Johnson, Stanley Morison and Graham Pollard. HGP writes: 'A corpus of type specimens was projected in 1937. The work of definition, etc, was done after dinner in Ellic Howe's Gloucester Road flat. A.F. Johnson and I did most of the work in compiling the list. The project was taken up by John Dreyfus in 1963'. (See next item but one.)

'The Scope for further Typographical Analysis'. *Thomas J. Wise, Centenary Studies,* ed. W.B. Todd, 1959, 64–79.

'Monuments of Typography' (unsigned review of *Type Specimen Facsimiles,* ed. John Dreyfus). *TLS* 26 April 1963.

AUTHOR BIBLIOGRAPHY

'Pirated Collections of Byron'. *TLS* 16 October 1937.

Contributions to *Cambridge Bibliography of English Literature,* 1940:

'Allan Ramsay'. ii, 969–72; 'George Crabbe', ii 345–7; 'George Gordon Byron, Baron Byron', iii, 187–212, revised in *New C.B.R.L.* iii (1969), 270–309; 'John Ruskin', iii, 691–707.

'The Early Poems of George Crabbe and *The Lady's Magazine*'. *Bodleian Library Record* v (July 1955), 149–56.

'Wise and Ruskin' (unsigned review of facsimile reprint, 1964, of T.J. Wise, ed., *A Complete Bibliography of John Ruskin*, 1893). *TLS* 22 October 1964.

'Indexes' (subjects and names). *SM, A Handlist of the Writings of Stanley Morison*, compiled by John Carter, Cambridge University for private distribution, 1950, 41–6.

'John Meade Falkner 1858–1932' (Some Uncollected Authors xxv). *Book Collector* ix (autumn 1960), 318–25.

ON PARTICULAR BOOKS

'The Bibliographical History of Hall's Chronicle'. *Bulletin of the Institute of Historical Research* x (1933), 12–17.

'Tennyson's "A Welcome"' (letter). *TLS* 15 March 1934.

'Thomas Hobbes, *Leviathan*, 1651'. Unsigned notes to items 71 and 72 in Birrell & Garnett, general catalogue 20 (1929). HGP writes: 'The three editions with the imprint of 1651 were here first distinguished and dated.'

'The Gutenberg Bible.' *TLS* 15 June 1940.

NINETEENTH CENTURY FORGERIES

All except the first and last items and *Centenary Studies* were written in collaboration with John Carter

'Mrs Browning's Sonnets, 1847' (letter). *TLS* 31 May 1934.

An Enquiry into the Nature of Certain Nineteenth Century Pamphlets, Constable, 1934. Unauthorised reprint by Haskell House, New York, 1971.

'More Light on the Wise Forgeries' (unsigned review of Fannie E. Ratchford, ed., *Letters of Thomas J. Wise to John Henry Wrenn*). *TLS* 28 April 1945.

The Firm of Charles Ottley, Landon & Co., footnote to an enquiry, Hart-Davis, 1948. (Corrections and additions, bifolium, 1967.) HGP says that this was almost entirely written by John Carter.

Thomas J. Wise, Centenary Studies, ed. William B. Todd, 1959. HGP contributed: 'Thomas J. Wise, Letter to Sir Edmund Gosse, 16 February 1897', with commentary, 30–7; 'The Case of *The Devil's Due*', 38–44; 'The Scope for Further Typographical Analysis', 64–79.

Working Papers for a second edition of 'An Enquiry into the Nature of Certain Nineteenth Century Pamphlets', distributed for the authors by Blackwell's of Oxford.

1. 'Precis of Paden or The Sources of "The New Timon"', 1967. Published February 1967; p.2 of wrapper reads, '140 copies... printed of which 105 are for sale.' Reprinted with minor corrections July 1967; p.2 of wrapper reads, 'Printed February 1967 (96 copies for sale), reprinted July 1967 (200 copies for sale)'.
2. 'The Forgeries of Tennyson's Plays', 1967. Published February 1967 and reprinted in July; numbers printed as for no. 1.
3. 'The Mystery of "The Death of Balder",' 1969. 200 copies printed for sale.
4. 'Gorfin's Stock', 1970. 400 copies printed for sale.

'Introduction'. *Buxton Forman*, Bernard Quaritch's catalogue 926, 1973, 1–4.

NEWSPAPER HISTORY

'From Press to Reader, distribution problems: Road, Rail and Air'. *The Times*, 150th anniversary number, 1 January 1935.

'The Press Club Newspaper Collection' (unsigned). *TLS* 3 October 1935.

'English Newspapers in the Bodleian' (unsigned review of R.T. Milford and D.M. Sutherland, *A Catalogue of English Newspapers in the Bodleian Library*, 1622-1800, Oxford Bibliographical Society, iv, 2). *TLS* 9 January 1937.

'Defoe as a Journalist' (unsigned review of *Defoe's 'Review' reproduced from the Original Editions*, ed. A.W. Secord). *TLS* 8 July 1939.

'The Gentleman's Magazine' (unsigned review of C. Lennart Carlson, *The First Magazine*). *TLS* 9 December 1939.

Contributions to *Cambridge Bibliography of English Literature*, 1940: 'News-Sheets and News-Books 1641–1659', i, 736–63; 'Dialogue Papers, 1676–1718', ii, 656–60; 'Magazines and Reviews, 1679-1800', ii, 668-88; 'The Newspaper (1660–1800)', ii, 688–739; 'Newspapers and Magazines (1800–1900)', iii, 779–846.

Lectures on the History of the Newspaper, Birkbeck College, London, 19, 26 April, 3, 10, 17 May 1940; reported in *The Times* 20 and 27 April 1940. Letter ('Fleet Street History') 13 May 1940.

Letters in *The Times* about the date of the first appearance of *Berrow's Worcester Journal* 30 December 1940, 3 and 11 January and 23 July 1941.

Article on the bicentenary of the *Birmingham Gazette* in that paper 17 November 1941. Corrigendum in (Birmingham) *Evening Despatch*, same date.

SERIALS

'Serial Fiction'. *New Paths in Book Collecting*, ed. J. Carter, 1934, 247-77. Issued separately ('Aspects of Book-Collecting') with corrigenda on back wrapper.

'Introduction'. I.R. Brussel, *Anglo-American First Editions 1826-1900 East to West*, 1935, 1–31.

'Novels in Newspapers: some unpublished letters of Captain Mayne Reid'. *Review of English Studies* xviii (1942), 72-85.

'The Beginnings of the Number Trade' (unsigned review of R.M. Wiles, *Serial Publication in England before 1750*). *TLS* 9 October 1959.

BOOK TRADE HISTORY

'Account of the expense of printing the Paston Letters'. *Bulletin of the Institute of Historical Research* xi (1934), 105-7.

'General Lists of Books printed in England'. *Bulletin of the Institute of Historical Research* xii (1935), 164-74.

'Books in Shropshire' (unsigned review of L.C. Lloyd, *The Book Trade in Shropshire*). *TLS* 24 October, 1936.

'The Company of Stationers before 1557'. *Library* 4 ser., xviii (1937/8), 1–38.

'The Early Constitution of the Stationers' Company'. *Library* 4 ser., xviii (1937/8), 235-60.

'Lettou's Address: a correction'. *Library* 4 ser., xviii (1937/8), 335-7.

'The English Book Trade' (unsigned review of Marjorie Plant, *The English Book Trade*). *TLS* 22 July 1939.

Contributions to *Cambridge Bibliography of English Literature*, 1940: 'Book Production and Distribution 1500-1600', i, 345-64; 'Book Production and Distribution 1660-1800', ii, 81-107; 'Book Production and Distribution 1800-1900', iii, 70-106.

'Notes on the Size of the Sheet'. *Library* 4 ser., xxii (1941/2), 105-37.

The Earliest Directory of the Book Trade, by John Pendred, 1785, ed. with introduction and appendix. Bibliographical Society's *Transactions*, suppt. 14, 1955.

'Historiography of the Book Trade' (unsigned review of Norma Hodgson and Cyprian Blagden, *The Notebook of Thomas Bennet and Henry Clements, 1686-1719*, Oxford Bibliographical Society, 1956). *TLS* 27 September 1957.

The English Market for Printed Books (Sandars Lectures, Cambridge, 3, 4, 10, and 11 February 1959), reproduced from typewriting, 1959.

The Distribution of Books by Catalogue from the Invention of Printing to A.D. 1800, based on material in the Broxbourne Library. Cambridge, printed for presentation (by Albert Ehrman) to members of the Roxburghe Club, 1965. The first chapter, 'The Fifteenth Century', was written by A. Ehrman.

'Introduction'. *Hodson's Booksellers, Publishers and Stationers Directory 1855*, facsimile of copy in the Bodleian Library. Oxford Bibliographical Society, Occasional Publication 7, 1972.

MEDIEVAL OXFORD

'Notes for a Directory of Cat Street, Oxford, before A.D. 1500'. Three typescripts, March 1937; copies in the British Library and the Bodleian. Addenda and corrigenda, March 1938.

'William de Brailles'. *Bodleian Library Record* v (1956), 202–9.

'The University and the Book Trade in Mediaeval Oxford'. *Beiträge zum Berufsbewusstsein des Mittelalterlichen Menschen, Miscellanea mediaevalia* iii (1964), 336–44.

'The Medieval Town Clerks of Oxford'. *Oxoniensia* xxxi (1968), 43–76.

'The Oldest Statute Book of the University'. *Bodleian Library Record* viii (1972), 69–91.

'Epilogue to the Medieval Archives of the University of Oxford'. *The Register of Congregation 1448–1463*, edd. W.A. Pantin and W.T. Mitchell, appendix III. Oxford Historical Society, new ser., xxii (1972), 410–32, and description of the manuscript (University Archives, Reg. Aa5), ibid., 433–44.

'The Legatine Award to Oxford in 1214 and Robert Grosteste'. *Oxoniensia* xxxix (1974), 62–72.

BOOKBINDING HISTORY

'Booksellers' Bookbinding' (unsigned). *TLS* 10 March 1932.

'Changes in the Style of Bookbinding, 1530–1830'. *Library* 5 ser., xi (1956), 71–94.

'The Construction of English Twelfth-century Bindings'. *Library* 5 ser., xvii (1962), 1–22.

'The Churchwardens' Accounts of South Newington, bibliographic description'. *South Newington Churchwardens' Accounts 1553–1684*, Banbury Historical Society 6 (1964), xxi–xxii. (On an agenda format binding by Garret Pilgrim at Oxford c. 1535.)

'The Names of some English Fifteenth-Century Binders'. *Library* 5 ser., xxv (1970), 193–218.

'Some Anglo-Saxon Bookbindings'. *Book Collector* xxiv (spring 1975), 130–59. (Issue honouring Howard Nixon.)

'Describing Medieval Bookbindings'. *Medieval Learning and Literature, essays presented to Richard William Hunt*, edd. J.J.G. Alexander and M.T. Gibson, 1975, 50–65.

BIRRELL & GARNETT CATALOGUES

HGP writes: 'The firm of Birrell & Garnett, antiquarian, new and foreign booksellers, was started by Francis Birrell and David Garnett at 19 Taviton Street, Bloomsbury, in the autumn of 1920. In 1921 they were joined by Ralph Wright, then of the National Central Library, and moved to 30 Gerrard Street, Soho. In June 1923 before I sat for my final schools examination I bought David Garnett's third share in the firm. In 1927 Ralph Wright sold his share to Miss J.E. Norton, and the business was made into a limited liability company, which was voluntarily wound up in 1939.

'The firm issued 45 catalogues. Two different catalogues were numbered 37 and 44. Nos 5, 21 (a quarto type-specimen catalogue) and 36 were not numbered. There were three sizes: small octavo, demy octavo, and quarto.

'The small octavo series (1–9, 13–15, 17, 19, 20, 22, 23, 25, 28, 32, 37, 40–44) were general, though arranged under subjects. Nos 22 and 25, arranged by Jane Norton, contained a notable series on economic theory and social conditions of the early nineteenth century.

'Of the demy octavo series (10–12, 16, 18, 24, 26, 27, 29–31, 33, 35, 37–39, 44) the first five were each given to a period of English literature from Elizabethan to the middle of the nineteenth century; 26, 31, and 44 were devoted to early newspapers, 37 to cookery, and 38 to colonial printing.

'The quarto series hardly got started. The only one printed was (21), the type specimen catalogue mentioned above on page 380. The second of the series was to have been of early writing books, and a very handsome stock of them had accumulated when W.M. Ivins of the Metropolitan Museum of Art in New York asked the firm to supply all the writing books which they considered important; this is why that institution now has what is probably the finest collection of such books. An uncorrected typescript of the catalogue still exists. The Italian portion, lent to A.F. Johnson, is now in the British Library; xerox copies of this have been made without permission.

'The third of the quarto series, a catalogue of catalogues, was never compiled. I gave some details in *The Distribution of Books by Catalogue*, pp. xvii–xviii.

'Three drawings by Duncan Grant were made for the front covers of Birrell & Garnett catalogues, (a) for 1–4 and 14; (b) for 7 and 15; (c) for (5), 6, 9, 13, 20, and 40, all in different coloured inks on different coloured paper.

The covers for 27 and 38 were drawn by Ronald Horton: the layout of the rest was mine.'

UNCLASSIFIED

'A forged Shelley Letter'. Letters in *TLS* 17 April, 8 May 1937, about postmarks.

'Mediaeval Loan Chests'. *Bulletin of the Institute of Historical Research*, xvii (1940), 113–9.

(Anon.) *Board of Trade Filing Manual, Restricted* 1949. Pp. 1–13 Introduction followed by 121 paragraphs of text (para. 100 cancelled by a gummed slip with revised text); p.13 Conclusion, with imprint Establishment Division, Board of Trade, Millbank, S.W.1, February 1949; pp. 14–6 Index. 10,000 copies. Inside front wrapper: 'This manual is the property of His Majesty's Government, and its contents must not be communicated to any person not holding an official position in His Majesty's service.'

Obituary of C.W. Dyson Perrins. *Library* 5 ser., xiii (1958), 129.

Obituary of Michael Sadleir. *Library* 5 ser., vol. xiii (1958), 129–31.

Review of Ray Nash, *American Writing Masters*. *Book Collector* ix (spring 1960), 92–9.

'The Bibliography of Butterflies' (unsigned review of Arthur A. Lisney, *A Bibliography of British Lepidoptera, 1608–1799*). *TLS* 4 November 1960.

'Bibliographical Society: memorandum on publishing policy, submitted by the President and accepted, as amended, by the Council on 6 October 1960' (unsigned). *Library* 5 ser., xvi (1961), 303–6.

Index

Abbey, John Rowland, 163
Ackers, Charles, 129
Adams, George, 228 n. 45
Adams, W. E., 359
Addams, Jesse, 347
Addison, Joseph, 195
Adventurer, 213
Agenzia Letteraria Internazionale, 359
Agustín, Antonio, 33–5, 37–43, 45–7
Ainsworth, William Harrison, 351
Alciati, Andrea, 34
Aldine Press, 157, 160
Aldrich, Henry, 134
Aleandro, Girolamo, 43, 48
Allen, Benjamin, 85
Allen, Mrs. Hanna, 84–6
Allot, Robert, 204
Altenberg, 269
Altona, 269
Ames, Joseph, 319, 328
Amsterdam
   Bookseller, *see* Wetstein
   Booksellers in Leipzig, 270
   Books published in, 100 n. 15
   Book trade in, 234–6
   Sale in, 317, 325
Amsterdam Gazette, 143–5
Anshelm, Thomas, 59 n. 87
Anspach, 269
Anthony, the *Eparch*, 38, 60 n. 96
Antwerp, 84, 235
Apostolis, Michael, 45
Apozeller, Jacob, 44, 50
Appleshaw, Hants, 91
Appleton, Berks, 91
Applin, Arthur, 376 n. 65
Arce, Juan de, 35, 43, 45–6, 49–50
Arch, John, 281
Arlenius, Arnoldus, 36–8

Aspley, William, 204–6
Astley, Thomas, 224 n. 2
Aston, Henry Harvey, 219
Atfield, Dr. Ambrose, 115 n. 24
Auctioneers, *see* Christie; Evans; Heath, J.; King, Thomas, jun; Leigh & Sotheby; Puttick & Simpson; Sotheby; Southgate
Augsburg. Book trade in, 269
   City Council, 45, 60
Authors' Syndicate, 359
Avignon, 234
Avington, Hants, 92

Backhouse, John, 65, 68
Baldwin, Richard, 200
Bale, Charles, 280
Bamberg, 269
Banbury, 78
Barber, Frank, 227 n. 23
Barcelona, 235
Barclay, Robert, 222, 223
Barnes, John, 97
Barnes, Joseph, 95
Barnes, Roger, 87 n. 20
Barr, Amelia Edith, 372 n. 15
Baskerville, John, 341
Baskett, John, 120
Basle, 37
   Booksellers from, 270
   Books published in, 34, 40, 54 n. 23
Bath, 81
Batsford, Richard, 344
Bauzen, 269
Bayreuth, 269
Beaumarchais, Pierre Augustin Caron de, 275
Beaumont, Francis, copyright, 195, 201
Beaver, John, 164, 165

387

INDEX

Becket, Thomas, 234
Beckford, John, 136
Bell, John, 341
Bembo, Pietro, 41
  his library, 38, 49
Bensley, Thomas, 279
Bentham, William, 281
Bentley, Mrs. Katherine, 202
Bentley, Richard, 202–5
Berger and Boedner, 235
Berlin, 354
  Book published in, 265
  Book trade in, 234–5, 269
Bernard, Edward, 134
Berne, 270, 354
Besançon, 233
Besant, Sir Walter, 365
Bessarion, John, 38, 48, 49
Bettesworth, Arthur, 197, 198, 206
Bewick, Thomas, 349 n. 20
Bibliotheca Parisiana, 330, 336
Binder, J., 18, 27
Bindley, James, 281
Binns, Ottwell, 377 n. 82
Birch, Thomas, 215, 225 n. 11
Birckmann, *heirs of Arnold*, 61 n. 111
Birmingham, 219
Birt, Samuel, 201
Black, William, 372 n. 14
Blackstone, Sir William, 119, 132
Blackthorn, Oxon., 74
Blado, Antonio, 44, 46
Blamire, R., 234
Bloome, Jacob, 74
Bloome, Manasses, 74
Blount, Edward, 204–6
Bluett, Henry, 87 n. 20
Boehme, Jacob, 82
Boissond, Col., 145
Bologna, 236
  Book published in, 172
  S. Domenico Library, 33
Bolognini, Luigi, 33
Bolton, 352, 357, 358
Bolton Evening News, 352
Bolton Weekly Journal, 369
Bonnardel, *frères*, 235
Bonner, William, 183

Bookbinders, *see* Barnes, R.; Binder J.; Bloome, M.; Bluett, H.; Bonnor, W.; Brindley, J.; Cavey, R.; Chapman, C.; Chapman, G.; Chastelaine, G.; Coke, C.; Cope, D.; Crucifer binder; Dawson, T.; Derome, J.; Elliott, T.; Gilbert, T.; Good, J.; Graves, J.; Hokyns, T.; Huggins, T.; Jacobus; Kemsyn, J.; Lewis, C.; Lisleie, A.; Mearne, S.; More, J.; Peerse, F.; Pembroke, T.; Reynes, J.; Rovert; Salisbury binder; Scales binder; Sedgley, R.; Sheen binder; Sparks, W.; Steel, J.; Steel, R.; Stephens, J.; Uffington, T.; Webb, W.
Bookplates, 281, 320, 327, 330, 337, 339
Booksellers, *see* Becket; Berger and Boedner; Bettesworth; Birt; Bloome; Bonnardel; Burn; Carr; Clay; Cochran; Cripps; Darby; de Hondt; Donaldson; Elmsley; Fickus; Garbrand; Gilbert; Goddard; Good; Goodwin; Graves; Herkes; Hone; Huggins; Hurd; King; Lawford; Mearne; Merkus; Nourse; Osborn; Overton; Pagliarini; Payne; Payne and Foss; Philibert; Pickering; Pott; Potter; Reycends; Rodd; Schreuder; Simco; Simmons; Smith; Sparke; Stephens; Swalle; Techener; Thorpe; Treuttel; Triphook; Vaillant; Vasse; Waisenhaus; Webb; Wellington, J.; Wellington, R.; Wetstein
Boone, Mr., 73
Boone, William, 282
Bordeaux, 233
Börsenverein der deutschem Buchhändler, 237
Boswell, James, 219, 222, 224
Bourdeaux, E., 235
Bourges, 42
Bowman, Francis, 81
Bowyer, Jonas, 179
Bowyer, William, 129, 219, 224 n. 2

388

INDEX

Boydell, John, 344
Boydell, Josiah, 344
Boyer, Abel, 144
Boyle, Frederick, 373 n. 24
Boze, Claude Gros de, 280
Bradford & District Newspaper Co. Ltd., 359
Bradshaw, Henry, 48
Brandenburg, 269
Brander, Gustavus, 318, 319, 331, 339
Bratislava, 270
Breitkopf, J. G. J., 235
Bremen, 269
Brerewood, Edward, 78, 79
Breslau, 268, 270
Brettell, Mrs., 345
Brettell, John, 345–7
Brewster, Edward, 204, 205
Brienne, Loménie de, 238
Brimelow, William, 357
Brindley, John, 184–6, 200
Brindley, Joshua, 184
Bristol, 81–3
Britwell Library, 281
Brocas, John, 141
Brown, Curtis, Ltd., 355, 356, 359
Browne, Daniel, 199, 200
Bruges, 338
Brunswick, Book trade in, 235, 269
Brussels, Book trade in, 234, 235
Buchanan, Robert, 359
Buchhandlung der Gelehrten, 237
Buck, Thomas, 155
Buckeridge, John, *Bishop of Rochester*, 63, 66, 68
Bulmer, Blackett, 347 n. 3
Bulmer, Charles, 343
Bulmer, Eleanor, 348 n. 6
Bulmer, Mrs. Eliza, 342, 343
Bulmer, Mrs. Elizabeth, 345–7
Bulmer, Sir Fenwick, 345, 346
Bulmer, Henry Morgan, 346
Bulmer, John, 347 n. 4
Bulmer, Joseph, 343
Bulmer, Ralph, 342
Bulmer, Thomas, 347 n. 4
Bulmer, William, 279, 341–9
Bulmer, William Frederick, 343

Bulmer, William Kirsop, 342, 343
Burghers, Mr., *engraver*, 130
Burland, John Burland Harris, 377 n. 75
Burn, Jacob Henry, 320
Bute, 3rd Earl of, 224
Butter, Alban, 64, 68
Butler, Richard, *archdeacon of Northampton*, 63, 66, 68
Butzaw, 235
Byfield, Nicholas, 79

Cadel, Thomas, 222
Caen, 233
Caine, Sir Thomas Henry Hall, 362
Calder, John, 329
Calladon, Germain, 58 n. 75
Calne, Wilts., 147
Cambridge
    Bookbinders in, *see* Bonner; Dawson
    Books bound in, 154
    Bookseller, *see* Crownfield
    Books printed in, 155
    Fitzwilliam Museum, 17, 26
    Letters written from, 66
    Magdalene Coll. Pepys Library, 183
    Pembroke Coll., 13, 23
    Price of boards in, 77
    Printer, *see* Buck
    St. John's Coll., 161, 163, 194
    University Library, 34, 47, 48, 183
    University Press, 129
Cameron, Emily Lovett, 371
Campana, Francesco, 42
Campbell, Sir Gilbert, 377 n. 78, 377 n. 87
Campbell, John, 326, 328
Canisio, Egidio, 44, 59
Canterbury Binder *see* Kemsyn, John
Canterbury Scribe, 17
Cappello, Carlo, 44
Cardiff, 82
Caroline, *Queen-consort of George II*, 184–6
Carr, Samuel, 159
Carter, John, 332
Caslon, Thomas, 200
Cassel, 269
Cassilis, Ina Leon, 372 n. 13

389

INDEX

Cassington, Oxon., 95
Cave, Edward, 212, 219, 220
Cavey, Robert, 87 n. 20
Caxton, William, 282, 338
Caylus, Comte de, 338
Cesena, 45
Cesi, Pietro Donato, 46, 50
Chalmers, Alexander, 212, 219
  Biographical Dictionary, 344
Chandler, Richard, 199
Chapman, Christopher, 154, 161, 162, 164–7, 172, 174–82
Chapman, George, 176
Chapman, Livewell, 83, 85, 86
Charlett, Dr. Arthur, 116, n. 28
Chastelaine, George, 19
Chatto & Windus, 359
Chauncy, Charles, 330, 336
Cheddleton, Staffs., 184
Chemnitz, 269
Chester, 79
Chesterfield, 4th Earl of, 212
Chetwynd, Philip, 204, 205
Cheyney, John, 126
Chichester 67, 68
Child, Francis, 281
Chiswell, Richard, 204, 205
Cholmondeley, Mary, 359
Christies (Christie, Manson and Woods, Ltd.), 223
Clagett, N., 179
Clarendon, 1st Earl of, 137
Clark, W., 200
Clarke, *London bookseller*, 282
Clarke, Samuel, *architypographus*, 120
Clavell, Walter, 327, 328
Clay, Francis, 197, 198, 206
Clements, Henry, 95, 96, 154
Cleriac, France, 144
Cleve, 269
Cobb, Thomas, 359
Coburg, 269
Cochran, John, 317, 324, 333, 338
Coke, Christopher, 19, 28
Coles, John, 224 n. 2
Colier, William, 97
Collins, Robert, 200
Collins, Wilkie, 360, 367

Cologne, 47, 269
Combe, Dr. Charles, 331
Combe, Taylor, 324
Combe Martin, Devon, 70 n. 27
Comers, Mrs., 338
Cook, Dutton, 372 n. 19
Cope, Damian, 71–6
Cope, Hugh, 74
Cope, John, 72, 74, 77
Cope, John, *of Blackthorn*, 74
Copenhagen. Booksellers in, 235–6, 269, 270
Copyright, 195–209, 237, 276, 353–71
Corbett, Charles, 198–200
Corelli, Marie, 372 n. 18
Corfield, William Henry, 163
Corfu, 326
Cork, 141
Cotes, Mrs. E., 204
Cotes, Richard, 204
Cotes, Thomas, 204
Cotta, J. G., 235
Cox, Peter, 97
Coxe, Henry Octavius, 22
Cramer, *frères*, 233, 235
Crawford, Francis Marion, 359
Cremona, 174
Crevenna, Pietro Antonio Bolongaro, 281, 317, 325, 328, 331, 332, 333
Cripps, Henry, *jun.*, 85, 86
Cripps, Henry, *sen.*, 71, 83–6
Crisp, Tobias, 84, 86
Critical Review, 215
Croce, Mr., 165
Crooke, Andrew, 204
Crosley, John, 87 n. 5
Crownfield, Cornelius, 158, 159, 191
Crucifer Binder, 17, 26
Cruttenden, Henry, 94, 95, 96
Cutler, Benjamin, 96, 97

Daily Courant, 143
Danvers, Sir Robert, 150 n. 15
Danzig, 269, 270
Darby, John, 197, 198, 206
Darlington, 360
Dartmouth, 1st Earl of, 141
Davenant, Sir William, 201

INDEX

Davis, Richard, 97
Dawe, Carlton, 377 n. 81, 377 n. 89
Dawkes' News-Letter, 142
Dawson, Henry, 348 n. 9
Dawson, Thomas, 158, 159, 190, 191
Debray, Nicolas Antoine Gabriel, 237
Debure, Guillaume François, 280
Decker, G. J., 235
De Hondt, Peter Abraham, 234, 235
Delafaye, Charles, 139–49
Delafaye, Lewis, 140
Delafaye, Capt. Lewis, 141
Delgardno, George, 132
Denon, Baron, 334
Derome, Jacques Antoine Nicolas Denis, *the younger*, 326
Diaz de Pastrana, Hernan, 45
Dibdin, Thomas Frognall, 279–314, 345, 348 n. 10, 349 n. 17
Dickens, Charles, 351
Digby, Long & Co., 359
Dr. Williams's Library, 329
Dod, Benjamin, *executors of*, 200
Dodd, Robert Borrodale, 343
Dodsley, Robert, 211, 213, 214
Donaldson, Alexander, 235
Dorchester, 1st Marquis of, 147
Dorigny, Sir Nicholas, 162
Douce, Francis, 281
    his MSS, 315–40
Drake,—,*gardener*, 344
Dresden, 235, 269
Drummond, Dorothy, 344
Drummond, James, 344
Drury, Henry, 324
Dryden, John, 195
Dublin, 141, 146, 342
Duchesne, Mme., 232
Dunton, John, 281
Dusouley, Peter, 150 n. 32

Eastwood, Mark, 359
Edinburgh, 235
Edmonton, M'sex, 167
Edwards, George, *bookseller*, 73–6
Edwards, George, *manciple of New Inn Hall*, 96, 97
Edwards, Jonathan, 129

Edwards, Richard, 74
Egan, Pierce, *the elder*, 351
Egan, Pierce, *the younger*, 351
Egelston, Mr., 75, 76
Egerton, Thomas and James, 321
Eisenach, 269
Elia, Stefano, 235
Elliott, Robert, 166
Elliott, Thomas, 154, 159, 162–78, 180–2
Elliott, Mrs. Thomas, 169
Ellis and Elvey, Messrs., 184
Ellis, G., 339
Ellwood, Samuel, 342
Elmes, Thomas, 66
Elmsley, Peter, 234
Elzevir, 155
Episcopius, Nikolaus, 34
Erbery, William, 82, 83
Erfurt, 269
Erlangen, 269
Errym, Malcolm J., *pseud. of M. J. Rymer*, 351
Escorial, 46, 55 n. 32
Esslinger, J. G., 235
Estienne, Robert, 37
Eton College, 19, 20
Eugubinus, *Bishop*, see Steuco, A.
Evans, Robert Harding, 282, 317, 320–3, 326, 328
Evening Post, 143
Everett-Green, Evelyn, 376 n. 69
Examiner, 143
Eynsham, Oxon, 95, 101 n. 38

Fairfax, Bryan, 281
Farmer, Mr., 334
Farmer, Richard, 281, 344
Feales, William, 196–9, 201, 203
Felice, F. B., 235
Fell, John, *Bishop of Oxford*, 86, 96, 120–2, 124–6, 133
Felton, John, 14
Fez, skins from, 164
Fickus, Thomas, 92, 93
Fiesole, 39, 40
Finch, Leopold, 100 n. 16
Fishtail Binder *see* Coke, Christopher
Fléchier, Esprit, 238

INDEX

Flensburg, 269, 270
Flesher, Miles, 203
Fletcher, John, 195, 201
Fletcher, Joseph Smith, 359
Floral Binder, see Uffington, Thomas
Florence, 36–7, 39, 236, 328
    Books published in, 39, 55 n. 29, 57 n. 67, 161
    Medici Library (San Lorenzo, Laurenziana), 34, 39–41, 50, 61
    Palazzo Vecchio, 33, 42
    San Gallo [sic], 40, 59
    San Marco, 39, 50
    Santa Croce, 40, 59
    Santa Maria del Carmine, 40, 59
    Santa Maria della Annunziata, 39, 59
    Santa Maria novella, 39, 59
    Santo Spirito, 40, 59
Flying Post, 143
Foa, Moyse Benjamin, 235
Fonvive, John de, 144
Forrest, Edward, 82
Forrest, John, 97
Fortescu, Hugh, 70 n. 27
Foster, J. Monk, 363, 364
Fradin, François, 53 n. 2
Frankfurt am Main
    Books printed in, 79, 228 n. 56
    Book trade in, 234–7, 268, 269
Frankfurt a.d. Oder, 269
Froben, H., 34, 37
Frowde, Ashburnham, 146
Fruit and Flower Binder, see Chastelaine, George
Fugger, Ulrich, 57 n. 69
Fulham, 342, 345
Furnis, Mr., 72
Fust and Schoeffer, 160

Gaignat, Louis Jean, 325, 336
Galatino, Pietro, 59 n. 84
Gallon, Tom, 359
Garbrand, Master, *bookseller*, 78
Garbrand, Mrs., *of Oxford*, 77
Gazeius, Gulielmus, 61 n. 113
Gazette de Londres, 140, 142, 147
Geneva
    Booksellers from, 270
    Books published in, 77, 80
    Book trade in, 234–6
Genoa
    Booksellers, 235
    Books published in, 59 n. 87
Gentleman's Magazine, 212, 219
George I, *King of England*, 186
Gerard, Morice, *pseud.*, 359
Gesner, Conrad, 36, 41
    Bibliotheca universalis, 280
Gibraltar, 164, 165
Gibson, John, 171, 179, 180
Gibson, Strickland, 12, 22, 71
Giessen, 269
Gilbert, Thomas, 92, 97
Giolito, Gabriel, 37, 38
Girardot de Préfond,—,281
Giunta, Lucantonio, 57 n. 67, 157, 162
    his heirs, 38
Glasgow University. Hunterian Library, 160, 163, 194
Gleditsch, J. F., 235
Glogau, 268, 270
Gloucester. College (now the King's) School, 77, 78
Goddard, T., *Norwich bookseller*, 337
Goldsmid, John Louis, 326, 339
Goldsmith, Oliver, 215
González de Mendoza, Cardinal D. Pedro, 45
Good, James, 92
Goodwin, Bethel, 197
Goodwin, Tim., 100 n. 17
Goold, John, 15
Goslin, William, 146
Gosling's Bank, 211
Gosse, P. Fred., 235
Gothe, 269
Göttingen, 269
Gough, Richard, 329, 330, 331, 332, 335, 337, 340
Gould, Nat., 375 n. 58
Gozzi, Gasparo, 236
Graham, George, 215
Graham, Thomas, *of Newcastle upon Tyne*, 342, 345
Grainger, James, 215
Granby, Marquis of, 147, 150 n. 15

INDEX

Graunte, Thomas, 65, 68
Graves, John, 158
Great Haseley, Oxon, 91
Greifswald, 269
Grenville, George, 229 n. 75
Greyhound Binder, 19, 28
Griffith, George, 378 n. 95
Grolier Club, New York, 279
Groot, Isaac de, 227 n. 26
Grotius, Hugo, 80, 81
Guardian, 141, 143
Guernsey, 141
Guilford, 5th Earl of, 326, 333
Guyon, Capt., 145
Guyon, Jean Baptiste Denis, *Seigneur de Sardière*, 335

Haarlem Gazette, 144
Hagenau, 59 n. 87
Hague, The
    Book trade in, 234, 235
    Sale in, 324
Halberstadt, 269
Halifax, 1st Earl of, 336
Halifax, 3rd Earl of, 336
Hall, John, 126-9
Hall, Peter, 320
Hall, Ronald, 283
Hall, William, *apprentice*, 126
Halle, Book trade in, 235, 269
Haloander, Gregor, 33, 34, 38, 40
Halton, Timothy, 100 n. 16
Hamburg, 269
Hamilton Palace, 163
Hampton Court, 162
Hanau, 269
Hanauer neuer Bücher-Umschlag, 275
Hanborough, Oxon, 95
Hanmer, Sir Thomas, 200
Hanover, 269
Hanrott, Philip Augustus, 317
Hardwicke, 1st Earl of, 225 n. 11, 226 n. 18
Hardy, Thomas, 362, 372 n. 20
Harleian Library, 153-94, 220, 228 n. 56
Harley, Margaret, 154
Harmanszoon, Harman, 125
Harmsworth, Messrs., 378 n. 90

Harris-Burland, John Burland, 376 n. 75
Harte, Francis Bret, 374 n. 48, 377 n. 80
Harvard University Library, books in, 279, 280, 283
Harvey, Francis, 81, 83
Haslewood, Joseph, 328
Hatton, Joseph, 377 n. 79
Haude and Spencer, 235
Hawes, L., 200
Hawkins, Richard, 203-5
Hearne, Thomas, 129, 155, 327
Heath, A. M., & Co. Ltd., 368
Heath, John, 328
Heathcote, Robert, 334
Heber, Richard, 281, 282
Hedges, Sir Charles, 141, 147, 150 n. 15
Hedley, Anna, 343, 345
Hedley, Mary, *dau. of Mrs. Mary*, 344
Hedley, Mrs. Mary, 343
Heilbronn, 269
Heinemann, William, Ltd., 372 n. 14
Helmstadt, 269
Henderson, John, *actor*, 321
Henderson, John, *of Charlotte St.*, 321
Henry, *of Walton, Archdeacon of Richmond*, 66
Herbert, William, 320
Herkes, Mrs. Anne, 78
Herkes, Richard, *bookseller*, 78
Herman, Henry, 357, 373 n. 22
Herringman, Henry, 203-5
Herwagen, Johann, 40, 54 n. 23
Hibbert, George, 330
Higgs, William Simonds, 281, 319, 337
Hildburghausen, 269
Hill, Headon, *pseud.*, 377 n. 83
Hirschfeld, 269
Hitch, Charles, 200
Hobson, Geoffrey Dudley, 12, 22, 163
Hodgkin, Thomas, 94
Hof, 269
Hohendorf, George Guillaume, Baron de, 324
Hokyns, Thomas, 14, 23
Holles, Lady Henrietta Cavendish, 157
Hollis, Thomas, 215
Holloway, Mr., 73, 74
Hone, William, 334

393

INDEX

Hope, Sir William Henry St. John, 327
Horey, Mary, 344
Huggins, Thomas, 71, 77, 78
Hume, Fergus, 365
Humphreys, Mrs. Desmond, 359
Huntington Library, 20, 30, 163
Hurd, Philip, 334
Hurley Priory, 66
Hurtado de Mendoza, Diego, 33, 36, 37, 38, 46, 49, 50
Hutchinson, J. R., 357
Hutchinson & Co., 360
Hyde, James, 347

Ideas, 378 n. 91
Illins, Pâris d', 238
Imprints, *see* Amsterdam; Basle; Bologna; Cambridge; Cologne; Cremona; Florence; Geneva; Genoa; Hagenau; Lérida; London; Lyons; Mainz; Milan; Naples; Nuremberg; Oxford; Paris; Rome; Seville; Toledo; Venice; Vilna; Wittenberg; Zürich
Inglis, John Bellingham, 338
Innys, William, 224 n. 2
International Union for the Protection of Literary and Artistic Works, 354
Ireland, Samuel, 228 n. 56
Irving, Henry, 228 n. 56
Isle of May, Fife, 67
Islington, 342

Jackman, Isaac, 344, 345
Jackman, Susan, 344, 345
Jackman, William, 344
Jacob, Edward, 332
Jacobus, *bookbinder*, 338
Jadis, Henry, 321
Jaggard, Mrs. Dorothy, 204
Jaggard, Isaac, 204-6
James, Louis, 351
James, Robert, 212
Jaubert, Pierre, 236
Jena, 269
Jennings, Edward, 75

Jennings, Mrs. Joan, 74, 75
Jenson, Nicholas, 162
Jervaulx Abbey, 67
Johnson, Arthur, 204
Johnson, Elizabeth, 95
Johnson, John Mordaunt, 328
Johnson, Michael, 228 n. 54
Johnson, Samuel, 200, 211-30
Johnston, William, 200, 214
Jones, Herschel V., 163
Jonson, Ben, 195
Justinian
    Basilica, 34, 44, 46, 51
    Codex, 33, 34, 37, 42, 46, 47
    Digest, 42
    Novellae constitutiones, 33, 34, 37, 38, 40, 46, 51
    Pandects, 33, 35, 37, 38, 42
Juxon, William, 67

Karlsruhe, 269
Kemsyn, John, 17, 25-6
Kensall, Mrs., *of Oxford*, 73, 74
Kent, 141, 142
Ker, Neil Ripley, 72, 73
Kilkenny, 141
King, *bookseller*, 332
King, R. E., & Co. Ltd., 359
King, Robert, *Bishop of Oxford*, 67
King, Thomas, *jun.*, 324
King's Printer, 120, 121
Kirkup, John, 349 n. 20
Kirsopp, Margaret, 347 n. 3
Knapton, John and Paul, 224 n. 2
Königsberg, 269, 270
Köthen, 269
Krünitz, J. G., 265
Kymer, Gilbert, 16, 22

Lafreri, Antonio, 46
Lambarde, William, 327
Lambe, Sir John, 64, 66
Lamoignon, Charles de, 42
Lang, Robert, 316, 319, 322, 323, 332
Langensalze, 269
Langford, Oxon., 117 n. 38
Langley, John, 77, 78

INDEX

Langton, Bennet, 222, 223
La Rue, Gervais de, 324
Lauban, 269
Laud, William, 63–70
Laurenti, Nicolaus, 39
Lausanne, 270
La Vallière, Duc de; Sale, 281, 317, 325, 331, 333, 334, 335, 336
Lawford, George, 282
Leake, William, 203
Legate, John, 204
Leghorn, 237
Leiden
  Booksellers from, 270
  Books printed in, 81
  Publishers, 236
Leiden Gazette, 144, 145, 149 n. 3
Leigh and Sotheby, 318, 325
Leipzig
  Book published in, 265
  Book trade in, 234–7, 268–74, 363
Le Jay, *publisher*, 232
Leng, Sir William Christopher, & Co., 359, 374 n. 45
Lenigo, 269
Lepard, John, 282
Lérida, 47
Leselabart, 330
Lesnes Abbey, 66, 68, 333, 336
Levet, Robert, 227 n. 23
Lewis, Charles, 281, 282, 334, 335
Lewis, George, 282
Lhuyd, Edward, 318, 333
Lichfield, 213, 220, 221, 223
Lichfield, John, 79
Lichfield, Leonard, 83, 93–6
Liège, 236
Liegnitz, 268, 270
Ligorio, Pirro, 46
Lincoln Cathedral, 282
Lindau, 269
Lingen, William, 141, 148
Lintot, Henry, 200, 219, 224 n. 2
Lisbon, 234–6
Lisleie, Andrew, 19
Lister, Anthony, 283
Literary Fund Society, 345
Literary Magazine, 221

Lloyd, C., 229 n. 75
Lloyd, Edward, 351
Lloyd, Thomas, 281
Lobo, Jeronymo, 211
London
  Books published in, 81, 94, 95, 100 n. 16, 179, 185, 186, 338
  British Museum Library, 206, 279, 304, 329
  King's Library, 157, 160, 162, 172, 185, 193[6]
  MSS, 14, 17, 18, 49, 56 n. 109, 68, 283, 320
  Letter from 84
  St. Paul's School, 78
  University. New College Library, 228 n. 56
  Will proved at, 347
London Chronicle, 214
London Gazette, 139, 142, 147
  French edition, *see Gazette de Londres*
Longman, Thomas, *firm*, 200, 206 n. 1, 282, 330
Looe, West (Westlow), Cornwall, 150 n. 15
Lottin, Augustin Martin, 231
Lowndes, Thomas, 200
Lübeck, 269
Lucca, 236
Luchtman, S. and J., *frères*, 233, 235
Lüneburg, 269
Lyons
  Bookseller from, 270
  Books printed in, 53 n. 2, 60 n. 107, 61 n. 113, 82, 161, 323
  Book trade in, 233, 269

Macbean, Alexander, 227 n. 24
MacCarthy-Reagh, Count Justin, 325, 326, 327, 331, 335, 336, 339
McCreery, John, 279
Madan, Falconer, 91, 116 n. 28, 116 n. 31, 127, 128, 132, 133, 315, 327
Madden, Samuel, 212
Madrid, 234
Magdeburg, 269
Magnes, James, 202, 203
Magnes, Mrs. Mary, 202, 203

INDEX

Magnes, Samuel, 202, 203
Mainz, Books printed in, 160, 163
Maitland, Mrs. Ann, *of Dublin*, 342
Maitland, Frederick, 342
Manchester Society of Book Collectors, 283
Manetti, Giannozzo, 41
Mannheim, 269
Marburg, 269
Marchmont, Arthur Williams, 370, 371, 377 n. 88
Maríotti, Augusto, 48, 61 n. 109
Markland, James Heywood, 281
Marryat, Frederick, 351
Marseilles, 233
Marsh, Richard, 366
Martyn, John, 203, 204
Masius, Andreas, 45, 51
Matal, Jean, 33-61
Maunsell, Andrew, 280
Maxwell, William, 224
Mazochius, Jacobus, 46
Mead, Robert, 203, 281
Meade, L. T., *pseud.*, 359
Mearne, Samuel, 159
Mede, William, 13
Meighan, Richard, 204, 205
Menander, Carl Friderich, 276
Mendoza, Jacob, *see* Hurtado de Mendoza
Meon, Dominique Martin, 323
Meredith, Christopher, 203
Merignac, Mme. Marie, 144
Merignac, Peter, 144, 145, 149
Merignac, Pierre, 144
Merkus, Mme, 235
Merton, Oxon., 73-5
Mervin, —, 148
Metellus, Johannes, *see* Matal, Jean
Midwinter, Daniel, 224 n. 2
Mietau, 269, 270
Milan
　Agency in, 359
　Books published in, 57 n. 66, 162, 163
　Book trade in, 233, 235, 236
Milbourne, Robert, 83
Millar, Andrew, 214
Miller, (unidentified), 281
Miller, Esther, 377 n. 90

Miller, William, *of Albourn Green*, 345
Millington, Edward, 95
Milton, John, 195, 201, 344
Miromesnil, Marquis de, 232
Missy, Caesar de, 336
Moetjens, Adriaen, 235
Molloy, Fitzgerald, 360
Monke, George, 147
Moore, Frank Frankfort, 365
More, John, 14, 23, 24
Morel-Vindé, Charles Gilbert, Vicomte de, 339
Morning Leader, 360
Mosely, Humphrey, 195
Moutard, *printer*, 232
Moxon, Joseph, 135
Moyes, James, 321
Munby, Alan Noel Latimer, 47 n. 1, 279, 315, 316, 322, 324
Münster, 269
Murdocke, John, 147
Murphy, Arthur, 221, 225 n. 5
Murray, David Christie, 373 n. 25
Murray, John, 206 n. 1
Musculus, Wolfgang, 45, 51

Nancy, 233
Nantes, 233
Naples, 59 n. 88, 234, 235, 236
Neal, John, 160
Neaulme, Jean, 235
Neele, John, 13
Neuchâtel, Société typographique, 233
Neville, Sir Thomas, 147
New, John, 200, 201
New, Nathaniel, 96, 97
Newark-on-Trent, 65
Newbery, John, 213-15
Newcastle, 1st Duke of, 157
Newcastle upon Tyne, 342-5, 347-9
Newcastle Weekly Chronicle, 359
Newcome, John, 161, 163
Newenham, —, 148
Newnes, George, Ltd., 359
Newport, Mon., 82
Newspaper Features Ltd., 360
New York, 361
Nicholls, Mr., *of Oxford*, 72, 73

INDEX

Nichols, John, 217, 219, 224 n. 2, 279
Nicholson, Edward Williams Byron, 315
Nicol, Mrs., *of Pall Mall*, 345
Nicol, George, 282, 348 n. 11
Nicol, Harriet, 344
Nicol, William, *of the Shakespeare Printing Office*, 344
Nicol, William Bulmer, 344
Noel, Nathaniel, 180, 181
Nordhausen, 269
Nördlingen, 269
Norris, William Edward, 363
North, Frederick, *see* Guilford
North, John, 281
Northampton, St. Andrew's Priory Library, 65, 68
Northern Echo, 360
Norton, John, 205
Norwich, 324, 337
Nourse, John, 234, 235
Nuremberg
   Books published in, 33, 38
   Book trade in, 234, 269

Observator, 143
Odhams Press Ltd., 359
Oldham, James Basil, 3, 12, 18, 164
Oppenheim, Edward Philips, 359
Ord, Craven, 321
Ormonde, 2nd Duke of, 140, 141
Orsini, Fulvio, 45
Osboond, Richard, 73, 74
Osborn, John, *of Paternoster Row*, 200, 201, 206 n. 1
Osborne, John, *of Merton*, 74
Osborne, Thomas, 158, 160-3, 172, 174, 179, 186, 192, 193[6], 194, 224 n. 2, 281
Oswald, John, 201
Otway, Thomas, 201
Ouida, *pseud.*, 359, 376 n. 68
Overton, Henry, 85, 86
Oxford
   All Souls, manciple, 96
      MSS, 14, 15, 134
   Bodleian Library, MSS, 13-20, 22, 24-29, 66, 125 and n., 134, 280, 281, 283, 315-40, 353

Printed books, 134, 172, 279, 315, 321, 322
Books published in, 79, 82, 93-5, 121-38, 200
Brasenose, 77, 82, 320
Chancellor's Court, 95, 128
Christ Church, 154
Corpus, MSS., 18, 19, 27
Durham College, 15, 20
Exeter, MS, 67
Jesus, books, 71; MSS., 84, 86 n. 2
Magdalen College, 13, 14, 15, 17, 18, 19, 20, 22, 23, 24, 28, 67, 71, 73
Magdalen Hall, 78
Merton, 19, 25, 81
New College, 96
New Inn Hall, manciple, 96
Oriel, 87 n. 5
Queen's, 82
R.C. Press, 116 n. 28
St. John's, 63-8, 70 n. 18
Sheldonian Press (Fell's), 120, 124, 125, 126
University College, 15, 20, 21, 24, 28, 30, 67
University Press, 119-38, 200
Worcester, 79
Oxford, Edward Harley, 2nd Earl of, 153-194
Oxford, Robert Harley, 1st Earl of, 153, 154, 156
Oxlad, Francis, *sen.*, 93

Page, Gertrude, 376 n. 59
Pagliarini, *frères*, 48, 61 n. 109, 235
Palencia, 35, 46
Pardis, —, 82
Paris
   Acts of, 354
   Booksales in, 323, 335, 339
   Books published in, 40, 69 n. 8, 77, 232, 237, 319, 337
   Book trade in, 231-5, 275
Paris-à-la-Main, 143, 144
Paris Gazette, 145, 146
Parliamentary Votes, 142, 147
Parma, 236
Parrhasius, Janus, 45

397

INDEX

Partridge, Anthony, *pseud.*, 378 n. 93
Paulmy, Marquis de, 331
Payne, John Thomas, 282, 320, 322, 330
Payne and Foss, 322–3
Payzant, James, 141, 144
Peerse, Francis, 87 n. 20
Pembroke, Thomas, 95
Pendred, John, 233, 237
Pepys, Samuel, 156
Percy, Thomas, 222, 223
Perkins, John, 222, 223
Perrin, Antoine, 232
Petroni, Prospero, 48, 51, 61 n. 109
Peyton, V. J., 227 n. 24
Philibert, C., 235
Phillipps, Sir Thomas, 230 n. 80, 321, 322, 323
Pickering, Edgar, 361, 374 n. 46
Pickering, William, 317, 325, 333
Pierpont Morgan Library, 166
Pillet, P. A. J. F., 237
Pinelli, Maffeo, 238
Pinker, James B., 359
Pirie, Robert S., 283
Plomer, Henry Robert, 91, 233, 234
Plot, Robert, 124
Plumptre, Annabella, 324, 337
Plumptre, Anne, 324, 337
Poliziano, Angelo, 33
Pollard, (Henry) Graham. Works mentioned
  Articles in *The Library*, 8, 338
  Changes in the Style of Bookbinding, 86 n. 4
  Contributions to C.B.E.L., 279
  Distribution of Books by Catalogue, 8, 60 n. 96, 60 n. 108, 231, 279
  Earliest Directory of the [English] Book Trade, 232
  English Market for Printed Books, 8
  Introduction to I. R. Brussel. *Anglo-American First Editions*, 376 n. 60
  List of Writing Books . . ., 7
  Medieval Book Trade in Oxford, 8
  Medieval Town Clerks of Oxford, 7
  Names of some English Fifteenth-Century Binders, 11, 12, 18, 19, 22, 23, 27
  Notes for a Directory of Cat St., 7
  On the Design of Forms, 6
  Serial Fiction, 8, 352
  Typefounders' Specimens, 7
Pollard, Robert, 344, 345
Pollein, Christopher, 65, 68
Pope, Alexander, 206
Porcelli, J. M., 235
Portarlington, Ireland, 145
Porter, Lucy, 219
Portland, 2nd Duke of, 154
Portland Papers at Welbeck, 153–5, 158, 161, 164, 180, 183, 185
Portsmouth, 342
Post Boy, 143
Post-Man, 143
Pott, Stephen, 68
Potter, Mr., 77
Potter, Christopher, 78
Potter, George, *bookseller*, 78
Poulson, John, 197–9
Powle, Henry, 335
Prague, 269
Precious, Jane, 344
Press Photographic Agency Ltd., 359
Pressburg, 268
Prest, Thomas Peckett, 351
Printers and Publishers *see* Ackers, C.; Aldine Press; Anshelm, T.; Barnes, J.; Baskerville, J.; Bensley, T.; Bentley, R.; Bettesworth, A.; Birckmann; Blado, A.; Blamire, R.; Bourdeaux, E.; Bowyer, W.; Brettell, J.; Brindley, J.; Browne, D.; Buck, T.; Bulmer, W.; Cave, E.; Caxton, W.; Chandler, R.; Chatto & Windus; Cheyney, J.; Clagett, N.; Clarke, S.; Clay, F.; Corbett, C.; Cotta, J. G.; Cramer; Cruttenden, H.; Darby, J.; Decker, G. J.; Duchesne; Elzevir; Episcopius, N.; Estienne, R.; Felice, F. B.; Forrest, E.; Froben, H.; Fust and Schoeffer; Gazeius, G.; Giolito, G.; Giunta; Heinemann, W.; Herwagen, J.; Hitch, C.; Hodgkin, T.; Hutchinson & Co.; Jenson, N.; Johnson, M.; Kirkup, J.; Lafreri, A.;

INDEX

Printers and Publishers (*cont.*)
    Laurenti, N.; Le Jay; Lintot, H.; Luchtman; McCreery, J.; Magnes, S.; Mazochius, J.; Mosely, H.; Moutard; Moyes, J.; Neaulme, J.; Newbery, J.; Nichols, J.; Oxford University Press; Priscianese, F.; Regnault, F.; Reich, P. E.; Rey, M. M.; Rouillé, G.; Ruault, N.; Rumball, E.; Schoeffer, P.; Silber, M.; Smith, S.; Stephens, J.; Strahan, W.; Sweynheim and Pannartz; Thistlethwaite, G.; Tonson; Tournes, J. de; Turner, W.; Walker, O.; Walther, G. C.; Webb, W.; Weld, J.; Wellington; Wetstein, J. H.; Worde, W. de
Priscianese, Francesco, 38
Prise, Sir John, 14
Prothero, John Keith, *pseud.*, 374 n. 46
Prynne, William, 79, 80
Purser, William, 83
Puttick and Simpson, 282

Quedlinburg, 269
Queensberry, 2nd Duke of, 141

Raffa, Peter, 146
Rambler, 213, 220, 221
Randolph, Francis, 119
Raphael, 162
Rawlinson, Richard, 126, 167, 328
Reed, Isaac, 344
Reed, John Watson, 321
Reeves, Helen Mathers, 372 n. 17
Regensburg, 269
Regnault, François, 40
Reich, Philipp Erasmus, 235
Renato, Cardinal Giuseppe, 333
Rennes, 233
Renouard, Antoine Augustin, 338
Retford, East, Notts., 150 n. 15
Rey, M. M., 235
Reycends, *frères*, 235
Reynes, John, 21, 30
Reynolds, Mr., 80, 81
Reynolds, Edward, 78
Reynolds, George William MacArthur, 351
Richardson, Mrs. Ann, 343
Richardson, Samuel, 214, 221, 224 n. 2
Richardson, Stephen, 129, 132
Richmond, Surrey, 147
Ridolphi, Cardinal Niccolò, 44, 49, 51
Riga, 269, 270
Rintelm, 269
Rita, *pseud.*, 359
Ritson, Joseph, 336, 337
Rivington, Charles, 216, 224 n. 2
Rivington, John, 200
Roberts, John, 70 n. 27
Rochester, 66, 68
Rodd, Ralph, *pseud.*, 378 n. 91
Rodd, Thomas, *jun.*, 332
Rodd, Thomas, *sen.*, 282, 333, 339
Rojas, Juan de, 45
Rolt, Richard, 213
Rome, 45, 46
    Books printed at, 38, 44, 46, 59 n. 87, 162, 333
    Book trade in, 234, 235
    Copyright Act, 354
    Epigraphy, 46
    San Marcello, 43, 49
    Sant' Agostino, 44
    Santa Maria della Pace, 43, 49
    Santa Maria del Popolo, 43, 49
    Santa Maria in Ara Coeli, 43
    Santa Maria sopra Minerva, 43, 49
Rostock, 235, 269
Rotterdam Gazette, 144, 145
Rouen, 233
Rouillé, Guillaume, 60 n. 107
Rovert, *bookbinder*, 159
Rowe, Nicholas, 206
Roxburghe Club, 279, 282, 344
Roxburghe, 3rd Duke of, 281
Royal Society of London. *Transactions*, 344
Roydon, Roger, 83
Ruault Nicolas, 232
Rumball, E., 203
Russell, Dora, 374 n. 45
Ryngrose, John, 66
Rynolds, Frances, 224

INDEX

Sainte-Palaye, Jean Baptiste La Curne de, 338
Sala, George Augustus, 372 n. 16
Salamanca, 45
Sales La Terrière, Fenwick Bulmer de, 346
Sales La Terrière, Mary Ann de, 346
Sales La Terrière, Mrs. Mary Anne Adams de, 344-6
Sales La Terrière, Peter de, 344, 345
Sales La Terrière, Peter Philip de, 346
Sales La Terrière, William James Bulmer de, 346
Salisbury Binder, 16, 25
Salmoni, Generoso, 235
Salviati, Cardinal Giovanni, 44, 49
Salzburg, 235
Sarpi, Paolo, 212, 219
Saugrin, Claude Marin, 231
Savage, Richard, 212, 219
Sawbridge, Thomas, 93, 94
Say, Charles, 224 n.2
Sayer, George, 142, 147, 148
Scales Binder, 11-13, 15, 21
Schmieder, Herr, 272
Schoeffer, Peter, 160
Schreuder, J., 235
Scott, Robert, 204
Seaman, Lazarus, 280
Sebright, Sir John, 318, 327, 333, 336
Sebright, Sir Thomas, 327, 333, 336
Sedgley, Henry, 157
Sedgley, Richard, 155-8
Seripandi, Antonio, 45
Serra, Mr., 165
Seville, 59 n. 88
Shakespeare, William, 195-208, 214, 215, 220, 344
Shakespeare Printing Office, *St. James*, 344
Sheen Binder, 13-14, 22
Sheffield Telegraph, 359
Sheffield Weekly Telegraph, 378 n. 91
Shifford, Oxon., 74
Shrewsbury, Duke of, 140
Shrewsbury School Library, 21, 164
Sibford, Oxon., 74
Sidelmann, Erasmus, 228 n. 56

Silber, Marcello, 59 n. 87
Simco, John, 318, 330
Simmons, Nevill, 146
Simms, Valentine, 85
Singer, Samuel Weller, 323, 328, 332
Smart Set Publishing Co., 372 n. 14
Smethwick, Francis, 203
Smethwick, John, 203-5
Smith, Charles; *map seller*, 345
Smith, George Frederick, 347
Smith, John, *of Merchant Taylors' Co.*, 184
Smith, Samuel, 100 n. 18, 228 n. 54
Sobieska, Princess Maria Clementina, 320
Society of Antiquaries, 17, 26, 167
Society of Authors, 370
Solms of Münzenberg, John Georg, Count, 228 n. 56
Sorau, 269
Sotheby & Co., 163, 193[28], 281, 282, 320, 337, 338
Soubise, Charles de Rohan, Prince de, 329, 339
Southgate, J. W., 334
Sparke, Michael, 80
Sparke, Thomas, 129, 132
Sparkes, Nathaniel, 176
Sparkes, William, 176
Spectator, 141
Spencer, 2nd Earl of, 282
Spenser, Edmund, 195
Stamford, Lincs., 150 n. 15
Stanislas, *of Mogila*, 319
Stannard, Mrs. Arthur, 359
Stationers' Company, 120-5, 167
Steel, Mrs. Jane, 159-63, 172, 191
Steel, Robert, 159, 166
Steele, Richard, 141, 143, 195
Steevens, George, 281, 344
Stephens, Anthony, *bookseller*, 91-117
Stephens, Rev. Anthony, 91
Stephens, John, 182
Stephens, Mrs. Martha, 92
Stettin, 269
Steuco, Agostino, 43, 49
Stockholm
    Booksellers from, 269, 270
    Book trade in, 234, 236

INDEX

Stowe, Mr., 148
Strahan, William, 129, 211, 213–24
Strasburg
    Book trade in, 233
    Dealers from, 268, 270
Stratford, Dr. William, 154
Stuart, Francis, 229 n. 61
Stuttgart, 235, 269
Suffolk, 150 n. 15
Sunday Chronicle, 378 n. 91
Sunderland, 3rd Earl of, 140, 141
Sussex, Duke of, 320
Swalle, Abel, 94
Swann, Annie S., 373 n. 21
Sweynheim and Pannartz, 162
Sykes, Sir Mark Masterman, 281
Sykys, Nicholas, 65, 68

Tatler, 141, 143
Tauchnitz, *Firma*, 363
Taylor, Isaac, 349 n. 20
Taylor, Mrs., 75
Taylor, John, 142
Techener, Josèphe J. and Son, 319, 322, 323
Tempest, Mary Drewe, 378 n. 92
Temple, Bessie, 373 n. 23
Temple Printing Office, 321
Term catalogues, 280
Thackeray, William Makepeace, 351
Theobald, Lewis, 200, 220
Thistlethwaite, Giles, *architypographus*, 128
Thomas, Leigh, 345
Thomas, Thomas, *of Bristol*, 83
Thompson, Richard, 142, 148
Thomson, George, 96, 97
Thorpe, Thomas, 320–2, 329, 335
Thou, de, *family*, 329
Thrale, Henry, 217, 223, 227 n. 34
Thrale's Brewery, 223
Tilenus, Daniel, 77
Tileslye, Richard, *Archdeacon of Rochester*, 66, 68
Tillotson, Mary, 357
Tillotson, William Frederic, 352, 357–8
Tilson, George, 151 n. 43

Tinsley, Lily, 371
Tiverton, 147
Toledo, 59 n. 88
Tonson, Jacob [not differentiated], 94, 195, 196, 200–6, 214, 215, 220, 221, 224 n. 2
Tonson, Richard, 200, 201
Torelli, Lelio, 33–4, 37–8, 41, 46
Torrentino, Lorenzo, 55 n. 29
Torres, Francisco, 35, 37, 39, 60
Toulouse, 233, 326
Tournes, Jean de, 61 n. 113
Towneley, John, 330
Traile, John, 148
Trattner, J. Thom., 235
Treuttel, *Parisian bookseller*, 330
Triphook, Robert, 282, 326, 330, 333, 339
Troubridge, Lorna, Lady, 359, 360
Tubingen, 269
Turin, 235
Turner, Dawson, 280, 282
Turner, William, 79, 80, 81, 82, 95
Turrianus *see* Torres, Francisco
Tutet, Mark Cephas, 319, 328
Twysden, Sir Roger, 68, 318, 327, 336
Tyrius, Maximus, 77
Tyrrel, John, 146, 148
Tyssen, Samuel, 327, 329
Tytler, Sarah, *pseud.*, 359

Uffington, Thomas, 18, 27
Ulm, 269
Umpire, The, 378 n. 91
Universal Chronicle, 214, 226 n. 12
Upcott, William, 318

Vaillant, Paul, 234
Valade, *publisher*, 232
Valencia Cathedral, 60 n. 102
Valladolid, 45
Vanbrugh, Sir John, 201
Vance, Louis Joseph, 359, 368
Vanity Fair, 359
Varrentrap, Frz., 235
Vasse, *frères*, 235

401

INDEX

Vatican Library, 34, 37, 42, 44, 46
  Bibliotheca Graeca, 42, 48, 49, 51
  Bibliotheca Latina, 42, 48, 49
  Parva Secreta, 42, 43, 48, 49
  Secreta Major, 42, 43, 45, 48
Venice
  Book bought in, 45
  Books published in, 33, 161, 163, 172, 194
  Book trade in, 234, 236
  Marciana Library, 33, 37, 38, 49, 51
Vettori, Piero, 41
Vienna
  Book trade in, 235, 269
  Decree from, 275
Vilna, 70 n. 27
Votes, see *Parliamentary Votes*

Waisenhaus, 235
Waite, Victor, 359
Walker, John, 98
Walker, Obadiah, 116 n. 28
Walker, Robert, 200, 201
Walker, Thomas, 67
Walkley, Thomas, 203, 204
Walmesley, Gilbert, 219
Walpergen, Peter de, 125
Walter, John, 345, 346, 347
Walther, G. Conrad, 235
Wanley, Humfrey, 69, 153-90
Ward, Aaron, 206 n. 1
Ward, John, 206 n.1
Waring, Samuel, 142
Warren, Thomas, 219
Warsaw, 236
Warton, Joseph, 225 n. 5
Watermarks, 56 n. 117-19, 48-51, 329
Watt, A. P., 359
Watts, John, 224 n. 2
Webb, Philip Carteret, 338
Webb, William, 71, 80, 82, 83
Weekly Times & Echo, London, 378 n. 98
Weimar, 269
Welbeck, see Portland Papers
Weld, John, 100 n. 16
Wellington, Bethel, 197, 199, 200, 206
Wellington, James, 197, 199, 200, 206

Wellington, Mrs. Mary, 197, 198
Wellington, Richard, *jun*., 197, 199-202, 206
Wellington, Richard, *sen*., 197, 198, 201, 203, 205
Werken, Theodoricus Nicolaus, 14
West, George, 96
West, James, 174
Westminster Abbey, Books from, 64-6, 68
Westminster, St. Stephen's Chapel, 68
Westowre, Richard, 66
Wetstein, Johann Heinrich, 131, 135
Weymouth, 1st Viscount, 146
Whalley, George, 65
Wheeler, Maurice, 124
White, John, 325
White, Thomas, *M.P.*, 150 n. 15
Widdowes, Giles, 80
Wilbraham, Roger, 329
Wilcox, Thomas, 219
Williams, Mrs. Anna, 221
Williams, Theodore, 323, 334
Wilson, William, 281
Wimpole Hall, Cambs., 154, 157-9, 172-7, 183
Winchester College, 20
Windsor, Royal Library, 185
Winter, John Strange, *pseud*., 359
Wismar, 235, 269
Witt, Richard, 128
Wittenberg, 73, 269
Wolvercote Paper Mill, 96, 124, 136
Wood, Anthony, 136
Woodburn, Henry, 320
Woodburn, Samuel, 320
Woodfall, Henry, 200, 224 n. 2
Worcester, 148
Worde, Wynkyn de, 282
Wouwerus, Johannes, 81
Würzburg, 269

Yate, Thomas, 120-2, 124-8
Yorkshire, 141, 142
York, Cardinal of, 320
Young, Henry, 347
Yverdon, 235

INDEX

Zanchi, Basilio, 44, 50
Zarotus, Antonius, 57 n. 66
Zell, 269
Zittau, 269
Zola, Emile, 376 n. 70

Züllichau, 235, 269
Zürich, 41, 270
Zurke, Herman, 16–17
Zwichem, Viglius van, 34, 40